# APPLIED DATA COMMUNICATIONS

## A Business-Oriented Approach

### FOURTH EDITION

**James E. Goldman**
**Phillip T. Rawles**
*Purdue University*

www.wiley.com/college/goldman

**Phillip T. Rawles/*To Cheri' and Hunter***

**James E. Goldman/*To Susan, Eric, and Grant***

| | |
|---|---|
| ACQUISITIONS EDITOR | Beth Lang Golub |
| ASSOCIATE EDITOR | Lorraina Raccuia |
| EDITORIAL ASSISTANT | Ame Esterline |
| MARKETING MANAGER | Gitti Linder |
| ASSOCIATE PRODUCTION MANAGER | Kelly Tavares |
| PRODUCTION EDITOR | Sarah Wolfman-Robichaud |
| MANAGING EDITOR | Kevin Dodds |
| DESIGNER | Jennifer Wasson |
| ILLUSTRATION COORDINATOR | Benjamin Reece |
| ILLUSTRATOR | Curtis A. Snyder |
| COVER DESIGN | Jennifer Wasson |
| COVER IMAGE | Copyright © Javier Dauden/CORBIS |

This book was set in 10/12 Palatino by Leyh Publishing LLC and printed and bound by RR Donnelley & Sons Company. The cover was printed by Phoenix Color Corp.

This book is printed on acid-free paper. ∞

U.S. ISBN: 0-471-34640-3
WIE ISBN: 0-471-45177-0

Printed in the United States of America

10 9 8 7 6 5 4 3 2 1

# PREFACE

## ■ NEW TO THE FOURTH EDITION

The field of data communications continues to evolve at a rapid pace. To provide the reader with the most timely and important information possible, several changes have been made to the fourth edition while preserving those unique aspects of the three previous editions that contributed to its wide acceptance and popularity. Among the significant changes to the fourth edition are the following:

- All new case studies match the material in every chapter.

- Increased technical depth, as well as breadth of coverage, have been added throughout the text.

- The data communication concepts chapter (chapter 2) has been expanded to include theory from all areas of data communication.

- The overarching application upon which data communication technologies are introduced has been changed from a dial-up-modem-based application to a LAN/DSL/cable modem application to resonate better with today's students (chapter 3).

- The local area networking materials have been consolidated into one chapter (chapter 4) that also includes complete coverage of wireless local area networks.

- Coverage of wireless communication technologies has been integrated throughout the text rather than compartmentalized in a single chapter. This better represents the state of wireless technology integration in the industry.

- Coverage of IP and the Internet has been increased substantially in the fourth edition. There are now two chapters that directly cover this material: an introductory chapter on network protocols and IP fundamentals (chapter 7) and a chapter on IP network design (chapter 8).

- Materials on network operating systems and remote access have been extensively revised.

- There is more coverage of wavelength division multiplexing and optical switching in the WAN chapter (chapter 6).

- The entire text is organized with an emphasis on the OSI 7 layer model.

## ■ THE NEED FOR THIS BOOK

The field of information systems has undergone major paradigm shifts over the past several years from mainframe-oriented, hierarchical information systems architectures through distributed, LAN-based, client-server information systems architectures, to browser/Internet-based information systems. However, this transition is far from complete because information systems architectures continue to evolve to include seamless integration with World Wide Web and Internet technologies such as application service providers, as well as more transparent interoperability with legacy or mainframe systems. Today's resultant information systems architecture is composed of a complicated array of interacting technologies combining elements of client-server, Web-based, Internet, intranet, legacy applications, and database management systems. Data communications is the key building block to all of these interacting technologies.

Designing, implementing, and managing a successful data communications system requires sophisticated business-oriented analysis, design, and problem-solving skills. Furthermore, the collaborative computing and multimedia applications that are likely to be executed on these information systems are highly dependent on properly designed networks for successful delivery of interactive content. The interdependency of application and network development required for successful deployment of distributed information systems is all too often overlooked by information systems professionals.

In order to effectively design today's highly integrated, distributed data communications networks, a comprehensive systems engineering approach that incorporates business analysis, application development, database systems integration, distributed network design, and structured technology analysis is required. Such a business-first, technology-last, top-down model was introduced in the first edition of *Applied Data Communications: A Business-Oriented Approach.* The highly successful subsequent editions of *Applied Data Communications,* combined with *Local Area Networks* and *Client Server Information Systems* texts, have solidified the top-down approach as the preferred design methodology for complex network-based information systems.

Unlike many of the currently available books and texts on data communications that seem to be either too broadly focused and conceptual or too narrowly focused and technical, this text strikes a balance between the two extremes, while offering the reader a structured approach to data communications analysis and design from initial business considerations through final technology choices.


## ■ DESCRIPTION

*Applied Data Communications: A Business-Oriented Approach; 4th ed.* provides a thorough explanation of the analysis, design, integration, and technology choices involved with deploying, managing, and securing effective data communications systems, local area networks, internetworks, and wide area networks.

The text is flexibly organized so as to cater to a variety of course orientations. The general organization and key features of the text are as follows:

- Text is divided into four major sections to maximize flexible use by a wide variety of course orientations:

  - Part 1: Data Communication Fundamentals
  - Part 2: Network Transmission Technologies
  - Part 3: Network Protocols and Administration
  - Part 4: Network Development and Management

- Thirteen chapters of manageable length allow instructors to pick and choose chapters as appropriate for course content, focus, length, and intended audience.

- The text is written in a logical, problem-solving style applauded by both students and faculty from academia and industry.

- The text material is organized into overall architectures or models. By providing students with the "big picture" first, the text assists students in understanding how particular individual topics relate to other topics and to the overall scheme of things.

- The text stresses analytical questioning and problem-solving skills as the key to successful design of information systems.

- The text provides working models into which students can organize their problem-solving approach. These models are reinforced and used throughout the text. Examples include

  ○ Top-down model
  ○ TCP/IP model
  ○ OSI model

- Business cases for each chapter are included on the book's support Web site. Questions guide students toward development of analytical skills and business-oriented client-server information systems design capabilities.

The text equips students with real-world skills. In a fashion similar to Professor Goldman and Rawles' previous texts, *Applied Data Communications: A Business-Oriented Approach; 4th ed.* teaches students how to do data communications design, rather than merely reading about it.

## ■ APPROACH

The reviews and current level of adoptions of the first three editions of *Applied Data Communications: A Business-Oriented Approach,* the first two editions of *Local Area Networks: A Business-Oriented Approach*, and *Client/Server Information Systems: A Business-Oriented Approach* indicate that the same proven, practical approach should be applied to the fourth edition of *Applied Data Communications: A Business-Oriented Approach.* The text follows the top-down model, examining the many options, standards, interfaces, implications, advantages, and disadvantages in each of the top-down model's five layers:

- Business

- Application

- Data

- Network

- Technology

Concept roadmaps are located throughout the text, stressing the relationship between chapters and a data communications systems architecture, as well as between topics within chapters.

Each chapter begins with an outline of new concepts introduced, previous concepts reinforced, and the learning objectives for that chapter. Section and paragraph headings help students organize and identify key concepts introduced in each chapter. End-of-chapter material includes chapter summaries, key term listings, and abundant review questions.

As previously mentioned, business cases based on the material in each chapter are included on the book's Web site at www.wiley.com/college/goldman, along with associated analysis questions to be answered by students or used as the basis for classroom discussion.

A liberal use (two to three times as many as competing texts) of clear, concise diagrams add to the usability of the text and to the understanding of the students.

## ■ TARGET AUDIENCES/COURSES

Due to the modular nature of this text, a variety of audience/courses could be well served. Among the courses as potential adopters of this text are the following:

- *An introductory level course on data communications.* The practical nature of the text would be appealing, as would its broad coverage and architectural orientation. Advanced sections of the text could be easily avoided. This course could also serve as the foundation course for a concentration or degree program in data communications/telecommunications and networking technology.

- *A business-oriented course in data communications as part of an MBA program.* This would especially be useful for those with concentrations in MIS.

- *Continuing education or industrial seminars offered in fundamentals of data communications.* Professional development courses are becoming more common as individuals and companies seek to maintain a competitive edge.

## ■ SPECIAL FEATURES

Although some of these features have been mentioned previously, they are repeated here to stress the unique nature of this text as a purveyor of practical, business-oriented data communications analysis skills and problem-solving abilities, rather than a mere collection of concepts and facts.

- Modular approach allows flexible use of text to fit instructor and course needs.

- Real business case studies available on the book's Web site stress the business impact of data communications, thereby assisting students in sharpening their analysis and problem-solving skills. Directed questions accompanying each case stimulate classroom discussion as well.

- "In Sharper Focus" sections highlight more detailed, more advanced, or background information for concepts introduced within a chapter. These sections can be included or excluded at the instructor's discretion.

- "Managerial Perspective" sections take a "bottom-line" approach to client server information systems analysis and design. The potential impact of management decisions in a variety of situations is highlighted in these sections and may be of particular interest to M.B.A. audiences.

- "Applied Problem Solving" sections of chapters focusing on the use of analytical models for "Applied Problem Solving" activities are highlighted for the benefit of both instructors and students. By stressing problem-solving activities, students can be assured of learning how to do data communications analysis and design.

- Emphasizing the practical nature of the text, instances of practical advice or warnings are highlighted in order to call the reader's attention to important but often overlooked information.

## ■ OSI NETWORK REFERENCE MODEL ORGANIZATION

Previous editions of *Applied Data Communications* have attempted to strike a balance between stressing a systems integration approach to teaching data communications against a strict organization of material according to the seven layers of the OSI Network Reference Model. The authors feel that the key to comprehending data communications lies in the understanding of the interfaces between OSI layer components rather than in the categorization of components according to OSI layer. As a result, although the material in the text is loosely organized according to the layers of the OSI model, the key theme to the overall organization of the text is the appreciation of how data communications components must be integrated in order to produce a functional end-to-end system. As an aid for those instructors wishing to organize their course according to the OSI model, the following table provides a cross-reference.

| OSI Model Layer | Topics | Chapter(s) |
|---|---|---|
| Layer 1—Physical | Media, signaling, modulation | 2, 3 |
| Layer 2—Datalink | LAN architectures | 4 |
| | PSTN architectures | 5 |
| | WAN architectures | 6 |
| Layer 3—Network | Network protocols | 7, 8 |
| Layer 4—Transport | Network protocols | 7, 8 |
| Layer 5—Session | Network protocols | 7 |
| Layer 6—Presentation | Network protocols | 7 |
| Layer 7—Application | Network protocols | 7 |

## ■ ANCILLARY MATERIALS

Student Web site www.wiley.com/college/goldman:

- Contains business case studies for each chapter

- Contains PowerPoint slides for each chapter

- Links to relevant Web sites

Instructor Web site www.wiley.com/college/goldman:

1. Instructor's Manual: This contains answers to all review questions featured at the end of each chapter in the text. In addition, solutions to case study questions will be provided.

2. Test Bank and Computerized Test Bank: The test bank is a comprehensive resource for test questions; it contains a mix of about seventy multiple choice and true–false questions per chapter. The questions are provided in Word documents and in a computerized format that allows instructors to create their own exams.

3. Lecture Slides in PowerPoint: This series of slides for each chapter is designed around the content of the chapter, incorporating key points and illustrations from the text.

These Instructor's Resources are also available on CD.

## ABOUT THE AUTHORS

### Phillip T. Rawles, Principal Author

Phillip T. Rawles is an associate professor of Computer Information Systems and Technology for Telecommunications and Networking in the nationally prominent Department of Computer Technology at Purdue University. Professor Rawles has won various student- and faculty-selected teaching awards for his performance in the classroom and for his work in developing and delivering courses in local area networking, systems administration, enterprise network management, and enterprise network design.

Professor Rawles is also the author of *Local Area Networks: A Business-Oriented Approach; 2nd ed.* (2000) and *Client/Server Information Systems: A Business-Oriented Approach.* Professor Rawles has active research and consulting practices.

### James E. Goldman

James E. Goldman is professor of Computer Information Systems and Associate Department Head for Telecommunications and Networking in the nationally prominent Department of Computer Technology at Purdue University. An award-winning teacher, in 1999 Professor Goldman was named as a University Faculty Scholar at Purdue.

Professor Goldman is also the author of *Local Area Networks: A Business-Oriented Approach; 2nd ed.* (2000) and *Client/Server Information Systems: A Business-Oriented Approach.* Professor Goldman maintains an active consulting practice.

# ■ ACKNOWLEDGMENTS

We are indebted to a number of people whose efforts were crucial in the development of this book.

For the outstanding-quality illustrations that appear in the book, as well as for his unwavering support, we'd like to thank Curt Snyder, our wonderful and talented illustrator.

For their support and help in developing materials in the wireless networking and wide area networking areas, we'd like to thank Lance Hassan and Scott Williams.

For their collaborative efforts in turning a manuscript into a published book, we'd like to thank the following professionals at John Wiley & Sons, Inc. and Leyh Publishing LLC:

Beth Golub, Acquisitions Editor

Lorraina Raccuia, Associate Editor

Kevin Dodds, Managing Editor

## Reviewers

A special debt of gratitude is owed to the professionals who were kind enough to review the manuscript of this book prior to publication. It is through your effort that an accurate text of high quality can be produced.

Mary Brabston, University of Manitoba

Thomas P. Cavaiani, Boise State University

Mark Dishaw, University of Wisconsin–Oshkosh

Lance Hassan, Purdue University

Hassan Ibrahim, University of Maryland–College Park

Nory Jones, University of Maine

Boris Jukic, George Mason University

Cynthia A. Mason-Posey, Prince George's Community College

Michael J. Much, Hennepin Technical College

Mihir Parikh, University of Central Florida

Gary Parks, National University

Kari A. Wood, Bemidji State University

# CONTENTS

## CHAPTER 9
## Local Area Network Operating Systems and Remote Access    336

# PART 4
# Network Development and Management    375

## CHAPTER 10
## The Network Development Life Cycle    375

# CHAPTER 11
# Network Management   425

# THE DATA COMMUNICATIONS INDUSTRY

*Concepts Introduced*

Interacting components of the data communications industry
Regulatory process
Deregulation and divestiture
Standards-making process
Top-down model
Data communications as a profession

Data communications and information systems
OSI model
Internet suite of protocols model
I-P-O model
Protocols and compatibility
Job skills
Career opportunities

## OBJECTIVES

Upon successful completion of this chapter, you should:

1. Understand today's data communications industry as a system of interacting components.

2. Understand the current state of the data communications industry, as well as the major issues facing each of the industry's constituent components.

3. Understand the challenges and solutions to business-oriented data communications analysis.

4. Understand the importance of structured models such as the top-down model, the OSI model, and the I-P-O model to successful business-oriented data communications analysis.

5. Understand the relationship of network analysis and design to information systems analysis and design.

6. Understand career opportunities in data communications and the job skills required to succeed in this field.

## ■ INTRODUCTION

Data communications is a field of study and an industry in a most rapid state of change. This chapter familiarizes the reader with the current state of the data communications industry and introduces the reader to a series of models or thinking frameworks. These frameworks provide a mechanism to organize thoughts, facts, requirements, solutions, and technology to overcome the challenges faced by today's data communications professionals. By mastering these thinking models, the reader will be developing a business-oriented, technology-independent process for the analysis and design of data communications systems. These models are used extensively throughout the remainder of the text to further familiarize the reader with them.

To better appreciate the wonderful professional opportunities available in data communications, it is important to understand how network analysis relates to information systems analysis in general, as well as the types of skills required for success in this most exciting field.

## ■ THE BEST WAY TO APPROACH DATA COMMUNICATIONS

Since the field of data communications is in a state of constant change—some would even refer to it as chaos—how can you study data communications and keep your sanity? The primary points to remember are:

- You will never know all there is to know about data communications.
- Be honest with yourself concerning what you don't know.

If you can accept these laws as facts, you will be well on your way to survival in this most exciting and rewarding field.

What, then, can you expect to master in a one-semester course in data communications based on this textbook? After successful mastery of the material contained in this text, you should be able to:

- Hold an intelligent conversation on a variety of data communications topics.
- Analyze networking requirements, evaluate networking options, ask appropriate networking questions, and know where to seek answers to those questions.

Understand, however, that you will not necessarily possess all of the answers. Nor will you necessarily be qualified to design networks. However, you will possess enough information to ask the essential questions and to keep yourself from getting in over your head.

### What Is Data Communications?

Data communications can be viewed as a foreign language. Just as the mastery of any foreign language requires practice in speaking and writing that language, so it is with data communications. As when learning a foreign language practice is a key factor for success. Try to speak the language as often as possible. Don't be afraid of making mistakes. Form informal study groups if possible and review key concepts by forcing yourself to speak data communications. You will be pleasantly surprised at the speed at which you become comfortable with this new language.

A classic definition of **data communications** might be "the encoded transmission of data via electrical, optical, or wireless means between computers or network processors." Traditionally, data communications is viewed as a subset of **telecommunications,** which encompasses the transmission of voice, data, and video. Throughout the text we'll see that the fields of telecommunications and data communications are becoming so intertwined that it's difficult, if not impossible, to differentiate between them. Voice, video, image, and fax transmission all currently fall within the domain of the data communications analyst.

In truth, any functional definition is really just a goal or outcome of a much larger process of interacting system components collectively known as the data communications industry. By breaking down a system-oriented representation of the data communications industry into constituent components, interaction among components and the resultant state of the data communications industry can be more easily understood.

### ■ THE DATA COMMUNICATIONS INDUSTRY

To be an effective participant in the data communications industry, it is important to understand the industry forces at work behind the scenes. In this manner, enlightened professionals can be proactive in their decision making rather than being at the mercy of an industry that at times seems to be beyond reason and out of control.

Figure 1-1 shows one way of breaking the complex world of data communications into a group of interacting components. As can be seen from the diagram, data communications is the sum total of the interacting components outlined. There is no distinct beginning or end. No single component is more important than another.

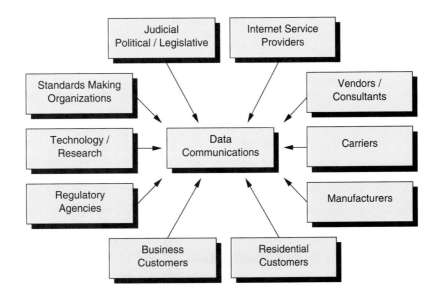

*Figure 1-1*   The Data Communications Industry: A Series of Interacting Components

## The Regulatory Process

Two tightly dependent components in a constant and ongoing state of change are the **regulatory** and **carrier** components. The regulatory component represents local, state, and federal agencies charged with regulating telecommunications, while the carrier component represents companies such as telephone and cable TV companies that sell transmission services.

To fully understand these two important components of today's data communications environment, we must focus on their interaction, those forces that join them and influence their present status. This interaction is a rather formal process of a series of proposals, also known as tariffs. Tariffs are submitted to state and federal regulatory agencies by carriers, and rulings and approvals are issued in return. This relationship is illustrated in Figure 1-2.

### Basic Telecommunications Infrastructure

To understand the changing regulatory relationship between different phone companies and their associated regulatory agencies, it is important to understand the physical layout of a basic telecommunications infrastructure and the names of the interacting components and service boundaries contained therein. Figure 1-3 illustrates the major components of the **public switched telephone network (PSTN)** required to support long distance dial-up service for data communications.

**Local access transport areas (LATA)** were established as a result of the breakup of AT&T to segment long-distance traffic. Originally all phone traffic within a LATA (intra LATA traffic) was reserved for the local phone company, also known as a **local exchange carrier (LEC).** Although recent rulings and legislation have made the distinction between intra-LATA and inter-LATA calls less significant, the LATA structure is still important to the overall telecommunications architecture.

A LATA is sometimes, but not always, equivalent to the geographic region covered by a given area code. However, there can be several LATAs per area code. Another key difference between LATAs and area codes is that a LATA can cross state boundaries, but an area code cannot. Figure 1-4 illustrates both the area codes and LATAs for the state of Indiana.

Residences or businesses are connected to the PSTN via circuits known as **local loops.** Local loops run between the residence or business location and the local **central office (CO),** a facility belonging to the local phone company in which calls are switched to their proper destination. Any phone traffic destined for locations outside of the local LATA must be handed off to the long-distance or **inter-exchange carrier (IXC)** of the customer's choice. Competing long-distance carriers wishing to do business in a given LATA maintain a switching office in that LATA known as a **point of presence** or **POP.** This POP handles billing information and routes the call over the long-distance carrier's switched network to its POP in the destination's LATA. The

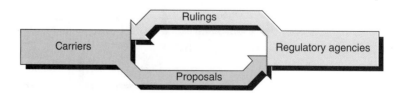

*Figure 1-2*   Systems Relationship of Regulatory Agencies and Carriers

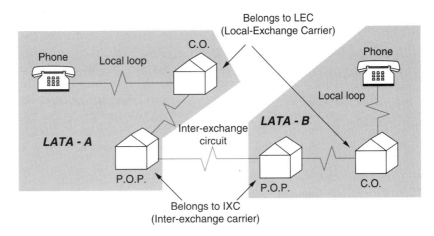

Figure 1-3    Basic Telecommunications Infrastructure

circuit between the POPs may be via satellite, microwave, fiber optic cable, traditional wiring, or some combination of these media. Depending on traffic levels on the long-distance carrier's network, calls may be routed through any combination of switches before reaching their final destination.

**Deregulation and Divestiture: 1980s**    After one understands the overall interaction of carriers and regulatory agencies as well as the basic infrastructure of today's telecommunications industry, the historical aspects of this regulatory relationship must be explored to better understand how today's regulatory environment evolved. Today's competitive telecommunications industry in the United States is largely the

Figure 1-4    Area Codes vs. LATAs

result of rulings by the Justice Department in the early 1980s. These rulings are generally referred to as **deregulation** and **divestiture.** These two terms are related but not synonymous.

Before deregulation and divestiture, America's telecommunications needs (data and voice, hardware and services) were supplied, with few exceptions, by a single vendor: American Telephone and Telegraph (AT&T). At that time, homeowners were not allowed to purchase and install their own phones. AT&T owned all equipment connected to the PSTN. Customers rented their phones from AT&T.

Local Bell operating companies provided local service but were still part of AT&T. All telephone service, both local and long distance, was coordinated through one telecommunications organization. Most indoor wiring was also the responsibility of AT&T, not the owner of the building in which the wiring existed. This top-to-bottom integration allowed for excellent coordination and interoperability. It was easy to know who to call for new service or a repair problem because installation and maintenance of hardware, as well as long-distance and local service for voice or data were all coordinated through one company. On the other hand, the total control of the telecommunications industry by one company severely limited customer choice. If you wanted a telephone, you became an AT&T customer. If you were not happy with AT&T's service or pricing, the only option was to terminate your service. This top-to-bottom control of the telecommunications industry was seen as a monopoly, especially by other vendors wishing to compete in the telecommunications industry.

The single company telecommunications industry model came to an end through deregulation and divestiture in the late 1970s and early 1980s. It is important to note that the initial divestiture and deregulation of the telecommunications industry was not the result of a purely regulatory process. This enormously important event was primarily a judicial process, fought out in the courtrooms and largely fostered by one man, Bill McGowan, former president of MCI.

Although the Federal Communications Committee (FCC), a federal regulatory agency, initially ruled in 1971 that MCI could compete with AT&T for long-distance service, it was McGowan's 1974 lawsuit that got the Justice Department involved and led to the actual breakup of the telecommunications monopoly in the United States. AT&T was declared a monopoly and broken into several smaller companies in a process known as divestiture as set forth by Federal Judge Harold Greene in the 1982 **Modified Final Judgment (MFJ).** By interpreting the MFJ, Judge Greene effectively controlled the U.S. telecommunications industry from the original ruling in 1982 until the Telecommunications Act of 1996 expressly ended his control.

Divestiture broke up the telephone network services of AT&T into separate long-distance and local service companies. AT&T would retain the right to offer long-distance services, while the former local Bell operating companies were grouped into new regional Bell operating companies **(RBOCs)** to offer local telecommunications service. Figure 1-5 illustrates the RBOCs and their constituent former Bell operating companies (BOCs) after divestiture through 1996.

Deregulation introduced an entirely different aspect of the telecommunications industry in the United States: the ability of "phone companies" in America to compete in an unrestricted manner in other industries such as the computer and information systems fields. Before deregulation, phone companies were either banned from doing business in other industries or were subject to having their profits and/or rates monitored or "regulated" in a fashion similar to the way in which their rates for phone service were regulated.

**Figure 1-5**  Post Divestiture/Pre-Telecommunications Act of 1996 RBOC and BOC Alignment

As a result of deregulation, both AT&T and the RBOCs were allowed to enter into other industries by forming additional subsidiaries. For the first time, phone companies were competing in a market-driven, customer-dictated economy. A common misconception about deregulation is that phone companies became totally deregulated and could charge whatever the market would bear for phone services. This is not the case. Phone companies today have both regulated and deregulated portions of their business, which are often segregated into separate companies.

Network services offered by phone companies are still regulated. New rate proposals from phone companies are filed as tariffs with state or federal regulatory authorities. Local service rate changes are filed on the state level with a particular state's Public Utilities Commission and on a federal level with the FCC for interstate service proposals and rate change requests. These commissions must balance objectives that are sometimes contradictory:

- Basic phone service must remain affordable enough that all residents of a state can afford it. This guarantee is sometimes known as **universal service** or **universal access.**

- Phone companies must remain profitable to be able to afford to constantly reinvest in upgrading their physical resources (hardware, cables, buildings) as well as in educating and training their human resources.

The divestiture and deregulation activities of the 1980s allowed competing long-distance carriers such as MCI and US Sprint to sell long-distance services on a level playing field with AT&T thanks to a ruling known as **equal access.** This means that all long-distance carriers must be treated equally by the local BOCs in terms of access to the local carrier switching equipment, and ultimately to their customers.

From the end-user's perspective, the divestiture and deregulation activities of the 1980s enabled freedom of choice for long-distance carriers. The competition for business and residential customers' long-distance business has forced down prices for long-distance service. On the other hand, the simplicity of ordering, installing, and maintaining services from one company was replaced by a series of services from multiple companies.

This loss of coordinated installation and troubleshooting is perhaps the biggest loss to telecommunications users as a result of deregulation and divestiture. Service problems can often result in finger-pointing between hardware vendors, local service carriers, and long distance carriers while the telecommunications users are left rather helplessly in the middle.

**Deregulation, Divestiture, and Realignment: 1990s**    In September 1992, the FCC enacted additional rulings that enabled limited competition in the local loop. The competition was limited to leased or private lines that bypass the phone company's switching equipment. Before these rulings, only the RBOCs were allowed to transport calls from a residence or business to the local central office and ultimately to the point of presence of any of the long-distance carriers.

After this ruling, a company could use a leased line to transport voice and/or data between corporate locations on a 24 hours/day, 7 day/week basis. Leased lines have no dial tone. They are private, point-to-point, "pipes" into which customers can transport voice and data to only the predetermined ends of those pipes. The differences among all of the various switched and leased voice and data services are explored further in Chapters 3 and 6.

Through a mandated process known as **co-location,** RBOCs had to allow alternate local loop carriers to install their equipment in the RBOC's CO. In return, RBOCs were allowed to charge **access charges** for co-location of the alternate carrier's equipment in their COs. End-users could also co-locate networking equipment in the RBOC's CO. Businesses could now build their own virtual private networks by co-locating their own networking equipment in local phone company COs.

Remembering that this ruling only affected leased line traffic, only those businesses that had a need for point-to-point or multipoint leased lines, usually for data transmission, were likely to benefit from this ruling. However, this local loop leased line deregulation was but a shadow of things to come.

In 1995, AT&T reacted to a changing marketplace in an unusual manner. To free its various divisions to seek business opportunities without regard for the interests of other AT&T divisions, AT&T split into three separate companies. Whereas the divestiture of AT&T in the 1980s was vigorously fought by AT&T and eventually government-imposed, the trivestiture of AT&T in 1995 was self-imposed. The three companies are as follows:

- AT&T—The carrier services, wireless services, and half of Bell Labs retain the AT&T name.

- Lucent Technologies—Data, voice, and networking equipment and the other half of Bell Labs.

- NCR—Known as AT&T Global Information Solutions after the 1991 takeover, NCR is once again an independent computer manufacturer.

**The Telecommunications Act of 1996** sought to encourage competition in all aspects and markets of telecommunications services including switched and dedicated local and inter-LATA traffic, cable TV, and wireless services such as paging, cellular, and satellite services. The legislation directs the FCC to produce the rules that will allow LECs and IXCs to compete in each other's markets. Companies that wish to offer local access service in competition with RBOCs are known as **competitive local exchange carriers (CLEC).**

Perhaps most importantly the law completely changed the regulatory environment of the telecommunications marketplace by expressly preempting the authority of Judge Greene to dictate the operation of the telecommunications industry in the United States. As a result of the act, the FCC has been given the task of establishing a fair and equitable market environment in which a variety of companies can compete in a deregulated manner. The goal of the Telecommunications Act of 1996 can be summarized in three words: *free market economy.* Figure 1-6 summarizes the major implications of the Telecommunications Act of 1996 from a variety of perspectives.

Managerial
Perspective

### TELECOMMUNICATIONS ACT OF 1996 IMPACT

In addition to its primary goal of creating competition in all aspects of the U.S. telecommunications market, the Telecommunications Act of 1996 has had several other effects on the various players in the marketplace. One of the most visible impacts is the merger and acquisition of telecommunications vendors in an attempt to gain competitive advantage. Because traditional long-distance carriers (IXCs) can potentially enter their marketplace, RBOCs have merged to increase territory size, capitalize major new ventures, and create a more formidable competitor for IXCs. The major RBOC realignments are as follows:

- NYNEX and Bell Atlantic combined as Bell Atlantic to control the northeast corridor region from Washington D.C. to Boston.

- Bell Atlantic and GTE combined operations to expand their service offerings under the Verizon brand name.

- PacTel (Pacific Telesis) and Southwestern Bell combined as SBC Communications to control telecommunications in the Texas to California high-tech region.

- SBC then merged with Ameritech to add a large section of the Midwest to their portfolio.

Similarly traditional long-distance companies are merging to consolidate market position and capitalize on research and development dollars. In addition to mergers within the long-distance company ranks, IXCs have merged with companies that cover other sectors of the telecommunications industry.

- European based WorldCom communications purchased UUNET, a leading Internet carrier.

- MCI merged with WorldCom to form MCI-WorldCom.

- America Online is currently trying to acquire Sprint.

- MCI-WorldCom acquired SkyTel, a leading two-way pager service provider.

- AT&T has acquired TCI cable systems to expand its presence in the cable television and high-speed Internet via cable marketplaces.

- Various IXCs are merging with or acquiring wireless carriers.

| Perspective | Implication/Importance |
|---|---|
| **Strategic Intent** | • Provides for a procompetitive deregulatory national policy framework by opening all telecommunications markets to competition<br>• Directs the FCC to create rulemakings to produce this deregulated environment |
| **FCC** | • Imposes a significant burden on the FCC to produce new rules so that the deregulated market operates fairly for all competitors<br>• Examines all regulations imposed on carriers and eliminates any that no longer serve a productive purpose |
| **IXCs** | • Eliminates the need for long distance carriers to file tariffs; rates are determined by competitive pricing and the free market<br>• Can enter into local access markets, thereby gaining access to local loops on a national basis<br>• Will likely resell access to RBOC's local networks rather than building their own |
| **CLECs** | • Gain access to RBOCs local loop markets<br>• Will likely resell access to RBOC's local networks rather than building their own<br>• Looking at wireless solutions as an alternative to using the RBOC's local loops |
| **LECs** | • Can compete for IXC business within their own region as long as they can prove there is at least potential for competition in the local loop<br>• Can enter into equipment manufacturing businesses |
| **Cable TV Companies** | • Can enter telephone business but must wait until cable rates are deregulated |
| **Users** | • Will be offered more opportunities for bundled services from a single vendor<br>• May regain single source for voice and data services lost in original divestiture/deregulation<br>• Increased competition in a variety of markets may produce lower costs |

*Figure 1-6*   Telecommunications Act of 1996

Although the resulting companies do not have the market position of the pre-breakup AT&T, the market seems to be moving toward a scenario in which a few companies can offer all types of communications services from traditional telephony to wireless telephony, cable television, and Internet service. These companies, also known as **universal carriers,** hope that by bundling various services together, they can become a one-stop solution for all of their customers' communications needs.

One of the key aspects of the Telecommunications Act of 1996 was that it opened the door for competition in the local phone service market. However, progress in this area has proven to be slow. Some state regulatory agencies delayed the ability for CLECs to enter the market. In those states that have successfully allowed CLECs to compete, the mid-2003 market share of CLECs ranges from around 30% in Michigan to under 3% in New Mexico.

The main reason that CLECs are having trouble entering the local service marketplace is local loop access. A CLEC can deliver local telephone access in two ways: lease the existing loop from the incumbent local service provider or provide an alternate means of customer connection.

If the CLEC chooses to lease local loop access from the incumbent LEC, it is limited to a retailer's profit, as the Act ensures the incumbent LEC of a reasonable profit for maintaining the local loops by setting the cost of local loop access to wholesale levels. The economics of this model simply have not spawned much interest in local access competition. However, new wireless technologies are making the second option, providing an alternate connection to the customer, far more viable. By implementing fixed-point wireless solutions, a CLEC can offer customers not only multiple lines of local telephone service, but also high-speed Internet access. By combining these new technologies with traditional local loop service, CLECs are aggressively beginning to enter the local service marketplace.

Interestingly, this competition in the local service marketplace is welcomed by the incumbent LECs. According to the Act, LECs cannot enter the highly lucrative long-distance marketplace until they can show meaningful competition in the local service marketplace. In this case, the potential profit lost on local service (which is usually fixed) will be more than made up for in increased revenue from long-distance services.

Another key player in the industry that has been affected by the Act is the cable television (CATV) industry. The CATV industry has an inherent advantage over traditional local service providers: Its connection to the user natively provides significantly greater bandwidth than the traditional telephone local loop. This increased bandwidth allows multiple phone lines and high-speed Internet access to be bundled with traditional cable service.

Although they are well positioned from a cable plant basis to deliver service in the local market, most cable companies are poorly positioned economically to do so. Bearing large debt loads as a result of rapid expansion, CATV providers are too undercapitalized to make the required investment to upgrade their traditional one-way analog networks to support the two-way digital transmission required to deliver local telephone service. Besides the economic issue, CATV providers also lack expertise in switching environments to implement telephony over the cable infrastructure. These issues are currently driving multiple mergers and partnerships between CATV companies and traditional long-distance carriers. The combined companies can offer bundled local and long-distance service along with television and Internet access.

The importance of the Internet and the ability to offer high-speed Internet access to telephone service providers cannot be overstated. New technologies such as Voice Over IP (VOIP) have the potential to replace traditional circuit-switched telephone technologies with packet-switched voice. The impact of such a shift will likely be more dramatic on the telecommunications industry than all legislative and regulatory rulings combined.

Due to the distance insensitivity of packet-switched Internet telephone technologies, the concept of pay per minute long distance could become obsolete. Instead it might soon be possible to pay a monthly fee for access to long-distance network and make an unlimited number of calls to anywhere in the world for no additional charge. Several IXCs including MCI and AT&T are experimenting with using Internet technologies in the core of their network between POPs to leverage the distance insensitivity of packet-switched voice.

The ability of Internet telephony to compete with traditional telephone networks may ultimately depend as much on the regulatory environment as it does on the quality and reliability of the technology. It remains to be seen what influence, if any, the FCC will have on packet-switched Internet telephony. Recent rulings are inconclusive because the FCC has expressed concern about the impact of such technologies on universal access, but has yet to place any new barriers to their implementation.

## The Standards Process

While the regulatory process is most important to carriers and their customers, the standards process is important to all constituencies of the data communications industry. Without standards, data communications would be nearly impossible, as single-vendor, customized transmission solutions would probably be the only way to achieve end-to-end transmissions. **Standards** allow multiple vendors to manufacture competing products that work together effectively. End-users can be confident that devices will operate as specified and will interoperate successfully. Standards can have a tremendous potential economic impact on vendors of data communications equipment, and the standards-making process is affected by both political and financial influences.

Although the charter of each standards-making organization dictates the exact procedure for standards development, the process can be generalized as follows:

1. Recognition of the need for a standard

2. Formation of some type of committee or task force

3. Information/recommendation gathering phase

4. Tentative/alternative standards issued

5. Feedback on tentative/alternative standards

6. Final standards issued

7. Compliance with final standards

**Standards-Making Organizations**  Standards-making organizations for the data communications industry fall into two major categories:

- Officially sanctioned

- Ad hoc

Some of the most significant officially sanctioned standards-making organizations, whose standards are referred to throughout the book, are listed in Figure 1-7.

Because of the lag time often required to produce standards in an officially sanctioned standards-making organization, or perhaps in response to the ever-broadening scope of data communications-related technology, many ad hoc standards-making organizations continue to be formed. Known by a variety of terms including *task forces, user groups, interest groups, consortium, forum, alliances,* or

| Organization Name | Abbreviation | Authority/Charter | Mission/Contribution |
|---|---|---|---|
| International Organization for Standardization | ISO | International; voluntary | OSI 7 layer model |
| Comite Consultif International Telegraphique et Telephonique | CCITT | International; U.N. chartered | Telecommunications standards |
| International Telecommunications Union | ITU-T | International; U.N. chartered | Parent organization and successor to CCITT |
| American National Standards Institute | ANSI | U.S. government representative to ISO | Information systems standards |
| Institute of Electrical and Electronics Engineers | IEEE | Industrial professional society | Local area network standards |
| Internet Engineering Task Force | IETF | International, open | Design protocol and other standards for the Internet |
| Internet Architecture Board | IAB | International, open | Oversees the standards process for Internet standards as developed by the IETF |
| Internet Society | ISOC | International, open | Parent organization of the IETF and IAB |
| Electronics Industries Association | EIA | Trade organization | Electrical signaling standards, wiring standards |

*Figure 1-7* Officially Sanctioned Standards-Making Organizations

*institutes*, these groups have developed standards for specific areas of the data communications industry.

Although these ad hoc organizations are able to produce standards faster, in most cases, than official standards-making organizations, their existence and operation pose a few potential problems. Vendor-initiated ad hoc standards-making organizations are occasionally organized into opposing camps, with users left as victims caught between multiple standards for a single item. These vendor-driven consortia do not necessarily have the best interests of end-users as their highest priority. Some ad hoc standards groups do not produce final standards, but rather seek to expedite the standards-making process by hammering out technical debates and issuing unified recommendations to official standards-making organizations for official sanction and ratification.

**Business Impacts of Standards** The standards-making process is important to manufacturers and they monitor it closely and participate in it actively. The development of new technology most often precedes its standardization. The development process is usually performed by either individual manufacturers or groups of manufacturers as part of their research and development work. Competing manufacturers may propose differing technological solutions for a given opportunity. It is often only after these competing technologies are about to come to market that the need for standardization prompts the formation of a standards committee.

It should be obvious that competing manufacturers have a strong desire to get their own technology declared as "the standard." To capture early market share and thereby influence the standards-making process, manufacturers often produce and sell equipment before standards are issued. Make no mistake about it: standards making can be a very political process. Furthermore, by the time standards are actually adopted for a given technology, the next generation of that technology is sometimes ready to be introduced to the market. Figure 1-8 attempts to illustrate this time lag between technological development and standards creation.

## PROPRIETARY STANDARDS

Purchasers of data communications equipment should be wary of buying equipment that complies with proprietary prestandards. Have accommodations been made to upgrade the equipment to comply with official standards once they are issued? Will there be a charge for this upgrade? Will the upgrade require a return to the factory, or is it a software upgrade that can be downloaded and installed in the field?

In general, standards work to the advantage of the data communications consumer, as they allow interoperability of equipment manufactured by a variety of vendors. However, users should be aware of at least two standards-related issues that can cause confusion and potentially lead to bad purchase decisions and operational nightmares.

**Standards Extensions**   Recalling the potentially competitive nature of the standards-making process, it should come as no surprise that final standards are sometimes "least common denominator" implementations of competing proposals. To differentiate their own product offerings, vendors are likely to offer "extensions" to a given "standard." Naturally, one vendor's "extensions" do not necessarily match all the other vendors' "extensions." Users must be careful not only to make sure that a particular vendor's equipment meets industry standards, but also to know *how* the equipment meets the standards and whether or not the vendor has implemented extensions to the standard.

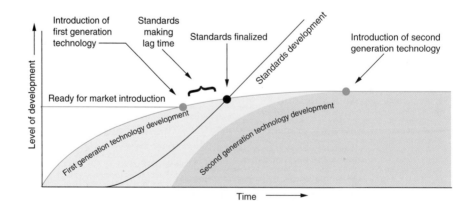

*Figure 1-8*   Technology Development and Standards Creation

The Jargon Jungle   Unfortunately, standards do not apply to the vocabulary used by salespeople and marketing agencies to describe data communications hardware and software technology. There is no standards-making body to regulate data communications vocabulary and its use. As a result, the data communications user is trapped in a situation sometimes referred to as the "jargon jungle." Competing manufacturers often call similar features or operational characteristics by different names, leaving it to the data communications consumer to sort out the differences.

The best way to prevent being lost in the "jargon jungle" is to ask lots of questions. Be prepared to determine functionality of equipment based on operational characteristics rather than on package labels.

## Manufacturing, Research, and Technology

Just as the regulatory and carriers components of the data communications environment were grouped together based on their respective interactions, many of the remaining component entities portrayed in Figure 1-1 can be legitimately grouped together based on their most important interactive force: business.

Supply and Demand   Unlike the formal interactions of proposals and rulings that join regulatory and carrier components, the interacting forces that join the remaining components as well as carriers are supply and demand, basic economic concepts. That's right, *data communications is business.* Figure 1-9 attempts to graphically illustrate the complex relationship among these many data communications environment components. The present status and near-term trends of any particular component are directly related to the net effect of the supply and demand forces of all other components combined.

This same phenomenon is sometimes referred to as **technology push/demand pull.** In a technology push scenario, new technologies may be introduced to the market to spawn innovative uses for this technology and thereby generate demand. Conversely, business needs may create a demand for services or technological innovation that are not currently available. However, the demand pull causes research and development efforts to accelerate, thereby introducing the new technology sooner than it would have otherwise been brought to market.

As an example, business and users may demand faster transfer of data. However, if research has not supplied the technology to accomplish these faster transfers, then manufacturers cannot produce and supply (sell) these products to business and users. Nor can vendors and consultants distribute and recommend their use.

Available technology also plays a key role in the relationship between business and carriers. Understanding that the phone companies are in business to make a profit and therefore need to sell the network services that business is willing to buy at a price business is willing to pay, it should follow that these enabling technologies tie the business demand for network services to the carrier's supply of network services. Stated another way, a carrier cannot provide the network services that businesses demand unless the proper technology is in place. Carriers can afford to invest in new technology only through profitable operations. This dynamic relationship can be expressed in the following equation:

Business Demand + Available Technology = Emerging Network Services

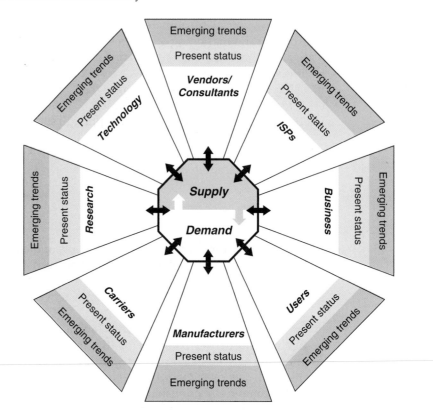

*Figure 1-9*    Supply and Demand as Driving Forces of the Data Communications Industry

## ■ CHALLENGES AND SOLUTIONS TO BUSINESS-ORIENTED DATA COMMUNICATIONS ANALYSIS

Having explored the interacting components of the data communications industry to gain an appreciation of its dynamic nature, the network analyst must next identify the key challenges to success in the data communications field and the potential solutions to those challenges. One of the most important things to realize is that corporations are not interested in investing in technology merely for technology's sake. Rather, implemented technology must produce measurable impact on business goals and requirements. Ensuring and accounting for this technological impact on business goals is a significant challenge.

### Challenge: Information Technology Investment vs. Productivity Gains, Ensuring Implemented Technology Meets Business Needs

In the past decade, over $1 trillion dollars has been invested by business in information technology. Despite this massive investment, carefully conducted research indicates that there has been little if any increase in productivity as a direct result of this investment. This dilemma is known as the **productivity paradox.** How did so much money get invested in technology that failed to deliver increases in productivity? What was the nature of the analysis and design process that recommended the purchase of this technology? Clearly, something is wrong with an analysis and design process that recommends technology implementations that fail to meet the strategic business objective of increased productivity.

What are the characteristics required of an analysis and design process that has the potential to overcome the productivity paradox? How can a network analyst remain properly focused on business requirements while performing technology analysis? Bringing this general investment in technology issue down to a particular investment in data communications and networking, it may be safe to say that: If the network doesn't make good business sense, it probably makes no sense.

To overcome the productivity paradox, a structured methodology must be followed to ensure that the implemented network technology meets the communications and business needs of the intended business, organization, or individual. The top-down approach and benchmarking are two potential solutions to the productivity paradox.

Applied Problem
Solving

## SOLUTION: THE TOP-DOWN APPROACH

One such structured methodology is known as the top-down approach. Such an approach can be graphically illustrated in a **top-down model** shown in Figure 1-10. Use of the top-down approach as illustrated in the top-down model is relatively straightforward. Insisting that a top-down approach to network analysis and design is undertaken should ensure that the network design implemented meets the business needs and objectives that motivated the design in the first place.

This top-down approach requires network analysts to understand business constraints and objectives, as well as information systems applications and the data on which those applications run, before considering data communications and networking options.

Notice where the network layer occurs in the top-down model. It is no accident that data communications and networking form the foundation of today's sophisticated

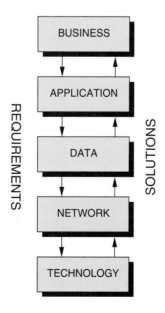

*Figure 1-10*  The Top-Down Model

information systems. A properly designed network supports flexible delivery of data to distributed application programs, allowing businesses to respond quickly to customer needs and rapidly changing market conditions.

**The Top-Down Model**    How does the proper use of the top-down model ensure effective, business-oriented network analysis and design? Figure 1-11 lists the analysis processes associated with each layer of the top-down model. One must start with the *business* level objectives. What is the company (organization, individual) trying to accomplish by installing this network? Without a clear understanding of business level objectives it is nearly impossible to configure and implement a successful network. In many cases, businesses take this opportunity to critically reexamine their business processes in an analysis methodology known as **business process reengineering (BPR).**

Once business level objectives are understood, one must understand the *applications* that will be running on the computer systems attached to these networks. After all, it is the applications that will be generating the traffic that will travel over the implemented network.

Once applications are understood and have been documented, the *data* that the applications generate must be examined. In this case, the term *data* is used in a general

| Top-Down Model Layer | Associated Analysis Processes |
|---|---|
| **Business Layer** | • Strategic business planning<br>• Business process reengineering<br>• Identify major business functions<br>• Identify business processes<br>• Identify business opportunities |
| **Applications Layer** | • Applications development<br>• Systems analysis and design<br>• Identify information needs<br>• Relate information needs to business processes and opportunities |
| **Data Layer** | • Database analysis and design<br>• Data modeling<br>• Data distribution analysis<br>• Client/server architecture design<br>• Distributed database design<br>• Relate data collection and distribution to information and business needs |
| **Network Layer** | • Network analysis and design<br>• Logical network design (what)<br>• Network implementation planning<br>• Network management and performance monitoring<br>• Relate logical network design to data collection and distribution design |
| **Technology Layer** | • Technology analysis grids<br>• Hardware software-media technology analysis<br>• Physical network design (how)<br>• Physical network implementation<br>• Relate physical network design to logical network design |

*Figure 1-11*    Analysis Processes of the Top-Down Model

sense, as today's networks are likely to transport a variety of payloads including voice, video, image, and fax in addition to true data. Data traffic analysis must determine not only the amount of data to be transported, but also important characteristics about the nature of that data.

Once data traffic analysis has been completed, the following should be known:

- Physical locations of data                          (Where?)

- Data characteristics and compatibility issues       (What?)

- Amount of data generated and transported            (How much?)

Given these requirements as determined by the upper layers of the top-down model, the next job is to determine the requirements of the *network* that will possess the capability to deliver this data in a timely, cost-effective manner. These network performance criteria could be referred to as *what* the implemented network must do to meet the business objectives outlined at the outset of this top-down analysis. These requirements are also referred to as the **logical network design.**

The *technology* layer analysis, in contrast, determines *how* various hardware and software components are combined to build a functional network that meets the pre-determined business objectives. The delineation of required technology is referred to as the **physical network design.**

Overall, the relationship between the layers of the top-down model can be described as follows: analysis at upper layers produces requirements that are passed down to lower layers, while solutions meeting these requirements are passed back to upper layers. If this relationship among layers holds true throughout the business oriented network analysis, then the implemented technology (bottom layer) should meet the initially outlined business objectives (top layer). Hence, the name, top-down approach.

## SOLUTION: BENCHMARKING

Applied Problem
Solving

If using the top-down approach ensures that implemented technology meets business objectives, how can the impact of implemented technology on business objectives be measured? Without measurement, the top-down approach can't be proven to be any more effective at overcoming the productivity paradox than any other analysis and design methodology. In the age of limited professional staffs and operating budgets, network managers must be able to prove the strategic importance of networking resources to achieve overall business objectives. Without such proof, network managers may soon find themselves and their staffs replaced by outside contractors.

One way to demonstrate the impact of implemented technology is to tie networking costs to business value through a process known as **benchmarking.** Benchmarking can be summarized into the following three major steps:

1. Examine and document quantifiable improvements to business processes.

2. Perform surveys to measure customer satisfaction with deployed network services.

3. Compare actual implementation costs with the cost to purchase similar services from outside vendors (outsourcing) or examine other companies in the same vertical market to compare costs.

Benchmarking the impact of networking technology is not an exact science. Although costs are relatively easy to quantify, the same cannot be said for benefits. Controlling all variables affecting business improvement is difficult at best. For example, how can improved business performance be directly attributed to network improvements while eliminating such variables as an improved economy or a reduction in competition?

## Challenge: Analysis of Complex Data Communications Connectivity and Compatibility Issues

Assuming that the proper use of the top-down model will ensure that implemented technical solutions will meet stated business requirements, the more technical challenges of network analysis and design must be addressed.

**Introduction to Protocols and Compatibility**    Solving incompatibility problems is at the heart of successful network implementation. Compatibility can be thought of as successfully bridging the gap or communicating between two or more technology components, whether hardware or software. This logical gap between components is commonly referred to as an **interface.**

Interfaces may be physical (hardware to hardware) in nature:

- Cables physically connecting to serial ports on a computer.

- A network interface card physically plugging into the expansion bus inside a computer.

Interfaces may also be logical or software-oriented (software to software):

- A network operating system client software (Novell Netware) communicating with the client PC's operating system (Windows).

- A client-based data query tool (Microsoft Access) gathering data from a large database management system (Oracle).

Finally, interfaces may cross the hardware to software boundary:

- A network operating system specific piece of software known as a driver that interfaces to an installed network interface card (NIC).

- A piece of operating system software known as a kernel that interfaces to a computer's CPU chip.

These various interfaces can be successfully bridged to support compatibility between components because of **protocols.** Protocols are nothing more than rules for how communicating hardware and software components bridge interfaces or talk to one another. Protocols may be proprietary (used exclusively by one or more vendors) or open (used freely by all interested parties). Protocols may be officially sanctioned by international standards-making bodies such as the International Organization for Standardization (ISO), or they may be purely market driven (de facto protocols). Figure 1-12 illustrates the relationship between interfaces, protocols, and compatibility.

For every potential hardware-to-hardware, software-to-software, and hardware-to-software interface, there is likely to be one or more protocols supported. The sum of all of the protocols employed in a particular computer is sometimes referred to as

**Hardware to Hardware Interface**

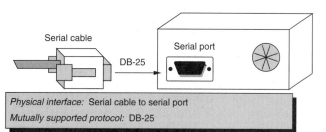

The serial cable is compatible with the serial port.

**Software to Software Interface**

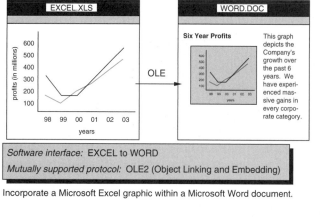

Incorporate a Microsoft Excel graphic within a Microsoft Word document.

**Software to Hardware Interface**

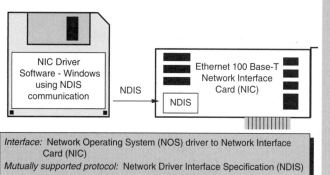

Implementing mutually supported protocols allows interfacing hardware and/or software technology to communicate, thereby ensuring compatibility.

*Figure 1-12*    Interfaces, Protocols, and Compatibility

that computer's **protocol stack.** Successfully determining which protocols must be supported in which instances for the multitude of possible interfaces in a complicated network design is likely to mean the difference between the success or failure of a network implementation.

How can a network analyst possibly keep track of all potential interfaces and their associated protocols? What is needed is a framework in which to organize the various interfaces and protocols in complicated network designs. More than one such framework, otherwise known as communications architectures, exists. Two of the most popular communications architectures are the seven-layer OSI model and the four-layer Internet suite of protocols model.

## SOLUTION: THE OSI NETWORK REFERENCE MODEL

Choosing the technology and protocols that can meet the requirements as determined in the logical network design from the network layer of the top down model requires a structured methodology of its own. Fortunately, the ISO has developed a framework for organizing networking technology and protocol solutions known as the open systems interconnection (OSI) network reference model or OSI model for short. The following section offers the reader only a brief introduction to the overall functionality of the OSI model as a network analysis tool; more detailed information on the model is provided throughout the remainder of the text. The OSI model should be looked on as a powerful, but somewhat complex, tool.

The **OSI Model** consists of a hierarchy of 7 layers that loosely group the functional requirements for communication between two computing devices regardless of the software, hardware, or geographical differences between the devices. The power of the OSI Model, officially known as ISO Standard 7489, lies in its openness and flexibility. It can be used to organize and define protocols involved in communicating between two computing devices located in the same room as effectively as two devices located on opposite sides of the world.

Each layer in the OSI Model relies on lower layers to perform more elementary functions and to offer total transparency as to the intricacies of those functions. At the same time, each layer provides incrementally more sophisticated transparent services to upper layers. In theory, if the transparency of this model is supported, changes in the protocols of one layer should not require changes in protocols of other layers. A **protocol** is a set of rules that govern communication between hardware and/or software components.

**Physical Layer**    The **physical layer,** also known as layer 1, is responsible for the establishment, maintenance and termination of physical connections between communicating devices. The physical layer transmits and receives a stream of bits. There is no data recognition at the physical layer.

Specifically, the physical layer operation is controlled by protocols that define the electrical, mechanical, and procedural specifications for data transmission. The RS232-C specification for serial transmission is an example of a physical layer protocol. Strictly speaking, the physical layer does not define the specifications for connectors and cables that are sometimes referred to as belonging to Layer 0. The physical layer will be covered in detail in chapter 3.

**DataLink Layer**    The **data-link layer** is responsible for providing protocols that deliver reliable point-to-point connections. The data-link layer is of particular interest to the study of local area networks as this is the layer in which network architecture standards are defined. These standards are debated and established by the **Institute of Electrical and Electronic Engineers (IEEE) 802** committee and will be introduced and explained later in this chapter. The number 802 is derived from the date of the committee's formation in 1980 (80) in the month of February (2).

The data-link layer provides reliability to the physical layer transmission by organizing the bit stream into structured **frames** which add addressing and error checking information. Additional information added to the front of data is called a **header,** while information added to the back of data is called a **trailer.** Data-link layer protocols provide error detection, notification, and recovery.

The data-link layer frames are built within the **network interface card** installed in a computer according to the pre-determined frame layout particular to the network architecture of the installed network interface card. Network interface cards are given a unique address in a format determined by their network architecture. These addresses are usually assigned and pre-programmed by the NIC manufacturer. The network interface card provides the connection to the LAN, transferring any data frames that are addressed to it from the connected network media to the computer's memory for processing.

The first two layers of the OSI model, physical and data link, are typically manifested as hardware (media and NICs, respectively) whereas the remaining layers of the OSI model are all installed as software protocols. The Data-Link layer will be covered in detail in chapter 4.

In order to allow the OSI Model to more closely adhere to the protocol structure and operation of a local area network, the IEEE 802 committee split the data-link layer into two sub-layers.

*Media Access Control*    The **media access control** or **MAC sub-layer** interfaces with the physical layer and is represented by protocols which define how the shared local area network media is to be accessed by the many connected computers. As will be explained more fully later is this chapter, Token ring (IEEE 802.5) and Ethernet (IEEE 802.3) networks use different media access methodologies and are therefore assigned different IEEE 802 protocol numbers. Unique addresses assigned to NICs at the time of manufacturer are commonly referred to as MAC addresses or MAC layer addresses.

*Logical Link Control*    The upper sub-layer of the data-link layer which interfaces to the network layer is known as the **logical link control** or **LLC sub-layer** and is represented by a single IEEE 802 protocol (IEEE 802.2). The LLC sub-layer also interfaces transparently to the MAC sublayer protocol beneath it. The advantage to splitting the data-link layer into two sub-layers and to having a single, common LLC protocol is that it offers transparency to the upper layers (network and above) while allowing the MAC sub-layer protocol to vary independently. In terms of technology, the splitting of the sub-layers and the single LLC protocol allows a given network operating system to run equally well over a variety of different network architectures as embodied in network interface cards.

*Network Layer*    The **network layer** protocols are responsible for the establishment, maintenance, and termination of **end-to-end network links.** Network layer protocols are required when computers that are not physically connected to the same LAN must communicate. Network layer protocols are responsible for providing network layer (end-to-end) addressing schemes and for enabling inter-network routing of network layer data **packets.** The term packets is usually associated with network layer protocols while the term frames is usually associated with data-link layer protocols. Unfortunately, not all networking professionals or texts adhere to this generally accepted convention. Addressing schemes and routing will be thoroughly reviewed in the remainder of the text.

Network layer protocols are part of a particular network operating system's protocol stack. Different networking operating systems may use different network layer protocols. Many network operating systems have the ability to use more than one network layer protocol. This capability is especially important to heterogeneous, multi-platform, multi-vendor client/server computing environments. The network layer will be covered in detail in chapter 7.

**Transport Layer**    Just as the data-link layer was responsible for providing reliability for the physical layer, the **transport layer** protocols are responsible for providing reliability for the end-to-end network layer connections. Transport layer protocols provide end-to-end error recovery and flow control. Transport layer protocols also provide mechanisms for sequentially organizing multiple network layer packets into a coherent **message.**

Transport layer protocols are supplied by a given network operating system and are most often closely linked with a particular network layer protocol. For example, NetWare uses IPX/SPX in which Internet Packet Exchange (IPX) is the network layer protocol and Sequenced Packet Exchange (SPX) is the transport layer protocol. Another popular transport/network protocol duo is TCP/IP in which TCP (Transmission Control Protocol) is the transport layer protocol that provides reliability services for IP (Internet Protocol), the network layer protocol. The transport layer will be covered in detail in chapter 7.

**Session Layer**    **Session layer** protocols are responsible for establishing, maintaining, and terminating sessions between user application programs. Sessions are interactive dialogues between networked computers and are of particular importance to distributed computing applications in a client/server environment. As the area of distributed computing is in an evolutionary state, the session layer protocols may be supplied by the distributed application, the network operating system, or a specialized piece of additional software designed to render differences between computing platforms transparent, known as middleware. RPC, or remote procedure call protocol, is one example of a session layer protocol. The session layer will be covered in detail in chapter 7.

**Presentation Layer**    The **presentation layer** protocols provide an interface between user applications and various presentation-related services required by those applications. For example, data encryption/decryption protocols are considered presentation layer protocols as are protocols that translate between encoding schemes such as ASCII to EBCDIC. A common misconception is that graphical user interfaces such as Microsoft Windows and X-Windows are presentation layer protocols. This is not true. Presentation-layer protocols are dealing with network communications whereas Microsoft Windows and/or X-Windows are installed on end-user computers.

**Application Layer**    The **application layer,** layer 7 of the OSI Model is also open to misinterpretation. Application layer protocols do not include end-user application programs. Rather, they include utilities and network-based services that support end-user application programs. Some people include network operating systems in this category. Strictly speaking, the best examples of application layer protocols are the OSI protocols X.400 and X.500. X.400 is an open systems protocol that offers interoperability between different e-mail programs and X.500 offers e-mail directory synchronization among different e-mail systems. DNS, Domain Name Service, which is an Internet protocol that resolves a computer's common or domain name to a specific IP address, is also considered an application layer protocol.

Figure 1-13 offers a conceptual view of the OSI Model and summarizes many of the previous comments.

Network analysts literally talk in terms of the OSI model. When troubleshooting network problems, inevitably the savvy network analyst starts with the physical layer (layer 1) and ensures that protocols and interfaces are operational at each layer before moving up the OSI model. Another benefit of the OSI model is that it allows

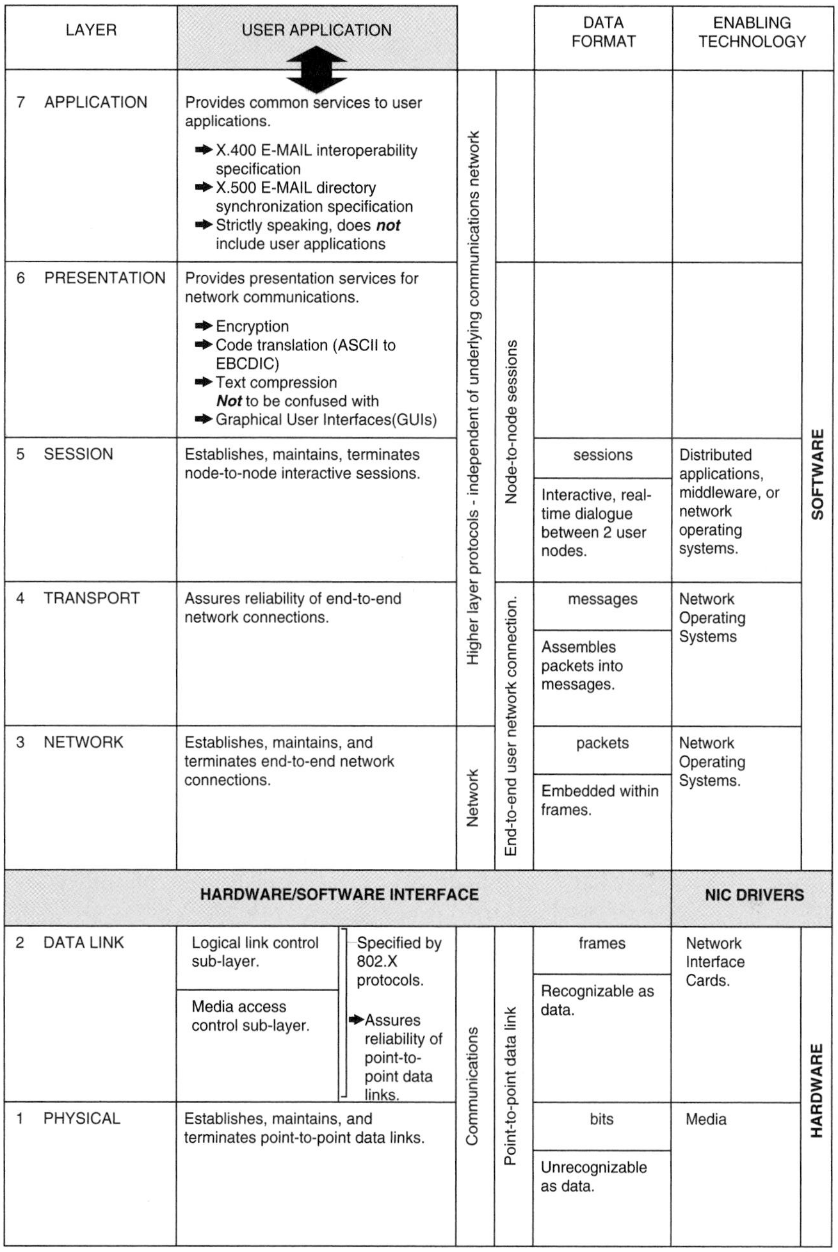

| LAYER | USER APPLICATION | | | DATA FORMAT | ENABLING TECHNOLOGY | |
|---|---|---|---|---|---|---|
| | ⬆ | | | | | |
| 7 APPLICATION | Provides common services to user applications. → X.400 E-MAIL interoperability specification → X.500 E-MAIL directory synchronization specification → Strictly speaking, does **not** include user applications | Higher layer protocols - independent of underlying communications network | Node-to-node sessions | | | SOFTWARE |
| 6 PRESENTATION | Provides presentation services for network communications. → Encryption → Code translation (ASCII to EBCDIC) → Text compression **Not** to be confused with → Graphical User Interfaces(GUIs) | | | | | |
| 5 SESSION | Establishes, maintains, terminates node-to-node interactive sessions. | | | sessions / Interactive, real-time dialogue between 2 user nodes. | Distributed applications, middleware, or network operating systems. | |
| 4 TRANSPORT | Assures reliability of end-to-end network connections. | | End-to-end user network connection. | messages / Assembles packets into messages. | Network Operating Systems | |
| 3 NETWORK | Establishes, maintains, and terminates end-to-end network connections. | | Network | packets / Embedded within frames. | Network Operating Systems. | |
| **HARDWARE/SOFTWARE INTERFACE** | | | | | **NIC DRIVERS** | |
| 2 DATA LINK | Logical link control sub-layer. / Media access control sub-layer. | Specified by 802.X protocols. / → Assures reliability of point-to-point data links. | Communications / Point-to-point data link | frames / Recognizable as data. | Network Interface Cards. | HARDWARE |
| 1 PHYSICAL | Establishes, maintains, and terminates point-to-point data links. | | | bits / Unrecognizable as data. | Media | |

*Figure 1-13*   OSI Model—A Conceptual View

data communications technology developers and standards developers to talk about the interconnection of two networks or computers in common terms without dealing in proprietary vendor jargon.

These "common terms" are the result of the layered architecture of the seven-layer OSI model. The architecture breaks the task of two computers communicating with each other into separate but interrelated tasks, each represented by its own layer. As can be seen in Figure 1-13, the top layer (layer 7) represents services offered to the application programs running on each computer and is therefore aptly named the application layer. The bottom layer (layer 1) is concerned with the actual physical connection of the two computers or networks and is therefore named the physical layer. The remaining layers (2–6) may not be as obvious but, nonetheless, represent a sufficiently distinct logical group of functions required to connect two computers, as to justify a separate layer. As will be seen later in the text, some of the layers are divided into sublayers.

To use the OSI model, a network analyst lists the known protocols for each computing device or network node in the proper layer of its own seven-layer OSI model. The collection of these categorized protocols is known as the protocol stack of the network node. For example, the physical media employed, such as unshielded twisted pair, coaxial cable, or fiber optic cable, would be entered as a layer 1 protocol, while Ethernet or token ring network architectures might be entered as a layer 2 protocol. As will be seen later in chapter 4, a given computer may employ more than one protocol on one or more layers of the OSI model. In these cases, such computers are described as supporting multiple protocol stacks or simply as multiprotocol.

The OSI model allows network analysts to produce an accurate inventory of protocols present on any given network node. This protocol profile represents a unique personality of each network node and gives the network analyst some insight into what **protocol conversion,** if any, may be necessary to allow any two network nodes to communicate successfully. Ultimately, the OSI model provides a structured methodology for determining the hardware and software technology required in the physical network design to meet the requirements of the logical network design.

Perhaps the best analogy for the OSI model is an assembly line producing an automobile. Although each process or step is independently managed and performed, each step also depends on previous steps to be performed according to standardized specifications or protocols for the overall process to be successful. Similarly, each layer of the OSI model operates independently while depending on neighboring layers to perform tasks according to specification while cooperating in the attainment of the overall task of communication between two computers or networks.

The OSI model is not a protocol or group of protocols. It is a standardized, empty framework into which protocols can be listed to perform an effective network analysis and design. As will be seen later in the text, however, the ISO has also produced a set of OSI protocols that correspond to some of the layers of the OSI model. It is important to differentiate between the OSI model and OSI protocols.

The OSI model is used throughout the remainder of the text as the protocol stacks of various network operating systems are analyzed and in the analysis and design of advanced network connectivity alternatives.

Applied Problem
Solving

### SOLUTION: THE INTERNET SUITE OF PROTOCOLS MODEL

Although the OSI model is perhaps more famous than any OSI protocol, just the opposite is true for the **Internet suite of protocols model** and its associated protocols. Also known as the **TCP/IP** protocol suite, or **TCP/IP** architecture, this communications architecture takes its name from **transmission control protocol/Internet protocol,** the de facto standard protocols for open systems internetworking. As can be seen in Figure 1-14, TCP and IP are just two of the protocols associated with this model.

Like the OSI model, the TCP/IP model is a layered communications architecture in which upper layers use the functionality offered by lower layer protocols. Each

| Layer | OSI | INTERNET | Data Format | Protocols |
|-------|-----|----------|-------------|-----------|
| 7 | Application | Application | Messages or Streams | TELNET FTP TFTP SMTP SNMP HTTP |
| 6 | Presentation | | | |
| 5 | Session | Transport or Host-Host | Transport Protocol Packets | TCP UDP |
| 4 | Transport | | | |
| 3 | Network | Internet | IP Diagrams | IP |
| 2 | Data Link | Network Access | Frames | |
| 1 | Physical | | | |

*Figure 1-14*    Internet Suite of Protocols vs. OSI

layer's protocols are able to operate independently from the protocols of other layers. For example, protocols on a given layer can be updated or modified without having to change the protocols in any other layers. A recent example of this independence is the new version of IP known as IPng (IP next generation) developed in response to a pending shortage of IP addresses. This proposed change is possible without the need to change all other protocols in the TCP/IP communication architecture. The exact mechanics of how TCP/IP and related protocols work are explored in greater depth in Chapter 7.

Figure 1-14 compares the four layer Internet suite of protocols model with the seven-layer OSI model. Either communications architecture can be used to analyze and design communication networks. In the case of the internet suite of protocols model, the full functionality of internetwork communications is divided into four layers rather than seven. Because of the fewer layers and the dominant market position of TCP/IP, some network analysts consider the internet suite of protocols model to be more simple and practical than the OSI model.

## SOLUTION: THE I-P-O MODEL

Applied Problem Solving

Once the protocols are determined for two or more computers that wish to communicate, the next step is to determine the technology required to deliver the identified internetworking functionality and protocols.

To understand the basic function of any piece of networking equipment, one really need only understand the differences between the characteristics of the data that came in and the data that went out. Those differences identified were processed by the data communications equipment.

This input-processing-output or **I-P-O model** is another key model used throughout the textbook to analyze a wide variety of networking equipment and opportunities. The I-P-O model provides a framework in which to focus on the difference between the data that came into a particular networked device (I) and the data that came out of that same device (O). By defining this difference, the processing (P) performed by the device is documented.

As a simple example of the use of the I-P-O model, let's assume that we wish to hook a particular PC to a particular printer. After some investigation, we discover that the PC can provide input (I) to the printer (O) only through the PC's serial port. However, the printer (O) only has a parallel interface. As a result, we have a serial interface (perhaps DB-25, RS-232) as an input and have a parallel interface (centronics connector) as an output. What is required is a device to provide the necessary (P) recessing to convert our serial input to the required parallel output. Such devices are readily available. However, before purchasing such a device, it is essential to have organized and documented the required electrical and mechanical protocols that must be interfaced and converted between. By organizing such interfaces in a simple I-P-O model, the exact conversions that must take place are immediately evident.

Although at first glance the I-P-O model may seem overly simplistic, it is another valuable model that can assist network analysts in organizing thoughts, documenting requirements, and articulating needs.

## ■ THE DATA COMMUNICATIONS PROFESSION

### Where Does Data Communications Fit in an Overall Information Systems Architecture?

How is a top-down approach to data communications analysis and design actually implemented in today's corporations? What is the overall information systems structure into which this top-down approach fits? Figure 1-15 illustrates one way in which a top-down approach could be implemented within the overall framework of an information systems architecture.

Several key points illustrated in the diagram are worth noting. Predictably, the entire information systems development process begins with the business analysis process. What is important to note, however, is that all major sections of the top-down approach model—business, applications, data, and network—take part in the business analysis process.

In some cases, a separate technology assessment group exists within a corporation and partakes in the business analysis phase of the information systems development process. In so doing, each layer of the top-down model is represented by trained individuals and complementary processes in the top-down approach to information systems development. This initial participation of all segments of the information systems development team in the business analysis portion of the process ensures that the implemented system will adequately support the business functions for which it was intended.

After this initial participation of all segments of the team in the business analysis phase, each segment develops its portion of the information system. However, merely knowing the business needs that an information system is trying to meet is an insufficient guarantee of successful implementation. It is essential that during the development process, the applications, database, network, and technology development teams continually communicate to ensure that their finished subsystems will interoperate effectively enough to support the identified business needs. This critical communication between subsystems as well as between the individuals who developed these subsystems is illustrated in Figure 1-15.

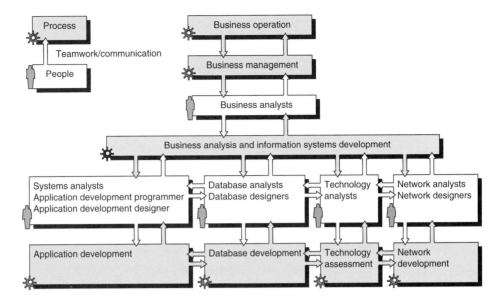

*Figure 1-15*    The Top-Down Approach to Information Systems Development

## Professional Development

The accomplishment of this communication between business, application, database, network, and technology analysts should not be taken for granted. These analysts must be able to speak each other's languages and jargon to communicate effectively. The need to understand all aspects of the information systems architecture has major implications for the proper training of data communications and networking professionals.

Unless one understands "the big picture" of the top-down model, one cannot effectively design and implement the data communications and networking foundation to support this same big picture. Put another way, data communications cannot be studied in a vacuum. The study of data communications and networking must be approached from "the big picture" perspective, ever-mindful of the tremendous potential effect that data communications and networking decisions have on this same big picture.

**Critical Skills for Data Communications Professionals**    To understand the critical skills required of data communications professionals, one must first thoroughly understand the business environment in which these professionals operate. Today's economic environment has been alternatively described as the information age or a knowledge-based economy. Characteristics of such an economy are the recognition of information as a corporate asset to be leveraged for competitive advantage and the need for highly reliable networks to support the mission-critical applications that deliver valuable information to key decision makers.

Such an economic environment requires data communications professionals who can move beyond their technical expertise and specialization by demonstrating the ability to solve business problems. In this role, data communications professionals will be seen increasingly as change agents and partners and less as technology experts and consultants.

So what do the current trends in data communications indicate in terms of employment opportunities? Given the recognition by business of the importance of networks and given the complicated nature of both the data communications technology and the integration of that technology to carrier-provided network services, job opportunities should be excellent for data communications professionals who:

- Understand and can speak "business."

- Demonstrate an ability to own and solve business problems in a partnership rather than consultative role.

- Demonstrate an ability to look outside their own expertise for solutions.

- Exhibit an understanding of the need for lifelong learning.

- Demonstrate an ability to evaluate technology with a critical eye as to cost/benefit and potential for significant business impact of that technology.

- Understand comparative value and proper application of available network services and can work effectively with carriers to see that implementations are completed properly and cost effectively.

- Communicate effectively, both verbally and orally, with both technically oriented people and business management personnel.

The multitalented nature of these data communications professionals is illustrated in Figure 1-16.

**The Certification Question**    Certification as an indication of mastery of a particular technology may be important in some employment situations. Figure 1-17 lists some of the certifications available to data communications professionals.

Some concerns with certification programs are

- The amount of practical, hands-on experience required to earn a given certification.

- The amount of continuing education and experience required to retain a certification.

- Vendor-specific certifications do not provide the broad background required for today's multivendor internetworks.

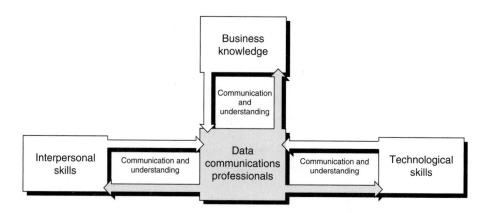

*Figure 1-16*    Critical Skills for Data Communications Professionals

| Vendor/Sponsor | Certification |
|---|---|
| **COMPTIA** | A+ (hardware), Network+ (network) |
| **Microsoft** | Certified systems engineer (MCSE) |
| **Novell** | Certified Novell engineer (CNE) |
| **Cisco Systems** | Cisco certified network associate (CCNA)<br>Cisco certified internetwork expert (CCIE) |

*Figure 1-17*    Vendor-Specific Certifications

**The Opportunity**    To say that these are exciting times in the field of data communications is an understatement of untold proportions. The opportunities are indeed significant for those individuals properly prepared. We invite you to enter the exciting world of data communications with us. We are confident that it is a journey you will not soon forget.

## SUMMARY

Today's data communications industry is characterized by an environment consisting of a group of interacting components such a business, technology and research, standards-making organizations, regulatory agencies, and common carriers. The state of the overall industry at any time is the product of the interaction of these components. To be an effective participant in the data communications field, one must be aware of the forces at work that are shaping the industry.

The data communications industry was traditionally tightly regulated. Although changes such as the breakup of AT&T in the early 1980s and the Telecommunications Act of 1996 have moved the marketplace toward a competitive model, local telephone and cable rates are still tightly regulated.

Data communications and networking are integral parts of an overall information systems architecture. The ultimate success of an implemented information system depends largely on the design of the network that forms the foundation of that system. This high degree of integration between networking and other information system architecture components is graphically illustrated in the top-down model.

The top-down model implies that any information system design must begin with a thorough understanding of business requirements before subsequent issues such as applications, data, networking, and technology are addressed.

The integrated nature of the network layer of an information systems architecture is mirrored in the skills required of today's data communications professionals. The demand is high for individuals well versed in business analysis, information systems, and networking design combined with outstanding written and verbal communications skills.

Remember—if the network does not make good business sense, it probably makes no sense at all.

## KEY TERMS

access charges
benchmarking
business process reengineering
carriers
central office

CLEC
CO
co-location
competitive local exchange carriers
data communications

demand pull
deregulation
divestiture
equal access
I-P-O model

interexchange carriers
interface
Internet suite of protocols model
IXC
LATA
LEC
local access transport area
local exchange carrier
local loops
logical network design
MFJ
Modified Final Judgment
OSI seven-layer model

outsourcing
physical network design
point of presence
POP
productivity paradox
protocol conversion
protocol stack
protocols
PSTN
public switched telephone
    network
RBOC
regional Bell operating companies

regulatory agencies
standards
TCP/IP
technology push
telecommunications
Telecommunications Act of 1996
top-down model
transmission control
    protocol/Internet protocol
universal access
universal carriers
universal service

## REVIEW QUESTIONS

1. What are the major interacting components that make up today's data communications industry?
2. What are the specific interaction scenarios between the following components: manufacturers and standards-making organizations; business and manufacturers; carriers and regulatory agencies; carriers and political/judicial/legislative?
3. Where does data communications and networking fit in an overall information systems architecture?
4. What is the role of business requirements analysis in network analysis and design?
5. What is the top-down model and how is it employed in network analysis and design?
6. Define the relationship between the following terms: inter-LATA and intra-LATA, CO and POP, local loop and RBOC.
7. What is the overall intent of the Telecommunications Act of 1996?
8. What has been the impact of the Telecommunications Act of 1996 on the traditional telecommunications players?
9. What skills are required of today's data communications professional?
10. What is divestiture and how does it differ from deregulation?
11. What is an RBOC?
12. Why is the data communications industry in such a state of change?
13. What is the Modified Final Judgment and why is it important?
14. What are the key events that led up to divestiture and deregulation?
15. Who were the big winners and losers as a result of divestiture?
16. From a data communications user's perspective, what have been the most important impacts of divestiture and deregulation?
17. Explain how carriers can engage in both regulated and unregulated business ventures.
18. Which agencies are responsible for regulation of carriers on both a state and federal level?
19. What is the OSI model and why is it important?
20. Why is the standards-making process so politically charged at times?
21. Why do standards often lag behind technological development?
22. What are the possible business impacts of standards on a manufacturer of data communications equipment?
23. How do the laws of supply and demand apply to the data communications industry? Give examples.
24. What is benchmarking and how is it related to the top-down model?
25. What is the I-P-O model and of what value is it?
26. What are the major processes performed by most data communications equipment?
27. Distinguish between and give an example of each of the three types of interfaces discussed in the chapter.
28. What is the relationship between interfaces, protocols, and standards?
29. What is meant by the statement, "Data communications solutions are business solutions"?
30. What is the Internet suite of protocols model?
31. Describe the similarities and differences between the OSI model and the Internet suite of protocols model.
32. What are the benefits and shortcomings of certification?
33. What are the major differences between logical network design and physical network design?
34. Explain how the processes associated with each layer of the top-down model contribute to effective information systems development.

35. How can one avoid wasting money on technology that does not improve productivity?

36. What kinds of opportunities are available in the data communications industry for properly trained graduates?

37. How can equations such as "Business Demands + Available Technology = Emerging Network Services" remain useful to you in the future?

38. What is the productivity paradox and why should a network analyst be concerned with it?

**Case Study:** For a business case study and questions on the data communications industry, go to www.wiley.com/college/goldman.

# CHAPTER 2

# DATA COMMUNICATIONS CONCEPTS

### *Concepts Reinforced*

I-P-O model                    Protocols & compatibility

### *Concepts Introduced*

Data digitization                    Analog vs. digital communications
Half-duplex vs. full-duplex          Synchronous vs. asynchronous
Data compression                         transmission
Modulation techniques                Baud rate vs. transmission rate
Packetization                        Multiplexing
Error detection and correction       Flow control
Circuit vs. packet switching         Connectionless vs. connection-
Serial vs. parallel communications       oriented networks

## OBJECTIVES

Upon successful completion of this chapter, you should be able to:

1.  Distinguish between the following related concepts and understand the proper application of each of the following terms:

    - analog
    - synchronous
    - full duplex
    - serial
    - bps
    - error detection
    - circuit switching
    - connectionless

    - digital
    - asynchronous
    - half duplex
    - parallel
    - baud rate
    - error correction
    - packet switching
    - connection-oriented

2.  Understand the concepts, processes and protocols involved with completing an end-to-end data communications session, including the following:

    - character encoding
    - modulation/demodulation
    - data switching

3.   Understand the impact and limitations of various modulation techniques.

4.   Understand the impact and limitations of various multiplexing techniques.

## ◼ INTRODUCTION

This chapter introduces the basic concepts and vocabulary of data communications. The concepts and terms introduced in this chapter form the foundation for the data communication technologies introduced later in the book so it is critical to develop a thorough understanding of the material before reading further. Discussions of specific technology will be kept to a minimum in this chapter, concentrating instead on the conceptual aspects of the "how" of data transmission. The in-depth study of communications technology, including its business impact, will begin in chapter 3.

### Overall Data Communication Architecture

Figure 2-1 serves as a roadmap for all of the concepts to be studied in the chapter. An end-to-end communication session between two computers across the Internet offers a framework into which most data communication concepts can be introduced. Each concept will be introduced individually and then explained in terms of its contribution to the overall end-to-end communication.

In this chapter, basic data communications concepts are introduced in a generic manner. These concepts are implemented in specific data communications technologies in different ways, depending on the environment the technology is intended to operate. Multiple technologies including modems, cable modems, and digital subscriber line (DSL) technologies can be used as the actual mechanism for gaining access to the Internet. These technologies, along with the manner in which they implement the basic data communication concepts, will be discussed in chapter 3.

This chapter will focus on the basic data communications concepts used in each of the areas defined in Figure 2-1. The technologies used to implement each portion of the overall end-to-end communication link will be introduced in the following chapters:

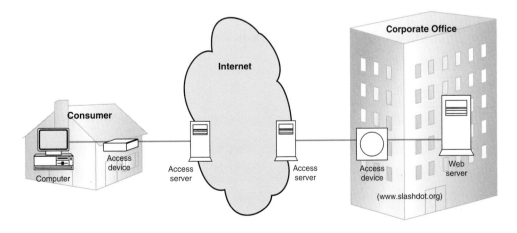

*Figure 2-1*   Basic Data Communications Concepts Used to Access the Internet

- PC to access device and access device to access server—chapter 3
- Local area networks—chapter 4
- Access device to access device across the Internet—chapter 6
- Network protocols used end-to-end—chapters 7 and 8

## ■ DATA DIGITIZATION

Before it can be sent across a data network, information must be converted from its native human interpretable form into a format native to computers. Humans operate in an analog world. Sounds have varying frequency and loudness, pictures have varying colors and shapes, and each character of text can be one of several options, depending on the language being used.

Computers operate in a digital world: the only values they understand are one and zero. All data must be represented as a series of these two basic values. Each one or zero in the data stream is known as **bit.** The digital data-bit stream is usually broken into chunks of 8 bits, known as a **byte or octet.** The significance of 8 bits to a byte is based on the number of bits required to represent a single character in the most common encoding schemes discussed later in this section.

The process of converting analog human interpretable data into digital data for use by computers is known as *digitization.* There are many different techniques available to digitize data. For audio and video information, specialized computer programs known as CODECS (COder/DECoder) are used. Examples of data streams produced by CODECs include MP3, AAC, and DIVX. In addition to simply providing a means of converting analog data to a digital format, most CODECs provide a means of compressing the data. This compression happens prior to the data entering the data communication system and should not be confused with online data compression techniques discussed later in this chapter. Although a thorough discussion of CODECs and the data conversion algorithms they employ is beyond the scope of this book, their importance to modern data communications systems cannot be overestimated.

For textual information, the process of transforming humanly readable characters into machine-readable code is known as **character encoding.** Using an encoding scheme, characters are turned into a series of ones and zeroes. There are multiple protocols or standards that can be used to code characters. The most commonly used standards include ASCII, EBCDIC, and UNICODE.

### ASCII

**American Standard Code for Information Interchange (ASCII)** is one standardized method for encoding humanly readable characters. Standardized by ANSI, ASCII uses a series of 7 bits to represent 128 ($2^7 = 128$) different characters, including uppercase and lowercase letters, numerals, punctuation and symbols, and specialized control characters. One use of control characters will be explained further in chapter 4. An eighth bit, known as a parity bit, is added to 7-bit ASCII for error detection. Error detection and parity checking will also be described in chapter 4. Figure 2-2 is an ASCII table that illustrates the relationship between characters and their associated ASCII codes.

| | | | Bit 6 | 0 | 0 | 0 | 0 | 1 | 1 | 1 | 1 |
|---|---|---|---|---|---|---|---|---|---|---|---|
| | | MSB | Bit 5 | 0 | 0 | 1 | 1 | 0 | 0 | 1 | 1 |
| | | | Bit 4 | 0 | 1 | 0 | 1 | 0 | 1 | 0 | 1 |
| **LSB** | | | | | | | | | | | |
| Bit 0 | Bit 1 | Bit 2 | Bit 3 | | | | | | | | |
| 0 | 0 | 0 | 0 | NUL | DLE | SP | 0 | @ | P | | p |
| 1 | 0 | 0 | 0 | SOH | DC1 | ! | 1 | A | Q | a | q |
| 0 | 1 | 0 | 0 | STX | DC2 | | 2 | B | R | b | r |
| 1 | 1 | 0 | 0 | ETX | DC3 | # | 3 | C | S | c | s |
| 0 | 0 | 1 | 0 | EOT | DC4 | $ | 4 | D | T | d | t |
| 1 | 0 | 1 | 0 | ENQ | NAK | % | 5 | E | U | e | u |
| 0 | 1 | 1 | 0 | ACK | SYN | & | 6 | F | V | f | v |
| 1 | 1 | 1 | 0 | BEL | ETB | | 7 | G | W | g | w |
| 0 | 0 | 0 | 1 | BS | CAN | ( | 8 | H | X | h | x |
| 1 | 0 | 0 | 1 | HT | EM | ) | 9 | I | Y | i | y |
| 0 | 1 | 0 | 1 | LF | SUB | * | : | J | Z | j | z |
| 1 | 1 | 0 | 1 | VT | ESC | + | ; | K | [ | k | { |
| 0 | 0 | 1 | 1 | FF | FS | , | < | L | \ | l | | |
| 1 | 0 | 1 | 1 | CR | GS | | = | M | ] | m | } |
| 0 | 1 | 1 | 1 | SO | RS | . | > | N | ^ | n | ~ |
| 1 | 1 | 1 | 1 | SI | US | | ? | O | - | o | DEL |

*Figure 2-2*　ASCII Table

## EBCDIC

**Extended Binary Coded Decimal Interchange Code (EBCDIC)** is an IBM proprietary 8-bit code capable of representing 256 different characters, numerals, and control characters ($2^8 = 256$). EBCDIC is the primary coding method used in IBM mainframe applications. Figure 2-3 is an EBCDIC table that illustrates the relationship between characters and their associated EBCDIC codes.

Practical Advice
and Information

### USING ASCII AND EBCDIC TABLES

Using ASCII or EBCDIC tables to interpret character encoding is relatively straightforward. The tables are arranged according to groups of bits otherwise known as *bit patterns*. The bit patterns are divided into groups. In the case of ASCII, bits 6 through 4 are known as the most significant bits (MSB) while bits 3 through 0 are known as the least significant bits (LSB). In the case of EBCDIC, bits 0 through 3 are known as the MSB and bits 4 through 7 are known as the LSB.

In order to find the bit pattern of a particular character, one needs to just combine the bit patterns that intersect in the table at the character in question, remembering that most significant bits always come before least significant bits. In the case of

| | | 0000 | 0001 | 0010 | 0011 | 0100 | 0101 | 0110 | 0111 | 1000 | 1001 | 1010 | 1011 | 1100 | 1101 | 1110 | 1111 |
|---|---|---|---|---|---|---|---|---|---|---|---|---|---|---|---|---|---|
| **MSB** | Bit 0 | 0 | 0 | 0 | 0 | 0 | 0 | 0 | 0 | 1 | 1 | 1 | 1 | 1 | 1 | 1 | 1 |
| | Bit 1 | 0 | 0 | 0 | 0 | 1 | 1 | 1 | 1 | 0 | 0 | 0 | 0 | 1 | 1 | 1 | 1 |
| | Bit 2 | 0 | 0 | 1 | 1 | 0 | 0 | 1 | 1 | 0 | 0 | 1 | 1 | 0 | 0 | 1 | 1 |
| | Bit 3 | 0 | 1 | 0 | 1 | 0 | 1 | 0 | 1 | 0 | 1 | 0 | 1 | 0 | 1 | 0 | 1 |

**LSB**

| Bit 7 | Bit 6 | Bit 5 | Bit 4 | | | | | | | | | | | | | | | | |
|---|---|---|---|---|---|---|---|---|---|---|---|---|---|---|---|---|---|---|---|
| 0 | 0 | 0 | 0 | NUL | DLE | DS | | SP | & | - | | | | | | | | | 0 |
| 1 | 0 | 0 | 0 | SOH | DC1 | SOS | | | | | | a | j | | | A | J | | 1 |
| 0 | 1 | 0 | 0 | STX | DC2 | FS | SYN | | | | | b | k | s | | B | K | S | 2 |
| 1 | 1 | 0 | 0 | ETX | DC3 | | | | | | | c | l | t | | C | L | T | 3 |
| 0 | 0 | 1 | 0 | PF | RES | BYP | PN | | | | | d | m | u | | D | M | U | 4 |
| 1 | 0 | 1 | 0 | HT | NL | LF | RS | | | | | e | n | v | | E | N | V | 5 |
| 0 | 1 | 1 | 0 | LC | BS | EOB | UC | | | | | f | o | w | | F | O | W | 6 |
| 1 | 1 | 1 | 0 | DEL | IL | PRE | EOT | | | | | g | p | x | | G | P | X | 7 |
| 0 | 0 | 0 | 1 | | CAN | | | | | | | h | q | y | | H | Q | Y | 8 |
| 1 | 0 | 0 | 1 | | EM | | | | | | \ | i | r | z | | I | R | Z | 9 |
| 0 | 1 | 0 | 1 | SMM | CC | SM | | >> | ! | | : | | | | | | | | |
| 1 | 1 | 0 | 1 | VT | | | | . | $ | , | # | | | | | | | | |
| 0 | 0 | 1 | 1 | FF | IFS | | DC4 | < | * | % | @ | | | | | | | | |
| 1 | 0 | 1 | 1 | CR | IGS | ENQ | NAK | ( | ) | | | | | | | | | | |
| 0 | 1 | 1 | 1 | SO | IRS | ACK | | + | ; | > | = | | | | | | | | |
| 1 | 1 | 1 | 1 | SI | IUS | BEL | SUB | | | - | ? | | | | | | | | |

*Figure 2-3*    EBCDIC Table

ASCII, this means that bits are arranged from bit 6 to bit 0, while EBCDIC is arranged from bit 0 to bit 7. As an example, representative characters, numerals, and control characters and their bit patterns are highlighted with shading in the ASCII and EBCDIC tables and are displayed in Figure 2-4 in humanly readable, ASCII, and EBCDIC formats.

| Humanly Readable | ASCII | EBCDIC |
|---|---|---|
| A | 1000001 | 11000001 |
| x | 1111000 | 10100111 |
| 5 | 0110101 | 11110101 |
| LF (Line Feed) | 0001010 | 00100101 |

*Figure 2-4*    Human readable characters and their corresponding ASCII and EBCDIC codes

## UNICODE and ISO 10646

ASCII and EBCDIC coding schemes have sufficient capacity to represent letters and characters familiar to people whose alphabets use the letters A, B, C, and so on. However, what happens if the computer needs to support communication in Cantonese or Arabic? It should be obvious that 128 or 256 possible characters will not suffice when other languages and alphabets are considered.

To resolve this issue, two different efforts were undertaken to establish a new coding standard that could support many more alphabets and symbols than ASCII or EBCDIC. The efforts were ultimately combined and a single standard, **International Standards Organization (ISO) 10646,** also known as **UNICODE** Version 1.1 was released in 1993.

UNICODE is a 16-bit code supporting up to 65,536 possible characters ($2^{16} =$ 65,536). It is backward compatible with ASCII because the first 128 characters are identical to the ASCII table. In addition, UNICODE includes more than 2,000 Han characters for languages such as Chinese, Japanese, and Korean. It also includes Hebrew, Greek, Russian, and Sanskrit alphabets as well as mathematical and technical symbols, publishing symbols, geometric shapes, and punctuation marks.

Application programs that display text on a monitor must encode characters according to an encoding scheme understood by the computer's operating system. It is up to the operating systems vendors to include support for particular encoding schemes such as UNICODE/ISO 10646. Windows NT, 2000, and XP, along with most major UNIX variants, support UNICODE.

## ■ DATA TRANSMISSION TECHNIQUES

There are several concepts that apply to all data transmission technologies. This section introduces these key building blocks that will be used throughout the book to define data transmission technologies.

### Serial vs. Parallel Transmission

The bits that represent human-readable characters can be transmitted in either of two basic transmission methodologies: either simultaneously (**parallel transmission**) or in a linear fashion, one after the other (**serial transmission**). The difference between each of these transmission methodologies is illustrated in Figure 2-5.

As illustrated in Figure 2-5, parallel communication is natively faster than serial communication as multiple bits are sent concurrently. There is a key limiting factor to the application of parallel communication, however: The multiple signal lines running in parallel tend to create interference with each other in an electrical transmission environment. The changing electrical signal on one wire creates a magnetic field that induces a ghost copy of the signal onto the surrounding wires. When multiple lines are running in parallel, this tends to quickly muddle the signal. This phenomenon is worsened by transmission speed and distance, thus limiting the application of parallel transmission to fairly short distances.

A common application for parallel communication is communicating between subsystems within a computer. In this application, distance is limited and the system designers can include many ground lines along the bus to bleed off any induced

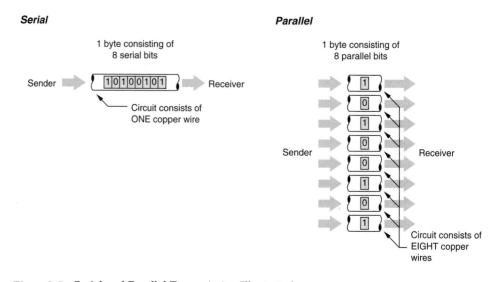

*Figure 2-5*    Serial and Parallel Transmission Illustrated

voltage, thus increasing signal quality. The term bus is often used to refer to a parallel communication channel in this application as in process bus, memory bus, or expansion bus. Common examples of this type of parallel communication include the PCI bus and IDE/ATA and SCSI hard drive connections.

Serial communication is typically used between computers and external devices. In this application the reduced number of wires required to carry the signal means that cables are less expensive and more flexible. For this reason, all local area and wire area network connections are serial in nature. As electronic signaling and sensing components have increased in speed and sensitivity modern serial standards can operate at speeds that can surpass that of their parallel counterparts allowing high-speed serial technologies such as serial ATA to replace older parallel based technologies.

The advantages, limitations and typical applications of parallel and serial transmission methodologies are summarized in Figure 2-6. Most data-communication technologies use serial transmission techniques, all technologies throughout the book can be assumed to use serial communication techniques unless otherwise stated.

| Transmission Characteristic | Serial | Parallel |
|---|---|---|
| Transmission Description | One bit comes after another, one at a time | All bits in a single character are transmitted simultaneously |
| Comparative Speed | Slower | Faster |
| Distance Limitation | Farther | Shorter |
| Application | Between two computers, from computers to external devices, local and wide area networks | Within a computer along the computer's busses, between a drive controller and a hard drive |
| Cable Description | All bits travel down a single wire, one bit at a time | Each bit travels down its own wire simultaneously with other bits |

*Figure 2-6*    Serial Transmission vs. Parallel Transmission Summary

## Synchronous vs. Asynchronous Transmission

When devices are communicating, they are exchanging some sort of detectable signal that represents the data. Unless the devices are so busy that they never stop talking, there will be a time when no signal is being sent across the communication channel. During these "dead" times there is no data being sent across the channel. Later when there is additional data to be sent the sending device will begin signaling again. When this happens there must be a way for the destination device to know when to begin looking for data: The two devices must establish and maintain some type of timing between them so that signals are produced, transmitted, and detected accurately. There are two main alternatives to establishing and maintaining the timing for the sampling of the signals. These two timing alternatives are known as **asynchronous** and **synchronous** transmission.

Figure 2-7 summarizes some important characteristics about asynchronous and synchronous transmission methods for 8-bit character-based data transmission. The most noticeable difference is the manner in which signal synchronization is maintained. In asynchronous communication the synchronization is reestablished with the transmission of each character via the use of start and stop bits. Depending on the technology used there may be 1, 1.5, or 2 stop bits. In synchronous communication the synchronization is maintained by a special synchronization bit in each block of data provided by a clocking signal supplied by the communication devices or the signal carrier. Due to the fewer number of bits used to maintain synchronization in synchronous communication; it is more efficient than asynchronous communications.

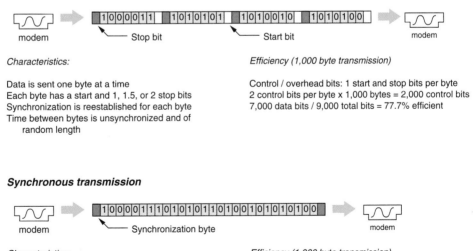

**Asynchronous transmission**

modem → [1|0|0|0|0|1|1] [1|0|1|0|1|0|1] [1|0|1|0|0|1|0] [1|0|1|0|1|0|0] → modem

    — Stop bit       — Start bit

*Characteristics:*

Data is sent one byte at a time
Each byte has a start and 1, 1.5, or 2 stop bits
Synchronization is reestablished for each byte
Time between bytes is unsynchronized and of
   random length

*Efficiency (1,000 byte transmission)*

Control / overhead bits: 1 start and stop bits per byte
2 control bits per byte x 1,000 bytes = 2,000 control bits
7,000 data bits / 9,000 total bits = 77.7% efficient

**Synchronous transmission**

modem → [1|0|0|0|0|1|1|1|0|1|0|1|0|1|1|0|1|0|0|0|1|0|1|0|1|0|1|0|0] → modem

    — Synchronization byte

*Characteristics:*

Data is sent as a block of uninterrupted bytes
Synchronization bytes precede and follow the
   data block
Synchronization is maintained whether data is
   actually being sent and detected or not
Modems remain synchronized during idle time

*Efficiency (1,000 byte transmission)*

Control / overhead bits: 48 total control bits per block
   using HDLC
48 control bits per block x 1 block = 48 control bits
7,000 data bits / 7,048 total bits = 99.3% efficient

*Figure 2-7*    Asynchronous vs. Synchronous Transmission

A second key difference between synchronous and asynchronous transmission is what happens when the line is idle with no data being transmitted. In asynchronous communications all data transmission stops and the communicating devices fall out of synchronization. In synchronous communication the communicating devices continue to transmit special null characters and thus stay in synchronization. The difference between synchronous and asynchronous communications is further illustrated in Figure 2-7.

## Half vs. Full Duplex Communication

Data communications sessions are bidirectional in nature. Even if the objective of the communication is to send a file from the sender to the destination some communication must go from the destination back to the sender. This reverse direction data includes error detection and correction information (covered later in this chapter). There are two environments available for handling this bidirectional traffic: full and half duplex.

In a full duplex communications environment, both devices can transmit at the same time. This is analogous to an in-person conversation: the communications environment allows you to both listen and talk at the same time. In a half duplex environment you can only hear *or* talk at any given point in time. This is similar to a conversation taking place via a walkie-talkie: you can only listen until you push the talk button to transmit. Once you press the talk button you can only transmit until you release it to begin listening again. Similarly, when two data communication devices are communicating in a half duplex environment, one device must be the transmitter and the other the receiver. In order to enable bidirectional communication they periodically have to reverse roles.

This role reversal is known as **turnaround time** and—depending on the environment—can take two-tenths of a second or longer. This might not seem like a very long time, but if this role-reversal needed to be done several thousand times over the course of a communications session, it can significantly affect efficiency and, by extension, cost. Most communication technologies support full duplex communication in some manner, although it is often a configurable choice. Given the choice of full or half duplex, it is usually better to choose full duplex unless there is a significant penalty in transmission speed associated with full duplex.

## Modulation/Demodulation

Although all modern data communications systems transmit digital data, depending on the type of communication channel used for the transmission it might have to be converted to an analog signal for transmission. In this case, the communication equipment at the sending end must convert the signal from its native digital format to an analog signal and transmit it to the destination. The communication equipment at the destination then takes the incoming analog signal, converts it back into a digital signal and relays it to the destination device. The process of converting digital data into an analog signal is known as modulation. Conversely, the process of converting a modulated analog signal back into a digital format is known as demodulation. These processes are illustrated in Figure 2-8.

Communications equipment that handles this conversion of data between digital and analog formats is known as a MOdulator/DEModulator, or **modem.** As shown in Figure 2-9, modems are placed at each end of the analog communication channel between the sending device and the channel.

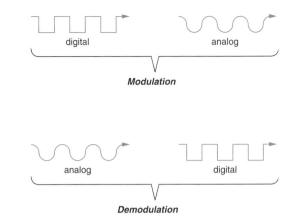

*Figure 2-8*  Modulation vs. Demodulation

**Carrier Waves**  An analog communication channel is used to transmit data in the form of an analog wave. In order to represent the discrete-state ones and zeroes, or bits of digitized data on an analog communication channel it must be converted into different types of waves. A "normal" or "neutral" wave must exist to start with, that can be changed to represent these ones and zeroes.

This "normal" or "neutral" wave is called a **carrier wave.** A sample carrier wave, along with its characteristics, is illustrated in Figure 2-10. Modems generate carrier waves that are altered (modulated) to represent bits of data as ones and zeroes. Before they can communicate, two modems must establish a carrier wave between themselves. Once the carrier wave has been established, the actual data transmission can begin as the modems manipulate the carrier wave to represent ones and zeroes.

How can the carrier wave be manipulated to represent ones and zeroes? There are three physical characteristics of a wave that can be altered or modulated:

- **Amplitude**
- **Frequency**
- **Phase**

As will be seen later in this section, in some modulation schemes more than one of these characteristics can be modulated simultaneously.

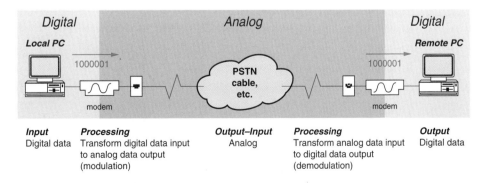

*Figure 2-9*  I-P-O Analysis: Modem Based Communication Channels

**Carrier wave**

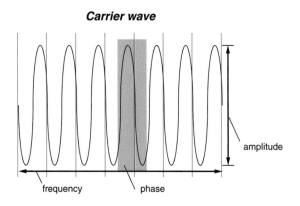

*Figure 2-10* Carrier Wave

**Amplitude Modulation** Figure 2-11 illustrates **Amplitude Modulation** of a carrier wave. Only the amplitude changes; the frequency and phase remain constant. In this example, the portions of the wave with increased height (altered amplitude) represent ones and the unaltered lower wave amplitude represent zeroes. Together, this portion of the wave would represent the letter "A" using the ASCII-7 character encoding scheme.

Each of the vertical lines in Figure 2-11 separates opportunities to identify a one or zero from another. These timed opportunities to identify ones and zeroes by sampling the carrier wave are known as signaling events. The proper name for one signaling event is a **baud.**

**Frequency Modulation** Figure 2-12 represents **frequency modulation** of a carrier wave. Frequency modulation is often referred to as **frequency shift keying,** or **FSK.** The frequency can be thought of as how frequently the same spot on two subsequent waves pass a given point. Waves with a higher frequency will take less time to pass while waves with a lower frequency will take a greater time to pass.

The distance between the same spots on two subsequent waves is called the **wavelength;** the longer the wavelength, the lower the frequency and the shorter the wavelength, the greater the frequency. In Figure 2-12 the higher frequency (shorter wavelength) part of the wave represents a 1 and the lower frequency

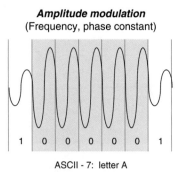

*Figure 2-11* Amplitude Modulation

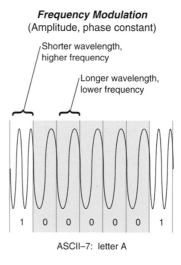

Figure 2-12 Frequency Modulation

(longer wavelength) part of the wave represents a 0, while amplitude and phase remain constant. Again, the entire bit stream represents the letter A in ASCII-7.

**Phase Modulation**   Figure 2-13 illustrates an example of **phase modulation,** also known as **phase shift keying** or **PSK.** Although the phase varies, the frequency and amplitude remain constant. Phase modulation can be thought of as initiating a shift or departure from the "normal" continuous pattern of the wave. In Figure 2-13, the normal carrier wave would follow the broken line, but instead the phase suddenly shifts and heads off in another direction. This phase shift of 180 degrees is a detectable event with each change in phase representing a change in state from 0 to 1 or 1 to 0 in this example.

*Measuring Phase Shift*   In Figure 2-13, the detected analog wave was either the base carrier wave with no phase shift, or it was phase shifted 180 degrees. Given that phase shifts are measured in degrees, there are multiple amounts of phase shift that can be applied to a carrier wave. By increasing the number of possible phase shifts, the number of potential detectable events can be increased. As illustrated in Figure 2-14, when there are just two potential detectable events (no phase shift or

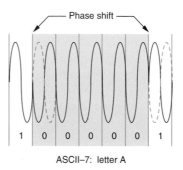

Figure 2-13   Phase Modulation

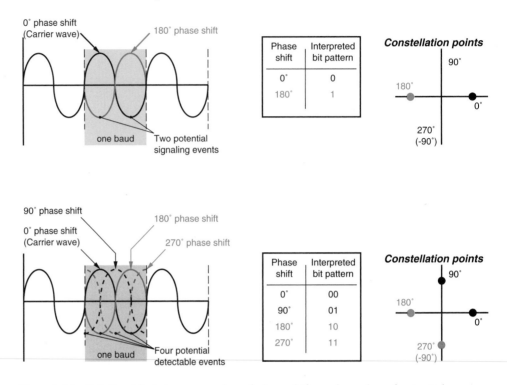

*Figure 2-14*    Relationship between number of phase shifts and number of potential detectable events

180-degree phase shift), the two events represent either a one or a zero, respectively. However, by introducing four potential phase shifts (0, 90, 180, 270), 2 bits can be associated with each detectable event.

A simpler and perhaps clearer way to represent phase shifts as illustrated in Figure 2-14 is through the use of **constellation points.** Using a four-quadrant representation of the 360 degrees of possible phase shift, individual points represent each different shifted wave. Note that when represented in a constellation diagram, a phase shift of 270 degrees is represented as –90 degrees. Phase shift modulation with four different phases is more properly referred to as **quadrature phase shift keying** or **QPSK.**

**Baud Rate vs. Transmission Rate**    The number of signaling events per second is more properly known as the **baud rate.** Although baud rate and **bps** (bits per second) or **transmission rate** are often used interchangeably, the two terms are in fact related, but not identical. In the first illustration in Figure 2-14, only two detectable events were possible meaning that only one bit was interpreted at each signaling event (one bit/baud). Therefore, in this case the baud rate was equal to the transmission rate as expressed in bps (bits per second).

However, in the second illustration in Figure 2-14, four detectable events are possible for each signaling event, making it possible to interpret 2 bits per baud. In this case, the bit rate or transmission rate as measured in bps would be twice the baud rate.

More sophisticated modulation techniques are able to interpret more than one bit per baud. In these cases, the bps is greater than the baud rate. For example, if the baud rate of a modem was 2,400 signaling events per second and the modem was able to interpret 2 bits per signaling event, then the transmission speed would be

4,800 bps. Mathematically, the relationship between baud rate and transmission rate can be expressed as follows:

$$\text{Transmission rate (bps)} = \text{Baud rate} \times \text{bits/baud}$$

## MORE THAN ONE BIT/BAUD

There are really only two ways in which a given modem can transmit data faster:

1. As mentioned previously, increase the signaling events per second, or baud rate.

2. Find a way for the modem to interpret more than one bit per baud.

By modifying a phase modulation technique such as that illustrated in Figure 2-14, a modem can detect, interpret, and transmit more than one bit per baud. The mathematical equation that describes the relationship between the number of potential detectable events and the numbers of bits per baud that can be interpreted is as follows:

$$\text{Number of states} = \text{Number of potential detectable events}^{\text{bits/baud}}$$

- Number of states = always 2 (Data are either a 1 or 0)
- Number of potential detectable events = 4 different phase angles (0, 90, 180, 270) as illustrated in the second illustration in Figure 2-14

To solve:

- To what power must 2 (the number of states) be raised to equal 4 (the number of different detectable events)?

The answer is 2, meaning that 2 bits/baud can be interpreted at a time. Two bits at a time are known as a dibit. By extending the mathematical equation above, it should be obvious that:

| Number of Potential Detectable Events | Number of bits/baud | Also known as |
|---|---|---|
| 8 | 3 | tribit |
| 16 | 4 | quadbit |
| 32 | 5 | |
| 64 | 6 | |
| 128 | 7 | |
| 256 | 8 | |
| 512 | 9 | |

Figure 2-15 shows the encoding of an ASCII A using dibits in differential Quadrature Phase Shift Keying. In this differential approach the phase change is measured in relationship to the previous baud rather than from the original carrier phase. Before

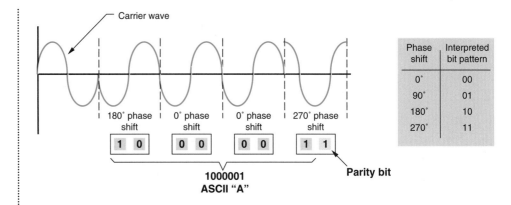

*Figure 2-15*   Differential Quadrature Phase Shift Keying

the ASCII A can be encoded, an eighth bit must be appended to make the total number of bits divisible by 2. This eighth bit is known as a parity bit and is further explained later in the chapter.

Comparing Figure 2-15 with Figure 2-13 shows the increased efficiency of QPSK over simple PSK. Using QPSK, only four baud periods are required to transmit the ASCII "A" using dibits, compared to the seven baud periods required for two-state phase modulation. Given a constant frequency, the data can be transmitted almost twice as fast.

Quadrature Amplitude Modulation   As illustrated in the previous example, increasing the number of phase shifts increases the efficiency (and, by extension, the transmission rate) of the communication channel. Depending on the type and quality of the analog transmission line, it may be possible to further increase the number of phase shifts that can be detected. If the communication channel was good enough to support sixteen different measurable phase shifts (phase shifts of as little as 22.5 degrees) the effective speed of the line could once again be doubled.

However, there is a method of further increasing the efficiency of the communication channel even if it does not support the reliable detection of more than four phase shifts. By combining the modulation of two aspects of the carrier wave, it is possible to add additional signaling events. When modulating multiple aspects of a carrier wave it is most common to modulate the phase and amplitude, while leaving the frequency steady. By varying both phase and amplitude sixteen different detectable events can also be produced. This technique is known as **quadrature amplitude modulation** or **QAM.**

**16QAM,** with sixteen different potential detectable events, allows 4 bits/baud or quadbits to be produced or detected per signaling event, resulting in a transmission rate four times the baud rate. Figure 2-16 illustrates a representative set of constellation points and associated quadbits for a QAM modulation scheme. Differences in phase are represented in degrees around the center of the diagram, while differences in amplitude are represented by linear distance from the center of the diagram. Each point is uniquely identified by combining one of three potential amplitudes (.311V, .850V and 1.161V) with one of twelve potential phase shifts (15, 45, 75, 105, 135, 175, −165, −135, −105, −75, −45, −15 degrees). Obviously, all potential combinations of these two sets of variables are not used in 16QAM.

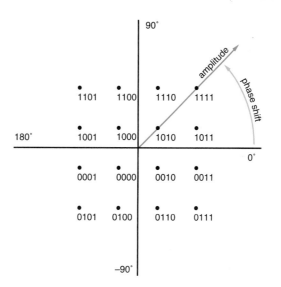

Figure 2-16    QAM Constellation Points and Quadbits

In Sharper Focus

## NYQUIST'S THEOREM AND SHANNON'S LAW

What are the underlying factors that limit the carrying capacity of a given circuit? The work of Harry Nyquist and Claude Shannon helps to answer that question.

**Nyquist's Theorem**    The constellation points illustrated in Figure 2-16 are sometimes referred to as symbols. As the number of constellation points (symbols) increases and symbols are in closer proximity to each other on the constellation diagram, the chance for a modem to misinterpret constellation points increases. Interference between symbols that can cause misinterpretation is known as **intersymbol interference.** Nyquist investigated the maximum data rate (measured in bps) that can be supported by a given bandwidth (measured in Hz) due to the effect of intersymbol interference. He found the relationship between bandwidth ($W$) and maximum data rate ($C$) to be

$$C = 2W$$

However, this fails to account for the ability of modern modems to interpret more than 1 bit per baud by being able to distinguish between more than just two symbols or potential detectable events. Taking this ability into account with the number of potential detectable events represented as $M$, Nyquist's Theorem becomes

$$C = 2W \log_2 M$$

A practical example of Nyquist's theorem is that of a modem that uses dial-up telephone lines. The bandwidth of an analog voice transmission channel is 3,100 Hz. Modern dial-up modems allow for sixteen detectable events per baud using QAM. Therefore, Nyquist states that maximum throughput of a voice-grade analog communications channel is $2(3,100) \times \log_2(16)$, or 24,800 bps.

**Shannon's Law**    The data rates theorized by Nyquist's Theorem are often not achievable in practice due to the presence of noise in the analog communication channel.

Noise is measured as a ratio of the strength of the data signal to the strength of the background noise. This ratio is known as the **signal to noise ratio (S/N)** and is computed as follows:

$$(S/N)_{dB} = 10 \log (\text{signal power}/\text{noise power})$$

S/N is expressed in decibels ($_{dB}$). Decibels are a logarithmic measurement using a reference of $0_{dB}$ for comparison. As a result, a noise level of $10_{dB}$ is 10 times more intense than a noise level of $0_{dB}$, a noise level of $20_{dB}$ is 100 times more intense than a noise level of $0_{dB}$, and a noise level of $30_{dB}$ is 1,000 times more intense than a noise level of $0_{dB}$.

Shannon found that the higher the data rate, the more interference is caused by a given amount of noise, thus causing a higher error rate. This should make sense because at higher data rates, more bits are traveling over a circuit in a fixed length of time, and a burst of noise for the same length of time will affect more bits at higher data rates. By taking into account the signal-to-noise ratio, Shannon expresses the maximum data rate of a circuit ($C$) as

$$C = W \log_2 (1 + S/N)$$

To make calculating Shannon's Law easier for calculators that aren't capable of calculating a $\log_2$, this equation is mathematically equivalent to

$$C = 3.32 \, W \log 10 \, (1 + S/N)$$

Considering a voice-grade circuit: if $W$ = 3,100 Hz and the S/N = 30dB, then $C$ = 30,894 bps. Depending on the value inserted into Shannon's Law for S/N or for $W$, $C$ will vary accordingly. 24,000 bps is also a common value for $C$ using Shannon's Law. As illustrated by substituting different values for $W$ and for S/N, the data channel capacity ($C$) can be more drastically affected by changes in bandwidth ($W$), than by changes in the signal to noise ratio (S/N).

Finally, it should be noted that there are numerous other line impairments such as attenuation, delay distortion, and impulse noise that Shannon's Law does not take into account. As a result, the data channel capacity ($C$) derived from Shannon's Law is theoretical and is sometimes referred to as error-free capacity.

## Data Compression

In the world of data communication, speed is expensive. The faster the data need to be sent, the more the equipment and services are required to send it cost. One way to get additional data throughput is to employ data compression. Data compression involves the sending device replacing large strings of repeating character patterns with a special code that represents the pattern. The code is then sent to the destination device. From that point forward, the sending device replaces any instances of the original pattern with the code. As the code is significantly smaller than the pattern it represents, the amount of data sent between the two devices is reduced as compared to sending the raw data. This reduction, up to 400 percent under optimal conditions, results in an increased amount of data being sent between the sending device and the receiving device (also known as throughput). Figure 2-17 illustrates the difference between throughput and transmission rate.

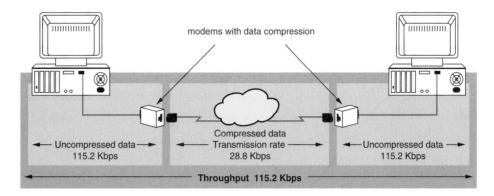

*Figure 2-17*    Data Compression: Transmission Rate vs. Throughput

Given the transmission of compressed data in which a single character may "uncompress" into many characters, the importance of error prevention, detection, and correction when using data compression cannot be overstated. An erroneously transmitted character could be referenced in the receiving device's library of repetitive patterns and incorrectly "uncompressed" into the wrong data stream.

It is important to understand how data compression works and the fact that all of the data does not actually travel across the communication channel. It is equally important to understand that data compression only works if both the sending and receiving data communication devices support the same data compression standard. Data compressed by the sending device must be uncompressed by the receiving device using an identical algorithm or methodology.

Obviously, the more "repetitive patterns" the data compression algorithm can find in the data, the higher the compression ratio that can be expected. Thus, some data streams are more compressible than other data streams and therefore yield a higher data compression ratio. It is also important to note that all data compression technologies use a similar process. If the raw data stream has already been compressed through the use of a CODEC such as an MP3 file or a compression utility such as a zip file, no gain will be realized by the data communication device's compression algorithm. In fact, in such an environment it is possible that the amount of data transmitted could slight increase if data compression is enabled.

Practical Advice
and Information

## SOFTWARE VS. HARDWARE DATA COMPRESSION

The data compression techniques discussed so far are hardware based, implemented in the communication devices themselves. Many data-communication software solutions (such as Microsoft Windows Dial-up networking and many virtual private network solutions) also include data compression. If both software and hardware compression are available, software compression is usually more effective because the software packages are typically optimized for the type of data being sent. Hardware compression must be generic as the device designers have no idea of the type of data the might be transmitted. Regardless of whether hardware or software compression is chosen, both hardware and software compression should never both enabled at the same time.

**Principle of Shifting Bottlenecks**    The ability to compress data introduces another key data communications issue: the **Principle of Shifting Bottlenecks.** Just as a chain is only as strong as its weakest link, a data communications system is only as fast as its slowest link—its bottleneck. If the existing bottleneck is eliminated (by employing data compression or any other technique), then the next slowest link becomes the bottleneck. Before investing in resolving one bottleneck, it should be determined what the next bottleneck would be. If investing in a solution to remove the first bottleneck will only result in a small increase in overall throughput before the next bottleneck becomes the limit, it might not make economic sense to do anything.

## ■ DATA COMMUNICATION TECHNIQUES

### Packetization

Packetization is the process of dividing the data stream flowing between devices into structured blocks known as packets. A **packet** can be defined as a group of bits organized in a predetermined, structured manner consisting of a piece of the overall data stream to which overhead or management information is added to assure error-free transmission of the data to its destination. These packets may be referred to as messages, sessions, frames, cells, blocks, data units, or several other names, depending on which layer of the OSI Network Reference Model they are located. The packetization process is illustrated in Figure 2-18.

The predetermined, structured nature of a packet is critical. At the lowest level the packet itself consists of nothing more than a series of ones and zeroes; there is nothing in the packet itself that explicitly indicates what any of the bits mean. Rather, the bits have implicit meaning; through the use of standards the two communicating devices know the number of bits assigned to the fields in the header, data section, and trailer of the packet. Fields used in the header to enable the seamless communication of data include destination and source addresses, sequence numbers, and error checks.

### Encapsulation/De-encapsulation

Once the data is packetized, it is placed in protocol containers for transmission across the network. As illustrated in Figure 2-19, a data message emerges from an application

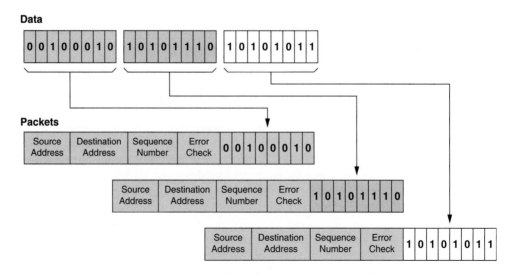

*Figure 2-18*   Packetization Process

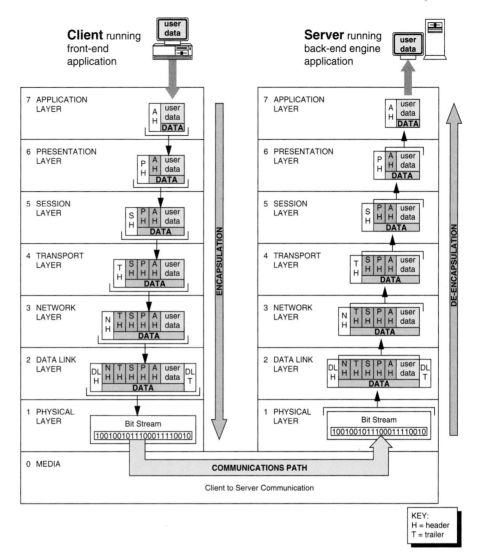

*Figure 2-19*  Encapsulation and De-encapsulation in the OSI Network Reference Model

and proceeds down the protocol stack of the network operating system in a process known as **encapsulation.** Each successive layer of the OSI model adds a header according to the syntax of the protocol that occupies that layer. In the case of the data-link layer, both a header and trailer are added. The bit stream is finally passed along the media that connects the two computing devices. Although the OSI model may seem to imply that given layers in a protocol stack talk directly to each other on different computers, the fact is that the computers are only physically connected by the media and that is the only layer where there is a direct communications link between computers.

When the full bit stream arrives at the destination computer, the reverse process of encapsulation, known as **de-encapsulation,** takes place. Each successive layer of the OSI model removes headers and/or trailers and processes the data that was passed to it from the corresponding layer protocol on the source computer until the data is given to the destination application running on the destination computer. While Figure 2-19 focused on the OSI network reference model, the same concepts are utilized in all other protocol models including the TCP/IP model.

## Multiplexing

Multiplexing is the process of sharing the bandwidth of a data line among multiple communication sessions. As illustrated in Figure 2-20, a long-distance parcel shipping analogy can be used to illustrate the underlying technical concept of multiplexing.

*Multiplexing* refers to taking a single communication channel and breaking it into subchannels that can be used to carry independent messages. This is shown in Figure 2-20; after the data is packetized, the packets are multiplexed into a single truck for transmission. In data communications, a multiplexer (also known as a **MUX**) takes data packets and packages them for transmission over a shared connection along with data packages from other sources. Once the package is received at the destination address, the data packets are de-multiplexed and forwarded to their respective destinations. These destinations represent the applications and services that require connectivity. Examples include web browsing and instant messaging.

Three basic techniques are employed in multiplexing digitized traffic across electrical physical connections where bits of data are transmitted as discrete voltages of electricity:

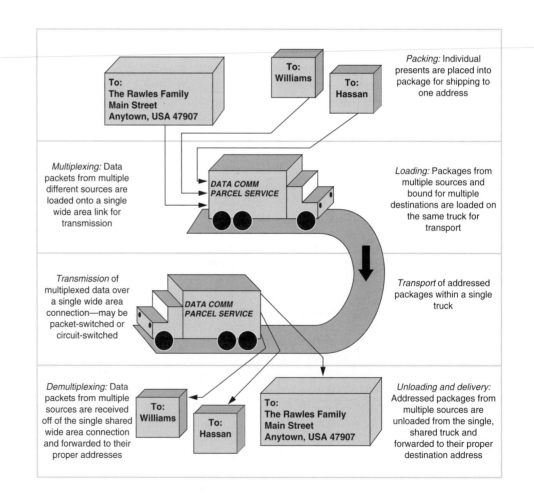

*Figure 2-20*   Multiplexing: A Parcel Shipping Analogy

- **Frequency Division Multiplexing (FDM)**

- **Time Division Multiplexing (TDM)**

- **Statistical Time Division Multiplexing (STDM)**

When optical transmission is used, bits of data are represented by bursts of light energy of varying wavelengths. In this environment, a relatively new multiplexing technique known as **wavelength division multiplexing (WDM)** has been developed. WDM technology is deployed primarily by telecommunications carriers with extensive long distance fiber optic networks in order to increase transmission capacity up to tenfold without the need to install additional fiber. WDM will be discussed in more detail in chapter 6.

**Frequency Division Multiplexing**   In frequency division multiplexing, multiple input signals are modulated to different frequencies within the available bandwidth of a single circuit and subsequently demodulated back into individual signals on the output end of the composite circuit. Sufficient space in between these separate frequency channels is reserved in **guardbands** in order to prevent interference between the two or more input signals that are sharing the single circuit. Figure 2-21 illustrates a simple frequency division multiplexing configuration.

The device that implements frequency division multiplexing is known as a frequency division multiplexer or FDM. An FDM can be either a stand-alone unit or it can be integrated into another piece of data communications equipment such as a cable or DSL modem.

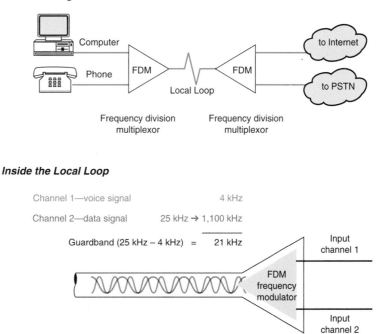

*Figure 2-21*   Frequency Division Multiplexing

In FDM, the total bandwidth of the composite channel is divided into subchannels by frequency. FDM works in the same manner as a cable television system; each channel is given a specific amount of bandwidth on the cable. By changing the frequency the television samples different channels are tuned for viewing.

In an FDM implementation, each channel is available 100 percent of the time, just as in a dedicated circuit. As a result, the timing of signals between a connected terminal or device and the centralized processor are not affected. However, the amount of bandwidth available in each channel is limited to the bandwidth devoted to the channel. If one channel is not using all of its available bandwidth there is no way to allow it to be used by another channel.

Common uses of FDM include modern Internet access technologies such as DSL (digital subscriber line) and cable modem services. In a DSL solution, FDM is used to multiplex a high-speed data signal over the same physical pair of copper wires used for dial-up telephone calls. In a cable modem solution, the high-speed data signal is multiplexed onto the same physical coaxial cable used to deliver television programming from the cable company. More detail on DSL and cable modems is presented in chapter 3.

**Time Division Multiplexing**    In a sense, time division multiplexing (TDM) works just the opposite of FDM. Rather than breaking the bandwidth into channels of lesser capacity that are available at all times, TDM creates channels by allowing the data communications devices to use all of the available bandwidth for short periods of time. This is similar to playing a game of "hot potato"; when you have the potato you can use all of the bandwidth but you have to wait to transmit until you have the potato. The portion of time available to each connected input device (known as the **time slot**) is constant and controlled by the Time Division Multiplexer. Unlike FDM, where a percentage of the available bandwidth is lost to guardbands, in a TDM environment all of the bandwidth is available for use. However, because each device can only transmit during its timeslot the timing of communications between the devices becomes more complicated.

Another key point to understand about time slots in a TDM environment is that a fixed portion of time, measured in milliseconds, is reserved for each attached input device whether the device is active or not. As a result, efficiency is sacrificed for the sake of simplicity. Just as in FDM, if a channel (time slot) is not being fully utilized there is no way to give that bandwidth to another channel that is using all of its bandwidth; a device with nothing to transmit is given its full time allotment while other busy devices must wait their turn to transmit. Figure 2-22 illustrates simple time division multiplexing.

As can be seen in Figure 2-22, each input channel has a fixed amount of buffer memory into which it can load data. Flow control is used to tell each device to stop transmitting to the buffer when it fills. A **central clock** or timing device in the TDM gives each device its allotted time to empty its buffer into an area of the TDM where the combined data from all of the polled input devices is conglomerated into a single message frame for transmission over the composite circuit. This process of checking on each connected terminal in order to see if any data is ready to be sent is known as **polling.**

If a device is inactive with nothing in its input buffer to contribute to the consolidated message frame, its allotted space in the **composite message frame** is filled with blanks. The insertion of blanks, or null characters, into composite message links is the basis of TDM's inefficient use of the shared composite circuit connecting the

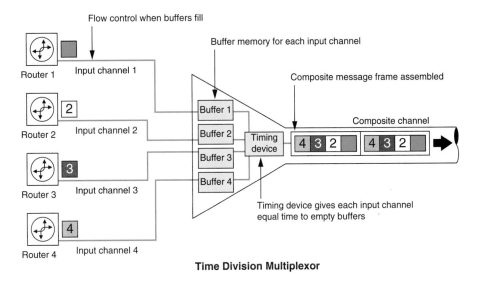

**Time Division Multiplexor**

*Figure 2-22* Time Division Multiplexing

two TDMs. Although the data from the devices is combined into a single message frame, each individual device's data is still identifiable by its position in the composite message frame. This is important since once the composite message frame has finished its journey across the transmission link, it must be re-segmented back into the individual device data streams.

**Statistical Time Division Multiplexing** Statistical time division multiplexing (STDM) is a variant of FDM that seeks to offer more efficient use of the composite bandwidth than simple TDM by employing increased monitoring and manipulation of input devices to accomplish two major goals:

- Eliminate "idle time" allocations to inactive terminals.
- Eliminate padded blanks or null characters in the composite message blocks.

In STDM, time slots are dynamically allocated to input devices rather than being fixed. As devices become more active, they get more time slots to use. As devices become less active, the STDM MUX polls them less frequently. This dynamic time slot allocation takes both processing power and additional memory. Statistics are kept as to terminal activity over time and hence the name: *statistical time division multiplexing.* Specially programmed microprocessors and additional buffer memory are key components of STDMs and contribute to their increased costs over the simpler TDMs.

To increase the efficiency of use of the composite link, padded blanks and null characters are not inserted into message frames for inactive terminals. In an STDM, rather than assign space to input devices in the composite message frame by position regardless of activity, the STDM adds control information to each terminal's data within the composite message frame that indicates the source device and how many bytes of data came from that device. Figure 2-23 illustrates composite message block construction in STDMs.

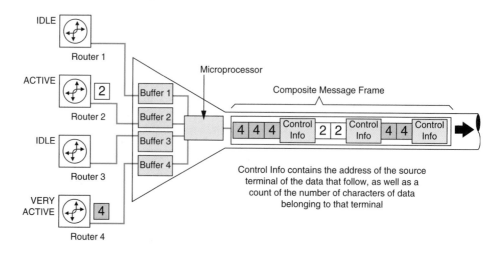

*Figure 2-23*     STDMs Make Efficient Use of Composite Bandwidth

Practical Advice
and Information

### NETWORK TIMING CONSIDERATIONS

The dynamic allocation of time afforded to individual end-devices by the STDM can interfere with the timing between these devices. It is particularly important to utilize a common synchronous *building integrated timing source* (BITS) clock to maintain synchronization across the entire network.

## Switching

If a device wishes to communicate with another device to which it has a direct connection, it is relatively simple to establish a connection and begin transmitting data. In this case the local device knows that any data sent out the specified interface will be travel directly to the destination across the direct connection, or circuit, between the two devices. However, when a device wishes to communicate with another device to which it does not have a direct connection, the process becomes significantly more difficult. Before the local device can begin sending data to the destination, a connection must be established to the destination. As shown in Figure 2-24, this connection must go through intermediate devices that create a path to the destination. Depending on the technology and protocols used, these intermediate devices may be known as exchanges, bridges, LAN switches, or routers.

Switching allows temporary connections to be established, maintained and terminated between sources and destinations, sometimes referred to as **data sinks.** There are two primary switching techniques employed in switching architectures:

- Circuit switching
- Packet switching

In circuit-switched networks, users get dedicated bandwidth on circuits created solely for their use. In packet-switched networks, users' packetized data is transported across circuits between packet switches, along with the data of other users of the same packet switched network.

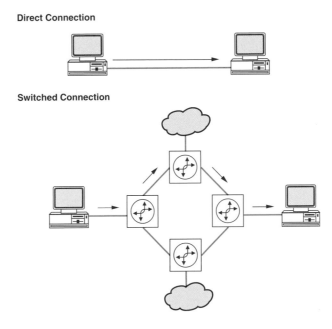

*Figure 2-24*    The Need for Switching

**Circuit Switching**    In a **circuit-switched network,** the work to create a signal path is done up front; a switch fabric creates a direct electrical or optical path between the source and the destination. After the circuit is established, communication takes place just as if the temporary circuit were a permanent direct connection: The switched dedicated circuit established on circuit-switched networks makes it appear to the user of the circuit as if a wire has been run directly between the communicating devices. The physical resources required to create this temporary connection are dedicated to that particular circuit for the duration of the connection. If system usage should increase to the point where insufficient resources are available to create additional connections, additional requests for connection are denied.

Traditionally, the most common example of a circuit-switched network is the telephone system or Public Switched Telephone Network (PSTN). When making a call over the PSTN the user dials the address of the destination device to which they wish to communicate and the telephone switches create a circuit between the source and destination handsets. Signals leaving the source handset are directly sent across this dedicated circuit to the destination handset where they are reconstituted into the voice of the calling party.

**Packet Switching**    In a **packet-switched network,** packets of data travel one at a time from the message source to the message destination. A packet switched network, otherwise known as a **public data network (PDN),** is usually represented in network diagrams by a cloud symbol. Figure 2-25 illustrates such a symbol as well as the difference between circuit switching and packet switching. The cloud is an appropriate symbol for a packet-switched network because all that is known is that the packet of data goes in one side of the network and comes out the other. The physical path taken by one packet may be different than that taken by the other packets in the data stream and in any case, is unknown to the end user. Inside the

**Circuit Switching**

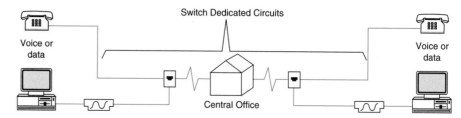

All data or voice travel from source to destination over the *same* physical path

**Packet Switching**

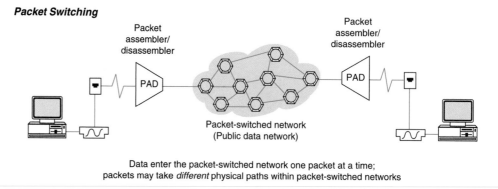

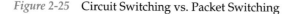

Data enter the packet-switched network one packet at a time;
packets may take *different* physical paths within packet-switched networks

*Figure 2-25*    Circuit Switching vs. Packet Switching

cloud is a series of **packet switches** that pass packets among themselves as they travel from source to destination.

Packets are specially structured groups of data that include control and address information in addition to the data itself. These packets must be assembled (control and address information added to data) somewhere before entry into the packet switched network and must be subsequently disassembled upon leaving the packet switched network before delivery to their destination. This packet assembly and disassembly is done by devices known as **PADs** or **packet assembler/disassemblers.** PADs may be standalone devices or may be integrated into other data communication devices such as modems or multiplexers. The PADs may be located directly at an end-user location, or may be located further along the communication path at the entry point to the packet-switched data network.

Another way in which packet switching differs from circuit switching is that as demand for transmission of data increases on a packet-switched network, additional users are not denied access to the packet-switched network. Overall performance of the network may suffer, errors and retransmission may occur, or packets of data may be lost, but all users experience the same degradation of service because in the case of a packet-switched network data travels through the network one packet at a time; traveling over any available path within the network rather than waiting for a switched dedicated path as in the case of the circuit-switched network.

*Connectionless vs. Connection-Oriented Networks*    In order for any packet switch to process any packet of data bound for anywhere, it is essential that packet address information be included on each packet. Each packet switch then reads and processes the packet by making routing and forwarding decisions based on the packet's current location, destination address, and network conditions.

Because an overall data message is broken up into numerous pieces by the packet assembler, these message pieces may arrive out of order at the message destination if they take different paths across the packet switched network. The data message must be pieced back together in proper order by the destination PAD before final transmission to the destination address. These self-sufficient packets containing full source and destination address information, plus a sequence number, are known as **datagrams.** Figure 2-26 illustrates the packet assembly/disassembly process.

A **connectionless** packet network is a switching methodology in which each datagram is handled and routed to its ultimate destination on an individual basis, resulting in the possibility of packets traveling over a variety of physical paths on the way to their destination.

There are no error control techniques applied by a datagram-based or connectionless packet-switched network. Such a network requires the end devices (computers) to provide adequate error control. This lack of inherent error control is the reason that connectionless packet networks are also known as **unreliable** packet networks.

In contrast to unreliable connectionless packet networks, **connection-oriented,** or **reliable,** packet networks offer built-in error control provided by the packet network itself. This removes the requirement that the end user devices provide this functionality. Figure 2-27 contrasts connectionless and connection-oriented packet-switched networks.

## ■ ERROR CONTROL TECHNIQUES

The objective of every data communications session is to efficiently and accurately transmit the desired data. However, just as in communication between two people,

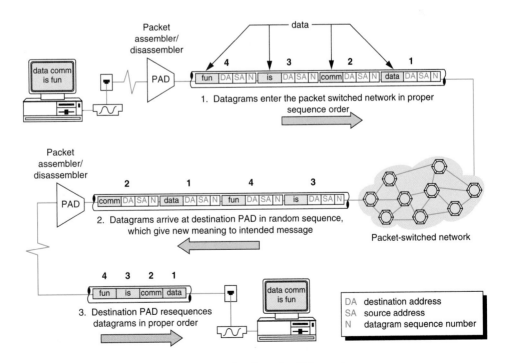

*Figure 2-26*   Datagram Delivery on a Packet-Switched Network

| | Overhead | Greatest Strength | Call Set-up | Addressing | Also Known as... | Error Correction | Flow Control |
|---|---|---|---|---|---|---|---|
| Connectionless | Less | Ability to dynamically reroute data | None | Global | Datagram unreliable | Left to end-user devices | Left to end-user devices |
| Connection-oriented | More | Reliability | Yes | Local logical channel number | Reliable Virtual circuit | By virtual circuit | By virtual circuit |

*Figure 2-27*   Connection-Oriented vs. Connection Packet-Switched Networks

there are times when the message sent is not the message received due to inaccuracies in the transmission or reception equipment or anomalies in the communications channel. For a data communication session to be useful, there must be a means of handling any transmission problems to ensure the reliable transmission of accurate data.

## Error Prevention

Data transmission errors occur when received data are misinterpreted due to noise or interference on the communication lines over which the data message traveled. Errors can be prevented by employing filters, amplifiers, and repeaters in the communication channel to improve the signal to noise ratio to reduce the likelihood of an error occurring. A detailed analysis of amplifiers and repeaters is provided in chapter 3.

Another way in which errors can be prevented during data transmission is through the use of **adaptive protocols.** Adaptive protocols adjust transmission session parameters such as base transmission speed in response to varying line conditions. The techniques available to help prevent errors vary, depending on the data transmission technologies being used. However, errors are inevitable; no amount of error prevention can eliminate them.

## Error Detection

Once everything possible has been done to prevent errors, the focus shifts to reliably detecting the errors that do occur. Remembering that transmitted data, on the most elementary level, is merely a stream of ones and zeroes, the role of error detection can be defined as providing the assurance that the receiving computer receives the same ones and zeroes in the exact sequence that they are transmitted by the transmitting computer.

This assurance is achieved through the cooperative efforts of the transmitting and receiving data communication devices. In addition to transmitting the actual data, the transmitting device must also transmit some type of verifiable bit or character that the receiving device can use to decide whether the transmitted data was received correctly. Figure 2-28 illustrates this overall process shared by all error-detection techniques.

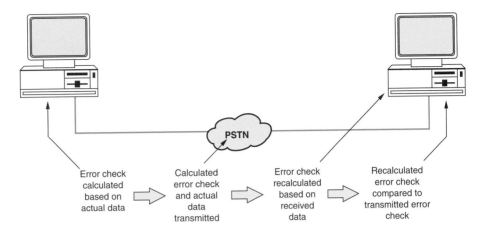

*Figure 2-28*    The Overall Error Detection Process

This generalized error detection process can be summarized as follows:

- The transmitting and receiving devices agree on how the error check is to be calculated.

- The transmitting device calculates and transmits the error check along with the transmitted data.

- The receiving device re-calculates the error check based on the received data and compares its newly calculated error check to the error check received with the data.

- If the two error checks match, everything is fine. If they do not match, an error has occurred.

Several error detection techniques of varying degrees of complexity have been developed. The following error detection techniques will be discussed further:

- Parity (VRC)

- Longitudinal Redundancy Checks (LRC)

- Checksums

- Cyclic Redundancy Checks (CRC)

**Parity**    **Parity,** also known as a (**vertical redundancy check** or **VRC**), is the simplest error-detection technique. Parity works by adding an error check bit to each character. For example, since the ASCII 7-bit code for the letter A is 1000001, a parity bit is added as the eighth bit. Whether this bit should be a 0 or a 1 depends on whether odd or even parity has been defined or agreed upon in advance by communicating devices. These devices can also agree to data transmission with no parity. Examples of the letter A with odd and even parity are illustrated in Figure 2-29.

As can be seen in Figure 2-29, when the letter A is transmitted with odd parity, the parity bit is set to 1 so that there is an odd number of ones in the 8-bit character. Conversely, when even parity is used, the parity bit is set to 0 so that there is an even

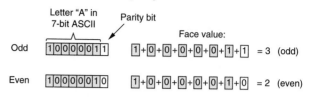

*Figure 2-29* Odd and Even Parity

number of ones in the 8-bit character. If even parity is chosen and the receiving computer detects an off number of ones in the character, then it knows that a transmission error has occurred.

Parity checking has a limitation. It can only detect odd numbers of bit-substitution errors. If an even number of bit-substitution errors occur, the received character will pass the parity check, even though the character received was not the character sent. Figure 2-30 illustrates parity checking's inability to detect even numbers of bit-substitution errors within the same character.

As can be seen in Figure 2-30, the received character has an even number of ones so that the receiving computer thinks everything is fine. However, a letter Q was received instead of the letter A that was sent.

**Longitudinal Redundancy Checks**   **Longitudinal redundancy checks (LRC)** seek to overcome the weakness of simple, bit-oriented, one-directional parity checking. One can think of LRC as adding a second dimension to parity. Figure 2-31 illustrates LRC with even parity in two dimensions.

As can be seen in Figure 2-31, LRC is a block-oriented parity-checking mechanism that adds an entire parity character following a block of data characters. The bits of the parity character are set to establish property parity for each bit position within the block of data characters. In the example illustrated in Figure 2-31 both the parity bits of individual characters (VRC) as well the parity bits of the LRC character would be checked to be sure that even parity existed in both directions.

**Checksums**   **Checksums** are also block-oriented error detection characters added to a block of data characters. However, rather than checking the number of ones in the block, as was the case with the LRC, a checksum is calculated by adding the decimal

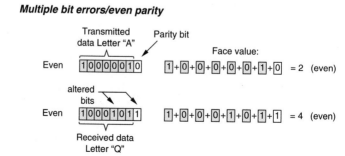

*Figure 2-30*   Parity Checking's Inability to Detect Multiple Bit Errors

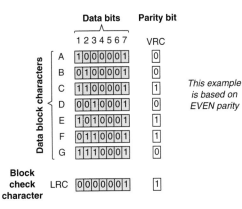

Figure 2-31   Longitudinal Redundancy Checks

face values of all of the characters sent in a given data block and sending only the least significant byte of that sum. The receiving computer generates its own checksum based on the data it has received, and compares the locally calculated checksum with the transmitted checksum.

## CHECKSUM CALCULATION

The formula for calculating a checksum is as follows:

- Add the ASCII decimal face value of each of the 128 characters in the block.
- Divide this number by 255.
- Determine the remainder. The remainder is the checksum character to be transmitted to and verified by the receiving computer.

In order to understand the inner workings of this formula, it is necessary to further understand the ASCII table, first introduced in Figure 2-2. Every value in the ASCII table has a decimal equivalent computed by transforming the ones and zeroes of any character, into their Base2 column values and adding the decimal values of those Base2 columns in which ones appear.

Example:

The 7-bit ASCII code for the Capital letter A is 1000001.
Now assign Base 2 place values to each column.

| Power of 2 | 7 | 6 | 5 | 4 | 3 | 2 | 1 | 0 |
|---|---|---|---|---|---|---|---|---|
| Decimal Value | 128 | 64 | 32 | 16 | 8 | 4 | 2 | 1 |
| Letter "A" Code | | 1 | 0 | 0 | 0 | 0 | 0 | 1 |

There is a 1 in the 64 column and a 1 in the 1 column. Adding these place values, yields 64 + 1, or 65 (Base 10), or decimal 65. Therefore, the ASCII decimal face value of the capital letter A is 65. Some ASCII and EBCDIC tables supply only decimal values rather than binary values, as illustrated in Figures 2-2 and 2-3.

If 128 capital A's were transferred as a single block of data, the total ASCII face value of the block would be 128 x 65 = 8,320. Dividing the total ASCII face value by 255 yields 8,320/255 = 32 r 160. So the remainder is 160. This remainder is also known as the *least significant byte.*

In order to represent the remainder (160) as a single checksum character in binary format, use the decimal values chart of the powers of 2.

| Power of 2 | 7 | 6 | 5 | 4 | 3 | 2 | 1 | 0 |
|---|---|---|---|---|---|---|---|---|
| Decimal Value | 128 | 64 | 32 | 16 | 8 | 4 | 2 | 1 |
| Binary Value of 160 | 1 | 0 | 1 | 0 | 0 | 0 | 0 | 0 |

Thus, the transmitted checksum character would be 10100000.

When dividing our total ASCII face value by 255, the highest remainder possible would be 254. Decimal 254 would be represented in binary and transmitted in a single checksum character (8 bits) as 11111110.

**Cyclic Redundancy Checks**    **Cyclic redundancy checks (CRC)** seek to improve on the error detection capability of checksums and LRCs. A CRC is really a more sophisticated form of a checksum. In order to understand CRCs, binary division is required. In cyclic redundancy checking, the entire message block of ones and zeroes, even if its 1,000 bits long, is treated as a single, gigantic binary number. This gigantic string of ones and zeroes is divided by a predetermined prime binary number one bit longer than the desired number of bits in the CRC value. Remembering that if these divisors are prime (only divisible by 1 and themselves) they will produce a remainder one bit shorter than themselves. Common lengths for CRCs are 16 and 32 bits. A 16-bit CRC uses a 17-bit divisor and a 32-bit CRC uses a 33-bit divisor.

This remainder is then attached to the actual data message (the original string of ones and zeroes to be transmitted) and transmitted to the receiving device where the received data string is again divided by the same divisor. The remainder calculated at the receiving device is compared to the remainder received from the transmitting device.

Using this technique, a error bursts up to one bit less than the CRC (15 bits for a 16-bit CRC and 31 bits for a 32-bit CRC) can be detected 100 percent of the time, and larger error bursts at $100 - 1/2^{(number\ of\ bits\ in\ the\ CRC)}$ percent of the time. Using this formula to compute the overall percentage for a 16-bit CRC yields an error detection rate of 99.999984742 percent.

## Error Correction

Once it is understood how data transmission errors can be detected, they must be reliably and efficiently corrected. In simple terms, error correction amounts to this:

- The receiving device detecting the error and requesting a re-transmission

- The transmitting device retransmitting the data containing the error

The differences in sophistication between the various error correcting protocols are centered on a few variables:

- How is the retransmission requested?

- How much data must be retransmitted?

- How is retransmission time minimized?

**Automatic Retransmission Request (ARQ)**     **ARQ** or **Automatic Retransmission Request** is a general term that really describes the overall process of error detection using one of the previously described methods, as well as the subsequent automatic request for retransmission of that data. As noted above, the actual request for retransmission can occur in different ways.

**Discrete ARQ—ACK/NAK**     **Discrete ARQ** is sometimes also known as *"stop and wait"* ARQ. In a protocol using Discrete ARQ, the transmitting device sends a block of data and waits until the remote receiving device does the following:

- Receives the data
- Tests for errors
- Sends an **acknowledgment (ACK)** character back to the transmitting device if the transmitted data were free of errors or
- Sends a **negative acknowledgment (NAK)** character if the data were not successfully received

After waiting for this **ACK/NAK,** the transmitting device does the following:

- Sends the next block of data if an ACK was received or
- Retransmits the original block of data if a NAK was received

This entire process repeats itself until the conclusion of the data transmission session. Using this technique the transmitting device spends a significant amount of time idly waiting for either an ACK or a NAK to be sent by the receiving device. This is inefficient, so other ARQ methods have been devised that take a different, more efficient approach to error detection and correction.

**Continuous ARQ**     A variation of ARQ known as **continuous ARQ,** eliminates the requirement for the transmitting device to wait for an ACK or a NAK after transmitting each block before transmitting the next block of data, eliminating a great deal of idle time and increasing overall data throughput.

With continuous ARQ, also known as a **sliding window protocol,** a **sequence number** is appended to each block of data transmitted. The transmitting device continuously transmits blocks of data without waiting for ACK or NAK from the receiving device after each block of data sent. However, there is often a block limit to prevent a device from transmitting indefinitely without having received either an ACK or a NAK. The receiving device still checks each block of data for errors, just as it did with discrete ARQ. However, when the receiving device detects an error in a block of data, it sends the sequence number along with the NAK back to the transmitting device. The transmitting device now knows which particular block of data was received in error, slides the transmission window back to the NAK'd block, and resumes transmission from that point.

**Selective ARQ**     Continuous ARQ's requirement to retransmit *all* blocks of data from the NAK'd block forward is more efficient than discrete ARQ but can still be made more efficient. **Selective ARQ** increases efficiency by requiring only the retransmission of the blocks received in error rather than the block in error and all subsequent blocks.

### Flow Control

When a data communication device receives data it is placed in a special place in memory known as buffer memory (or simply a **buffer**) until it can be sent to the attached destination device. To ensure the data are sent to the destination device in the proper order, they are stored in the order they were sent. The amount of memory available in the buffer is finite: once the buffer is full no more data can be stored and any data that come in will be discarded. The process of discarding data because the buffer is full is known as a buffer **overflow,** although data communication professionals will sometimes refer to it as placing data in the **bit bucket.** Obviously, discarding data because the buffer is full is an undesirable situation.

To prevent buffer overflows, the receiving device sends a signal to the sending device that says, in effect, "shut up for a minute while I catch up." This is not unlike students raising their hand to ask the professor to wait before changing slides or erasing the board so they can finish taking notes. When it occurs in a data communication application, this process is known as **flow control.** The flow control software constantly monitors the amount of free space available in buffer memory and tells the sending device to stop sending data when there is insufficient storage space. When the buffer once again has room, the sending device is told to resume transmitting.

## SUMMARY

Key concepts used in all types of data communication technologies were introduced in this chapter.

Data must be in a digital form before it can be sent across a data network. CODECs and character encoding standards such as ASCII and UNICODE are used to convert analog data into a digital format prior to transmission.

The two main types of data transmission are parallel and serial. In parallel transmission, multiple bits are sent concurrently across multiple signal wires, while in serial transmission the bits are sent one at a time across one signaling wire. Parallel transmission is typically used inside a computer while serial transmission is typically used between computers.

Although all data sent across a data communications network must be in a digital form, it is often sent using analog signal signaling. For the digital signal to be sent across an analog transmission link it must be modulated using techniques such as AM, FM, PM, and QAM.

A data stream must also be packetized into chunks for transmission. These chunks are then embedded into protocols in a process known as encapsulation before being sent across the communications link. At the destination the protocols are un-encapsulated and the data de-packetized before being delivered to the destination application.

To enable efficient use of the communications link, multiplexing is often used to allow multiple communication sessions to share a single link. The most commonly used multiplexing techniques are FDM, TDM, and STDM.

When building a network, some means of creating links between the source and destination devices is required. There are two basic approaches to this: circuit switching and packet switching. In circuit switching, a physical circuit is connected between the devices. In packet switching, the packetized data between the devices is routed across shared circuits to the destination. In modern networks, packet switching is used almost exclusively.

To ensure accurate reception of transmitted data, error control is implemented. There are three basic parts of error control: error prevention, error detection, and error correction. Error prevention includes activities such as line conditioning to lessen the chance of an error occurring, error detection includes technologies such as parity and CRCs to allow errors to be detected, and error correction includes the processes used to request re-transmissions of packets that contain errors.

Flow control is used to ensure that the data is not sent faster than the receiving device can process it. Flow control techniques provide a means for the receiver to tell the sender to wait before transmitting an additional data.

## KEY TERMS

ACK
adaptive protocols
amplitude
amplitude modulation
ARQ
ASCII
asynchronous transmission
baud
baud rate
bit
bit bucket
bps
buffer
buffer overflow
byte
carrier wave
central clock
character encoding
checksum
circuit switching
composite message frame
connectionless communication
connection-oriented
    communication
constellation points

continuous ARQ
CRC
data sinks
datagram
discrete ARQ
duplex
EBCDIC
flow control
frequency
frequency division multiplexing
frequency modulation
FSK
guardbands
intersymbol interference
longitudinal redundancy check
modem
modulation
multiplexing
NAK
octet
packet switches
packet switching
packetization
PAD
parallel transmission

parity
phase
phase modulation
polling
principle of shifting bottlenecks
PSK
public data networks
QAM
QPSK
sequence number
serial transmission
signal to noise ratio
sliding window
statistical time division
    multiplexing
synchronous transmission
time division multiplexing
time slot
transmission rate
turnaround time
UNICODE
vertical redundancy check
wavelength
wavelength division multiplexing

## REVIEW QUESTIONS

1. What are the three major character encoding standards?
2. Why isn't there a single encoding standard?
3. What is character encoding and why is it necessary?
4. What is the importance of encoding standards such as Unicode/ISO 10646?
5. What is a disadvantage of encoding standards such as Unicode/ISO 10646?
6. What is a bit and how is it represented within a computer?
7. What are the primary differences between serial and parallel transmission?
8. Which type of transmission (serial or parallel) is most often used in data communications and why?
9. What is a UART and what role does it play in the overall process of getting data from a local PC to a remote PC?

10. What is the difference between analog transmission and digital transmission?
11. What is the difference between asynchronous transmission and synchronous transmission? Which is more efficient?
12. Modem is actually a contraction for which two words?
13. What is a carrier wave?
14. What three characteristics of a carrier wave can be varied?
15. How are the number of detectable events related to the baud rate and bits per second (bps)?
16. What is the importance of signal to noise ratio in terms of modem design and operation?
17. What is the advantage of varying more than one characteristic of a carrier wave?

18. What is the difference between full-duplex and half-duplex data transmission?

19. What is the difference between bps and baud rate?

20. Explain in simple terms how a circuit-switched or dial-up call is established.

21. Complete an I-P-O chart illustrating the required functionality of a modem.

22. What role does a carrier wave play in data transmission over an analog communications link?

23. What is the relationship between wavelength and frequency?

24. What is a signalling event?

25. Which transmission methodology requires an external clocking source? Why?

26. How are handshaking and turnaround time related to full-duplex and half-duplex transmission?

27. Give an example of how physical interfaces or connectors don't necessarily imply a transmission protocol.

28. What is a constellation point?

29. What is intersymbol interference and what impact does it have on modulation scheme design?

30. Why are standards important when it comes to data compression?

31. What is packetization?

32. Why is packetization important in a data communication network?

33. What is multiplexing?

34. Explain frequency division multiplexing.

35. Explain time division multiplexing.

36. Explain statistical time division multiplexing.

37. Which multiplexing technique is most efficient?

38. Why is switching a requirement for a data communication network?

39. Compare and contrast circuit and packet switching.

40. What is a packet assembler/dis-assembler and what is its purpose?

41. What is a datagram?

42. Why are connectionless networks considered unreliable?

43. Elaborate on the relationship between Error Prevention, Error Detection, and Error Correction.

44. What is the difference between discrete ARQ and continuous ARQ?

45. What inefficiency is inherent in a data transmission session utilizing discrete ARQ over a full duplex circuit?

46. Explain how multiple bit errors can remain undetected using simple parity checking.

47. Explain how LRC overcomes parity checking's inability to detect multiple bit errors.

48. Explain in simple terms how checksums and CRCs detect transmission errors.

49. What is meant by a sliding window protocol?

50. How are block sequence numbers related to sliding window protocols?

51. What role does buffer memory play in the implementation of sliding window protocols?

52. Why is flow control important?

**Case Study:** For a business case study and questions that relate to the data communications concepts in this chapter, go to www.wiley.com/college/goldman.

CHAPTER **3**

# Basic Data Communication Technology

*Concepts Reinforced*

Top-down model
Modulation techniques
Transmission services

I-P-O model
Protocols and compatibility
Multiplexing

*Concepts Introduced*

Communications media
Wireless point-to-point
   technologies
Dial-up modem technologies

Cable modem technologies
Serial technologies
Internet service providers
DSL technologies

## OBJECTIVES

After mastering the material in this chapter, you should:

1. Understand the types of communication media available and the limitations and applications of each.

2. Be able to compare and contrast basic point-to-point communication technologies such as RS-232, USB, IEEE-1394/Firewire, and Centronics parallel.

3. Understand the applications and limitations of wireless point-to-point communication technologies, including IrDA and Bluetooth.

4. Understand the role of an Internet service provider.

5. Understand modem operation, comparative modem features, the importance of modem standards, and the cost/benefit analysis of various modem purchases.

6. Understand the architecture and operation of digital subscriber line (DSL) technologies.

7. Understand the architecture and operation of cable modem technologies.

8. Be able to analyze and select the best Internet access technology for a given location.

## ■ INTRODUCTION

This chapter begins an in-depth analysis of the OSI Network Reference Model layers that is carried forward through chapter 8. As detailed in chapter 1, the OSI Network Reference Model can easily be mapped onto other protocol models such as the TCP/IP model. This mapping will be detailed throughout the coming chapters.

This chapter introduces communication media, basic point-to-point data communications technologies, and Internet access technologies. It takes the basic concepts introduced in chapter 2 and maps them to real-world technologies that a typical student interacts with on a daily basis. In addition to technical details, emphasis is placed on the application and business implications of the technologies introduced.

## ■ PHYSICAL LAYER

The first layer of the OSI Network Reference Model, the **physical layer,** is responsible for the establishment, maintenance, and termination of physical connections between communicating devices. The physical layer transmits and receives a stream of bits. There is no data recognition at the physical layer. The physical layer is mapped onto the TCP/IP model as the bottom part of the network access layer that also contains the OSI datalink layer.

Specifically, physical layer operation is controlled by protocols that define the electrical, mechanical, and procedural specifications for data transmission. Strictly speaking, the physical layer does not define the specifications for media and connectors. These specifications are sometimes referred to as belonging to layer zero of the model, as they underlie layer one.

## ■ COMMUNICATIONS MEDIA

Although communications media are technically not part of the OSI Network Reference or TCP/IP models, their importance cannot be understated. Without some sort of connection between two devices they will not be able to communicate; regardless of the hardware and protocols used. In this way media is analogous to a highway; it does not do you any good to have a Ferrari if you need to travel across a swamp that has no roads.

When two devices that have been working flawlessly cease to operate, there is a very good chance that the problem can be directly attributed to problems with the media connecting the devices. Perhaps the first mantra of network troubleshooting should be, "Check the physical layer."

There are many different types of data communications media. This section details commonly used media, their characteristics, and typical application.

### Not Twisted Pair

The type of phone wire installed in most homes built prior to the mid-1990s consists of a tan plastic jacket containing four untwisted wires: red, yellow, green, and black. This cable is typically referred to as **four conductor station wire** or **RYGB.** While capable of carrying an analog telephone call, this type of wire is not suitable for data transmission and should not be confused with unshielded twisted pair (UTP).

Another popular type of phone wiring is **flat gray modular** cable, also known as *gray satin* or *silver satin*. Inside this flat gray jacket are two, four, six, or eight wires, which are crimped into either RJ-11 (4-wire), RJ-12 (6-wire), or RJ-45 plugs (8-wire) using a specialized crimping tool. Premises phone wiring (as well as phones), crimp tools, RJ plugs, and flat gray modular wire are attainable at nearly any hardware or department store.

Flat gray modular wire is not the same as twisted pair and is suitable only for carrying data at fairly slow speeds over short distances. For instance, this type of cable is often used between a PC or workstation and a nearby RJ-11 jack for access to the telephone system or to carry RS-232 serial communication signals.

## Unshielded Twisted Pair

Twisted-pair wiring consists of one or more pairs of insulated copper wire twisted around each other at varying lengths ranging from 2 to 12 twists per foot. The twisting is used as a mechanism to reduce interference between pairs and from outside sources such as electric motors and fluorescent lights that can cause data errors and necessitate retransmission. These individually twisted pairs are then grouped together and covered with a plastic or vinyl jacket, or sheath. No additional shielding is added before the pairs are wrapped in the plastic jacket. Thus, the completed product is known as **unshielded twisted pair** or **UTP.** The most common numbers of pairs combined to form the unshielded twisted pair cables are 2, 3, 4, and 25 pairs of twisted copper wire.

All UTP cables are not created equal. One of the common appeals of UTP is that it is often already installed in modern buildings for the purpose of carrying voice conversations from telephone handsets to a voice PBX. Most often, when the twisted-pair wiring for the voice PBX was installed, extra pairs were wired to each office location. Some people jump to the conclusion that they don't need to invest in any new wiring to carry data transmission throughout their building—they can just use the extra pairs of the existing UTP wiring. The problem lies in the fact that there are six different categories of UTP as specified by **EIA/TIA 568** (Electronics Industry Association/Telecommunications Industry Association). EIA/TIA 568 also specifies the following:

- The topology, cable types, and connector types to be used in EIA/TIA 568 compliant wiring schemes

- The minimum performance specifications for cabling, connectors and components—such as wall plates, punch down blocks, and patch panels to be used in an EIA/TIA 568 compliant installation

Although category 1 UTP, otherwise known as voice-grade, need only carry voice conversations with reasonable clarity, categories 3 to 6 (data-grade) cable must meet certain predefined electrical characteristics that assure transmission quality and speed. Before assuming that the UTP in a building is adequate for data transmission, have its transmission characteristics tested to be certain that these characteristics meet the listed data-grade UTP specifications. Figure 3-1 summarizes the specifications for categories 1 to 6 UTP. It is important to note that a higher category of cable can be used for applications that require a lower cable category.

| UTP Category | Maximum Data Speed | Attenuation /NEXT limit | Applications |
|---|---|---|---|
| **Cat 1 UTP** | < 1 Mbps | | Telephone lines |
| **Cat 2 UTP** | 4 Mbps | 4 MHz | 4 Mbps token ring over UTP |
| **Cat 3 UTP** | 16 Mbps | 16 MHz | 10BaseT Ethernet. Tested for attenuation and near-end crosstalk up to 16 MHz. |
| **Cat 4 UTP** | 20 Mbps | 20 MHz | 16 Mbps token ring over UTP. Tested for attenuation and near-end crosstalk up to 20 MHz. |
| **Cat 5 UTP** | 100 Mbps (2 pair) 1 Gbps (4 pair) | 100 MHz | 100BaseT (fast) Ethernet, 155 Mbps ATM, gigabit Ethernet |
| **Cat 5e UTP** | 100 Mbps (2 pair) 1 Gbps (4 pair) | 100 MHz | 100BaseT (fast) Ethernet, 155 Mbps ATM, gigabit Ethernet Category 5e cable has a tighter quality control standard than standard cat 5 cable. |
| **Cat 6 UTP** | 2.5 Gbps (2 pair) potentially up to 10 Gbps (4 pair) | 200 MHz | None that **require** cat 6 at the time of this writing; the IEEE is working on a copper 10 Gbps Ethernet standard that would require cat 6 if released |

*Figure 3-1*   Unshielded Twisted Pair Specifications

Wire thickness is measured by gauge and represented with the unit **AWG** (American Wire Gauge). The higher the gauge number, the thinner the wire. UTP wiring of different categories must meet specifications for resistance to different forces that interfere with signal strength. Two of the more common sources of interference or loss of signal strength are as follows:

- **Attenuation** is the decrease in the power of signal over a distance in a particular type of wire or media.

- **Near-End Crosstalk** (**NExT**) is signal interference caused by a strong signal on one-pair (transmitting) overpowering a weaker signal on an adjacent pair (receiving). Near End Crosstalk and Attenuation to Crosstalk Ratio (ACR) are both measured in dB or decibels. A decibel is a logarithmic rather than linear measurement of the ratio between two powers, often a data signal and some type of noise or interference.

Practical Advice and Information

### BEYOND CAT 6

Although no official category 7 cable has become standardized, media vendors are attempting to develop cable that is capable of carrying data at frequencies of up to 600 MHz. Some such attempts are not truly unshielded twisted pair but rather are FTP or foil-twisted-pair cable that is more closely related to shielded twisted pair. Buyers must be wary of so-called category 7 cable by focusing on whether the cable is truly UTP and whether it is a specified EIA/TIA standard.

Anixter, a major cabling manufacturer, has proposed a program to define performance characteristics for cabling tested beyond the 100 MHz required for cat 5. Since higher-speed network architectures such as fast Ethernet and gigabit Ethernet require four pair of UTP to be transmitting power simultaneously, it was determined

| Level | Highest Test Frequency | Required Frequency in MHz for Attenuation to Crosstalk Ratio (ACR) at 10dB (Powersum Bandwidth) |
|-------|------------------------|-------------------------------------------------------------------------------------------------|
| 5 | 200 MHz | 80 MHz |
| 6 | 350 MHz | 100 MHz |
| 7 | 400 MHz | 160 MHz |

*Figure 3-2*   UTP Level 5, 6, and 7 Performance Specifications

that crosstalk should be measured by taking into account the crosstalk influence from all pairs in the cable (whether 4-pair or 25-pair) rather than just crosstalk between adjacent pairs, or pair-to-pair, as had been required for cat 5 certification. This type of crosstalk test is called **Powersum Crosstalk.** Key performance specifications for Level 5, 6, and 7 are detailed in Figure 3-2.

Regardless of the final standard for category 7 cable, it is likely that the standard will not support the venerable RJ-45 connector. The design of the RJ-45 simply promotes too much crosstalk to effectively support the higher data speeds associated with category 7. However, changing the cable could spell the end of the category 7 project. If the connector changes, then it would not be possible to use category 7 cable and connectors with existing data communication technologies such as fast and gigabit Ethernet. Without this backward compatibility, many buyers might simply choose to migrate their cable plants directly to fiber-optic cable to take advantage of its even higher bandwidth.

## COMMON UTP INSTALLATION MISTAKES

Practical Advice
and Information

Strict adherence to EIA/TIA 568 installation standards is essential to successful transmission at 100 Mbps or higher over UTP cabling. Because a less-than-perfect installation will probably transport 10 Mbps traffic without any problem, issues with noncompliant installations may not surface until upgrades to higher-speed network architectures are attempted. The most common installation mistakes are:

- Untwisting the UTP wire more than the maximum 13 mm in order to secure the UTP to wall plates or punch-down blocks. Exceeding the maximum bend radius specified for UTP. Overbending the wire increases crosstalk between stretched pairs of wires.

- Bundling the groups of UTP together too tightly with cable ties. Excessively pinching the UTP together increases crosstalk between pairs.

### STP-Shielded Twisted Pair

Data transmission characteristics, and therefore the data transmission speed, can be improved by adding **shielding** around each individual pair and the entire group of twisted pairs. This shielding may be a metallic foil or copper braid. The function of the shield is simple. It "shields" the individual twisted pairs as well as the entire cable from either Electromagnetic Interference (EMI) or Radio Frequency Interference (RFI). However, installation of shielded twisted pair can be tricky.

The shielding is metal and therefore a conductor. Often, the shielding is terminated in a drain wire that must be properly grounded on one end of the cable. It is critical that the shield be grounded on only one end or a *ground loop* can occur. In a ground loop a small current flows across the shield from the ground connector at one end of the cable to the ground connector at the other end of the cable. This current can actually decrease performance by inducing noise directly into the signal wires—quite the opposite of why the shielding was added.

Shielded twisted pair is becoming much less common. STP was commonly specified for token ring installations. However, recent technologies such as high-speed Ethernet, ATM, and other high-speed network architectures have specified category 5+ UTP rather than STP.

## Coaxial Cable

Coaxial cable, more commonly known as **coax** or cable TV cable, has specialized insulators and shielding separating two conductors, allowing reliable, high-speed data transmission over relatively long distances. Figure 3-3 illustrates a cross-section of a typical coaxial cable. Coax comes in various thicknesses and has been historically used in Ethernet network architectures. In some cases, these network architecture specifications include required characteristics of the (physical layer) coaxial cable over which the (data-link layer) MAC layer protocol is transmitted.

Modern local area network implementations rarely use coaxial cable. However, coaxial cable is still a key component of the cable television system. With the advent of cable modems and the use of the cable television system as a mechanism to provide high-speed Internet connectivity to homes coaxial cable continues to play an important role in data communication.

## Fiber-Optic Cable

Fiber-optic cable is the current reliability and performance champion of the data communication world. Although the most expensive media choice currently available, fiber-optic media delivers data transmission speeds measured in gigabytes (billions of characters) per second over distances often measured in miles.

Fiber-optic cable is also one of the most secure of all media, as it is relatively untappable, transmitting only pulses of light, unlike all of the aforementioned media, which transmit varying levels of electrical pulses. Because fiber optic is really a thin

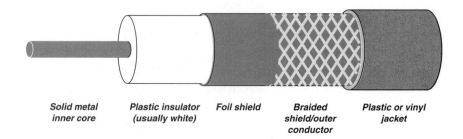

| Solid metal inner core | Plastic insulator (usually white) | Foil shield | Braided shield/outer conductor | Plastic or vinyl jacket |

*Figure 3-3*    Coax Cable: Cross-Section

fiber of glass, it is immune to electro-magnetic interference, contributing to its high bandwidth and data transmission capabilities. Another important thing to remember is that fiber-optic cable requires more careful handling than copper media. Figure 3-4 illustrates a cross-section of a fiber-optic cable.

**Light Transmission Modes**    Once a pulse of light enters the core of the fiber-optic cable, it will behave differently, depending on the physical characteristics of the core and cladding of the fiber-optic cable. In a **Multimode** or **Multimode Step Index** fiber-optic cable, the rays of light will bounce off of the cladding at different angles and continue down the core while others will be absorbed in the cladding. These multiple rays at varying angles cause distortion and limit the overall transmission capabilities of the fiber. This type of fiber-optic cable is capable of high bandwidth transmission but usually over fairly short distances.

By gradually decreasing a characteristic of the core known as the refractive index from the center to the outer edge, reflected rays are focused along the core more efficiently yielding higher bandwidth over several kilometers. This type of fiber-optic cable is known as **Multimode Graded Index Fiber.**

The third type of fiber-optic cable seeks to focus the rays of light even further so that only a single wavelength can pass through at a time, in a fiber type known as **single mode.** Without numerous reflections of rays at multiple angles, distortion is eliminated and bandwidth is maximized. Single mode is the most expensive fiber-optic cable, but can be used over the longest distances.

**Core Thickness**    The thickness of fiber-optic cable's *core* and *cladding* is measured in microns (millionths of an inch). The three major core thicknesses are 50, 62, and 100 microns with their associated claddings being 125, 125, and 140 microns, respectively. The increasing core thicknesses generally allow transmission over longer distances at a greater expense, however.

**Light Source Wavelength**    The wavelength of the light that is pulsed onto the fiber-optic cable is measured in nanometers (nm), with the optimal light transmitting wavelengths coming in three distinct windows of 820 nm, 1,310 nm, and 1,500 nm; 820nm and 1,310nm are most often used for local and campus-wide networking such as gigabit Ethernet, while 1,310 nm and 1,500 nm are used by carriers to deliver high bandwidth fiber-based service over long distances. The higher-frequency light-emitting sources carry a higher price tag.

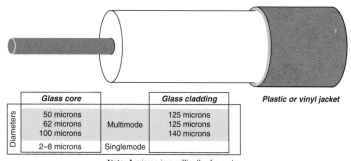

| | Glass core | | Glass cladding | | Plastic or vinyl jacket |
|---|---|---|---|---|---|
| Diameters | 50 microns<br>62 microns<br>100 microns | Multimode | 125 microns<br>125 microns<br>140 microns | | |
| | 2–8 microns | Singlemode | | | |

Note: A micron is a millionth of a meter

*Figure 3-4*    Fiber-Optic Cable: Cross-Section

Applied Problem
Solving

| Media Type | Also Called | Bandwidth | Distance Limits | Connectors | Comments/Applications | Ethernet | Fast Ethernet | Gigabit Ethernet | ATM |
|---|---|---|---|---|---|---|---|---|---|
| | | | | | | | **Architectures** | | |
| 4-wire phone station wire | Quad RYGB | 3 Kbps | 200 feet | RJ-11 jacks | 4 insulated wired-red,green, yellow, black. Home phone wiring; voice Applications | | | | |
| Flat gray modular | Flat satin, telephone cable, silver satin | 14.4 Kbps | 10-20 feet | RJ-11 or RJ-45 plugs | Comes with 4,6,8 conductors; used for short data cables using modular (mod-tap) adapters | ■ | | | |
| Unshielded twisted pair | UTP | 100 Mbps | 100 feet | RJ-45 | 5 Designated categories. Twists prevent interference, increase bandwidth; voice grade usually not suitable for data | ■ | ■ | ■ | ■ |
| Shielded twisted pair | STP | 16 Mbps | 100 feet | RJ-45 or IBM data connectors | Shielding reduces interference but complicates installation | ■ | ■ | | ■ |
| Coax- thick | Frozen yellow garden hose | 10 Mbps | 500 feet | AUI (attachment unit interface) | Original Ethernet cabling | ■ | | | |
| Coax-thin | RG-58, thinnet, cheapernet | 10 Mbps | 200 feet | BNC connector | Looks like cable TV cable. Easier to work with than thick coax | ■ | | | |
| Coax-thin | RG-62 | 2.5 Mbps | 200 feet | BNC or IBM data connector | Similar to RG-58 (thinnet) but different electrical characteristics make these cables NOT interchangeable | | | | |
| Fiber-optic cable | Fiber Glass | Several Gbps | Several kilometers | SI or SMA 905 or SMA 906 | Difficult to install but technology is improving. High bandwidth, long distance, virtually error free, high security | ■ | | ■ | ■ |

*Figure 3-5*   LAN Media Technology Analysis

## ■ POINT-TO-POINT DATA TRANSMISSION TECHNOLOGIES

The most basic data communication technologies are those used to directly connect two devices. These connections can be used to connect a computer to peripheral devices such as modems, scanners, PDAs, and so on, or as the basis for a directly connected computer-to-computer data connection. Operating at layer one of the OSI Network Reference Model, these technologies provide a physical connection that can be used to carry many higher-level protocols.

### Serial Transmission Standards

Serial transmission is the basis of most data communication between computers. There are several different serial communication standards available for use in modern computers, including RS-232, USB, and IEEE 1394 (Firewire).

**RS-232**  RS-232 is currently the most commonly used serial standard for modem communication. Standardized by the Electronics Industries Association (EIA), RS-232 is currently in its third release (RS-232-C). The prevalence of RS-232 in the PC marketplace is so great that the term serial port has come to mean an RS-232 serial connection. Although newer serial standards threaten to replace RS-232 as the pre-dominate serial standard in the not too distant future, it still merits a close inspection.

RS-232 uses electrical signals to transmit the ones and zeroes of the digital datastream. The RS-232 standard defines voltages of between +5 and +15 volts DC on a given pin to represent a logical zero, otherwise known as a space, and voltages of between 5 and 15 volts DC to represent logical ones, otherwise known as a *mark*.

RS-232 can be implemented on a multitude of data connectors. In the case of the DB-25 connector illustrated in Figure 3-6, the presence or absence of an electrical charge on each of these 25 pins has been designated as having a specific meaning in data communications. These standard definitions are officially known as **RS-232-C.** They were issued by the EIA, and are listed in Figure 3-8.

Although all 25 pins are defined, in most cases, 10 or fewer of the pins are actu-ally used in the majority of serial transmission applications. On some PCs, such as

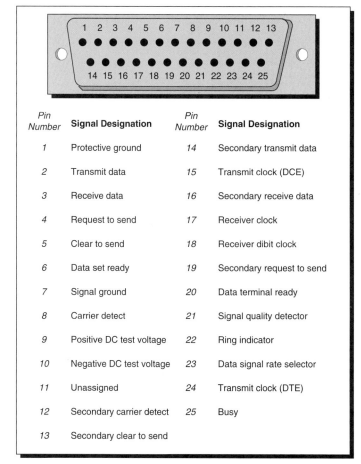

| Pin Number | Signal Designation | Pin Number | Signal Designation |
|---|---|---|---|
| 1 | Protective ground | 14 | Secondary transmit data |
| 2 | Transmit data | 15 | Transmit clock (DCE) |
| 3 | Receive data | 16 | Secondary receive data |
| 4 | Request to send | 17 | Receiver clock |
| 5 | Clear to send | 18 | Receiver dibit clock |
| 6 | Data set ready | 19 | Secondary request to send |
| 7 | Signal ground | 20 | Data terminal ready |
| 8 | Carrier detect | 21 | Signal quality detector |
| 9 | Positive DC test voltage | 22 | Ring indicator |
| 10 | Negative DC test voltage | 23 | Data signal rate selector |
| 11 | Unassigned | 24 | Transmit clock (DTE) |
| 12 | Secondary carrier detect | 25 | Busy |
| 13 | Secondary clear to send | | |

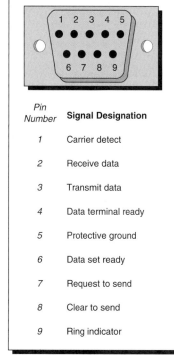

| Pin Number | Signal Designation |
|---|---|
| 1 | Carrier detect |
| 2 | Receive data |
| 3 | Transmit data |
| 4 | Data terminal ready |
| 5 | Protective ground |
| 6 | Data set ready |
| 7 | Request to send |
| 8 | Clear to send |
| 9 | Ring indicator |

*Figure 3-6*  RS-232 Serial Transmission Protocol as Defined for DB-25 and DB-9 Connectors

personal computers as well as many notebook and laptop computers, the serial port has only 9 pins (DB-9 connector) and the RS-232 serial transmission protocol is supported as listed in Figure 3-6. Other RS-232 implementations rely on mini-DIN connectors or phono-plug style connectors. Pictures of common RS-232 connectors are shown in Figure 3-7.

**Practical Advice and Information**

## PHYSICAL INTERFACES VS. TRANSMISSION PROTOCOLS

It is important to distinguish between those standards that describe the connectors or physical interfaces that are used to connect appropriate cables to a computer's physical ports, and the standards that describe the electrical characteristics, or transmission protocols used.

*RS-232 Cables*    To connect devices via RS-232, a multi-wire cable must be used. The cable has several small, insulated wires within an outer jacket. Each signal to be carried, or RS-232 pin to be supported, requires its own individual inner wire.

The number of signals that must be transmitted across an RS-232 connection between two devices will depend on the software used. The number of signals required can vary from as few as two for one-way communication to twelve for a full-duplex modem connection. Figure 3-8 summarizes the signals that are most commonly included in modem cables and designates which signals are assigned to which pins on both DB-9 and DB-25 connectors. The signals are arranged in logical pairs in order to increase understanding rather than in order of pin number.

*DCE vs. DTE*    The original application of RS-232 was to connect computing devices to modems. To make cabling this "standard" solution easier, two classifications of RS-232 devices were created. The pin-outs for these classifications were established so that the cable could be "straight through" in nature, where each pin is connected to the same pin on the other end of the cable. Pin 1 will connect to pin 1, pin 2 to pin 2, and so on. The PC and the modem in our scenario are examples of these two classifications: **data terminal equipment (DTE)** and **data communications equipment (DCE)**, respectively. DCE can also expanded as **data circuit terminating equipment.**

Although this approach made sense for modem applications, the use of RS-232 has expanded to include all sorts of electronic equipment ranging from modems to personal digital assistants (PDAs) to advanced television remote controls. It is therefore critical to establish exactly which signals are associated with each pin on the connector. It is impossible to rely on any standard mapping, as each device might have deviated from the loosely enforced standard if they even use a "standard" connector.

DB-25 connector (female)

DB-9 connector (female)

*Figure 3-7*    Common RS-232 Connectors

| RS-232 Signal | DB-25 Pin | DB-9 Pin | Abbr. | From | To | Explanation |
|---|---|---|---|---|---|---|
| Protective Ground | 1 | 5 | PG | | | A reference voltage used to protect circuit boards inside PC |
| Signal Ground | 7 | 5 | SG | | | A reference voltage used to determine proper signal voltage for ones and zeroes |
| Transmit Data | 2 | 3 | TXD | DTE | DCE | Discrete voltages representing characters encoded as 1s and 0s are transmitted on this pin to deliver the actual data message |
| Receive Data | 3 | 2 | RXD | DCE | DTE | Discrete voltages representing characters encoded as ones and zeroes are received on this pin to receive the actual data message |
| Request to Send | 4 | 7 | RTS | DTE | DCE | Used in conjunction with CTS to perform modem-to-modem flow control allowing modems to take turns transmitting to each other |
| Clear to Send | 5 | 8 | CTS | DCE | DTE | Used in conjunction with RTS to perform modem-to-modem flow control allowing modems to take turns transmitting to each other |
| Data Set Ready | 6 | 6 | DSR | DCE | DTE | Used for initial handshaking between local modem and local PC to indicate local modem is functional |
| Data Terminal Ready | 20 | 4 | DTR | DTE | DCE | Used for initial handshaking between local modem and local PC to indicate local PC is functional |
| Transmit Clock | 15 | | TC | DTE | DCE | Clocking signal transmitted on this pin; required for synchronous modems only |
| Receive Clock | 17 | | RC | DCE | DTE | Clocking signal received on this pin; required for synchronous modems only |
| Carrier Detect | 8 | 1 | CD | DCE | DTE | Indicates that the local modem has successfully contacted the remote modem and is ready to transmit data |
| Ring Indicator | 22 | 9 | RI | DCE | DTE | Indicates to the local modem that a call is incoming and that the modem should auto-answer the call |

*Figure 3-8*   Most Commonly Used RS-232 Signals

*Serial/Parallel Conversion: UARTs*   Data travel via parallel transmission within a PC over the PC's main data bus. The data emerging from the serial port must be in serial format. Therefore, somewhere inside the PC a parallel to serial conversion must be taking place. A specialized computer chip known as a **Universal Asynchronous Receiver Transmitter (UART)** acts as the interface between the parallel transmission of the computer bus and the serial transmission of the serial port. UARTs differ in performance capabilities based on the amount of on-chip buffer memory. The commonly used 16550 UART chip contains a 16 byte on-chip buffer memory for improved serial/parallel conversion performance.

In Sharper Focus

| Standard Name | Standards Body | Physical Interface Connector | Description |
|---|---|---|---|
| **RS-422** | EIA | DB9 DB25 DB37 | An electrical specification usually associated with RS-449 (DB37 Connector). Each signal pin has its own ground line (balanced) rather than sharing a common ground. Up to 10 Mbps over 1,200 meters. Use of DB25 or DB9 is also possible. |
| **RS-423** | EIA | DB9 DB25 DB37 | An electrical specification is usually associated with RS-449 (DB37 Connector). Signal pins share a common ground wire (unbalanced signaling). Up to 10 Mbps over 1,200 meters. Use of DB25 or DB9 is also possible. |
| **RS-449** | EIA | DB37 plus DB9 | A physical/mechanical specification for a DB-37 (37-pin connector), plus an additional DB-9 if required. Usually associated with either RS-422 or RS-423 electrical specifications. |
| **RS-485** | EIA | DB9 DB25 DB37 | Can be used in multipoint applications in which one computer controls multiple (up to 64) devices. Often used in computer-integrated manufacturing operations or in telecommunications management networks. |
| **RS-530** | EIA | DB25 | A physical/mechanical specification that works with RS-422 or RS-423 over a DB-25 connector rather than a DB-37 connector. Allows speeds of up to 2 Mbps. |
| **V.35** | ITU | M-Block | An international standard for serial transmission up to 48 Kbps defined for an M-block connector. Often used on data communications equipment that must interface to high-speed carrier services. |

*Figure 3-9*    Other Traditional Serial Transmission Standards

## OTHER TRADITIONAL SERIAL TRANSMISSION STANDARDS

RS-232 is officially limited to 20 Kbps (kilobits per second) for a maximum distance of 50 feet. In reality, depending on the type of media used and the amount of external interference present—RS-232 can be transmitted at higher speeds and/or over greater distances. However, modern hardware typically supports speeds up to 115 Kbps using 16550 family UARTS.

To resolve the speed and distance limitations of RS-232, several other serial transmission standards have been developed. Some of these standards also include the ability to connect more than two devices at the same time. A serial standard that can connect three or more devices together concurrently is known as a multipoint serial communications standard. A list of common serial standards is provided in Figure 3-9.

**Universal Serial Bus (USB)**    Although RS-232 is historically the most widely implemented serial standard, a new standard serial communication standard has virtually replaced RS-232 in all but the most basic applications. This is because three basic architectural limitations in the RS-232 technology limit its application to new devices such as scanners, digital cameras, video cameras, and personal digital assistants: RS-232 is slow (only up to 115 Kbps), only supports one device per port, and requires significant configuration to attach a device.

The **universal serial bus** (**USB**) is a high-speed, multipoint serial communications technology developed by the USB Implementer's Forum to resolve RS-232's shortcomings. There are two versions of USB currently available—the original USB 1.1 specification and a newer, higher-speed USB 2.0 specification. USB 2.0 is backward compatible with USB 1.1. However, to gain the higher speeds offered by USB 2.0, devices must be attached either directly to the computer or to a USB 2.0 compatible hub.

USB version 1.1 operates at either 1.5 Mbps or 12 Mbps. That equates to more than 1,000 times the maximum speed of RS-232. USB 2.0 can operate at even higher speeds, up to 480 Mbps. This increased speed is significantly important when supporting such high data devices as scanners and digital cameras. As covered in chapter 4, it is even possible to connect to a local area network (LAN) via a USB network interface card (NIC).

Both USB 1.1 and USB 2.0 use electrical signals to transmit the ones and zeroes of the digital datastream. Unlike RS-232, which is ground referenced (uses voltages of +5Vdc and 0Vdc for ones and zeroes), USB uses a differential electrical signal. A digital 1 is represented when D+ signal line voltage is 200 mv greater than the D– signal voltage. Similarly, a digital 0 is represented by the D+ signal voltage being 200 mV less than the D– signal voltage. Differential signaling offers more noise resistance than ground referenced signaling while greatly reducing the potential impact of ground loops.

When connected to a computer, low-speed USB devices such as joysticks and PDAs create virtual serial ports. These ports are typically assigned as if they were physical RS-232 com ports (COM2, COM3, etc.) Since each of these ports can only use up to 115 Kbps of bandwidth, they can easily be multiplexed over the same physical USB connection with no loss of performance. However for high-speed devices such as scanners and video cameras, it is better to connect them to one of the computer's USB ports.

USB can support up to 126 devices on each port. Some devices come with two USB ports so that the user can simply "daisy-chain" the devices together. Although this solution is functional for a couple of devices, a better solution for larger implementations is to use a USB hub. As illustrated in Figure 3-10, a USB hub is a device that connects directly to the computer's USB port and offers multiple ports to connect other USB devices.

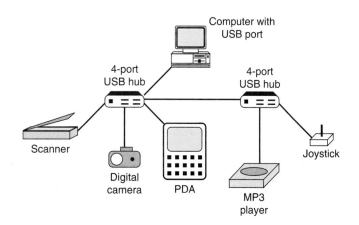

*Figure 3-10*   USB Hub Implementations

To reduce the configuration hassles traditionally associated with serial connectivity using RS-232, USB is designed to be *plug and play*. Devices are automatically given an address, assigned a speed, and identified by the computer's operating system. As long as the operating system supports USB plug and play, all that is required to connect a device is to plug it into either the computer or to a USB hub connected to the computer.

To make the process of attaching devices even easier, the USB ports and cables also include the power to the device, eliminating the need to have a separate power supply for each peripheral. When using powered USB devices it is important that the power consumption of the attached devices does not exceed that of the computer port or USB hub to which the devices are attached. While the USB specification requires 500 milliamps of power, in an effort to save battery life some notebook computer vendors have reduced the USB power output to lower levels. In these cases, some combinations of devices may not work without adding an externally powered USB hub.

There are two connector types associated with USB. The USB "A" connector is used to connect to computers and the USB "B" connector is used to connect to the devices. The ability to disconnect the USB cable at the device end of the connection makes it significantly easier to change devices compared to having to reach behind the computer to disconnect the cables. Figure 3-11 shows the USB A and B connectors.

**IEEE-1394/Firewire**   Another high-speed serial standard is **IEEE-1394.** Originally developed by Texas Instruments and implemented by Apple Computer Inc. as the proprietary **Firewire,** the interface was standardized by the IEEE in 1995. Sony has trademarked the name **i.Link** for their implementation of IEEE-1394, and that moniker seems to be gaining popularity, at least among Japanese consumer electronics manufacturers.

Similar to USB, IEEE-1394 is a multipoint serial bus–based solution. Devices can be added or removed from the live bus. Devices can be daisy chained or connected to an IEEE-1394 hub for connectivity between more than two devices. Although similar to USB in many ways, IEEE-1394 is not intended to directly compete with USB but rather to complement USB. USB offers a low- to medium-speed serial solution while IEEE-1394 offers a high-speed solution. By having two separate serial standards, each can be optimized for specific applications.

IEEE-1394 uses electrical signals to transmit the ones and zeroes of the digital datastream. Like USB, IEEE-3194 uses differential signaling to provide better performance and noise abatement over longer distances. Unlike USB, IEEE-1394b is also capable of operating over fiber-optic media, offering higher speeds and greatly increased distances.

USB-A (on left) and USB-B (on right) connectors

*Figure 3-11*   USB Connectors

IEEE-1394 is a high-speed serial solution ranging in speed from 400 Mbps (original specification) to 800 Mbps (1394b). One of the key differentiators between IEEE-1394 and other serial bus standards is that, in addition to standard asynchronous communication, IEEE-1394 includes support for isochronous communication. *Isochronous communication* guarantees data delivery at a constant, predetermined rate. This allows IEEE-1394 to be used in time critical multimedia solutions. The constant data delivery rate reduces the need to buffer data, thereby greatly reducing the cost of implementing the technology compared to a traditional asynchronous solution.

Taking advantage of its isochronous capabilities, the main applications of IEEE-1394 at the current time are in the transmission of digital data between consumer electronics devices. IEEE-1394 has been adopted by the digital VCR Manufacturers Association as its standard interconnection technology. The ongoing conversion of television from an analog format to digital HDTV technologies will increase the marketplace for IEEE-1394 technologies in the consumer electronics marketplace.

IEEE-1394 ports are also being introduced in multimedia-capable computers. In addition to allowing the computer to connect to digital camcorders and VCRs, IEEE-1394 ports will allow data network solutions to be deployed. To support the use of IEEE-1394 on computer platforms, the IEEE-1394 Trade Association released an updated version of the standard known as IEEE-1394b in 2002. The IEEE-1394b standard increases speeds to 800 Mbps at 100 meters and reduces latency by streamlining the protocol. Also known as Firewire 800, IEEE-1394b is designed to be backward compatible with the original IEEE-1394 standard.

IEEE 1394 uses two different connectors: a four-wire connector that supports full-duplex data transmission and a six-wire connector that also provides power to a connected device. Figure 3-12 shows these two interface connectors.

## Parallel Transmission

Parallel transmission is primarily limited to transmission of data within a computer, although the release of the IBM personal computer included an 8-bit parallel interface designed to connect the computer to a printer. Common physical interfaces associated with this parallel transmission technology are the DB-25 connector and the Centronics connector. The Centronics connector is a 36-pin parallel interface. In addition to the physical plug and socket, the Centronics parallel standard defines electrical signaling for parallel transmission and is a de-facto standard. DB-25 and Centronics parallel physical interfaces are illustrated in Figure 3-13.

IEEE-1394 Connectors

*Figure 3-12*   IEEE-1394 Connectors

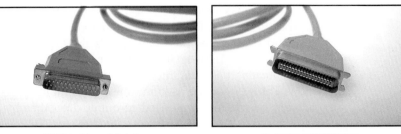

DB-25 (male) parallel interface        Centronics parallel interface

*Figure 3-13*    Parallel Transmission Physical Interfaces

Initially intended for connecting a printer, the parallel port on personal computers later saw duty as a means of connecting medium-speed peripheral devices such as scanners, tape drives, and video cameras due to its relatively high speed as compared to RS-232. However, with the proliferation of USB and IEEE-1394, use of the Centronics parallel port has significantly trailed off to the point that some notebook computer vendors are no longer including parallel ports on their products.

## Wireless Technologies

One of the largest hassles with the explosion of modern computing devices is the series of cables required to connect them. This is even more of a problem when traveling. If you have a notebook computer, a PDA, a cell phone, and an MP3 player, you could potentially need three different data cables to connect them, in addition to the requisite power supplies and cords. Two technologies have been developed as wireless cable replacements: infrared (IRDA) and radio (Bluetooth).

Infrared (IrDA)    The Infrared Data Association (**IrDA**) is an international standards body responsible for creating standards that apply to the use of infrared (Ir) light to provide wireless connectivity for devices and/or to locations that would typically require more traditional wire-based solutions. IrDA signals are point-to-point nature, have a narrow angle (30 degree cone), are limited to around meter, and have a throughput of 9,600 bps to 4 Mbps. IrDA has proven to be a popular technology, with compliant ports currently available in an array of devices, including embedded devices, pagers, phones, modems, cameras, watches, computers (PCs) and laptops, PDAs, printers, and other computer peripherals.

There are two widespread IrDA versions: IrDA 1.0 and 1.1. Designed as a direct RS-232 serial port replacement, IrDA 1.0 (also known as SIR) offers data speeds of 9.6, 19.2, 38.4, 57.6, and 115.2 Kbps. IrDA 1.1 (FIR) increases the list of available speeds to include 576 Kbps, as well as 1.152 and 4.0 Mbps. A third version of the standard (FIR) that supports data speeds up to 16 Mbps was ratified but has not seen widespread use. Regardless of version, IrDA ports are addressed as RS-232 serial ports.

Despite widespread acceptance, infrared has some significant limitations to its use. In general, IrDA is a point-to-point protocol; only two devices can communicate at any given time. If a session is live between two devices and a third device attempts to initiate a session, the initial session will be dropped. There is a derivative of IrDA that supports multi-point communication (IrLAN), but it has not achieved widespread adoption and probably will not due to the evolution of Bluetooth technologies.

Another key limitation of IrDA is that there must be a direct line of sight between the two communicating devices. If either is moved, the communication session will be dropped. This limitation effective prevents IrDA from being used in many applications such as connecting a PDA to the Internet through a cell phone in a belt holster. Using IrDA, the phone must be out on a table right in front of the PDA. Between these limitations and the limited speed available, IrDA is likely to be replaced by Bluetooth as that standard matures.

Bluetooth **Bluetooth** is the name given to an emerging wireless radio frequency (RF) communication standard. Originally developed by Erickson, Bluetooth is currently backed by Bluetooth Special Interest Group (SIG), a collection of Bluetooth promoters that includes 3COM, IBM, Intel, Microsoft, and Nokia, among others, with the purpose of developing and promoting the use of the Bluetooth technology.

Bluetooth uses radio frequency communication in the unlicensed 2.4–2.4835 GHz band using *frequency hop spread spectrum* (FHSS). As its name suggests, FHSS hops from one frequency to another throughout the allowable frequency range. The pattern of frequency hopping must be known by the wireless receiver so that the message can be reconstructed correctly. A given wireless transceiver's signal is on a given frequency for less than 1 second. By constantly changing frequency, the transmission tends to be less affected by interference, an especially desirable characteristic for mobile computing applications.

Bluetooth offers data speeds of up to 1 Mbps up to 10 meters. Unlike IrDA, Bluetooth supports a LAN-like mode where multiple devices can interact with each other. Due to the limited size of the Bluetooth coverage area, the terms *piconet* and *personal area network* (PAN) have been coined to describe a Bluetooth coverage zone.

The key limitations of Bluetooth are security and interference with wireless LANs. The fact that Bluetooth doesn't require line-of-sight to communicate cuts both ways: while it makes it possible to use your PDA with your cellular phone that is stashed in your briefcase, it also makes it possible for someone else with a device hidden from view to attempt to gain illicit access to your computing devices. Bluetooth attempts to mitigate this risk through the use of strong authentication and encryption technologies. Because Bluetooth uses the same frequency range as IEEE 802.11b wireless networks, simultaneous use of both technologies greatly affects performance. This concept is covered further in chapter 4.

Devices hitting the market that include Bluetooth include cellular phones, PDAs, headphones, and mobile gaming platforms. Although the technology is too new to guarantee widespread success, it shows great promise as a way to eliminate the spaghetti bowl of cords that beleaguers mobile workers.

## ■ INTERNET ACCESS TECHNOLOGIES

After connecting to peripheral devices, most people want to connect their computer to the Internet. While a technical discussion of the Internet is beyond the scope of this chapter, suffice it to say that it is a large, international network that offers a wide-ranging selection of data services to any connected computer including e-mail, instant messaging, Web pages, and streaming media. More detail on the technical "how" of the Internet will be provided in chapters 7 and 8.

The process of connecting to the Internet is conceptually straightforward: All you have to do is create a link between your computer and a device connected to the

Internet. The traffic from the local computer that needs to go to the Internet will be sent across this link. The problem is the distance between the local computer and the Internet-connected device.

Although the point-to-point data communications technologies previously discussed provide a means to connect a computer to a local device or even another computer located in close physical proximity, they are not capable of dealing with the distance between the local computer and the remote Internet connection device. A whole new class of data communication technologies is required to meet the distance and speed requirements for Internet access. The Internet access architecture is illustrated in Figure 3-14.

## Internet Service Providers

In most cases, an individual wishing to connect to the Internet will initiate a link to a company whose business is extending the Internet to individuals. These companies, known as **Internet service providers (ISPs)**, take a high-speed connection to the Internet and—using a collection of Internet access technologies—offer Internet connectivity to individual users.

ISPs range in size from a local provider that focuses on meeting the needs of a geographically limited area to national and international providers such as America Online (AOL), which provide service across large geographic areas. In addition to the area they service, ISPs vary widely in the access technologies offered, data speeds provided, and pricing methods.

Managerial
Perspective

### SELECTING AN ISP

Regardless of size, ISPs all provide access to the same Internet. When selecting an ISP it is important to look at four key criteria:

- *Service hosting*—Do you need the ISP to host your Web pages, e-mail addresses, and so on?

- *Performance*—What types of access technologies does the ISP support? What data rates are offered? What is the confirmed information rate (CIR—the

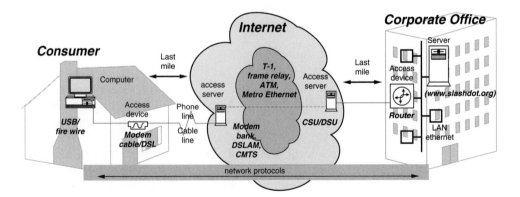

*Figure 3-14*   Internet Access Architecture

amount of throughput the ISP guarantees, which is usually significantly slower than the base speed)?

- *Cost*—What is the monthly cost of the service? What is the cost per megabyte per second? Are there service caps after which surcharges apply?

- *Reliability*—Does the ISP have a generator on site to maintain connectivity in the event of a power failure? Does the ISP have multiple links to the Internet so that if one fails you still have access? Does the ISP offer multiple links to your location to protect from the failure of a single link?

## Dial-Up Modems

The first and most basic method for connecting a home computer to the Internet is to use a dial-up modem. A dial-up modem creates a circuit-switched connection across the public switched telephone system (PSTN) to another modem that is connected to the Internet.

**Architecture**   A switched or **dial-up** line is the type of phone line typically installed in a home or place of business. To place a call, you pick up the receiver or handset, wait for a dial tone, and dial the number of the location you wish to call. This ordinary type of phone service is sometimes called **POTS** or **Plain Old Telephone Service.** More formally, the phone network is referred to as the **Public Switched Telephone Network (PSTN)**. Figure 3-15 illustrates the major components of the PSTN.

As introduced in chapter 1 and detailed in chapter 5, the phone set is connected to a large switch in a telephone company building called a central office or CO via a local loop. When a call is dialed, the telephone switch connects the phone set to the destination set by finding an available circuit or path.

**Technology**   Calls placed over dial-up lines through CO switches that have connections built from available circuits are called **circuit-switched connections.** In order to interface transparently to the PSTN, modems must be able to dial and answer phone calls to and from other modems.

The next important characteristic related to transmitting data over a dial-up phone line has to do with how the data are represented on that phone line. First, it is

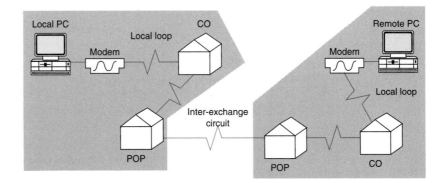

*Figure 3-15*   PSTN Architecture

important to realize that today's dial-up phone network was originally designed to carry voice conversations efficiently and with reasonable sound quality. This "efficiency of design with reasonable sound quality" meant reproducing a range of the frequencies of human speech and hearing just wide enough to produce reasonable sound quality. That range of frequencies, or **bandwidth,** is 3,100 Hz (From 300 Hz to 3,400 Hz), and is the standard bandwidth of today's voice-grade dial up circuits (phone lines). Hz is the abbreviation for hertz. One hertz is one cycle per second. The higher the number of hertz or cycles per second, the higher the frequency. Frequency, wavelength, hertz, and cycles per second were introduced in chapter 2.

This 3,100 Hz is all the bandwidth with which the modem operating over a dial-up circuit has to work. Because the dial-up phone network was designed to be able to mimic the constantly varying tones or frequencies that characterize human speech, only these continuous, wave-like tones or frequencies can travel over the dial-up phone network in this limited bandwidth.

The challenge for the modem is to represent the discrete, digitized ones and zeroes from the input (PC) side of the modem in a continuous or analog form within a limited bandwidth so that the data may be transmitted over the dial-up network. Figure 3-16 summarizes the results of I-P-O analysis involving modems and the PSTN.

The modem's job is to convert digital data into analog data for transmission over the dial-up phone network and to convert analog data received from the dial-up network into digital data for the terminal or PC. As previously discussed in chapter 2, the proper names for these processes are *modulation* and *demodulation*. In fact, the word *modem* is actually a contraction for modulator/demodulator.

Most local loops that are used for connection to the PSTN to supply switched, dial-up phone service are physically described as *two-wire circuits*. Since one of these two wires serves as a ground wire for the circuit, that leaves only one wire between the two ends of the circuit for data signaling. Dial-up or switched two-wire circuits generate a dial tone.

Given that two-wire dial-up circuits only have one wire for data signaling, only one modem could be transmitting at a time while the other modem could only be receiving data. This one direction at a time transmission is known as half-duplex.

Modems that interfaced to a dial-up circuit had to support this half-duplex transmission method. What this meant was that once the two modems completed initial

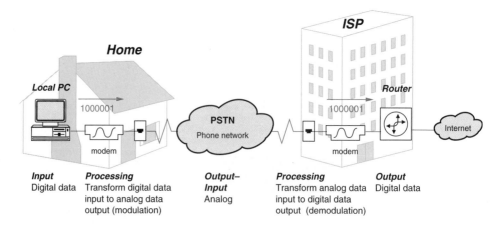

*Figure 3-16*   I-P-O Analysis: Modems and the PSTN

**handshaking,** one modem would agree to transmit while the other received. In order for the modems to reverse roles, the initially transmitting DTE (terminal or computer) drops its RTS (request to send) RS-232 Pin #4 and the transmitting DCE (modem) drops its CTS (clear to send) RS-232 Pin #5, and perhaps its carrier wave. Next, the initially receiving DTE must raise RTS, the initially receiving DCE (modem) must generate a carrier wave and raise CTS, and the role reversal is complete.

This role reversal is known as **turnaround time** and can take two-tenths of a second or longer. This might not seem like a very long time, but if this role-reversal needed to be done several thousand times over a long-distance circuit, charged by usage time, it might have a large dollar impact.

Full-duplex transmission supports simultaneous data signaling in both directions. Full-duplex transmission might seem to be impossible on two-wire circuits. Until the advent of the V.32 9,600 bps full-duplex modem, the only way to get full-duplex transmission was to lease a four-wire circuit. Two wires (signal and ground) were for transmitting data and two wires (signal and ground) were for receiving data. There was no "role reversal" necessary and therefore, no modem turnaround time delays. Modems manufactured to the CCITT's V.32 standard (and the later V.34 standard) can transmit in full-duplex mode, thereby receiving and transmitting simultaneously over dial-up two-wire circuits using a sophisticated **echo cancellation** technique.

Echo cancellation takes advantage of sophisticated technology known as **digital signal processors** (**DSP**) that are included in modems that offer echo cancellation. By first testing the echo characteristics of a given phone line at modem initialization time, these DSPs are able to actually distinguish the echoed transmission of the local modem from the intended transmission of the remote modem. By subtracting or canceling the echoed local transmission from the total data signal received, only the intended transmission from the remote modem remains to be processed by the modem and passed on to the local PC.

Standards   In order for modems manufactured by different vendors to interoperate successfully, they must adhere to common operational standards. These standards must define methods of modulation, data compression, error correction, and autodialing, and must provide backward compatibility with older standards. Figure 3-17 summarizes significant dial-up modem standards of the last twenty years.

The V series standards featured in Figure 3-17 are officially sanctioned by the International Telecommunications Union—Telephony Sector (ITU-T). The Bell standards listed in Figure 3-17 are pre-divestiture standards from the time when AT&T dictated modem specifications in the United States and compliance with international standards was not an option. The suffix "bis" refers to the second standard issued by a given standard committee, while the suffix "ter" refers to the third standard issued by that same committee.

## NON-STANDARD STANDARDS

In an effort to gain market share during the time when standards-making organizations are deliberating new standards, vendors often introduce proprietary versions of pending standards. Before the standardization of V.90 there were two proprietary 56 Kbps modem technologies: X2 from 3COM/US Robotics and K56flex from Lucent Technologies.

One very important point to keep in mind when purchasing pre-standard data communications equipment is the ability of the vendor to upgrade that equipment to

Practical Advice
and Information

| Modem Standard | Transmission Rate | Baud Rate | Data Compression | Error Correction | Modulation Method |
|---|---|---|---|---|---|
| **V.90** | 56 Kbps down, 28.8 Kbps up | 3,200, 3,000, 2,400, 2,743, 2,800, 3,429, baud | V.42bis/MNP5 | V.42/MNP4 | Digital downlink & 9QAM & TCM uplink |
| **V.34** | 28.8 Kbps 33.6 Kbps (optional) | 3,200, 3,000, 2,400, 2,743, 2,800, 3,429, baud | V.42bis/MNP5 | V.42/MNP4 | 9QAM & TCM |
| **V.32 ter** | 19.2 Kbps | 2,400 baud | V.42bis/MNP5 | V.42/MNP4 | 8QAM & TCM |
| **V.32 bis** | 14.4 Kbps | 2,400 baud | V.42bis/MNP5 | V.42/MNP4 | 6QAM & TCM |
| **V.32** | 9.6 Kbps | 2,400 baud | V.42bis/MNP5 | V.42/MNP4 | 4QAM & TCM |
| **V.22 bis** | 2,400 bps | 600 baud | V.42bis/MNP5 | V.42/MNP4 | 4QAM & TCM |
| **Bell 212A** | 1,200 bps | 600 baud | | | 4PSK |
| **Bell 103** | 300 bps | 300 baud | | | FSK |

*Figure 3-17* Modem Standards

meet the specifications of the official standard once it is issued. In some cases, software upgrades are possible, while in other cases, hardware upgrades or chip replacement is required. In some cases, these upgrades may be free and easily accomplished via the Internet, while in other cases, the upgrade may involve returning the equipment to the factory, involving upgrade fees of several hundreds of dollars. Be sure to understand all of the details regarding standards compliance upgrades before ever purchasing pre-standards data communications equipment.

*V.34* V.34 offers a transmission rate of up to 33.6 Kbps (33,600 bps) over the standard analog local loop. The highest required speed for a V.34 compliant modem is 28.8 Kbps. The 33.6 Kbps speed is available for modems that make use of an optional baud rate. As shown in Figure 3-17, the higher speed is achieved by using a lower baud rate with more bits per baud than the required 28.8 Kbps speed.

It is important to note that although modulation standards have changed in order to produce higher transmission rates, the associated data compression and error correction standards have remained constant. The V.34 modem standard instituted a variety of technical innovations in order to achieve this transmission rate over dial-up lines of variable quality. The overall effect of these technical innovations is that the V.34 modem is better able than any previous modem standard to easily and dynamically adjust to variable line conditions in order to optimize transmission rate.

In Sharper Focus

## V.34 TECHNICAL INNOVATIONS

Figure 3-18 summarizes the technical innovations introduced with the V.34 modem standard and their associated importance or implication.

Although all of the technical innovations listed in Figure 3-18 are considered part of the V.34 standard, it is not safe to assume that they are all included in any V.34 modem. In addition, several other optional features may or may not be supported on any given V.34 modem:

- Support of leased lines as well as dial-up lines

- Inclusion of four-wire as well as two-wire physical interfaces

- Password protection and callback security

| V.34 Technical Innovation | Importance/Implication |
| --- | --- |
| **Multiple baud rates/ Carrier frequencies** | The V.34 standard specifies three required baud rates (3,200, 3,000, 2,400) and three optional baud rates (3,429, 2,800, 2,743). Multiple potential baud rates increase the V.34 modem's ability to adapt to variable line conditions. Each baud rate supports two different carrier frequencies in order to optimize transmission speed on dial-up lines of variable quality. |
| **Baud rates greater than 2,400** | The V.34 standard is the first to attempt baud rates of greater than 2,400. The 28.8Kbps transmission rate is achieved by interpreting 9 data bits per baud at a baud rate of 3,200. The 33.6 Kbps transmission rate is achieved by interpreting 12 bits per baud at a baud rate of 2,800. |
| **Auxiliary management channel** | An auxiliary or side channel, separate from the data channel, is available for transmission of management or configuration data. This channel would be particularly important if the V.34 modem were attached to a router or similar internetworking device that might require monitoring or management without disrupting the main data traffic. |
| **Asymmetric transmit/ receive speeds** | Some applications such as database queries/responses, or Web requests/downloads, may require wide bandwidth in one direction only. V.34 specifies a method for allocating the data with a larger bandwidth in one direction than the other. |
| **Adaptive line probing** | Adaptive line probing tests the characteristics of the transmission line not just at call initiation time, but throughout the transmission. Changes in baud rate, carrier frequency, constellation size and shape and other parameters can be changed in order to optimize transmission rate. |
| **Precoding and nonlinear encoding** | Reduces high-frequency line noise and increases immunity to interference on analog to digital conversion by plotting constellation points in areas with less interference. |
| **Fallback/fallforward** | Although many modem standards support fallback, V.34 supports fall-forward features that allow increases in transmission rates as line conditions improve. |
| **Trellis coded modulation** | A forward error correction methodology that helps support higher baud rates on dirty phone lines by predicting the location of a given constellation point. Can add significant processing overhead. |
| **V.8 Training specification** | Also known as fast-training, this specification allows two V.34 modems that support V.8 training to set-up and initialize a call faster than modems that do not support V.8. |

*Figure 3-18* V.34 Technical Innovations

- Ability to connect to fax machines via the V.17 FAX standard

- Ability to auto-dial via the V.25bis autodial standard

- Auto-dial backup for failed leased lines or lost carrier

- Auto restoral to repaired leased lines

This lack of assurance as to the exact features supported on any given V.34 can lead to interoperability problems among V.34 modems. The best solution to this dilemma is to purchase identical modems from a single manufacturer. If this is not practical, then the time invested to carefully investigate which features of the V.34 standard are implemented in a given modem would be a wise investment indeed.

*V.90*   According to Shannon's Law the highest V.34 transmission rate of 33.6 Kbps should be the maximum transmission rate that a voice-grade telephone line can support. However, Figure 3-17 claims that modems that adhere to the V.90 standard are capable of transferring data in at least one direction at speeds up to 56 Kbps per second. How can this be? Were telecommunications engineers able to change the laws of physics?

The answer is obviously no. Shannon's law is still intact for data transmission across the PSTN. The telecommunications engineers instead changed the paradigm in order to alleviate one of the largest components of noise in a traditional modem implementation. The resulting standard, known as **V.90,** is a hybrid analog/digital standard that offers transmission rates of almost double V.34 levels.

A preview of chapter 5 shows that the majority of the telephone system is currently digital in nature with the local loops from the central offices to the end users being the only remaining analog connections. An analog telephone signal is converted into a digital signal at the Central Office (CO) for transmission across this digital telephone system then converted back into an analog signal at the destination CO for transmission to the destination telephone across the destination local loop.

The limiting factor in exceeding V.34 speeds is the quantization noise associated with the conversion of the analog signal to a digital signal for transmission across the digital telephone system. In order to exceed V.34 speeds, this analog to digital conversion and its associated quantization noise must be eliminated. Fortunately the digital nature of the modern PSTN makes this possible.

## QUANTIZATION NOISE

In Sharper Focus

Conversion of a signal from an analog format to a digital format imparts "noise" into the signal. This can be readily explained by considering the nature of both analog and digital signals. Analog signals can consist of any possible level. Digital signals can consist only of fixed levels.

As shown in Figure 3-19, when an analog signal is sampled and converted into a digital signal, a certain level of detail is lost. When the digital signal is converted back into an analog signal at the destination end of the call, the resulting analog waveform is not exactly equal to the source waveform. This error is known as **quantization noise** or **quantization error.**

While quantization noise is not perceivable by humans on normal telephone calls, it affects the ability of modems to use the entire bandwidth of the call, thus limiting the potential transmission rate. It is important to note that quantization noise is created by the analog to digital conversion process, although it does not manifest itself until subsequent digital to analog conversion.

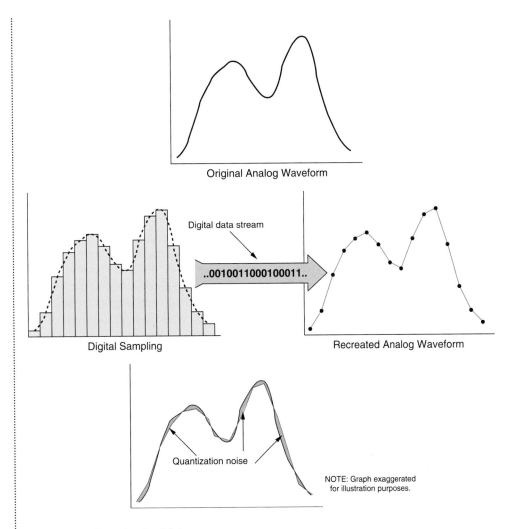

*Figure 3-19* Quantization Noise

The V.90 modem standard makes use of the digital PSTN to overcome quantization noise by replacing the analog modem on one end of the connection with a digital server. This server connects directly to its Central Office (CO) via a digital connection such as an ISDN PRI or T-1 line. By using a direct digital connection, the server avoids any analog to digital conversions for outgoing transmission, thereby eliminating quantization noise. At the other end of the connection the CO converts the digital signal into a clean analog signal and transmits it to the destination modem. This process is illustrated in Figure 3-20.

By using this technique, a theoretical transmission rate of 56 Kbps can be achieved from the server to the modem. Note that this is a theoretical rate. An FCC limit on the amount of power allowed on the local loop reduces this theoretical limit to around 53 Kbps. Physical limitations in the local loop—including the distance from the modem to the CO, the number of connections or splices in the local loop, and the overall quality of the local loop—can limit the actual transmission rates further. In the authors' experience it is far more common to achieve transmission rates of around 44 Kbps, although connections at rates in excess of 50 Kbps have been noted.

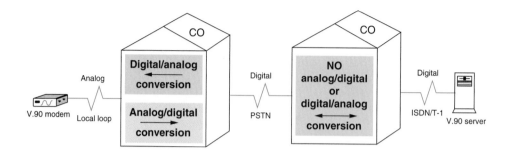

*Figure 3-20* V.90 Implementation

A close examination of Figure 3-20 shows that the increased speed offered by V.90 is limited to the half of the connection originating at the server and terminating at the modem. The other half of the connection, originating at the modem and terminating at the server, must undergo an analog to digital conversion and therefore incurs quantization error, limiting speeds to V.34 levels. Because the speeds are different in each direction, V.90 is said to be an **asymmetrical transmission** technology.

Fortunately, the asymmetrical characteristic of V.90 matches the asymmetrical nature of the most common modem application: accessing the Internet. In a normal Internet session, a user sends a fairly short request (such as the address of a Web page) to a server. The server responds with a much larger collection of data (such the text and graphics that make up the Web page) to the user, making V.90 a natural fit for Internet access.

As with all modern modem standards, V.90 compliant modems are backward compatible with earlier standards. When a connection is initially made, the modem will attempt to connect at the highest possible V.90 speed. It will then drop back to slower V.90 levels, then resort to V.34 levels, V.32 levels, and so on, until a carrier wave can be established. Because of this automatic rate fallback strategy, it is common for first-time users to comment on the long time required for a V.90 modem to establish a carrier and begin communicating.

**Data Compression and Error Correction Standards** By operating more efficiently, modems are able to offer more transmitted data in a given amount of time. Although several factors can lead to increased modem efficiency, data compression can have the most significant impact in the amount of data actually delivered by a given modem in a given amount of time.

*Data Compression* As introduced in chapter 2, data compression replaces large strings of repeating character patterns with a special code that represents the pattern. The code is then sent to the other modem. From that point forward, the sending modem sends the code instead of the original pattern. As the code is significantly smaller than the pattern it represents, the amount of data sent between the two modems is reduced, up to 400 percent under optimal conditions. The process of data reduction is similar in concept to having more than one bit per baud, as covered in the previous chapter.

By using data compression, a 28.8 Kbps (V.34) modem could optimally transfer 115.2 Kbps (28.8 Kbps × compression factor of 4:1) of data across a dial-up phone line. In this scenario, the 115,200 bps is known as *throughput*, while the transmission rate remains at or below the V.34 maximum of 28.8 Kbps.

*V.42bis and MNP 5*   The two predominant data compression standards are V.42 bis and MNP5. Most modems try to negotiate with each other to implement V.42bis data compression at initialization. The less-efficient MNP5 protocol is commonly used as a second option.

**V.42bis** uses a data compression algorithm known as the Lempel Ziv algorithm. Ideally, it can compress files, and thereby increase throughput by a 4:1 ratio. Proprietary improvements to this algorithm by modem manufacturers can be achieved in two ways:

- Increase the amount of memory dedicated to the library, also known as the dictionary (1.5KB standard, some modems use up to 6KB)

- Increase the size of the pattern of characters, also known as string size, which can be stored in the dictionary (32 bytes standard, some modems support strings up to 256 bytes)

Proprietary improvements to standards such as V.42bis are only effective when both modems involved in a transmission are identical. It should also be noted that most independent modem testing suggests that compression ratios in the range of 2.5:1 are most likely, despite higher optimal claims.

**MNP Class 5** yields data compression ratios in the range of between 1.3:1 and 2:1. MNP5 uses two data compression algorithms:

- *Huffman encoding* is a special character encoding scheme that re-encodes ASCII characters. Frequently used characters such as "a", "e", and "s", are encoded with only 4 bits, while rarely occurring characters such as "x" or "z" are encoded using as many as 11 bits. Overall, the effect of Huffman encoding in that more characters are transmitted using fewer bits.

- *Run-length encoding* exams a datastream in search of repeating characters. When any character repeats more than three times, the run-length encoding algorithm replaces the entire string of repeated characters with only three repetitions of the character followed by a count field indicating how many times the character is actually repeated. For example, a data string containing ten consecutive repetitions of the same character would be replaced by three repetitions of that character followed by a 1-byte count character. This would reduce the string in question from 10 bytes to 4 bytes, for a savings of 60 percent. Repeated characters can include nonprinting characters such as spaces, carriage returns, and line feeds.

Improving the reliability of the data transmission link between two modems will ultimately make that data transmission faster and more efficient. Fewer retransmissions due to data errors will reduce the overhead associated with correcting errors, thus reducing the time necessary to transmit a given message. This will minimize the cost of the data transmission.

*Error Prevention*   Data transmission errors occur when received data is misinterpreted due to noise or interference on the phone lines over which the data message traveled. Errors can be prevented by

- Reducing the amount of noise or interference on a given transmission line

- Employing modulation techniques that are able to adapt to and overcome noisy lines

*Line Conditioning, Repeaters, and Amplifiers*    **Line conditioning** is a value-added service available for analog leased lines from the phone company. Various levels of conditioning are available at prices that increase proportionally to the level of conditioning, or noise reduction, requested. Conditioning represents a promise from the phone company in terms of the noise levels or interference present on a given analog leased line. In order to deliver on this promise, the phone company might have to install additional equipment.

A **repeater** is often used by a phone company to assure signal quality over the entire length of a circuit. As a signal travels through a medium such as copper wire, it loses some of its strength due to the resistance of the wire. This loss of signal strength or volume is known as attenuation.

A repeater on an analog circuit, sometimes called an **amplifier,** strengthens and repeats the signal. Unfortunately, on an analog circuit the amplifier cannot distinguish between the voice or data signal and the background noise. As a result, the amplifier strengthens and repeats both signal and the background noise.

Repeaters on digital circuits are able to distinguish the digital signals from the background noise. Therefore, digital repeaters can retransmit a digital signal free of noise, ensuring that the signal will reliably arrive at its destination without the need for specialized line conditioning.

*Adaptive Protocols*    Another way in which errors can be prevented during data transmission is through the use of **adaptive protocols.** Adaptive protocols adjust transmission session parameters in response to varying line conditions. The MNP Classes of networking protocols offer several examples of such adaptive protocols.

**Adaptive Size Packet Assembly** is an **MNP Class 4** protocol that can increase or decrease the amount of data sent in each packet according to the current condition of the transmission circuit. A packet that includes data and overhead information is analogous to a handwritten message (the data) plus a sealed, addressed envelope (the overhead). This protocol tries to optimize the amount of data per packet by building packets containing the greatest amount of data that can be transmitted reliably and therefore, not require retransmission.

Optimal packet size is a moving target, changing with line conditions. Each packet of data contains overhead. Therefore, if line conditions are good, it makes sense to use large packets to maximize the data to overhead ration. Returning to the previous analogy, it would be advantageous to write as long a letter as possible for each envelope. Too little data per packet and time is wasted processing overhead (opening envelopes in the analogy).

However, if line conditions are poor, errors will occur. Because the error detection process can only determine that an error occurred in the packet rather than the exact bit in error, the entire packet containing the error must be retransmitted. The larger the packets are, the more data that must be retransmitted for each error. In our analogy this correlates to receiving, rewriting and remailing letters for insufficient postage. Adaptive Size Packet Assembly solves the data per packet dilemma by adapting the amount of data included in each packet according to varying line conditions. When errors are detected, packet size is reduced. When no errors are detected over a period of time, packet sizes are increased.

**Dynamic Speed Shifts** is an **MNP Class 10** adaptive protocol that allows two modems to change speeds up or down (faster or slower) in the midst of their data transmission in response to varying line conditions. The adaptive nature of this protocol assures that the highest practical transmission speed will be used at all times, dependent upon current line conditions. This adaptive protocol is especially useful in cellular phone environments in which line quality can vary significantly over short periods of time.

## ADAPTIVE PROTOCOLS CAN MASK PROBLEMS

Dynamic Speed Shifts or any adaptive protocol can be a double-edged sword, however. In the event of degraded line quality, MNP 10 modems may automatically downgrade their transmission speeds. Unless a personnel procedure is in place to take note of the lower transmission speed, the problem might go undetected and unreported to the carrier for an extended period of time.

*Forward Error Correction*  Sophisticated error correction techniques exist that send sufficient redundant data to the receiving modem to enable it to not only detect, but also to correct data transmission errors without the need for retransmission. Forward error correction works in a similar manner to the data correction techniques previously explained. On the transmitting side, the incoming data signal is processed and redundant code bits are generated based on that incoming signal. These additional redundant bits are added to the original signal and transmitted to the receiving device. The receiving device processes the incoming data signal in the same manner as the transmitting device and regenerates the redundant code bits. The transmitted redundant code bits are compared with the redundant code bits regenerated by the receiving modem. If they match, then no errors have occurred on the incoming signal. If they don't match, the forward error correction circuitry at the receiving device uses the transmitted redundant bits to correct the incoming data signal, thereby correcting transmission errors without the need for retransmission.

However, there is a downside to forward error correction. In data communications, just as in life, you can't get something for nothing. In order to give the receiving modem sufficient redundant data to be able to correct its own detected errors, the overall throughput of informational data on the circuit is reduced. This process, known as **forward error correction,** tries to favorably balance how much redundant data can be sent *up front,* thereby avoiding retransmissions, to maximize overall throughput on the circuit. It's a bit of a gamble, really:

- If not enough redundant data are sent, the overall throughput is reduced due to retransmissions.

- If too much redundant data are sent, the overall throughput is reduced because the redundant data is taking up space and processing power that could be occupied by "new" non-redundant data.

*Trellis Coded Modulation*  Trellis coded modulation (**TCM**) is another way in which transmission errors can be overcome without the need for retransmission. Modems that employ TCM are able to overcome twice as much noise on a given circuit as QAM modems that don't employ TCM. Intersymbol interference can cause a modem to detect the wrong constellation point and subsequently interpret that constellation point into an incorrect sequence of bits. Using a sophisticated technique known as **convolutional encoding,** TCM adds a redundant bit that limits the possible valid constellation points for the current transmission. By limiting the number of possible constellation points that are potentially valid for any given symbol received, the modem is able to avoid misinterpreting symbols that would ordinarily lead to retransmissions in order to correct the error.

For example, if we wanted to send 6 data bits per baud, we would ordinarily require a 64-point constellation ($2^6$). However, by adding a 7th TCM code bit to each 6 data bits, a 128-point constellation would be generated ($2^7$). But remember, only 64 constellation points are required to transmit the original 6 data bits per baud, so only 64 of the 128 possible detectable constellation points are defined as valid. If one of the invalid constellation points is detected, the TCM circuitry selects the most likely valid constellation point and its associated pattern of bits. In this manner, TCM reduces errors and the need for retransmission due to line impairments. However, error detection and correction techniques must still be employed.

The sophistication of a given TCM scheme is measured by the number of potential trellis codes or states. The greater the number of TCM states, the higher the required processing power in the modems, and the higher immunity to inter-symbol interference due to line noise. TCM was first introduced as part of the V.32 modem standard and is supported by V.34 and V.90 modems.

*MNP4*    The MNP error control standards were originally developed by Microcom, a modem manufacturer. The MNP standards include Classes 2, 3, and 4. These error control standards optimize the full-duplex transmission of data over dial-up lines through Adaptive Size Packet Assembly and the elimination of redundant or overhead information from transmissions.

*V.42*    Not to be confused with the CCITT V.42bis standard for data compression, **V.42** incorporates MNP Class 4 Error Control as the first of two possible error control protocols. In addition, a second error control protocol known as **Link Access Protocol for Modems,** or **LAP-M,** adds Selective ARQ to the capabilities of MNP Class 4 Error Control protocol. Selective ARQ, described earlier, only requires retransmission of specific blocks received in error rather than all blocks subsequent to the block in which the error was detected. V.42 also provides for negotiation during modem handshaking to allow two modems to decide whether they will implement MNP 4 or LAP-M as an error control protocol for their data transmission.

Practical Advice
and Information

## HARDWARE VS. SOFTWARE ERROR CONTROL

MNP4 and V.42 are error control protocols implemented within modems. Using these protocols, the modems themselves assure error-free transmission. There is no need for additional error control protocols that can be supplied by communications software packages running as an application program on a PC.

*Flow Control*    There are two basic approaches to implementing flow control in a modem environment: hardware and software flow control. Hardware flow control is dependent on the use of the RS-232 serial communication standard. When using hardware flow control the Request to Send (RTS) and Clear to Send (CTS) signals are used to perform the essential elements of flow control. A transmitting device will only send data into buffer memory as long as Clear to Send is "held high" (has a 5-volt signal). As soon as Clear to Send is "dropped" (goes to zero volts), the transmitting device immediately ceases transmitting data.

A second flow-control mechanism is to carry embed flow control flags within the datastream itself. Special data sequences, known as flags, that mean "Stop Sending Data" (XOFF) and "Resume Sending Data" (XON) are defined. When a device cannot receive data any longer, it sends an XOFF signal to the sending device. When it can resume receiving data, it sends an XON flag to the sending device.

Practical Advice
and Information

## SOFTWARE VS. HARDWARE FLOW CONTROL

When using RS-232 hardware flow control is usually more reliable and faster than software flow control. Software flow control is nothing more than transmitted characters susceptible to the same transmission problems as normal data. Occasionally, an XOFF might be transmitted in error and might stop a data transmission session for no apparent reason. Second, because XON and XOFF are sent in the datastream along with all the "normal" data and must be differentiated from that data. This process takes time (adds latency) and is subject to error.

*Application*    While the most ubiquitous, Internet Access Technology, dial-up modems are the least attractive from a pure performance perspective. With best case, real-world data speeds limited to around 45 Kbps downstream and 33 Kbps upstream, dial-up modems are simply too slow to truly provide adequate service for an increasingly multimedia Internet.

At this point dial-up modems have three applications in the Internet access paradigm:

- *Travel*—PSTN lines are available at residences, hotels, and even modern pay phones. When combined with a national ISP, a dial-up modem can provide Internet access just about anywhere.

- *Cost*—Dial-up modems continue to be the least expensive Internet access technology in terms of base monthly fee. However, when looking at the cost/MB of data downloaded, dial-up trails faster technologies by a significant margin. If a full-time connection is required, the cost of a second phone line can quickly drive the cost of dial-up higher than faster alternatives.

- *Last resort*—Dial-up Internet access is available virtually everywhere, even those places where other, faster alternatives are not yet available. In some cases, it is simply dial-up or nothing.

Beyond the Internet access paradigm, dial-up modems have other applications, including serving as a backup connection for other technologies such as the wide area networking connections detailed in chapter 6. If the primary connection fails, a dial-up connection is established to the destination to enable business to continue. However, due to the reduced speed of a dial-up connection, care must be taken to ensure that the limited bandwidth is used for the mission-critical applications by preventing other, less critical applications from using the connection.

Managerial
Perspective

## LEASED LINE BACKUP

Coping with leased-line failure requires a business decision. The technology is available to backup failed leased lines by automatically establishing connections via dial-up lines between points on the failed circuit. However, there are at least two incremental costs involved in this automatic backup. First, there is the cost of the additional technology necessary to detect the leased-line failure and establish the dial-up connection. Second, dial-up circuits must be available for the auto dial backup unit to utilize in the event of a leased line failure. These dial-up circuits would incur both installation and monthly charges, whether they are used or not.

In addition, if the established dial backup connection is long distance, then per-minute usage charges for the dial-up lines could amount to a significant incremental cost. The other side of the cost/benefit equation would require the following question to be asked, "What is the cost of the business lost during the time that the leased line is down?" If that lost business can be translated into lost sales dollars in excess of the incremental cost of establishing and maintaining the dial-up backup for the failed leased line, then the acquisition of the equipment and phone lines to enable automatic backup would constitute a prudent business decision.

## Digital Subscriber Line (DSL)

As the Internet has matured, so has the sophistication of the content it carries. With Web pages growing in size due to the addition of animation and graphics, the explosion of file sharing using networks such as Kazaa, and the promise of real-time voice and video communication, dial-up modems have become too slow to meet the needs of the Internet consumer and are being phased out in favor of "broadband" access technologies. Broadband has many definitions, but the simplest is to consider any access technology that provides access to the Internet at greater that 56 Kbps to be a **broadband** technology.

One of the faster broadband technologies currently available is **Digital Subscriber Line (DSL)**. DSL provides an "always on" connection to the Internet over the same copper wires that provide dial-up telephone service.

**Architecture**   DSL uses the same physical local loop connection as the local phone service used in POTS, as illustrated in Figure 3-15. When a local loop is used for DSL frequency division multiplexing is used to separate the existing voice service from the DSL service. As detailed earlier in this chapter, a POTS line uses only the bottom 4 KHz of bandwidth on the copper loop. All of the bandwidth above is available for an alternate service, such as DSL.

As illustrated in Figure 3-21, DSL operates above the POTS frequency range. In the figure the DSL service operates between 25 Khz and 1,100 Khz. This frequency range is further broken into two parts for upstream and downstream data. Upstream uses between 25 Khz and 100 Khz. Downstream data uses 110 Khz to 1100 Khz. This is

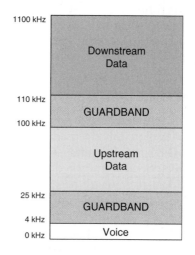

*Figure 3-21*   Frequency Division Multiplexing in DSL

an example of an asynchronous link. Because the amount of bandwidth given to the downstream link is larger than that given to the upstream link, the connection supports a proportionally higher downstream data transfer speed. This type of DSL service is commonly referred to as an **Asymmetrical Digital Subscriber Line (ADSL)**.

Because DSL uses the same copper loop as a POTS line, it reduces the cost to the DSL provider. If additional copper wires are needed to deliver service, the DSL provider would have to send out a technician to install the additional wire, increasing the cost of installation with a corresponding increase in DSL service cost.

In order to support DSL service, additional equipment must be installed in the central office (CO) and the customer home (also known as the customer premises). As illustrated in Figure 3-22, this equipment includes a DSL modem at the customer premises and a **Digital Subscriber Line Access Multiplexer (DSLAM)** at the central office.

A DSL modem is installed at the customer's premises. This modem works like the dial-up modems discussed earlier in the chapter in that it takes digital signals from your computer and converts it to analog signals for transmission over the local loop to the central office using the same digital to analog modulation technologies as a dial-up modem. The key differences are that the DSL modem doesn't need to "dial up" the central office equipment every time you want to connect to the Internet: the central office is always at the other end of the local loop connection.

When the modem is initially powered on, it communicates with the DSLAM at the central office. The two devices then determine the optimal speed based on the quality of the connection over the copper pair and establish a connection. This connection is a point-to-point connection between the modem and the central office. The customer is the only person using the local loop between the central office and the customer premise. The connection remains live until the modem is powered down.

A DSL modem connects to any phone jack at the customer premise using a standard RJ-11 phone connection to receive the analog data signal from the DSLAM. The DSL modem then un-modulates the signal and provides it to your computer (or other network device) via a second port. The majority of the DSL modems in use today use a standard Ethernet for this connection. The Ethernet port would be connected to an Ethernet network interface card (NIC) in your PC or other network device use as a firewall/router. Some DSL modems may use a USB connection to

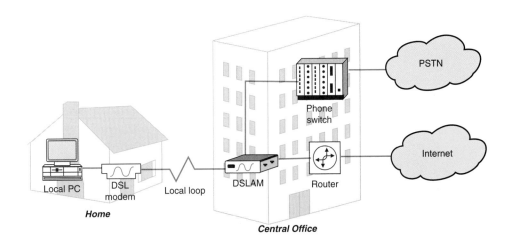

*Figure 3-22* DSL Architecture

connect to the computer in place of the Ethernet connection. If the modem only supplies a USB connection it must be connected to a computer rather than another network device.

A DSLAM is installed on the central office. This device is analogous to a modem bank in a dial-up environment. It takes multiple incoming DSL local loops, demodulates their datastreams, and multiplexes them onto a high-speed connection for transmission to the ISP. These high-speed connections can vary from a T1 to frame relay, to an OC-3 SONET connection. For more information about these technologies, please refer to chapter 6. After stripping the data signal from the local loop the DSLAM sends the underlying POTS signal to the dial-up telephone switch.

DSL modems and DSLAMs are layer two devices: they simply pass the data between them without interpreting it. From the perspective of the user at the customer premises the DSL modem and DSLAM are invisible.

**Standards and Technology**   Unlike dial-up modems, there is little standardization in the DSL world. Different vendors have developed different solutions that use different frequencies and modulation schemes. Fortunately, the only two devices that have to agree on the DSL technology used are the DSL modem and the DSLAM. For this reason, most DSL service providers require customers to rent or purchase DSL modems directly from them. This is diametrically opposite the approach taken in cable modem environments.

There are several different DSL standards deployed. The key differences between these technologies are the data transmission speeds they provide, the distance over which they travel, and their reliability and resistance to noise. A matrix of commonly available DSL services is provided in Figure 3-23.

| DSL Technology | Maximum Speed | Pairs of copper needed | Distance Limitation | Application |
|---|---|---|---|---|
| ADSL (Asymmetrical DSL) | Up to 8 Mbps downstream 640 Kbps upstream | 1 | Up to 18,000 ft. | Consumer Internet access |
| IDSL (ISDN DSL) | 144 Kbps downstream 144 Kbps upstream | 2 | Up to 18,000 ft. (additional equipment can extend distance) | ISDN replacement and business Internet access |
| SDSL (Symmetrical DSL) | 1.544 Mbps downstream 1.544 Mbps upstream | 1 | Up to 10,000 ft. | Business Internet access |
| HDSL (High bit-rate DSL) | 1.544 Mbps downstream 1.544 Mbps upstream | 2 | 12,000 to 15,000 ft. | T-1 replacement and business Internet access |
| VDSL (Very high bit-rate DSL) | up to 34 Mbps upstream and downstream, if symmetric | 1 | Max. of 4,000 ft. | Business Internet access |

*Figure 3-23*   DSL Comparison Matrix

**Implementation and Performance**    A few items affect the speed of DSL services. The first item is the copper local loop. The quality of the copper in the ground is a major factor. If you live in an area built in the early 1950s, the copper installed in the ground is older and might have degraded over time. If you live in a newly constructed area, the copper could be newer and made with more modern manufacturing techniques. The quality of the copper is something you may not be able to fix, but it is something you need to be aware of when dealing with DSL.

Another item that affects the speed of DSL is the distance you are from the central office. The farther you are from the central office, the longer the analog signal needs to travel over the copper. As analog signals travel over copper over a distance, the signal degrades in power. This signal loss affects the speed at which DSL operates. In areas where the DSL modem is close to the central office, the DSL modem may run near its theoretical speeds. In locations where you are farther away from the central office, the DSL modem will not operate at the theoretical speeds, but will generally operate at a speed faster than dial-up modems.

*Splitter and Media Filters*    A **splitter** would be installed on the outside of the house by the telephone company. The goal is to separate the data service from the voice service. This was needed due to the nature of how phone service works. When a phone goes off hook, a power spike is caused by the contacts opening up on the phone switch. The power spike sends a frequency blip over the entire frequency spectrum allowed to pass over the copper pair. The frequency blip, if not stopped, would cause the DSL modem to "momentarily" drop connection with the DSLAM in the central office. This would cause data to be lost and the modem would have to reestablish their connection.

Early DSL modems required these splitters to be installed to eliminate the possibility of phone calls affecting the data service. The splitter separated the wiring inside the house to a phone set of connections and a single data connection. The phone connection also had a device installed to eliminate the power spike. The installation of the splitter increased the cost of the service due to the labor of the person from the telephone company being required to visit each residence to install the splitter. A consumer installation method was required that would eliminate the *truck roll*, thus lowering the cost and decreasing the time it took to turn up each service. The solution was found in the use of **media filter.**

Media filters are sent with the DSL modem and installed by the consumer. Media filters are wire-wrapped magnets that are installed on each phone in the house that is connected to the phone line the DSL is on. The goal of the filter is to suppress the high-voltage spike that occurs when a traditional phone is taken "off hook." Media filters absorb the frequency blip and allow the DSL modem to work without interruption.

*Consumer Class vs. Business Class DSL*    As discussed above, DSL can be used for both business and consumer access to the Internet. As you would expect, business-class DSL costs more than consumer-class service. Consumer-class DSL usually uses DHCP for IP addressing and usually allocates one IP address per DSL modem. The bandwidth allocation is generally more in the downstream direction and the upstream direction. This matches the wants of most consumers: they need to get more information from the Internet than they send.

Business-class DSL generally allocates a static IP address to the business. Additional IP addresses can be purchased, for a cost. Businesses generally want to run a Web site from their location, so the data requirements are different than the "standard" consumer. Bandwidth allocation is generally more symmetrically with speed moving toward T1 speeds (1.544 Mbps upstream and downstream). The business might also want the ISP to supply e-mail services for all their employees. This will also increase the cost.

If a consumer needs some of the features that a business would need, the providers are more than happy to sell them a business class DSL connection. The only catch is that they will pay the same cost as the business would. Some providers do offer a more cost-effective consumer solution that deletes some of the other key features that a business user would need.

**Future of DSL**   The future of DSL is focused on providing new services over the DSL modem. DSL providers would like to provide audio and video-on-demand services over the DSL modem. Both of these services will require the need for quality of service (QoS) to allow them to work effectively. QoS will allow the user to make voice calls over the Internet, stream video to PC, and download files at the same time without the voice or video quality suffering from the file download.

## Cable Modems

A second provider of high bandwidth connectivity to customer premises is the television cable company. In fact, the cable provider's infrastructure offers a significantly higher bandwidth to the consumer than the local loop provided by the telephone company due to the coaxial cable media used for cable television transmission.

**Architecture**   Cable systems were originally designed to provide one-way communication between the programming source, known as the head end, to the consumer's television set. Analog television programming was broadcast across the network to any and all television receivers connected to the system via coaxial cable. Splitters and amplifiers were placed in the system where needed to allow the system to grow to meet the needs of the community served. This type of cable television network looks like a tree: the head end is the root and the branches continually are split off and fed into neighborhoods.

Modern cable networks have evolved to support two-way communication in addition to one-way, broadcast communication with increased bandwidth available. The increased bandwidth can be used by the cable company to offer a larger number of television channels in either analog or digital form, offer on-demand television where a customer can request movies to be sent directly to their home, and offer interactive Internet access.

To offer bi-directional Internet access, frequency division multiplexing is used to reallocate the bandwidth for one television channel (in the 50 to 750 MHz range) for downstream traffic and another channel (in the 5 to 42 MHz band) is reallocated to carry upstream signals. A single downstream 6-MHz television channel can support up to 27 Mbps of downstream data throughput using 64 QAM (quadrature amplitude modulation) transmission technology. Speeds can be boosted to 36 Mbps using 256 QAM. Upstream channels may deliver 500 Kbps to 10 Mbps from homes using 16QAM or QPSK (quadrature phase shift key) modulation techniques, depending on the amount of spectrum (number of channels) allocated for service and the relative noise on the line.

Once the bandwidth to be used for Internet access has been allocated, equipment must be installed at the head end and at the customer premises. Cable modem service providers use a **Cable Modem Termination System (CMTS)** to add data transmission capabilities to the existing CTV infrastructure. The CMTS is capable of providing throughput to multiple homes at rates of up to 50 Mbps. However, throughput is usually less than 27 Mbps due to the way data are transmitted to homes from the cable modem service provider.

As can be seen in Figure 3-24 the CTMS is capable of serving multiple distribution hubs, which, in turn, serve multiple fiber nodes. Each fiber node serves a *neighborhood,* or physical grouping of homes. Most groupings range from 500 to 2,000 homes on a modern HFC network. This architecture typically results in speeds to the home of between 500 Kbps and 1.5 Mbps, depending on network congestion. Between the fiber nodes and the homes in the neighborhood, the upstream and downstream bandwidth is shared by the active data subscribers connected to a given cable network segment. A device known as a **diplexer** is used to both separate and combine the upstream and downstream signals and is located at the fiber node.

Once the coaxial cable reaches the subscriber's home, a frequency splitter is used to separate the TV signals from the data signals. Assuming the home is pre-wired for CTV, the existing wiring is used for the CTV signals. The "new" wire is connected to a cable modem, which, in turn, connects to the subscriber's PC via 10 Mbps Ethernet or, optional in newer cable modems, a USB connection. Figure 3-25 illustrates this configuration.

The function of a cable modem is essentially the reverse of the CMTS: to modulate and demodulate upstream and downstream signals, respectively. As mentioned, the CMTS uses the same techniques on the upstream and downstream signals at the head end. Downstream data is modulated at the headend using the 64-QAM modulation technique. The data occupies a 6-MHz channel somewhere in the 50 to 750 MHz range. The signal is demodulated at the cable modem side.

Upstream signals are handled differently. Like their downstream counterparts, they are modulated at the cable modem side and transmitted back to the CMTS. Because multiple cable modems must share the upstream bandwidth to the CMTS, a

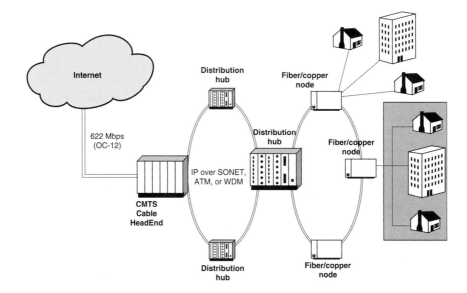

*Figure 3-24*  Cable Data Network Architecture

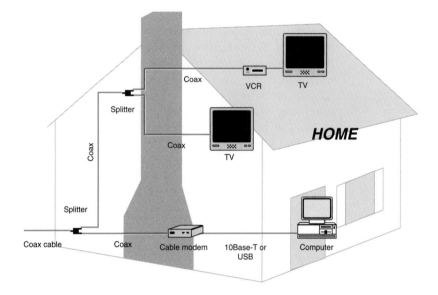

*Figure 3-25*    Typical Cable Modem Installation

multiple access multiplexing scheme must be used. Time Division Multiple Access (TDMA) and Frequency Division Multiple Access (FDMA) are commonly used to allow multiple cable modems to communicate to the CMTS concurrently. Before a cable modem can transmit to the CMTS, it must request and receive a bandwidth allocation. This is usually handled as part of the initial power-on handshaking between the cable modem and the CMTS.

**Standards and Technology**    Initially, there were no standards that defined the modulation schemes used between cable modems and the CMTS. As a result, cable modem customers were locked into the cable modems offered by their cable company. In 1996, several cable operators commissioned the development of a standard, which would control compatibility of cable modem equipment, both on the user side, the cable company side, and the wiring in between. The resulting **Data Over Cable Service Interface Specification** (**DOCSIS**) standard defines the protocol stack used in transmissions, modulation techniques for the CMTS, and cable modem and line speeds. Both cable modems and CMTS systems can be certified as DOCSIS-compliant, which indicates all aspects of the specification are adhered to and ensures interoperability between vendors. As long as the CMTS is DOCSIS compliant, the consumer can purchase any DOCSIS-compliant cable modem with certainty that it will work with their cable system.

The DOCSIS standard also includes some security enhancements for the privacy of data. This basic privacy specification is called the BPI, or Baseline Privacy Interface. BPI allows for the use of encryption algorithms to assure the privacy of data when traveling between the user's cable modem and the cable company. It should be noted, however, that the BPI was developed to benefit the provider, not the user. The implementation of the encryption is done at the cable company, meaning subscribers have no control over whether encryption is activated or not for their shared "ring."

When activated, encryption provides several benefits, including authentication of users' modems (preventing theft of service), and virtually eliminates the sniffing threat between the cable modem and the CMTS at the cable company.

An extension to the BPI, BPI+, extends the capabilities of BPI to eliminate cloning of cable modems. Prior to the implementation of BPI+ it was possible for software or hardware to clone a cable modem and have it communicate successfully to a CMTS. BPI+ allows increased authentication by incorporating the cable modem's physical address into the encryption scheme.

**Implementation and Performance**   In many ways, a cable modem system has more in common with an Ethernet local area network than it does with a dial-up modem or DSL system. Unlike dial-up or DSL, where the bandwidth between the customer premises and the central office is dedicated to the customer, cable modem systems require that everyone on the cable segment share a fixed amount of bandwidth. Because of this, users might find that the service that was blazingly fast when only a few people shared the segment has grown increasingly slower as more of their neighbors connect. This shared bandwidth scenario also has security ramifications: the downstream traffic destined for one cable modem is received by all cable modems on the segment. Although each cable modem normally ignores traffic not destined for it, if placed in promiscuous mode the cable modem will pass all incoming traffic to the attached computer. For more information about broadcast shared media networks, please refer to chapter 4.

Cable modems themselves come is three forms: external, internal, and set-top box. External cable modems, by far the most popular, are physically distinct. Like all cable modems, they translate the data signal between the coaxial cable that the cable company supplies and the 10Base-T Ethernet signal the user's PC expects. This flavor of modem allows for multiple PCs to share the connection but requires a separate Ethernet network card to be installed in the subscriber's PC.

Internal cable modems are packaged as a PCI card installed in the subscriber's PC. Internal cable modems are less expensive than their external counterpart, but they are not "plug" compatible with laptop computers and Macintosh machines.

The final cable modem form factor is the set-top box, which provides network access on the subscriber's television. Set-top implementations require a separate upstream method, usually a standard dial-up modem for return signals. Typically, this type of implementation was only used for older, broadcast-only cable systems rather than modern bi-directional systems.

**Future of Cable Modems**   Cable modems offer the highest Internet access connection speeds currently available. Although the shared media approach used in cable modems requires the bandwidth on an individual cable segment to be shared among the users on the segment, most cable modem customers receive excellent data speeds. As cable companies gain experience in the data communications marketplace, they are in an excellent position to leverage their existing cable plans to provide additional interactive services to consumers.

## Other Internet Access Technologies

Several other Internet access technologies are under development. One of the most interesting is fixed-point wireless. In a **fixed-point wireless** environment, the service provider places a series of transmitters on a tower. Each transmitter is directional in nature and covers a portion of the 360 degrees around the tower. Consumers place a receiver unit in their home that connects to the tower via radio waves. Depending on their distance from the tower, consumers may need a directional external antenna to establish a radio link. Once the link is established, the consumer can access the Internet.

There are several different wireless access schemes under development, ranging from variants of IEEE 802.11 wireless LANs to licensed spectrum solutions. For more information on IEEE 802.11 networks, please refer to chapter 4.

Originally thought to best fit into urban/suburban settings, wireless Internet access is instead making its initial market penetration in rural areas. Upon closer inspection, rural areas are perfect for wireless access: there are few tall buildings to create multi-path interference in the radio signal and there are typically few competing broadband access technologies because cable and DSL providers have been focusing on more densely populated areas. Some smaller rural towns have begun proactively seeking wireless access providers to remain competitive at attracting new residents to their tax base. It is becoming increasingly common to see an antenna array installed on the top of grain elevators in small towns across the country.

Cellular telephone companies are working to develop faster Internet access technologies to serve their mobile customers. Although the cost of these services is currently too high to make them a viable choice for non-mobile users, it is too soon to rule them out as potential players in the market. These technologies are discussed in detail in chapter 5.

There are many different wide area network services available that can be used to provide Internet access. While these solutions are normally considerably more expensive than the previously discussed solutions, they offer the advantage of being dedicated to your use. A complete discussion of wide area network technologies is presented in chapter 6.

Applied Problem
Solving

## INTERNET ACCESS TECHNOLOGY SELECTION FRAMEWORK

There is no one "best" Internet access technology solution for everyone. To help decide the best solution for a given situation the following series of questions should be answered:

- What types of service are available at the location? There may be only one choice available.

- How much bandwidth is required/desired?

- Which of the available services can meet the bandwidth requirements?

- Will Internet services such as the Web and e-mail be hosted on premises?

    ○ If so, an "always on" broadband service such as DSL, cable, or a wide area network solution is required.

    ○ Be sure to check the usage rules for any service considered. Some cable companies, for instance, have chosen to block incoming Web traffic to prevent users from running their own Web servers.

After analyzing your needs and the available solutions, it is not uncommon to find a clear winner. For those people fortunate enough to have multiple viable solutions, monthly cost and data speeds should be the deciding factors.

## SUMMARY

By focusing on how data communications devices of any type deliver on pre-determined business requirements and objectives, one can avoid purchasing technology that may be appealing or cleverly marketed, but which lacks the ability to deliver a positive impact on business objectives.

LAN media can differ significantly in cost, supported speeds, ease of use, and network architectures supported. Although fiber optic cable was at one time considered to be the only media suitable for speeds of 100 Mbps and greater, Category 5 Unshielded Twisted Pair seems to be a common media option for high speed network standards. New advanced testing techniques have been developed to assure that UTP will be capable of transmitting high speed network architectures such as Gigabit Ethernet.

Point-to-point data communication occurs in either a serial or parallel manner. Modern connections are almost exclusively serial in nature. Common standards include RS-232, universal serial bus (USB) and IEEE-1394 (Firewire).

Using the transmission of data between a computer and the Internet as an example of a simple data communications system, many key concepts from the last chapter were show in context in this chapter. These technologies include dial-up modems, digital subscriber line modems, and cable modems.

Current modem standards include V.34 and V.90. V.34 is the newest analog modem standard offering transmission speeds up to 33.6 Kbps in both directions. V.90 is a hybrid analog/digital standard that offers an asymmetrical transmission rate of up to 56 Kbps from a remote server to the modem and up to 33.6 Kbps from the modem to the server.

Current modulation standards such as V.34 and V.90 can deliver even more throughput over dial-up lines when compression standards such as MNP5 or V.42bis are applied. As this increasing sophistication in dial-up modems has yielded ever faster transmission speeds over dial-up lines, the types of network services offered by carriers have also evolved.

Regardless of the modem technology used dial-up data calls have limited data carrying capacity. To access the power of the Internet, a faster means of connecting is required. Often referred to as broadband, these faster connections currently use two basic technologies: DSL and cable modems.

Digital subscriber line (DSL) technologies use frequency division multiplexing to add a high speed data signal to the existing telephone local loop. The data is modulated and multiplexed in a DSL modem that is connected directly to the telephone wiring in the home. At the central office the signals are de-multiplexed by a DSL access multiplexer (DSLAM). DSL offers data speed in excess of 1 Mbps over an existing direct connection to the home.

Cable modem technologies use frequency division multiplexing to add high a high speed data signal to the existing cable television cable coming into the home. Similar to DSL, a cable modem handles the modulation/demodulation at the home and a cable modem termination system (CMTS) handles it at the cable head end. However, unlike DSL the cable modem communication channel is shared among all of the users on the cable node.

New Internet access technologies such as fixed point wireless and 3G digital cellular systems promise to further improve the availability of high speed data connectivity to the home.

## KEY TERMS

| | | |
|---|---|---|
| adaptive protocols | asymmetrical transmission | cable modem termination system (CMTS) |
| adaptive size packet assembly | attenuation | circuit-switched connection |
| amplifier | bandwidth | convolutional encoding |
| Asymmetrical Digital Subscriber Line (ADSL) | Bluetooth | data circuit terminating equipment |
| | broadband | |

data over cable service interface
   specification
DCE (data communications
   equipment)
dial-up line
Digital Signal Processors (DSP)
Digital Subscriber Line (DSL)
Digital Subscriber Line Access
   Multiplexer (DSLAM)
diplexer
DOCSIS
DTE (data terminal equipment)
dynamic speed shifts
echo cancellation
EIA/TIA 568
Firewire
fixed point wireless
flat gray modular
forward error correction

four conductor station wire
handshaking
IEEE-1394
i.Link
Internet service provider (ISP)
IrDA
Link Access Protocol for Modems
   (LAP-M)
media filter
MNP Class 4
MNP Class 5
MNP Class 10
Multimode
Multimode Graded Index Fiber
Multimode Step Index Fiber
Near-End Crosstalk (NExT)
physical layer
Plain Old Telephone Systems
   (POTS)

Powersum Crosstalk
Public Switched Telephone
   Network (PSTN)
quantization noise
RYGB
repeater
single mode
splitter
trellis coded modulation (TCM)
turnaround time
Universal Asynchronous Receiver
   Transmitter (UART)
universal serial bus (USB)
unshielded twisted pair (UTP)
V.34
V.42
V.42bis
V.90

## REVIEW QUESTIONS

1. How can the top-down model remain useful given the rate of rapidly changing technology?
2. Why is twisted pair twisted?
3. What is the importance of EIA/TIA 568?
4. What is the most common type category of UTP installed today and why?
5. Why is UTP category 5 favored over shielded twisted pair, coax, and fiber optic cable for many high-speed network architectures?
6. Why is shielded twisted pair considered trickier to install than UTP?
7. What is the difference between Powersum Crosstalk and pair-to-pair crosstalk?
8. How are Levels 5, 6, and 7 different from Category 5?
9. Why are testing and certification specifications required beyond CAT 5?
10. What are the key advantages of fiber optic media over copper media?
11. List the two main types of fiber optic media and the advantages of each.
12. List the ten most commonly used RS-232 pins including name, abbreviation, and DCE/DTE orientation.
13. What is the name of the device employed to monitor and manipulate RS-232 signals?
14. At what speeds does USB operate?
15. List three advantages of USB over RS-232.
16. List the currently available versions of USB and the maximum data speeds offered by each.

17. Differentiate between IEEE-1394, Firewire, and i.Link.
18. At what speeds does IEEE-1394 operate?
19. What is currently the primary application for IEEE-1394?
20. List the currently available versions of IEEE-1394 and the maximum data speeds offered by each.
21. Which point-to-point serial transmission standards offer power to attached devices?
22. What is modulated to provide wireless connectivity via IrDA?
23. What are some of the significant limitations associated with IrDA?
24. Which IrDA standard offers multi-point communication?
25. What is the size and data transmission speed offered by Bluetooth?
26. What type of radio frequency communication does Bluetooth use?
27. What is a piconet?
28. What types of devices are likely to include Bluetooth capability?
29. What is the purpose of the I-P-O model and how can it be used to model both ends of given circuit?
30. What is an Internet service provider (ISP)? What types of services does an ISP provide?
31. What is the potential throughput of a V.34 modem with V.42bis data compression?
32. Why are standards important when it comes to data compression?

33. What is meant by an adaptive protocol? Give at least two examples.
34. What are the key differences between V.32 and V.32bis?
35. What does "bis" stand for?
36. What is the difference between V.42 and V.42bis?
37. How does a V.90 modem system overcome the 33.6 Kbps limit as dictated by Shannon's Law?
38. What is quantization error?
39. Explain why V.90 is asymmetrical in nature?
40. How fast can a V.90, 56 Kbps modem actually transfer data?
41. Will a V.90 modem provide faster speeds than a V.34 modem in all cases? Why or why not?
42. What are the major differences between repeaters and amplifiers?
43. Explain the differences between hardware and software flow control.
44. What is forward error correction and what is the trade-off involved in such a protocol?
45. Differentiate between MNP5 and V.42bis.
46. Differentiate between MNP4 and V.42
47. What are the main applications of dial-up Internet access today?
48. What does the term broadband mean in the context of Internet access?
49. What existing communication link into the home does DSL use?
50. What piece of equipment is required at the central office to enable DSL use?

51. What are the maximum speeds and distance limitations of the most commonly available DSL services?
52. Why are splitters or media filters required in DSL implementations?
53. What is the difference between consumer and business class DSL offerings?
54. Is DSL a shared or dedicated connection into the home?
55. What type of multiplexing is used by a cable modem?
56. In a cable modem deployment how many television channels are eliminated to provide bi-directional data services?
57. What piece of equipment is required at the cable system head end to enable cable modem usage?
58. Is cable modem access a shared or dedicated connection to the home?
59. What is a cable node and what is its relevance to cable modem services?
60. What is a diplexer and what is its purpose in a cable modem installation?
61. What is DOCSIS and why is it important?
62. What are the technologies developed to improve security in a cable modem deployment?
63. What are the three most common form factors for a cable modem? List the advantages of each.
64. Which offers higher data rates: DSL or cable modems?
65. What is fixed-point wireless and where is it initially being deployed?

**Case Study:** For a business case study and questions that relate to using data communications technology, go to www.wiley.com/college/goldman.

# LOCAL AREA NETWORKS

### *Concepts Reinforced*

| | |
|---|---|
| OSI model | Top-down model |
| Hardware/software compatibility | Protocols and standards |
| Local area networks | |

### *Concepts Introduced*

| | |
|---|---|
| Access methodologies | Logical topologies |
| Physical topologies | LAN architectures |
| IEEE 802 standards | LAN technology architectures |
| Ethernet | Wireless LANs (WiFi) |
| LAN hubs | LAN switches |

## OBJECTIVES

After mastering the material in this chapter, you should:

1. Understand the value of the OSI model in the analysis of network architecture alternatives.

2. Understand how access methodologies, logical topologies, and physical topologies combine to form alternative network architectures.

3. Understand the interaction between the various hardware and software components of the local area network technology architecture.

4. Understand the major local area network technologies and their applications.

5. Understand basic wireless local area network technology architectures.

6. Understand how to implement, secure, and manage wireless local area networks.

7. Understand the differences between switched LAN architectures and shared-media LAN architectures.

8. Understand the comparative differences between and proper application of available network interface cards.

9. Understand the comparative differences between and the proper application of hubs, concentrators, bridges, and switches.

10. Understand how proper LAN analysis can help determine which network architecture is most appropriate in any given situation.

# ■ INTRODUCTION

Chapter 4 explores local area network hardware and software technologies in wired and wireless environments. One of the key distinguishing characteristics of a particular local area network is the network architecture adhered to by a particular LAN. In order to understand the role of LAN switches in network architectures, the differences between switched-based and shared-media LAN architectures are outlined, followed by a detailed review of local area network hardware alternatives.

# ■ LAYER 2: THE DATALINK LAYER

The second layer of the OSI Network Reference Model is the *datalink layer.* The datalink layer provides point-to-point connectivity between devices over the physical connections provided by the underlying physical layer. In order for two devices to communicate at the datalink layer there must be some sort of physical communication channel in place between them; data sent from the datalink layer of one device must be automatically delivered to the datalink layer of the destination device by the physical layer. The manner in which this communication takes place can be over a physical circuit (as in a modem to modem connection) or a logical circuit (as in a shared media local area network such as Ethernet).

The datalink layer breaks a data stream into chunks called *frames,* or *cells,* depending on the technology used, and then transmits them to the destination device. These frames of data have a header that contains a start delimiter and information about the frame followed by the data itself, then some sort of stop delimiter to note the end of the frame.

In Sharper Focus

### FRAMES, CELLS, AND PACKETS

It is important to note the difference in the terminology used to describe the data being transmitted at each of these layers of the OSI Network Reference Model. The datalink layer (layer two) transmits *frames* or *cells* of data. The network layer (layer three) transmits *packets* of data.

The datalink layer provides a *reliable* communications link between devices. As detailed in chapter 2, a reliable communications link provides three key functions: error detection, error correction, and flow control. Error detection in the datalink layer is provided by some sort of checksum (normally a cyclical redundancy check). The checksum is calculated based on the contents of the frame by the sending device and placed in the header of the frame. When the destination device receives the frame it recalculates the checksum and compares it to the received checksum. If they match, then no errors occurred during transmission and the correct. It they do not match, then there were errors in transmission and the frame is bad.

The receiving device then sends either an acknowledgment (ACK—the data received was good) or negative acknowledgment (NAK—the data received was bad) back to the sender. Based on this information, the sender will either re-send the frame or send the next frame in the sequence. In most cases a sliding window protocol (as detailed in chapter 2) is used to increase data throughput.

Flow control is also implemented to ensure that the data are not sent faster than the destination device can process it. Once again, details on flow control concepts and techniques are available in chapter 2.

In local area networks, the datalink layer can be broken down into two sublayers: media access control (MAC) and logical link control (LLC). Most local area network technologies are based on a shared media architecture where each device on the network "hears" all of the data transmitted. In this scenario, the media access control layer negotiates access to the media so that only one device is attempting to use the media at any given point in time. Several different approaches to media access control are covered later in this chapter.

Logical link control provides a way to create logical links across the network. Each of these links is viewed by layer three and above as a separate entity used to carry specific types of data. From a practical perspective, logical link control provides a manner of marking each frame as to the type of layer three data it contains. In this manner, a single network can be used to carry multiple layer three network protocols such as IP and IPX concurrently.

Although the datalink layer is implemented in software in some wide area network solutions (detailed in chapter 6), this chapter focuses on local area networks where it is implemented in hardware as part of the network interface card (NIC).

## Datalink Layer Addressing

In the shared media local area network architecture, each device on a network segment hears all of the traffic transmitted on the segment, regardless of the source and destination. This is analogous to trying to send a message to a friend located across a crowded room; whatever you say will be heard by everyone else in the room. If you are trying to send a message across the room to your friend, you need to get their attention to let them know that the message is for them, and you need to let everyone else know the message is not for them. You do this by using name, such as, "Hey Joe—it's Phil. How are you doing?" Similarly there needs to be a way for devices on a shared media network to identify who the sender of the data frame is and for which devices the data are intended. This is done through the use of addresses known as physical or MAC addresses.

As illustrated in Figure 4-1, each device on the network must have a unique physical address that uniquely identifies them on the network. For the most commonly used LAN technologies, the physical (MAC) address of a network interface card is programmed at the factory at the time of manufacture. The MAC address is a 48-bit address where the first 2 bits identify the type of address, the next 22 bits identity the manufacture of the NIC, and the last 24 bits are a unique serial number of the card. In this manner, each NIC in the world is assigned a unique MAC address, eliminating the need to assign specific MAC addresses to each NIC. Although this usually works well, it is possible to override this default value by locally administering MAC addresses. However, when using locally administered addresses, it is your responsibility to ensure that they are unique within each network segment.

Going back to the analogy of conversation across a crowded room, there might be times when you want to send a message to everyone in the room, such as, "Hey, listen up—the food will be served in five minutes." Similarly there are occasions when a device on a local area network wants to send a broadcast message to every other device on the segment. To send a broadcast message, the device sets the destination MAC address to a value of all ones. Each device on the network will listen to messages sent to this special address as well as their unique address.

In general, devices will ignore any messages unless they are explicitly set to process all messages. This setting, also known as **promiscuous mode,** tells the NIC to

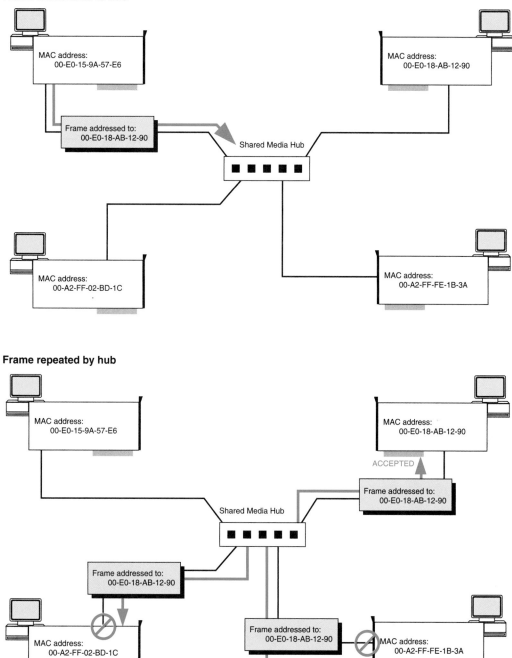

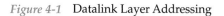

*Figure 4-1*  Datalink Layer Addressing

process all data frames regardless of destination address. Due to the increased load on the NIC, promiscuous mode results in a reduction in overall network device performance and is typically used only when troubleshooting the network with network analyzer software. Such software is commonly referred to as a **sniffer** based on the name of the original device from Data General that offered this capability.

In Sharper Focus

## NETWORK SEGMENTS VS. SUBNETS VERSUS COLLISION DOMAINS VS. BROADCAST DOMAINS

The collection of network devices on a local area network are referred to by several terms, including *network segment, subnet, collision domain,* and *broadcast domain.* The general term, *network segment,* is the least precise and will be used in this book as a general term to mean all of the devices on a local area network that can be addressed directly without the use of a router or other layer three device. Often, people will use the term *IP subnet,* or simply *subnet,* interchangeably with network segment. However, as detailed in chapter 7, an IP subnet is technically a subdivision of an IP address space that may or may not map directly to a network segment in modern switched networks.

Two other terms with more specific meanings will be used throughout the book: *collision domain* and *broadcast domain.* A collision domain is the collection of devices that share media directly; only one can transmit at a time. A broadcast domain is the collection of devices that will hear a broadcast message sent at the datalink layer regardless of network structure. In a true shared media network, the entire network segment is a single collision domain and a single broadcast domain. As detailed later this chapter, the use of bridges and LAN switches allow a single network segment to be broken into multiple collision domains although they remain part of a single broadcast domain.

## ■ THE LOCAL AREA NETWORK ARCHITECTURE MODEL

Although not all network architectures are standardized by the IEEE or some other standards making organization, all network architectures are made up of the same logical components. In order to accurately describe a given network architecture, one needs to know the following:

- Access methodology
- Logical topology
- Physical topology

Numerous network architectures are evaluated later in the chapter. Each architecture will be examined from these three perspectives. The only other variable added to the network architecture of choice is the particular media over which a given network architecture can operate. As will be seen, most network architectures are able to operate over a variety of media types. Although networking vocabulary is by no means standardized, the previously mentioned combinations of variables can be summarized in the following manner:

- Network  architecture  =  access  methodology  +  logical  topology + physical topology
- Network configuration = network architecture + media choice

## Access Methodology

If a medium is to be shared by numerous PC users, then there must be some way to control access by multiple users. Realizing that more than one user is likely to be sending requests onto the shared local area network media at any one time, there is an obvious need for some way to control when and which users get to put their messages onto the network. These media sharing methods are properly known as **access methodologies.** Sharing the media is an important concept to local area networks, also referred to as **media sharing LANs.**

Logically speaking, there are really only two philosophies for controlling access to a shared media. An analogy of access to a crowded freeway vividly illustrates these access methodology choices.

**CSMA/CD**    One philosophy says, "Let's just let everyone onto the medium whenever they want and if two users access the medium at the exact same split second, we'll work it out somehow." Or, in the analogy of a crowded freeway, "Who needs stop lights! If we have a few collisions, we'll work it out later!"

The access methodology based on this model is known as **carrier sense multiple access with collision detection,** or **CSMA/CD** for short. A clearer understanding of how this access methodology works can be achieved by examining the name of this access methodology one phrase at a time.

First, look at the phrase *carrier sense:* The PC wishing to put data onto the shared media listens to the network to see if any other users are "on the line" by trying to sense a neutral electrical signal known as a *carrier.* If no transmission is sensed, then *multiple access* allows anyone onto the media with no further permission required. Finally, if two user PCs should both sense a free line and access the media at the same instant, a collision occurs. *Collision detection* lets the PCs know that their data were not delivered and controls retransmission in such a way as to avoid further data collisions. Another possible factor leading to data collisions is the **propagation delay,** or the time it takes a signal from a source PC to reach a destination PC. Because of propagation delay, it is possible for a workstation to sense that there is no signal on the shared media, when in fact another distant workstation has transmitted a signal that has not yet reached the carrier sensing PC.

In the event of a collision, the station that first detects the collision sends out a special jamming signal to all attached workstations. Each workstation—or, more precisely, the network interface card in the workstation—stops all transmission instantly and waits a random amount of time before re-transmitting, thus reducing the likelihood of reoccurring collisions. If successive collisions continue to occur, the random time-out interval is doubled.

CSMA/CD is obviously most efficient with relatively little contention for network resources. The ability to allow user PCs to access the network easily without a lot of permission requesting and granting reduces overhead and increases performance at lower network usage rates. However, as usage increases the increased number of data collisions and retransmissions can negatively affect overall network performance.

**Token Passing**    The second philosophy of access methodology is much more controlling. It says, "Don't you dare access the media until it's your turn. You must first ask permission, and only if I give you the magic token may you put your data onto the shared media." The highway analogy would be the controlled access ramps to freeways in which a driver must wait at a stoplight and somehow immediately get to 65 mph in order to merge with the traffic.

**Token passing** assures that each network node has 100 percent of the network channel available for its data requests and transfers by insisting that no PC accesses the network without first possessing a specific packet of data known as a **token.** The token is passed among the network nodes until a host would like to access the network.

At that point, the requesting host seizes the token, changes the token status from free to busy, puts its data frame onto the network, and doesn't release the token until it is assured that its data were delivered successfully. Successful delivery of the data frame is confirmed by the destination host setting **frame status flags** to indicate successful receipt of the frame and continuing to forward the original frame around the ring to the sending host. Upon receipt of the original frame with frame status flags set to "destination address recognized, frame copied successfully," the sender resets the token status from busy to free and releases it. The token is then sent to the next node on the network, which might either grab the free token or pass it along.

Token passing adds a measurable amount of overhead to the network due to each host having to wait until it receives the token to transmit. This overhead tends to add a small amount of latency when traffic levels are low. However, because all hosts on a token passing access control network are well behaved and always have the magic token before accessing the network, there are, by definition, no collisions. This makes token passing a more efficient access methodology at higher network utilization rates.

## CSMA/CD VS. TOKEN PASSING

Much has been made of the differences between CSMA/CD and token passing over the years. What once burned as a holy war between Ethernet and token ring advocates (see the In Sharper Focus section on "Ethernet vs. Token Ring" for more details) has been reduced to academic discussion due to marketplace dynamics.

However, there are real differences in the performance of networks using these two media access techniques. CSMA/CD requires less overhead and is more efficient than token passing at low traffic levels. At higher traffic levels, the inherent collisions and retransmissions make token passing more efficient. Although the exact traffic level where token passing becomes more efficient than CSMA/CD depends on factors such as frame size and segment length, the overall relationship will always look very similar to that shown in Figure 4-2.

In Figure 4-2, the horizontal axis represents the demand for network capacity (or bandwidth) as a percentage. The vertical axis represents the actual capacity delivered

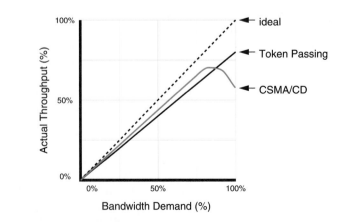

*Figure 4-2* CSMA/CD vs. Token Passing

by the media access control technique. Ideally, a one-to-one mapping, or a line running at a 45-degree angle up the chart, would be possible. However, the overhead associated with each technique makes that impossible.

As shown in the figure, CSMA/CD provides nearly perfect efficiency until the number of collisions and retransmits starts to erode the performance. This phenomena starts to seriously affect performance around 60 percent bandwidth demand and increases until performance actually deteriorates with additional bandwidth demand. Simply put, the collisions starts to outnumber the successful transmissions.

The structured media access approach used in token passing does not suffer this same fate. Because transmission is tightly controlled, performance is predictable up until 100 percent of the bandwidth is demanded. However, the overhead associated with token passing makes is less efficient than CSMA/CD at lower levels of demand.

## Logical Topology

Once a data message is placed onto the network media shared among multiple workstations, the next thing that must be determined is how the message will be passed from workstation to workstation until ultimately reaching its intended destination workstation. The particular message-passing methodology employed is more properly referred to as the network architecture's **logical topology.** An analogy used to describe logical topologies has to do with how best to put out a fire in a PC user's wastebasket.

**Sequential**  The first logical topology or method of delivering data is known as **sequential access.** In a sequential logical topology, also known as a **ring** logical topology, data are passed from one PC (or node) to another. Each node examines the destination address of the data packet to determine if this particular packet is meant for it. If the data were not meant to be delivered at this node, the data are passed along to the next node in the logical ring.

This is analogous to the bucket-brigade method of putting out a fire in a PC user's wastebasket. A bucket of water is filled by one PC user and passed to the neighboring PC user. That user determines if his or her wastebasket is on fire. If it is, the user douses the flames with the bucket of water. Otherwise, the user passes the bucket along to the next user in the logical ring.

**Broadcast**  The second logical topology or method of delivering data are known as **broadcast access.** In a broadcast logical topology, a data message is sent simultaneously to all nodes on the network. Each node decides individually if the data message was directed toward it. If not, the message is simply ignored. There is no need to pass the message along to a neighboring node. They received the same message at the same time.

This is analogous to the sprinkler-system method of putting out a fire in a PC user's wastebasket. Rather than worry about passing a bucket of water around a logical ring until it finally reaches the engulfed wastebasket, the water is just broadcast over the entire network, with the result being that the wastebasket that was on fire will know that the water was meant for it.

To summarize, in order to appreciate the key difference between sequential and broadcast logical topologies, focus on the role or responsibility of the intermediate workstations to which a destination message is not actually addressed. In the case of sequential logical topology, the non-recipient workstation has a job to do. It must continue to pass the message along to its next sequential neighbor. However, in the case of a broadcast logical topology, the non-recipient workstation has no further responsibilities and simply ignores the message.

## Physical Topology

Finally, the clients and servers must be physically connected to each other according to some configuration and must be linked by the shared media of choice. The physical layout of this configuration can have a significant impact on LAN performance and reliability, and it is known as a network architecture's **physical topology.** There are three basic physical topologies: bus, ring, and star.

A **bus** topology is a linear arrangement with terminators on either end with devices connected to the *bus* via connectors and/or transceivers. The purpose of the terminator is to close off the ends of the bus topology, thereby completing the electrical circuit and allowing the data signals to flow. In a **ring** topology, each host is an active part of the ring, passing data packets in a sequential pattern around the ring.

Although bus and star physical topologies were common in the past, all modern LAN designs use a star physical topology. In a star topology, a central device is used to interconnect all of the hosts on the network. Depending on the underlying network architecture and sophistication of the device, it may be called a *hub,* a *wiring center,* a *concentrator,* a *MAU* (multiple access unit), a *repeater,* or a *switching hub.*

Since all network data in a star topology are going through this one central location, it is an ideal location to add system monitoring, security, or management capabilities. The other side of the coin is that since all network data are going through this one central location, it makes a marvelous networking no-no known as a **single point of failure.** The good news is, any node can be lost and the network will be fine. The bad news is, lose the hub and the whole network goes down. Fortunately, vendors have risen to the occasion by offering such reliability extras as redundant power supplies, dual buses, and "hot swappable" interface cards.

## ■ THE LOCAL AREA NETWORK TECHNOLOGY MODEL

In general terms, any local area network, regardless of network architecture, requires the following components:

- *A central wiring concentrator of some type that serves as a connection point for all attached local area network devices.* Depending on the particular network architecture involved and the capabilities of the wiring center, this device can be known alternatively as a **hub, MAU, concentrator, LAN switch,** or a variety of other names.

- *Media such as shielded or unshielded twisted pair, coaxial cable, or fiber optic cable.* These must carry network traffic between attached devices and the hub of choice.

- *Network Interface Cards.* **Network interface cards** (**NIC**) are installed either internally or externally to client and server computers in order to provide a connection to the local area network of choice.

- *Network interface card drivers.* These software programs bridge the hardware/software interface between the network interface card and the computer's network operating system.

Figure 4-3 summarizes the key components of the LAN technology architecture.

## Implications of LAN Technology Choices

Within each of the major categories of LAN technology illustrated in Figure 4-3, numerous alternatives exist as to the specific make, model, and manufacturer of the technology. It is important to note that choosing a particular technology in one LAN technology category may have significant implications or limitations on available technology choices in other LAN technology categories. It is also important to fully understand the implications of a given technology decision prior to purchase. Figure 4-4 portrays some of the relationships and dependencies between technology choices in a variety of LAN technology categories.

## Network Interface Cards

**Functionality**   NICs are the physical link between a client or server PC and the shared media of the network. Providing this interface between the network and the PC or workstation requires that the network interface card have the ability to adhere to the access methodology (CSMA/CD or token passing) of the network architecture (Ethernet, token ring, FDDI/CDDI, ATM etc.) to which it is attached. These software rules, implemented by the network interface card, control the access to the shared network media. They are known as media access control (MAC) protocols and are represented on the MAC sublayer of the datalink layer (Layer 2) of the OSI 7 layer reference model.

Since these are MAC layer interface cards and are, therefore, the keepers of the MAC layer interface protocol, it is fair to say that it is the NICs themselves that determine network architecture and its constituent protocols. If you take an Ethernet NIC out of the expansion slot of a PC and replace it with a token ring NIC, it becomes a token ring workstation. In this same scenario, the media may not even need to be changed because Ethernet, token ring, and FDDI/CDDI often work over the same media.

A network interface card is a bit like a mediator or translator. On one side it has the demands of the client or server PC in which it is installed for network-based services, while on the other side it has the network architecture with its rules for

**Logical Diagram**

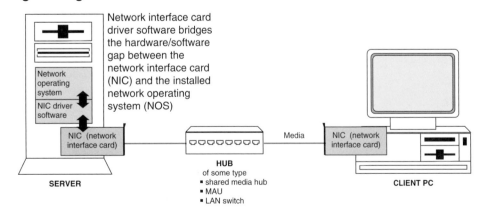

*Figure 4-3*   Local Area Network Technology Architecture

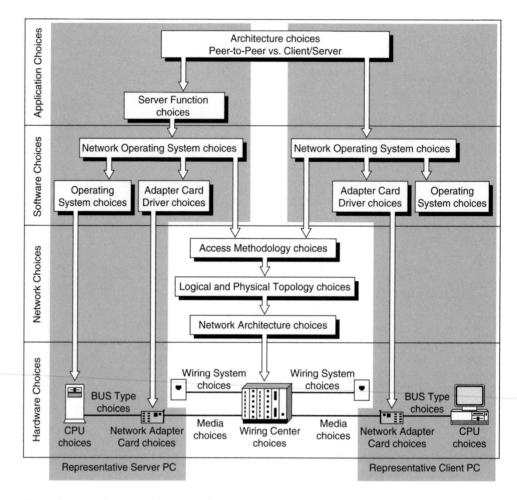

*Figure 4-4*    Implications of LAN Technology Choices

accessing the shared network media or LAN switch. The network interface card's job is to get the PC all of the network services it desires while adhering to the rules (MAC Layer Protocols) of the network architecture.

Applied Problem
Solving

## NETWORK INTERFACE CARD TECHNOLOGY ANALYSIS GRID

A *technology analysis grid* is a structured analysis tool for mapping functional networking requirements, as identified by the logical network design of the networking layer in the top-down model to the technical capabilities and characteristics of available technology. In this manner, technology can be comparatively evaluated in an objective fashion. Recalling the basic premise of the top-down model and assuming that each lower layer offers solutions that meet the requirements of the immediate upper layer, then the chosen technology incorporated in the physical network design should meet the original business goals and objectives as identified in the business layer.

As a practical example, whereas servers will need to transfer large quantities of data more quickly than client PCs, technology analysis should be performed in order to purchase more powerful, faster NICs for servers than for clients in order to minimize potential bottlenecks. Figure 4-5 illustrates a network interface card technology analysis grid.

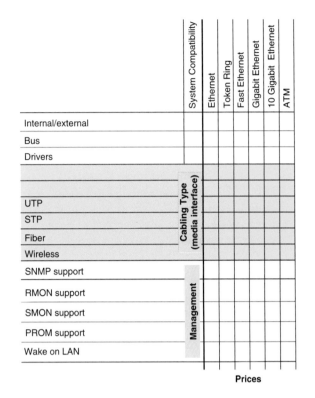

*Figure 4-5*  Network Interface Card Technology Analysis Grid

**Network Interface Card Drivers**  Ensuring that a purchased network interface card interfaces successfully with both the bus of the CPU and the chosen media of the network architecture will also ensure hardware connectivity. Full interoperability, however, depends on compatibility between the NIC and the network operating system installed on a given computer and is delivered by **NIC drivers.** Any driver software must be compatible with the hardware card itself, which is why many NIC manufacturers ship numerous drivers from which to choose with their NICs. A given network interface card may also be required to be compatible with a number of different network operating systems. The network operating systems use the NIC drivers to communicate with the NICs and the network beyond. Without the proper NIC drivers, there can be no communication through the NIC and, as a result, there is no network. The installation and configuration of NIC drivers was once a complicated task. Newer operating systems that support plug and play, along with bus interfaces such as PCI and CardBus, have combined to make NIC installation virtually effortless.

## ■  LOCAL AREA NETWORK ARCHITECTURES

### Ethernet (Traditional)

The invention of **Ethernet** is generally credited to Robert Metcalfe, who later went on to become the founder of 3COM Corporation. Although Ethernet and **IEEE 802.3** conflict from a strict standards viewpoint, the term *Ethernet* is commonly used to refer to any IEEE 802.3 compliant network. Differences between the two standards will be outlined shortly. Traditional Ethernet can be defined as follows:

- Access methodology: CSMA/CD

- Logical topology: Broadcast

- Physical Topology: Historically—bus, currently—star

**Standards**    The first Ethernet standard was developed by Digital, Intel, and Xerox corporation in 1981 and was known as DIX 1.0, sometimes referred to as Ethernet I. This standard was superseded in 1982 by DIX 2.0, the current Ethernet standard, also known as Ethernet II. The frame layouts for **Ethernet II** and IEEE 802.3 are illustrated in Figure 4-6.

As illustrated in Figure 4-6, both Ethernet II and IEEE 802.3 frames can vary in length from 64 to 1,518 octets in length.

*Ethernet II*    The Ethernet II frame layout consists of the following fields:

- The Ethernet II frame starts with a preamble of eight octets. The purpose of the preamble is to alert and synchronize the Ethernet network interface card to the incoming data.

- The destination and source addresses are each six octets long and are also known as MAC layer addresses. These addresses are permanently burned into the ROM (read-only memory) of the Ethernet II network interface card at the time of manufacturer. The first three octets of the address identify the manufacturer of the network interface card and are assigned by the IEEE. The last three octets are assigned by the manufacturer, producing unique MAC layer addresses for all Ethernet network interface cards.

- The type field identifies which network protocols are embedded within the data field. For example, if the data field contained Network IPX/SPX protocols, then the type field would have a value of 8137 (hexadecimal) and if the

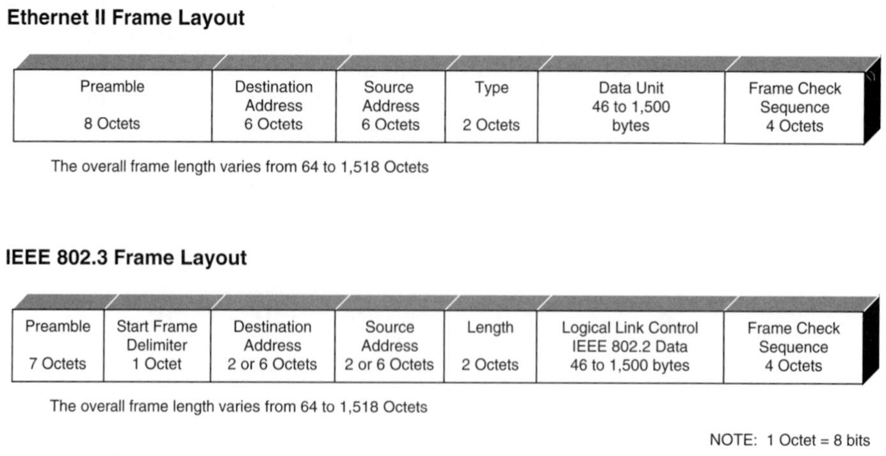

**Ethernet II Frame Layout**

| Preamble | Destination Address | Source Address | Type | Data Unit | Frame Check Sequence |
|---|---|---|---|---|---|
| 8 Octets | 6 Octets | 6 Octets | 2 Octets | 46 to 1,500 bytes | 4 Octets |

The overall frame length varies from 64 to 1,518 Octets

**IEEE 802.3 Frame Layout**

| Preamble | Start Frame Delimiter | Destination Address | Source Address | Length | Logical Link Control IEEE 802.2 Data | Frame Check Sequence |
|---|---|---|---|---|---|---|
| 7 Octets | 1 Octet | 2 or 6 Octets | 2 or 6 Octets | 2 Octets | 46 to 1,500 bytes | 4 Octets |

The overall frame length varies from 64 to 1,518 Octets

NOTE: 1 Octet = 8 bits

*Figure 4-6*   Ethernet and IEEE 802.3 Standards

data field contained TCP/IP protocols then the type field would contain a value of 0800 (hexadecimal). These type values are assigned by the IEEE. The type field is important in order to enable multiple protocols to be handled by a single network interface card that enables multiple protocol stacks to be loaded in a given client or server. Once the network interface card identifies which protocol is embedded within the data field, it can forward that data field to the proper protocol stack for further processing. Multiple protocol stacks allow communication between clients and servers of different network operating systems which is essential to transparent distributed computing.

- The data unit field contains all of the encapsulated upper layer (network through application) protocols and can vary in length from 46 to 1,500 bytes. The 46-byte minimum data field length combines with the 18 octets of fixed overhead of all of the other fields to produce the minimum frame size of 64 octets.

- The **frame check sequence** (**FCS**) is an error-detection mechanism generated by the transmitting Ethernet network interface card. A 32-bit *cyclical redundancy check* (CRC) is generated over the address, type, and data fields. The receiving Ethernet network interface card regenerates this same CRC on the address, type, and data fields in the received frame and compares the regenerated CRC to the transmitted CRC. If they match, the frame was received error free. A 32-bit CRC has the ability to detect error bursts of up to 31 bits with 100 percent accuracy.

*IEEE 802.3*    The IEEE 802.3 frame layout is very similar to the Ethernet II frame layout. Highlights of the IEEE 802.3 frame layout are as follows:

- The seven-octet preamble plus the one-octet starting frame delimiter perform the same basic function as the eight-octet Ethernet II preamble.

- Address fields are defined and assigned in a similar fashion to Ethernet II frames.

- The two-octet length field in the IEEE 802.3 frame takes the place of the type field in the Ethernet frame. The length field indicates the length of the variable-length IEEE 802.2 LLC (Logical Link Control) data field that contains all upper-layer embedded protocols.

- The type of embedded upper-layer protocols is designated by a field within the LLC data unit and is explained more fully in the "In Sharper Focus" section below.

- The frame check sequence is identical to that used in the Ethernet II frame.

### IEEE 802.2

In order for an IEEE 802.3 compliant network interface card to be able to determine the type of protocols embedded within the data field of an IEEE 802.3 frame, it refers to the header of the **IEEE 802.2** LLC data unit.

More specifically, the types of protocols embedded within the data unit are identified within the destination and source service access point fields (**DSAP** and **SSAP**). These fields are analogous to the type field in the Ethernet frame. SAP codes that identify a particular protocol are issued by the IEEE to those companies that register their

IEEE-compliant protocols. For example, an SAP code of E0 identifies a Novell proto-col and an SAP code of 06 identifies a TCP/IP protocol. NetWare frames adhering to this standard are referred to as NetWare 802.2 (802.3 plus 802.2).

*Technology*     Fast Ethernet uses the same frame layout as its predecessors. In its common 100baseTX form, fast Ethernet supports a maximum network diameter of 210 meters with up to two repeaters/hubs between end nodes. 100baseTX can be implemented as a shared-media LAN using hubs or as a switched LAN using LAN switches, as detailed later in this chapter.

Fast Ethernet NICs are also referred to as **10/100 NICs** because they can support either 10baseT or 100baseT. However, an NIC can only operate at one speed at any given time. Fast Ethernet networks can only interoperate with 10 Mbps Ethernet with the help of internetworking devices such as bridges, switches, or routers. Most Ethernet switches have the capability to auto-sense, or distinguish between, 10baseT and fast Ethernet traffic and then change the speed of the port to match that of the connected NIC. Figure 4-7 illustrates a representative fast Ethernet installation.

*Ethernet Speed*     Originally operating at 1 Mbps, Ethernet has evolved to speeds of up to 10 Gbps. Although traditional Ethernet operates at 10 Mbps, the current base speed of traditional Ethernet is 100 Mbps, known as fast Ethernet. Fast Ethernet represents a family of standards offering 100 Mbps performance and adhering to the CSMA/CD access methodology. The details of the operation of fast Ethernet are in the **IEEE 802.3u** standard. Fast Ethernet is most widely implemented over category 5 or greater twisted pair cable in 100baseTX form. In addition to 100baseT, a fiber-based version of fast Ethernet, 100baseFX, is available. They key reason to implement 100baseFX is the additional distance supported by the fiber media.

## ETHERNET NOMENCLATURE

In Sharper Focus

Often Ethernet is referred to as XbaseY. Using this nomenclature, the X refers to the speed of the network in Mbps, the *Base* refers to **baseband transmission,** meaning that the entire bandwidth of the media is devoted to one data channel, and the Y refers to the type of media if not coaxial cable or the maximum transmission length in hundreds of meters if coaxial cable. For instance the Ethernet standard known as **10baseT** runs at 10 Mbps over twisted pair cable. Faster Ethernet standards include 100baseT and 1000baseSX.

*Full-duplex Ethernet*     Switched LAN architectures depend on specialized LAN hubs known as LAN switches. They are able to provide dedicated point-to-point links between communicating clients and servers. In the case of Ethernet switches, for example, since the point-to-point link between two communicating PCs is dedicated, there can be no data collisions; therefore there is no longer any need for an access methodology such as CSMA/CD, as no other workstations can contend for this dedicated bandwidth. As a result, the two computers that serve as the endpoints of this switched dedicated connection could send and receive data simultaneously. This switch-dependent capability is known as **full duplex Ethernet** and requires compliant NICs, NIC drivers, and Ethernet switches. Typically, Ethernet switches automatically sense full-duplex operation when they negotiate speed. If both the switch and the NIC support full-duplex operation, it will be automatically enabled.

In theory, full-duplex Ethernet should allow twice the normal Ethernet performance speed. In practice, the throughput, or actual data transferred, on full-duplex Ethernet connections is usually not double the base speed. Chief among the reasons for

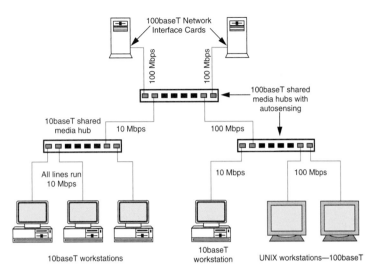

*Figure 4-7*  Typical Fast Ethernet Implementation

this is that the amount of network transmission is a product of application program design. Most distributed application programs tend to exhibit short requests for services from clients to servers, followed by large transfers of data from the server back to the client. However, this is not to say that the technology lacks the ability to deliver higher performance. Controlled tests involving high bandwidth applications have produced double the base throughput. The most likely implementation scenario for full-duplex Ethernet is in switch-to-switch connections and switch-to-server connections.

Since the full-duplex NIC installed in the computer is sending and receiving data simultaneously, a multithreaded operating system and a network operating system are required to take full advantage of this technology. Examples of such multithreaded operating systems and network operating systems are Windows 2003, XP, 2000, and NT, NetWare 4, 5, and 6, as well as most varieties of UNIX including Linux.

In Sharper Focus

## DUAL SPEED HUBS

Traditionally a bridge or LAN switch was required to interconnect 10 and 100 Mb Ethernet nodes. However, as Ethernet technologies made their way into the home marketplace, vendors introduced dual-speed hubs. A dual-speed hub is simply a two-sided Ethernet bridge with one bus operating at 10 Mbps and the other operating at 100 Mbps. The hub auto-senses the speed of the node attached to each port and connects the port to the appropriate internal hub. Frames that must go between the two busses must cross the bridge. As the speed of true LAN switches continues to fall, they will rapidly replace dual-speed hubs in the marketplace.

Application    The potential for collisions and retransmission on an Ethernet network has already been mentioned. In some cases, Ethernet networks with between 100 and 200 users barely use the available capacity of the network. However, the nature of the data transmitted is the key to determining potential network capacity problems. Character-based transmissions, such as typical data entry, in which a few characters at a time are typed and sent over the network, are much less likely to cause network capacity problems than the transfer of graphical user interface, screen-oriented transmissions such as Windows-based applications. Streaming media applications are even more bandwidth intensive.

A key advantage to Ethernet is scalability. High-speed Ethernet network architectures have been developed that allow for a hierarchy of network capacity. The fact that these higher-speed Ethernet implementations maintain the standard Ethernet frame structure allows traffic to be quickly bridged or switched onto these higher capacity networks without having to reformat the data. Details on bridging and switching are presented later in this chapter.

## High-Speed Ethernet

As previously mentioned, Ethernet has increased in speed beyond the wildest dreams of its creators. Although these faster versions of Ethernet have little in common with traditional Ethernet in many areas, they maintain the standard Ethernet frame. This common frame structure enables a network engineer to use high-speed solutions in the core of the network while using slower, less expensive solutions for workstation connectivity. The concept of this bandwidth hierarchy will be discussed in detail in a later section.

## Gigabit Ethernet

Ethernet continued to increase in speed. In 1998, the IEEE released another tenfold increase in Ethernet speed: Gigabit Ethernet.

**Standards**    **Gigabit Ethernet,** also known as 1000baseX, is an upgrade to fast Ethernet that was standardized as **IEEE 802.3z** by the IEEE on June 25, 1998. The standard defined the following configurations:

- **1000baseSX:** uses short wavelength (850 nanometers) laser multimode fiber optic media, primarily used for horizontal building cabling on a given floor.

- **1000baseLX:** uses long wavelength (1,300 nanometers) laser single mode fiber optic media, primarily for high-speed campus backbone applications.

- **1000baseCX:** uses copper twinaxial cable and transceivers for distances of only 25 meters, used primarily to link servers within a data center or high-speed network devices within a wiring closet. The subsequent release of 1000baseTX has effectively killed 1000baseCX.

- **1000baseTX:** uses four pair of category 5 unshielded twisted pair with a maximum distance of 100 meters.

Specifics of the gigabit Ethernet standard are listed in Figure 4-8. It should be pointed out that the maximum recommended distance over FDDI style multimode fiber optic cable is only 220 meters.

**Technology**    Initially, most gigabit Ethernet switches and network interface cards only supported either the 1000baseSX or 1000baseLX fiber-optic-based standards. With the introduction of the 1000baseTX standard in mid-1999, vendors have rapidly added support for the copper-based standard. Among vendors of gigabit Ethernet

| Standard | Media | Fiber Core Diameter | Bandwidth | Range |
|----------|-------|--------------------|-----------|-------|
| **1000baseTX** | 4 Pair category 5 UTP (unshielded twisted pair) | N/A | N/A | 100 m |
| **1000baseSX** | Multimode fiber | 62.5 microns | 160 | 2 m to 220 m |
| **1000baseSX** | Multimode fiber | 62.5 microns | 200 | 2 m to 275 m |
| **1000baseSX** | Multimode fiber | 50.0 microns | 400 | 2 m to 500 m |
| **1000baseSX** | Multimode fiber | 50.0 microns | 500 | 2 m to 550 m |
| **1000baseLX** | Multimode fiber | 62.5 microns | 500 | 2 m to 550 m |
| **1000baseLX** | Multimode fiber | 50.0 microns | 400 | 2 m to 550 m |
| **1000baseLX** | Multimode fiber | 50.0 microns | 500 | 2 m to 550 m |
| **1000baseLX** | Single-mode fiber | 9 microns | N/A | 2 m to 5 km or more |

*Figure 4-8*   Gigabit Ethernet Fiber-Dependent Configurations

switches and NICs are familiar names such as 3Com, Cabletron, Intel, Lucent, Cisco, Hewlett-Packard, and Nortel, as well as new names such as Foundry, Extreme Networks, and Packet Engines. As with any relatively new technology, multi-vendor interoperability is a major concern as subtleties of implementation of the gigabit Ethernet standard are ironed out. Also, beware of switches that merely introduce gigabit Ethernet interfaces without upgrading the bandwidth of the aggregate switch backplane. Appropriately sized switches should have backplane capacity in the tens of gigabits per second, and tens of millions of packets per second.

The importance of the IEEE 802.3ab 1000baseT gigabit Ethernet over copper standard cannot be overstated. Although the fiber-based standards offer a high bandwidth alternative for campus networks, metropolitan area networks, and data centers, the vast majority of installed network media is UTP copper. The introduction of the 1000baseTX standard was delayed to resolve technical issues associated with maximum transmission distance. The majority of buildings are currently wired with maximum cabling distances up to 100 meters, the distance supported by the existing 10baseT and fast Ethernet over UTP standards. The final 1000baseTX standard meets this de-facto distance requirement.

Although the 1000baseTX standard supports category 5 UTP, it is important to note that in order to squeeze gigabit data transfer rates into the limited bandwidth available, the cable installation must be exactly to standard. Unlike the slower 10baseT and fast Ethernet standards that use only two pair, 1000baseTX requires all four pairs. Organizations that chose to "split pairs" on their existing wiring to carry either two Ethernets or Ethernet and a telephone line on one cable will be forced to rewire their cable plants. A category 5 wiring plant that exhibits excellent performance under the fast Ethernet standard might not work at all with gigabit Ethernet. Just as NICs that automatically adjusted speed to either 10 or 100 Mbps Ethernet became the de-facto standard, 10/100/1000 tri-speed copper NICs are entering the marketplace.

Although most organizations will implement gigabit Ethernet in a switch-based configuration, the CSMA/CD MAC protocol was retained for backward compatibility with 10baseT and fast Ethernet based full duplex, shared-media Ethernet implementations. In addition, the minimum and maximum Ethernet frame size has not changed. However, to maintain the required slot time (see In Sharper Focus section earlier in this chapter, "Timing Issues and 100baseT Network Diameter") given the tenfold increase in speed over fast Ethernet would have reduced maximum cable lengths to only 10 meters. As a solution, gigabit Ethernet increases the slot size, but not the minimum frame size, from 64 bytes to 512 bytes in a process called *carrier extension.*

**Application**     Gigabit Ethernet offers two key advantages over previous Ethernet standards: speed and maximum transmission distance when using single-mode fiber optic cable. These two advantages directly map to the applications for gigabit Ethernet.

Support for single-mode fiber that can run up to 5 km makes gigabit Ethernet an excellent candidate for campus networks and metropolitan area networks. For networks that do not require bandwidth splitting between telephony and data payloads, gigabit offers a unique combination of speed, distance, cost, and compatibility with existing Ethernet networks. With the imminent demise of FDDI, most FDDI rings will be converted to gigabit Ethernet over the next few years. If streaming media technologies such as VOIP continue to evolve, the domain of gigabit Ethernet in campus and MAN networks may increase to include converged data and voice networks. For more on VOIP and network convergence see chapter 5.

The raw speed of gigabit Ethernet makes it a natural fit for bandwidth constrained servers and building backbones. By simply adding a gigabit capable switch and gigabit NICs, most server bandwidth constraints can be resolved. However, as the principle of shifting bottlenecks states, fixing one limitation in a network will undoubtedly uncover another. For most applications, both the backbone and server connections must be upgraded to gigabit Ethernet to practically solve bandwidth limitations.

## 10 Gigabit Ethernet

The next speed step in the Ethernet hierarchy is 10 gigabit Ethernet.

**Standards**     10 gigabit Ethernet was approved in June 2002 as the IEEE 802.3ae standard by the IEEE 802.3ae subcommittee of the IEEE 802.3 Ethernet Working Group. The standard allows for data to be transmitted at 10 Gbps over fiber in the following configurations:

- **10GbaseSR/SW** uses short wavelength (850 nanometers) laser multimode fiber (MMF) optic media, primarily for horizontal building cabling on a given floor.

- **10GbaseLR/LW** uses long wavelength (1,310 nanometers) laser single mode fiber (SMF) optic media, primarily for metro area backbone applications.

- **10GbaseER/EW** uses extra long wavelength (1,550 nanometers) laser single mode fiber (SMF) optic media, primarily for long haul carrier backbone applications.

- **10GbaseLX4** uses wave division multiplexed (1,310 nanometers) laser multimode fiber (MMF) or single-mode fiber (SMF) optic media.

The difference between the xR's and the xW's is their intended use. The xR's are used with dedicated fiber (most likely in a campus on metropolitan area network) while the xW standards are designed to connect to SONET-based switching equipment. For detailed information on SONET, please refer to chapter 6.

Specifics of the 10 gigabit Ethernet standard are listed in Figure 4-9. One key limitation of 10 gigabit Ethernet is that the maximum recommended distance over FDDI-style 62.5 micron multimode fiber optic cable is only 26 meters using 10baseSR/SW and 300 meters using 10GbaseLX4.

**Technology**    The key goals of IEEE 802.3ae task group were as follows:

- *Preserve the 802.3 Ethernet frame format and minimum/maximum frame sizes.* This allows for compatibility with legacy Ethernet at the MAC level. By maintaining these characteristics, packets can freely move though routers from 10 Gbps to 10 Mbps without being reformatted, thus reducing the latency through network devices such as routers and switches. Another key benefit is that this allows technicians knowledgeable with standard Ethernet to use existing skills to troubleshoot 10 Gbps.

- *Support full duplex only.* This is a change over 1 Gbps Ethernet. Since the application of this technology is for very high throughput, there is no need to support the slower half duplex mode. This also enables additional performance gains by removing the requirement to support the legacy CSMA/CD media access control algorithm.

- *Support star-wired local area networks.* Just as in gigabit Ethernet, all devices must connect to a LAN switch.

- *Support various types of fiber at different distances.* Unlike gigabit Ethernet, 10 gigabit Ethernet only supports fiber. Using current technology, copper cannot currently support 10 Gbps speeds. Even if it were possible to achieve 10 Gbps speeds over copper, the distance limitation would be only a few meters.

- *Define two families of physical interfaces (PHY).*

  ○ LAN PHY—This is the local area network physical interface that support a data rate of 10 Gbps.

  ○ WAN PHY—This is the wide area network interface. Since the majority of high-speed long-haul WANs are SONET based, the specification was written to be compatible with the existing OC-192c specification. This specification

| Standard | Media | Fiber Core Diameter | Bandwidth | Range |
|----------|-------|---------------------|-----------|-------|
| **10GbaseSR/SW** | Multimode fiber | 62.5 and 50.0 microns | 10 Gb | 26 m to 100 m |
| **10GbaseLR/LW** | Single-mode fiber | 5 to 8 microns | 10 Gb | Up to 10 km |
| **10GbaseER/EW** | Single-mode fiber | 5 to 8 microns | 10 Gb | Up to 40 km |
| **10GbaseLX4** | Multimode and single-mode fiber | 62.5 or 50.0 micro for MMF; 5 to 8 microns for SM | 10 Gb | Up to 300 m MMF Up to 10 km SMF |

*Figure 4-9*    10 Gigabit Ethernet Fiber Dependent Configurations

defines a payload capacity of 9.58464 Gbps. The WAN PHY constrains the data being sent over the WAN to the payload capacity of OC-192c.

Managerial
Perspective

## ETHERNET AS A WAN STANDARD

The 10 Gbps Ethernet standard further extends the life of Ethernet in the local area network and provides a migration path for it to become a key standard for wide area networks. Although only time will tell if Ethernet can become a dominate wide area network standard, the adage "Don't bet against the success of Ethernet" has never been more true.

**Application**   The applications for 10 gigabit Ethernet include those of gigabit Ethernet: datacenter and building backbones, campus networks, and metropolitan area networks. The initial application for 10 gigabit Ethernet is to upgrade existing gigabit Ethernet backbones that are under pressure from ever-increasing traffic levels driven by the explosive growth of Internet and intranet traffic. Increases in the amount of traffic to Web hosting and application hosting sites—along with the bandwidth-intensive applications like high-quality video—are combining to exceed the capacity of older Ethernet standards.

The extension of the Ethernet frame to 10 Gbps speeds allows Ethernet to be used as the common transport protocol from LAN, to MAN, and back to LAN. The standardization of the WAN PHY allows 10 Gbps to travel easily over both SONET and dense wave division multiplexing (DWDM), opening a new marketplace for Ethernet in the WAN environment.

10 gigabit Ethernet can also be used in storage area networks (SANs). As the popularity and amount of data stored on SANs increases, the sheer speed of 10 Gbps Ethernet—combined with its inherent ability to operate transparently in the MAN—position it well for expansion into this booming market space.

In Sharper Focus

## ETHERNET BEYOND 10 GIGABIT SPEEDS

Although 10 gigabit Ethernet is in its infancy, researchers are already working on higher-speed Ethernet derivatives. According to Cisco Systems, 40 gigabit Ethernet is in the design stage with deployment expected by mid-2005. With the continued growth of the Ethernet speed hierarchy, Ethernet (or at least the Ethernet frame) is going to be a major LAN standard for a long time to come.

## Token Ring

The credit for the first token ring network architecture has been attributed to Olaf Soderblum, who proposed such a network in 1969. IBM has been the driving force behind the standardization and adoption of token ring, with a prototype in IBM's lab in Zurich, Switzerland, serving as a model for the eventual **IEEE 802.5** standard. Token ring can be defined as follows:

- Access methodology: Token passing

- Logical topology: Sequential

- Physical topology: Star

**Standards**  The token ring network architecture, adhering to the IEEE 802.5 standard, utilizes a star configuration, sequential message delivery, and a token passing access methodology scheme. Unlike IEEE 802.3, Ethernet networks whose speed is specified as part of the IEEE standard, the IEEE 802.5 token ring standard does not include a speed specification. IBM, the leading advocate of the token ring network architecture, specified token ring network architectures that operate at 4 Mbps and 16 Mbps. Later a group of vendors developed the high-speed token ring standard that supported 100 Mbps transmission.

Managerial
Perspective

## TOKEN RING IS DEAD, LONG LIVE TOKEN RING

Discussions as to the relative merits of token ring or Ethernet network architectures were conducted at one time with all the fervor of a religious war. There seems to be no argument now as Ethernet has clearly won the war. Even the final stronghold of token ring (IBM minicomputer and mainframe integration) is no longer working in token ring's favor because the mainframe/minicomputer world has evolved to embrace open systems; namely, TCP/IP and Ethernet.

In the end, price and the scalability of Ethernet from the nominal 10 Mbps speed, through 100 Mbps, and gigabit (1000 Mbps) to 10 Gigabit and beyond allowed Ethernet to win the war, despite token ring's superior media access architecture. It doesn't matter that token ring can squeeze more data into a given amount of bandwidth if 10 times the bandwidth is available for half the money with Ethernet.

### ATM on the LAN

ATM (asynchronous transfer mode) is a switched network technology originally developed for wide area network applications. ATM has been defined at speeds ranging from 25 Mbps to several gigabits per second. Network interface cards are available for both workstations and servers. Additional detail on ATM can be found in chapter 6.

If all computers that need to communicate support ATM, then it is relatively easy to configure ATM for LAN data transport. However, if ATM-based computers need to communicate with non–ATM-based computers, a process known as LAN emulation must be implemented.

**Technology**  Since ATM acts as a layer two switching service, and since layer two LAN switches support virtual LANs, it would stand to reason that ATM switches ought to be able to support virtual LANs as well. In fact, through a process known as **ATM LAN emulation,** virtual LANs are able to be constructed over an ATM-switched network regardless of the geographic scope of that network. ATM LAN emulation is considered a bridging solution, like LAN switch-based virtual LANs, because traffic is switched based on MAC layer addresses. Unlike LAN switch-based virtual LANs, however, MAC layer addresses must be translated into, or resolved into, ATM addresses in a process known as **ATM address resolution.** In ATM LAN emulation, the ATM switching fabric adds an entire layer of its own addressing schemes, which it uses to forward virtual LAN traffic to its proper destination.

## ATM LAN EMULATION

It is important to understand that ATM LAN emulation, like other virtual LAN architectures built on layer two switching, is basically a bridged topology that suffers from the same limitations as other layer two switched networks:

- Flat network topology

- Broadcast storms (although limited to a particular virtual LAN)

- No layer three filtering for security or segmentation

On the other hand, because it does not discriminate between network layer (layer three) protocols, ATM LAN emulation is able to support, or transport, multiple network layer protocols between virtual LANs.

Perhaps more importantly, however, ATM LAN emulation offers no routing capability. As a result, each virtual LAN that is emulated using ATM emulation must still have a dedicated connection to a router that is able to process layer three addresses and make appropriate route determination and forwarding decisions between virtual LANs.

**Application**   Moreover, in order for applications to take full advantage of ATM's speed and features, they must be *ATM aware*. ATM was once a fairly popular choice for high-speed backbone networks in the data center, but it is rapidly being displaced in favor of high-speed Ethernet. ATM is now used almost exclusively in applications where its predictable performance is a requirement, such as video editing.

Managerial
Perspective

## IT'S THE CONCEPT, NOT NECESSARILY THE TECHNOLOGY, THAT ULTIMATELY WINS THE WAR

One of the original selling points for ATM on the LAN was the promise of standardizing the layer two data unit on the ATM cell across the LAN, Backbone, and WAN. Having such a standard data unit offers faster data transmission, as data can simply be switched at layer two rather than having to remove the layer three packet and repackage it in a different layer two frame/cell. (For more detail on data encapsulation/de-encapsulation see chapter 7.)

This vision was realized, but not in the manner intended by ATM supporters. Instead of ATM moving from the WAN to the LAN and standardizing on ATM cells, Ethernet has moved from the LAN to the WAN in its gigabit and 10 gigabit variants, and the industry has standardized on Ethernet frames. This simply goes to prove that it's the concept that ultimately wins the war, not necessarily the technology.

## Wireless LANs

Once the stuff of science fiction, wireless LANs have rapidly become an integral part of most organizations' network structure. In fact, for small offices and many homes, wireless networks have evolved to be the only network structure.

**Standards**   The evolution of the IEEE 802.11 family of standards in the late 1990s set in motion a surprising adoption rate for wireless LANs. The standard meant interoperability between vendors was possible for the first time; a user could now buy equipment from different manufactures that supported the 802.11 standards and ensure they would work together.

*Underlying Physical Access Techniques*  Regardless of the exact network standard used, there are three basic approaches to utilizing the spectrum available to the Wireless LAN: FHSS, DSSS, and OFDM.

- **Frequency–hopping spread spectrum (FHSS)** hops from one frequency to another throughout the allowable frequency range. The pattern of frequency hopping must be known by the wireless receiver so that the message can be reconstructed correctly. A given wireless transceiver's signal is on a given frequency for less than 1 second. Another desirable effect of all of the hopping from one frequency to another is that the transmission tends to be less effected by interference, an especially desirable characteristic for mobile computing applications.

- **Direct sequence spread spectrum (DSSS)** transmits at a particular frequency within the allowable range. In order to distinguish between transmissions from multiple wireless workstations, DSSS adds at least 10 bits to the data message in order to uniquely identify a particular transmission. DSSS receivers must be able to differentiate between these bits, known as chips, in order to properly distinguish transmissions. The addition, removal, and interpretation of chips in DSS add complexity, cost, and processing overhead. Nonetheless, DSSS generally delivers superior throughput to FHSS.

- **Orthogonal frequency division multiplexing (OFDM)** spreads the data over multiple carrier frequencies at the same time. These multiple carrier frequencies are spaced so that they don't interfere with each other. Multiple data bits are sent per carrier. This allows OFDM systems to send more data over a specific bandwidth, which makes the bandwidth more efficient. Think about this being a "virtual parallel cable" where multiple bits are sent at one time from transmitter to receiver.

*802.11 Overview*  The IEEE commissioned the 802.11 subgroup in 1990 to look into wireless local area networks (Wireless LANs). The goal of the group was to determine the over-the-air interfaces between wireless clients and base stations at the physical and media access control layers of the OSI Network Reference Model.

The resulting standard defines how data are transmitted between nodes at these layers. For the physical layer, supported technologies include direct spectrum spread spectrum (DSS), frequency-hopping spread spectrum (FHSS), and infrared pulse position modulation (IR). The media access control layer was standardized as **CSMA/CA (carrier sense multiple access with collision avoidance)**.

CSMA/CA is similar in approach to the CSMA/CD approach used in wired Ethernet in that each node listens to see if anyone is using the bandwidth (in this case, the airborne carrier frequency) before transmitting. The key difference between the two is in how they deal with contention on the media. In a wireless environment it is difficult to detect a collision, so CSMA/CA seeks to avoid collisions by waiting a predetermined amount of time after determining the media are available. The source then sets up a point-to-point wireless circuit to the destination node and transmits the data frame. The wireless point-to-point circuit remains in place until the source receives an acknowledgment from the destination that the message was received error free. At that point in time, the circuit is destroyed and the process repeats.

802.11 frames are very similar to wired Ethernet frames, with both containing source and destination MAC addresses. Wireless access points translate between the two frame types when they bridge data from a wired network to the wireless network, and vice versa.

802.11 networks are identified by a **service set identifier** (**SSID**), a 32-character unique identifier for the wireless LAN. Also known as a network name, SSIDs are user configurable and are used to differentiate one wireless LAN from another. For two devices to be able to communicate on a wireless LAN they must both be configured to use the same SSID. The 802.11 standard mandates the SSID be sent as plain text in the header of the packets on the wireless network. In this manner, wireless devices learn of the wireless networks available to them in a given location. In some early implementations, the SSID was used as a security mechanism by not broadcasting the SSID but instead requiring the clients know the correct SSID before allowing them to connect. However, this violates the 802.11 standard and has since fallen out of favor.

The original 802.11 standard was accepted in 1997 and allowed for 1 or 2 Mbps transmission using the 2.4 GHz band. Extensions to the original 802.11 standard have been developed that increase network speed using additional unlicensed spectrum. All extensions to the 802.11 standard are given lowercase letters to differentiate them.

*802.11b*    Ratified in 1999, 802.11b uses direct sequence spread spectrum encoding in the 2.4 GHz – 2.485 GHz frequency band. The standard offers up to 11 Mbps of theoretical throughput while allowing for fallback to lower speeds (5.5 Mbps, 2 Mbps, and 1 Mbps) as distances increase and signal strength decreases.

As shown in Figure 4-10, the standard divides the available bandwidth into eleven overall channels, three of which are non-overlapping. As detailed later in the chapter, overlapping channels share common frequencies and cause interference that lowers the throughput of the users. When deploying a network as illustrated in Figure 4-13, channels must be assigned to APs so that APs with the same channels are not near each other. Two APs with the same channel near each other will cause interference problems, greatly reducing the throughput on the network.

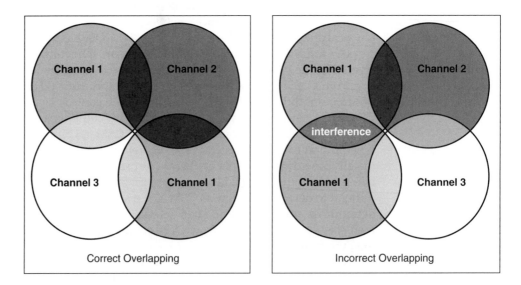

*Figure 4-10*    802.11b Overlapping Channels

Like all other wireless LAN technologies 802.11b is a shared media technology, so overall throughput drops as the number of users increases. Despite the theoretical capacity of 11 Mbps, real-world practice shows that most users will see actual performance in the range of around 4 Mbps.

In addition to 802.11b, the 2.4 GHz band is also used for other communications devices such as cordless phone handsets, baby monitors, and even Bluetooth enabled devices (see chapter 2). Microwave ovens also emit radiation in this frequency range. These devices can create significant interference with 802.11b networks, depending on their implementation and physical proximity to the wireless network nodes.

Despite the potential for interference, 802.11b has enjoyed widespread market acceptance and is currently the most commonly deployed wireless LAN technology.

*802.11g*    Ratified in June of 2003, 802.11g uses orthogonal frequency division multiplexing (OFDM) encoding in the 2.4 GHz to 2.485 GHz band. The standard offers up to 54 Mbps of theoretical throughput while allowing for fallback to lower speeds of 11 Mbps and 6 Mbps as signal strength decreases. 802.11g uses the same eleven channels as 802.11b with the same considerations for overlapping channels. In a practical application, 802.11g offers around 27 Mbps of usable bandwidth as long as no 802.11b devices are included on the network.

## 802.11G BACKWARD COMPATIBILITY WITH 802.11B

Many vendors state that 802.11g is *backwards compatible* to 802.11b. This is typically advertised as 802.11g access points being able to communication with 802.11b devices as well as 802.11g devices. In order to provide this backward compatibility 802.11g access points have two protection modes designed to allow them to share the available bandwidth between both DSSS and OFDM modulation schemes.

Although they are technically compatible, there is a significant performance penalty that occurs when an 802.11g access point must interoperate with 802.11b devices. Since the AP has to communicate with both 802.11g and 802.11b, it will need to accommodate both within its limited amount of bandwidth. Initial field testing has shown that a single 802.11b device on an 802.11g network reduces the throughput of the whole network to around 9 to 13 Mbps, depending on the protection mode used. Additional 802.11b devices added to the network further reduce the overall network throughput well into the single-digit Mbps range.

*802.11a*    Ratified in 2001, 802.11a delivers up to 54 Mbps of throughput using orthogonal frequency division multiplexing (OFDM) over unlicensed bandwidth in the 5 GHz range. Just as with 802.11b and 802.11g, the 802.11a standard allows for fallback to a lower speed (22 Mbps, 12 Mbps, and 6 Mbps) as signal strength degrades.

The standard initially offered eleven non-overlapping channels (eight of which were available in the United States), but the addition of additional spectrum as detailed below has allowed for twnety-four non-overlapping channels. Practical throughput for an 802.11a system is around 27 Mbps, with greatly reduced interference issues as compared to 802.11b/g.

## 5 GHZ WIRELESS WANS

In June of 2003, the Federal Communications Commission set aside an additional 250 MHz of bandwidth in the 5.47 to 5.725 GHz for a new class of wireless LANs and other wireless devices. This frequency band is used by the U.S. military, so some concessions were added around the topics of transmission power control (TPS) and dynamic frequency selection (DFS). These concepts are detailed in the 802.11h section below.

This change clears out frequencies that are available in other countries, ensuring that wireless LANs that operate at 5 GHz won't require different cards for different countries. The frequencies, from 5.15 to 5.350 GHz and from 5.725 to 5.825 GHz are collectively known as the Unlicensed National Information Infrastructure (U-NII). Compliant devices could include PCs and laptops with built-in or external radio receivers.

## 802.11A VS. 802.11G

After looking at the available wireless LAN standards, you may find yourself asking, "If I want to use the fastest wireless LAN available, should I purchase 802.11g or 802.11a devices?" Both standards state a throughput of 54 Mbps. 802.11g may seem to have an initial advantage as it offers a degree of backward compatibility with any existing 802.11b devices you may already have in place.

However, 802.11a will offer superior performance in almost all implementations. It operates in a less crowded (for now) frequency range and is less susceptible to interference from microwave ovens. Another advantage of 802.11a is the number of non-overlapping channels provided. Where 802.11g has only three non-overlapping channels, 802.11a offers twenty-four non-overlapping channels.

*802.11h*   802.11h is a new standard that allows 5 GHz wireless LANs to be used in Europe. The standard adds transmission power control (TPS) and the dynamic frequency selection (DFS) to the 802.11a standard. Adaptive power control allows the base station (access point) and the client to determine the minimum power needed to communicate and adjust transmit power to that level. Dynamic frequency allocation requires access points and clients to listen to the channel to ensure that nothing is using that piece of bandwidth. In the event that there is something else using the channel, the device must move to another channel and repeat the check until it finds an unused channel. The formal standard is scheduled to be ratified by the end of 2003.

Summarized comparisons between all of these standards are in Figure 4-11.

| Standard | Data Throughput (Theoretical) | Data Throughput (Practical) | Transmission Technology | Frequency band | Number of non-overlapping channels | Year Ratified |
|---|---|---|---|---|---|---|
| 802.11 | Up to 2 Mbps | 1 Mbps | DSSS or FHSS | 2.4 Ghz – 2.4835 Ghz | 3 (in DSSS) | 1997 |
| 802.11b | 11 Mbps | 6 Mbps | DSSS | 2.4 Ghz – 2.4835 Ghz | 3 | 1999 |
| 802.11g | 54 Mbps | 27 Mbps (g-only networks) 9–13 Mbps (b/g combination networks) | OFDM | 2.4 Ghz – 2.4835 Ghz | 3 | 2003 |
| 802.11a | 54 Mbps | 27 Mbps | OFDM | 5.12 Ghz – 5.25 Ghz, 5.47 Ghz – 5.725 Ghz, 5.725 Ghz – 5.825 Ghz | 24 | 2001 |
| 802.11h | 54 Mbps | 27 Mbps | OFDM *Requires TPS and DFS Technologies* | 5.12 Ghz – 5.25 Ghz, 5.47 Ghz – 5.725 Ghz, 5.725 Ghz – 5.825 Ghz | 24 | Scheduled for late 2003 |

*Figure 4-11*   Wireless LAN Standards Comparison Table

In Sharper Focus

## WIRELESS STANDARDS BEYOND 802.11A, B, AND G

The 802.11 committee chartered the High Throughput Study group (802.11n committee) in 2002 to work on increasing the raw data speed of wireless LANs and improve the end user experience. This group is looking at ways of increasing the maximum modulation rate from the current 54 Mbps up to 108 Mbps, or even 320Mbps. They are also looking at new antenna technologies designed to increase the range of wireless LAN products. Although some of their work looks promising, no new standards proposals are expected until 2005 or 2006.

Managerial
Perspective

## WI-FI ALLIANCE

To ensure that wireless LAN hardware from different vendors in interoperable the **Wi-Fi Alliance** was formed in 1999 to ensure the interoperability of wireless LAN products based on the 802.11 specification. Their original work was with 802.11b devices. The group runs vendors' wireless LAN equipment through rigorous testing to ensure products from multiple vendors work together. Since their origin in 1999, they have become the de-facto group for certifying wireless LAN products. The majority of the wireless LAN vendors use the Wi-Fi Alliance to certify their equipment. They have since expanded their scope to include 802.11a and 802.11g products. They have also become involved with interoperability testing for Wi-Fi Protect Access (WPA). If two products have Wi-Fi Alliance labels on their packaging, it is guaranteed they will work together.

Technology    There are two basic types of Wireless LAN architectures: **ad-hoc** or **infrastructure.** Ad-hoc networks are "on the fly" networks where multiple devices with wireless LAN cards are configured to communicate directly with each other. There is no central point in which all the devices communicate through; each device talks to the other devices directly.

Ad-hoc networks are primarily used for file sharing between two users or for playing games in mobile locations. Although they require no hardware except two hosts with wireless NICs, there are significant limitations associated with ad-hoc networks:

- No automatic IP addressing available; addresses must be manually set for each host on the network (see chapter 7 for more details on IP addressing)

- No ability to limit access to the network through the use of MAC address filtering or other security techniques

- No ability to connect the wireless network to a wired network

For these reasons, ad-hoc networks represent a small number of the networks in use today. Even most home users have implemented infrastructure networks using access points.

In an infrastructure network configuration, wireless hosts communicate through access points (APs). An access point, sometimes referred to as a base station, is a device that connects to a wired network and bridges traffic between the wired and wireless networks. In addition to providing a connection point to a wired network, access points also provide a centralize point to control access to the wireless network by employing technologies such as **MAC address filtering.** When in an infrastructure network each wireless network client must *associate* with an access point on the network and relay all outgoing traffic through that access point which in turn forwards the traffic to the next hop along the way to its destination.

Although the most common use for an access point is to allow wireless clients to access the wired network, access points can also be used to bridge two wired networks across a wireless link. Uses of access points are illustrated in Figure 4-12.

In Sharper Focus

## ACCESS POINTS VS. WIRELESS GATEWAYS

For home users, manufactures have combined access points into other home networking devices. For many home users the access point is the first piece of networking equipment they purchase as the addition of wireless technologies allow them to create a LAN. This is especially true for apartment dwellers and owners of older homes, as they typically do not (and in some cases cannot) easily install a wired network.

The most common combination device is the wireless gateway: a combination wireless access point and Internet firewall/router that also includes the ability to perform network address translation (see chapter 8 for more details on NAT). By implementing a wireless gateway and a cable or DSL modem, a homeowner can instantly provide broadband Internet access to all of the computers in their home. Given the relatively low cost (around $100) and widespread availability of these devices, manufacturers such as Linksys and D-Link are selling millions of them.

The wireless gateway phenomenon is typically limited to the home market space, however. Enterprises typically have switches, routers and firewalls already installed and merely add access points to extend their network to wireless clients.

Another key aspect of infrastructure networks is that they provide a means to transparently extend the range of the wireless network beyond that of a single access point. As shown in Figure 4-13 multiple access points can be set up in a grid so that no matter where they are in the service area they will be within range of an access point.

Each wireless client will associate with the access point that has the strongest signal, usually the closest one. When a client is moved away from its associated access point toward another access point, the client has the ability to change its association from the old access point to the new access point that is providing a stronger signal. This ability to roam between access points allows for transparent access throughout the wireless network's coverage area.

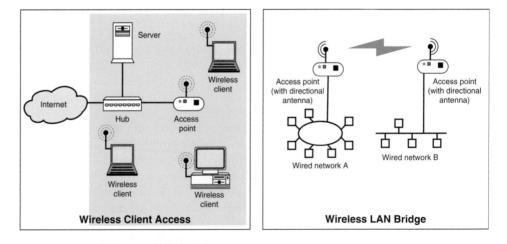

*Figure 4-12*   Access Point Applications

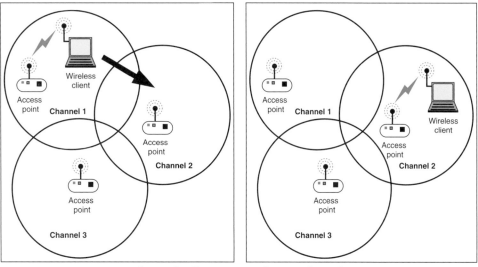

**Accessing the nearer or stronger channel**

*Figure 4-13*   Multiple Access Points and Roaming

In Sharper Focus

## MOBILE IP

Although most wireless access point vendors support roaming between different access points, each access point must be on the same network segment so that the client's IP address remains on the correct network segment. This can be done by connecting each access point to the same physical LAN switch or by using virtual LANs (these concepts are covered in detail later in this chapter and in chapter 7). **Mobile IP** removes the requirement that each access point be connected to the same network segment by providing a means of dynamically changing IP addresses as the client roams between access points.

Mobile IP employs two pieces of software in order to support roaming:

- A mobile IP client is installed on the roaming wireless client workstation

- A mobile IP home agent is installed on a server or router on the roaming user's home network

The mobile IP client keeps the mobile IP home agent informed of its changing location as it travels from network to network. The mobile IP home agent forwards any transmissions it receives for the roaming client to its last reported location.

When deploying access points, care must be exercised to ensure that the coverage of each access point encompasses the desired area. The coverage area of an access point is affected by the materials in the building, and the type of antenna used. Building materials such as metal or concrete walls, water pipes, metal tinted windows, etc. can dramatically reduce the coverage of an access point. The coverage area of an access point is also affected by the type of antenna used. Depending on the frequency the wireless LAN uses, antennas usually come in several different shapes that can be used to tailor the access point's coverage area.

*Wireless LAN Security*    Security is another item that needs to be considered when configuring a wireless LAN. Since wireless LANs extend the "wired LANs" in most configurations, access to the wireless LAN must be secured to ensure that unauthorized people do not have access to the network. The ability to transparently connect to the network without having to find an available network cable cuts both ways: it eases use of the network for unauthorized people as well as the people for whom the network was implemented to service.

Since the radio frequencies used in wireless LANs go through walls, the coverage of the wireless LAN likely extends outside of the building as well. Not only do you have to be aware of unauthorized users inside the facility, but of those outside the building yet in range of the wireless LAN. If a hacker connects to an access point with an Ethernet connection to the private LAN, the hacker could compromise data on devices connected to the wired network as well as data being transported on the wireless LAN. Proper security measures should be used to keep unauthorized users from accessing the network.

**MAC address filtering** was one of the first mechanisms deployed to control access to the wireless LAN. In an enterprise network where all traffic must traverse an access point before reaching its destination, MAC address filtering serves to limit use of the access point to only those wireless NICs explicitly authorized in a table maintained in the access point. By using MAC address filter it is possible to reduce the likelihood that an unauthorized client can connect through the access point to resources on the wired LAN.

MAC address filtering is limited in its capabilities, however. Because it is not an encryption technique, it provides no defense against unauthorized users capturing data from the wireless network. MAC address filtering is not even a foolproof method of limiting access to the access point. Most NICS allow the administrator to manually set the MAC address, so a user can listen in on the wireless network, capture an authorized MAC address, and then use it to gain access to the access point once the real user of the MAC address is no longer on line. Despite these limitations, MAC address filtering is a good first step in securing a wireless LAN.

**Wired equivalent privacy (WEP)** was the initial 802.11 encryption solution that debuted with 802.11b. Unfortunately, WEP has proven to have significant vulnerabilities. Although WEP supports adequately long cipher keys that would ideally prove hard to break, initial wireless NIC implementations only used a 40-bit key, forcing administrators to choose between the higher security of longer key lengths versus the cost of replacing older wireless NICs. Anther key weakness with WEP is that the single shared encryption key is static. Because the key never changes, it is possible to crack the key if a hacker collects enough frames of encrypted data. There are many tools freely available on the Internet that take advantage of the vulnerabilities in WEP to crack the key. Once the key is broken, an unauthorized device can be configured with the key, and it will instantly have the ability to fully decode all traffic crossing the wireless network. Despite these vulnerabilities WEP still has a place in the wireless security arsenal.

When the flaws in WEP became apparent, two efforts were launched to develop a better encryption solution of wireless LANs: an interim solution known as WPA and a complete new security architecture known as 802.11i. **Wi-Fi protected access (WPA)** provides a method of authentication as well as an improved encryption solution. Authentication is provided through the use of the **extensible authentication protocol (EAP)** and 802.1x, while a dynamic key exchange based on the **temporal key integrity protocol (TKIP)** replaces the static keys used in WEP. WPA was designed to work with existing wireless access points through a firmware upgrade. However, the dynamic key exchanges of TKIP may cause a performance hit in older wireless LAN hardware devices and might not even work in some older PDA devices due to the increased processor capacity required to perform the key exchange in the device.

While WPA provides a quick security improvement, the IEEE 802.11 committee chartered a new task force to develop a new security architecture for Wireless LANs. The IEEE 802.11i task force is working on a draft of a new solution that formally standardizes the use of WPA and provides a new encryption algorithm based on the **advanced encryption standard** (**AES**). AES is the new U.S. government standard to protect sensitive, unclassified information that uses up to a 256-bit cipher key to encrypt data. Due to the additional processor power needed to encrypt and decrypt packets using keys this long, legacy wireless LAN devices will likely be unable to support the new standard and will need to be replaced with new devices. The standard is expected to be ratified in 2004.

*Performance*    Performance on a wireless LAN is difficult to quantify due to the large number of factors that affect the propagation of the radio signal between devices. As previously mentioned, many items a network engineer has no control over—such as building, materials, and construction techniques—can dramatically affect the range and speed of a wireless network. Other RF devices can also affect the throughput of wireless LANs. If a device operates at the same frequency as the wireless LAN, it will cause interference. This interference reduces the throughput of the wireless LAN, and could cause problems for the other RF device. Items such microwaves, cordless phones, light control systems, satellite radio, and other wireless devices have the potential to affect the throughput of the wireless network in unpredictable manners.

Despite the extreme variability of these issues there are two basic factors that consistently affect wireless network performance in a predictable manner: the number of devices communicating directly and the distance between devices.

Wireless LANs are the embodiment of shared media networks: there is a limited amount of spectrum devoted to all of the devices on the network to share and only one can use it at time. As the number of devices increase, the effective throughput available to each device decreases. Just as in a wired shared media Ethernet LAN, the amount of bandwidth available to each client depends on the number of clients on the network sharing the bandwidth.

The second factor is distance between devices. The closer a device is to the access point, the faster the device can send data. As the device moves farther from the access point, data speeds are reduced until the device is no longer in range and able to communicate. The concept of using multiple access points on non-overlapping channels resolves this problem by providing a non-interfering signal from a second access point for the device to use when it starts to lose the signal from the original access point.

Applications    Wireless LANs based on the 802.11b standards have been one of the brightest areas in the telecommunication industry in the early 2000s. Interestingly enough, the initial market for Wireless LANs was in the home rather than in the business sector. The demand for home wireless LANs was originally fueled by two separate, yet aligned trends: multiple computers in the home and the widespread availability of broadband Internet service.

Whether fueled by buying a new computer and wanting to keep the old one, purchasing another computer for the children, or bring home a notebook computer from work the number of households with more than one computer has continued to rise. With multiple computers in the home people want to connect them to share files and printers, share a broadband connection to the Internet, and play interactive games. Traditionally, the biggest obstacle of creating home networks was the lack of an appropriate cable infrastructure. Most homes simply are not wired for Ethernet, and the homeowners are not willing to incur the cost of retrofitting them with Ethernet cabling. The availability of inexpensive wireless networks removed that obstacle and freed home users to interconnect their machines easily.

The growth of broadband access, the increase in two (or more) PC households, and the low cost of wireless LAN components from Linksys, D-Link, and Netgear among others has created an explosion of wireless LAN implementations in the consumer space. Hardware firewalls with 802.11b access points built in are widely available for under $100. The wireless LAN allows for multiple PC in multiple rooms to be connected to the broadband connection in the house without running wiring to each PC.

The growth of wireless LANs in the consumer space has also fueled the use of Wireless LANs in the enterprise space. Business users with laptop that work from home with wireless LANs have bought cards to use at home to connect to their broadband connection. With the use of a VPN, they are able to connect to their enterprise resources as well. The use of wireless LANs allows the business user to roam anywhere inside the house and be connected. This allows the business user to work in family rooms while watching the kids, or outside on their decks.

Enterprises are beginning to see the benefits in allowing users with laptops to roam between meeting while being connected. It increases the productivity of their employees. The productivity gains can be seen in having online information readily available in meetings for quick decision making. How many times have you been in a meeting and heard someone say, "I will need to get back to you because I don't have that information with me?"

Even with these benefits, the Wireless LAN deployment in the enterprise has been relatively slow, with security and cost being the major limiting factors. Despite these concerns, however, many enterprises have embraced the technology and deployed wireless LANs. In order to address the security considerations, some have isolated the wireless LAN from the production network and required the users to establish a VPN connection to the corporate network to gain access. Others have deployed interim fixes such as WEP, and proprietary security solutions until WPA and AES are available.

Enterprises see another major gain in the use of Wireless LANs in a small or branch offices with few users. The cost of wiring such an office with LAN cabling is expensive. Some companies are also deploying Wireless LANs to reduce the cost of building a new building or moving an old office to another location.

Managerial
Perspective

## WIRELESS LAN "HOTSPOTS"

One of the fastest-growing areas of wireless networking is offering free or low-cost Internet access through wireless LANs to business customers. Retail companies, particularly those at which people gather, such as coffee shops and restaurants, are trying to find way to distinguish themselves from their competitors by offering Internet access for their patrons. Hotels and airports are also adding wireless Internet access to people at locations throughout their facilities as a way of gaining new business or as a second profit center in itself. These open wireless networks are known as **hotspots.**

A *hotspot* is a geographic area in which an 802.11 access point has been set up and connected to a broadband Internet connection. These geographic areas are generally within a single building and provide patrons who have wireless LAN capable devices access to the Internet to check e-mail, check stock quotes, and so on, on their own laptop computers. Although some businesses offer hotspot service as a free perk for their customers, the majority offer the service for a fee, where the user signs up for a monthly (or daily) contract with the provider.

Examples of hotspots include Starbucks, Borders bookstores, and McDonald's. By the end of 2003, all Starbucks are to be hotspot capable through a service provided by mobile phone carrier T-Mobile. McDonald's is also piloting hotspot services in selected areas. Although the final pricing plans have yet to be determined at the time of this writing, one option calls for a free hour of access included with every extra value meal sold, with additional time available at a fee. The phrase, "I'll take a Big Mac and an hour of Internet" might not be far from our daily lexicon.

## FUTURES IN WIRELESS LANS

Practical Advice and Information

Despite their rapid deployment rate, Wireless LANs are still in their infancy. IEEE has just released their first set of standards with the promise of faster and cheaper technologies to come. Some analysts say that wireless LANs may virtually replace wired LANs for client access in all but the largest facilities. As wireless LAN hotspots continue to appear, the possibility of their replacing the struggling wireless WAN technologies, based on cellular phones, is increasing.

A second area to watch is the development of wireless LAN *switching*. Wireless LAN switching refers to the deployment of low-cost "dumb" access points attached to LAN switches that contain the "smarts" of the network such as the configuration of the radio (power, SSID, etc.). This approach allows for centralized management of multiple access points with a single management system capable of sending a change to the switch, which updates all of the access points. This approach further reduces the cost of access points, making it more economical to upgrade to faster wireless LAN standards as they are released. A third benefit is a reduction in the likelihood of access-point theft, as access points are useless unless they are connected to the proper LAN switch.

Another interesting area is the development of combination network cards. Wireless NICs that support both 802.11b and 802.11a are coming on the market. Since the standardization of 802.11g, combo cards that are 802.11b but capable of being flash upgraded to 802.11g are beginning to appear in the marketplace. Some vendors are looking at combining wireless LAN and wireless WAN technologies on the same card to provide a single solution for remote access.

Another development on the horizon is software tunable radios in wireless LAN cards. These cards promise to have a tunable radio chip that can change the radio frequency it operates at with a change in software, thus reducing the number of radio chips needed to support multiple technologies, which will reduce the amount of power required by the NIC while providing for software upgrades to as yet undeveloped wireless LAN standards. Expect to see software-tunable radios by 2006.

## ■  LAN INTERCONNECTION HARDWARE

The most common network physical topology employed today is the star topology and the heart of the star topology is the wiring center. A hub is simply a box that has multiple connections, or ports, that can be attached to different computers or other pieces of network hardware. The hub handles the transmission of data received on one port to its destination. Each port is connected either to a computer, another interconnection box, or another piece of network equipment such as a router or access point. Routers are covered in more detail in chapters 7 and 8.

A hub may also be known as a *concentrator, repeater, switch,* or one of a variety of other terms, depending on the LAN technology supported and the manner in which it internally interconnects the ports. For the purposes of this chapter we will use the term *hub* as a generic term for all types of interconnection devices, *shared media hub* to refer to a hub that implements shared media access control, and *switch* to refer to a hub capable of more sophisticated data transmission and media control.

## Hub Categories

In terms of functionality and features, hubs can be separated into three broad categories: stand-alone hubs, stackable hubs, and enterprise hubs.

**Stand-alone Hubs**   **Stand-alone hubs** are self-contained units offering a limited number (usually twelve or fewer) of ports of a particular type of network architecture (Ethernet, token ring, ATM, etc.) and media. They are fully configured and include their own power supply but are not generally expandable, do not include management software, and are the least expensive of the three hub categories. Stand-alone hubs typically have the ability to be linked together, or cascaded, via the same media used in the normal data connections. The actual method used to connect the hubs depends on the network architecture. Ethernet hubs are cascaded via uplink ports, while token ring hubs are cascaded via ring in and ring out ports. Stand-alone hubs are usually used in small networks such as those found in small offices and home environments.

**Stackable Hubs**   **Stackable hubs** add expandability and manageability to the basic capabilities of a stand-alone unit by allowing multiple units to be interconnected via a process known as stacking or **cascading.** Stackable hubs can be linked together to form one larger virtual unit of a single type of network architecture and media. When stacked, the entire stack appears as a single large wiring center. In general, cascading ports are proprietary in nature, thereby making it impossible to cascade hubs of different vendors together. Specialized cascading cables may also be required, and the maximum allowable distance between stacked hubs often varies as well. Stackable hubs also vary as to stackability, with the number of stackable hubs ranging from four to twenty and the total number of stacked ports ranging from roughly twenty-four to the thousands. Due to their ability to support increased numbers of ports, stackable hubs are usually used in mid-sized networks and at the edge of large networks.

**Enterprise Hubs**   **Enterprise hubs,** also known as **modular hubs** differ from stackable hubs in both their physical design and offered functionality. Rather than being fully functional self-contained units, enterprise hubs are modular by design, offering a chassis-based architecture to which a variety of different modules can be inserted. An enterprise hub starts with a fairly empty, box-like device called a *chassis.* The chassis contains one or more redundant power supplies and a "built-in" network backplane. Network modules are inserted into the backplane. Backplane design within enterprise hubs is proprietary and, as a result, modules are not interoperable between vendors. Therefore, it is important to assure that the enterprise hub purchased supports all the required types of modules in terms of network architecture, media type, management, internetworking, WAN interfaces, or security.

Higher-end units support the insertion and removal of modules while the unit remains powered-up, a capability known as **hot-swappable.** Modules can be of the same, or in some cases different, LAN technology. Additional modules may allow data traffic from this "network in box" to travel to other local LANs via bridge or router add-on modules. Bridges and routers will be discussed later in the chapter. Communication to remote LANs or workstations may be available through the addition of other specialized cards, or modules, designed to provide access to Wide Area Network services purchased from common carriers such as the phone company (see chapter 6 for more detail on WAN technologies). Enterprise hubs are usually used at the network core and at the edge of large networks where port densities are high enough to justify their differential price over stackable switches.

These broad category definitions and labels are not standardized and are not universally adhered to by manufacturers. Signaling standards defined as part of the IEEE or ANSI LAN standards allow hubs and NICs of different vendors to interoperate successfully in most cases. Figure 4-14 illustrates some of the physical differences between the three major categories of hubs, while Figure 4-15 differentiates between the functionality of the major categories of hubs.

## Stackable hubs

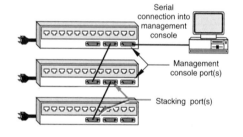

- Each hub has a fixed number of ports
- Hubs are stackable
- Single network architecture and media
- Provides management software and link to network management console
- Logically one large hub/switch

## Stand-alone hubs

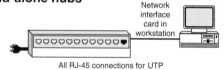

- Fixed number of ports
- Single network architecture
- Hubs are cascadable
- Single media type

## Enterprise hubs

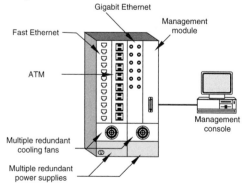

- Modular chassis-based design
- Supports multiple network architectures and media types
- Integrated management module
- May include internetworking or WAN modules

*Figure 4-14*    Major Categories of Hubs

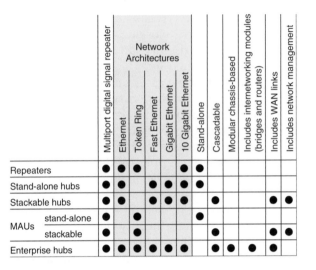

| | Multiport digital signal repeater | Network Architectures | | | | | Stand-alone | Cascadable | Modular chassis-based | Includes internetworking modules (bridges and routers) | Includes WAN links | Includes network management |
| | | Ethernet | Token Ring | Fast Ethernet | Gigabit Ethernet | 10 Gigabit Ethernet | | | | | | |
|---|---|---|---|---|---|---|---|---|---|---|---|---|
| Repeaters | ● | ● | ● | | | | ● | ● | | | | |
| Stand-alone hubs | ● | ● | | ● | ● | ● | ● | | | | | |
| Stackable hubs | ● | ● | | ● | ● | ● | | ● | | | ● | ● |
| MAUs stand-alone | ● | | ● | | | | ● | | | | | |
| MAUs stackable | ● | | ● | | | | | ● | | | ● | ● |
| Enterprise hubs | ● | ● | ● | ● | ● | ● | | ● | ● | ● | ● | |

*Figure 4-15*   Hub Functional Comparison

## Hub Management

Since all traffic must pass through the wiring center, it is an ideal place for the installation of management software to both monitor and manage network traffic. As previously stated, stand-alone hubs rarely support management capabilities. In the case of stackable and enterprise hubs, two layers of management software are most often involved:

- Proprietary **local management software** is usually supplied by the vendor to support configuration and management of the device. Traditionally this software is usually designed to run on a network-attached computer that talks to the device via proprietary protocols. Currently there is a strong trend toward placing the management software in the device itself and making it available via a Web interface. This approach is usually taken with stand-alone and some stackable hubs.

- Since these hubs are just a small part of a vast array of networking devices that might have to be managed on an enterprise basis, most stackable and enterprise hubs are also capable of sharing management information with **enterprise network management systems** such as Computer Associates Unicenter, HP OpenView, Tivoli NetView, and SunNet Manager.

Although chapter 11 will cover network management in more detail, a small explanation here as to how this management information is fed to the Enterprise Network Management system is appropriate.

Network management information transfer between multi-vendor network devices and enterprise network management systems must be characterized by standards-based communication. The standards that govern this network management communication are part of the TCP/IP family of protocols, more correctly known as the Internet Suite of Protocols. Specifically, network management information is formatted according to **Simple Network Management Protocol** or the **SNMP.** The types of information to be gathered and stored have also been defined as **Management Information Bases** or **MIBs.** There are actually numerous MIBs defined with the most often used one for network monitoring and management known as the **RMON (Remote MONitoring) MIB.** RMON collects data from a single network segment. The newest addition to the SNMP family of monitoring standards is **SMON (Switch MONitoring)**. SMON expands RMON's monitoring ability by offering a mechanism to collect data from all network segments connected to a LAN switch.

Network statistics and information is gathered in the first place and packetized in SNMP format by specialized software known as **agents** that reside within the monitored network device and are supplied by the network device's manufacturer. Enterprise network management systems, such as HP OpenView, are able to interpret, consolidate, and display information and alarms from a variety of different networking equipment manufactured by a variety of different vendors, thanks to standards-based communication protocols. Figure 4-16 illustrates the relationship of the various aspects of the standards-based network management communications protocols

Practical Advice
and Information

### STACKABLE HUB MANAGEMENT

Some hub management issues are particular to stackable and/or enterprise hubs. For example:

- Many stackable hubs offer network management capabilities as an optional hardware or software upgrade. It is important to fully understand the ease with which this upgrade can be accomplished and whether or not the hubs must be powered off while doing so.

- The network management traffic may exit the hub via a separate serial port or travel along a separate bus within the hub so as not to diminish the amount of bandwidth available for data. These options are sometimes referred to as out-of-band management connections.

- The entire stack of hubs should be viewed, monitored, and managed by the network management software as a single, virtual hub.

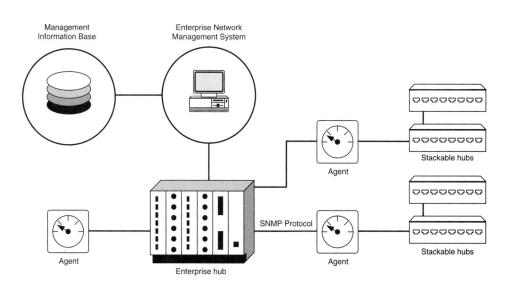

*Figure 4-16*   Standards-Based Network Management Communications Protocols

- If at all possible, management modules or upgrades should be included with the original purchase in order to avoid potential upgrade hassles. Buying management modules at purchase time is often more economical than buying upgrades later, thanks to vendor discount packages.

Applied Problem
Solving

## HUB TECHNOLOGY ANALYSIS

Some of the major technical features to be used for comparative analysis are listed in Figure 4-17. Before purchasing a hub of any type, consider the implications of the various possible features listed in the Hub Technology Analysis.

| Hub Characteristic | Implications/Options |
| --- | --- |
| Expandability | Most stand-alone hubs are cascadable via the same network technology as is used to connect nodes to the wiring center. Stackable hubs are cascadable via proprietary cabling that allows the entire stack to appear as one large hub and enterprise hubs are expandable by adding additional modules. Enterprise hubs vary in the number of open slots, from approximately five to twenty. Total backplane capacity (speed) is important, as this is the shared capacity that must be shared by all attached modules. |
| Network Architectures | Options: Ethernet, token ring, gigabit Ethernet, ATM, etc. Not all enterprise hubs have all types of network architecture modules available. |
| Media | Options: UTP, STP, thin coax, thick coax, fiber-optic cable. Modules also differ according to supported media. Remember that an NIC is on the other end of the connection to the module. Is this module media type and connector compatible with installed NICs? |
| Terminal Communications | Can "dumb" asynchronous terminals be connected directly to the wiring center? What is the physical connector and serial transmission specification? (DB-25, RS-232?) |
| Internetworking | Are bridging and or routing modules available that can redirect traffic from module to module? Across different types of network architecture modules? Across which different network architecture modules will traffic need to be bridged? |
| Wide Area Networking | Is this hub connected to others through the use of carrier-based data services? If so, which WAN services are supported? Options include frame relay, ISDN, switched 56K, digital leased lines, SONET, etc. |
| Management | Is a local management program available? Are SNMP management protocols supported? Can individual ports be managed? Is monitoring software included? What security services are available? Can ports be remotely enabled/disabled? Can the device be controlled by a port attached workstation or only by a special management console? Can the device be controlled remotely? Via modem? Are management statistics and alarms graphically displayed? How are alarm thresholds set? How are faults managed? Can port access be limited by day and/or time? What operating systems can the management software run on? Can a map of the network be displayed? |
| Reliability | Is an integrated UPS included? Are power supplies redundant? Are modules hot-swappable? Are cooling fans redundant? Which components are capable of being replaced by the user? |

*Figure 4-17*  Hub Technology Analysis

## Shared-Media Hubs

The most basic form of hub is the shared media hub. Shared media hubs are simply multi-port digital signal repeaters. As discussed in chapter 3, repeaters and shared media hubs operate at layer one, or the physical layer of the OSI Network Reference Model. They do not make logical decisions based on the addresses or content of frames; they merely take each bit of digital data received on port and retransmit, or "repeat" it on all of the other ports. This repeating action "cleans up" the digital signals by retiming and regenerating them before passing this repeated data from one attached device or LAN segment to the next.

The terms *shared media hub* and "*concentrator*" or *intelligent concentrator* are often used interchangeably. The type of media connections and network architecture offered by the hub is determined at the time of manufacture. Shared media hubs can only link devices or LAN segments of similar network architectures. For example, a 100baseTX Ethernet hub will offer a fixed number of RJ-45 twisted-pair connections for an Ethernet network. Additional types of media or network architectures are not supported.

Although a shared media hub is a quick and easy way to interconnect nodes on a network, it has some major limitations. Because a shared media architecture in effect puts every attached node onto the same piece of wire, or the same collision domain, media access control becomes a serious issue. If there are only a few nodes on the network, there might be enough bandwidth to go around. As the number of nodes grows, there is more and more contention of the media, which results in longer waits to use the network. If the number of nodes grows too large or the existing nodes on the network increase, the amount of data they need to transmit to the network can literally come to a halt because no one has the chance to talk.

Practical Advice
and Information

### ZERO PORT HUBS OR CROSS-OVER CABLES

In the case of twisted-pair-based Ethernet, a two-node network can be easily created by simply connecting them together with a special cable that crosses the transmit and receive pairs so that one computer's send pair connect to the other's receive pair and vice versa. Known as **cross-over cables,** these cables can also be used to connect two hubs or switches together, as long as the rules limiting the maximum network diameter are not violated.

To create an Ethernet cross-over, cable pins one and two must be crossed with pins three and six. Please see the discussion on twisted-pair wiring in chapter 3 for more detail on creating twisted-pair cables.

## LAN Switches

As client/server information systems and distributed computing applications have put increasing demands on the local area network infrastructure in terms of the amount of data traffic to be transferred, network architects and technology providers have responded with alternative solutions. As detailed earlier in the chapter, one solution to the network bandwidth crunch is to offer higher-speed shared-media network architectures such as gigabit Ethernet.

A second approach is to break a large shared media LAN into smaller sections. Switched LAN architectures depend on hubs called **LAN switches** or **switching hubs,** which resolve the one-at-a-time limitation of shared-media LAN architectures by offering all attached workstations access to a switching matrix that provides point-to-point connections between any two ports. Each port on the LAN switch is effectively a dedicated LAN segment with dedicated bandwidth offered to the attached devices. Each port on the LAN switch might be assigned to a single work-station or to an entire LAN segment linked by a media-sharing network architecture (non-switching) hub.

Although shared-media LAN segments can link to a LAN switch to take advantage of its dedicated connections and guaranteed bandwidth, there is no shared media or shared bandwidth within the switched LAN architecture itself. The limiting factor in a switch-based LAN architecture is the number of simultaneous point-to-point connections that a given switch can support, commonly referred to as switch **backplane capacity.** Figure 4-18 contrasts the differences in hub functionality between media-sharing and switch-based LAN architectures.

**Switching Process**   Switching is a datalink layer process, making forwarding decisions based on the contents of layer two frame addresses (the MAC address in the case of Ethernet). Switches are transparent devices, receiving every frame broadcast

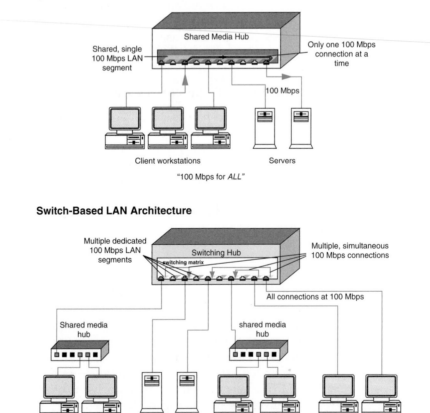

*Figure 4-18*   Switched LAN versus Media-Sharing LAN Hub Functionality

on a given port. Rather than merely transferring all frames to all ports like a shared media hub, a switch reads the *destination address* (MAC layer address of destination NIC) of each data frame received and forwards it to the port to which the destination device is attached. In the case of a broadcast frame the switch would forward it to all ports.

But how does the switch know to which port the node with the destination address is attached? As described earlier in the chapter, layer two protocols such as Ethernet contain a *source address* as well as the destination address within the frame header. A switch checks the source address of each frame it receives and adds that source address to the **local address table** (LAT) for the port. In doing so, the switch is learning, without having to be manually reconfigured, about new workstations that might have been added to the network.

After each destination address is read, it is compared with the contents of the local address tables for the other ports on the switch to determine to which port the frame should be forwarded. Figure 4-19 illustrates the use of datalink layer frame addresses by switches.

Once the correct destination port is identified, there are two basic approaches to the process of forwarding data from one port to another. Using **store-and-forward switching** the entire frame is read into a shared memory area in the switch. The contents of the transmitted Frame Check Sequence field is read and compared to the locally recalculated Frame Check Sequence. If the results match, then the switch consults the address lookup table, builds the appropriate point-to-point connection, and forwards the frame. As a result, store-and-forward switching catches any bad frames/cells and does not forward them to the destination.

Using **cut-through switching** only the address information in the frame header is read before beginning processing. After reading the destination address, the switch consults an address lookup table in order to determine which port on the switch this frame should be forwarded to. Once the address lookup is completed, the point-to-point connection is created and the frame is immediately forwarded. Cut-through switching is very fast. However, because the frame check sequence on the forwarded frame was not checked, bad frames are forwarded. As a result, the receiving station must send a request for retransmission, followed by the sending station retransmitting the original frame leading to overall traffic increases.

**Error-free cut-through switching,** also known as **adaptive switching,** provides a means of automatically selecting the better of the two preceding switching technologies for each port. Using this process both the addresses and frame check sequences are read

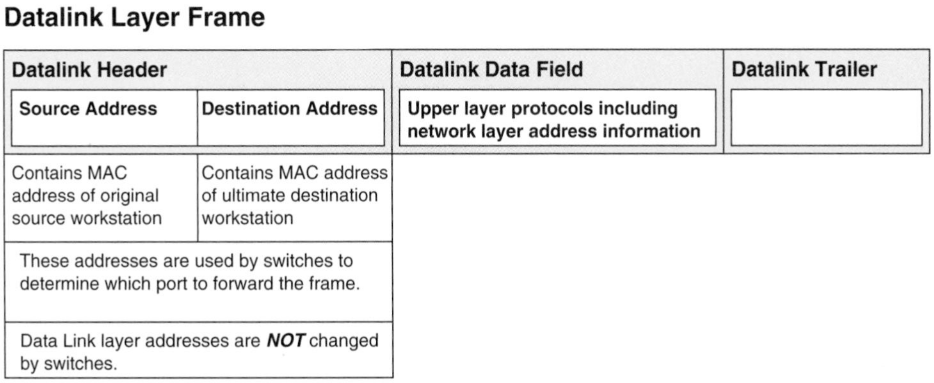

### Datalink Layer Frame

| Datalink Header | | Datalink Data Field | Datalink Trailer |
|---|---|---|---|
| **Source Address** | **Destination Address** | **Upper layer protocols including network layer address information** | |
| Contains MAC address of original source workstation | Contains MAC address of ultimate destination workstation | | |
| These addresses are used by switches to determine which port to forward the frame. | | | |
| Data Link layer addresses are **NOT** changed by switches. | | | |

*Figure 4-19*   Use of Datalink Addresses by LAN Switches

for every frame. Frames are forwarded immediately to destination nodes in an identical fashion to cut-through switches. However, should bad frames be forwarded, the error-free cut-through switch is able to reconfigure those individual ports producing the bad frames to use store-and-forward switching. As errors diminish, to pre-set thresholds, the port is set back to cut-through switching for higher performance throughput.

**Building a Bandwidth Hierarchy** LAN switches are essentially multi-port LAN bridges. Like a bridge, a switch has the ability to connect LANs running at different speeds. In this manner a LAN switch can transparently connect nodes or LAN segments running at different speeds. In the case of Ethernet a switch can interconnect nodes or segments running at 10 Mbps with nodes or LAN segments running at 100 Mbps or even gigabit speeds. As shown in Figure 4-20, exercising this multi-speed capability a network speed hierarchy can be developed that allows network traffic to be aggregated onto a high-speed backbone or a high-speed server link. This ability is essential to build a large network where many client nodes need to communicate with a limited number of centralized servers.

Managerial
Perspective

### ADVANTAGES OF SWITCHED LAN ARCHITECTURES

It is important to note that switched LAN architecture implementations only change the hub technology and, as a result, the manner in which workstations are able to set up point-to-point communications to each other. In other words, network interface cards, network interface card drivers, and media do not change. For this reason, installing a LAN switch is often the first and easiest alternative chosen when network bandwidth demands exceed current supply. In order to go from an Ethernet shared-media architecture to an Ethernet switch-based architecture, it is only necessary to replace the shared media hub with an Ethernet LAN switch.

With the cost of Ethernet switches down to as little as $5 or less a port, there is no reason to deploy shared media LANs at this point in time.

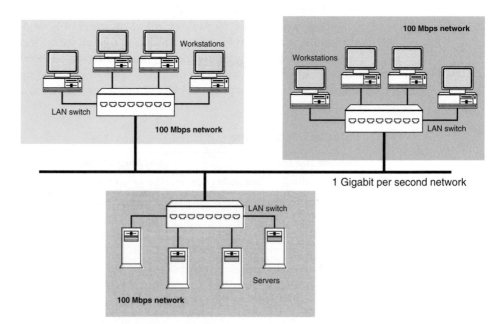

*Figure 4-20* Building a Bandwidth Hierarchy with a Switched LAN Architecture

## SWITCH TECHNOLOGY ISSUES

**Switch Flow Control**    Switches are very often employed to make switched connections between multiple network architectures. A common role of LAN switches is to provide switched connections between 10 Mbps and 100 Mbps network architectures. However, when servers on high-speed (100 Mbps) switched connections blast high-bandwidth data traffic back to clients on shared 10 Mbps port connections, data traffic can get backed up and data frames can be lost once buffers designed to hold overflow data become filled.

Switch vendors have attempted to respond to this situation in a variety of ways. Some switches include so-called deep buffers that allow more overflow traffic to be buffered before it is discarded. However, the dilemma with this approach is that memory is expensive, and it is difficult to determine how much buffer memory is enough while still keeping switch costs reasonable.

A second approach for Ethernet switches involves implementing a feedback mechanism known as **backpressure.** Backpressure prevents lost frames during overload conditions by sending out false collision-detection signals in order to get transmitting clients and servers to time-out long enough to give the switch a chance to forward buffered data. It is somewhat ironic that the CSMA/CD access methodology that the switch sought to overcome is being used to improve switch performance. The difficulty with backpressure mechanisms in the case of multiple device LAN segments being linked to a single switch port is that the false collision detection signal stops all traffic on the LAN segment, even peer-to-peer traffic that could have been delivered directly without the use of the switch. One possible solution to this shortcoming is to only enable backpressure on those switch ports that are connected to single devices such as servers.

*Switch Management*    Another major issue to be faced by network managers before jumping blindly onto the LAN switch bandwagon is the matter of how to monitor and manage switched-LAN connections. Unlike shared-media LAN management tools, which are able to access all network traffic from a single interface to the shared-media hub, switched architecture management tools must be able to monitor numerous point-to-point dedicated connections simultaneously. In a switched-LAN architecture, each port is the equivalent of a dedicated LAN, which must be individually monitored and managed. Switch vendors currently offer three basic approaches to the switch management dilemma:

- **Port mirroring** copies information from a particular switch port to an attached LAN analyzer. The difficulty with this approach is that it only allows one port to be monitored at a time.

- **Roving port mirroring** creates a roving RMON probe that gathers statistics at regular intervals on multiple switch ports. The shortcoming with this approach remains that at any single point in time only one port is being monitored.

- **Simultaneous RMON View** allows all network traffic to be monitored simultaneously. Such a monitoring scheme is only possible on those switches that incorporate a shared memory multi-gigabit bus, as opposed to a switching matrix internal architecture. Furthermore, unless this monitoring software is executed on a separate CPU, then switch performance is likely to degrade.

- **SMON** allows traffic to be monitored on a per-switch basis rather than a per-segment basis. SMON greatly reduces the bandwidth required to collect network statistics.

There is little doubt that properly deployed LAN switches can greatly improve network performance. However, management tools for LAN switches continue to evolve, and network managers should be wary of introducing technology into an enterprise network whose impact cannot be accurately monitored and managed.

Applied Problem
Solving

## LAN SWITCH TECHNOLOGY ANALYSIS

Some of the important analysis issues surrounding LAN switch selection are highlighted in Figure 4-21.

| LAN Switch Characteristic | Implications/Options |
|---|---|
| **Switching Architecture** | Options include cut-through, store-and-forward, and error-free store-and-forward. |
| **Token Ring Switches** | Some token ring switches also employ store-and-forward switching with buffering on the outbound port so that the outbound port has time to wait until the token reaches that switch port when multiple token ring devices are attached to a single switch port. Token ring switches are also able to reduce NetBIOS and source route bridging broadcast traffic by filtering. Some token ring switches also support full duplex token ring networking, also known as DTR (dedicated token ring), IEEE 802.5r. |
| **Network Architectures** | Switches may support one or more of the following: Ethernet, token ring, FDDI, fast Ethernet, gigabit Ethernet, and ATM. Network architectures may be available in a variety of different media types. |
| **Port Configuration** | Switches can vary in both the number of MAC addresses allowed per port as well as the total number of MAC addresses supported for the entire switch. Some switches only allow single devices to be attached to each LAN switch port. How easily can devices be assigned/re-assigned to switch ports? Can devices that are physically attached to different switch ports be assigned to the same virtual LAN? |
| **Full Duplex** | Some switches allow some ports to be enabled for full-duplex operation. Full-duplex switch ports will only communicate with full-duplex NICs whereas "normal" switch ports will communicate with existing NICs. |
| **Switch-to-Switch Connection** | Some switches use Ethernet or token ring switched ports, while others use higher-speed architectures such as FDDI or ATM. These inter-switch connections are sometimes referred to as the Fat Pipe. |
| **Internet-working** | In addition to merely establishing switched connections and forwarding traffic, some switches also have the ability to examine the addressing information contained within the data frames and perform bridging and routing functions. Token ring switches may or may not perform source route bridging which is specific to the token ring architecture. Some routing models can also examine embedded protocols and make routing and filtering decisions based on that criterion. |
| **Management** | Does the switch support both SNMP and the RMON MIB? Does the switch contain a management port and management software? Which type of RMON probe is supported? Is a separate CPU provided for processing system monitoring software? Does the local management software support Enterprise Network Management software such as HP OpenVew, IBM NetView, and Sun SunNet Manager? Is a port provided to which a protocol analyzer can be attached? |

*Figure 4-21*   LAN Switch Technology Analysis

Applied Problem
Solving

## NETWORK TECHNOLOGY SELECTION IN A NUTSHELL

There is no one "best" local area network technology solution. In order to decide which solution is best in any given situation, a top-down approach should be taken:

- Types of applications required to meet business objectives:

  - Multimedia?
  - Collaborative or distributed computing?
  - Large or frequent distributed database lookups?
  - Specialized applications such as CAD/CAM, medical imaging, or video editing?
  - Internet or IP-based telephony?

- Bandwidth and network delivery requirements of the data produced by these applications:

  - Are there high bandwidth needs?
  - Are guaranteed delivery times available for time-sensitive or streaming traffic?
  - Are there large database downloads or replications?
  - Do you need additional bandwidth? Additional bandwidth is not always the answer. Application or processing latency can vary independent of the amount of bandwidth. Understand bottlenecks well before designing your network.

- Preferred upgrade philosophy:

  - Replace all NICs, hubs, and possibly cabling?
  - Replace hubs and NICs in a gradual manner?
  - Replace just the hubs and leave the NICs and cabling alone? This option is really only available with switched network upgrades.

- Issues to note when considering an upgrade to a particular high-speed network architecture:

  - New NICs
  - Proper cabling to meet new cable specifications
  - New hubs
  - Management software
  - New distance limitations
  - New rules for cascading hubs or maximum number of repeaters between two end nodes
  - Availability of internetworking hardware such as bridges and routers compatible with the desired high-speed network architecture; without such hardware, the network will not be able to be extended beyond the immediate local network

## SUMMARY

The importance of protocol compatibility to network communications can be modeled using the OSI model as an open framework for protocol compatibility design. Of particular interest is the data link layer that serves as the home of the IEEE LAN standards and is sub-divided into the MAC and LLC sub-layers for that purpose.

The local area network architecture model distills network architectures into three basic components: access methodology, logical topology, and physical topology. Network architectures applied to a variety of media alternatives are known as network configurations.

While there are several LAN technologies available including Ethernet, token ring, FDDI, and ATM, Ethernet is the predominate player. Ethernet is a CSMA/CD based network architecture. Ethernet can run over several different media types, but most commonly is used over twisted pair wiring in a star physical topology. Twisted pair Ethernet supports speeds of 10, 100, and 1000 Mbps.

Gigabit Ethernet, 1000baseX, offers extremely high bandwidth over fiber optic cable and copper cabling. While 10 gigabit Ethernet only supports fiber optic cable, its high speed is rapidly making it the network architecture of choice for backbone and server connectivity applications. 40 gigabit Ethernet is in the planning phase to meet the ever increasing demand for higher LAN transmission speeds.

The fastest growing LAN technology area is that of wireless LANs (WLANs). Wireless LANs utilizing the IEEE 802.11 series of standards offer easy to configure wireless connectivity. There are currently three main IEEE 802.11 (also known as WiFi) standards: IEEE 802.11a, b, and g. IEEE 802.11 a is the fastest current standard providing up to 54 Mbps of bandwidth. IEEE 802.11g also promises 54 Mbps of bandwidth, but is limited by its backward compatibility with IEEE 802.11b which only offers 11 Mbps of capacity.

All IEEE 802.11 standards use a cellular approach to coverage. By arranging access points with non-overlapping channels in such a manner that the slightly overlap each other's coverage areas a user can roam between access points transparently. In this mode the access points hand off the users as they leave one access points range and enter another's.

Regardless of wireless standard, security is a key limitation of wireless networks. Wireless equivalent privacy (WEP) the original WiFi security standard has proven to offer weak security. Other solutions such as the use of VPN technologies, MAC address filtering, and WPA offer stop-gap solutions until the advanced encryption standard (AES) is fully deployed.

No one network architecture can be considered the best in all situations. Top Down analysis examining business, application, and data issues is required before determining which network architecture is most appropriate in each situation.

With the exception of wireless LANs, a hub of some sort must be implemented to connect the network nodes together. Types of hubs include: stand-alone hubs, stackable hubs, and enterprise hubs. Hub management software should be able to tie into Enterprise network management software.

LAN switches offer multiple simultaneous connections to attached workstations as opposed to the one-at-a-time access schemes of the shared media hubs. Similar in concept to a multi-port bridge, a LAN switch is capable of creating short term, direct connections between two ports. In this manner different ports can be communicating simultaneously on a LAN switch without creating contention on the medium.

## KEY TERMS

| | | |
|---|---|---|
| 10 gigabit Ethernet | 100baseTX | access methodologies |
| 10/100 NIC | 10baseT | adaptive switching |
| 1000baseSX | 802.11a | ad-hoc wireless infrastructure |
| 1000baseTX | 802.11b | advanced encryption standard |
| 100baseFX | 802.11g | AES |

agents
ATM address resolution
ATM LAN emulation
backplane
backpressure
baseband transmission
broadcast access
bus topology
carrier sense multiple access with
    collision avoidance
carrier sense multiple access with
    collision detection
cascading hubs
cell
concentrator
cross-over cable
CSMA/CA
CSMA/CD
cut-through switching
direct sequence spread spectrum
DSAP
EAP
enterprise hubs
enterprise network management
    systems
error-free cut-through switching
Ethernet
Ethernet II
extensible authentication protocol
frame
frame check sequence
frame status flag
frequency hopping spread
    spectrum

full duplex Ethernet
gigabit Ethernet
hotspot
hot-swappable
hub
IEEE 802.11
IEEE 802.2
IEEE 802.3
IEEE 802.3u
IEEE 802.5
infrastructure wireless architecture
LAN switch
LAN switches
LANE
LAT
LLC
local address table
local management software
logical link control
logical topology
MAC address filtering
management information base
MAU
media sharing LAN
MIB
modular hubs
multiple access unit
network interface card
NIC
NIC driver
orthogonal frequency division
    multiplexing
packet
physical topology

port mirroring
promiscuous mode
propagation delay
remote monitoring
ring
ring topology
RMON
roving port mirroring
sequential access
service set identifier
simple network management
    protocol
simultaneous RMON view
SMON
sniffer
SNMP
SSAP
SSID
stackable hubs
stand alone hubs
store and forward switching
switch monitoring
switching hubs
temporal key integrity protocol
TKIP
token
token passing
token ring
WEP
WiFi alliance
Wi-Fi protected access
wired equivalent privacy
WPA

## REVIEW QUESTIONS

1. Why is the data link layer of particular interest to LAN network architectures?
2. Define the relationship between the two data-link layer sub-layers.
3. What does the introduction of data-link layer sub-layers offer in terms of increased interoperability options?
4. In general, what are the purposes of the header and trailer added to data-link layer frames.
5. Where are data link layer frames built and why is this an appropriate place?
6. What are the three elements which make up any network architecture?
7. List the broad functions and inter-relationships of each of the major categories of technology cited in the LAN Technology Architecture.

8. Compare and contrast CSMA/CD and token passing as access methodologies.
9. What are two different potential causes of collisions in Ethernet networks?
10. What actually is a token?
11. What is the difference between a logical and a physical topology?
12. Differentiate between the broadcast and sequential logical topologies.
13. Differentiate between the bus, star, and ring physical topologies.
14. Differentiate between Ethernet II and IEEE 802.3 Ethernet.
15. What is the relationship between IEEE 802.2 and IEEE 802.3?

16. Differentiate between the various media-specific alternative configurations of 10 Mbps Ethernet.
17. What are the unique characteristics of a token ring network architecture?
18. Differentiate between Ethernet and Token Ring in terms of performance at various traffic levels.
19. What is the advantage of dual homing?
20. What is the advantage of buying 10/100 NICs?
21. What is a dual-speed hub?
22. What are the advantages and disadvantages of gigabit Ethernet?
23. Over what type(s) of media does 10 gigabit Ethernet run?
24. What is the main application(s) for 10 gigabit Ethernet?
25. 10 gigabit Ethernet does not use CSMA/CD. Why is it still considered Ethernet?
26. What were the key goals of the IEEE 802.3ae task group?
27. What are the three underlying physical access techniques used in wireless LANs? Briefly explain each.
28. What is an SSID?
29. Is IEEE 802.11g as fast as IEEE 802.11a? Explain your answer.
30. What is the role of the WiFi Alliance?
31. Explain the difference between ad-hoc and infrastructure wireless networks.
32. Differentiate between a wireless access point and a wireless gateway.
33. In terms of a wireless LAN, what is roaming?
34. Why are non-overlapping channels important in a wireless LAN?
35. What functionality does Mobile IP add to a wireless network?
36. List three ways to improve wireless network security.
37. What is AES?
38. What is a wireless hotspot?
39. What applications are full duplex network architectures especially well suited for?
40. What roles can ATM play in a local area network?
41. How can "legacy LANs" be integrated into an ATM network?
42. What are the unique capabilities of ATM which account for all of the interest in this technology?
43. What is LAN emulation and why is it important?
44. What is the meaning of the phrase: "The NIC is the keeper of the MAC layer protocol."?
45. Differentiate between a shared-media network architecture and a switch-based network architecture in terms of advantages and disadvantages of each.
46. What are some of the potential drawbacks or cautions to upgrading to a LAN switch?
47. Differentiate between the three major implementation scenarios for LAN switches in terms of delivered functionality and corresponding required switch technology.
48. What are the advantages and disadvantages of full duplex network architectures?
49. What do full duplex architectures require, in terms of both hardware and software, beyond normal switch-based LAN architectures?
50. What is a zero port hub?
51. Differentiate between the three major categories of hubs in terms of delivered functionality and required technology features.
52. What important advantages does an active management MAU offer?
53. Why can't modules from one vendor's enterprise hub be used in another vendor's enterprise hub even though the modules both support the same network architecture?
54. What are the differences between the two levels of management software which hubs should support.
55. How is it possible for an enterprise network management system to compile statistics from networking equipment manufactured by a variety of different vendors?
56. What are the major functional differences between how LAN switches process and forward packets? What are the advantages and disadvantaged of each method?
57. In what types of LAN switch implementations is backpressure likely to be an issue?
58. Why is traffic monitoring and management more of a challenge in LAN switches than in shared-media hubs?
59. Differentiate between the three major LAN switch traffic monitoring and management techniques.
60. What are the advantages and disadvantages of assigning multiple workstations per switch port?

**Case Study:** For a business case study and questions on LANs, go to www.wiley.com/college/goldman.

CHAPTER 5

# VOICE COMMUNICATION CONCEPTS AND TECHNOLOGY

*Concepts Reinforced*

Top-down model                    Protocols and interoperability
OSI model

*Concepts Introduced*

Voice digitization                Data/voice integration
Voice compression                 Voice network concepts
PBX functionality and architecture    Computer telephony integration
Voice transmission alternatives   Voice over the Internet

## OBJECTIVES

After mastering the material in this chapter, you should be able to:

1. Understand the underlying technical concepts for voice transmission, voice digitization, voice compression, and data/voice integration.

2. Understand currently available voice-related technology including PBXs, voice digitizers, and voice/data multiplexers and modems.

3. Understand the functionality, standards, business impact, and technology involved with computer telephony integration.

4. Understand the functionality, concepts, standards, business impact, and technology involved with voice network services, voice transmission alternatives, and voice/data integration.

## ■ INTRODUCTION

Network analysts must be qualified to design networks that are capable of carrying voice as well as data. Before designing such networks, it is essential for the network analyst to understand the nature of voice signals, as well as how voice signals can be processed and integrated into a cohesive network with data transmissions.

Once based exclusively on analog transmission, voice communication is rapidly becoming dependent on digital transmission technology. Once the voice signal has been digitized, a wide variety of transmission services can potentially be employed to complete the transmission of the voice signal to its designated destination. As is the case with any type of communications system involving the interoperability of multiple pieces of hardware and software technology, standards play an essential role in assuring end-to-end interoperability.

Although traditional telephony continues to be the bearer of most voice calls, alternatives such as voice over IP (VOIP) promise equal quality at significantly lower cost. Technologies such as H.323 and SIP, combined with broadband Internet technologies, have the potential to replace the modern telephone network architecture and revolutionize how calls are placed and billed.

One of the fastest-growing areas of telecommunications is wireless telephony. With the development of higher capacity, better-sounding digital networks cellular phone use has grown exponentially in the United States and worldwide. In addition to voice communication, these networks are capable of carrying digital data to a spate of new handheld devices. As these wireless digital networks continue to evolve, new applications that take advantage of their better interoperability and higher data speeds will continue to be developed.

A private branch exchange (PBX) acts as a local phone switch for an organization. The PBX allows for calls to be made inside the organization without using the PSTN, while allowing for calls to be made between the internal extensions and the PSTN. Newer PBX features allow for the integration of VOIP and wireless technologies into the PBX.

## ■ VOICE TRANSMISSION BASIC CONCEPTS

The modern telephone system is commonly known as the **public switched telephone network,** or **PSTN.** A voice conversation consists of sound waves that are of varying frequency and amplitude and are represented as a continuously varying analog waveform. The **POTS (plain old telephone service)** network employed analog transmission methodologies to transmit the voice signals from source to destination.

But how does this analog waveform get from a person's mouth, the human transmitter, onto the PSTN and subsequently into the ear, the human receiver, of the person who was called? Figure 5-1 illustrates the mechanics of a typical phone handset, which consists of both transmitter and receiver components.

The telephone handset, consisting of both a transmitter and receiver, is really a fairly simple device that works largely based on the properties of electromagnetism. The *transmitter,* or mouthpiece, contains a movable diaphragm that is sensitive to changes in voice frequency and amplitude. The diaphragm contains carbon granules that have the ability to conduct electricity. Because the human voice spoken into the transmitter varies, the amount of carbon granules striking the electrical contacts in the mouthpiece varies, sending a varying analog, electrical signal out onto the voice network.

This constantly varying analog electrical wave is transmitted over the voice network to the phone of the receiving person. The *receiver* or earpiece portion of the handset basically works in the opposite fashion of the mouthpiece. The varying electrical waves produced by the transmitter are received at the receiver at an electromagnet. Varying levels of electricity produce varying levels of magnetism that, in

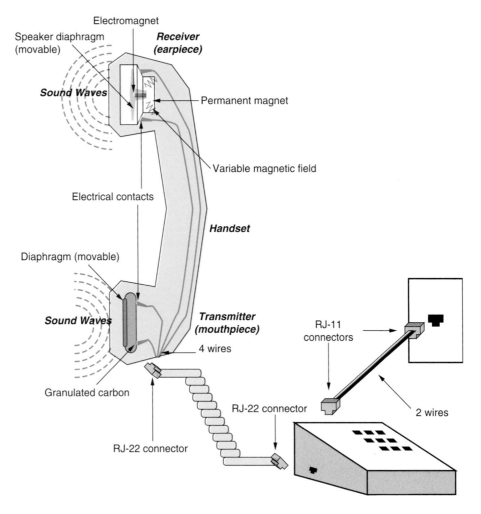

*Figure 5-1*  Getting Voice onto and off of the Network

turn, cause the diaphragm to move in direct proportion with the magnetic variance. The moving diaphragm produces varying sound waves that correspond to the sound waves that were input at the transmitter. The electromagnetically reproduced sound produced at the receiver resembles the actual sound waves input at the transmitter closely enough to allow for voice recognition by the receiving party.

## Voice Bandwidth

Although the approximate range of hearing of the human ear is between 15,000 to 20,000 Hz, significantly less bandwidth is used to transmit the electromagnetic representations of analog voice signals over the analog PSTN. POTS uses a bandwidth of 4,000 Hz including two *guardbands* to prevent interference from adjacent frequencies from interfering with the voice signal. As a result, the usable bandwidth on the local loop circuit connecting an individual's home or business to the phone company's central office for dial-up analog voice transmission is 3,000 Hz, from 300 to 3,300 Hz.

Figure 5-2 illustrates the comparative bandwidths of human speech and the analog phone network. This limited bandwidth is why people sound less lifelike on the telephone than in person.

## ■ VOICE NETWORK CONCEPTS

Telephone calls are connected from source via circuit switching. Circuit switching is an analog telecommunications term that originally meant that a physical electrical circuit was created from the source telephone handset to the destination telephone handset. In the early days of the telephone system, a telephone system operator manually connected these connections at a switchboard. Later the rotary telephone and automatic switching was introduced.

A better definition of a switched connection in the modern phone system is a reserved bandwidth connection between two telephone handsets. Although there is no longer a physical circuit in place between the handsets, the capacity on the telephone network required to deliver the call is reserved for the exclusive use of the call: The same amount of telephone system capacity is used by two people who are being perfectly quiet as is used by two people who are talking at the same time. The capacity is dedicated to the call as soon as it is placed.

### Basic Telecommunications Infrastructure

Figure 5-3 illustrates the major components of the PSTN. The circuits between a residence or business and the local **central office** or **CO** are known as **local loops.** A central office is a facility belonging to the local phone company in which calls are switched to their proper destination. As covered in chapter 1, the LATA is an area

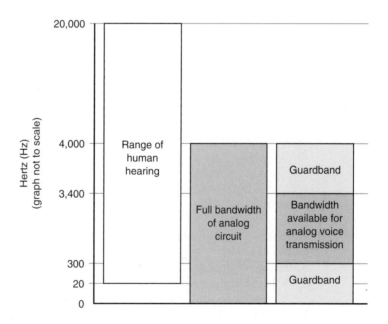

*Figure 5-2*  Voice Bandwidth

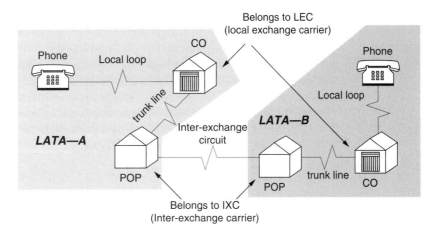

*Figure 5-3*  Basic Telecommunications Infrastructure

within which the local carrier completed all of the calls during the time period between the break-up of AT&T and the Telecommunications Act of 1996.

Telephone calls are established by a device located at the local telephone companies CO known as a **telephone switch.** The telephone switch is directly connected to the customer's telephone handset via the local loop. The telephone switch routes calls to the destination telephone handset. Requested destinations for phone calls are indicated to the telephone switch by dialing a series of numbers. These numbers tell the telephone switch whether the call will be local, intra-LATA, or inter-LATA, and subsequently, which circuits must be accessed and combined to complete the call as requested.

All voice traffic destined for locations outside of the local LATA, and some traffic within the LATA, must be handed off to the long distance or **inter-exchange carrier (IXC)** of the customer's choice. Competing long-distance carriers wishing to do business in a given LATA maintain a switching office in that LATA known as a **POP,** or **point of presence.** This POP handles billing information and routes the call over the long-distance carrier's switched network to its POP in the destination's LATA. The circuit between the POPs may be via satellite, microwave, fiber-optic cable, traditional wiring, or some combination of these media. Depending on traffic levels on the long-distance carrier's network, calls may be routed through any combination of switches before reaching their final destination.

In the basic infrastructure illustrated in Figure 5-3, the only analog links in the PSTN are the local loops running from the end points to the central offices. Once the voice signal hits the central office it is converted into a digital signal for transmission across the PSTN to the destination central office, where it is converted back into an analog signal for transmission across the local loop to the destination telephone. The processes used to convert the phone call from analog to digital signals are covered later in this chapter.

Because these local loops are the sole remaining analog links in the modern PSTN and cover relatively short distances, they are commonly referred to as the **last mile** in the telephone system. Throughout the next few chapters you will see how the analog local loops pose a serious limitation in terms of the rate of data transmission across the PSTN.

## PSTN Network Hierarchy

As can be seen in Figure 5-4, a residential or business call is first processed in the local central office, also known as an end office or local office. In terms of the network hierarchy, an end office is known as a **Class 5 office.** This local central office contains a switch that processes incoming calls, determines the best path to the call destination, and establishes the circuit connection.

Local calls come into the local central office via a local loop and travel to their local destination via a local loop. If a call is destined to another telephone on the

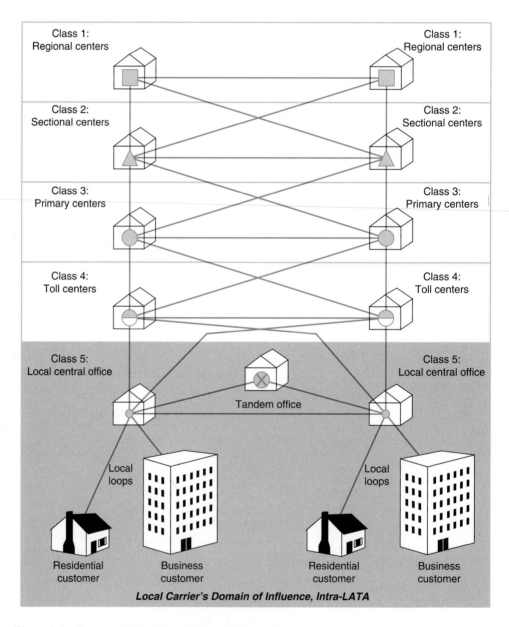

*Figure 5-4*   Representative Voice Network Hierarchy

same telephone switch, the call is switched at the CO to the destination local loop. Calls that are not local but are still within the same LATA are known as intra-LATA calls and are handled by the caller's selected intra-LATA carrier, most often an RBOC. Technically, these are long-distance calls, and a local CO may not have a direct trunk to the destination CO. In this case, the call is routed through a **tandem office** that establishes the intra-LATA circuit and also handles billing procedures for the long-distance call.

If the call is bound for a destination in another LATA, it must be turned over from the local carrier to a long-distance carrier such as AT&T, MCI, or Sprint. In most cases, the Inter-Exchange Carrier (IXC) will have been chosen by individual residential and business subscribers. The local CO still receives such inter-LATA calls from subscribers. However, rather than routing the call itself, the CO merely forwards the call to the local Point of Presence of the long-distance carrier of choice.

Such a long-distance switching office is also known as a POP, or a **Class 4 toll center.** The term *toll center* implies that long-distance billing calculation as well as switching activities are performed at these locations. A given local CO might have trunks to more than one toll center. As will be seen, circuit redundancy offering multiple alternative paths for call routing is a central premise of the voice network hierarchy. If the local toll center can find adequate space on a trunk headed to the destination CO, then the connection between source and destination COs is completed. If no paths to the destination are directly available to the local toll center, then the call is escalated up the network hierarchy to the next level of switching office. The overall desire is to keep the call as low on the hierarchy as possible. This provides both quicker call completion for the subscriber as well as maximization of the cost-effective use of the lowest and least-expensive switching offices possible.

Higher levels on the network hierarchy imply greater switching and transmission capacity, as well as greater expense. When calls cannot be completed directly, Class 4 toll centers turn to **Class 3 Primary Centers** that subsequently turn to **Class 2 Sectional Centers** that turn finally to **Class 1 Regional Centers.** These categories of switching and transmission centers were originally AT&T's, and not all inter-LATA or long distance carriers have such a five-level network hierarchy. However, the five-level hierarchy has become industry standard terminology.

## Telephone Number Plans

Telephone numbers are a hierarchical address method. U.S. telephone numbers can be broken into three basic parts: a three-digit area code, a three-digit exchange, and a four-digit subscriber number. To make a telephone call, at a minimum the exchange plus the subscriber number must be dialed. If the call is to a destination phone outside of the source phone's area code, the destination area code must be dialed as well.

Originally assigned to geographic areas, area codes are the top level of the hierarchy. When the U.S. telephone system was originally designed, all area codes had either a zero or a one as the center digit. Conversely, exchanges were not allowed to have a zero or a one as the center digit. This technique allowed the telephone switches at the central office to easily distinguish between area codes and exchanges. Because of this differentiation, long-distance calls placed within an area code could simply be dialed by adding a one to the beginning of the local telephone number.

This system worked well until the number of area codes increased to the point that all of the area codes with ones and zeros in the center were in use. At that point, there was no choice but to add an area code with a different number as the center digit. The first area code placed in service that did not have a one or zero as the center digit was the 770 area code that serves the area outside of Atlanta, Georgia.

The implementation of these nonstandard area codes originally caused some problems. Telephone switches and PBXs had to be reprogrammed to support the new number scheme. When the 770 area code first went into use, several areas could not place a call to it. This new area code number scheme created another problem. Because the telephone switch cannot tell the difference between an exchange and an area code based on number structure, it is now usually necessary to dial all ten digits when placing a long-distance call, even if the call is within the same area code.

Although the area code + exchange + subscriber number system is used in the United States, a broader ranging system is used internationally. To place an international call you must dial 011 + country code + city code + number. The numbering systems for country codes, city codes, and local numbers can vary between countries. It is important to carefully research the dialing pattern before placing an international call.

In Sharper Focus

### TELEPHONE NUMBER SHORTAGES AND NEW AREA CODES

The need for new area codes is driven from the increasing need for new telephone numbers. The proliferation of fax machines, cellular phones, pagers, and second lines for use to connect to the Internet has caused an exponential increase in the number of telephone numbers currently in use. Each exchange supports 10,000 telephone numbers. Each area code supports 1,000 exchanges, or 10 million separate telephone numbers. When the required amount of telephone numbers exceeds the available capacity, there is no choice but to add another area code to the geographic area served by the original area code.

There are two basic approaches to adding area codes. The geographic area served by the original area code can be broken into two smaller sections. One section would retain the original area code while the new section would be given a new area code. Although this approach is true to the original concept of an area code, the area code for half of the telephones in the old area code is changed. This change affects the calling patterns of every subscriber in the area code and of everyone who needs to place a long distance call to them. Each business that experiences an area code change must replace all of its business cards, letterhead, and any other items that contain its telephone number, often at a significant expense.

To resolve these issues, an alternate concept known as overlaying is becoming common. In a overlay solution, a new area code is added to the original area code's geographic area. New telephone numbers are simply assigned to this new area code. In this scenario, no existing customers are forced to change their area code. However, it is possible that your neighbor might be in a different area code than you. In this case, you would simply dial the full ten-digit telephone number to place a local call to your neighbor.

## System Signaling

In addition to carrying the actual voice signals, the telephone system must carry information about the call itself. This information is commonly referred to as **system signaling,** or **inter-office signaling.** At a bare minimum, system signaling needs to provide a means of accomplishing call set-up and call termination. Advanced functions are also available, including call waiting, caller ID, and three-way calling. Each of these functions requires the source telephone set to send data to the local phone switch or for the local phone switch to send data to the destination phone switch and telephone set in addition to the basic voice data transmission. There are two basic approaches to sending system signaling data across the PSTN: in band and out of band.

**In-Band Signaling**   In an **in-band signaling** system the signals are sent on the same channel as the voice data itself. This is the method used to send signals across the analog local loop for most home telephones. When you pick up the phone you listen for a **dial tone** to make sure the telephone switch at the CO is ready to serve you. At that point you dial (sending the phone number across in the voice bandwidth) and listen for the phone to ring. If the called party answers the phone, the remote telephone switch comes off the hook and the connection is established.

The destination telephone number can be communicated to the telephone switch in two ways. Older style rotary phones, like the one which was taken apart in order to draw Figure 5-1, have a round dial that causes a certain number of pulses of electricity to be generated, depending on the number dialed. Dialing a "1" produces one electrical pulse, dialing a "2" produces two electrical pulses, and so on. These pulses were used to physically operate relays in the first automatic phone switches. Modern phone switches no longer use mechanical relays and therefore do not require electrical pulses to indicate the destination telephone number.

Many of today's phones no longer have rotary dials on them. Instead, they contain twelve buttons that correspond to the ten numbers on the rotary dial plus two characters, the star (*) and the octothorpe (#—also known as the pound key in the US). A switch is often included that can be set to have the telephone set issue a series of **pulses** to emulate the dialing process of the older style of phone for areas where central office switches have not yet been upgraded to understand **touch-tone** dialing.

In Sharper Focus

## TOUCH-TONE DIALING

Touch-tone dialing is technically called **DTMF,** or **dual tone multi-frequency,** because the tone associated with each number dialed is really a combination of two tones selected from a matrix of multiple possible frequencies. Figure 5-5 illustrates the numbers and symbols found on a typical telephone touch panel and their associated dual tone frequencies. The two keys on either side of the 0 were officially named star (*) and octothorpe (#) by Bell Labs, although they have different commonly used names in different languages.

The tones generated by DTMF phones can be used for much more than merely dialing destination telephone numbers. As will be seen later in the chapter, these same tones can be used to enable specialized services from PBXs, carriers, banks, information services, and retail establishments.

When you decide to terminate the call, you hang up or change the status of your local loop to on-hook. At that time, the local telephone switch changes from off-hook to on-hook and the telephone switch knows you are off the phone and are ready to receive a telephone call. Call waiting, three-way calling, and caller ID all use similar in-band means to communicate information between the telephone handset and the local telephone switch.

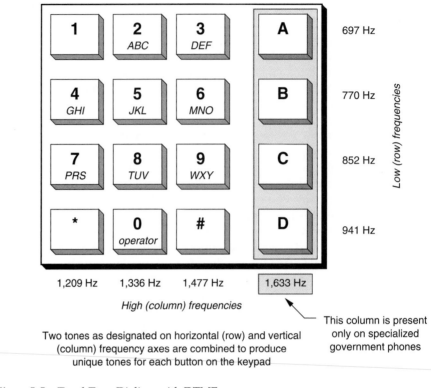

*Figure 5-5*  TouchTone Dialing with DTMF

**Out-of-Band Signaling**  While in-band signaling works well for communication between telephone handsets and the local telephone switch across the analog local loop, the inter-switch connections on the digital PSTN make use of a separate channel to carry system signaling data. This **out-of-band signaling** approach provides a means to manage the network itself by handling the routing of calls and circuit establishment as well as the monitoring of circuit status and notification and re-routing in the case of alarms or circuit problems. By moving the call setup and management data to a separate network it becomes easier to support transparent operation between different digital encoding mechanisms. The management data is readily available to each piece of telephone network equipment regardless of the encoding mechanism used.

The worldwide, CCITT approved standard for out-of-band signaling is known as **Signaling System 7 (SS7)**. SS7 controls the structure and transmission of both circuit-related and non-circuit related information via out-of-band signaling between central office switches. SS7 delivers the out-of-band signaling via a packet switched network physically separate from the circuit switched network that carries the actual voice traffic. Each node on the PSTN must connect to both the voice network and the SS7 network.

The SS7 network is really nothing more than a packet-switched network not unlike other suites of protocols that will be examined in chapters 7 and 8. Like most protocol suites, SS7 can be modeled in comparison to the OSI 7 Layer Reference Model. Figure 5-6 summarizes the major characteristics of the Signaling System 7 Protocols as well as comparing the SS7 Protocol Suite to the OSI model.

| OSI Model | Signaling System 7 | | |
|-----------|---|---|---|
| Application | O&MAP | | |
| | TCAP | | |
| Presentation | | | |
| Session | | | |
| Transport | | | |
| Network | SSCP | | |
| Datalink | | | MTP |
| Physical | | | |

| Protocol Name | Description/Function |
|---------------|---------------------|
| Operations Maintenance Application Part (O&MAP) | *O&MAP* provides standards for routing and management of messages related to network operations and maintenance |
| Transaction Capabilities Application Part (TCAP) | *TCAP* provides standards for routing and management of noncircuit related information for transaction processing applications requiring out-of-band signaling |
| Signaling Connection Control Part (SCCP) | *SCCP* provides standards for routing and management of signaling messages.  Not related to call set-up between switches.  A connection-oriented service providing reliable message delivery |
| Message Transfer Part (MTP) | *MTP* provides standards for routing of signaling messages between switches.  A connectionless, datagram service |
| Network Service Part (NSP) | *Another term for the combination of the SCCP and the MTP3* |

*Figure 5-6*    Signaling System 7 Protocols and the OSI Model

Signaling System 7 and the intelligent services that it enables are often described as part of an all-encompassing interface between users and the PSTN known as the **AIN** or **advanced intelligent network.** The AIN is sometimes simply referred to as the **intelligent network (IN)**.

The AIN provides a great deal of flexibility to customers. The use of AIN services provides a means of achieving many different applications:

- **Alternate billing service (ABS)**—This service allows a long-distance call to be billed to a calling card, to a third party, or to the receiver (collect call).

- **Custom local area signaling service (CLASS)**—A group of services that allows many services local access to the customer's telephone. Examples include call waiting, call forwarding, call blocking, caller ID blocking, busy number redial, and automatic redial of missed calls.

- **Enhanced 800 service**—This service allows 800-number portability. Originally, 800 numbers were tied to a specific area code and long-distance provider. This service resolves those limitations.

- **Intelligent call processing (ICP)**—Using this service customers are able to reroute incoming 800 calls among multiple customer service centers in a matter of seconds. This rerouting is done completely transparent to the calling customer. ICP allows multiple call centers geographically dispersed throughout the country to function as one logical call center, with the overall number of incoming calls distributed in a balanced manner across all centers.

User-oriented network services such as the AIN are being offered in response to user demands for in-house control over a key element of their business: their telecommunications systems and the links from those systems to the wide area PSTN. Catalog sales organizations are literally out of business without their phones and must have contingency plans in place in order to deal with and perhaps avoid possible catastrophes.

## Voice Digitization

The analog POTS system has largely been supplanted in the modern telephone system by a combination of analog and digital transmission technologies. While analog signaling is effective, it is limited in terms of quality, distance, and capacity. The longer the signal has to travel, the poorer the quality. There are also significant capacity issues associated with analog transmission. In general, only one voice conversation can be carried on a single set of wires using analog transmission. Although it is possible to partially overcome this limitation through the use of multiplexing, as illustrated in detail in chapter 2, digital transmission offers better quality and higher capacity than analog transmission over a given media. The modern voice network is almost entirely digital in nature.

Although the local loop between the local central office and a residence or place of business might be an analog circuit, it is highly unlikely that the continuously varying analog signal representing a person's voice will stay in analog form all the way to the destination location's phone receiver. Rather, it is very likely that high-capacity digital circuits will be employed to transport that call, especially between COs or carriers. The fact that carriers might be converting a voice conversation to digital format and converting it back to analog form before it reaches its destination is completely transparent to phone network users.

The basic technique for **voice digitization** is relatively simple. The constantly varying analog voice conversation must be sampled frequently enough so that when the digitized version of the voice is converted back to an analog signal, the resultant conversation resembles the voice of the call initiator. Most voice digitization techniques employ a sampling rate of 8,000 samples per second.

Recalling that a digital signal is just a discrete electrical voltage, there are only a limited number of ways in which the electrical pulses can be varied to represent varying characteristics of an analog voice signal:

- **Pulse amplitude modulation,** or **PAM,** varies the amplitude or voltage of the electrical pulses in relation to the varying characteristics of the voice signal. PAM was the voice digitization technique used in some earlier PBXs.

- **Pulse duration modulation (PDM),** otherwise known as **pulse width modulation (PWM),** varies the duration of each electrical pulse in relation the variances in the analog signal.

- **Pulse position modulation (PPM),** varies the duration between pulses in relation to variances in the analog signal. By varying the spaces in between the discrete electrical pulses on the digital circuit, PPM focuses on the relative position of the pulses to one another as a means of representing the continuously varying analog signal. Figure 5-7 illustrates these three voice digitization techniques.

**Pulse Code Modulation (PCM)**    Although any of the above methods may be used for voice digitization, the most common voice digitization technique in use today is known as **pulse code modulation** or **PCM.** Figure 5-8 illustrates the basics of PCM.

**PAM: Pulse Amplitude Modulation**

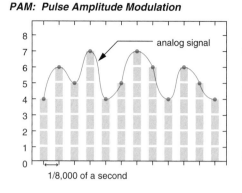

Variable: Pulse amplitude

Constants: Pulse duration, pulse position

Sampling rate = 8,000 times/second

**PDM: Pulse Duration Modulation**

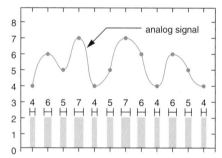

Variable: Pulse duration

Constants: Pulse amplitude, pulse position

**PPM: Pulse Position Modulation**

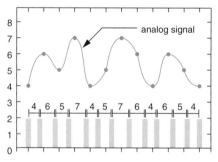

Variable: Pulse position

Constants: Pulse amplitude, pulse duration

*Figure 5-7*    Voice Digitization: PAM, PDM, PPM

As can be seen from Figure 5-8, 8 bits or 1 byte are required in order to transmit the sampled amplitude of an analog signal. Since an 8-bit code allows $2^8$ or 256 different possible values, each time the actual analog wave is sampled, it is assigned a value from 0 to 255, dependent on its location or amplitude at the instant it is sampled. Some simple mathematics will reveal the bandwidth required to transmit digitized voice using PCM. This computed required bandwidth will, by no coincidence, correspond exactly to a very common digital circuit bandwidth.

The device that samples the analog POTS transmission coming in from the local loop and transforms it into a stream of binary digits using PCM is known as a coder/decoder or **codec.** As mentioned in the following section, each codec outputs a digital signal at a data rate of 64 Kbps. This data rate, known as a DS-0, is the basic unit of voice data transmission in a PCM based telephone system. All higher speed

**Analog Signal to be Digitized**

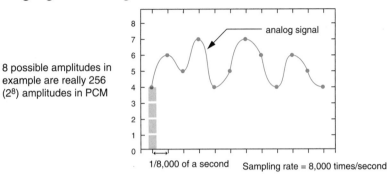

8 possible amplitudes in
example are really 256
($2^8$) amplitudes in PCM

1/8,000 of a second    Sampling rate = 8,000 times/second

**Step 1: Sample Amplitude of Analog Signal**

Amplitude in example at sample position 1 (the gray shaded box) is    4

**Step 2: Represent Measured Amplitude in Binary Notation**

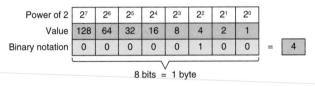

| Power of 2 | $2^7$ | $2^6$ | $2^5$ | $2^4$ | $2^3$ | $2^2$ | $2^1$ | $2^0$ |
|---|---|---|---|---|---|---|---|---|
| Value | 128 | 64 | 32 | 16 | 8 | 4 | 2 | 1 |
| Binary notation | 0 | 0 | 0 | 0 | 0 | 1 | 0 | 0 |

= 4

8 bits = 1 byte

**Step 3: Transmit Coded Digital Pulses Representing Measured Amplitude**

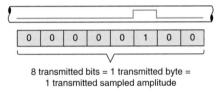

| 0 | 0 | 0 | 0 | 0 | 1 | 0 | 0 |
|---|---|---|---|---|---|---|---|

8 transmitted bits = 1 transmitted byte =
1 transmitted sampled amplitude

*Figure 5-8*    Voice Digitization: Pulse Code Modulation (PCM)

voice connections will operate at some multiple of this DS-0 speed. Codecs are usually deployed as part of a channel bank. A channel bank is a hybrid device consisting of twenty-four codecs and the circuitry required to place the digitized PCM voice signals onto a T-1 circuit. Codecs and channel banks may be integrated into telephone switches or purchased separately.

In Sharper Focus

## VOICE DIGITIZATION BANDWIDTH REQUIREMENTS

Since 8,000 samples per second are required to assure quality transmission of digitized voice and each sample requires 8 bits to represent that sampled bandwidth in binary (ones and zeroes) notation, the following equation reveals that 64,000 bits per sec is the required bandwidth for transmission of voice digitized via PCM. A DS-0 circuit has a transmission capacity of exactly 64 Kbps. Twenty-four DS-0s are combined to form a T-1, yielding the fact that a T-1 can carry 24 simultaneous voice conversations digitized via PCM. Following is the mathematical proof:

8,000 samples/sec × 8 bits/sample = 64,000 bits/sec (bps)

64,000 bits/sec = 64 Kbps = DS-0 Circuit

24 DS-0s = 24 × 64 Kbps = 1536 Kbps = 1.536 Mbps

Plus: 1 framing bit/sample × 8,000 samples/sec. = 8,000 framing bits/sec

8 Kbps + 1,536 Kbp = 1,544 Kbps = 1.544 Mbps = Transmission capacity of T-1 circuit

It is important to note that the maximum data-carrying capacity of a T-1 circuit is only 1.536 Mbps because the framing bits cannot be used to carry data.

ADPCM   A variation of this digitization technique known as **adaptive differential pulse code modulation,** or **ADPCM,** is most commonly used in Europe. ADPCM is a CCITT (ITU) standard that takes a slightly different approach to coding sampled amplitudes in order to use transmission bandwidth more efficiently; ADPCM requires roughly half the bandwidth for each digitized conversation as compared to PCM. By transmitting only the approximate difference or change in amplitude of consecutive amplitude samples, rather than the absolute amplitude, only 32 Kbps of bandwidth in required for each conversation digitized via ADPCM.

Using a specialized circuit known as an adaptive predictor, ADPCM calculates the difference between the predicted and actual incoming signals and specifies that difference as one of sixteen different levels using 4 bits ($2^4 = 16$). Since each voice channel can be represented by just 4 bits, ADPCM can support 48 simultaneous voice conversations over a T-1 circuit.

The ITU standard for 32 Kbps ADPCM is known as G.721 and is generally used as a reference point for the quality of voice transmission known as **toll quality.** G.721 has been superseded by other ADPCM standards that use less than 32Kbps per voice channel. For example. G.723 defines ADPCM for 24 Kbps and 40 Kbps while G.726 defines ADPCM for 40, 32, 24, and 16 Kbps.

Fortunately voice signals can be readily converted between any of these digital formats enabling transparent telephone conversations regardless of the voice digitization technique used at either end of the call.

## Voice Compression

ADPCM is also known as a **voice compression** technique because of its ability to transmit twenty-four digitized voice conversations in half of the bandwidth required by PCM. Other more advanced techniques employ specially programmed microprocessors known as **digital signal processors** that take the digitized PCM code and further manipulate and compress it. In doing so, DSPs are able to transmit and reconstruct digitized voice conversations in as little as 4,800 bps per conversation, an increase in transmission efficiency of more than thirteen times over PCM!

Numerous voice compression technological approaches exist. Voice compression can be performed by standalone units or by integral modules within multiplexers. The particular method by which the voice is compressed may be according to an open standard or by a proprietary methodology. Proprietary methods require that a given vendor's equipment must be present on both ends of the voice circuit in question. Each voice compression technique seeks to reduce the amount of transmitted voice information in one way or another.

Some voice compression techniques attempt to synthesize the human voice, other techniques attempt to predict the actual voice transmission patterns, while still others attempt to transmit only changes in voice patterns. Regardless of the voice compression technique employed, one thing is certain. The quality of compressed voice transmissions does not match the quality of an analog voice transmission over an analog dial-up line or a PCM-digitized voice transmission using a full 64 Kbps of digital bandwidth. The transmission-quality degradation will vary from one instance to another. However, only the end users of the compressed voice system can determine whether the reduced voice quality is worth the bandwidth and related cost savings.

## ■ VOICE TRANSMISSION ALTERNATIVES

Although the PSTN has traditionally been seen as the cheapest and most effective way to transmit voice, alternative methods for voice transmission do exist. Several such methods are briefly explored in terms of configuration requirements, advantages, and disadvantages.

### Voice over IP (VOIP)

Although this alternative voice transmission methodology is also commonly referred to as **voice over the Internet,** it is actually the underlying transport protocols of the Internet that deliver the voice conversations. Voice over IP refers to any technology used to transmit voice over any network running the IP protocol. The important point about VOIP technologies is that they are not exclusively confined to use on the Internet. They can be used just as effectively in any of the following topologies:

- Modem-based point-to-point connections
- Local area networks
- Private networks, also known as **intranets**

VOIP can be successfully deployed in any of the previously mentioned topologies provided that required technology is properly implemented. Figure 5-9 illustrates both the technology required to implement IP-based voice transmission as well as the alternative topologies possible.

Required client hardware and software technology for VOIP transmission includes the following:

- VOIP client software
- PC workstation with sufficiently fast CPU to digitize and compress the analog voice signal Sound card for local playback of received voice transmission
- Microphone for local input of transmitted voice signals
- Speakers for local output of received voice signals

Figure 5-10 summarizes many of the key features and functionality of VOIP client software.

**REQUIRED CLIENT TECHNOLOGY**

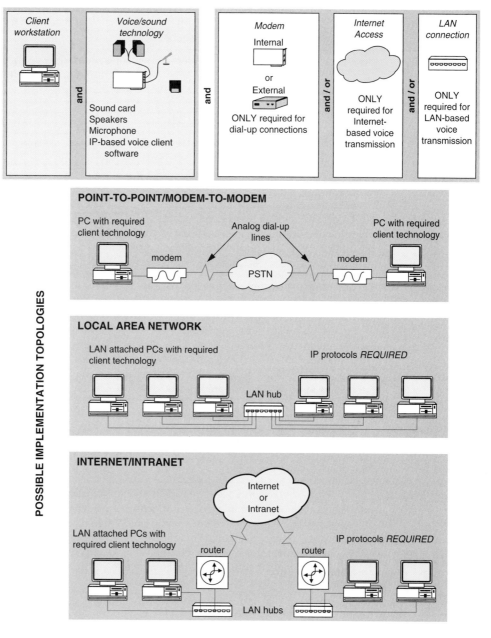

*Figure 5-9*   VOIP Transmission Technology and Topologies

**VoIP Alternatives to PCs: Wired Handsets and Wireless Handsets**   In addition to personal computers network manufactures are also selling wired and wireless handsets that support natively support VOIP technologies. These handsets look like a traditional telephone handset, but instead of having a local loop connection they have an Ethernet or a wireless LAN connection. Because they contain microprocessors, these IP handsets offer additional features not found on traditional phones, such as customizable ring

| Feature | Importance/Implication |
|---------|------------------------|
| **Client platform support** | Most IP-based voice transmission software supports Windows, with fewer packages supporting UNIX and Macintosh operating systems. |
| **Interoperability** | The **ITU H.323** standard for interoperability among client software for low bandwidth audio (voice) and video conferencing is supported by some, but not all, client IP-based voice transmission software. |
| **Transmission quality** | Although transmission quality has improved thanks to improved voice compression algorithms, the fact remains that shared IP networks were designed to carry data that could tolerate delays. Voice networks are designed with dedicated circuits offering guaranteed bandwidth and delivery times to voice transmissions. |
| **Multipoint audioconferences** | Some packages may employ proprietary methods while others may support the **T.120** conferencing standard. |
| **Addressing for call creation** | IP-based software packages employ a variety of different addressing techniques to create calls. In some cases, a directory server must be established listing all potential voice call destinations. In other cases, e-mail addresses or IP addresses may be used to initiate and IP-based voice call. Third-party directory services may also be supported. |
| **Bandwidth reservation on networks** | In order to more closely emulate the dedicated bandwidth circuits of the PSTN, an IP-based protocol known as **RSVP** (Resource Reservation Protocol) enables routing software to reserve a portion of network bandwidth known as a **virtual circuit.** This dedicated, guaranteed bandwidth is assigned to a particular IP-based voice transmission session, thereby minimizing transmission delay and increasing the quality of the transmission. Other quality of service (QoS) options are also available. Different hardware devices implement QoS in different ways, so you will need to consult the manufacturer for the best options. Some of the most popular options are Priority Queuing, Custom Queuing, VLANs, and Weighted Random Early Discard. |
| **Voice compression** | Depending on the particular codec algorithm used, voice compression can cause a major difference in required bandwidth. Among the more popular codec standards are high bandwidth **GSM** (Global Systems Mobile Communication) that uses 9,600–11,000 bps and low-bandwidth **RT24,** 2,400 bps. |
| **Auxiliary features** | Many IP-based voice packages support a variety of other functions that may be important to some organizations. Examples of such functions include: answering machine/recorded message capabilities, online rolodex with photographs of called parties, text-chat when sufficient voice quality cannot be maintained, electronic whiteboard for long distance brainstorming, file transfer and application sharing, incorporation of voice transmission into HTML documents for Web pages, API to integrate voice transmission in customized applications. |

*Figure 5-10*   Features and Functionality of VOIP Software

tones and specialized phone applications that can be written to connect to data residing on the network. Currently the costs of these new handsets are more expensive than a traditional telephone handset, but prices are steadily coming down. With the potential savings on long-distance toll calls associated with VOIP technologies, the additional cost might be easy to justify in many environments.

In a sign of the impending convergence in the telecommunication marketplace, some vendors are developing wireless handsets that support VOIP over wireless LANS along with digital cellular technologies such as those detailed later in this chapter. These phones will connect via the wireless LAN when in a building, then automatically switch to the digital cellular carrier when outside the wireless LAN coverage zone. In this manner, calls would be routed across the most cost-effective network available at any given time.

**SIP: A Replacement for H.323 Signaling**    **Session Initiation Protocol** (SIP) is a signaling protocol for Internet conferencing, telephony, presence, events notification and instant messaging developed by the IETF to be the standardized mechanism to send multimedia over the Internet. Although H.323 was the original protocol used for VOIP, SIP is gaining momentum as the communication protocol of choice for VOIP implementations. Many vendors such as Cisco and Microsoft, as well as carriers like MCI, have embraced SIP as the communication protocol of choice for VOIP applications.

Another emerging application for SIP is in third-generation cellular networks. The 3GPP (3rd Generation Partnership Project) has chosen SIP as the signaling protocol of choice for these emerging networks. For more information on 3G wireless, see the Digital Cellular section later on in this chapter.

**Voice Gateways: More than just a PBX**    As VOIP has matured, so have the devices that support it. VOIP has evolved from being just a "cool application" used by two or more computers on the Internet into a full-fledged alternative to traditional telephony. However, most organizations are not going to be able to simply replace all of their existing telephone technology overnight with a VOIP solution. Instead, mechanisms must be developed to integrate newer VOIP technologies into existing telecommunications infrastructures. For organizations that have an existing PBX, the preferred solution is to install a VOIP card that enables them to support VOIP software and handsets. Such an "IP enabled" PBX is also referred to as a **voice gateway.**

A voice gateway provides a means for the VOIP-enabled devices to access the traditional telephone network. The gateway can be set up to assign telephone numbers to IP devices so they can make traditional phone calls over the existing telephone network, have access to voicemail services, and other traditional phone features. By adding IP to the PBX, vendors can extend the use of the PBX into the new VOIP paradigm. For those organizations that do not have a PBX vendors such as Cisco Systems have introduced voice gateways that provide similar functionality. These devices have connections to both the data network and to the PSTN to route outgoing and incoming calls.

Managerial
Perspective

## COST/BENEFIT ANALYSIS FOR IP-BASED VOICE TRANSMISSION

Figure 5-11 identifies many of the potential costs associated with implementing an IP-based voice transmission network. All cost categories listed will not apply in all situations. Benefits will be most significant for those organizations with large domestic or international long distance calling expenses. However, it should be noted that such organizations often already have large-volume discounted rate contracts with their phone service providers that minimize or negate any potential savings that might be achieved by shifting to an IP-based voice transmission network.

A more subjective criteria that must be considered is the minimum acceptable transmitted voice quality. Higher transmission quality demands higher amounts of dedicated bandwidth. Lower amounts of shared bandwidth can cause transmission delays that will be manifested as voice drop-outs or clipped words.

| Costs | |
|---|---|
| **Client platforms** | |
| Workstation (with sufficiently fast CPU) if not already available | $ |
| Modem or other network access technology | $ |
| Speakers | $ |
| Microphone | $ |
| Sound card | $ |
| Client voice software | $ |
| **Other devices** | |
| Handset | $ |
| Wired | $ |
| Wireless | $ |
| **Total cost pervoice client** | $ |
| **Total cost for all voice clients** | $ |
| **Server platforms** | |
| Directory servers | $ |
| Directory server software | $ |
| **Total server costs** | $ |
| **Access charges** | |
| Internet access (monthly charge to ISP) | $ |
| Access line (paid to phone carrier) | $ |
| **Total access costs** | $ |
| **Other costs** | |
| Training & support | $ |
| Other costs | |
| **Total other costs** | $ |
| **Total costs** | $ |
| **Benefits** | |
| Savings from reduced phone bills to phone service provider | $ |

*Figure 5-11*   Cost/Benefit Analysis for IP-Based Voice Transmission

Typical delays on voice transmission networks such as PSTN are in the 50–70 milliseconds range, while IP-based voice transmission networks can exhibit delays of 500 milliseconds to 1.5 seconds. Many corporations may conclude that the current generation of IP-based voice transmission technology is sufficient for internal corporate communication but is unacceptable for external communication with clients and customers.

Finally, should large amounts of revenue begin to bypass phone carriers as a result of a massive use of IP-based voice transmission over the Internet, it is likely that the Federal Communications Commission might take steps to assure that Internet Service Providers (ISP) do not have an unfair competitive advantage.

## Voice over Frame Relay

IP-based voice transmission via the Internet is not the only alternative to traditional voice transmission over wide areas. Frame relay is another wide area transmission services that was primarily or initially deployed for data transmission but is now capable of delivering voice transmissions as well. Although Frame Relay will be discussed further in chapter 6, the implications of transmitting voice over this service will be detailed here.

In order to be able to dynamically adapt to transmit data as efficiently as possible, frame relay encapsulates segments of a data transfer session into variable length frames. For longer data transfers, longer frames with larger data payloads are used, and for short messages, shorter frames are used. These variable-length frames introduce varying amounts of delay due to processing by intermediate switches on the frame relay network. This variable-length delay introduced by the variable-length frames works very well for data but is unacceptable to voice payloads that are very sensitive to delay.

The FRAD or frame relay access device is able to accommodate both voice and data traffic by employing any or all of the following techniques:

- *Voice prioritization*—FRADs are able to distinguish between voice and data traffic and prioritize voice traffic over data traffic.

- *Data frame size limitation*—Long data frames must be segmented into multiple smaller frames so that pending voice traffic can have priority access. However, data must not be delayed to unacceptable levels.

- *Separate voice and data queues*—In order to more effectively manage pending data and voice messages, separate queues for data and voice messages can be maintained within the FRAD.

Voice conversations transmitted over Frame Relay networks require 4 to 16 Kbps of bandwidth each. This dedicated bandwidth is reserved as an end-to-end connection through the frame relay network known as a PVC, or permanent virtual circuit. In order for prioritization schemes established by FRADs to be maintained throughout a voice conversation's end-to-end journey, intermediate frame relay switches within the frame relay network must support the same prioritization schemes. At this point, voice conversations can only take place between locations connected directly to a frame relay network. There are currently no interoperability standards or network-to-network interface standards defined between frame relay networks and the voice-based PSTN. Figure 5-12 illustrates voice transmission over a frame relay network.

## Voice over ATM

Whereas frame relay is a switch-based WAN service using variable length frames, ATM (asynchronous transfer mode) is a switch-based WAN service using fixed-length frames, more properly referred to as cells. Fixed-length cells assure fixed-length processing time by ATM switches, thereby enabling predictable, rather than variable, delay and delivery time. Voice is currently transmitted across ATM networks using a bandwidth reservation scheme known as CBR, or constant bit rate, which is analogous to a Frame Relay virtual circuit. However, constant bit rate does not make optimal use of available bandwidth because, during the course of a given voice conversation, moments of silence intermingle with periods of conversation. The most common method for currently transmitting voice over an ATM network is

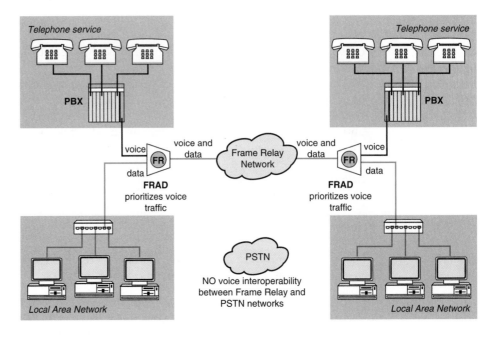

*Figure 5-12*    Voice Transmission over a Frame Relay Network

to reserve a CBR of 64 Kbps for one voice conversation digitized via PCM (pulse code modulation).

In Sharper Focus

## OPTIMIZING VOICE OVER ATM

More efficient use of ATM network capacity for voice transmission can be achieved in one of the following ways:

- *Voice compression*—The ITU standardized voice compression algorithms via the G series of standards. Algorithms vary in the amount of bandwidth required to transmit toll-quality voice (G.726: 48, 32, 24, or 16 Kbps; G.728: 16 Kbps; G.729: 8 Kbps). An important point to remember with voice compression is that the greater the compression ratio achieved, the more complicated and processing-intensive the compression process. In such cases , the greatest delay is introduced by the voice compression algorithm with the highest compression ratio, requiring the least bandwidth.

- *Silence suppression*—All cells are examined as to contents. Any voice cell that contains silence is not allowed to enter the ATM network. At the destination end, the nontransmitted silence is replace with synthesized background noise. Silence suppression can reduce the amount of cells transmitted for a given voice conversation by 50 percent.

- *Use of* **VBR (variable bit rate)** *rather than CBR*—By combining the positive attributes of voice compression and silence suppression, ATM-based voice conversations are able to be transmitted using variable-bit rate bandwidth management. By only using bandwidth when someone is talking, remaining bandwidth is available for data transmission or other voice conversations. Use of VBR is controlled via two parameters:

1. Peak voice bit rate controls the maximum amount of bandwidth a voice conversation can be given when there is little or no contention for bandwidth.

2. Guaranteed voice bit rate controls the minimum amount of bandwidth that must be available to a voice conversation regardless of how much contention exists for bandwidth.

Standards for voice transmission over ATM (VTOA) networks are being developed by the ATM Forum. Among the standards available or under development are the following:

- Circuit Emulation Standard (CES)—Defines voice transport over ATM networks using CBR (constant bit rate). Equivalent to PVCs over frame relay nets.

- VTOA–ATM—For use on private or public ATM networks, defines voice transmission using the following:

  ○ ISDN (integrated services digital network) as a voice source network

  ○ Transport of compressed voice over ATM

  ○ Virtual tunnel groups that are able to handle multiple calls simultaneously between two locations

- VTOA to the Desktop—Defines interoperability between ATM and non-ATM networks.

Figure 5-13 illustrates the transmission of voice conversations over an ATM network.

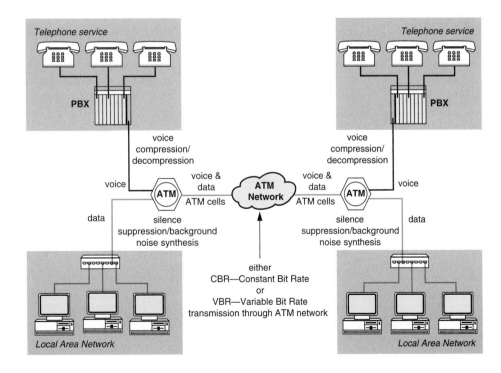

*Figure 5-13*   Voice Transmission over an ATM Network

## Voice/Data Multiplexers

As opposed to using a switch-based frame relay or ATM network for wide area transmission of voice and data, organizations have traditionally chosen to link combined voice and data transmission over long distances via leased digital transmission services such as T-1. From a business perspective, a key difference between switched services such as Frame Relay or ATM and leased services such as T-1 is that switched services are usually tariffed according to usage and leased services are usually tariffed according to a flat monthly rate. As a result, leased services are being paid for 24 hours/day, 7 days/week, whether they are being used or not.

Many corporations that once maintained a private network of **voice/data multiplexers** linked via T-1 or other high-speed digital services, have found that the usage-based pricing of frame relay networks can save them significant expense. A voice/data multiplexer is able to simultaneously transmit digitized voice and data over a single digital transmission service by assigning the voice and data transmissions to separate channels.

## ISDN

Integrated services digital network is a switched digital, rather than analog, service that is also capable of transmitting voice and data simultaneously. Rather than using modems, ISDN requires devices that are officially known as terminal adapters but that are frequently marketed as **ISDN data/voice modems.** ISDN BRI (Basic Rate Interface) service offers two 64 Kbps channels. One of these channels is used for data while the other is used to simultaneously transmit voice. Analog phones or fax machines can be interfaced to the ISDN data/voice modem in order to allow these analog devices to access ISDN's digital transmission service. Point-to-point ISDN connections require both ends of the transmission to be able to access ISDN services via ISDN data/voice modems.

ISDN is not nearly as available as switched analog voice phone service. In addition, pricing policies for ISDN can include both a monthly flat fee as well as an additional usage-based tariff Figure 5-14 illustrates the differences between simultaneous voice and data transmission using ISDN.

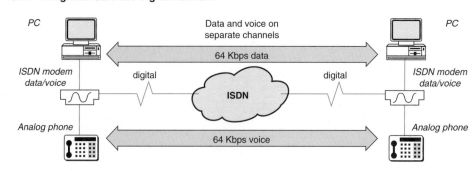

**ISDN—Integrated Services Digital Network**

*Figure 5-14*   Simultaneous Voice/Data Transmission with ISDN

### ■ WIRELESS VOICE TRANSMISSION

Modern wireless telephones are based on a cellular model. As shown in Figure 5-15, a wireless telephone system consists of a series of cells that surround a central base station, or tower. Cells are arranged so that no two adjoining cells use the same frequency. In this manner, there is a clear point of demarcation between cells. The term *cellular phone* or its abbreviation *cell phone* comes from the cellular nature of all wireless networks.

When turned on, a wireless phone is constantly communicating with the closest cell tower in the background. The point of this background communication is to let the cellular system know where the phone is so that incoming calls can be routed to the correct tower for transmission to the phone. When a phone makes or receives a call it initiates a connection between itself and the nearest tower. If over the course of the call the phone handset moves away from the current tower into a new cell the background communication link will be used to "hand off" the call from the tower in the old cell to the tower in the new cell. The handoff between the towers must be seamless to the end user and must carry forward the call information, such as air time, user ID, and so on, for proper billing. The connection of multiple cell sites, together with handoffs, allows a carrier to build a nationwide network in which calls can be made coast to coast.

### Analog Cellular

The traditional circuit-switched analog cellular network is more properly known by the transmission standard to which it adheres: the **advanced mobile phone service**

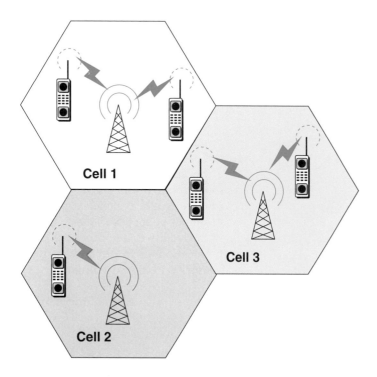

*Figure 5-15*   Cellular Phone System

(**AMPS**), which operates in the 800 MHz frequency range. Although AMPS networks currently have the broadest coverage of any network in the United States, they have significant limitations. Because the connection is analog in nature, AMPS calls offer relatively poor signal quality; static and interference are inherent with the system. Another key issue with analog AMPS networks is that they can handle relatively few concurrent calls per cell.

### Digital Cellular

To overcome these limitations, carriers have steadily moved to digital cellular systems. In a digital cellular system, the call is digitized at the telephone handset and sent in a digital format to the tower. Because this signal is digital in nature, quality is greatly improved. As long as you can get a signal, the call will sound perfect. However, as soon as the signal is lost, the call is dropped.

Another key feature from the perspective of wireless carriers is that the digital network allows more calls to share the common bandwidth in a cell concurrently, increasing capacity and billable minutes compared to analog cellular. This digital link is also better equipped to support wireless data transmission, paving the way for technologies such as Internet enabled phone handsets.

**Digital cellular** seeks to evolve an all-digital network architecture capable of delivering a variety of telecommunications services transparently to users at any time, regardless of their geographic location. Digital cellular is not a totally new "from the bottom up" telecommunications architecture. In fact, it is the integration of a number of existing telecommunications environments. Digital cellular seeks to combine the capabilities of the PSTN, otherwise known as the **landline telephone network,** with a new, all-digital cellular network, along with paging networks, and satellite communications networks.

The need for seamless delivery of a combination of all of the above services is easily illustrated by the plight of today's mobile professional. A single person has a phone number for his or her home phone, a voice and fax number for the office, a cellular phone number for the automobile, a pager phone number for a pager, and perhaps even another phone number for a satellite service phone for use outside of cellular phone areas. The premise of digital cellular is rather straightforward: one person, one phone number.

This **personal phone number** or **PPN** would become the user's interface to digital cellular and the vast array of transparently available telecommunications services. This personal phone number is a key concept to digital cellular. It changes the entire focus of the interface to the telecommunications environment from the current orientation of a number being associated with a particular location regardless of the individual using the facility to a number being associated with particular individual regardless of the location, even globally, of the accessed facility. Figure 5-16 illustrates the basic elements of digital cellular.

**Digital Cellular Standards**   Given the limited bandwidth (only about 140 MHz from 1.85 GHz to 1.99 GHz, referred to as the 2 GHz band) allocated to digital cellular and the potentially large number of subscribers needing to share that limited bandwidth, a key challenge for digital cellular is the ability to maximize the number of simultaneous conversations over a finite amount of bandwidth. Just as multiplexing was originally introduced in the study of wide area networks as a means of maximizing the use of wire-based circuits, two variations of multiplexing are being field tested as a means of maximizing the use of the allocated bandwidth of these air-based circuits.

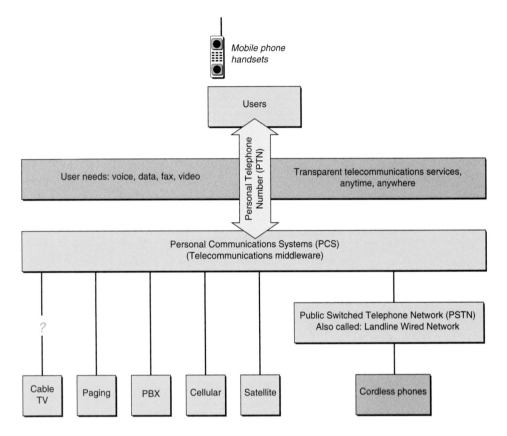

*Figure 5-16*   Basic Elements of Digital Cellular

TDMA (Time Division Multiple Access) and CDMA (Code Division Multiple Access) are the two access methodologies used in digital cellular systems. Both offer significant capacity increases compared to AMPS analog cellular systems. A TDMA-based digital cellular can support three times (some tests indicate six or seven times) the transmission capacity of analog cellular, while CDMA can offer as much as a tenfold increase. Note that the names of each of these techniques end in the words *multiple access* rather than *multiplexing*. The *multiple access* refers to multiple phone conversations having access to the same bandwidth and yet not interfering with each other. Figure 5-17 illustrates TDMA and CDMA.

TDMA achieves more than one conversation per frequency by assigning time slots to individual conversations. Ten timeslots per frequency are often assigned, with a given cellular device transmitting its digitized voice only during its assigned time slot. Receiving devices must be in synch with the time slots of the sending device in order to receive the digitized voice packets and reassemble them into a natural-sounding analog signal. TDMA should be able to transmit data at 9.6 Kbps. TDMA digital standards to handle call set-up, maintenance, and termination have been defined by the Telecommunications Industry Association (TIA) as follows:

- IS-130: TDMA Radio Interface and Radio Link Protocol 1

- IS-135: TDMA Services, Async Data, and FAX

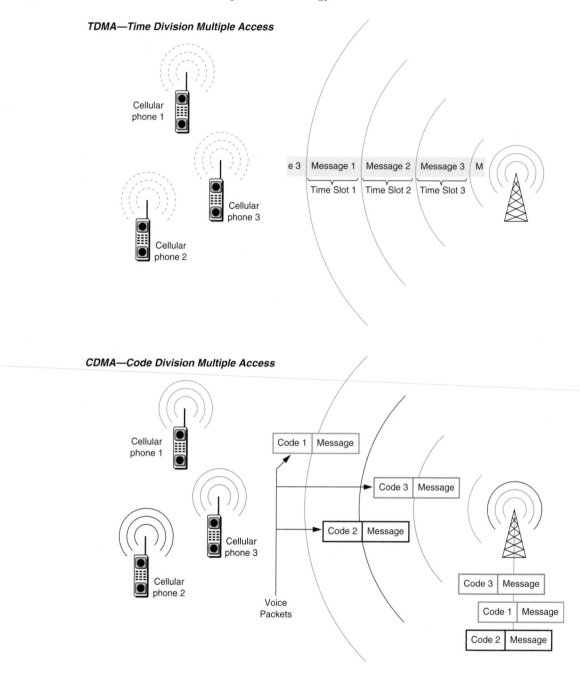

*Figure 5-17* Maximizing Minimum Bandwidth: TDMA and CDMA

**Global System for Mobile Communication (GSM)** is a new service layer that overlies TDMA. GSM provides a standardized billing interface and a means of offering enhanced data services. The standardized billing interface is particularly important to carriers because it simplifies the way they bill the consumer and provides a framework for seamless roaming between the GSM networks of different companies. Another key feature of GSM is the use of a SIM card to store the user's information, including their phone number, contacts, and so on. If users want to change phones, they need only move the SIM card from one device to another. Since the SIM card contains the entire user's information, no programming of the new phone is needed, thus reducing the service cost to the carrier. Most TDMA-based carriers are migrating to GSM.

CDMA attempts to maximize the number of calls transmitted within a limited bandwidth by using a spread spectrum transmission technique. Rather than allocating specific frequency channels within the allocated bandwidth to specific conversations as is done with TDMA, CDMA transmits digitized voice packets from numerous calls at different frequencies spread all over the entire allocated bandwidth spectrum.

To keep track of which voice packet belongs with which call, each is marked with a code. This technique is not unlike the datagram connectionless service used by packet switched networks to send packetized data over numerous switched virtual circuits within the packet switched network. By identifying the source and sequence of each packet, the original message integrity is maintained while maximizing the overall performance of the network. The CDMA standards defined by the TIA are IS-95a and IS-99: Data Services Option for Wideband Spread Spectrum Digital Cellular Systems, commonly known as CDMAone.

TDMA and CDMA networks are both deployed in the United States. In Europe and much of the rest of the world, GSM (based on TDM) is deployed, while **Personal Handyphone System** (**PHS**) is the digital cellular standard implemented in Japan. Currently, these various digital cellular transmission standards are not interoperable, thereby precluding the possibility of transparent global access to digital cellular services.

In Sharper Focus

## TDMA VS. CDMA: A TALE OF CAPABILITIES VS. PATENT ROYALTIES

An analysis of the technical details of TDMA and CDMA shows that CDMA is the better technology in almost all aspects. However, there is a business limitation associated with CDMA that has limited its deployment. CDMA is patented by Qualcom, based in San Diego, California. As the patent holder for the CDMA technologies, Qualcom currently requires an 8 percent patent royalty on all CDMA devices sold. Many manufacturers are not willing to reduce their profit margin to pay Qualcom, so they have instead chosen to use the more technically limited TDMA technology. Other vendors are actively working to develop an alternative CDMA-like technology implementation that is different enough that it will skirt Qualcom's patent rights.

The question a carrier has to ask itself is if it is worth the hassle and expense of licensing CDMA technology to realize the benefits of higher cell density and the faster data transmission speeds offered by CDMA-based 1xRTT and EV-DO, as described in the next section. While Verizon Wireless and Sprint have chosen to go with CDMA, other major carriers such as AT&T Wireless, Cingular, and T-Mobile have chose to stick with TDMA and avoid Qualcom's patents.

An early GSM draft standard called for GSM to operate over CDMA rather than TDMA networks. However, many vendors and carriers were not willing to standardize on a patented technology that required royalty payments to a single company. The lesson to be learned here is that the marketplace likes open standards and is willing to forgo potential technological benefits to eliminate the cost and limitations associated with licensing patented technology.

## MARKET ISSUES FACING WIRELESS TELEPHONE SYSTEMS

A key issue in the digital cellular market space is number portability. If a user decides to change from one cellular company to another, the person would be required to change their phone number. With the low cost of cellular services, some people have replaced their land line phone with cell phone. For these users, the pain of change numbers to change carriers held them "hostage" to one carrier. In mid-2003, the FCC won judicial approval for a ruling requiring that cellular companies allow a person to keep their phone number whenever they change carriers, effective November 2003. Although sure to have its deployment pains, cellular number portability ushers in a new level of consumer choice and carrier responsibility. No longer will customers be stuck with a carrier because they have advertised their cellular number.

Perhaps the most significant hurdles to the future of digital cellular services are the individual, conflicting, business missions of the various companies that must somehow produce a comprehensive, seamless, global, transparent digital cellular service for subscribers. Each of these firms must look out for their best interests while trying to work together for the betterment of the consumer.

Cellular telephony is a big business, with carriers investing $7.7 billion for auctioned spectrum in 1995 to 1996. It is estimated that somewhere between an additional $10 billion and $50 billion must be spent on digital cellular infrastructure before nationwide services can be achieved. The dilemma is that cellular vendors must price their services attractively enough to gain market share while maintaining adequate cash flow to service a tremendous amount of debt.

Ultimately the consumer will determine the future of cellular technologies. If recent trends continue to hold true, that future will be bright. The number of cellular phones continues to grow worldwide. In developing nations that never achieved a solid wired telecommunications infrastructure, carriers are skipping that step and rolling out cellular services instead. In countries that have a solid wired infrastructure, many consumers are choosing to forgo a traditional wired telephone and are choosing to use their cellular service as their primary telephone.

## ■ WIRELESS DATA SERVICES

Although wireless LANs offer mobility to users across a local scope of coverage, a variety of wireless services are available for use across wider geographic spans. These **wireless WAN services** vary in many ways including availability, applications, transmission speed, and cost. Among the available wireless WAN services that will be explained further are the following:

- Private packet radio
- Enhanced paging and two-way messaging
- Circuit-switched analog cellular
- CDPD—cellular digital packet data
- GPRS—general packet radio service
- CDMA (a.k.a 1xRTT)—code division multiple access or single carrier (1x) radio transmission technology

- EDGE—enhanced data for GSM evolution
- EV-DO—evolution data only

The key characteristics of these and other wireless WAN services are summarized in Figure 5-18.

## Wireless Data Service Generations

Often wireless data services are referred to by their generation: 1st Generation (1G), 2nd Generation (2G), Advanced 2nd Generation (2.5G), and 3rd Generation

| Wireless WAN Service | Geographic Scope | Directionality | Data Characteristics | Billing | Access Device | Standards |
|---|---|---|---|---|---|---|
| Enhanced Paging | National | One- or two-way relatively short messages | 100 characters or less | Flat monthly charges increasing with coverage area | Pagers | Mobetex |
| Private Packet Radio | Nearly national, more cities than CDPD but less than circuit-switched cellular | Full duplex Packet-switched digital data | 4.8 Kbps | Per character | Proprietary modem compatible with particular private packet radio service | Proprietary |
| Circuit Switched Analog Cellular | National | Full-duplex Circuit switched | 14.4 Kbps max | Call duration | Modems with specialized error correction for cellular circuits | Analog cellular |
| CDPD | Limited to large metropolitan areas | Full duplex Packet-switched digital data | 19.2 Kbps max | flat monthly charge plus usage charge per kilopacket | CDPD modem | CDPD |
| GPRS | National in large metro areas | Full duplex Packet-switched digital data | 30 Kbps to 40 Kbps | Monthly flat rate for business users; metered rated based on usage for consumer | Tethered cell phones and PCMCIA/CF cards | TDMA |
| IxRTT | National in large metro areas | Full duplex Packet-switched digital data | 40 Kbps to 56 Kbps | Monthly flat rate for business users; metered rated based on usage for consumer | Tethered cell phones and PCMCIA/CF cards | CDMA |
| EDGE | Limited metro areas | Full duplex Packet-switched digital data | Up to 384 Kbps | Monthly flat rate for business users; metered rated based on usage for consumer | Tethered cell phones and PCMCIA/CF cards | TDMA |
| EV-DO | Limited metro areas | Full duplex Packet-switched digital data | 600 Kbps to 2 Mbps | Monthly flat rate for business users; metered rated based on usage for consumer | PCMCIA cards | CDMA |

*Figure 5-18*    Wireless WAN Services Technology Analysis

(3G). Each of these generations can be defined by the services and data speeds they offer:

- 1G networks are defined as analog networks that carried just voice traffic such as AMPS.

- 2G networks are defined by technologies that use digital transmission between the handset and the tower, such as TDMA and CDMA. Most 2G systems provide 9.6–14.4 Kbps circuit-switched data service.

- 2.5G networks are defined as digital networks that provide between 56 Kbps and 115 Kbps of data capacity, such as GPRS and 1xRTT.

- 3G is an ITU specification for the third generation of mobile communications technology. The primary benefit of 3G is increased bandwidth ranging from 128 Kbps in a moving car to 2 Mbps for fixed applications. Examples of 3G network are EDGE and EV-DO; however, many other 3G network technologies are currently being developed.

## Circuit-Switched Analog Cellular

Transmitting data over AMPS analog cellular networks requires modems that support specialized cellular transmission protocols on both ends of the cellular transmission in order to maximize throughput. Examples of such protocols include **MNP-10 Adverse Channel Enhancements** and **Enhanced Throughput Cellular** (**ETC**). In some cases, cellular service providers have deployed modem pools of cellular enhanced modems at the **mobile telephone switching office** (**MTSO**) where all cellular traffic is converted for transmission over the wire line public switched telephone network (PSTN). Figure 5-19 illustrates data transmission over the circuit switched analog cellular network.

Using analog cellular, a call must be placed from the handset to a modem. From the perspective of the network this data call is just like a voice call and is billed based on call duration. Speeds for analog cellular are limited to a maximum of 14.4 Kbps with speed dependent on the quality of the connection.

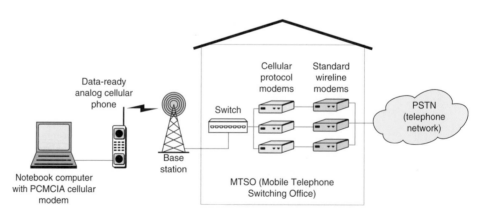

*Figure 5-19*  Data Transmission over the Circuit-Switched Analog Cellular Network

## CDPD

Once one of the most widely deployed technologies, **CDPD** is rapidly be phased out. AT&T Wireless, one of the largest CDPD network providers, has determined that the CDPD is not in its future. With the wireless carrier strapped for cash after buying spectrum for newer digital technologies, it has determined it is not financial viable to maintain two separate networks. AT&T has stated that existing CDPD users should migrate to EDGE, and AT&T Wireless will discontinue the CDPD service at the end of 2004. Other carriers are following suit, making CDPD a poor choice for new installations.

## GPRS and 1xRTT

Unlike analog cellular transmission, transmitting digital data from a notebook computer over digital cellular networks does not require modulation. As a result, computers can interface directly to digital TDMA and CDMA-based digital cellular phones via serial ports. A second advantage to digital cellular networks is that connections are practically instantaneous because there is no carrier to establish and call set-up is greatly simplified. Figure 5-20 illustrates data transmission over a digital cellular network.

**GPRS** and **1xRTT** are the two currently competing digital cellular data standards in the United States. Both networks were deployed in 2002/2003 across major metropolitan areas. GPRS is based on the TDMA model, while 1xRTT is based on the CDMA model. This means that mobile devices will only work on one type of network AT&T Wireless, Cingular, and T-Mobile support the GPRS standard, while Sprint and Verizon Wireless support the 1xRTT standard.

Side-by-side tests between GPRS and 1xRTT have shown that 1xRTT is currently faster. 1xRTT networks have shown data rates as high as 100 Kbps, while GPRS testing has shown a maximum of around 56 Kbps. However, a multitude of factors can affect throughput, including cell tower load, Internet traffic conditions, and signal strength. As the build-out of these services continues, overall speeds are expected to increase. Both technologies have the potential to offer data service at speeds upward of 200 Kbps.

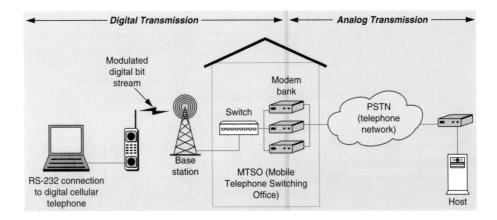

*Figure 5-20*   Data Transmission over a Digital Cellular Network

The build-out of GPRS and 1xRTT networks was not driven entirely by the need for wireless data. By deploying these technologies, wireless carriers were able to further increase the number of calls each cellular tower could handle while offering add-on features like downloadable ring tones, games, instant message, and multimedia messaging. These new features represent a new income stream for the carriers. Since the majority of a wireless carrier's revenue is based on consumer voice service, they initially marketed and priced the technology for consumers. Currently, business data users only make up a small percentage of a carrier's revenue stream, so they weren't targeted during the initial roll-out. The next upgrade to the technologies will increase the data throughput and be targeted more at business users.

## EDGE and EV-DO

**EDGE** and **EV-DO** are third generation (3G) wireless data transmission technologies for existing TDMA/CDMA network infrastructures. EDGE is the upgrade path for TDMA-based GPRS, while EV-DO is the upgrade path for CDMA-based 1xRTT solutions. As discussed in the GPRS and 1xRTT section, devices manufactured to work on a TDMA/EDGE network will not work on a CDMA/EV-DO network, and visa versa. However, EDGE device will be backward compatible with GPRS and TDMA, while EV-DO devices will be backward compatible with 1xRTT and CDMA.

EDGE networks have theoretical data speeds up to 384 Kbps, although early deployments have only provided around 100 Kbps. EV-DO networks have theoretical data speeds of up to 2 Mbps. However, just as in EDGE, early deployments have shown practical speeds much lower, in the 384 Kbps range.

These technology upgrades are focused on delivering high speeds for wireless data. Unlike the GPRS and 1xRTT build-out, the upgrades are focused more the business user than the consumer. The good news for carriers is that this upgrade is easier than the migration from TDMA/CDMA to GPRS/1xRTT. This upgrade generally includes software changes in the MTSO equipment and upgrades in the devices used to connect the network. This upgrade does not require all existing devices to be replaced. Users that need the extra data speeds can upgrade their equipment to the new standard, while users with older technology will be able to continue to work, albeit at their existing data speeds.

## Next Generation Wireless Services

The next generation of wireless will focus on specialized high-bandwidth wireless services. The standards for this next generation of wireless transmission services are most often grouped under the name of **3G (Third Generation) Mobile Telephony,** otherwise known as UWC-136 (Universal Wireless Communications). The ITU's overall initiative for 3G Wireless Telephony is known as IMT 2000 (International Mobile Telecommunications) and consists of three separate initiatives: UMTS (ETSI), UWC-136 (TIA), and CDMA2000 (TIA). These initiatives are summarized in Figure 5-21.

In addition to new 3G standards, there is ongoing research into what has been termed 4G. NTT DoCoMo in Japan has begun testing the next evolution of their W-CDMA network. The hope is for this new 4G network to work up to 100 Mbps. DoCoMo expects to have a commercial 4G network available by 2010.

| 3G Transmission Technology | Stationary Maximum Transmission Rate | Moving Upstream Transmission Rate | Moving Downstream Transmission Rate |
|---|---|---|---|
| W-CDMA—Wideband Code Division Multiple Access | 2 Mbps | 100 Kbps | 384 Kbps |
| UMTS—Universal Mobile Telecommunications System | 2 Mbps | 100 Kbps | 384 Kbps |
| CDMA 2000—Code Division Multiple Access 2000 | 2 Mbps | 100 Kbps | 384 Kbps |

*Figure 5-21*    3G Mobile Telephony Standards

Applied Problem
Solving

## A TOP-DOWN APPROACH TO WIRELESS WAN SERVICES ANALYSIS

Due to the many variable factors concerning these wireless WAN services, it is important to take a top-down approach when considering their incorporation into an organization's information systems solution. Questions and issues to be considered on each layer of the top down model for wireless WAN services are summarized in Figure 5-22.

As a practical example of how to use the top-down model for wireless WAN services analysis, start with the business situation that requires wireless support and examine the applications and data characteristics that support the business activity in question. For example, which of the following best describe the data to be transmitted by wireless means?

| Top-Down Layer | Issues/Implications |
|---|---|
| **Business** | • What is the business activity that requires wireless transmission?<br>• How will payback be calculated? Has the value of this business activity been substantiated?<br>• What are the anticipated expenses for the 6-month, 1-year, and 2-year horizons?<br>• What is the geographic scope of this business activity? Localized? National? International? |
| **Application** | • Have applications been developed especially for wireless transmission?<br>• Have existing applications been modified to account for wireless transmission characteristics?<br>• Have training and help-desk support systems been developed? |
| **Data** | • What is the nature of the data to be delivered via the wireless WAN service? short bursty transactions, large two-way messages, faxes, file transfers?<br>• Is the data time-sensitive or could transmissions be batched during off-peak hours for discounted rates?<br>• What is the geographic scope of coverage required for wireless data delivery? |
| **Network** | • Must the WAN service provide error correction?<br>• Do you wish the WAN service to also provide and maintain the access devices? |
| **Technology** | • Which wireless WAN service should be employed?<br>• What type of access device must be employed with the chosen WAN service?<br>• Are access devices proprietary or standards-based? |

*Figure 5-22*    Top-Down Analysis for Wireless WAN Services

- Fax

- File transfer

- E-mail

- Paging

- Transaction processing

- Database queries

The nature of the content, geographic scope, and amount and urgency of the data to be transmitted will have a direct bearing on the particular wireless WAN service employed. Unfortunately, no single wireless WAN service fits all application and data needs. Once a wireless WAN service is chosen, compatibility with existing local area network architectures and technology must be assured.

## ■ PBX AND CTI SERVICES

In order to provide flexible voice communications capability among people within a business organization as well as with the outside world, a switching device known as a **PBX,** or **Private Branch Exchange** is often employed. Sales of PBXs in the United States represent approximately a $4 billion annual market with service on these PBXs accounting for an additional $2 billion in revenue. The PBX market is currently dominated by Nortel (Northern Telecom) with its line of Meridian PBXs and by Lucent Technologies (formerly AT&T Global Business Communications Systems) with its line of Definity PBXs. Each of these two major players control about 25 percent market share. The major players in the PBX market and their approximate market shares are displayed in Figure 5-23.

### PBX Functionality and Architecture

As illustrated in the I-P-O (Input-Processing-Output) diagram of Figure 5-24, a PBX provides an interface between users and the shared private or public network connections available for carrying users' voice and data traffic. The additional intelligent services offered by a PBX allow users to use their phones more efficiently and effectively.

A PBX is really just a privately owned, smaller version of the switch in telephone company central offices that control circuit switching for the general public.

| Approximate PBX Market Share | PBX Vendors |
|---|---|
| 25–30% | Nortel, Lucent Technologies |
| 10–20% | NEC and Mitel |
| 5–10% | Siemens Rolm |
| 2–5% | Fujitsu, Intecom, Ericsson, Hitachi |
| Less than 2% | Toshiba, Executone, Tadrian, SRX, Harris Digital |

*Figure 5-23*   PBX Vendors and Market Share

| I (Input) | P (Processing) | O (Output) |
| --- | --- | --- |
| Users access PBX connections and services via desktop phones or access devices. | Necessary switching is provided to allow connections among PBX users or to outside network services. | Other local PBX connections or outside local loops and PSTN connections. Outside connections may also be to shared high-speed digital lines. |
| Input traffic may be voice, data, or video. | This Provides additional intelligent services to track PBX usage, offer conference calling, call-forwarding, least cost routing, automatic call distribution, automated attendant, and links to computer databases. | |

*Figure 5-24*    IPO Diagram of PBX Functionality

Depending on the requested destination, switched circuits are established, maintained, and terminated on a per-call basis by the PBX **switching matrix.**

Beyond the switching capabilities of a PBX, programmable features offer advanced functionality to users. These features and the overall performance of the PBX are controlled by software programs running on specialized computers within the PBX in an area sometimes referred to as the PBX CPU, stored program control or common control area.

Telephone sets in user offices are connected to the PBX via slide-in modules or cards known as **line cards, port cards,** or **station cards.** Connection to an outside network (usually the PSTN) is accomplished via **trunk cards.** Trunk cards vary in design from easily scalable cards to specialized cards for a particular type of network line.

Some PBXs allow any chassis slot to be used for any type of card or module, while other PBXs specify certain slots for line cards and others for trunk cards. Starting with an open chassis or cabinet with power supply and backbone or backplane, modules or cards are added to increase PBX capacity for either user extensions or connections to the outside network. Additional cabinets can often be cascaded to offer PBX expandability. Figure 5-25 illustrates the physical attributes of a representative PBX.

## PBX Technology Analysis

Before reviewing PBX technology, it is essential to have performed a thorough top-down analysis beginning with the business needs and functionality that must be met by the chosen PBX technology. Having identified those PBX features that are most important to a given business, the following information could be used as a representative sample of typical PBX features and services.

PBX features and services tend to fall into three broad categories:

- Features and services that provide users with flexible usage of PBX resources

- Features and services that provide for data/voice integration

- Features and services that control and monitor the use of those PBX resources

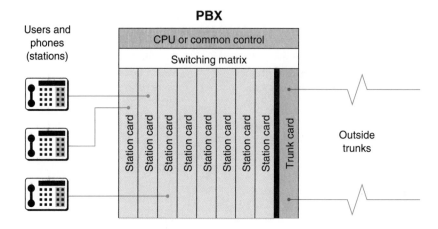

*Figure 5-25* PBX Physical Architecture

*Voice-Based Features and Services*  In the flexible usage category, features such as conference calling, call forwarding, call transfer, speed dialing, redialing and call hold are commonplace and shouldn't require further explanation. Other voice-based PBX features and services that support flexible usage of PBX resources are summarized in Figure 5-26.

| Feature/Service | Description |
| --- | --- |
| **Least Cost Routing (LCR)** | Using routing and pricing information supplied by the user, the PBX chooses the most economical path for any given call. This feature was especially important when WATS (Wide Area Telecommunications Service) lines were more prevalent. These days, thanks to competition and discount programs among long-distance carriers, PBXs can access any outgoing trunk rather than trying to get certain calls onto certain trunks. |
| **Automatic Call Distribution (ACD)** | Incoming calls are routed directly to certain extensions without going through a central switchboard. Calls can be routed according to the incoming trunk or phone number. Often used in customer service organizations in which calls may be distributed to the first available agent. |
| **Call Pickup** | Allows a user to pickup or answer another user's phone without the need to actually forward calls. |
| **Paging** | Ability to use paging speakers in a building. May be limited to specific paging zones. |
| **Direct Inward Dialing (DID)** | Allows calls to bypass the central switchboard and go directly to a particular user's phone. |
| **Hunting** | Hunt groups are established to allow incoming calls to get through on alternate trunks when a primary trunk is busy. For example, most businesses publish only one phone number even though they may have multiple incoming trunks. If the primary trunk is busy, the PBX hunts for an open trunk transparent to the user. |
| **Prioritization** | Individual extensions can be given priority access to certain trunks or groups of trunks. In most cases, PBXs are equipped with fewer outgoing trunks than internal extensions or station lines. If certain users must have access to outside lines, prioritization features are important. |
| **Night Mode** | Many companies close their switchboard at night but still have employees working who must be able to receive and make phone calls. |

*Figure 5-26*  Voice-Based PBX Features and Services

**Data/Voice Integration Features and Services** Data/Voice integration by PBXs is increasingly common although PBXs can vary significantly in the extent of support for data transmission. Differences in data interfaces and whether or not those interfaces and associated software represent an upgrade at additional cost should be investigated thoroughly before any PBX purchase. In some cases, data is transmitted through the PBX via a dedicated connection and in other cases a specialized hybrid voice/data phone is used to transmit both voice and data simultaneously over a single connection to the PBX. Data and data/voice integration related features and issues are summarized in Figure 5-27.

**Control and Monitoring Features and Services** Control and monitoring features range from the simple, such as limiting access to outside lines from certain extensions, to the complex, such as entire stand-alone **call accounting systems.** Call accounting systems are often run on separate system that interfaces directly to the PBX and execute specially written software. Accounting reports or bills sorted by department or extension can be run on a scheduled basis or on demand. Exception reports can be generated to spot possible abuses for calls over a certain length or cost, or calls made to a particular area code. Incoming as well as outgoing calls can be tracked. Call accounting systems can pay for themselves in a short amount of time by spotting and curtailing abuse as well as by allocating phone usage charges on a departmental basis.

The information on which such a call accounting system depends is generated by the PBX. In a process known as **SMDR** or **station message detail recording,** an individual detail record is generated for each call. This data record can then be transferred from the PBX to the call accounting system computer, usually from an RS-232 DB-25 port on the PBX to the serial port on the PC. Data records can be stored and summarized on the call accounting system computer, dependent on available disk space. Figure 5-28 illustrates the set-up of a call accounting system.

**Auxiliary Voice-Related Services** Just as call accounting systems are most often an add-on device for PBXs, other auxiliary systems exist to enhance PBX capability. The auxiliary nature of these systems implies that they are often not included as standard

| Feature/Service | Description |
| --- | --- |
| **ISDN Support** | Are WAN interfaces for ISDN (Integrated Services Digital Network) supplied or available as upgrades? ISDN BRI (Basic rate interface) service is two 64 Kbps channels. ISDN PRI service is twenty-three 64 Kbps channels. |
| **T-1 Support** | Are T-1 (1.544 Mbps) interfaces supported? Outside of North America, are E-1 (2.048 Mbps) supported? Are codecs included? Are channel banks included? |
| **Data Interfaces** | Are computer data interfaces included on the PBX? Are hybrid voice/data phones available? Are LAN interfaces such as ethernet and token ring as well as serial interfaces such as RS-232 supported? How many of the following services are supported: fax transmission, modem pooling, printer sharing, file sharing, video conferencing? |
| **PBX-to-Host Interfaces** | Prior to the advent of open systems computer telephony integration APIs such as TAPI and TSAPI, each PBX vendor had their own PBX-Host interface specification. How many of the following vendor-specific PBX-Host interfaces are supported? Nortel: Meridian Link; Rolm: CallBridge; IBM: CallPath; AT&T: Passageway; Siemens: Applications Connectivity Link (ACL); Mitel: NeVaDa (Networked Voice and Data). |

*Figure 5-27*   Data and Data/Voice Integration PBX Features and Services

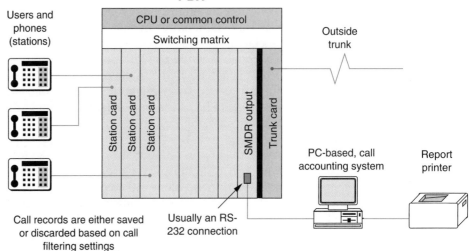

*Figure 5-28*   Call Accounting Systems Installation

features on PBXs but may be purchased separately from either the PBX vendor or third-party manufacturers. Sometimes these services are available as a combination of specialized PC boards and associated TAPI or TSAPI compliant software. Figure 5-29 lists and describes a few of the more popular auxiliary PBX systems.

| Service/Device | Description |
| --- | --- |
| **Automated Attendant** | A recorded message works with a touch-tone phone that requests callers to press the number of the extension they wish to reach. Those wishing to speak to an operator are transferred. |
| **Voice Mail** | Voice mail systems can vary widely in cost and sophistication. After recording an initial message for someone, voice mail systems may allow the voice mail to be handled like a written phone message. It can be forwarded, copied, appended to, saved, recalled, or deleted. |
| **Voice Response Units Interactive Voice Response** | Menu selections are offered to callers who use the touch pad to navigate through menu selections. Some answering machines include VRUs that allow the owner to check for messages remotely. Banks allows customers to make account inquiries and transactions via VRUs and airlines provide arrival and departure information via VRUs. |
| **Voice Processor** | Performs same basic functions as VRU but may also provide additional services based on voice response, speech recognition or tone detection. |
| **Voice Server** | A LAN based server stores, processes and delivers digitized voice messages. Often used as the processing and storage component of a voice mail system. |
| **Music/Ads on Hold** | When customers are put on hold, music plays, or alternatively, a tape-recorded sales message interrupts periodically with messages such as, "Your call is important to us, please stay on the line." |

*Figure 5-29*   Auxiliary Voice-Related Services/Devices

## Computer Telephony Integration (CTI)

**CTI** or **computer telephony integration** seeks to integrate the two most common productivity devices, the computer and the telephone, to enable increased productivity not otherwise possible by using the two devices in a nonintegrated fashion. CTI is not a single application, but an ever-widening array of possibilities spawned by the integration of telephony and computing. Figure 5-30 briefly describes some of the sub-categories of CTI applications.

**CTI Architectures**    Computer telephony integration is commonly implemented in one of the following three architectures:

- PBX-to-host interfaces
- Desktop CTI
- Client/server CTI

| CTI Application Category | Application Description |
| --- | --- |
| **Call Control** | • Using computer-based applications ,users are more easily able to use all of the features of their phone system or PBX, especially the more complicated but seldom used features.<br>• Includes use of features like on-line phone books, auto-dialing, click-and-point conference calls, on-line display and processing of voice mail messages. |
| **Automated Attendant** | • This allows callers to direct calls to a desired individual at a given business without necessarily knowing their extension number. |
| **Automated Call Distribution** | • Used primarily in call centers staffed by large numbers of customer service agents, incoming calls are automatically distributed to the first available rep, or in some cases, the rep that serves a given geographic region as automatically determined by the computer based on the incoming phone number. |
| **Audiotex** | • These systems deliver audio information to callers based on responses on the touch-tone keypad to prerecorded questions. Primarily used for information hotlines. |
| **Fax-On-Demand** | • By combining computer-based faxing with interactive voice response, users can dial in and request that specific information be faxed to their fax machine. |
| **Interactive Voice Response** | • Interactive Voice Response systems differ from audiotex systems in that IVR systems support on-line transaction processing rather than just information hotline applications. As an example, banks use IVR systems to allow users to transfer funds between accounts by using only a touch-tone phone. |
| **Outbound Dialing** | • Also known as **Predictive Dialing,** this merger of computing and telephony uses a database of phone numbers, automatically dials those numbers, recognizes when calls are answered by people, and quickly passes those calls to available agents. |
| **Unified Messaging** | • Perhaps the most interesting for the LAN-based user, unified messaging, also known as the **Universal In-Box** will allow voice mail, e-mail, faxes, and pager messages to all be displayed on a single graphical screen. Messages can then be forwarded, deleted, or replied to easily in point and click fashion. Waiting calls can also be displayed in the same Universal In-Box. |

*Figure 5-30*    Computer Telephony Integration Functionality

Traditionally, computer telephony integration was achieved by linking mainframes to PBX via proprietary PBX-to-host interfaces. Applications were required to be compatible with both the model of mainframe computer and PBX installed. In many cases, these systems actually linked to an ancillary device known as an **ACD** or **automatic call distribution** unit. These systems were very expensive and were usually only employed in large customer service call centers. In this CTI architecture, all phones are controlled by the CTI application running on the mainframe computer.

Desktop CTI, also known as **first-party call control** is a much less expensive and simpler alternative to the PBX-to-host interface architecture. In this CTI architecture, individual PCs are equipped with telephony boards and associated call control software. Each desktop CTI-equipped PC controls only the phone to which it is directly attached. There is no overall automatic call distribution across multiple agents and their phones, and there is no sharing of call-related data among the desktop CTI PCs.

Finally, client/server CTI offers the overall shared control of the PBX-to-host CTI architecture at a cost much closer to the desktop CTI architecture. In this CTI architecture, a CTI server computer interfaces to the PBX or ACD to provide overall system management while individual client-based CTI applications execute on multiple client PCs. The advantage to such an architecture is that multiple CTI applications on multiple client PCs can share the information supplied by the single CTI server. Figure 5-31 illustrates the various CTI architectures.

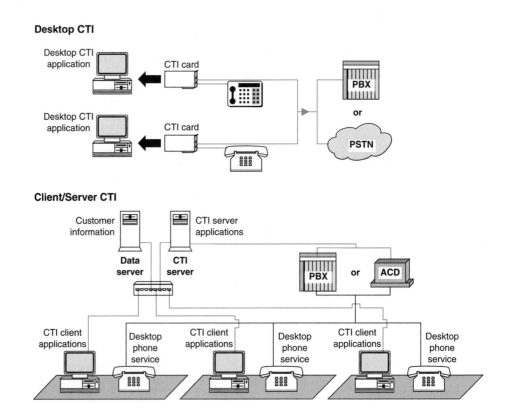

*Figure 5-31*   CTI Architectures

## SUMMARY

Network analysts must be qualified to design networks that are capable of carrying voice as well as data. Before designing such networks, it is essential for the network analyst to understand the nature of voice signals, as well as how voice signals can be processed and integrated into a cohesive network with data transmissions.

Voice bandwidth on the analog Public Switched Telephone Network (PSTN) is limited to 3,100 Hz. In order to combine voice with data over a single transmission link, voice signals must first be digitized. Pulse code modulation or one of its derivatives are the most popular voice digitization techniques. Depending on voice compression algorithms employed, digitized voice requires between 64 Kbps and 8 Kbps of bandwidth.

The voice network is comprised of a hierarchy of switching offices designed to offer fast, reliable service. Switches are able to communicate with each other via a common language known as Signaling System 7. End-users are able to now use SS7 to monitor and control their carrier-based transmission circuits through the Advanced Intelligent Network

While traditional switched services still carry the majority of telephone calls today, newer data network based alternatives have the potential to replace traditional telephony solutions. Using CODECs to encode an analog voice conversation into data packets, these alternatives promise to greatly reduce the cost of long distance calls while increasing the ability to integrate telephone service into computing infrastructures.

While these data network based alternatives can operate directly over data services such as frame relay and ATM, the leading alternative is to simply encode the data into IP datagrams that can be sent across any underlying data network. Technologies used to implement this vision include H.323 and SIP.

One of the fastest growing areas of telephony is wireless telephony. Using a cellular approach where a user can be handed off between towers, wireless telephony systems provide a seamless means of placing calls from mobile phones.

Where the cellular system was predominately analog under the AMPS standard, it has now evolved into digital networks using TDMA, GSM, and CDMA. These digital networks offer improved voice call quality while adding the ability to offer additional services such as wireless data transmission.

Modern wireless data transmission technologies are most commonly based on GSM/GPRS or CDMA/1xRTT. These 2.5G networks offer data speeds up to 100 Kbps in an "always on" mode. Newer 3G networks have the potential of greatly increasing data rates.

The PBX is the voice server or switch that links users' phones with their intended destinations. Today's PBXs have evolved from proprietary monolithic architectures to open, standards-based architectures.

PBXs are being increasingly seen as a specialized server for distributed client/server information systems. Computer telephony integration seeks to optimize the use of the telephone and the desktop computer by being able to share the information and functionality offered by each. Standardized APIs and PBX-to-host interfaces are required if CTI is to ever reach its full potential.

## KEY TERMS

| | | |
|---|---|---|
| 1xRTT | automatic call distribution | Class 4 toll center |
| 3G | call accounting systems | Class 5 office |
| ACD | CDMA | CO |
| adaptive pulse code modulation | CDPD | code division multiple access |
| ADPCM | central office | codec |
| advanced mobile phone service | Class 1 regional carrier | computer telephony integration |
| alternate billing service | Class 2 sectional center | CTI |
| AMPS | Class 3 primary center | custom local area signaling service |

dial tone
digital cellular
digital signal processors
DSP
DTMF
dual tone multi-frequency
EDGE
enhanced 800 services
enhanced throughput cellular
ETC
EV-DO
first party call control
global system for mobile
    communication
GPRS
GSM
H.323
in-band signaling
intelligent call processing
inter-exchange carrier
inter-office signaling
Intranet
landline telephone network
last mile
line cards
local loop
MNP-10 adverse channel
    enhancements

mobile telephone switching office
MTSO
out-of-band signaling
PAM
PBX
PCM
PDM
personal handyphone system
personal phone number
PHS
plain old telephone system
point of presence
POP
port cards
POTS
PPM
PPN
private branch exchange
PSTN
public switched telephone
    network
pulse amplitude modulation
pulse duration modulation
pulse position modulation
pulse width modulation
pulses
PWM
    pulse code modulation

session initiation protocol
signaling System 7
SIP
SMDR (station message detail
    recording)
SS7
station cards
switching matrix
system signaling
tandem office
TDMA
telephone switch
time division multiple access
toll quality
touch-tone
trunk cards
voice compression
voice digitization
voice gateway
voice over IP
voice/data multiplexers
VOIP
wireless WAN services

## REVIEW QUESTIONS

1. Why is it important for network analysts to be qualified to design voice networks?
2. How do the sound waves of the human voice actually get transferred onto and off of the voice network?
3. What is DTMF and what are its potential uses beyond assisting in completing a call?
4. What are the differences between the various voice digitization techniques?
5. How does PCM differ from ADPCM in terms of bandwidth requirements?
6. How is voice compression accomplished? What technology is involved?
7. What is the business motivation for voice compression? What is the potential trade-off?
8. What is the voice network hierarchy and what are the fundamental implications of such a hierarchical design?
9. What is out-of band signaling and of what importance is such a technical ability in terms of emerging network services?
10. Why might a voice conversation not be totally transmitted via analog transmission even if the source and destination loops are analog?

11. How does sampling rate in voice digitization relate to the quality of the transmitted voice signal?
12. How does ADPCM accomplish digitized voice transmission in less than 64 Kbps?
13. Why is DS-0 considered a standard circuit for transmission of digitized voice?
14. How does PCM differ from other voice digitization techniques such as PAM?
15. What are the benefits of PCM over other voice digitization methods?
16. What is the role of a CODEC in voice digitization?
17. Compare the bandwidth of the PSTN with that of human hearing.
18. What is a channel bank?
19. What is toll quality and how is it related to ADPCM?
20. Show the mathematical proof of why a T-1 circuit is 1.544 Mbps.
21. What is a Signaling System?
22. What is the AIN and what role does SS7 play in such a network?
23. What is a tandem office?
24. What is required to transmit voice over the Internet?

25. What are some important features of VOIP client software?
26. Differentiate between H.323 and SIP.
27. Does VOIP require a computer be in place at each end of the call?
28. Why is quality of service so important to VOIP?
29. What is a voice gateway?
30. How is voice compression related to bandwidth requirements and delay?
31. What characteristic of frame relay must be overcome for effective voice transmission?
32. What are some of the issues surrounding voice over ATM?
33. What is the difference between CBR and VBR for voice over ATM?
34. Differentiate between Peak voice bit rate and guaranteed voice bit rate.
35. How does a FRAD assist in optimizing voice transmission over frame relay?
36. In terms of wireless phones, what is a cell? How do cells inter-relate?
37. What are the key limitations of AMPS?
38. Differentiate between analog and digital cellular transmission systems in terms of data transfer capabilities and equipment requirements
39. Differentiate between TDMA and CDMA.
40. How is the notion of a personal phone number central to PCS and what changes in thinking about phone systems does it require?
41. What is GSM?
42. List six wireless data standards and their maximum speeds.
43. What are the requirements for a true 3G wireless network?
44. Compare and contrast GPRS and 1xRTT.
45. Compare and contrast EDGE and EV-DO.
46. What are the major architectural elements of a PBX?
47. Describe the basic architecture of a PBX. How is it like and unlike the switch in a CO?
48. What are some of the issues surrounding interoperability of PBXs from various vendors?
49. What are some important architectural trends in PBX design and what is the driving force behind these trends?
50. Explain how voice transmission can be integrated with computers to produce a service known as computer telephony integration.
51. What are some of the interoperability issues surrounding CTI?
52. How can the cost of call accounting systems be justified?
53. What are some the PBX features required to support a call accounting system?
54. What are some practical business applications of CTI?
55. What are some potential uses of voice processing or interactive voice response?

**Case Study:** For a business case study and questions on voice communication concepts and technology, go to www.wiley.com/college/goldman.

CHAPTER **6**

# WIDE AREA NETWORKING CONCEPTS, ARCHITECTURES, AND SERVICES

*Concepts Reinforced*

OSI model                  Top-down model
Multiplexing               Error detection and correction
Switching

*Concepts Introduced*

Wide area network architecture     Wide area network design
Wide area network services         T-1 services
Network convergence                Frame relay
X.25                               MPLS
SONET
Broadband transmission
  architectures

**OBJECTIVES**

After mastering the material in this chapter, you should:

1. Understand the drivers and issues surrounding WAN design and network convergence.

2. Understand the relationship between business motivation and available technology in creating wide area networking solutions.

3. Understand the advantages and limitations of WAN technologies.

4. Understand the importance of standards as applied to wide area networking.

5. Understand the interrelationships and dependencies of WAN architecture components.

6. Understand the digital services hierarchy.

7. Understand the principles of SONET and the synchronous digital hierarchy.

8. Understand frame relay and cell relay switching methodologies.

9. Be able to compare and contrast X.25 and frame relay.

10. Be able to compare and contrast ATM and MPLS.

## ■ INTRODUCTION

When network services must be distributed over large geographic areas, it is essential to have an understanding of the telecommunication systems on which such distribution depends. One of the most significant differences between wide area networks (WANs) and the local area networks (LANs) that were studied in previous chapters is the general dependency on third-party carriers to provide these transmission services. This chapter focuses on the telecommunication services offered by exchange carriers and the underlying transmission and switching technologies that enable them.

## ■ BUSINESS PRINCIPLES OF WIDE AREA NETWORKING

Wide area networking provides a means of connecting locations across large geographical distances. In order to master the services and technologies used in wide area networking, an understanding of the underlying business issues and architectures must be developed.

In order to better understand the technical principles of wide area networking, it is important to first comprehend the business drivers associated with this field of study. As in most areas of business, maximizing the impact of technology investments is essential. Figure 6-1 illustrates the underlying business motivation for wide area networking. Given five disparate systems that need to communicate over a long distance, there are two possible physical configurations. Either a dedicated WAN link can be utilized for each system-to-system connection or a single WAN link can be employed to provide communication between each of the five systems. Research indicates that WAN traffic nearly doubles annually; however, enterprise budgets for WAN services increase at an average rate of less than 10 percent annually. Given this information, a single WAN link between each of the five systems (Option B) is a wise business decision.

### Network Convergence

The number one WAN design consideration today is **network convergence.** Network convergence is the merging (or converging) of data, voice, and video traffic onto a single network architecture with as few layers as possible. In general, the more layers in the network architecture, the more equipment that is required to implement the end-to end solution. The addition of equipment to the network increases the overall cost of the telecommunications system and the **Capital Expense (CAPEX)** incurred to purchase the necessary hardware.

The amount of telecommunication hardware utilized in the network solution is also directly related to the amount of personnel required to implement the solution, manage it, and maintain it throughout its lifetime. Ultimately, network convergence is driven by senior IT management in an effort to reduce costs associated with the

**A.  Dedicated Multiple Wide Area System to System Connections**

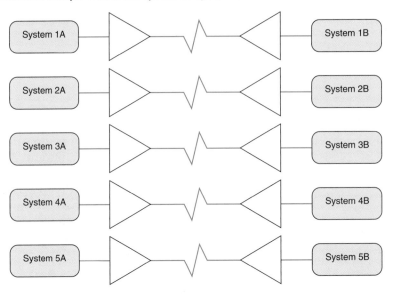

**B.  Single Wide Area Link Shared to Provide Multiple System to System Connections**

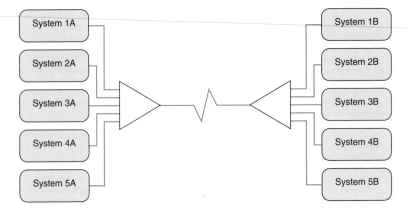

*Figure 6-1*    WAN Technical Principles Are Motivated by Business Principles

telecommunications systems that enable business and generate revenue. This, in turn, increases long-term profitability of the organization as the telecommunications system is amortized over time.

The key business drivers behind network convergence include:

- The volume of Internet traffic in the United States has surpassed the volume of voice traffic; however, much of the legacy voice systems are already paid for.

- An innovative market such as Internet telephony, which is expected to generate $3–4 billion by 2004, provides opportunities for companies to generate new revenue streams.

- The Telecommunications Act of 1996 increased competition among network service providers.

- Subscribers desire *one-stop shopping* for converged network services.

Managerial
Perspective

### NETWORK CONVERGENCE BOTTOM LINE

Network convergence strategies should start with a solid business case and not be driven by vendors trying to create a market for their newest technologies and services. It is essential that organizations have a clear understanding of what they hope to gain from network convergence, their current network architecture, and their traffic patterns before migrating to a converged telecommunications system. Without accurate documentation of the existing network architecture, and the various levels of telecommunications network hierarchy, it is impossible to develop a convergence migration strategy to eliminate unnecessary levels. Without a clear understanding of user requirements and associated traffic patterns, it will be impossible to assess the return on an investment in network convergence.

## Network Design Principles

Exercising principles of network convergence to share a WAN link would obviously lead to a reduction in network cost. Cost reduction is one design principle of wide area networking; however, there are numerous others, including the following:

- Performance

- Cost reduction

- Security/auditing

- Availability/reliability

- Manageability and monitoring

- Quality of service/class of service

- Support for business recovery planning

Optimizing the design for one of these principles may lead to a diminished focus on other network design principles. For example, if a WAN is to be optimized for availability and performance, it will not be optimized for cost. Senior business and technical managers typically decide which network design principles will take priority.

## ■ WIDE AREA NETWORK ARCHITECTURE

The major segments and interrelationships of overall wide area network architecture are defined in Figure 6-2. This is used to illustrate the need for existing and emerging wide area network technologies and services.

As can be seen in Figure 6-2, the **user demands** of businesses and residential customers are the driving force behind the evolution of wide area **network services.** The

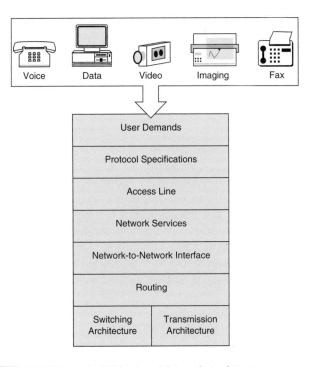

*Figure 6-2*   Major Components of a Wide Area Network Architecture

companies that offer these services are in business to generate profit by implementing network architectures that enable the desired WAN services at the lowest possible cost.

In order for users to take advantage of these network services, standardized **interface specifications** must be developed to ensure interoperability among different manufacturer's end-user equipment. For example, the T-1 protocol specification ensures that users can purchase T-1 multiplexers from any manufacturer and ensure connectivity to a circuit-switched network service. Once the user payload is encapsulated within a standard protocol specification, carrier network services can be accessed via an appropriately sized **access line** running from the customer to the entry-point or gateway to the carrier's network.

In order to assure transparent delivery of network services to customers, regardless of geographic location, several carrier architectures may need to interoperate. Customer traffic may be handed off between several carrier networks to provide end-to-end service for a given customer. The transparent interoperability of network services from different carriers requires standardized **network-to-network interfaces.**

**Switching architectures,** such as circuit switching or packet switching, assure the proper routing of information (data, voice, video, etc.) from source to destination. **Transmission architectures** provide the circuits or data highways over which the information is actually delivered. In wide area networks, the copper, fiber, microwave, and satellite links constitute the transmission architecture of wide area networks. The central-office switches that build connections from source to destination utilizing these transmission circuits constitute the switching architecture of the wide area network. The underlying infrastructure of the carrier networks enables the provisioning of WAN services to customers. The combination of switching architecture and transmission architecture that make up this infrastructure is also known as the **network architecture.**

## ■ WIDE AREA NETWORKING TRANSMISSION

There are two main physical WAN transmission techniques in use today: T-1 and SONET/SDH.

### T-1

Transmission standards are required to define the size and structure of digital communications links. This, in turn, enables connectivity between carriers and a standard means of network access for customers. The standard for digital transmission circuits in North America is known as a **T-1** with a bandwidth of 1.544 Mbps. The **E-1** standard for digital transmission utilized in other parts of the world provides a bandwidth of 2.048 Mbps.

**T-1 Framing**    The T-1 transmission standard is divided into twenty-four 64 Kbps channels, each of which is known as a DS-0. In order to allow more flexible use of the 1.544 Mbps of bandwidth, some of these twenty-four channels may be used for voice while others are used for data. Each channel consists of a group of 8 bits known as a **time slot.** Each time slot represents one voice sample or a byte of data to be transmitted through the T-1 switching architecture using time division multiplexing (TDM) techniques. A T-1 **frame** consists of a framing bit and twenty-four DS-0 channels, each containing 8 bits, for a total of 193 bits per frame. The **framing bits** provide a mechanism for maintaining synchronization between T-1 switching devices while allowing frames to be identified as they are transmitted and received in rapid succession. This frame structure is illustrated in Figure 6-3. For a review of TDM techniques refer to chapter 2.

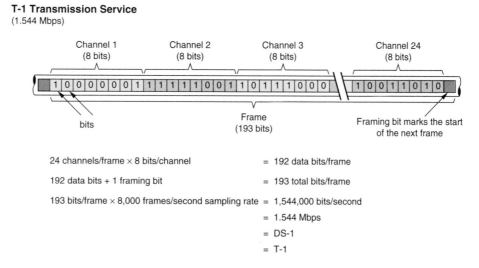

**T-1 Transmission Service**
(1.544 Mbps)

24 channels/frame × 8 bits/channel = 192 data bits/frame

192 data bits + 1 framing bit = 193 total bits/frame

193 bits/frame × 8,000 frames/second sampling rate = 1,544,000 bits/second

= 1.544 Mbps

= DS-1

= T-1

*Figure 6-3*    T-1 Frame Layout

As detailed in chapter 5, **pulse code modulation (PCM)** is used in the US to convert analog voice calls to digital signals. Using PCM, each voice sample is encoded with a byte-value proportionate to the amplitude of the analog voice signal. Each analog voice signal is sampled 8,000 times per second in order to assure its quality when converted back to an analog signal. This rate of 8,000 samples per second was determined by Nyquist sampling theory; therefore, the highest analog frequency passed through the low-pass filter must be less than 4 KHz or aliasing would occur. Since each voice sample requires eight bits to represent its amplitude, and the sample rate is 8,000 samples per second, 64 Kbps is the required transmission bandwidth for an analog signal digitized via PCM. This 64 Kbps bandwidth is the basis for the T-1 transmission standard.

The T-1 transmission standard groups subsequent frames for synchronization and management purposes. A group of twelve frames is known as a **superframe,** while a group of twenty-four frames is known as an **extended superframe (ESF).** Superframes and extended superframes are both illustrated in Figure 6-4. Within a **superframe,** the framing bits are primarily used to identify the beginning of a frame. However, techniques have been developed to utilize sequential framing bits into meaningful arrangements that provide management and error control capabilities for the T-1 transmission service. This development has been implemented with ESF systems to overcome the weakness of **robbed-bit signaling,** which was employed by older T-1 switching systems that made use of superframing. This older T-1 signaling technique "robbed" the least significant bit of each DS-0 in frames 6 and 12 of the superframe, which resulted in 56 Kbps of guaranteed bandwidth per channel.

**Digital Service Hierarchy**   The 1.544 Mbps standard is part of a hierarchy of standards known as the **digital service hierarchy,** or **DS** standards. The digital service standards are independent of the standards for transmission, which provide the

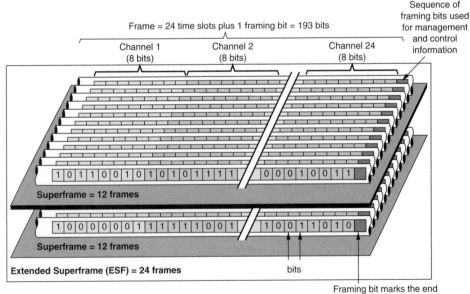

*Figure 6-4*   Superframes and Extended Superframes

bandwidth on the circuit. Technically speaking, a DS-1 is not the same as T-1 but the two terms are often used interchangeably. To be exact, a **T-1** transmission service modulates a **DS-1** signal on two twisted pair of wires. Figure 6-5 summarizes the digital service hierarchy for North America as well as the CCITT Standards for international digital services. Although numerous transmission services are listed in Figure 6-5, T-1 and T-3 are by far the most common service levels delivered. Although T-1 service is most often delivered via four copper wires (two twisted pair) and T-3 service is most commonly delivered via optical fiber, coaxial cable can be found in some older network implementations.

**T-1 Architecture**   Before the advent of high-speed packet services or high speed-modems, which worked over dial-up (circuit-switched) lines, leased lines were the only available means of high-speed data transfer over a wide area network. Network managers did their best to get the most out of these relatively expensive leased lines through the use of statistical time division multiplexers (STDM), as detailed in chapter 2. Although T-1 transmission services predate newer WAN services, they are still commonly used for corporate office connectivity to local-exchange networks. The local-exchange carrier (LEC) will either connect this circuit to an Internet service provider (ISP) or trunk the voice channels, contained within the T-1, to the public switched telephone network (PSTN).

T-1 circuits are examples of leased or private communication lines. As a dedicated service, the T-1 differs from circuit-switched lines in several ways: Leased lines do not provide dial tone; the circuit should remain up and operational at all

**Digital Service Hierarchy**

| Digital Service Level | Number of Voice Channels | Transmission Rate | Corresponding Transmission Service |
|---|---|---|---|
| DS-0 | 1 | 64 Kbps | DS-0 |
| DS-1 | 24 | 1.544 Mbps | T-1 |
| DS-1C | 48 | 3.152 Mbps | T-1C |
| DS-2 | 96 | 6.312 Mbps | T-2 |
| DS-3 | 672 | 44.736 Mbps | T-3 |
| DS-4 | 4,032 | 274.176 Mbps | T-4 |

**CCITT Digital Hierarchy**

| Digital Service Level | Number of Voice Channels | Transmission Rate | Corresponding Transmission Service |
|---|---|---|---|
| 1 | 30 | 2.048 Mbps | E-1 |
| 2 | 120 | 8.448 Mbps | E-2 |
| 3 | 480 | 34.368 Mbps | E-3 |
| 4 | 1,920 | 139.264 Mbps | E-4 |
| 5 | 7,680 | 565.148 Mbps | E-5 |

*Figure 6-5*   Digital Service Hierarchy and CCITT Standards

times. Since leased-line services are billed at a flat monthly rate regardless of usage, it is for important to cost-justify this expense with a sufficient amount of business-critical traffic during normal hours of operation. It should be of no surprise that the cost of leased-line services increases with the bandwidth provided. Another major difference between leased lines and circuit-switched connections becomes evident in the means by which they are established. Whereas circuit-switched connections can be established in a matter of seconds, leased lines take the LEC much longer to provision. In most cases, a 4- to 6-week lead time is required for the installation of a leased line.

In some cases, multiple 64 Kbps channels within a T-1 transport circuit are provided to a customer that does not require the full T-1 bandwidth. A service that offers such capability is known as **Fractional T-1** or **FT-1.** A FT-1 only provides a subset of the twenty-four available DS-0s within a T-1. In truth, the full T-1 circuit must be physically delivered to the customer premises; however. The customer only pays for the number of 64 Kbps channels that are enabled. A traffic analysis performed by the customer would provide an indication of the bandwidth required for the application. The ability of FT-1 to provide the bandwidth necessary for customer applications, in 64 Kbps increments, has made it very attractive service offering. Businesses and enterprise corporations alike have made use of FT-1 to provide physical transmission for frame-relay access networks with low bit-rate requirements.

**T-1 Technology**    In order to access a T-1 service offered by a local-exchange carrier, customers may use a variety of T-1 technologies. The fundamental piece of T-1 hardware is the **T-1 CSU/DSU** (channel service unit/data service unit). This device interfaces directly to the carrier's termination of the T-1 service at the customer premises. A T-1 is commonly delivered as a four-wire circuit (two wires for transmit and two for receive) physically terminated with a male **RJ-48c** connector. Most T-1 CSU/DSUs provide the corresponding RJ-48c female connector to interface with the male counterpart provided by the carrier. The T-1 CSU/DSU will transfer the 1.544 Mbps of bandwidth to local devices such as routers, PBXs, or channel banks over high-speed connections such as V.35, RS-530, RS-449, or Ethernet that are provided on the customer side of the CSU/DSU. Because the T-1 CSU/DSU plays such an important role in a corporation's wide area network, companies are often able to communicate status and alarm information to network management systems via the simple network management protocol (SNMP). For more information on SNMP, please refer to chapter 11.

**T-1 multiplexers** are able to aggregate low-speed data or voice channels into an aggregate T-1 link. T-1 multiplexers often have a built-in CSU/DSU to enable them to connect directly to the carrier. On the customer (tributary) side, all data input channels are required to be in a digital format that adheres to established transmission standards such as RS-232, RS-449, or V.35. Voice input to a T-1 multiplexer may be digitized with Foreign Exchange Office (FXO) or Foreign Exchange Station (FXS) tributary cards prior to being assigned to a DS-O channel. **Fractional T-1 multiplexers** are able to use less than the full 1.544 Mbps of composite T-1 output bandwidth. It makes good business sense to save on monthly leased-line charges when less than 1.544 Mbps of aggregate bandwidth is sufficient for network access. A **T-1 inverse multiplexer (IMUX)** is able to combine multiple T-1 output lines to provide high bandwidth requirements for such applications as LAN-to-LAN communication via routers or high quality videoconferencing. Currently, business use of inverse multiplexing is most commonly implemented within end systems such as IP routers or ATM switches.

Traditionally a special type of T-1 multiplexer, known as a T-1 **Channel Bank,** was used to digitize analog voice services and multiplex them into the DS-0 channels of a T-1 frame. These devices are commonly found in central office (CO) switching facilities owned and operated by local exchange carriers (LEC). With the Telecomm Act of 1996, and the increased competition that was created in the LEC market, incumbent local exchange carriers (ILEC) needed a means of providing a wider variety of services to compete with competitive local exchange carriers (CLEC). In doing so, vendors were pressured to develop additional cards that could be utilized within the T-1 channel bank. As a result, ISDN and DSL cards were created for use in these existing chassis. As a result, the line between the functionality provided by a T-1 channel bank and a T-1 multiplexer has become less distinct.

Currently, a T-1 channel bank is best defined as an open chassis-based piece of equipment with built-in CSU/DSUs to which a variety of data and voice channel cards can be flexibly added. The line-side of a T-1 channel bank typically provides a single T-1 interface; however, newer channel banks can provide M1-3 functionality to multiplex 28 T-1 services into an aggregate T-3.

Finally, companies wishing to build their own private wide area networks can employ T-1 switches. T-1 switches are able to switch entire T-1s or particular DS0s among and between T-1 interfaces. This provides flexibility in the delivery of voice and data to geographically dispersed corporate locations. Figure 6-6 illustrates the implementation of a variety of T-1 technology.

## SONET and SDH

**SONET (synchronous optical network)** is an optical transmission service that makes use of TDM techniques to deliver bandwidth in a similar manner as the T-1

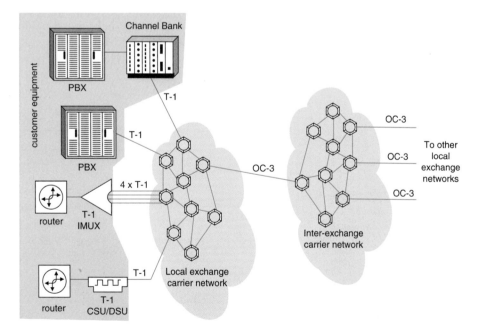

*Figure 6-6*   T-1 Technology Implementation

transmission service. The primary difference between T-1 and SONET transmission services is the higher transmission capacity of SONET due to its fiber optic media and the slightly different framing techniques used to create channels from this higher transmission capacity. SONET is defined by ANSI (American National Standards Institute) in the T1.105 and T1.106 standards.

Just as the digital service hierarchy defined levels of service for traditional digital services, optical transmission has its own hierarchy of service levels for both North American and international regions. In the United States, SONET is used; however, international countries use the **synchronous digital hierarchy** (**SDH**). Whereas the SONET hierarchy makes use of synchronous transport signals (STS), the SDH hierarchy makes use of synchronous transport modules (STM). These two service hierarchies utilize the same data rates, but at different service levels. Fortunately, service levels of the same transmission rate allow for interoperability between North American and international network systems.

As the North American Digital Signal Hierarchy utilized T-carrier levels for electrical transmission, optical transmission in North America is categorized by **optical carrier** (**OC**) levels. Accordingly, an STS-192 signal is called an OC-192 once a light source has been modulated with the STS and coupled to a fiber optic transmission media.

**SONET Framing**   In many ways, SONET framing is identical to T-1 framing. The basic purpose of each is to establish markers with which to identify individual channels. Because of the higher base speed of SONET (51.84 Mbps in an OC-1 vs. 1.544 Mbps in a T-1) and the potential for sophisticated mixed-media services, more overhead is reserved surrounding each frame than the single bit reserved per 193 bytes in a T-1 frame.

Rather than fitting twenty-four channels into a frame delineated by a single framing bit, a SONET frame or **row** is delineated by 3 octets of overhead for control information followed by 87 octets of payload. Nine of these 90 octet rows are grouped together to form a **SONET frame.** The 87 octets of payload per row in each of the time rows or the Superframe is known as the **synchronous payload envelope,** or **SPE.** The electrical equivalent of the **OC-1,** the optical SONET frame standard is known as the **STS-1** or **synchronous transport signal.** The SONET frame structure is illustrated in Figure 6-8.

**SONET and SDH Transmission Rates**

| SONET/SDH Level | Transmission Rate | |
|---|---:|---|
| STS-1/STM-0 | 51.84 | Mbps |
| STS-3/STM-1 | 155.52 | Mbps |
| STS-12/STM-4 | 622.08 | Mbps |
| STS-48/STM-16 | 2.488 | Gbps |
| STS-192/STM-64 | 9.953 | Gbps |
| STS-768/STM-256 | 39.81 | Gbps |

*Figure 6-7*   SONET and SDH Transmission Rates

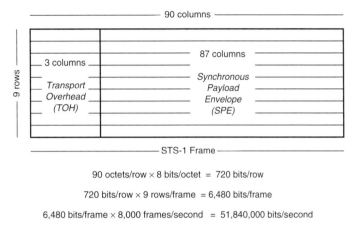

90 octets/row × 8 bits/octet  = 720 bits/row

720 bits/row × 9 rows/frame  = 6,480 bits/frame

6,480 bits/frame × 8,000 frames/second  = 51,840,000 bits/second

*Transfer Rate* of 51.84 Mbits/second

*Figure 6-8*    SONET Framing

**Virtual Tributaries in SONET**    Unlike the T-1 frame with its twenty-four pre-defined 8-bit channels, SONET is flexible in its definition of the use of its payload area. It can map DS-0 (64 Kbps) channels into the payload area just as easily as it can map an entire T-1 (1.544 Mbps). These flexibly defined channels within the payload area are known as **virtual tributaries,** or **VTs.** For instance, a T-1 would be mapped into a virtual tributary standard known as **VT-1.5,** with a bandwidth of 1.728 Mbps; the 1.544 Mbps T-1 combined with the required SONET overhead.

The virtual tributaries of SONET are equivalent to circuit-switched transmission services. In addition to the three octets per row of transport overhead in an OC-1, there is also a variable amount of path overhead imbedded within the SPE to keep track of where each virtual tributary starts within the SPE payload. This path overhead brings the total overhead to about 4 percent before any additional overhead embedded within the SPE payload is considered.

**SONET Architecture**    The architecture of a SONET network is based on a layered hierarchy of transport elements and associated technology. Understanding the differences between these various SONET transport elements is vital to understanding how to build a SONET network and how to decipher the contents of a SONET frame. Figure 6-9 summarizes the characteristics of the various SONET transport elements while Figure 6-10 shows SONET framing with detail as to the overhead associated with each SONET transport element.

Figure 6-10 adds detail to the SONET frame illustrated in Figure 6-8, highlighting where the overhead information for section, line, and path are stored.

**SONET Deployment**    SONET services are currently available within many major metropolitan areas. Accessing such services requires the local carrier to bring the fiber-based ring directly to a corporate location and to assign dedicated bandwidth to each SONET customer. Because of the limited geographic scope of most SONET services, it is most useful for those organizations with a very high bandwidth need (OC-1 to OC-192) between locations located in the SONET service area. Such companies would typically be employing multiple T-3s and looking at SONET as an attractive upgrade path.

| SONET Building Block | Function/Description |
|---|---|
| **Section** | Basic building block of a SONET network. A SECTION is physically built using a single fiber optic cable between two fiber optic transmitter/receiver. A transmitter/receiver is the most basic SONET technology. It is sometimes referred to as an optical repeater or designated as STE (Section Terminating Equipment). All sophisticated SONET technology includes this capability. |
| **Line** | Multiple sections combine to form a SONET LINE. A SONET Line is terminated with LTE (Line Terminating Equipment) such as an add/drop multiplexer. |
| **Path** | Multiple lines combine to form a SONET PATH. A Path is an end-to-end circuit most often terminating in SONET access multiplexers that have channel interfaces to lower speed or digital electronic transmission equipment. |

*Figure 6-9*   Hierarchy of SONET Transport Elements

Add-drop multiplexers, sometimes referred to as broadband bandwidth managers or cross-connect switches, are the customary type of hardware used to access SONET services. Such devices are often capable of adding several T-1 or T-3 digital signals together and converting those combined signals into a single, channelized, optical SONET signal, usually OC-3 or higher. In some cases, ATM switches are equipped with SONET interfaces for direct access to either a local SONET ring or commercial SONET services.

Another key advantage of SONET is the fault tolerance and reliability afforded by its fiber-based architecture. In the event of a network failure, traffic can easily be rerouted. Although numerous SONET architectures are possible, the two principal architectures for SONET deployment are **unidirectional path-switched rings (UPSR)** and **bi-directional line-switched rings (BLSR)**.

In a UPSR environment, all users share transmission capacity around the ring rather than using dedicated segments. UPSRs are most commonly used for in access networks and adhere to Bellcore standard GR-1400. UPSRs provide duplicate,

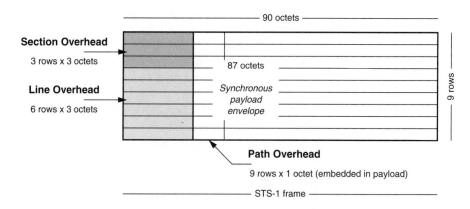

*Figure 6-10*   Section Line and Path Overhead in a SONET Frame

geographically diverse paths for each service, thereby protecting against cable cuts and node failures. As the data signal travels in one direction, a duplicate signal travels in the opposite direction for protection. The system automatically switches to the protection signal if there is a problem with the primary data signal. A UPSR SONET topology is illustrated in Figure 6-11.

In a BLSR environment, each user's traffic is specifically rerouted in the case of a fiber failure. BLSR architectures employ two fiber rings with bi-directional traffic flow with each ring's capacity divided equally (by STS) between working and protection bandwidth. BLSR provides survivability in the event of electronic, node, or cable failure by automatically routing traffic away from faults in as little as 50 ms. Blurs are most commonly used for inter-node, or carrier backbone networks, and adhere to Bellcore standard GR-1230. A BLSR SONET topology is illustrated in Figure 6-12.

**Wavelength Division Multiplexing**   SONET network capacity can be increased substantially using **wavelength division multiplexing.** By transmitting more than one wavelength (color) of light simultaneously on a given single-mode fiber, multiple optical signals, and the data contained therein, can be transmitted simultaneously. Wavelengths are between 50 and 100 GHz apart. When eight or more distinct wavelengths are simultaneously transmitted, the term **DWDM (dense wavelength division multiplexing)** is often used. DWDM should theoretically be able to produce transmission capacity on a single fiber in the Terabit per second (1,000 Gbps) range. Individual DWDM wavelengths are often referred to as **lambdas.**

**Conclusion: So What Is SONET?**   SONET is a service independent transport function that can carry the services of the future such as B-ISDN (Broadband ISDN) or HDTV (high-definition television), as easily as it can carry the circuit-switched traffic of today such as DS-1 and DS-3. It has extensive performance monitoring and fault-location capabilities. For instance, if SONET senses a transmission problem, it can switch traffic to an alternate path in as little as 50 milliseconds (1,000ths of a second). This network survivability is the result of SONET's redundant or dual ring physical architecture. Based on the OC hierarchy of standard optical interfaces, SONET can deliver multi-gigabyte bandwidth transmission capabilities to end users.

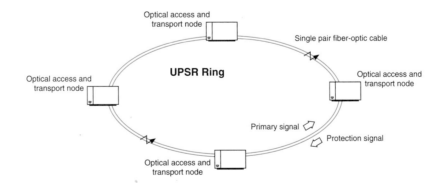

*Figure 6-11*   SONET UPSR Topology

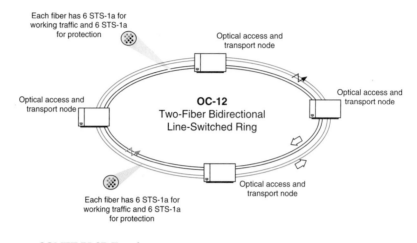

*Figure 6-12*    SONET BLSR Topology

Managerial
Perspective

## SONET AVAILABILITY

SONET availability is currently limited to large metropolitan areas in most cases. SONET availability implies that a high-capacity, dual-ring, fiber-optic cable-based transmission service is available between the customer premises and the carrier central office. SONET services cost about 20 percent more than conventional digital services of identical bandwidth. The benefit of the 20 percent premium is the network survivability offered by SONET's dual-ring architecture. Unless a corporation has identified mission-critical network transmissions requiring fault-tolerant circuits, SONET's benefits might not be worth the added expense.

## ■ WIDE AREA NETWORK SWITCHING

Once the underlying transmission technologies are in place, a means of providing logical connections across the WAN must be developed. Switching of some type or another is necessary in wide area network architectures because the alternative is unthinkable. To explain: Without some type of switching mechanism or architecture, every possible source of data in the world would have to be directly connected to every possible destination of data in the world, not a very likely prospect. Switching allows temporary connections to be established, maintained and terminated between message sources and message destinations, sometime called **sinks** in data communications. There are two primary switching techniques employed: circuit switching and packet switching.

### Circuit Switching

In a circuit-switched network, a switched, dedicated circuit is created to connect the two or more parties, eliminating the need for source and destination address information such as that provided by packetizing techniques explored earlier. The switched dedicated circuit established on circuit switched networks makes it appear to the user of the circuit as if a wire has been run directly between the phones of the calling parties. The physical resources required to create this temporary connection are dedicated to that particular circuit for the duration of the connection. If system usage should increase to the point where insufficient resources are available to create additional connections, users would not get a dial tone.

## Packet Switching

In a packet-switched network, packets of data travel one at a time from the message source to the message destination. A packet-switched network, otherwise known as a public data network (PDN), is represented in network diagrams by a symbol that resembles a cloud. Figure 6-13 illustrates such a symbol as well as the difference between circuit switching and packet switching. The cloud is an appropriate symbol for a packet-switched network because all that is known is that the packet of data goes in one side of the PDN and comes out the other. The physical path that any packet takes may be different than other packets and, in any case, is unknown to the end users. What is beneath the cloud in a packet-switched network is a large number of packet switches that pass packets among themselves as the packets are routed from source to destination.

Remember that packets are specially structured groups of data that include control and address information in addition to the data itself. These packets must be assembled (control and address information added to data) somewhere before entry into the packet switched network and must be subsequently disassembled before delivery of the data to the message destination. This packet assembly and disassembly is done by

**Circuit Switching**

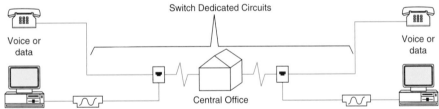

All data or voice travel from source to destination over the *same* physical path

**Packet Switching**

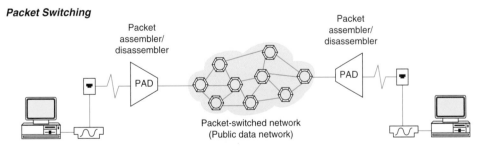

Data enter the packet-switched network one packet at a time;
Packets may take *different* physical paths within packet-switched networks.

*Figure 6-13* Circuit Switching vs. Packet Switching

a device known as a **PAD** or **packet assembler/disassembler.** PADs may be stand-alone devices or may be integrated into specially built modems or multiplexers. These PADs may be located at an end-user location, or may be located at the entry point to the packet-switched data network. The bottom portion of Figure 6-13 illustrates the latter scenario in which the end users employ regular modems to dial-up to the packet-switched network that provides the PADs to properly assemble the packets prior to transmission. This set-up is often more convenient for end users because they can still employ their modem for other dial-up applications as well.

The packet switches illustrated inside the PDN cloud in Figure 6-13 are generically known as **data-switching exchanges** (**DSE**s) or **packet-switching exchanges** (**PSE**s). DSE is the packet-switching equivalent of the DCE and DTE categorization that were first encountered in the study of modems and dial-up transmission.

Another way in which packet switching differs from circuit switching is that as demand for transmission of data increases on a packet-switched network, additional users are not denied access to the packet-switched network. Overall performance of the network may suffer, errors and retransmission may occur, or packets of data may be lost, but all users experience the same degradation of service. This is because, in the case of a packet-switched network, data travel through the network one packet at a time, traveling over any available path within the network rather than waiting for a switched, dedicated path, as in the case of the circuit-switched network.

**Connectionless vs. Connection-Oriented Packet-Switched Services**   In order for any packet switch to process any packet of data bound for anywhere, it is essential that packet address information be included on each packet. Each packet switch then reads and processes each packet by making routing and forwarding decisions based upon the packet's destination address and current network conditions. The full destination address uniquely identifying the ultimate destination of each packet is known as the **global address.**

Because an overall data message is broken up into numerous pieces by the packet assembler, these message pieces may actually arrive out of order at the message destination due to the speed and condition of the alternate paths within the packet-switched network over which these message pieces (packets) traveled. The data message must be pieced back together in proper order by the destination PAD before final transmission to the destination address. These self-sufficient packets containing full source and destination address information plus a message segment are known as *datagrams.* Figure 6-14 illustrates this packet-switched network phenomenon.

A switching methodology in which each datagram is handled and routed to its ultimate destination on an individual basis resulting in the possibility of packets traveling over a variety of physical paths on the way to their destination is known as a **connectionless** packet network. It is called *connectionless* because packets do not follow one another, in order, down a particular path through the network.

There are no error-detection or flow-control techniques applied by a datagram-based or connectionless packet switched network. Such a network would depend on end-user devices (PCs, modems, communication software) to provide adequate error control and flow control. Because datagrams are sent along multiple possible paths to the destination address, there is no guarantee of their safe arrival. This lack of inherent error-detection or flow-control abilities is the reason that connectionless packet networks are also known as *unreliable* packet networks.

*Virtual Circuits*   In contrast to the connectionless packet networks, **connection-oriented** or *reliable* packet networks establish **virtual circuits** enabling message

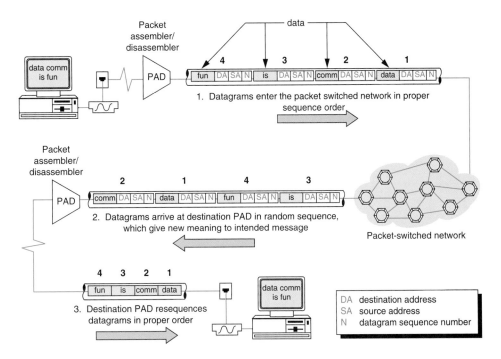

*Figure 6-14*  Datagram Delivery on a Packet Switched Network

packets to follow one another, in sequence, down the same connection or physical circuit. This connection from source to destination is set up by special packets known as **call set-up packets.** Once the call-set up packets have determined the best path from the source to the destination and established the virtual circuit, the message-bearing packets follow one another in sequence along the virtual circuit from source to destination.

Unlike a connectionless service, a connection-oriented service, because of the establishment of the virtual circuit, can offer checksum error-detection with ACK/NAK retransmission control and flow control. The packet network itself can offer these services; there is no need to depend on the end-user devices. Because connection-oriented packets all follow the same path, or **logical channel,** from source to destination, they do not require the full global addressing on each packet, as in the case of the connectionless datagram networks. Instead, connection-oriented network packets include an abbreviated **logical channel number,** or **LCN,** with each packet. The details that relate the LCN to a physical circuit consisting of an actual series of specific packet switches within the packet switched network are stored in a **virtual circuit table.**

Connection-oriented packet switching networks actually define two types of virtual circuits: **switched virtual circuits** (**SVC**) and **permanent virtual circuits** (**PVC**). The switched virtual circuit connection is terminated when the complete message has been sent and a special **clear request packet** causes all switched virtual circuit table entries related to this connection to be erased. The virtual circuit table of the permanent virtual circuit is not erased, making the PVC the equivalent of a "virtual" circuit-switched leased line.

Although the use of LCNs (as opposed to full global addressing) reduces overhead in connection-oriented packet networks, the following elements add to that overhead:

- Connection set-up

- Network-based, point-to-point error detection and flow control

Figure 6-15 contrasts the overhead of connectionless with connection-oriented packet-switched networks, as well as several other key differentiating criteria.

Managerial
Perspective

## A BUSINESS PERSPECTIVE ON CIRCUIT VS. PACKET SWITCHING

If the top-down model were applied to an analysis of possible switching methodologies, circuit switching and packet switching could be properly placed on either the network or technology layers. In either case, in order to make the proper switching methodology decision, the top-down model layer directly above the network layer—namely, the data layer—must be thoroughly examined. This raises key questions:

- What is the nature of the data to be transmitted, and which switching methodology will best support these data characteristics?

The first data-related criterion to examine is the data source:

- What is the nature of the application program (application layer) that will produce this data?

- Is the application program transaction-oriented or more batch update or file-oriented in nature?

A transaction-oriented program, producing what is sometimes called *interactive data,* is characterized by short bursts of data followed by variable-length pauses due to users reading screen prompts or pausing between transactions. This transaction-oriented traffic, best categorized by bursty banking transactions at an Automatic Teller Machine must be delivered as quickly and reliably as the network can possibly perform.

|  | Overhead | Greatest Strength | Call Set-up | Addressing | Also Known As... | Virtual Circuit | Error Correction | Flow Control |
|---|---|---|---|---|---|---|---|---|
| Connectionless | Less | Ability to dynamically reroute data | None | Global | Datagram unreliable | None | Left to end-user devices | Left to end-user devices |
| Connection-oriented | More | Reliability | Yes | Local logical channel number | Reliable Virtual circuit | Created for each call, virtual circuit table established | By virtual circuit | By virtual circuit |

*Figure 6-15*   Connection-Oriented vs. Connectionless Packet Switched Networks

Applications programs more oriented to large file transfers or batch updates have different data characteristics than transaction-oriented programs. Overnight updates from regional offices to corporate headquarters or from local stores to regional offices are typical examples. Rather than being bursty, the data in these types of applications usually flow steadily and in large amounts. These transfers are important, but often not urgent. If file transfers fail, error detection and correction protocols such as those examined in the study of communications software can retransmit bad data or even restart file transfers at the point of failure.

From a business perspective the two switching techniques vary as well. Although both circuit-switched and packet-switched services usually charge a flat monthly fee for access, the basis for usage charges differs. In general, circuit-switched connections are billed according to time connected to the circuit. Leased lines are billed with a flat monthly fee that varies according to circuit mileage. Packet-switched networks usually charge according to packet transfer volume.

To analyze further, if a company gets charged for connection time to the circuit-switched circuit whether they use it or not, they had better be sure that while they are connected, they are taking full advantage of the available bandwidth.

One other switching difference is worth noting before drawing some conclusions. In terms of the need to deliver bursty, transaction-oriented data quickly and reliably, call set-up time can be critical. With circuit-switched applications, a dial tone must be waited for, and the number must be dialed and switched through the network. With connection-oriented packet-switched networks, call set-up packets must explore the network and build virtual circuit tables before the first bit of data is transferred. Datagrams don't require call set-up but offer no guarantee of safe delivery.

By first carefully examining the characteristics of the data traffic to be transported, a network analyst can more reliably narrow the choices of possible network services to consider.

## Switching Technologies

There are multiple switching technologies available. Figure 6-16 illustrates the relationship between the available switching services.

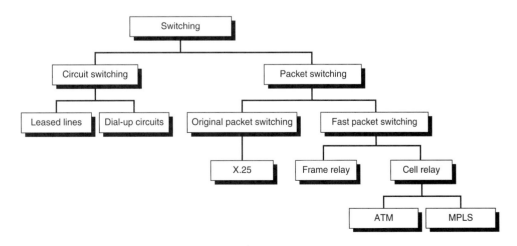

*Figure 6-16*  Switched Network Services

There are two basic circuit switched technologies: leased lines and dial-up circuits. The key performance differences between the two are availability and connection time. A leased line is available to carry data 24/7. As such there is no latency incurred when data needs to be sent. A dial-up line however must establish a connection before data can be sent, adding latency to the data transmission.

There are four basic packet switched technologies currently in use: X.25, frame relay, asynchronous transfer mode (ATM), and multiprotocol label switching (MPLS).

**X.25**   **X.25** is an international CCITT standard that defines the interface between terminal equipment (DTE) and any packet-switched network (the cloud). It is important to note that X.25 does *not* define standards for what goes on *inside* the cloud. One of the most common misconceptions is that the X.25 standard defines the specifications for a packet-switching network. On the contrary, X.25 only assures that an end-user can depend on how to get information into and out of the packet-switched network.

X.25 is a three-layer protocol stack corresponding to the first three layers of the OSI model. The total effect of the three layer X.25 protocol stack is to produce packets in a standard format acceptable by any X.25 compliant public packet-switched network. X.25 offers network transparency to the upper layers of the OSI protocol stack. Figure 6-17 illustrates the relationship of the X.25 protocol stack to the OSI model.

*Functionality*   The X.25 standard consists of a three-layer protocol that assures transparent network access to OSI layers 4 through 7. In other words, applications running on one computer that wish to talk to another computer do not need to be concerned with anything having to do with the packet switched network connecting the two computers. In this way, the X.25 compliant packet switched network is nothing more than a transparent delivery service between computers.

The physical layer (layer 1) protocol of the X.25 standard is most often RS-232 or some other serial transmission standard. The datalink layer (layer 2) protocol is

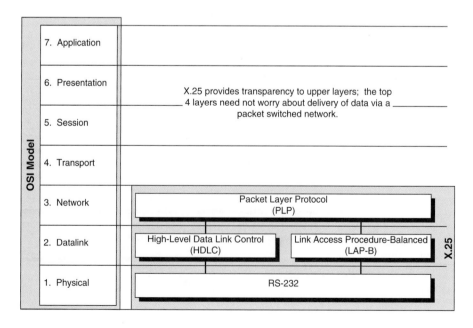

*Figure 6-17*   X.25 and the OSI Model

known as **HDLC,** or **high-level datalink control.** HDLC is very similar to IBM's SDLC in structure. Functionally, HDLC accomplishes the same things as any other datalink layer protocol such as Ethernet or token ring:

- It organizes data into structured frames that may contain more than one packet.

- It assures reliable delivery of data via error checking.

- It provides point-to-point data delivery between adjacent nodes.

Figure 6-18 illustrates an HDLC frame. In the case of HDLC and X.25, error checking is achieved via a 16-bit frame check sequence, while the control field transports important management information such as frame sequence numbers and requests for retransmission. Newer implementations of X.25 use **LAP-B,** or **link access procedure-balanced,** a subset and functional equivalent of the full HDLC frame, as a datalink layer protocol. The network layer (Layer 3) X.25 protocol is known as **PLP,** or **packet layer protocol.** Remembering that the job of any OSI layer 3 (network layer) protocol is the establishment, maintenance, and termination of end-to-end connections, PLP's main job is to establish, maintain, and terminate virtual circuits within a connection-oriented packet-switched network.

Figure 6-19 lists important standards related to X.25 and a brief explanation of their importance:

*Implementation*   X.25 requires data to be properly packetized by the time it reaches the cloud. Terminals and computers that do not possess the X.25 protocol stack internally to produce properly formatted packets communicate with the X.25 network through a **packet assembler/disassembler** (**PAD**). The PAD will packetize non-X.25

| Flag | Address field | Control field | Information field | Frame check sequence | Flag |
|------|---------------|---------------|-------------------|----------------------|------|
| 8 bits | 8 bits | 8 bits | Variable | 16 bits | 8 bits |

*Figure 6-18*   X.25 Datalink Layer Protocol: HDLC

| Standard | Explanation/Importance |
|----------|------------------------|
| **X.121: Global Addressing Scheme** | A global addressing scheme is necessary to access to X.25 networks. X.121 defines 14-digit international data number (IDN) addresses to uniquely identify the destination node. |
| **X.28 and X.32: Dial-up Access Directly into PADs** | X.28 (asynchronous) and X.32 (synchronous) standards allow users to dial into a PAD and place calls over the packet-switched network. |
| **X.75: Internetworking Packet-Switched Networks** | X.25 defined the interface from the end-user device into the packet-switched network cloud. A standard was required to define an interface between different packet-switched networks. X.75 is the PSN Gateway protocol that allows connectivity between PSNs. |

*Figure 6-19*   X.25 Related Standards

traffic for entry into the cloud. Such devices usually have a minimum of four RS-232 serial ports for input from PCs, terminals, or host computers that wish to communicate via a carrier's X.25 service. These input ports are typically asynchronous; however, the aggregate output port is synchronous. The data rate of all PAD interfaces is determined by the physical-layer specification used. RS-232 serial interfaces are limited to 115 Kbps; however, other aggregate interfaces can be utilized to provide more bandwidth on this link. Inside the carrier's network, X.25 switches are connected together in a mesh topology via high-speed digital transmission services such as T-1.

Although X.25 is a waning technology, existing X.25 networks continue to be used for out-of-band network management purposes. Since most network devices utilize RS-232 serial interfaces for console configuration, X.25 networks can be used to provide WAN connectivity to these devices. This becomes useful when in-band network management via SNMP or telnet is unavailable. Figure 6-20 illustrates this X.25 technology implementation.

**Frame Relay** In order to understand how these packet services could be made faster, the source of the overhead or slowness of the existing X.25 packet switching networks must first be examined. Recall from the previous discussion of connection-oriented packet-switched networks that error-checking and retransmission requests were done

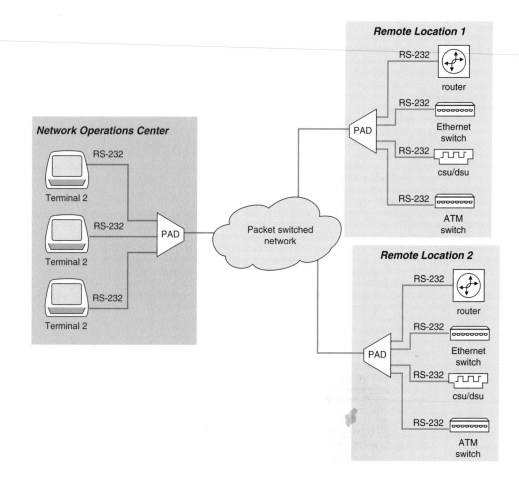

*Figure 6-20* X.25 Technology Implementation

on a point-to-point basis, between adjacent packet switches. This point-to-point error checking is sometimes also called hop-by-hop error checking.

At the time X.25 was first introduced about twenty or so years ago, the long-distance circuits connecting the X.25 packet switches were not nearly as error free as they are today. Transmission errors are measured by **bit error rate** (**BER**). To guarantee end-to-end error free delivery, it was necessary to check for errors and request retransmissions on a point-to-point or hop-by-hop basis at every X.25 packet switch in the network. Although necessary, this constant error checking and correction added significant overhead, and therefore delay, to the X.25 packet transmission process.

Today's long-distance digital transmission systems are largely fiber based and far less error prone. As a result, new packet-switching methodologies such as **frame relay** were introduced that sought to take advantage of the decreased bit error rate on today's transmission systems. The basic design philosophy is simple: Given the quality of the transmission system, stop all point-to-point error correction and flow control within the network itself and let the end-nodes worry about it.

The end nodes, such as PCs, servers, and mainframes, would use higher level (layers 4 through 7) protocols to perform their own error checking. In the case of a PC, this would likely be a sliding window file transfer protocol. This philosophy works fine as long as the basic assumption, the low bit error rate of today's transmission system, holds true. If not, then retransmissions are end-to-end spanning the entire network, rather than point-to-point between adjacent packet switches.

*Error Detection and Correction*    Error detection and correction were introduced in chapter 2. In this section, the application of these concepts to X.25 and frame relay are discussed. The difference and resultant processing time savings for frame relay occurs in the action taken upon the detection of an error. An X.25 switch will always send either a positive ACK or negative NAK acknowledgment upon the receipt of each packet and will not forward additional packets until it receives an ACK or NAK. If an NAK is received, the packet received in error will be retransmitted. Packets are stored in X.25 switches in case an NAK is received, necessitating retransmission. This is why X.25 packet switching is sometimes called a **store-and-forward** switching methodology.

On the other hand, if a frame relay switch detects an error when it compares the computed versus transmitted FCSs, the bad frame is simply discarded. The correction and request for retransmission of bad frames is left to the end node devices— PCs, modems, computers, and their error-correction protocols. Technically speaking, in frame relay, there is point-to-point error detection, but only end-to-end error correction. X.25 networks were typically limited to 9.6 Kbps, but frame relay networks typically offer transmission speeds of T-1 (1.544 Mbps) and occasionally T-3 (44.736 Mbps). Figure 6-21 illustrates point-to-point vs. end-to-end error correction.

In terms of the OSI model, the difference between X.25 packet switching and frame relay is simple. Frame relay is a two-layer protocol stack (physical and datalink) while X.25 is a three-layer protocol stack (physical, datalink, and network). There is no network layer processing in frame relay, which accounts for the decreased processing time and increased throughput rate.

***Flow Control***    Although end node devices such as computers can handle the error detection and correction duties shed by the frame relay network with relative ease, flow control is another matter. End nodes can only manage flow control between themselves and whatever frame relay network access device they are linked to. There is no way for end nodes to either monitor or manage flow control within the frame relay network itself. Some frame relay switch vendors have implemented their own

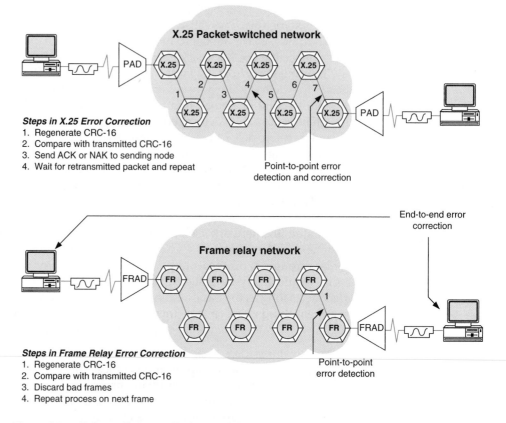

**Steps in X.25 Error Correction**
1. Regenerate CRC-16
2. Compare with transmitted CRC-16
3. Send ACK or NAK to sending node
4. Wait for retransmitted packet and repeat

**Steps in Frame Relay Error Correction**
1. Regenerate CRC-16
2. Compare with transmitted CRC-16
3. Discard bad frames
4. Repeat process on next frame

*Figure 6-21*    Point-to-Point vs. End-to-End Error Correction

flow control methodologies that work only if that particular vendor's equipment is used throughout the network.

Referring to the frame relay frame structure diagram in Figure 6-22, note that there are three bits in the frame definition known as **BECN, FECN, and DE.** These acronyms stand for **backward explicit congestion notification, forward explicit congestion notification,** and **discard eligibility.** BECN is sent back to the original source user to tell the FRAD to throttle back its transmission onto the frame relay network, while FECN warns the destination recipient of this frame of the congested network conditions. If the discard-eligible field is set, then the carrier managing the frame relay network is granted permission to discard such frames in order to relieve network congestion. These bits are the elements of a scheme to allow frame relay devices to dynamically adjust flow control. Some frame relay devices even have the ability to read or write to these fields.

## FRAME RELAY FLOW CONTROL COMPATIBILITY

The only problem is that the action that should be taken by a device in the event that any of these bits indicate a flow control problem has not necessarily been agreed upon or uniformly implemented by frame relay technology manufacturers. On one hand, unless you were responsible for setting up your own frame relay network, you might not think much of this problem. On the other hand, it represents the need to have a healthy dose of cynicism when shopping for data communications devices,

Practical Advice
and Information

even when those devices "support all applicable standards." If technology manufacturers do not uniformly implement standards, they are of little use.

In a similar manner to X.25 packet formation, frame relay frames are formatted within the FRAD, or in computers or PCs that have frame relay protocol software loaded to build frame relay frames directly. The frames that a frame relay network forwards are variable in length, with the maximum frame transporting nearly 8,000 characters at once. Combining these potentially large, variable-length frames with the low overhead and faster processing of the frame relay switching delivers a key characteristic of the frame relay network: High throughput with low delay.

Figure 6-22 illustrates the frame definition for frame relay networks. This frame definition is said to be a subset of the LAP-D protocol. **LAP-D** stands for **link access protocol—D channel,** where the D channel refers to the 16 Kbps delta channel in basic rate ISDN (BRI) or a 64 Kbps delta channel in primary rate ISDN (PRI).

The variable-length frames illustrated in Figure 6-22, can be a shortcoming, however. Because there is no guarantee as to the length of a frame, there can be no guarantee as to how quickly a given frame can be forwarded through the network and delivered to its destination. In the case of data, this lack of guaranteed timed delivery or maximum delay is of little consequence.

However, in the case of more time-sensitive information such as voice or video, it could be a real issue. Digitized voice or video can be packetized or put into frames like any other data. The problem arises when framed voice and video do not arrive in a predictable timed fashion for conversion back to understandable voice and video. As a result, frame relay is often described as a data only service. That is not exactly

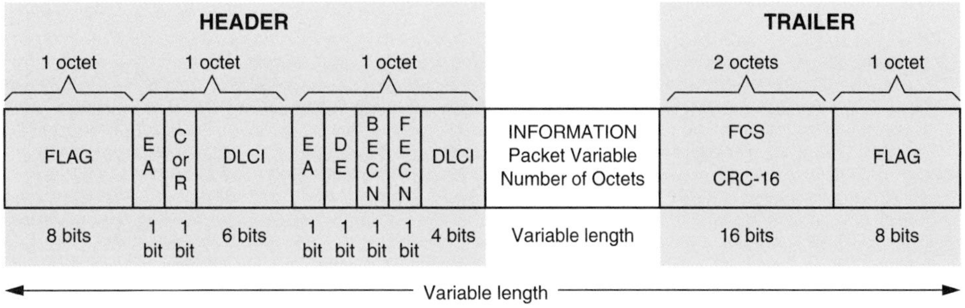

| FLAG | Unique bit sequence that indicates beginning of frame |
| EA | extended address—standard address is two octets, this bit setting can extend address to 3 or 4 octets |
| C or R | Command or response—application specific—not used by standard frame relay protocol |
| DLCI | Data-link connection identifier (address)—identifies particular logical connection over a single physical path |
| EA | Extended address—standard address is two octets, this bit setting can extend address to 3 or 4 octets |
| DE | Discard eligibility—used by frame relay switches for flow control |
| BECN | Backward explicit congestion notification—used by frame relay switches for flow control |
| FECN | Forward explicit congestion notification—used by frame relay switches for flow control |
| DLCI | Data-link connection identifier (address)—identifies particular logical connection over a single physical path |
| INFORMATION | Minimum number of octets—enough to make total frame at least 7 octets long; maximum number of octets is 8,000; carries upper layer data |
| FCS | Frame check sequence for error detection—also called cyclic redundancy check |
| FLAG | Unique bit sequence that indicates end of frame |

*Figure 6-22*   Frame Relay-Frame Layout

true. Options do exist to transport digitized, compressed voice transmissions via a frame relay network. However, most voice-over frame relay technology is proprietary, requiring all FRADs and/or switches that support voice-over frame relay to be purchased from the same vendor.

***Virtual Circuits*** Frame relay networks most often employ permanent virtual circuits (PVC) to forward frames from source to destination through the frame relay cloud. Switched virtual circuit (SVC) standards have been defined but are not readily available from all carriers. An SVC is analogous to a dial-up call; in order to transport data over an SVC-based frame relay network, tributary client-systems must communicate call set-up information to the frame relay network before sending information to or receiving information from a remote frame-relay device.

T-1 transmission rates are commonly seen in frame relay networks, with thousands of PVCs aggregated through the frame relay core. Frame relay services occasionally reach DS-3 data rates of 44.736 Mbps in the core; however, fractional T-1 implementations are much more commonly utilized to provide remote corporate offices access to enterprise networks. A key advantage of frame relay over circuit-switched technologies, such as leased lines, is the ability to have multiple virtual circuits supported from a single access line. This allows for the creation of a logical mesh through a frame relay core to geographically distributed locations. From a cost-justification standpoint, this allows a frame relay client to replace multiple leased-line connections with a single access line to a frame relay network. Figure 6-23 illustrates the concept of multiple PVCs per single access line.

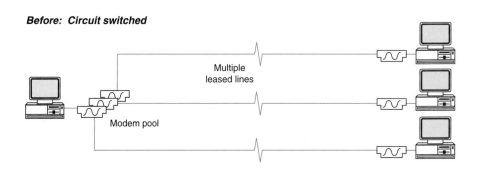

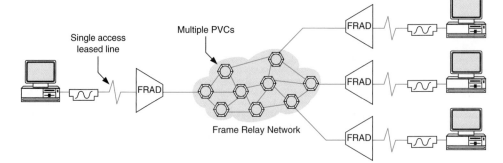

*Figure 6-23*    Multiple PVCs per Access Line

***Dynamic Bandwidth Allocation***    Another important characteristic afforded by the many transmission options available with the mesh network of the frame relay cloud is the ability to allocate bandwidth dynamically. In other words, up to the transmission limit of the access line and the circuits between the frame relay switches, the frame relay network will handle bursts of data by simply assembling and forwarding more frames per second onto the frame relay network, over multiple PVCs if required.

This ability to handle bursty traffic is especially appealing for LAN interconnection. Inter-LAN communication tends to be bursty with intermittent requests for data and file transfers. Remembering that this inter-LAN communication should be as transparent as possible, frame relay's ability to handle bursty traffic by dynamic bandwidth allocation is especially appealing. In the case of frame relay network access for LAN interconnection, the internetwork bridge or router is often integrated with a frame relay assembler/disassembler or frame relay protocol software.

A word of caution: *bursty* traffic is not easy to define. How large a burst, in terms of maximum bandwidth demand, and of what duration, is the frame relay network expected to be able to handle? An attempt has been made to structure burstiness with the following two terms:

- **CIR,** or **committed information rate,** refers to the minimum bandwidth guaranteed to users for "normal" transmission.

- **CBS,** or **committed burst size,** defines the extent to which a user can exceed its CIR over a period of time. If a user exceeds its CBS, the frame relay network reserves the right to discard frames in order to deliver guaranteed CIRs to other users.

***Protocol Independence and Network to Network Interface***    Another frame relay feature that is appealing for LAN interconnection is that fact that frame relay merely encapsulates user data into frames and forwards it to the destination. Frame relay is merely a delivery service. It does not process user data and is therefore protocol independent or protocol transparent. It can forward SNA/SDLC traffic just as easily as it can forward TCP/IP or Novell IPX traffic.

An issue hindering widespread global use of frame relay is the need for better coordination among the different frame relay network vendors in order to offer transparent access between them in a manner similar to the standard interfaces developed by phone companies for voice traffic. A conceptual standard known as **NNI,** or **network to network interface,** would be the functional equivalent of the X.75 internetwork standard for X.25 packet-switched networks.

*Implementation*    As can be seen in Figure 6-21, the technology configurations for the X.25 packet-switched network and the frame relay network are amazingly similar. In the case of the frame relay network, the access device is known as a **FRAD** or **FAD** (frame relay or frame assembler/disassembler) rather than a PAD, while the switching device is known as a **frame relay switch,** rather than a packet or X.25 switch. FRADs are also known as **frame relay access devices.** FRADs and frame relay switches are available in numerous configurations and integrated with numerous other internetworking devices such as bridges, routers, multiplexers, and concentrators.

*Conclusion: What Is Frame Relay?*    First, frame relay is a suite of network protocols. LAP-D is the datalink layer protocol that defines a frame structure containing destination address, error checking, control information, and user data, all within a single frame. It is this interface specification that allows faster processing to take place within the frame relay network.

Second, frame relay is a network service, offered by several exchange carriers primarily for the purpose of LAN interconnection. Frame relay's ability to dynamically allocate bandwidth over a single access line to the frame relay network make it particularly well-suited for the bursty nature of inter-LAN traffic. Private frame relay networks can be established as well.

Finally, frame relay could also be considered a switching architecture. What goes on inside the frame relay network cloud is really remains transparent to end-users, as long as the interface specification causes frame relay frames to enter the cloud and frame relay frames to exit the cloud. However, there are true frame relay switches designed specifically to forward frame relay frames at an optimal rate. A mesh network made up of these "native" frame relay switches could legitimately be considered a switching architecture.

**Asynchronous Transfer Mode (ATM)**    As seen in Figure 6-16, cell relay is another switching technology that has been a key layer of the exchange-carrier and service-provider network architectures. **Asynchronous transfer mode** (**ATM**) is currently the most widely accepted standard for cell-relay transmission services. The key physical difference between cell relay and frame relay is that, unlike the variable length frames associated with frame relay, cells have a fixed length. ATM cells are a fixed length of 53 octets. Although there are multiple ways of defining the format of an ATM cell as described below, most ATM networks utilize ATM Adaptation Layer (AAL) 5, which reserved 48 of the octets per cell for user data encapsulated from higher-layer protocols while 5 octets are reserved for the cell header.

*ATM Protocol Model*    Since ATM switches utilize very short, fixed-length cells, they can process information much faster than frame relay switches. Fixed-length cells allow for virtual circuits (VCs) to be forwarded in hardware, as opposed to utilizing processor cycles. In addition, the fixed-length cells are enhanced with connection-oriented services. Together, these two features of ATM enable predictable and consistent transfer of information between source and destination.

The predictability and consistency of transmission associated with ATM are the features that make this technology a good choice for transporting both real-time services (voice and video) as well as data. The lack of a predictable and consistent delivery of information was a key limitation of frame relay, which prevented the widespread use of this technology for converged applications.

Access to the ATM core is typically provided by T-carrier services (T-1 or T-3); however, SONET is used as the physical-layer protocol within the network core. As a result, the transmission rates associated with core ATM networks are only limited by the SONET standards. Concatenated OC-192c ATM services are common in large service-provider networks.

Like all other protocols, ATM can be mapped to the OSI Network Reference Model. Figure 6-24 shows how the lower three layers of the OSI model relate to ATM and Figure 6-25 conceptually illustrates how inputs of data, voice, or video can all be processed and transmitted as homogeneous ATM cells, while relating the layers of the ATM model to the layers of the OSI model.

***ATM Cell Structures***    An ATM cell header consists of several fields. Each of these fields has a specific purpose in ensuring data is efficiently delivered across the network to the destination. Figure 6-26 details the ATM cell header fields and provides a description of each.

| OSI Layer | ATM Layer | Description |
|-----------|-----------|-------------|
| **Network** | • Signaling | Fault management, performance management, connection management |
| | • Data | User data, voice, video input, which must be adapted into ATM cells |
| **Datalink** | • AAL—ATM adaptation layer convergence Sublayer<br>   ○ Segmentation and reassembly Sublayer | Converts input data, video, and voice into ATM cells |
| | • ATM—Asynchronous transfer mode | ATM cell-processing layer; flow control; address assignment and translation |
| **Physical** | • TCS—Transmission convergence sublayer | Cell delineation, header error check, path overhead signals, multiplexing |
| | • PMD—Physical medium dependent sublayer | Physical transport and connectivity, framing, bit timing, line coding, loopback testing |

*Figure 6-24*    ATM Layer Functionality

ATM is currently defined by two different cell formats. The first is called the **user-to-network interface** (**UNI**), which carries information between a client device and the core ATM network. The second cell format is known as **the network-to-network interface** (**NNI**). Cells with the NNI format are used to carry information between core ATM switches.

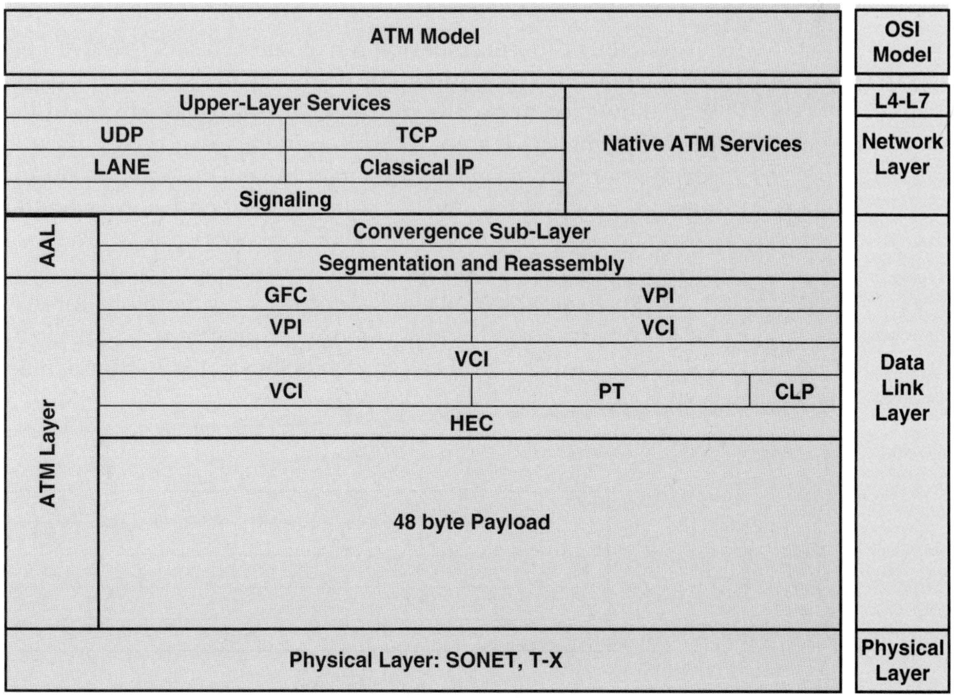

*Figure 6-25*    ATM Model vs. OSI Model

| ATM Cell Field Name | Description |
|---|---|
| GFC: Generic Flow Control | This is a means of providing flow control at the UNI point where tributary systems access the ATM core. Once the traffic is in the core, flow control is no longer necessary and this field is replaced with additional VPI bits in the NNI cell header. |
| VPI: Virtual Path Identifier | The VPI uniquely identifies the connection between two ATM network nodes. A VPI consists of several VCIs (see below). |
| VCI: Virtual Channel Identifier | Voice, video, and data channels can travel along the same logical path from one end of the ATM network to the other. The VCI uniquely identifies a particular channel of information within the virtual path. |
| PT: Payload Type | Indicates the cell's contents for prioritization purposes. These bits are considered by the queuing algorithm performed on an output buffer. |
| CLP: Cell Loss Priority | If an ATM transmission exceeds the bandwidth guaranteed by its class of service (CoS), which may include concessions for traffic bursts, a cells associated with this transmission can be "tagged" at ingress to an ATM switch. If congestion occurs on the ATM network, these tagged cells are the first to be discarded in a process known as *policing*. |
| HEC: Header Error Correction | Provides for the detection and correction of errors found in the cell header. Payload reliability is maintained by upper-layer protocols (TCP). |

*Figure 6-26*    ATM Header Field Descriptions

The key difference between two cell formats relates to how bits are assigned to the channel and path identifier fields. As illustrated in Figure 6-27, the UNI cell format allows for more bits in the ATM cell header to be utilized for virtual channel identification (VCI) since these identifiers are more prolific at the ATM network edge for distribution of information to tributary systems. In the ATM core, virtual channels are grouped into virtual paths. Virtual paths are used to logically group virtual channels requiring the same quality of service (QoS) or to logically group virtual channels that are bound for the same destination node.

Conversely the NNI cell header reserves more bits for virtual path identification (VPI) because the VPI field is more commonly used for grouping virtual circuits in the ATM core. The NNI cell format is illustrated in Figure 6-28.

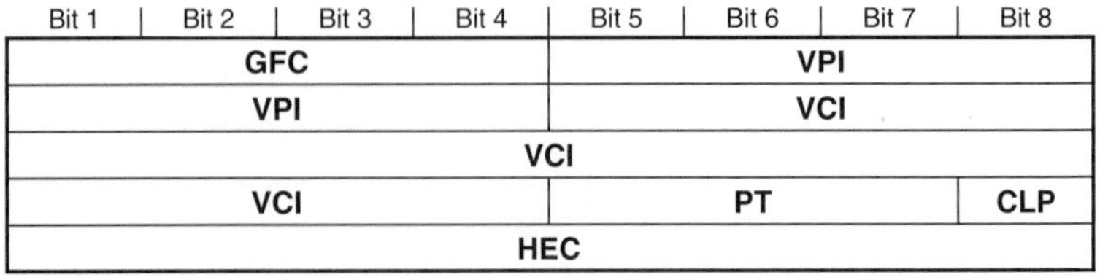

| Bit 1 | Bit 2 | Bit 3 | Bit 4 | Bit 5 | Bit 6 | Bit 7 | Bit 8 |
|---|---|---|---|---|---|---|---|
| GFC | | | | VPI | | | |
| VPI | | | | VCI | | | |
| VCI | | | | | | | |
| VCI | | | | PT | | | CLP |
| HEC | | | | | | | |

*Figure 6-27*    ATM UNI Cell Header

| Bit 1 | Bit 2 | Bit 3 | Bit 4 | Bit 5 | Bit 6 | Bit 7 | Bit 8 |
|-------|-------|-------|-------|-------|-------|-------|-------|
| VPI | | | | | | | |
| VPI | | | | | | | |
| VCI | | | | | | | |
| VCI | | | | PT | | | CLP |
| HEC | | | | | | | |

*Figure 6-28*    ATM NNI Cell Header

***ATM AAL Protocols***    User inputs of data, video, or voice must be processed into fixed-length ATM cells before they can be forwarded and delivered by ATM switches. This processing is done on the **ATM adaptation layer** (AAL). Depending on the type of input (voice, video, or data) a different type of adaptation process may be used and different types of delivery requirements or priorities can be assigned within the ATM network. After emerging from the ATM adaptation layer, all cells of a given AAL are in the identical format.

ATM adaptation layer protocols are designed to optimize the delivery of a wide variety of payload types. However, all of these different types of payload vary in a relatively small number of ways:

- *Delay sensitivity.* Can the traffic tolerate variable delay or must end-to-end timing be preserved?

- *Cell loss sensitivity.* Can the traffic tolerate the occasional cell loss associated with connectionless transmission services, or must connection-oriented transmission services be employed in order to avoid cell loss?

- *Guaranteed bandwidth.* Must the traffic receive a constant amount of guaranteed bandwidth or can it tolerate variable amounts of bandwidth?

- *Additional overhead required.* In addition to the 5 octets of overhead in the ATM cell header, some AAL protocols require additional overhead in order to properly manage payloads. This additional overhead is taken from the 48-octet payload. This can raise overhead percentages to as high as 13 percent.

To date, four different types of ATM adaptation protocols have been defined and are summarized in Figure 6-29.

***ATM Bandwidth Management***    The requirements vary for each type of converged service (voice, video, or data), and AAL protocols are utilized to accommodate these differences. As illustrated in Figure 6-29, there are currently four different AAL standards utilized to accommodate disparate payload types.

ATM classes of service (CoS):

- **Constant bit rate** (**CBR**) provides a committed information rate (CIR) to each virtual circuit. This produces the equivalent of a virtual leased-line. The negative side of CBR is that this bandwidth is reserved and it is wasted if not utilized. No other virtual circuit can utilize bandwidth reserved for CBR services.

- **Variable bit rate** (**VBR**) provides a minimum sustainable cell rate (MSCR), which guarantees a minimum amount of constant bandwidth. The bandwidth

| ATM AAL Protocol | Timing | Connectivity | Class of Service | Payload (octets) | Application/Notes |
|---|---|---|---|---|---|
| AAL-1 | Preserved | Connection oriented | CBR | 47 | Used for TDM services (e.g., T-1) |
| AAL-2 | Preserved | Connection oriented | VBR | 45–47 | Compressed video |
| AAL-3/4 | Variable delay | Connectionless | VBR | 44 | Connectionless data services |
| AAL-5 | Variable delay | Connection oriented | VBR | 48 | Most commonly used AAL. (a.k.a. the simple and efficient adaptation layer (SEAL) |

*Figure 6-29*    ATM AAL Protocols

available for a VBR service will not drop below the MSCR. However, as VBR traffic bursts often require more bandwidth than this guaranteed minimum, provisions are made for the maximum burst size (MBS) that VBR services may not exceed. VBR services are cheaper than CBR services, but there is a noticeable performance difference.

- **Available bit rate (ABR)** services provide access to the leftover bandwidth whenever it is not required by the variable bit rate traffic. This is the cheapest class of service and subscribers rely upon the statistical nature of this technology, assuming that VBR services will not frequently burst to consume all of the available bandwidth. The level of oversubscription on a carrier's network should be evaluated when considering this CoS. Regardless, this CoS should never be used for mission-critical data.

Figure 6-30 illustrates the relationship between CBR, VBR, and ABR.

*Implementation*    Key benefits of ATM networks are:

- The constant cell length affords faster and predictable delivery times.
- The predictable nature of ATM allows voice, video, and data to be transported effectively.
- ATM protocols are supported on both the LAN and the WAN; the availability of ATM NICs and WAN switches remove the need for multiple protocol conversions across the network.

An implementation of an ATM-based enterprise network would consist of ATM access devices as well as a "cloud" of ATM switches. The ATM access devices would take user information in the form of variable-length data frames from a LAN, digitized voice from a PBX, or digitized video from a video codec and format all of these various types of information into fixed-length ATM cells. The local ATM switch could route information to other locally connected ATM devices as well as to the wide area ATM network.

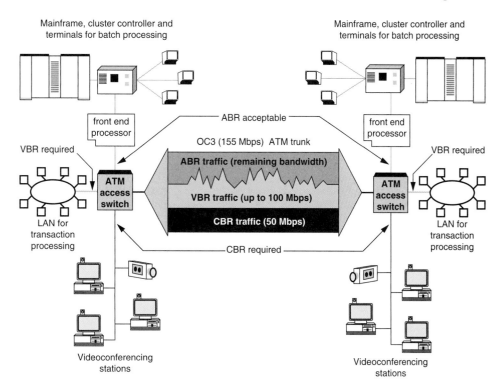

*Figure 6-30*    CBR, VBR, and ABR Bandwidth Management for ATM

In a sense, the general makeup of the ATM network is not unlike the X.25 or frame relay networks. Access devices assure that data are properly formatted before entering "the cloud" where the data are forwarded by switches specially designed to handle that particular type of properly formatted data. However, the functionality that an ATM network can offer far exceeds that of either the X.25 or frame relay networks. Figure 6-31 illustrates a possible implementation of a variety of ATM technology.

*Broadband ISDN*    Together, ATM and SONET form the underlying network architecture for **broadband ISDN (B-ISDN)**. ATM is the statistical multiplexing and switching architecture that enables B-ISDN to provide service differentiation and convergence for voice, video, and data services. SONET is the optical transmission mechanism by which broadband ISDN services are delivered. ATM provides the cell relay switching fabric providing bandwidth on demand for bursty data from any source (voice, video, etc.), while SONET's synchronous payload envelope provides empty boxcars for ATM's cargo. Simply stated, SONET possesses the flexibility to carry multiple types of data cargo (voice, video, etc.) simultaneously, while ATM has the ability to switch multiple types of data simultaneously. The fact that the complementary natures of the two architectures produce a network service known as B-ISDN should come as no surprise.

Much of the excitement that surrounded B-ISDN was due to its ability to support current (T-1, T-3) and emerging services (HDTV, medical imaging). The B-ISDN architecture has proven to meet the requirement for bandwidth on demand while supporting existing and emerging services; however, several limitations of ATM have identified the B-ISDN architecture as less than optimal. It is for this reason that

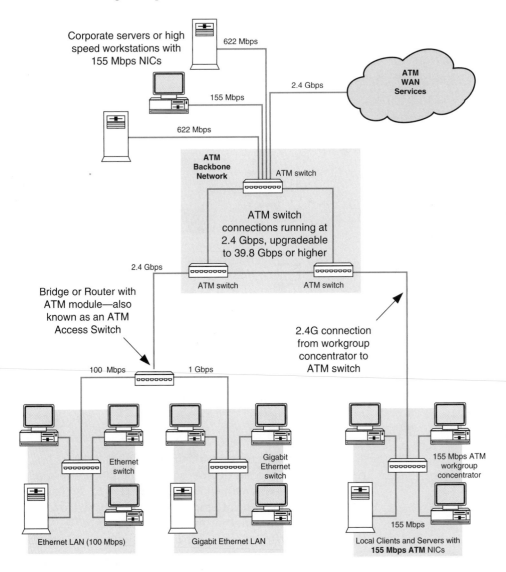

*Figure 6-31*    Implementation of ATM Technology

current WAN infrastructures are migrating to IP over MPLS. This new approach promises to be less complicated and more affordable than B-ISDN, while maintaining QoS levels mandated by customers.

**MPLS**    A second cell relay protocol is **multiprotocol label switching (MPLS)**. MPLS technologies have evolved with the strengths and weaknesses of ATM in mind. One of the biggest weaknesses attributed to ATM was the **cell tax.** This term refers to the fact that ATM cells generally impose 10 percent overhead to the transmission stream when AAL 5 is utilized. Additional bandwidth is also reserved for signaling between ATM network devices. This signaling information contains routing updates with network topology changes. Additional control information is necessary to establish and terminate switched virtual circuits. With all of the overhead added at the ATM layer of the protocol stack, many network engineers agree that ATM should be replaced with a protocol that requires less overhead, while providing connection-oriented services for variable-length frames.

The connection-oriented nature of ATM is maintained with MPLS due to the use of label switched paths (LSP). The LSP is the MPLS equivalent of the ATM switched virtual circuit. Although ATM utilized separate address architecture to route SVC through the network, MPLS is designed to integrate more tightly with the IP address architecture utilized at layer 3 of the OSI model. The 20-byte addresses utilized by ATM were considered cumbersome; one address scheme for global communication was deemed desirable. It is for this reason that MPLS has been designed to utilize IP for the global address architecture utilized to establish end-to-end LSPs.

From this discussion of MPLS functionality, it should be evident that this protocol has been designed to overcome the limitations of ATM: excessive overhead and complicated address architecture. It should also be evident that MPLS is designed to provide QoS, as did ATM, through connection-oriented services.

*Implementation*    Figure 6-32 illustrates the three-level architecture used to implement MPLS. The outer layer of the architecture is the **edge layer.** Devices contained in this layer are typically non-MPLS devices. Examples of such devices may include Ethernet switches, IP routers, or voice gateways. These non-MPLS devices are connected to **label edge routers** (**LER**) in the second layer of the MPLS network, the **access layer.** The LER is responsible for encapsulating traffic from the network edge within MPLS frames. The LER also establishes, maintains, and terminates label-switched paths through the network core for non-MPLS edge devices. The third level of the MPLS network architecture, the **MPLS network core,** is formed by a mesh of **label switch routers** (**LSR**).

The core MPLS network accepts requests for label-switched paths from the MPLS access layer. These requests are processed with layer 3 IP addresses to determine the best path through the MPLS core. Once the preferred path is determined, the next-hop LSR is contacted to determine if it has the resources necessary to meet the QoS requirements of the transmission. This negotiation process is repeated hop by hop through the MPLS core until the egress LSR is reached. At this point, the egress LSR communicates an accept message back through the MPLS core to the originating LSR, and the connection-oriented LSP is established. With the accept message from egress LSR to the originating LSR, and the establishment of the LSP, a **next-hop label forwarding entry** (**NHLFE**) is created within each LSR along the LSP. The NHLFE table in each LSR is utilized for established LSP connections. This precludes the need to process subsequent MPLS frames with the same label identifier at layer 3. The ability to switch MPLS frames in hardware enables shaping and policing of traffic through established connections, which ensures that QoS contracts are met for each customer.

## ■ WAN EVOLUTION

Modern WAN systems are evolving toward a network architecture that consists of four layers: photonic switching, time division multiplexing, statistical time division multiplexing, and routing. These four layers are illustrated in Figure 6-33.

Working from the bottom of the architecture up, the first layer is **photonic switching.** With the exponential growth of network traffic over time, many enterprise networks are fiber constrained and have few remaining pairs of optical fiber to accommodate additional increases in user traffic. Given the expense of laying optical

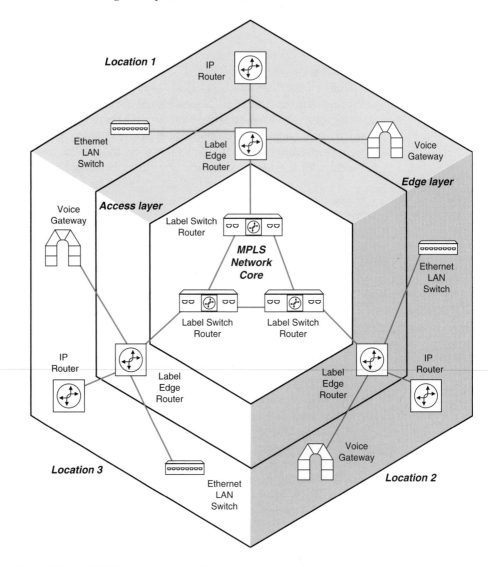

*Figure 6-32*    MPLS Three-Level Architecture

fiber in the ground, especially in urban areas, it is often more economical to increase the effective bandwidth of existing fiber as opposed to deploying additional fiber. The main method used to increase fiber bandwidth is dense wavelength division multiplexing (DWDM). As detailed earlier in this chapter, DWDM systems increase the effective bandwidth of optical WAN transmission systems using frequency division multiplexing (FDM) techniques. The ITU-standard channel frequencies utilized for DWDM are centered around 1,550 nm, above the infrared spectrum. The focus of this layer in the telecommunications network hierarchy is to provide massive amounts of bandwidth, up to several Terabits per second (Tbps) per fiber.

The current generation of telecomm switches is electronic or digital in nature, although optical transmission between these switching devices has been possible for more than a decade. As a result, optical signals must be converted to electrical signals before they can be switched. This introduces substantial latency to the

| Layer | Technologies |
|---|---|
| Routing | IP via RIP, OSPF, BEP |
| Statistical Time Division Multiplexing (STDM) | ATM MPLS |
| Time Division Multiplexing (TDM) | SONET |
| Photonic Switching | DWDM Optical cross-connects (OXC) |

*Figure 6-33*  Four-Layer Modern Network Architecture

end-to-end transmission. Clearly, substantial transmission gains can be achieved if this optical–electrical–optical (O–E–O) conversion can be avoided.

The future of photonic switching will allow for optical signals to be routed between source and destination without the need to for an O–E–O conversion for route processing in the electrical domain. Photonic switching is an enabler for the converged network of the future; it will provide for the marriage of functionality from the routing and photonic transmission layers of the model and potentially eliminate the need for intermediate layers of the telecommunications network hierarchy throughout the WAN core.

New **optical cross-connect (OXC)** switches have been produced that eliminate the need to de-multiplex optical signals into electronic cross-connects. DWDM wavelengths passing through an OXC can be switched from an input fiber to an output fiber. More advanced OXC technologies also allow for wavelength translation from the input wavelength on the input fiber to the output wavelength on the output fiber. This means the input wavelength can be switched to a different output wavelength when the input wavelength is already in use on the output fiber. Between input and output fibers, the light beams can be focused via lenses, redirected with mirrors, and filtered for wavelength translation or dropped with the use of an **optical add/drop multiplexer (OADM)**.

Photonic switching may be considered a circuit-switching technology because each wavelength is redirected from an input fiber to an output fiber. Optical wavelength inputs can be switched between wavelengths on different output fibers in 5 to 150 milliseconds, depending on the particular technology. DWDM may place hundreds of wavelengths on each fiber, and core WAN nodes may terminate hundreds of fiber pairs. Each of these input and output wavelengths on all fibers may be organized into a photonic switch-matrix to facilitate connectivity through the DWDM switching facility. This creates the need for OXC technologies that scale to provide matrices of $10^4 \times 10^4$ photonic cross-connections, and several vendors have offered products to address this requirement.

As shown in Figure 6-33, the second layer of the architecture is time division multiplexing (TDM). At this layer of the telecommunications network hierarchy, it is necessary to provide reliability for upper-layer services with the use of automatic protection switching (APS) and various ring-protection methods. In addition, legacy voice systems typically integrate at this layer of the telecommunications network hierarchy. Traditionally, SONET is used in North America to provide the functionality required of this layer.

The third layer of the architecture is statistical time division multiplexing (STDM). The STDM layer is traditionally implemented using Asynchronous Transfer Mode (ATM) technologies. ATM is generally utilized for several reasons: First, ATM provides for the efficient use of bandwidth provided at layers one and two. Second, ATM is connection-oriented; all information passed between a given source and destination will traverse the same path for the duration of the communication session. The connection-oriented nature of ATM, combined with the small (53 byte) cell size, allows for deterministic transport of encapsulated services with very little delay or delay variation, which is essential for real-time voice and video. Finally, this layer allows for the prioritization of one connection over another. The ability to prioritize connections allows a corporation to ensure the delivery of mission-critical information; connection prioritization also enables service providers to offer a wide variety of service-level agreements to their customers.

The top layer in the architecture is routing. The routing layer of the telecommunications network hierarchy provides a means for global addressing of all network devices and client systems. Traditionally, the Internet Protocol (IP) is used to provide this global address architecture. With this address architecture in place, protocols such as Routing Information Protocol (RIP), Open Shortest Path First (OSPF), and Border Gateway Protocol (BGP) can route packets of information from source to destination. For more information on IP routing protocols please refer to chapter 8.

## SUMMARY

In order to understand the basic technical principals of Wide Area Networking, one must really start by looking at the basic business principles. In wide area networking as in most areas of business, the desire to maximize the impact of any investment in technology is a central focus. Chief among the business principles of wide area networking is the desire to converge multiple connections onto a single wide area network link.

The two key aspects of a wide area network are transmission and switching. The most commonly used transmission technologies are the T-1 family and SONET. T-1 technologies provide a means of packaging data in time slots using time

division multiplexing. There are 24 time slots of 64 Kbps in a single T-1 frame. T-1 frames are then packaged into superframes and extended superframes. Using T-1 channel banks, multiplexers, and switches a complete T-1 network can be built.

SONET and SDH are optical transmission services. SONET is used in the United States while SDH is used in Europe. Fortunately, SONET and SDH have the ability to inter-operate. SONET packages voice and data into frames known as synchronous transport signals (STS-1). Unlike the T-1 family, SONET allows the payload to be flexibly defined using virtual tributaries. Using a counter-rotating ring architecture, SONET is error resistant and highly reliable.

SONET capacity can be extended through the use of dense wave division multiplexing (DWDM). DWDM takes the bandwidth of a single piece of fiber optic cable and divides it into different wavelengths of light, each capable of simultaneously carrying a different signal. Using DWDM it is possible to achieve bandwidths of up to a Terabit per second.

There are two types of switching used in wide area networking: circuit and packet switching. In a circuit switched network, a specific path is generated between the source and destination across the network. The bandwidth for this path is dedicated to that connection. There are two main types of circuit switched networks: leased lines and dial-up lines.

In a packet switched network, individual data packets are routed from the source to the destination across the network between packet switches. Because the bandwidth is not dedicated to a specific connection, a packet switched network can offer more usable bandwidth for a given investment. Packet switched networks can offer the ability to emulate a circuit switched network by creating a specific path across the network. These virtual circuits can either be dynamically built as needed (switched virtual circuits) or pre-defined (permanent virtual circuits).

There are four commonly available packet switched wide area network technologies: X.25, frame relay, ATM, and MPLS. X.25 is an older technology that uses point-to-point error correction. X.25 is a relatively slow technology that is rapidly being displaced in favor of higher speed solutions. However, X.25 is still commonly used as an out of band solution for network management traffic.

Frame relay is another packet switched network technology. Like X.25 frame relay uses variable length packets, known as frames in frame relay, to carry data. Unlike X.25 frame relay relies on end-to-end error detection and correction. Frame relay has two key data speeds: a confirmed information rate (CIR) which is the minimum amount of bandwidth available to a connection and a committed burst size (CBS) which is the extent to which a user can exceed their CIR for short periods of time. Frame relay is still a viable wide area network technology and is often used for international data links.

Asynchronous Transfer Mode (ATM) is a cell relay technology. Unlike X.25 and frame relay which use variable length packets, cell relay technologies such as ATM and MPLS use fixed length data units known as cells. By using a fixed length data unit it is easier to predict data flow and offer time dependent data services. There are two different types of ATM cells available. The UNI cell is used for a device to connect to an ATM device while the NNI cell is used between network devices.

ATM provides three levels of service: constant bit rate which is the CIR for each virtual circuit, variable bit rate which is the minimum bandwidth available, and available bit rate which is the left over bandwidth that is available on a first come, first served basis. The data payload in ATM is flexible as defined by ATM adaptation layers (AAL).

MPLS is a second cell relay switching technology. Compared to ATM, MPLS offers a more efficient (less overhead) solution that supports better quality of service options with a simplified addressing scheme. MPLS is typically implemented as a three level architecture. Data sources are in the edge layer and connect to label edge routers located in the access layer. The label edge routers in turn connect to label switch routers located at the network core.

## KEY TERMS

| | | |
|---|---|---|
| AAL | available bit rate | bit error rate |
| ABR | backward explicit congestion | BLSR |
| access layer | notification | broadband ISDN |
| access line | BECN | call set-up packet |
| asynchronous transfer mode | BER | CAPEX |
| ATM | bi-directional line switched ring | capital expense |
| ATM adaptation layer | B-ISDN | CBR |

CBS
cell tax
channel bank
CIR
clear request packet
committed burst size
committed information rate
connection-oriented
constant bit rate
data switching exchange
DE
dense wavelength division
    multiplexing
digital services hierarchy
discard eligibility
DS-1
DSE
DWDM
E-1
edge layer
extended superframe
FAD
FECN
forward explicit congestion
    notification
fractional T-1
FRAD
frame
frame relay
frame relay access device
frame relay
    assembler/disassembler
frame relay switch
framing bits
FT-1
global address
HDLC
high-level datalink control
IMUX
interface specification

label edge router
label switch router
lambda
LAP-B
LAP-D
LCN
LER
link access procedure-balanced
link access protocol–D channel
logical channel
logical channel number
LSR
MPLS
MPLS network core
multiprotocol label switching
network architecture
network convergence
network services
network to network interface
network-to-network interfaces
next hop label forwarding entry
NHLFE
NNI
NNI
OADM
OC
optical add/drop multiplexer
optical carrier
optical cross-connect
OXC
packet player protocol
packet switching exchange
PAD packet
    assembler/disassembler
permanent virtual circuit
photonic switching
PLP
PSE
pulse code modulation
PVC

RJ48-c
robbed-bit signaling
row
SDH
SONET
SONET frame
SPE
store-and-forward switching
STS-1
superframe
SVC
switched virtual circuit
switching architectures
synchronous digital hierarchy
synchronous optical network
synchronous payload envelope
synchronous transport signal
T-1
T-1 CSU/DSU
T-1 framing
T-1 inverse multiplexer
T-1 multiplexer
time slot
transmission architectures
UNI
unidirectional path switched ring
UPSR
user demands
user to network interface
variable bit rate
VBR
virtual circuit
virtual circuit table
virtual tributary
VT
VT-1.5
wavelength division multiplexing
X.25

## REVIEW QUESTIONS

1. What is network convergence?
2. What limitations in network design or operation would a lack of interoperability cause?
3. What is the difference between switching and transmission and how do the two architectures compliment each other?
4. What types of information are included in packets other than the actual data itself?
5. What is the difference between a T-1 and an E-1?
6. Differentiate between the following: time slot, frame, superframe, ESF.

7. What is the difference between a T-1 and a DS-1?
8. What is a fractional T-1 and what is the business motivation behind such as service?
9. What is a channel bank?
10. What is SONET and where does it fit in the wide area network architecture?
11. What is the relationship between SONET and SDH?
12. What is an STS-1?
13. What are the roles of the virtual tributaries in SONET?

14. Compare and contrast UPSR and BLSR.
15. What unique performance characteristics does SONET offer and what type of application might require such characteristics?
16. What is dense wavelength division multiplexing?
17. In terms of DWDM, what is a lambda?
18. What is the difference between circuit switching and packet switching?
19. Compare and contrast the two most common circuit switching technologies.
20. What are the four most common packet switching technologies?
21. What is the difference between a packet assembler/disassembler and a packet switch?
22. What is the difference between connectionless and connection-oriented packet service in terms of overhead, physical transmission path, and reliability?
23. What do connection-oriented services use in place of global addressing?
24. What overhead is involved with the establishment and maintenance of logical channel numbers?
25. What are the differences between a PVC and an SVC in terms of establishment, maintenance, and termination?
26. What part of the packet switched network does X.25 actually define?
27. What is meant by the term "bursty data" and what unique transmission challenge does it pose?
28. What is the most common source of bursty data?
29. What are some of the technological differences between an X.25 network and a frame relay networks?
30. What are some of the performance or architectural differences between an X.25 network and a frame relay network?
31. What are frame relay's underlying assumptions regarding transmission media and bit error rates?
32. How is flow control handled in a frame relay network?
33. What is the significance of frame relay's variable length frames in terms of the types of payload that can be effectively delivered?
34. Why is dynamic allocation of bandwidth an important feature of frame relay?
35. Why is multiple PVCs per access line an important feature of frame relay?
36. What are the primary differences between frame relay and cell relay in terms of architecture and network performance?
37. List the two most common implementations of cell relay?
38. Map ATM to the OSI Network Reference Model.
39. In terms of ATM, compare and contrast UNI and NNI.
40. What is the purpose of the AAL protocols? Which is most commonly used?
41. Differentiation between CBR, VBR, and ABR in terms of architecture and applications.
42. What are the key benefits of ATM networks?
43. What is broadband ISDN?
44. What is meant by the term cell tax as it relates to ATM networks?
45. What is MPLS and how does it relate to ATM?
46. What are the layers of the MPLS hierarchy? What type(s) of devices reside at each?
47. What is next-hop label forwarding entry?
48. What is photonic switching?
49. What is an optical cross-connect?
50. What technologies are most commonly implemented in the modern, four layer WAN network architecture?

**Case Study:** For a business case study and questions on TCP/IP network design, go to www.wiley.com/college/goldman.

# CHAPTER 7

# LOCAL AREA NETWORK COMMUNICATIONS PROTOCOLS

## Concepts Reinforced

OSI Network Reference Model     Protocol encapsulation
Datalink functionality     Network functionality

## Concepts Introduced

Network layer addressing     Address resolution
Routing     Packet fragmentation
Connectionless protocols     Connection-oriented protocols
Sessions     Ports
Sockets     Application functionality

## OBJECTIVES

After mastering the material in this chapter, you should:

1. Understand the concept of protocol encapsulation.

2. Understand address resolution and its role in the delivery of data.

3. Differentiate between packets and frames.

4. Understand the network, transport, and session layers of the OSI Network Reference Model.

5. Differentiate between connectionless and connection-oriented protocols.

6. Understand IPX/SPX protocols and their implementation.

7. Understand TCP/IP protocols and their basic implementation.

8. Understand the limitations and applications of the NetBEUI and DLC communication protocols.

## ■ INTRODUCTION

Local area network communications protocols can be thought of as the language of computer networks: They provide the language and grammatical rules that define communication. Just as humans have to agree on common languages to communicate, local area networks must agree on common protocols to communicate.

In this chapter, the general concepts of LAN communications protocols will be developed and specific protocol implementations will be discussed. This chapter focuses on local area network protocols, which control communication between hosts on inter-connected networks.

## ■ LAYER THREE: THE NETWORK LAYER

The third layer of the OSI Network Reference Model is the *network layer.* Analogous to the internetwork layer of the TCP/IP model, the network layer is primarily concerned with providing a means for hosts to communicate with other hosts on different network segments. As explained in chapter 4, the datalink layer provides a means for two hosts on a *common* network segment to communicate. Technologies such as *Ethernet* and *token ring* provide this intra-segment connectivity.

Network layer protocols expand the capabilities of the network by providing a means of delivering data (called *packets*) between network segments. A network layer protocol provides a means of addressing a host on the interconnected network and a means of delivering data across the network to destination hosts. *Addressing* is the process of defining where on the internetwork the host is located and *routing* is the process of determining the best path to the destination host and delivering the data.

### FRAMES AND PACKETS

It is important to note the difference in the terminology used to describe the data being transmitted at each of these layers of the OSI Network Reference Model. The datalink layer (layer two) transmits *frames* of data. The network layer (layer three) transmits *packets* of data.

### NETWORKS AND SEGMENTS

A constant source of confusion is the use of multiple terms to describe network architectures. Different sources commonly use different terms to mean the same thing. Regardless of terminology, there are two key levels of networking: single segments where every host receives every packet and multi-segment networks where some internetworking device forwards packets between network segments.

Single network segments are commonly referred to as segments, sub-networks, or subnets. Inter-connected segments are commonly referred to as networks or internetworks. Don't let these varying terms confuse you: if every host sees every frame of data on the LAN, it's a segment. If more than one segment is used, it's an internetwork.

Although this chapter focuses on the network layer of the OSI Network Reference Model, each protocol discussed is part of an overall protocol family that integrates protocols from layers three through seven of the OSI model.

## Network Layer Addressing

The role of network layer addresses is to provide a means to uniquely identify a host on the internetwork. The **network layer address** is used in the routing process to deliver a packet of data to the correct network segment for delivery. In this manner, network addresses are used for "end-to-end" or "inter-segment" communication.

There are two basic components to a network layer address: a network segment address and a host address. The **network segment address** identifies in which network segment the destination host is located. This address is used by the routing process to determine the destination network segment and deliver the packet to that segment. Once the packet has arrived at the correct network segment, the **host address** is resolved to a physical address and passed to the datalink layer for delivery. The relationship between address components and their purpose is illustrated in Figure 7-1.

Collectively, these two parts identify a host on the internetwork. The segment address must be unique to the internetwork to ensure that the packet is delivered to the correct network segment. Similarly, the host address must be unique *within a network segment*. As shown in Figure 7-2, it is possible to use the same host address on multiple segments. There is no chance for confusion between the hosts, as the packet will be routed to the network segment of the correct host based on the segment address.

Network layer addresses are assigned on a per-NIC basis. It is possible for a single device to contain more than one NIC. In this case, each NIC will have its own network layer address (segment address + host address). Devices that contain more than one NIC are said to be **multi-homed.**

There are several reasons to multi-home a device, including performance, reliability, and stability. However, the primary reason a device is multi-homed is to allow it to forward packets from one network segment to another. By definition a device that performs packet forwarding is known as a **router.** In Figure 7-2, the device in the center of the diagram that connects to all three network segments is functioning as a router; forwarding packets as needed from one segment to another.

## Network Layer vs. Datalink Layer Addressing

As previously mentioned, the network layer is primarily responsible for addressing hosts uniquely on an internetwork and providing a means of delivering data across network segments. The responsibility of moving data within a network segment is that of the datalink layer. As described in chapter 4, the datalink layer uses the physical address (also known as the MAC addresses for Ethernet and token ring technologies) of the NIC to deliver data rather than the network layer host address.

For the network and datalink layers to successfully interact to deliver data, a direct, one-to-one mapping must be made between the network layer address and the datalink layer physical address. Although the exact method used to make this

| Address Component | Layer | Purpose |
|---|---|---|
| Network Segment Address | Network | Used by routers to forward data to the correct network segment. |
| Host Address | Network | Identify a host within a network segment. Resolved to physical address for actual data delivery. |
| Physical Address | Datalink | Used to deliver data to the destination host. |

*Figure 7-1*  Network Address Components

## Physical Topology

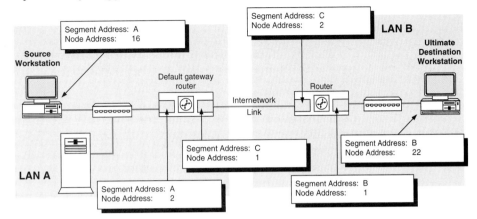

*Figure 7-2*    Host Addressing

mapping varies between the various network layer protocols, every network layer protocol has a standardized method for mapping its host address to the physical address associated with the NIC. The process of determining the physical layer address of a NIC from the network layer address is known as **address resolution.**

Each NIC is assigned a single data link layer physical address and one or more network addresses. The network layer address is used by upper-layer protocols to denote which host they wish to communicate with. The network layer is also used to transport (route) data through the network to the destination network segment. Once the data arrive at the destination network segment, the network layer address is resolved to a physical address and delivered to the destination host (NIC) by the data link layer.

The process of delivering data to a destination host is analogous to the method used to deliver a letter to a person's house. The street name (network segment address) is used to route the mail to the correct postal route. The mail carrier for that route then looks at the house number (host address) to determine the final destination of the letter. The mail carrier then resolves the house number to a physical mailbox location (physical address) for delivery. This relationship is shown in Figure 7-3.

## Protocol Encapsulation/De-encapsulation

Although different layer three protocols use different techniques for addressing and packet construction, a layer three packet will always contain at least three sections:

| Network Data Delivery | Mail Delivery |
| --- | --- |
| Network Segment Address | Street Name |
| Host Address | House Number |
| Physical Address | Physical Mailbox Location |

*Figure 7-3*    Network Data Delivery vs. Mail Delivery

source network address, destination network address, and data. The source and destination addresses are used in the routing process and the data is the reason the packet was sent. Packet construction will be detailed in subsequent sections for the most common network layer protocols currently in use.

Packets are sent through the network by encapsulating them in datalink layer frames. As illustrated in Figure 7-4, a packet of data from the network layer is placed in the data section of a datalink layer frame. Known as **encapsulation,** this process adds both a header and trailer to the packet. The bit stream is finally passed along the shared media that connects the two computing devices. When the full bit stream arrives at the destination server, the reverse process of encapsulation, **de-encapsulation** takes place. In this manner, the destination datalink layer strips the layer two header and trailer and passes the packet to network layer for processing.

## Fragmentation

Every protocol has a maximum overall packet (or frame) length. This length is the maximum size of a packet (or frame) including the header and data. The maximum size of a packet or frame of data is known as the **Maximum Transmission Unit** (MTU).

In the event that a higher-level packet will not fit into a lower layer's available payload area, the higher-level packet is broken into two or more packet fragments. These packet fragments are sent across the network and re-assembled into a single packet before being sent back up the protocol stack on the destination host. **Fragmentation** allows large quantities of data to be sent across the network in smaller, more manageable "chunks" of data.

Data fragmentation is required between the application layer and the network layer for large quantities of application layer data (such as a 10 MB file) to be sent across a network. However, data fragmentation between the network layer and the datalink layer represents additional overhead and should be avoided if at all possible. Fragmenting network layer packets is required when the underlying layer two frame's data payload is not capable of transporting the entire layer three packet. Such fragmentation requires the layer three packet be broken into multiple layer two frames of data that are sent across the physical network and re-assembled at the layer two destination host.

The impact of network layer packet fragmentation is illustrated in Figure 7-5. When the source creates a packet that is larger than the underlying layer two transport protocols, each router on path between the source and destination must break

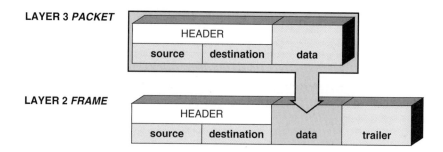

*Figure 7-4*    Protocol Encapsulation

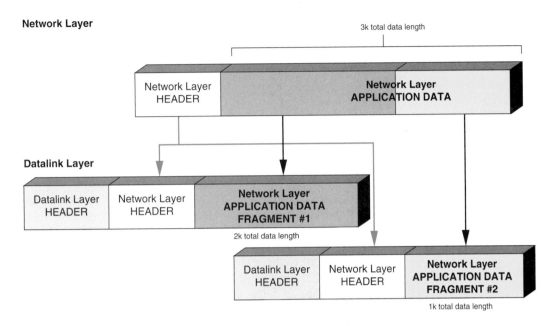

*Figure 7-5* Layer Three Packet Fragmentation

the packet into multiple fragments, sending each fragment across the layer two link to the next router. Each frame that contains a fragment of the packet must also contain a copy of the packet's header to ensure that the packet is properly reassembled.

The next router must collect the fragments, re-assemble them into the original network layer packet, and repeat the process for the next hop. Such repeated packet fragmentation and reassembly places a large processing burden on routers, effectively reducing their overall routing capacity.

Compare Figure 7-5 to Figure 7-6. Figure 7-6 represents the same network, but the layer three packet size has been set equal to or lower than the underlying layer two frame data payload. In Figure 7-6, each router merely has to package each network layer packet into a single layer two frame and send it along the route to its destination. Packet fragmentation is currently one of the key capacity limitations on

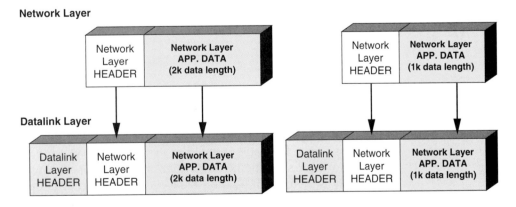

*Figure 7-6* Layer Three Packet Fragmentation Eliminated

most routed networks, especially when the network includes WAN links, which typically use much smaller frame sizes than LAN links.

## Routing

**Routing** is the process of moving data across network segments toward its final destination. Routers receive frames of data, de-encapsulate the layer three packet, examine the network layer packet header, determine the next hop of the packet, package the packet into a new data frame and transmit the new frame.

Going back to the mail example in the previous section, the routing process is analogous to the method used by the post office to deliver a letter. Someone places a sheet of paper (data) in an envelope (packet), addresses it, places it in a mailbox, and raises the flag (transmits the packet). The postman picks up the letter and places it in a mail bag (data frame) and takes it to the post office (default gateway). At the post office, the letter is taken out of the mail bag (data frame), and the zip code (network segment address) is used by the post office to determine where to send the letter (routing). After the next hop is determined, the letter is placed into a new mail bag (data frame) for transmission to the destination post office (router on the destination network segment). This process continues until the letter reaches the post office that services the destination zip code (router to the destination segment).

At the destination post office, the letter is removed from the mail bag and placed into the mail bag of a mail carrier that services the destination street address. The mail carrier then places the mail in the mailbox of the destination street address for final delivery to the recipient.

## Routing Is Address Processing

Although routing will be explained in detail in chapter 8, it is important to understand some basic routing concepts in order to appreciate routing protocol functionality. Perhaps the most important thing to understand about routing is that it is nothing more than address processing performed when messages need to travel beyond the local LAN. By keeping track of the following address-related issues, the entire routing process can be largely demystified. As illustrated in Figure 7-7, the only thing that changes throughout the routing process is that the source and destination physical addresses are changed during each hop on the way to the destination host. For this example, network layer addresses are given in the format Letter:Number where Letter is the segment address and number is the host address.

The first logical step in the routing process is for the source workstation to fill in the source address field in the network layer header with its own network layer address and the destination address field in the network layer header with the network layer address of the ultimate destination workstation. Since the destination workstation is not on the local LAN, the packet must be forwarded to the local gateway, or router, which will have sufficient information to forward this packet properly.

The source workstation looks in its network layer configuration information in order to determine the network layer address of its default gateway. The default gateway is the default path off the local LAN. In order to deliver this packet to the router for further processing, the packet must be wrapped in a datalink layer frame such as Ethernet or token ring. Addresses that are included in the datalink layer

## Physical Topology

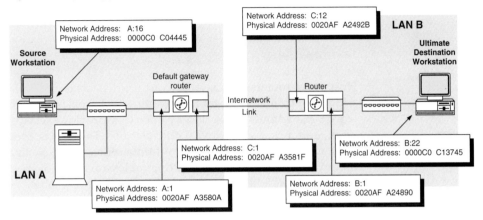

## Address Processing

From source workstation to default gateway router found on LAN A:

| Datalink | | Network | |
|---|---|---|---|
| source 0000C0  C04445 | destination 0020AF  A3580A | source A:16 | destination B:22 |

From LAN A router to next hop router towards ultimate destination as noted in routing table:

| Datalink | | Network | |
|---|---|---|---|
| source 0020AF  A3581F | destination 0020AF  A2492B | source A:16 | destination B:22 |

From LAN B router to locally attached ultimate destination workstation:

| Datalink | | Network | |
|---|---|---|---|
| source 0020AF  A24890 | destination 0000C0 C13745 | source A:16 | destination B:22 |

*Figure 7-7*   Routing Is Address Processing

header are known as physical addresses. Although the source workstation has the network address of the default router in its network configuration file, it does not know the physical address of that router. The source workstation determines the physical address of the router through address resolution.

Once the source workstation determines the physical address, it encapsulates the network layer packet in a datalink layer frame. The physical address associated with its own NIC is placed in the source address field of datalink layer frame and the physical address of the default gateway is placed in the destination address of the datalink layer frame.

The default gateway or local router receives the datalink layer frame explicitly addressed to it and examines the ultimate destination address held in the packet. The router then consults its routing tables to see if it has an entry for a known path to the ultimate destination workstation. That known path may be via another router, or the ultimate destination workstation may be part of a different LAN connected to this same router through a different NIC. In either case, the packet and its addresses are not modified but are instead re-encapsulated in a fresh datalink layer frame with the physical layer destination address of either the ultimate destination workstation, or of the next router along the path to that workstation. The source address field on the fresh datalink layer frame is filled in with the physical address of the default router that has just completed processing the packet.

## Routing Tables

Hosts and routers decide where to send packets by looking up the destination address in their **routing table.** A routing table consists of a series of destination networks, the address of the local router that provides service to the destination network, and a cost associated with the route. The cost is used to determine the best route in the event that there are multiple routes to the destination available. In addition to these required items, routing tables are protocol specific with different layer three protocols adding different fields to the routing table.

Regardless of protocol, there should always be a special entry in the routing table for the **default router** or **gateway of last resort.** This is the router where a packet should be sent if there is not a route listed in the local routing table for the destination network. You can think of the default router as the "out of town" slot at your local post office: it gets the packets that leave the scope of the local router. You have no idea of how it is going to get to the destination, but trust that the default router will find a path for it.

## Routing Protocols

In the previous example, it was assumed that each router intuitively knew where to send a packet to get it to its destination. However, when a router is initially started, it only knows about the interfaces connected to it, or **static routes** that have been configured by an administrator. In order for a network to dynamically build comprehensive routing tables that automatically add new routes and remove old ones, a routing protocol must be used. Routing protocols provide routers a means of automatically exchanging routing tables to ensure that each router knows where to route packets for a given destination.

Individual routing protocols will be discussed in detail in chapter 8, but a brief introduction is required to understand the routing capabilities of the various network layer protocols discussed in this chapter.

There are two basic classes of routing protocols: interior gateway protocols and exterior gateway protocols. The difference between interior and exterior gateway protocols is the scope of the routing information they distribute. Interior gateway protocols distribute routing information within a hierarchical address space such as that assigned to a single organization. As shown in Figure 7-8, these hierarchical address spaces, also known as **autonomous units,** can be interconnected into an internetwork.

When autonomous units are connected into an internetwork, exterior gateway protocols are used to distribute information about the various autonomous units between the routers that provide connectivity between them. If we expand the postal analogy from Figure 7-3 to include exterior gateways, we would add the name of the city to the process. Just as the post office first needs to get a letter to the right city before worrying about the street names and house numbers, an internetwork must get a packet to the autonomous unit that contains the destination network segment and host. Exterior gateway protocols provide this capability. Once the packet containing the destination arrives at the gateway router for the autonomous unit, the job

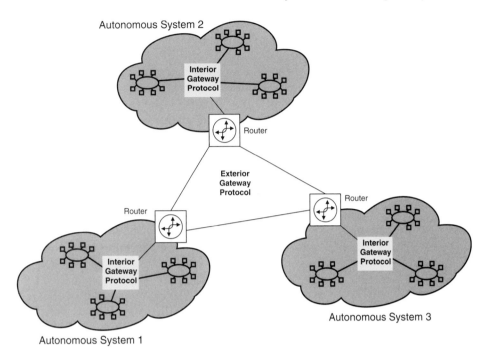

*Figure 7-8*    Interior vs. Exterior Gateway Protocols

of the exterior gateway protocol is complete. For the remainder of this chapter we will focus within an autonomous unit. Exterior gateway protocols are discussed in more detail in chapter 8.

There are two major categories of interior routing protocols: distance vector and link state. Distance vector protocols broadcast their entire routing table periodically. In this manner, changes to the network routing tables slowly make their way through the network. A router using a distance vector algorithm knows nothing about the make-up of the network beyond the next hop to the destination—merely that by sending a packet of data to the next hop, it should eventually make it to the destination.

Link state protocols transmit a more complete picture of the network between routers. Through the use of link state packets (LSP), each router learns the structure of the entire network. In this manner, the link state algorithm can make better routing decisions. Link state routing reacts quicker to changes in the routing structure than distance vector routing while using less bandwidth maintaining routing tables.

## LAYER FOUR: THE TRANSPORT LAYER

The fourth layer of the OSI Network Reference Model is the *transport layer*. The OSI transport layer maps to the bottom half of the TCP/IP model transport or **host-to-host** layer and is primarily concerned with creating, maintaining, and tearing down end-to-end network connections. When an application needs to send data to a remote network host, the transport layer is responsible for determining the correct network layer address and initiating the connection to the remote host. The transport layer also performs error control and correction and flow control for host to host connections. This includes ensuring that all packets arrive at the destination host without errors caused by dropped packets, duplicate packets, packets arriving out of order, or packets corrupted in transmission.

The transport layer can be thought of as being responsible for creating a communication channel between two hosts on an internetwork. Although the network layer actually transports the packets between the two hosts, the transport layer ensures that the packets flow as a data stream rather than a series of independent packets. From the perspective of higher level protocols, the connection is a pipeline directly to the other host, independent of the routers and network links that must be traversed. For this reason the transport and all higher levels are collectively known as end-to-end layers.

Unlike network layer protocols that are **connectionless** in nature, transport layer protocols are usually **connection-oriented** and therefore provide reliable data transmission. Each packet is assigned a sequence number that uniquely identifies it in the data flowing through the connection. By referencing the sequence numbers, the destination host can ensure packets are arriving in the proper order and that no packets have been dropped. The destination host must then respond to each packet with either an acknowledgment (ACK) of correct receipt or a negative acknowledgment (NAK) to indicate an error condition.

As illustrated in Figure 7-9, the destination host acknowledges the correct receipt of each packet by sending an ACK back to the sender that includes the sequence number of the packet. If a packet fails the error check upon receipt, the destination host responds with a NAK for the sequence number. If a packet arrives out of order, the destination host examines the sequence number, realizes it is not the correct next packet, and responds with an NAK for the missing sequence number. The sending host also keeps track of the time since a packet was sent. If the destination host doesn't respond

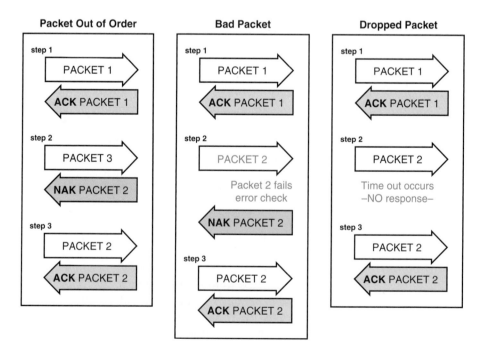

*Figure 7-9* Connection-Oriented Error Correction

with an ACK within a preset time period, the sending host assumes that packet was dropped and re-sends that packet with the original sequence number. This is referred to as a packet timing-out or a time-out error.

Data sent via a connection-oriented transport layer protocol will either arrive at their destination safely or the sending application will be alerted that the transmission failed. Because of their reliability, most data streams make use of connection-oriented transport protocols. However a connection-oriented protocol adds overhead to the communication process. A connection must be built between the two hosts before any data are transmitted. The process of building a connection can require multiple packets of data to be exchanged between the two hosts. Each packet that is sent via the connection requires an ACK packet in response. At the end of the communication the transport layer must also exchange packets to tear down the connection.

In Sharper Focus

## CONNECTIONLESS OR CONNECTION-ORIENTED?

Although connection-oriented protocols require more overhead than connectionless protocols, they provide an assurance that the data will accurately reach its destination. This reliability is important for most data streams because the data they carry are important or they would not have been sent in the first place. It would certainly make sense for a bank to use a connection-oriented protocol to carry financial transaction data—you wouldn't want any packets to be dropped without notice and error correction!

However, there are cases in which the use of a connection-oriented protocol may not be required. For messages that can be contained in a single packet, the overhead of establishing and tearing down a connection and processing ACKS can add more overhead than the message is worth. An example of a nonurgent, single-packet message is a routing protocol packet. Because routing protocol packets are routinely sent between routers, dropping a single packet is not a catastrophic event. It makes more sense to risk an occasional dropped packet than to add the overhead associated with a connection-oriented protocol for this application.

Another common application for connectionless protocols is streaming media. Streaming multimedia application layer protocols that can carry audio and video data across data networks are now commonplace. For these protocols to provide clear sound and pictures, it is important that every packet be accurately delivered to the destination. However it is inevitable that packets will be dropped from the media stream at some point regardless of the protocol used. The issue is what to do when a packet is dropped. Is it worth the additional overhead of a connection-oriented protocol to re-send dropped packets, or is it better to simply miss an occasional second of the stream?

## ◼ LAYER FIVE: THE SESSION LAYER

The fifth layer of the OSI Network Reference Model is the *session layer*. The session layer maps to the top part of the TCP/IP transport or host-to-host layer and is responsible for establishing, maintaining, and terminating logical sessions between applications. In the event of session failure, the session layer is responsible for reestablishing the session.

The session layer builds on the functionality of the transport layer by adding a mechanism to differentiate between applications at each end of a connection. It ensures that a packet gets to the correct application on the remote host after it crosses the connection. If there are two different communications sessions running between two hosts (such as a Telnet session and a WWW session), the session layer identifies the packets for each session and keeps them separated.

Session layer protocols identify sessions through the use of **ports** and **sockets.** Although these terms have slightly different meanings depending on the protocol, they represent the "address" of an application on a host. Each application on a host is assigned a unique port number. Most session layer protocols make use of fixed port numbers for commonly used services. This greatly simplifies the establishment of sessions between these services. Other application protocols may use a range of ports that are dynamically assigned. Regardless of the manner in which port numbers are assigned, no two applications can concurrently use the same port. To ensure that a packet is delivered to the correct address on the correct destination host, both the network layer address and port number must be specified.

Going back to the letter addressing example used earlier in this chapter, the port or socket number is analogous to the person's name on the letter. The network layer is only concerned with getting the letter to the correct mailbox. It is the responsibility of the session layer to get the letter to the correct person in the house (application).

Although the functionality of the session layer is distinct from that of the transport layer, most protocol suites merge transport and session layer functionality into a single protocol.

## ■ LAYERS SIX AND SEVEN: THE PRESENTATION AND APPLICATION LAYERS

Although they are not technically part of a network protocol suite, the sixth and seventh layers of the OSI Network Reference Model are usually tied to the underlying layer three protocol and can be mapped to the TCP/IP model application layer. The sixth layer is the *presentation layer.* The presentation layer is responsible for formatting data for transmission across the network. The presentation layer performs encryption and compaction of data and converts between data communication codes as required.

The seventh layer of the OSI Network Reference Model is the *application layer.* The application layer is responsible for providing data transmission services to user applications. The application layer provides these services via an Application Programming Interface (API). Any application that makes calls to the API can use the services of the application layer and its underlying layers for data communication. Presentation layer functionality is closely related to application layer functionality, and both are commonly integrated into a single protocol. For the remainder of this chapter, the presentation and application layers will be grouped as upper-layer protocols.

Each protocol suite takes significant liberties in the assignment of functionality to protocols above the network layer. In practical terms it is impossible to match single end-to-end protocols with a specific layer of the OSI Network Reference Model. However the protocols of a particular protocol suite collectively provide the complete functionality as described in the OSI model.

## ■ LOCAL AREA NETWORK PROTOCOLS

There are many different network layer protocols. IPX, IP, and AppleTalk are the three most commonly used protocols for local and wide area network traffic. The remainder of this chapter will cover these protocols in depth and illustrate the key implementation and maintenance considerations for each.

## NetWare (IPX/SPX) Protocol Suite

The IPX/SPX protocol suite was originally developed by Novell for its NetWare network operating system. IPX/SPX has also found its way to Microsoft operating systems and is commonly used to support network computer games due to its ease of configuration.

**Network Layer Protocol—IPX**    **Internet Packet Exchange (IPX)** was developed for and is still most commonly used in NetWare environments. While the I in IPX stands for *internet,* don't confuse it with the Internet (capital I). The Internet uses IP rather than IPX as its network layer protocol.

IPX, like most network layer protocols, serves as a basic delivery mechanism for upper-layer protocols such as SPX, RIP, SAP, and NCP. This delivery mechanism is accomplished through encapsulation whereby upper-layer protocols are encapsulated within properly addressed IPX "envelopes." Network layer protocols are generally characterized as:

- **Connectionless**—implying individual, fully addressed packets, or datagrams, are free to negotiate their way through the network in search of their final destination.

- **Unreliable**—implying that the network layer does not require error checking and acknowledgment of error-free receipt by the destination host.

The entire IPX packet is, in turn, encapsulated within a datalink layer frame, which corresponds to the installed network interface card. For example, if the workstation in question has a token ring card, then the entire IPX packet will be inserted into the data field of the token ring frame. If an ethernet card is present, then the encapsulation of the IPX packet will be into the data field of the designated type of ethernet frame.

IPX is a fairly small, easily configured protocol primarily designed to support local area network configurations. IPX is supported by many operating systems including Novell NetWare and Microsoft Windows. While IPX was once the default network layer protocol for both NetWare and Windows networking, it has seen its usage decline with the explosion of IP-based Internet.

**Addressing**    Addressing in IPX is straightforward and relatively easy. The segment address and host address are kept separate and are automatically determined by most hosts on the network.

*Network Segment Address*    IPX uses a 32-bit segment address that is usually displayed in hexadecimal (base 16). This gives an available IPX address space ranging from 0000 0000 to FFFF FFFF, which corresponds to 4.29 billion different network segments. Segment addresses are hierarchical in nature, allowing easier routing within IPX networks.

Assignment of segment address to IPX network hosts is a two-part sequence. Routers are assigned a segment address by a network administrator. In addition to physical routers, any Novell NetWare servers running IPX also serve as an IPX router, even if they only contain one NIC.

Once the routers are properly configured they will broadcast the IPX segment address to the remaining hosts on the network as part of the normal routing protocol update process. Segment addresses are sent in Routing Information Protocol (RIP) packets that are sent every 60 seconds by all IPX routers. Upon receiving an initial RIP packet, network hosts that are not IPX routers, read the segment address and configure themselves accordingly. This process is illustrated in Figure 7-10.

The process of broadcasting network addresses makes IPX extremely easy to set up initially. The only configuration required is to set the segment address on any IPX routers on the segment and the remaining hosts will be automatically configured. However, it is critical that each router on a network segment be assigned the same network address. If a single router is misconfigured, it will broadcast incorrect address information to any unconfigured hosts on the network segment, resulting in a large collection of hosts that cannot communicate with any correctly configured hosts on the network. This is the most common mistake made in IPX network configuration.

*Host Address*    As mentioned earlier in this chapter, a network layer host address is associated with a NIC card and must correlate with the underlying NICs physical address (the MAC address for Ethernet and token ring NICs). To keep configuration of IPX networks as simple as possible, the designers of the IPX protocol simply use the NIC's MAC address as the IPX host address.

As mentioned in chapter 4, MAC addresses are six bytes long and are usually reported as six sets of two hexadecimal numbers (such as 00-A0-24-51-3C-D0). Since MAC addresses are by design unique (no two NICs can have the same MAC

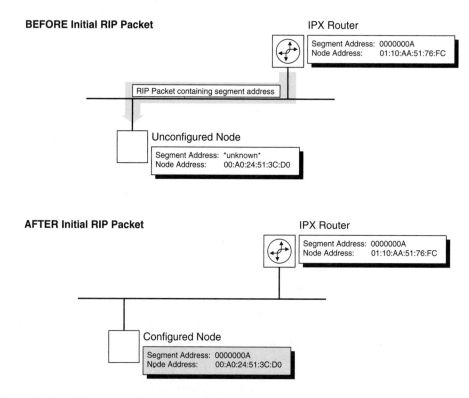

*Figure 7-10*   IPX Segment Address Assignment

address), each host address on an IPX segment is therefore unique. In addition to eliminating the need to configure each host on an IPX network, this design also eliminates the need to resolve IPX layer three host addresses to physical addresses: The host address *is* the physical address.

*Socket Address* In addition to the required segment and host address, IPX also provides a socket address. Technically a transport layer function, the socket address indicates which process on the destination host is to process the packet. IPX supports up to fifty sockets per computer. Upper-layer protocols to which IPX transfers data frequently via encapsulation such as NCP, SAP, RIP, and NetBIOS have reserved socket numbers. Together the segment address, host address, and socket address make up a complete IPX address.

**Packet Construction** IPX packets can carry a payload of up to 546 bytes of encapsulated data. Packet delivery is controlled with a 30-byte packet header consisting of multiple fields. The packet layout for IPX is shown in Figure 7-11 and a detailed description of the fields and their roles is presented in Figure 7-12.

In Sharper Focus

## IPX LIMITATIONS

Every network layer protocol is limited by its construction and the information carried in its header fields. In the case of IPX, the key limitations are the overall packet length and the transport control limit.

Due its relatively small size of 576 bytes, IPX loses some efficiency in a common Ethernet based local area network. As described in chapter 4, Ethernet frames have a payload capacity of 1,508 bytes. However, as only a single layer three packet can be encapsulated in one Ethernet frame, IPX cannot make full use of Ethernet's capacity, resulting in extra overhead. This can be easily understood by taking a look at a message consisting of 1,152 bytes. While this message could theoretically fit into a single Ethernet frame, it must be broken into two IPX packets, each of which will require separate Ethernet frames, resulting in increased overhead.

The other key limitation of IPX is the hard coded maximum transport control value of 16. This limitation directly affects maximum network diameter, as it is not possible to pass an IPX packet across more than fifteen routers. Even if a large IPX network is designed to only require fourteen hops on the longest run, it is still possible to drop packets if one of the links along the shortest run fails and the backup run requires more than fifteen hops.

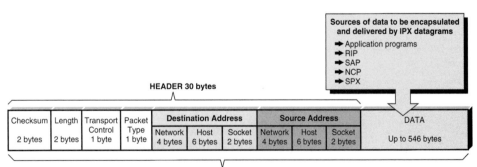

*Figure 7-11* IPX Packet Layout

| IPX Packet Fields | Function/Importance |
| --- | --- |
| Checksum | Not used by IPX. No error checking in IPX, hence its "unreliable" characterization. IPX depends on upper-layer protocols such as SPX for error checking and proper sequencing of messages and file transfers which span multiple IPX packets. |
| Length | Length of the entire IPX packet in bytes. |
| Transport Control | Also known as a hop-counter or "time-to-live" timer. Assures that free-floating datagrams do not meander infinitely around the network occupying bandwidth. Every time a router processes the IPX packet, this counter is incremented by 1. When this field reaches 16, the packet is deleted to avoid further aimless wandering. This is one of the reasons why IPX packets may never reach their intended destination. |
| Packet Type | As illustrated in Figure 7-11, the data field of an IPX packet may contain a variety of different upper-layer protocols each of which needs to processed in its own unique way. By identifying the embedded upper-layer protocol in the header's Packet Type field, the upper-layer protocols can be properly processed. |
| Addressing | Both source and destination addresses are composed of three segments:<br>• Network segment address<br>• Host (computer) address<br>• Socket address |
| Data | As previously described and illustrated in Figure 7-11, upper-layer protocols are encapsulated within the data field. |

*Figure 7-12*   IPX Header Fields

**Transport/Session Layer Protocols**   Although IPX is technically a network layer protocol it also provides session layer addressing via sockets. An application layer protocol can directly address a remote application using only IPX as long as it specifies the socket number of the application on the destination host. For simple communication between two hosts such as exchanging routing information, IPX may be the only protocol required. Applications that require a reliable network transport mechanism require the use of SPX.

**SPX**   **Sequenced Packet Exchange (SPX)** is a transport/session layer protocol that can be used with IPX to provide reliable communication. The key characteristics of SPX are:

- **Connection-oriented,** implying that specific paths known as **virtual circuits** are explored and determined prior to the first packet being sent. Once the virtual circuit is established directly from the source host or host to destination host, then all packets bound for that address follow each other in sequence down the same physical path. Virtual circuits are especially important when the source host and destination host reside on different networks.

- **Reliable,** implying that SPX requires error checking and acknowledgment in order to assure reliable receipt of transmitted packets. Because transfer of a single file may be broken up across multiple IPX packets, SPX adds sequence numbers to assure that all pieces are received and that they are reconstructed in the proper order. In order to assure that packets are not lost accidentally due to hosts or routers suffering from buffer overflow, SPX also has mechanisms to institute flow control.

SPX provides reliability by adding sequence numbers and acknowledgments to IPX. Figure 7-13 illustrates an SPX packet including the fields in the SPX header and shows the relationship between SPX and IPX. As can be seen, SPX is encapsulated within IPX and therefore depends on IPX for delivery to the destination workstation via the local network interface card. The role of each field in the SPX packet layout is detailed in Figure 7-14.

## Support Application Layer Protocols and Services

**IPX Routing Protocols**    IPX supports two basic interior routing protocols: RIP and NLSP. NetWare's **Routing Information Protocol (RIP)**, is a router-to-router protocol used to keep routers on a NetWare network synchronized and keep them up to date. RIP information is delivered to routers via IPX packets. In terms of generated network traffic, one of the undesirable qualities of RIP is that every router broadcasts its entire routing table every 60 seconds to all other routers to which it is directly attached. As will be seen, this shortcoming has been dealt with in newer versions of NetWare. One desirable quality of NetWare's RIP protocol is that routing table entries to particular networks can be updated and replaced if faster delivery routes are discovered based on the contents of the number of ticks field. Routing logic will be reviewed in-depth in chapter 8.

**NLSP** or **NetWare Link Services Protocol** was introduced in NetWare 4.1 in an effort to overcome the inefficiencies introduced by RIP. When dealing strictly with local area networks and their megabit-per-second bandwidths, protocols such as RIP, which broadcast every 60 seconds, are really nothing more than a slight nuisance. However, when expensive, limited bandwidth WAN links are involved, chatty protocols such as RIP become intolerable.

To be specific, the major problem with RIP is that all RIP-based IPX routers broadcast their entire routing table every 60 seconds, whether or not anything has changed since the last broadcast. In contrast, NLSP only broadcasts as changes occur, or every

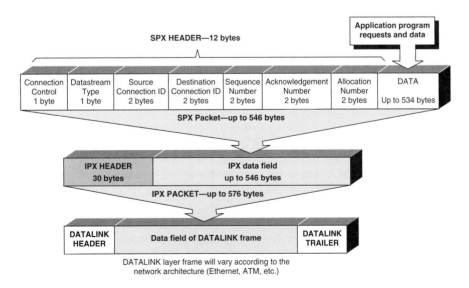

*Figure 7-13*    SPX Packet Layout and Encapsulation

| SPX Packet Fields | Function/Importance |
|---|---|
| **Connection Control** | Different 1-byte flags inserted into this field assist with the overall flow control and reliability for which SPX is responsible. Examples include end of message flags and acknowledgment request flags. |
| **Datastream Type** | This 1-byte field allows upper-layer protocols to offer hints as to the protocols or information contained within the SPX data field so that it might be processed more efficiently. This field is analogous to including an Attention: line on the outside of an envelope. It allows that envelope to be properly routed for processing without having to examine the contents (data) contained within the envelope. |
| **Connection IDs** | Source and Destination Connection IDs are used to identify communication sessions between two communicating processes. A connection ID is another layer in the hierarchical addressing scheme introduced in IPX. Just as multiple-socket IDs were possible for each host ID, multiple connection IDs can be associated with each socket ID. |
| **Sequence Number** | As the name implies, this field is used to assure the proper sequencing of packets in multipacket file transfers. |
| **Acknowledgment Number** | This field is incremented by the destination host as it receives sequenced packets. When the next packet is received, it will be error checked and the acknowledgment will be sent to the source workstation with this number included. |
| **Allocation Number** | This number is used in the implementation of the flow control mechanism. It is used to inform the source workstation of the number of buffers that the destination workstation can afford to allocate to SPX connections. |

*Figure 7-14* SPX Header Fields

2 hours at a minimum. Real-world implementations of NLSP have reported 15 to 20 times (not %) reduction in WAN traffic. Novell claims that up to a fortyfold decrease in router-to-router traffic is possible. Obviously, these data traffic reductions are only possible if communicating routers both support NLSP. Novell's multiprotocol router currently supports NLSP, but other vendor's routers need to be carefully reviewed.

Another limitation of RIP was its maximum of sixteen hops before the RIP packet was discarded. This sixteen-hop limit effectively limited the physical size of the internetwork linking IPX LANs. NLSP has also addressed this shortcoming by increasing the maximum hop count to 128. NLSP is interoperable or backward compatible with RIP allowing gradual migration by network segment to the more efficient NLSP. This feature is especially important to large internetworks manned by typically small networking staffs.

In addition to reducing the amount of broadcast traffic required to share routing updates, NLSP addressed the chatty nature of SAP. In order to eliminate the every 60-second broadcast of SAP packets, an associated feature of advanced IPX known as **SAP filtering,** assures that SAP broadcasts are synchronized to take place only with NLSP updates.

SAP   The **Service Advertising Protocol (SAP)** is used by network servers to advertise the services they provide. Servers broadcast this information every 60 seconds. Networked servers receiving SAP broadcasts store that information for future reference. Local workstations requiring a particular service are able to query their local server, which consults its list to provide the latest information as to the closest availability of any network service. SAP uses IPX packets as its means of delivering its service advertising requests or responses throughout the network. Figure 7-15 illustrates a physical representation of the uses of SAP while Figure 7-16 illustrates the header fields of a SAP packet.

In a manner similar to RIP, information regarding multiple servers can be either requested or supplied within a single SAP packet. Although only one operation type field per SAP packet is permitted, the remaining six fields can be repeated up to seven times in a single SAP packet. The role of each field in the SAP packet layout is detailed in Figure 7-17.

## The Internet Suite of Protocols: Overall Architecture and Functionality

**TCP/IP** (**Transmission Control Protocol/Internet Protocol**) is the term generally used to refer to an entire suite of protocols used to provide communication on a variety of layers between widely distributed different types of computers. Strictly speaking,

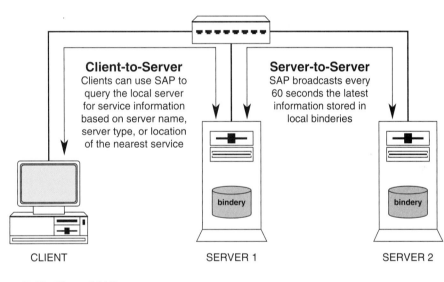

*Figure 7-15*   Uses of SAP

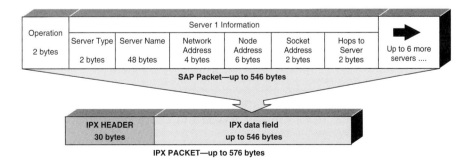

*Figure 7-16*   SAP Packet Layout and Encapsulation

| SAP Packet Fields | Function/Importance |
|---|---|
| **Operation Type** | This field defines whether this SAP packet contains a request for service information or a broadcast of existing or changed information. Only one operation type is allowed for each SAP packet. |
| **Server Type** | This field identifies the particular type of service offered by a server. One server can offer multiple different services. The valid service types are defined by Novell and are identified by unique hexadecimal values in this field. Following are a few of the defined service types and their hex values: |
| **Server Name** | This field identifies the server or host offering the type of service identified in the service type field. |
| **Network Address** | This is the address of the network on which the server resides. |
| **Host Address** | This is the address of the server itself. |
| **Socket Address** | This is the socket address on this particular server to which requests for this particular type of service must be addressed. |
| **Hops to Server** | This field indicates how far from the local server this particular service is located. This field is used on queries from workstations desiring the nearest available service of a particular type. |

Within the Server Type cell:

| Service Type | Hex Value |
|---|---|
| File server | 4 |
| Job server | 5 |
| Gateway | 6 |
| Print server | 7 |
| Archive server | 9 |
| SNA gateway | 21 |
| Remote bridge server | 24 |
| TCP/IP gateway | 27 |
| NetWare access server | 98 |

*Figure 7-17*   SAP Header Fields

TCP and IP are just two of the protocols contained within the family of protocols more properly known as the **Internet Suite of Protocols.** TCP/IP was developed during the 1970s and widely deployed during the 1980s under the auspices of **DARPA,** or Defense Advanced Research Projects Agency, in order to meet the Department of Defense's need to have a wide variety of different computers be able to inter-operate and communicate. TCP/IP became widely available to universities and research agencies and has become the de-facto standard for communication between heterogeneous networked computers.

**Overall Architecture**   TCP/IP and the entire family of related protocols are organized into a protocol model. Although not identical to the OSI Network Reference Model, the TCP/IP model is no less effective at organizing protocols required to establish and maintain communications between different computers. Figure 7-18 illustrates the TCP/IP model, its constituent protocols, and its relationship to the OSI Network Reference Model.

As illustrated in Figure 7-18, the OSI model and TCP/IP model are functionally equivalent, although not identical, up through the transport layer. Although the OSI model continues with the session, presentation, and applications layers, the TCP/IP

| Layer | OSI | INTERNET | Data Format | Protocols |
|-------|-----|----------|-------------|-----------|
| 7 | Application | Application | Messages or Streams | HTTP SSH TELNET FTP TFTP SMTP SNMP |
| 6 | Presentation | | | |
| 5 | Session | | | |
| 4 | Transport | Transport or Host-Host | Transport Protocol Packets | TCP UDP |
| 3 | Network | Internet | IP Diagrams | IP |
| 2 | Datalink | Network Access | Frames | |
| 1 | Physical | | | |

*Figure 7-18*   The TCP/IP Model

model has only the application layer remaining, with utilities such as Telnet (terminal emulation) and FTP (file transfer protocol) as examples of application layer protocols. As illustrated in Figure 7-18, the functionality equivalent to the OSI model's session, presentation, and application layers is added to the TCP/IP model by combining it with the Network File System (NFS) distributed by Sun Microsystems. As a result, in order to offer equivalent functionality to that represented by the full OSI model, the TCP/IP family of protocols must be combined with NFS, sometimes known as the Open Network Computing (ONC) environment.

**Individual Protocols: Architecture and Functionality**   Figure 7-19 illustrates the placement of many of the TCP/IP family of protocols into their respective layers of the TCP/IP model. Each of these protocols, as well as several others, will be explained in detail. Many protocols involved with network management, routing, and remote

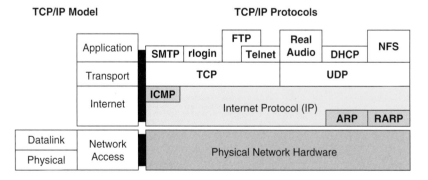

*Figure 7-19*   TCP/IP Family of Protocols

access do not logically fit into any of the layers of the TCP/IP model and are therefore not listed. The same lack of a proper layer into which to place such protocols is true in the OSI model as well.

IP Version 4   The most commonly used network layer protocol is IP, or the **Internet Protocol.** As its name would indicate, IP is the protocol used on the World Wide Web (WWW). All WWW browsing, e-mail exchanging, and media streaming on the Internet is carried by IP.

The Internet Protocol was the first packet switched protocol. Originally developed to allow communication on the ARPAnet, IP has continually evolved and remains the most important layer three protocol currently in use. The version of IP most currently used is version four, or IPv4. However, as IP continues to gain acceptance and the size and traffic levels on the Internet continue to grow, IPv4 is hitting its limits. To resolve these issues, the Internet Engineering Task Force (the standard bearers for IP) has created an updated version of IP: IPv6, also known as **IPng** (for Next Generation). This chapter will introduce IP. Additional details on IP network design and IPv6 are covered in chapter 8.

## IP Addressing

Rather than breaking the segment and host portions of the network layer address into separate units, as was done in IPX, IP combines the two into a single hierarchical IP address. Although the hierarchical nature of IP addresses makes routing of IP packets easier, it makes understanding IP addressing somewhat confusing.

IPv4 addresses are 32 bits long and are represented as a sequence of four **octets.** Each octet is a decimal representation of an 8-bit section of the overall IP address. As shown in Figure 7-20, each 8-bit section of the overall IP address is converted to its decimal value and separated by a period. This is commonly referred to as a dotted decimal approach to representing IP addresses. Although people commonly refer to sections of an IP-based network by the IP address, it is important to remember that its the binary value that determines how the address is parsed and utilized.

IP Address Classes   Because the IP address contains both the network segment and host addresses, there must be a means of differentiating which bits belong to which each part. The original IPv4 specification provided this differentiation through the use of **address classes.** There are three basic address classes used for addressing normal network hosts that vary in the number of hosts that can be located on the

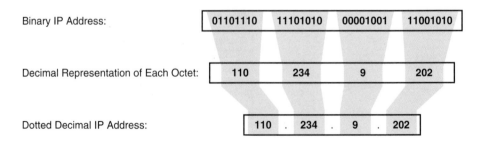

| Binary IP Address: | 01101110 | 11101010 | 00001001 | 11001010 |

| Decimal Representation of Each Octet: | 110 | 234 | 9 | 202 |

| Dotted Decimal IP Address: | 110 . 234 . 9 . 202 |

*Figure 7-20*   IP Address Construction

network segment. The relatively few class A networks support the largest number of hosts, class B networks offer more segments of fewer hosts and class C networks offer many segments of relatively few hosts. As illustrated in Figure 7-21, these **classful** addresses are broken apart on octet boundaries.

In addition to these basic address classes, two additional classes, class D and class E, can be used for IPv4 addressing. class D addresses are reserved for multicast systems such as routers, while class E addresses are reserved for future use. As shown in Figure 7-21, the class of an address can be identified by examining the first few bits of the address. Based on the class of the network, it is easy to determine which bits of the IP address represent the network segment and which bits represent the host address.

The assignment of address classes and network ID ranges to a particular organization wishing to connect to the Internet is the responsibility of the Internet Architecture Board (IAB). The IAB assures that all organizations using the Internet for network communications have unique IP addresses for all of their workstations. If an organization has no intention of ever accessing the Internet, then there may not be a need to register with the IAB for an IP address class and range of valid network IDs. However, even in this case, all workstations on all communicating networks must have IP addresses unique within the internal corporate network.

**Subnetworking**   One of the strengths of the IP protocol is its ability to support network **subnetworking.** If we only use classful addresses there is relatively little flexibility in the use of the address space. An organization with only ten hosts that needs to be on the Internet must be given at least a class C network. The unused addresses cannot be used elsewhere on the Internet and are wasted. This problem is compounded if the organization has three locations that each need ten hosts. In a true classful addressing scheme the organization would require at least three class C

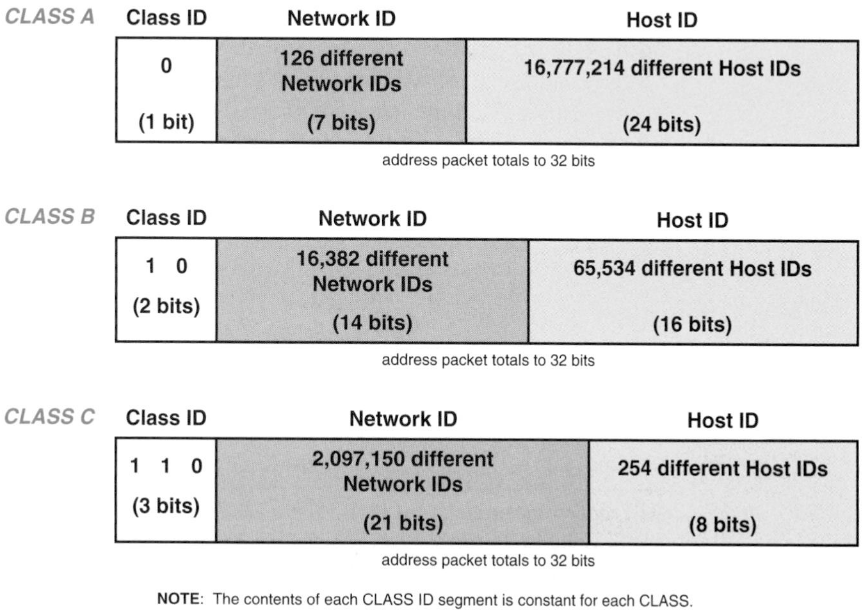

| CLASS A | Class ID | Network ID | Host ID |
|---|---|---|---|
| | 0 | 126 different Network IDs | 16,777,214 different Host IDs |
| | (1 bit) | (7 bits) | (24 bits) |

address packet totals to 32 bits

| CLASS B | Class ID | Network ID | Host ID |
|---|---|---|---|
| | 1  0 | 16,382 different Network IDs | 65,534 different Host IDs |
| | (2 bits) | (14 bits) | (16 bits) |

address packet totals to 32 bits

| CLASS C | Class ID | Network ID | Host ID |
|---|---|---|---|
| | 1  1  0 | 2,097,150 different Network IDs | 254 different Host IDs |
| | (3 bits) | (21 bits) | (8 bits) |

address packet totals to 32 bits

NOTE: The contents of each CLASS ID segment is constant for each CLASS.

*Figure 7-21*   IPv4 Address Classes

networks be assigned even though there are theoretically enough addresses in a single class C network to meet their needs.

Ideally, there would be a way to take the address space available in a classful network and break it into multiple subnetworks that each contain a limited number of hosts. For instance, a given organization could be issued a single class B network ID address with its associated 65,534 host IDs. This host section could be broken into multiple subnetworks (or **subnets**) and be distributed across multiple, geographically distributed locations.

The solution to the above dilemma is subnetworking. By applying a 32 bit subnet mask to their assigned class B IP address, a portion of the bits which make up the host ID can be reserved for denoting subnetworks, with the remaining bits being reserved for host IDs per subnetwork. If the first 8 bits of the host ID were reserved for subnetwork addresses and the final 8 bits of the host ID were reserved for hosts per subnetwork, this would allow the same class B address to yield 254 subnetworks with 254 hosts each, as opposed to one network with 65,534 hosts. Figure 7-22 provides examples of subnet masks. The overall effect of subnetworking is to create multiple network segments within the address space given by the IAB.

Subnetworking allows multiple network segments to be created within a single IP network address space. By creating such subnetworks, routing is also easily extended. From the perspective of a host outside the network, all hosts on any of the subnetworks appear to be on the original single network. Therefore these hosts simply route the packets to the gateway router for the network regardless of the actual destination subnetwork. The gateway router is configured to understand the subnetworking method used and routes the packets across the subnetworks to their intended destination. This process is illustrated in Figure 7-23 where the gateway router accepts all packets destined for the 10.x.x.x network and routes them based on class B subnetworking where the second octet has been made part of the network address rather than part of the host address. Subnetworking is covered in more detail in chapter 8.

**Subnet Masks**   As previously mentioned, an IP address contains both a segment address and a host address for a host, with the first $X$ bits representing the segment address and the remaining $32-X$ bits representing the host address. As long as addresses are used in a classful manner, the location of the split between the segment address and the host address can be determined by the first few bits of the IP address.

| | Binary Subnet Mask | Decimal Subnet Mask | Number of Subnetworks | Number of Hosts per Subnetwork |
|---|---|---|---|---|
| **Default Class B Subnet Mask** | 11111111 11111111 00000000 00000000 | 255.255.0.0 | 1 | 65,534 |
| **Alternative Subnet Mask Used to Subnet Class B Network** | 11111111 11111111 11111111 00000000 | 255.255.255.0 | 254 | 254 |

*Figure 7-22*   IPv4 Subnetworking

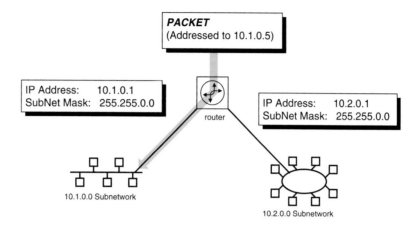

*Figure 7-23*   Routing with Subnetworking

However, when a classful network segment is subnetworked, this is no longer possible. The segment address becomes the original network address plus the subnetwork address, with the remaining bits used for the host address. Because there is no way of knowing if an address has been subnetworked or how many bits have been "stolen" from the original host section to create subnetworks, there is no way to know exactly how many bits are used for each merely by looking at the IP address. This problem is illustrated in Figure 7-24.

To resolve this problem there must be a way of identifying which bits are used for each portion of the overall address. This is accomplished via a **subnet mask.** A subnet mask is a 32-bit binary sequence that divides the IP address by using a one to indicate that the corresponding position in the IP address is part of the segment address and by using a zero to indicate that the corresponding portion in the IP address is part of the host address. Because the segment address is the first $x$ bits and the host address is the remaining bits, a subnet mask will always consist of $x$ ones followed by 32-$x$ zeroes. The effect of using varying subnet masks on an IP address is shown in Figure 7-25. Just like IP addresses, subnet masks are usually referred to in dotted decimal format.

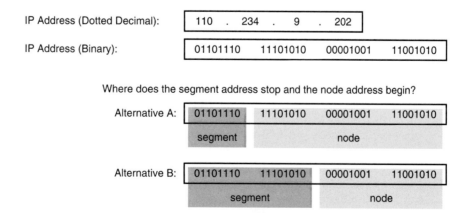

*Figure 7-24*   IP Segment Address vs. Host Address

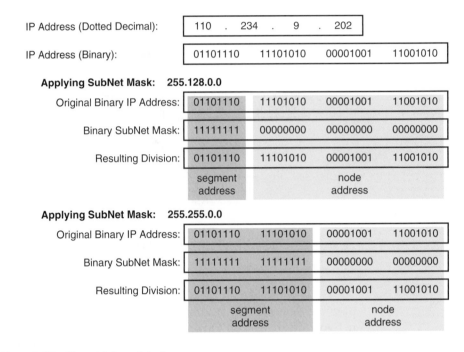

*Figure 7-25*   Use of Subnet Masks

**Special Host Addresses**   Once an IP address had been divided into a segment address and a range of host addresses through the application of a subnet mask, the resulting IP addresses may be assigned to the hosts on the network segment. However there are two reserved host-section addresses that may not be assigned to a host—the address that corresponds to all ones in the host section and the address that corresponds to all zeroes in the host section. Using all ones in the host section of the IP address denotes the **broadcast address** for the segment. This address is used to send a single message to every host on the network segment. All zeroes in the host section of the IP address is the address of the network segment itself. This address is used by routers to refer to the network in their routing tables. For a class C network these addresses correspond to x.x.x.255 and x.x.x.0, respectively.

**Default Gateway (Router)**   For IP networks that consist of a single network segment, the specification of an IP address and a segment mask is adequate to ensure proper packet delivery. However, most IP networks have multiple segments; in fact, support for multiple segments is one of the key reasons to use IP in the first place.

For IP networks that consist of multiple network segments, each host must also be configured with a **default gateway** (sometime referred to as a **gateway of last resort**). The default gateway address represents a router that should be used to route packets on remote network segments. The default router must reside on the same network segment as the host. If the host cannot talk to remote segments without a default gateway, how could it talk to a default gateway on a remove segment?

Although any valid address within a network segment can be declared the default router, it is common to use either the largest valid host address or the smallest valid host address. As mentioned earlier in this chapter, all zeroes in the host section of the IP address denotes the address of the network segment itself and all ones in the host section of the IP address denotes the broadcast address for the network segment. Therefore, the default router is usually set at either all zeroes with a one in the least significant bit or all ones with a zero in the least significant bit. For a class C network segment this would correspond to either x.x.x.1 or x.x.x.254, respectively. Regardless of which approach is taken, it is best to be consistent in terms of default gateway address across the internetwork. If x.x.x1 is the default router on one segment, it should be the default router on *all* segments.

**IP to Datalink Address Resolution**    Unlike IPX, an IP host address has no direct relationship with its associated NIC datalink (MAC) address. Therefore, a mechanism to resolve IP addresses to datalink addresses is required to deliver packets within a local area network. This process is analogous to the use of directory assistance services in order to find a desired phone number. There are two protocols that resolve between IP addresses and datalink addresses: ARP and RARP.

**Address Resolution Protocol** or **ARP** (RFC 826) is used if an IP address of workstation is known but a datalink layer address for the same workstation is required. Each host on the network uses ARP to determine the datalink address for each destination.

**Reverse Address Resolution Protocol** or **RARP** is used if the datalink layer address of the workstation is known but the IP address of the same workstation is required. RARP is most commonly used to provide configuration information to hosts at boot time.

ARP and RARP are broadcast protocols. The requests for addresses are broadcast to an entire IP network segment. It should be obvious that this could represent a significant traffic burden. Routers do not rebroadcast ARP or RARP packets and thereby act as a filter to prevent infinite propagation of ARP/RARP broadcasts. Responses to ARP and RARP requests are sent directly to the requesting workstation rather than being broadcast to all attached workstations. The ARP response is sent by the workstation whose IP address is found in the destination address field of the broadcast ARP packets. To reduce the overhead required by ARP requests, ARP responses are stored in an ARP cache so that it will not be necessary to rebroadcast for the same address.

**Packet Construction**    IP packets have a minimum length of 576 bytes and a maximum length of 64 Kbytes. Depending on the underlying layer two protocol(s) used to deliver the packet, an IP packet may be broken into smaller packet fragments as described earlier in this chapter. As shown in Figure 7-26, the IP header can be either 20 or 24 bytes long, resulting in an effective data payload of 552 to 65,516 bytes. Packets are sent with the bits transmitted in **network byte order** (from left to right). The IPv4 packet layout is illustrated in Figure 7-26 and a detailed description of each field in the IP header is presented in Figure 7-27.

## IMPROVING WINDOWS INTERNET ACCESS BY REDUCING FRAGMENTATION

The network functionality of the Microsoft Windows family of operating systems was primarily designed to connect clients to local servers. Because of this focus, the default maximum transmission unit for IPv4 is 1,500 bytes. Although this setting provides increased efficiency on Ethernet networks by reducing packet header overhead, it usually results in fragmented packets when accessing the Internet.

If the primary network connectivity issue for a computer is Internet access through a modem to an ISP, reducing the IP MTU to 576 can potentially increase

In Sharper Focus

Internet connectivity speed. By setting the MTU to 576, the ISP's gateway router no longer needs to fragment and re-assemble every packet transmitted between the router and the remote host. Changes to the IP MTU can be made through the registry editor. Instructions are available at many locations on the Internet.

## Private Addressing and Network Address Translation

As mentioned earlier IP address depletion has resulted from the explosion of the Internet as well as the inefficient use of existing IP addresses forced by Classful addressing. One way to cope with the rapid depletion of IP addresses is through the use of **private addressing.**

When organizations connect to the Internet, the IP addresses that they send out over the Internet must be globally unique. In most cases, an organization's Internet service provider specifies these globally unique addresses.

However, traffic that remains only on an organization's private network does not need to be globally unique. It only needs to be unique across that organization's private network. In support of this, the Internet Assigned Numbers Authority (IANA) has set aside the following three ranges of private IP addresses:

- 10.0.0.0 through 10.255.255.255    (equal to a single class A Network ID)

- 172.16.0.0 through 172.31.255.255    (equal to 16 contiguous class B Network IDs)

- 192.168.0.0 through 192.168.255.255    (equal to 256 contiguous class C Network IDs)

Traffic using any of the above address ranges must remain on the organization's private network. Since anyone is welcome to use these address ranges, they are not globally unique and therefore cannot be used on the Internet. Computers on a network using the Private IP address space can still send and receive traffic to/from the Internet by using **network address translation** (**NAT**). There are two basic types of NAT—Static NAT and dynamic NAT with dynamic NAT the most commonly implemented.

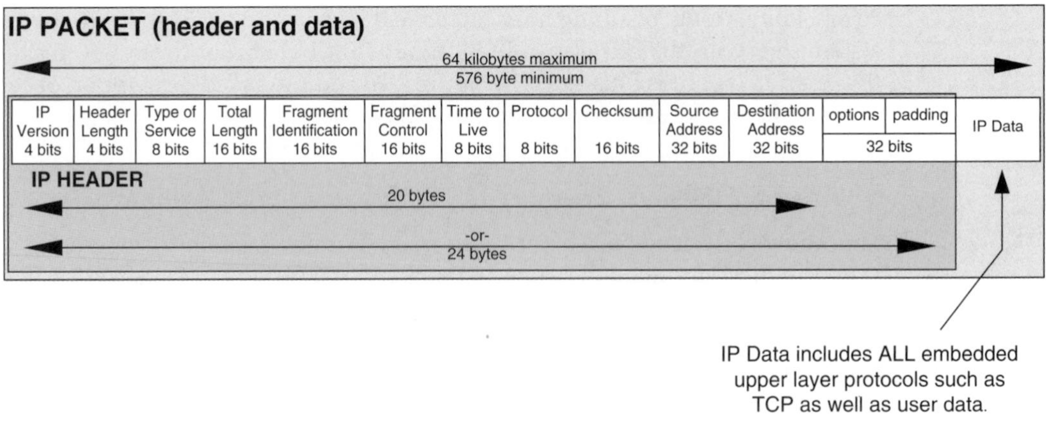

*Figure 7-26* IPv4 Packet Layout

| IP Packet Field | Function/Importance |
|---|---|
| **IP Version** | It is important for computers and internetwork devices processing this IP packet to know the version of IP with which it was written in order to preclude any potential cross-version incompatibility problems. |
| **Header Length** | The header can be either five or six 32-bit words (20 or 24 bytes), depending on whether the options field in activated. |
| **Type of Service** | The flags in this field can be used to indicate eight levels of precedence as well as different types of service for low delay, high throughput, or high reliability. Unless routers are able to read this field and respond accordingly, they are of no use. |
| **Total Length** | This is the total length of the IP packet, including the header and the IP data. |
| **Fragment Identification** | This is a 16-bit integer ID of a fragment. IP packets must be fragmented as dictated by the limitations of lower layer (data-link) network architectures. |
| **Fragment Control (Flags and Offset)** | Fragment flags (3 bits) are used to indicate the last fragment of an original datagram, as well as if a datagram should not be fragmented. Fragment offset (13 bits) indicates the relative position of this fragment in the original IP datagram. |
| **Time to Live** | This field is a simple hop counter that is decremented every time this IP packet is handled by a router. When the Time to Live counter reaches 0, the packet is discarded so that it does not wander around the network infinitely, monopolizing bandwidth. The counter can be initialized as high as 255, but is more typically set to 32 or 16. |
| **Protocol** | This is an important field because it indicates which protocol is embedded with the IP data area. By reading this field, the IP software is able to forward the IP data to the proper transport layer protocol stack for further processing. Typical values and their corresponding protocols are as follows:<br>17 – UPD<br>6 – TCP<br>1 – ICMP<br>8 – EGP<br>89 – OSPF |
| **Checksum** | This field is more correctly known as the IP Header Checksum because it only provides error detection for the IP header. Reliability checks for the IP data are provided by upper-layer protocols. |
| **Source Address** | This is the 32-bit IP address of source computer. |
| **Destination Address** | This is the 32-bit IP address of the ultimate destination computer. |
| **Options** | Used for diagnostics purposes, these fields are sometimes set by other TCP/IP family utilities such as Ping or Trace Route. Security and source routing options can also be set using this field. All workstations and routers in a given network must support these features in order to be implemented fully and effectively. |
| **Padding** | Depending on how many options are selected, padding of zeroes may need to be added in order to bring the IP header to the full $6 \times 32$-bit word (24 byte) length. |

*Figure 7-27* IP Header Fields

Regardless of the approach used, NAT is provided by a router (such as Internet gateway devices from Linksys and D-Link among others) or by a stand-alone network translation software package running on a multi-homed server. A multi-homed server is the term used to describe a server that would have one network interface card that was a member of the internal private IP address space network and one network interface card that was assigned a globally unique IP address. A version of such a program that is included as a networking feature of Linux is known as IP Masquerade, while a version included with Windows is known as Internet Connection Sharing (ICS). For the purposes of this section we will refer to any device or server than provides NAT services as a "NAT box."

A static NAT (SNAT) solution has multiple public IP addresses defined on the external NIC on the NAT server. The server then statically binds a public address with a private address from the internal network. The SNAT process is shown in Figure 7-28:

1. Outbound traffic from the internal host is sent to the NAT box.

2. The source address is translated from the private address of the internal host to the public address assigned to the internal host.

3. The packet is forwarded to the destination host on the Internet.

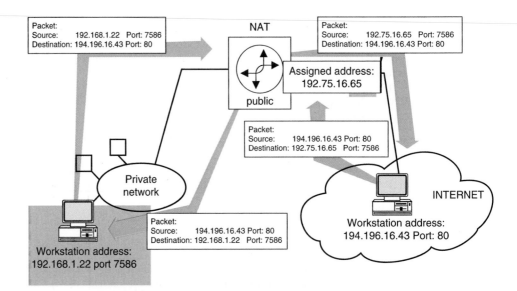

## NAT Source/Destination Table

| Private Source IP Address | Assigned Public Address |
| --- | --- |
| 192.168.1.22 | 192.75.16.65 |
| 192.168.1.23 | 192.75.16.66 |
| 192.168.1.24 | 192.75.16.67 |
| 192.168.1.25 | 192.75.16.68 |
| ...and so on... | ...and so on... |

*Figure 7-28* Static Network Address Translation (SNAT)

The destination doesn't know anything about the NAT process and simply responds to the source address/port in the packet it received. When the reply packet arrives at the NAT box:

1. The packet's destination address is examined to determine to which private host the packet is truly intended.

2. The destination address is changed to the private address of the destination.

3. The packet is forwarded on the private network to the destination host.

Dynamic NAT (DNAT), also known as Port Address Translation, takes the concept of NAT further by allowing a single public address to serve multiple private addresses. This is accomplished by translating port numbers as well as source addresses. As shown in Figure 7-29, the DNAT process consists of the following steps:

1. Outbound traffic from the internal host is sent to the NAT box.

2. The source address is translated from the private address of the internal host to the public address of the NAT box.

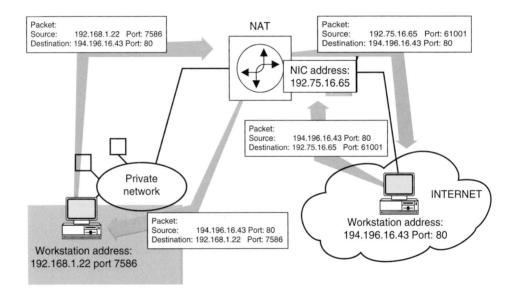

### NAT Source/Destination Table

| Private Source IP Address | Private Source Assigned Port ID |
|---|---|
| 192.168.1.22 | 61001 |
| 192.168.1.23 | 61002 |
| 192.168.1.24 | 61003 |
| 192.168.1.25 | 61004 |
| ...and so on... | ...and so on... |

*Figure 7-29*   Dynamic Network Address Translation (DNAT)

3. The source port number is changed from its original value to a value that represents the internal host.

4. The NAT box makes a table in which ports are assigned to each internal address.

5. The packet is forwarded to the original destination.

Just as in SNAT, the destination doesn't know anything about the NAT process and simply responds to the source address/port in the packet it received. When the reply packet arrives at the NAT box:

1. The packet's destination port is examined and compared to the port translation table to determine which internal host for which the packet is really destined.

2. The destination address and port are translated to the internal address of the destination host.

3. The packet is forwarded to the internal host.

Because it allows a single public IP address to service multiple internal hosts, DNAT is used far more often than SNAT. Because of this, unless a NAT solution specifically says that it is using SNAT, you should assume that it is a DNAT implementation.

## ICMP: Internet Control Message Protocol

Although IP is, by definition, an unreliable transport mechanism, it does have a mechanism to deliver error and status messages. The **Internet Control Message Protocol (ICMP)** delivers a variety of error status and control messages related to the ability of IP to deliver its encapsulated payloads. ICMP uses IP as a transport mechanism and is able to deliver a variety of error and control messages through the use of type and code fields as illustrated in Figure 7-30.

ICMP carries thirteen different message types as detailed in Figure 7-31.

The most common use of ICMP from the user's perspective checking for network connectivity between two hosts. The ping application is used to generate and process ICMP echo/reply packets, commonly referred to as "ping" packets. The process of checking for connectivity in this manner is commonly referred to as "pinging" the address.

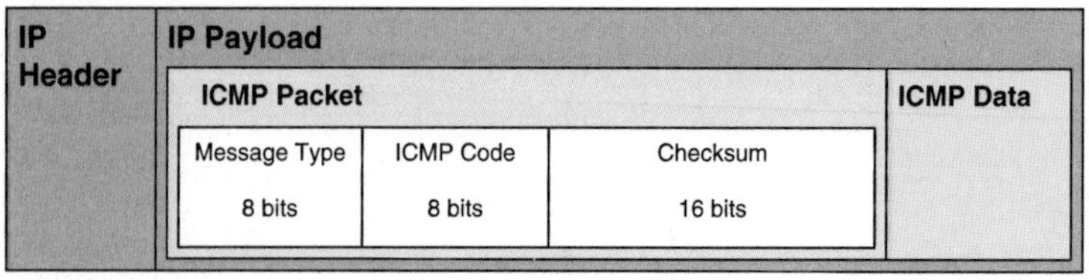

| IP Header | IP Payload | | | |
|---|---|---|---|---|
| | ICMP Packet | | | ICMP Data |
| | Message Type | ICMP Code | Checksum | |
| | 8 bits | 8 bits | 16 bits | |

*Figure 7-30*   ICMP Protocol Layout

| ICMP Type | Name | Explanation/Use |
|---|---|---|
| 0 | Echo Reply | This is the ICMP message expected from a workstation that has been "pinged" by an ICMP Type 8 message. |
| 3 | Destination Unreachable | A router would return this message to the source workstation or router along with a code indicating a more specific reason why the destination was unreachable. In this case, unreachable means that the network identified in the IP address could not be found. Possible reason codes include:<br>0—Network is unreachable.<br>1—Host is unreachable.<br>2—Protocol is unreachable.<br>3—Port is unreachable.<br>4—Fragmentation needed, but the "Do not fragment" bit is set.<br>5—Source route failed. |
| 4 | Source Quench | This is how IP's version of flow control is implemented. The source quench message is a request from a computer or router to a source of IP datagrams to slow down the flow of IP datagrams in order to avoid data loss. |
| 5 | Redirect a route | Also known as route change request, this ICMP message is used only by routers when they receive an IP packet that they believe could be handled more quickly or efficiently by a different router. In that case, the originating workstation or router is notified of the new suggested route, and the original message is also forwarded to the preferred router in order to expedite the delivery of the original IP packet. |
| 8 | Echo request to a remote station | This is the ICMP message sent out by the Ping utility. ICMP message type 0 is the expected return from a successful Ping. |
| 11 | Time exceeded for datagram | This message is usually sent from routers to originating workstations if the Time to Live field (TTL) in the IP header has been decremented to 0. This can be caused if a hop count has been exceeded or if a network failure has occurred, causing an IP packet to be processed by more routers than usual. |
| 12 | Parameter problem with a datagram | This message is fairly serious, as it indicates that a parameter within the IP header could not be understood. Luckily, the message includes an indication of where the parameter problem occurred in the IP header in order to more easily diagnose the problem. |
| 13 | TimeStamp request | This message is used to request the time of day from a networked host. |
| 14 | TimeStamp reply | This is the reply message type for message type 13 requests. |
| 15 | Information request | This message is used to request the network number of the network to which the requesting host is attached. The most likely scenario when a host wouldn't know the network to which it is attached is in remote access situations using SLIP or PPP. |
| 16 | Information reply | This is the ICMP message type used to reply to ICMP message type 15. |
| 17 | Address Mask request | This message type is used to request the subnetwork mask of the network to which a host is connected. It is likely to be used in the same situations as ICMP message type 15. |
| 18 | Address Mask reply | This is the ICMP message type used to reply to ICMP message type 17. |

*Figure 7-31*   ICMP Message Types

## Transport Layer Protocols

As previously mentioned, Internet protocols implement OSI network model functionality in a slightly modified manner. As illustrated in Figure 7-18, Internet transport or host-to-host protocols implement both transport layer functionality and session layer addressing functionality. The remaining OSI session, presentation, and application layer functionality are implemented by Internet application layer protocols. This chapter will focus on Internet protocols through the transport layer. Application layer protocols will be covered in subsequent chapters on network operating systems.

**UDP—User Datagram Protocol**    The **User Datagram Protocol** (**UDP**) is used to provide unreliable, connectionless messaging services for applications. The header has two main purposes:

- It allows UDP to keep track of which applications it is sending a datagram to and from through the use of port addresses.

- It passes those messages along to IP for subsequent delivery.

Because UDP does not provide reliable connection-oriented services, the UDP packet header is small. UDP uses only an 8-byte header as illustrated in Figure 7-32. A description of the UDP header fields is presented in Figure 7-33.

Due to the small size of UDP packet headers and the fact that they require no acknowledgments from the receiving host, UDP is the perfect transport/session layer protocol for delivering streaming media packets. The overhead associated with a connection-oriented protocol would greatly reduce the number of clients that a streaming media server could support when compared with the relatively efficient UDP protocol.

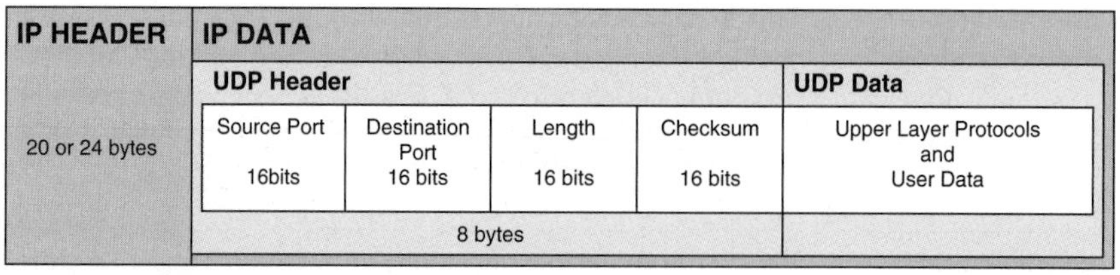

| IP HEADER | IP DATA | | | | |
|---|---|---|---|---|---|
| | **UDP Header** | | | | **UDP Data** |
| 20 or 24 bytes | Source Port<br><br>16bits | Destination Port<br><br>16 bits | Length<br><br>16 bits | Checksum<br><br>16 bits | Upper Layer Protocols<br>and<br>User Data |
| | 8 bytes | | | | |

*Figure 7-32*    UPD Header Layout

| UDP Header Field | Function/Importance |
|---|---|
| **Source Port** | Port address of the application on the source host that sent the packet |
| **Destination Port** | Port address of the application on the destination host that is to receive the packet |
| **Length** | Overall length of the UDP datagram |
| **Checksum** | Checksum calculated on both the UDP header and data |

*Figure 7-33*    UDP Header Fields

**TCP—Transmission Control Protocol**    The majority of network traffic requires a more reliable connection than UDP offers. To provide connection-oriented, reliable data transmission, the **Transmission Control Protocol (TCP)** is the transport/session layer protocol of choice. Reliability is assured through the additional fields contained within the TCP header that offer flow control, acknowledgments of successful receipt of packets after error checking, retransmission of packets as required, and proper sequencing of packets.

The fact that TCP is considered connection-oriented implies that a point-to-point connection between source and destination computers must be established before transmission can begin and that the connection will be torn down after transmission has concluded. This is accomplished through the use of TCP flags. When an originating host needs to establish a connection with another host, it sends a TCP packet containing an SYN flag and a sequence number to the destination. This sequence number is used as the starting point for the stream of TCP packets from the source to the destination.

When the destination host receives the initial SYN packet, it responds by sending an ACK of the SYN packet's sequence number with a SYN packet and sequence number to establish the return half of the connection. The originating host then sends an ACK to the destination host's SYN packet and the connection is established. Subsequent packets in each direction increment the sequence numbers. When communication is complete the originating host sends an FIN flag to the destination and tears down the connection. This process is illustrated in Figure 7-34.

The TCP header layout is illustrated in Figure 7-35 and the header fields are explained in Figure 7-36.

**UDP and TCP Port Numbers**    UDP and TCP provide session layer addressing through the use of **ports.** Ports are specific 16-bit addresses that are uniquely related to particular applications. Source port and destination port addresses are included in the UDP/TCP header. The unique port address of an application combined with the unique 32-bit IP address of the computer on which the application is executing is

### TCP Connection Creation

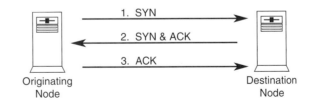

### TCP Connection Tear-Down

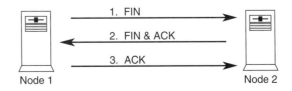

*Figure 7-34*    Connection Creation and Tear Down

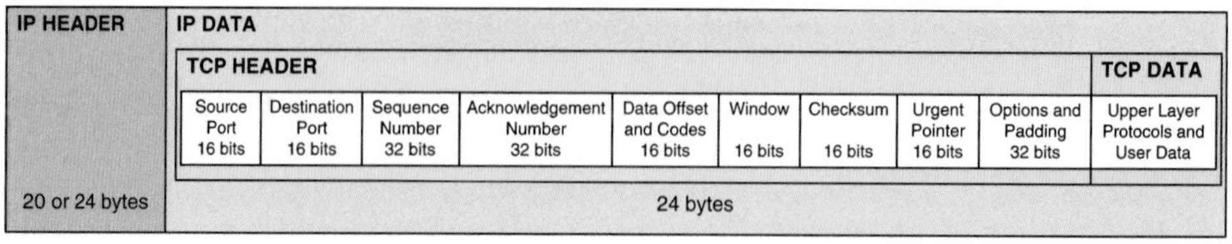

| IP HEADER | IP DATA | | | | | | | | | | |
|---|---|---|---|---|---|---|---|---|---|---|---|
| | **TCP HEADER** | | | | | | | | | | **TCP DATA** |
| | | Source Port 16 bits | Destination Port 16 bits | Sequence Number 32 bits | Acknowledgement Number 32 bits | Data Offset and Codes 16 bits | Window 16 bits | Checksum 16 bits | Urgent Pointer 16 bits | Options and Padding 32 bits | Upper Layer Protocols and User Data |
| 20 or 24 bytes | 24 bytes | | | | | | | | | | |

*Figure 7-35*    TCP Header Layout

known as a **socket.** Some typical port numbers for popular TCP/IP applications are listed in Figure 7-37.

## Support Application Layer Protocols and Services

Although the following protocols and services are not part of the TCP/IP standard themselves and are not required to make an IP-based network function, they offer services that greatly increase the usability and manageability of IP-based networks.

**Automatic IP Address Assignment**    Each host on an IP-based network must have a unique IP address. Traditionally, these addresses were statically assigned to each host through an interactive process. Although this is an effective manner to assign IP addresses, it does represent some problems:

- Someone must serve as the central authority to ensure that each host has a unique IP address. From a practical perspective it makes sense to have the DNS administrator perform this task as they keep track of all IP addresses while managing the DNS tables.

- When the IP address of a host is changed, it requires administrator intervention in assigning a new IP address.

To resolve these issues two services have been developed to automatically assign IP addresses to network hosts: BOOTP and DHCP. **BOOTP,** the boot protocol, is a static address assignment method. When a host is configured to use BOOTP it broadcasts a datalink layer frame to the network segment requesting an IP address. A BOOTP server on the network then looks up the physical (MAC) address of the requesting station in a table and replies with the correct IP address. Through the use of BOOTP relay agents the requirement that each network segment contain a BOOTP server can be eliminated. A BOOTP relay agent listens for BOOTP requests and forwards them to the server. The server looks up the IP information and sends it to the relay agent, who replies to the requesting host.

Although BOOTP was a step in the right direction for solving manual IP address assignment problems, it still requires one-to-one mapping between hosts and IP addresses. This is especially a concern given the explosive growth of the Internet. With hosts connecting to the Internet on an occasional dial-in basis, it is terribly inefficient to assign each host a unique IP address, especially considering the fact that IPv4 address space is rapidly running out.

To resolve this issue, the **Dynamic Host Control Protocol (DHCP)** was developed. An extension of the original BOOTP protocol, the Dynamic Host Configuration

| UDP Header Field | Function/Importance |
|---|---|
| **Source Port** | The port address that uniquely identifies the particular application from which this packet is sent. |
| **Destination Port** | The port address that uniquely identifies the particular application to which this packet is addressed. |
| **Sequence Number** | The sequence number of the first octet of data in this segment. This allows TCP at the destination address to properly re-sequence the data stream if IP happens to deliver the segments out of order. |
| **Acknowledgment Number** | In order to meet its objective of assuring reliable transmission, the transmitting computer must know the sequence number of the segment that was last successfully received by the receiving computer. The transmitted acknowledgment number is, in fact, the segment number of the last successfully received segment plus one. This lets the transmitting computer know which segment the receiving computer is waiting for. If the acknowledgment number does not increment before a preset retransmission timer expires, then the transmitting computer assumes that the repeated acknowledgment number's segment never arrived and that it must retransmit that segment. |
| **Data Offset** | The length of the TCP header in terms of the number of 32-bit words before the start of the TCP data. The entry in this field would be 5 (20 bytes) if options and padding are not enabled, or 6 (24 bytes) if they are enabled. |
| **Reserved** | Set to all zeroes. |
| **Codes** | Also known as flags, codes are used for connection setup, management, and termination. There are six possible codes:<br>• *SYN*—Used to initially set up connections and to synchronize sequence numbers.<br>• *ACK*—Indicates validity of acknowledgment number, especially important at connection setup time.<br>• *URG*—Indicates validity of urgent pointer field.<br>• *PSH*—The Push flag is used to cause TCP to flush data buffers immediately in order to push this packet directly to the application whose port number is indicated in the TCP header.<br>• *FIN*—Used to terminate connections normally.<br>• *RST*—Used to reset the connection, thereby forcing a connection termination. |
| **Window** | The window field is used by TCP as a means of a sort of flow control. The window value is sent from a destination host to a source host advertising how many bytes of free buffer space are available on the destination host for this connection. This number then becomes the limit as to how much data can be sent by the source before receiving an acknowledgment from the destination host. |
| **Checksum** | This is a calculated checksum on the TCP header and data that are transmitted to the destination host for error detection purposes. |
| **Urgent Pointer** | This tells the destination where to look in the data field for an urgent message, such as a break signal or some other type of interrupt. |
| **Options and Padding** | The only option typically set with TCP is a value for maximum segment size that lets the destination host know the largest acceptable segment length. Padding is used to extend the options field to a full 32-bit word, and is only used if options are set. |

*Figure 7-36*   TCP Header Fields

| TCP/IP Application | Port Number |
|---|---|
| HTTP | 80 |
| Telnet | 23 |
| FTP | 21 |
| SMTP | 25 |
| BootP client | 68 |
| BootP server | 67 |
| TFTP | 69 |
| Finger | 79 |
| NetBIOS session service | 139 |
| X.400 | 103 |
| SNMP | 161 |

*Figure 7-37*   Selected Port Numbers

Protocol allows special servers to dynamically assign TCP/IP addresses to hosts. A DHCP server references a database of available IP addresses and can dynamically assign available addresses to requesting clients. IP addresses issued by DHCP are leased, rather than being permanently assigned. The length of time that IP addresses can be kept by DHCP clients is known as the lease duration. Dial-in users are typically assigned an IP address only for the duration of their call. In addition to dynamically assigning IP addresses, DHCP can statically assign addresses in a manner similar to BOOTP through the use of address reservations.

Practical Advice
and Information

### USE OF DHCP FOR SERVERS

DHCP can greatly reduce IP addressing issues for network clients. Servers should always be assigned permanent IP addresses to ensure that clients can locate them on the network. DHCP can still be used to assign IP addresses to servers, but DHCP reservations should be used to ensure each server maintains a consistent network address.

**Domain Name System**   IP addresses are used to uniquely identify hosts on an IP-based network. However, 32-bit IPv4 addresses are difficult for humans to memorize and work with, even in dotted decimal form. To make identifying host addresses easier for people, the **Domain Name System (DNS)** was created. DNS provides the following key services:

- Uniquely identifies all hosts connected to the Internet by name

- Resolves, or translates, host names into IP addresses (and vice versa)

- Identifies which services are offered by each host such as gateway or mail transfer, and to which networks these services are offered

DNS is a hierarchical naming structure, with the hierarchical layers being separated by periods—for example, www.company.com. DNS addresses are listed in inverse order with the hostname being the first word and the domain name being the following words. In the www.company.com example, *www* is the hostname and *company.com* is the domain name. The last section of a domain name is called the top-level domain. Top-level domains are carefully managed to ensure that there is no confusion between DNS domains. To make DNS as intuitive as possible, consistent naming conventions have been established. For hosts connected directly to the Internet, standard top-level domains such as .edu for educational institutions, .com for commercial entities, and .gov for government agencies are used. Private institutions not directly connecting to the Internet are welcome to establish their own naming schemes for use within their corporate networks.

DNS is physically implemented in a client/server architecture in which client-based DNS software known as the DNS or name **resolver,** sends requests for DNS name resolution to a **DNS** (or name) **server.** The address of the nearest (primary) DNS server, as well as at least one backup (secondary) DNS server, is entered into a configuration file when TCP/IP is installed on the local client. Networks that connect to the Internet must supply both a primary and backup DNS server in order to process name queries from Internet attached hosts. DNS is a hierarchical service in that if a given DNS server cannot resolve a name as requested, it will reply with the address of a DNS server of a higher authority that may have more available information. Alternatively, the local DNS server may contact the higher authority DNS server itself, thereby increasing its own knowledge while meeting the client request in a process known as **recursion.** The scope of coverage, or collection of domains, for which a given DNS server can resolve names is known as a DNS **zone.**

**IP Interior Routing Protocols**    In order for IP-based routers to automatically update their routing tables a routing protocol must be implemented. Although they are tied directly to a specific layer three protocol, routing protocols themselves are considered application layer protocols supporting the routing application. There are two basic, nonproprietary IP interior routing protocols: RIP and OSPF. RIP is a distance vector protocol, while OSPF is a link state protocol. RIP and OSPF are detailed in chapter 8.

## ■ STAND ALONE TRANSPORT LAYER PROTOCOLS

### NetBEUI (NBF)

**NetBEUI Frame (NBF)** is a simple transport/session layer protocol that does not provide any network layer functionality. The lack of network layer addressing results in a non-routable protocol limited to use on networks consisting of a single network segment.

As the expansion of NetBEUI (NetBIOS Extended User Interface) implies, NetBEUI is an extended version of the original NetBIOS API used in Microsoft LAN Manager and OS/2 LAN Server. NetBEUI is a connection-oriented, reliable protocol that makes use of sequence numbers and acknowledgments to ensure correct data transmission. NBF improves on NetBEUI's data transfer performance in connection-oriented sessions by adopting an adaptive sliding window protocol that allows for more efficient data transfer. As will be seen, the word *window* in the name of this protocol is not related to the term *window* as in Windows NT.

NBF is able to adjust how many packets can be sent by the sending computer before an acknowledgment must be received. Ideally, the sending computer wants to send the maximum number of packets possible while avoiding the need to retransmit packets due to transmission errors. The number of packets allowed to be sent before the receipt of an acknowledgment determines the size of the **send window.** Should a negative acknowledgment be received, thereby necessitating a packet retransmission, the sending window will slide back to the packet that was received in error and retransmit it.

The second major improvement of NBF over NetBEUI has to do with **session limits.** Since NetBEUI is NetBIOS-based, it was forced to support the 254 session limit of NetBIOS. The source of this limit is a variable within NetBIOS known as the **local session number.** The local session number is a 1-byte (8-bit) field with a limit of only 256 possible entries (2 to the eighth = 256, less reserved numbers = 254). Since Windows NT servers using the NBF communications protocol could easily need to support more than 254 sessions, some way needed to be found to overcome the 254 session limit. The key to the solution is a two-dimensional matrix maintained by NBF that maps 254 logical session numbers against the network address of each computer with which it may establish a session. (A detailed explanation of the mathematical algorithms behind this solution is beyond the scope of this chapter.) The end result of the maintenance and translation of the various matrices is that each client to server connection can support 254 sessions, rather than a grand total for all connections of 254 sessions.

Practical Advice
and Information

### USE OF NETBEUI

NetBEUI has two selling points: efficiency and ease of configuration. Because NetBEUI is not routable, there is no need to assign network addresses or to reserve space in the packet header to carry them. However, these points are overshadowed by the fact that NetBEUI is non-routable.

The only reason to use NetBEUI is connection with legacy equipment that requires its use. At this point in time, there is no reason to install a new NetBEUI based network.

### DLC

**Datalink Control** or **DLC** is a communication protocol traditionally reserved for communication with IBM mainframe computers. DLC is used by Microsoft SNA Gateway for Windows NT to allow transparent interoperability between Windows NT clients and IBM mainframe computers. By using a gateway server, the Windows NT clients do not require any hardware or software modifications in order to communicate with the IBM mainframe. DLC has also been adopted as a means to communicate between print servers and printers directly attached to the network through network interface cards such as Hewlett-Packard JetDirect cards.

Similar to NetBEUI, DLC is a transport-layer-only protocol that is nonroutable and is only applicable to single segment networks. DLC does adheres to the OSI model principal of independence of the functional layers by running equally well over ethernet or token ring network interface cards and attached network architectures. In addition, DLC is also compatible with the IEEE 802.2 LLC (Logical Link Control) specification and frame layout.

## NETWORK PRINTERS AND DLC

Although DLC is a viable protocol solution for network attached printers, only a single print server can attach to a DLC connected printer at a time. Combined with the requirement that the print server be physically located on the same network segment as the printer, this greatly limits network printing scalability.

If IP is in use on the network a better solution to connect to network attached printers is the LPR protocol. Most network printer cards support this protocol that allows multiple servers to attach to a single printer. Since LPR is an application layer protocol that runs over IP, it allows print servers throughout the network to print to network attached printers.

## SUMMARY

The network layer of the OSI Network Reference Model is concerned with addressing and routing data packets between nodes on connected internetworks. All data from higher level protocols is encapsulated in network layer protocols for transmission across network segments.

Each node must be given a fully qualified network layer address consisting of both a network segment address and a node address. This fully qualified network layer address is resolved to an underlying NIC physical address when the layer three packet is encapsulated in a layer two frame for transmission at the datalink layer of the OSI model.

The transport layer of the OSI Network Reference Model is concerned with the creation, maintenance, and destruction of logical network connections between nodes. Typically connection-oriented in nature, packets sent across a transport layer connection are subject to error correction and flow control.

The session layer of the OSI Network Reference Model is concerned with addressing data streams to particular applications running on each node. These connections, know as sessions, are typically identified via ports and sockets.

There are two major network layer protocol suites currently in use: IPX/SPX and TCP/IP. IPX/SPX is the traditional network layer protocol for Novell NetWare systems and provides an easy to configure inter-network protocol.

IPX is the network layer protocol responsible for end to end communication across the internetwork. IPX also provides a means of addressing the applications on each host through the use of a socket address. SPX is an optional transport layer protocol that adds reliability to IPX.

TCP/IP is the protocol suite used to transmit data across the Internet. The TCP/IP suite consists of three major protocols: IP, TCP, and UDP. The current version of the IP protocol is IPv4.

There are three basic classes of IP addresses used to address hosts on an IP network: class A, B, and C addresses. A fourth address type, class D, is used to address multicast data flows. When classful addresses are used the first few bits in the address defines which part of the address is the network segment address and which part is the host address.

Subnetworking provides a means of breaking a classful IP address into smaller units to make better use of the address space. When subnetworking some of an addresses host bits are stolen to create a subnet address. When subnetworking the entire classful address must be subnetworked. A subnet mask is used to tell where the break between the extended network segment address and the host address is located.

UDP is a connectionless protocol used to add port addressing to IP. Due to its unreliable nature, UDP is best used for single packet messages and data streams that can tolerate packet loss. Examples of traffic flows that are appropriate for UDP include DHCP, routing messages, and media streams such as VOIP phone calls.

TCP is a connection-oriented transport layer protocol that adds reliability and port addressing to IP. TCP uses a three step handshake to build reliable connections between hosts. The majority of IP based application layer traffic uses TCP to take advantage of its reliability.

NetBEUI and DLC are non-routable protocols. NetBEUI was traditionally used for Microsoft Windows peer-to-peer networks while DLC was traditionally used for mainframe or printer connectivity. Both should not be used in modern networks unless required for backward compatibility.

## KEY TERMS

address resolution
Address Resolution Protocol (ARP)
Boot Protocol (BOOTP)
broadcast address
classful
connectionless protocols
connection-oriented protocols
Datalink Control Protocol (DLC)
de-encapsulation
default gateway
distance vector protocol
Domain Name System (DNS)
Dynamic Host Control Protocol (DHCP)
encapsulation
fragmentation
host-to-host
Internet Control Message Protocol (ICMP)

Internet Packet Exchange (IPX)
Internet Protocol (IP)
link state protocol
Maximum Transmission Unit (MTU)
multicasting
multi-homed
multi-homed
NetBEUI Frame (NBF)
NetWare Link Services Protocol (NLSP)
network segment address
node address
octet
Open Shortest Path First (OSPF)
Point-to-Point Protocol (PPP)
Port
Recursion
resolver
Reverse Address Resolution Protocol (RARP)

reverse poison
router
Routing Information Protocol (RIP)
Sequenced Packet Exchange protocol (SPX)
Service Advertising Protocol (SAP)
slow convergence
socket
split horizon
subnet mask
subnetworking
Time To Live (TTL)
Transmission Control Protocol/Internet Protocol (TCP/IP)
triggered updates
tuple
zone

## REVIEW QUESTIONS

1. What are the two components of a network layer address?
2. Explain the concept of protocol encapsulation.
3. Explain the concept of address resolution.
4. What layer's address is used to deliver data across an inter-network (end to end delivery)?
5. What layer's address is used to deliver data to a NIC within a network segment (point to point delivery)?
6. What is meant by protocol fragmentation?
7. What is the implication of fragmentation between the network and datalink layers of the OSI Network Reference Model?
8. What does a router do?
9. What address does a router use to make routing decisions?
10. Why are routing protocols used?

11. What is the difference between a distance vector routing protocol and a link state routing protocol?
12. Explain the difference between connectionless and connection-oriented protocols
13. Why are all connectionless protocols considered unreliable?
14. What is a session?
15. Explain the purpose of ports and sockets.
16. List the protocols in the IPX/SPX protocol suite. What is the primary purpose of each protocol?
17. How are IPX network segment addresses assigned to IPX routers?
18. How are IPX network segment addresses assigned to non-routing IPX nodes?
19. How are IPX node addresses assigned?
20. What is the address resolution process used to resolve physical addresses from IPX addresses?

21. What is a socket?
22. What is the MTU of an IPX packet?
23. What field in an IPX packet prevents a packet from wandering through an inter-network forever?
24. What is the distance vector routing protocol used with IPX?
25. What is the link state routing protocol used with IPX?
26. List the protocols in the TCP/IP protocol suite. What is the primary purpose of each protocol?
27. How is address resolution accomplished within the IP network layer protocol?
28. Explain the concept of subnetworking.
29. What are the first three bits of a class C IP address?
30. Break the IP address 192.168.101.4 (subnet mask 255.255.255.0) into its network segment and node address components?
31. What class of IP address is 172.16.1.254?
32. What is the broadcast address for the network that contains the node with IP address 192.168.5.68 (subnet mask 255.255.255.0)?
33. Given the class A IP network address 10.x.x., how many subnetworks of how many nodes can be created by applying a subnet mask of 255.255.0.0?
34. What is the maximum and minimum MTU of IPv4?
35. What are the major problems associated with version four of the IP protocol?

36. What field in an IP header prevents a packet from wandering around an IP network infinitely?
37. What two fields are always present in a network layer packet header regardless of the protocol?
38. What is the purpose of ICMP?
39. Explain the purpose of the Domain Name System?
40. What is the distance vector routing protocol used with IP based networks?
41. What is the link state protocol used with IP based networks?
42. What is the purpose of the hop count (or metric) field in a routing table?
43. What is the difference between broadcasting and multicasting?
44. Explain the process of building a TCP connection. What flags are sent and why?
45. For what applications is UDP a better choice than TCP?
46. In terms of IP, what is the difference between a port and a socket?
47. When is NetBEUI a viable primary LAN protocol?
48. For what applications is DLC commonly used?
49. What is the network layer protocol traditionally used with Novell NetWare?
50. What network layer protocol is used on the Internet?

**Case Study:** For a business case study and questions on LAN communication protocols, go to www.wiley.com/college/goldman.

CHAPTER 8

# ADVANCED TCP/IP NETWORK DESIGN

*Concepts Reinforced*

Classful addressing
Subnet masks

*Concepts Introduced*

Classless addressing
Reserved subnets
Extended Network Prefixes
Route summarization
Internet structure
RIP, OSPF, and BGP4

Variable-length subnet masks
Classless inter-domain routing
Longest match lookups
IPv6
Routing processes
Routing evolution

## OBJECTIVES

After completing this chapter, the reader should be able to:

1. Define proper classful subnet masks for a given IP address that will meet network design requirements.

2. Understand the advantages and proper use of variable length subnet masking.

3. Define proper variable length subnet masks for a given IP address that will meet network design requirements.

4. Understand the advantages and proper use of classless inter-domain routing addresses.

5. Understand the IPv6 protocols and the various methods of transitioning to IPv6.

6. Understand the structure of the Internet.

7. Understand the IP routing process and be able to differentiate between routing and layer three switching.

## ■ INTRODUCTION

Having thoroughly introduced TCP/IP from a conceptual standpoint in chapter 7, this chapter seeks to inform the reader on how network design is actually performed in a TCP/IP-based network. The key issues in this chapter are the importance of how to use IP addressing to properly define subnet masks and how the logical distribution of IP addresses must correlate to the physical topology of the network. Issues that are critical to network design in the real world—such as the shrinking pool of IP addresses and the need to minimize the size of routing tables—are analyzed, and potential solutions are provided. By the completion of this chapter, the reader should be comfortable designing IP-based networks in both a classful and classless addressing environment.

## ■ NETWORK DESIGN WITH CLASSFUL IP ADDRESSING

### Address Classes

Classful addresses are broken apart on octet boundaries. Therefore, there are three basic classes of addresses. As illustrated in Figure 8-1, these classes are known as class A, B, or C networks. To distinguish between classes, the first few bits of each segment address is used to denote the address class of the segment. The class ID plus network ID portions of the IP address are also known as the network prefix, the network number, or the major network. As illustrated in Figure 8-1, class A addresses have an 8-bit network prefix, sometimes referred to as "/8" (slash eight); class B addresses have a 16 bit network prefix and are sometimes referred to as /16

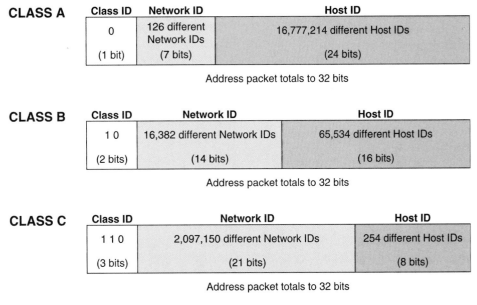

*Figure 8-1*   IPv4 Address Classes

addresses, and class C addresses have a 24-bit network prefix and are sometimes referred to as /24s.

As illustrated in Figure 8-1, class A addresses can be identified if the first bit is a 0 in binary notation, or has a decimal value between 1 and 126. class B addresses can be identified if the first two bits are 10 or if the first decimal octet is between 128 and 191. The first octet address of 127 is reserved for loopback tests on network interface cards and routers. class C addresses can be identified if the first three bits in binary notation are 110 or if the first octet's decimal value is between 192 and 223, inclusive.

In addition to these basic address classes, there are two additional classes, class D and class E that can be used for IPv4 addressing. class D addresses are reserved for multicast systems such as routers while class E addresses are reserved for future use.

The assignment of address classes and network ID ranges to a particular organization wishing to connect to the Internet is the responsibility of the Internet Architecture Board (IAB). The IAB assures that all organizations using the Internet for network communications have unique IP addresses for all of their workstations. If an organization has no intention of ever accessing the Internet, then there might not be a need to register with the IAB for an IP address class and range of valid network IDs. However, even in this case, all workstations on all communicating networks must have IP addresses unique within the internal network.

**Subnetting**   When the IP address classes were established in the early 1980s, computer networks were composed of a relatively small number of relatively expensive computers. However, as time went on and the personal computer exploded into local area networks, the strict boundaries of the classful addressing address classes became restrictive and forced an inefficient allocation of addresses. More specifically, a class C address with its limit of 254 hosts (computers) per network is too small for most organizations, while a class B address with its limit of 65,534 hosts per subnet is too large. Unfortunately, class B addresses were given out to organizations that would never need the 65,534 addresses.

A second issue came about as organizations' networks grew and needed to be divided or segmented in order to improve traffic flow. *Routers* join two separate networks. Networks that are separated by routers must have different network IDs so that the router can distinguish between them. This would require all organizations that needed to install a router-based internetwork to go back to the IAB for more addresses, thereby accelerating the depletion of IP addresses.

In order to address both of these concerns, RFC 950 was defined in 1985. It gave users a way to **subnet,** or provide a third layer of organization or hierarchy between the existing network ID and the existing host ID. Since the network IDs were assigned by IAB and could not be altered, the only choice was to "borrow" some of the host ID bits that were under the control of the organization to which the address had been assigned. These "borrowed" bits constitute the subnet portion of the address. A subnet mask identifies which particular bits are used for the subnet ID.

Subnetting allowed organizations to use the one network ID assigned by the IAB and create multiple subnets within their private network. Although their internal routers needed to remain aware of all of the internal subnets in order to properly deliver data, the Internet routing tables did not need to be concerned about that since all of these subnets existed behind the original network ID assigned by the IAB. As a result, organizations could build router-based internetworks without asking for additional network IDs and the Internet routing tables did not need to be overloaded with all the information about routes to all of the internal subnets.

## Subnet Masks

By applying a 32-bit subnet mask to a class B IP address, a portion of the bits that make up the host ID can be reserved for denoting subnetworks, with the remaining bits being reserved for host IDs per subnetwork. If the first 8 bits of the host ID were reserved for subnetwork addresses and the final 8 bits of the host ID were reserved for hosts per subnetwork, this would allow the same class B address to yield 254 subnetworks with 254 hosts each as opposed to one network with 65,534 hosts. Figure 8-2 provides examples of subnet masks. The overall effect of subnetworking is to create multiple network segments within the address space given by the IAB.

As illustrated in Figure 8-2, to create a subnet mask, each bit position is reserved for either a network ID or a host ID. By default, in the case of a class B address, the first 16 bits are reserved for network ID and the second 16 bits are reserved for host ID. Of the 16 bits originally reserved for host ID, we can reserve those bits that we wish to use for a subnet ID by placing a one in that bit position. If we wish to retain the use of a bit position for host ID, then we reserve that bit position with a zero. In the example illustrated in Figure 8-2, we borrowed 8 of the 16 bits set aside for host ID and reassigned their function as subnet ID by reserving those 8-bit positions with a one in the subnet mask. Converting the binary place holder values to decimal yielded the decimal subnet mask 255.255.255.0.

This subnet mask yields 8-bit positions for subnet IDs and 8-bit positions for host IDs. Two to the eighth power is 256. However, as will be explained further, the all-zeroes and all-ones subnet and host IDs are reserved, thereby leaving 254 available subnets and 254 available host IDs as listed in Figure 8-2.

**Extended Network Prefix**   The **extended network prefix** is the classful network prefix (/16 in the case of a class B address) plus the number of bits borrowed from the host ID. In the case of the example illustrated in Figure 8-2, the extended network prefix would be /24 (/16 network prefix + /8 subnet mask). As an example, if we were given the class B address of 128.210. 49. 213/24 what would we know? Figure 8-3 illustrates the network prefix, extended network prefix, subnet mask in binary and decimal, network ID, subnet ID, and host ID.

**The TCP/IP Subnet Definition Chart**   Once the theory behind how subnet masks are defined is understood, it would be nice to be able to define appropriate subnet

| | Binary Subnet Mask | Decimal Subnet Mask | Number of Subnetworks | Number of Hosts per Subnetwork |
|---|---|---|---|---|
| **Default Class B Subnet Mask** | 11111111 11111111 00000000 00000000 | 255.255.0.0 | 1 | 65,534 |
| **Alternative Subnet Mask Used to Subnet Class B Network** | 11111111 11111111 11111111 00000000 | 255.255.255.0 | 254 | 254 |

*Figure 8-2*   IPv4 Subnetworking

|  | Decimal | Network Prefix | Subnet ID | Host ID |
|---|---|---|---|---|
| IP Address | 128.210.49.213 | 10000000.11010010 | 00110001 | 11010101 |
| Subnet Mask | 255.255.255.0 | 11111111.11111111 | 11111111 | 00000000 |
|  |  | ← Extended Network | Prefix =/24 → |  |

*Figure 8-3*    Extended Network Prefix

masks without having to perform binary arithmetic. Figure 8-4 provides a chart that can be quickly used to define the proper subnet mask dependent on the class of the original network ID, the number of required subnets, and the number of required hosts per subnet.

## Working with Subnet Masks—Subnet Design

In order to illustrate the use of the TCP/IP Subnet Definition Chart, let's take a practical example:

> The university where you work has six administrative offices, each on its own subnet and each requiring between 15 and 25 hosts. For your class C address, you create the subnet mask 255.255.255.240. How well does this solution address the problem? Explain.
>
> Referring to the TCP/IP Subnet Definition Chart, we can see that if 6 subnets are required, then the last octet in the subnet mask should be 224, not 240, which would yield 30 hosts per subnet. In the example, the defined subnet of 240 would yield 14 subnets but only 14 host per subnet, which would not meet the requirement.
>
> The correct answer, 224, has 3 ones in the subnet mask borrowed from the host ID. A class C address is a /24 subnet mask by default. Adding the

| Number of Ones in Last Octet of Subnet Mask | Subnet Mask Octet | Address Block Size | Number of Subnets | Number of Class C Hosts | Number of Class B Hosts | Number of Class A Hosts |
|---|---|---|---|---|---|---|
| 2 | 192 | 64 | 2 | 62 | 16,382 | 4,194,302 |
| 3 | 224 | 32 | 6 | 30 | 8,190 | 2,097,150 |
| 4 | 240 | 16 | 14 | 14 | 4,094 | 1,048,574 |
| 5 | 248 | 8 | 30 | 6 | 2,046 | 524,286 |
| 6 | 252 | 4 | 62 | 2 | 1,022 | 262,142 |
| 7 | 254 | 2 | 126 | N/A | 510 | 131,070 |
| 8 | 255 | 1 | 254 | N/A | 254 | 65,534 |

*Figure 8-4*    Classful IP Subnet Definition Chart

3 ones yields a correct subnet mask of 255.255.255.224 or a correct extended network prefix of /27 (24 + 3).

In order to properly define a subnet mask for a given classful address, one must know the following information:

- What is the address class of the assigned network ID? This is important because knowing the address class tells you how many bits are available for "borrowing" from the host ID for the subnet ID. class A: 24 bits, class B: 16 bits, class C: 8 bits. Obviously, you can't borrow all of the available bits for the subnet ID because there won't be anything left for the host ID.

- How many subnets are required both now and in the future? Future considerations are important. Although more flexible subnet definition alternatives will be examined later in the chapter, classful subnet definition needs to be done exactly the same across all subnets in a given network ID.

- How many host IDs per subnet are required now and in the future? Again, you must define your subnet mask based on worst anticipated scenario. That is to say, what is the largest number of hosts that you anticipate having to support on your largest subnet? Remember, you can't just choose an arbitrarily large number of host IDs since every bit that gets reserved for host IDs means one less bit available for subnet IDs.

Let's try another example:

A retail chain of eighty stores expects to expand by twenty stores per year for the next eight years. Only one computer connected to a router at each site (total of two host IDs) will be needed to upload the daily sales figures to corporate headquarters. The IP address is 165.32.0.0. What should the subnet mask be? Explain.

The given IP address is 165.32.0.0. This is a class B or /16 address, which means we have 16 bits available with which to define the subnet mask. In order to determine the number of required subnets, we take the 80 current stores and add 160 more (20 per year × 8 years) for a total anticipated number of stores or subnets of 240. We only need two host IDs per subnet. Using the TCP/IP Subnet Definition Chart, we see that in order to have 240 subnets, we will need 8 bits in the subnet mask. Adding the subnet mask to the default for a class B address yields 255.255.255.0 or an extended network prefix of /24 (/16 + 8).

**Defining Subnet Numbers**   Once the subnet mask for a given major network or network prefix has been defined, the next job is to define the individual subnet numbers that are associated with the assigned major network number. From the previous example, the assigned major network was 165.32.0.0. We know we are going to use the next 8 bits, or the entire third octet, for the subnet ID. The subnet mask of 255.255.255.0 tells us this is so. Notice how the third octet, which is normally reserved for host ID is a class B address, is all ones (255) in the subnet mask indicating that it will be used for defining the subnet ID. Since 2 raised to the eighth power is 256, we should be able to define 256 different subnet IDs. In fact, we can. However, as we'll soon see, two of those subnet addresses are reserved, yielding 254 available subnet IDs, as stated on the TCP/IP Subnet Definition Chart. Figure 8-5 shows how individual subnet IDs are defined.

**Reserved Subnet Numbers** Two subnet numbers, the all-zeroes subnet and the all-ones subnet are typically reserved, especially in routers that support classful routing protocols. The all-zeroes subnet is labeled as Subnet 0 and the all-ones subnet is labeled as Subnet 255 in Figure 8-5. As can be seen in Figure 8-5, the full address of subnet 0 (165.32.0.0) is identical to the Assigned network ID of 165.32.0.0. In order to differentiate between the two, one would have to know the extended network prefix in each case. Since routers supporting classful routing protocols don't exchange extended network prefixes, there is no way for them to differentiate between the assigned major network ID, sometimes referred to as the default route, and subnet 0 of the major network, leading the subnet 0 address to be declared reserved. The all-ones subnet ID is reserved because it has a special meaning to classful routing protocol routers—namely, broadcast to all subnets. Later in the chapter, we will talk about other types of routing protocols that are able to share extended network prefixes thereby allowing routers to distinguish between the pairs discussed above and listed in Figure 8-6.

**Defining Host Addresses for a Given Subnet** In the current example the network ID with extended network prefix is 165.32.0.0/24. That tells us that the last octet, or last 8 bits, has been reserved to define host IDs. Host IDs are defined within a given subnet. In Figure 8-7, we have chosen to define host IDs for subnet 1. As a result, we know that all host IDs will have the same first three octets in dotted decimal format, namely, 165.32.1. The only part that will vary will be the fourth octet, which will contain unique host IDs. Since there are 8 bits in the fourth octet, we should be able to define 2 to the eighth power, or 256 different host IDs per subnet. However, as was the case with subnet IDs, we have two reserved host IDs, as well leaving us with 254 usable host IDs.

**Reserved Host Addresses** As mentioned in chapter 7, there are reserved host IDs. Regardless of the length (number of bits) of the host ID, the all-ones host ID is reserved as the broadcast address for a given subnet and the all-zeroes host ID is

| | Network Prefix | Subnet Number | Reserved for Host ID | Decimal with Extended Network Prefix |
|---|---|---|---|---|
| Assigned Network ID | 10100101.00100000 | 00000000 | 00000000 | 165.32.0.0/16 |
| Subnet 0 | 10100101.00100000 | 00000000 | 00000000 | 165.32.0.0/24 |
| Subnet 1 | 10100101.00100000 | 00000001 | 00000000 | 165.32.1.0/24 |
| Subnet 2 | 10100101.00100000 | 00000010 | 00000000 | 165.32.2.0/24 |
| Subnet 3 | 10100101.00100000 | 00000011 | 00000000 | 165.32.3.0/24 |
| Subnet 254 | 10100101.00100000 | 11111110 | 00000000 | 165.32.254.0/24 |
| Subnet 255 | 10100101.00100000 | 11111111 | 00000000 | 165.32.255.0/24 |

*Figure 8-5*  Defining Subnet Numbers

| | Decimal with Extended Network Prefix |
|---|---|
| Assigned Network ID | 165.32.0.0/16 |
| All-Zeroes Subnet | 165.32.0.0/24 |
| Broadcast | 165.32.255.0/16 |
| All-Ones Subnet | 165.32.255.0/24 |

*Figure 8-6*  Reserved Subnet Numbers

| | Extended Network Prefix | Host ID | Decimal |
|---|---|---|---|
| Host 1 | 10100101.00100000.00000001 | 00000001 | 165.32.1.1/24 |
| Host 2 | 10100101.00100000.00000001 | 00000010 | 165.32.1.2/24 |
| Host 3 | 10100101.00100000.00000001 | 00000011 | 165.32.1.3/24 |
| Host 4 | 10100101.00100000.00000001 | 00000100 | 165.32.1.4/24 |
| Host 5 | 10100101.00100000.00000001 | 00000101 | 165.32.1.5/24 |
| Host 253 | 10100101.00100000.00000001 | 11111101 | 165.32.1.253/24 |
| Host 254 | 10100101.00100000.00000001 | 11111110 | 165.32.1.254/24 |

*Figure 8-7*  Defining Host IDs for a Given Subnet

reserved as identifying the subnet number itself. As a result, the broadcast address for the number one subnet used in Figure 8-7 would be 165.32.1.255.

**Determining if IP Addresses Are Part of the Same Subnet**   In the example we have been using, the entire third octet was used for the subnet ID, so the subnet number is immediately evident just by reading the dotted decimal address. For example, the subnet ID in the address 165.32.2.46/24 is 2 and the subnet ID in the address 165.32.1.23/24 is 1. What would happen if this were not the case? What if the entire third octet were not reserved for the subnet ID? How would we, or the routers for that matter, be able to determine what the real subnet address was when all we are given is the dotted decimal format?

Given the network ID 192.210.165.0 from the IAB, we need to define a subnet ID that will yield thirty subnets with up to six hosts per subnet. Noting that we are dealing with a class C address and referring back to the Subnet Definition Chart (Figure 8-4), we should see that we need the last octet to be 248. Since this is a class C or /24 address and we are reserving 5 or the remaining 8 bits for subnet ID, it should be evident that the extended network prefix will be /29 or the subnet mask in dotted decimal format would be equivalently expressed as 255.255.255.248. Figure 8-8 shows how the subnets would be defined.

Notice how in Figure 8-8 there are only 5 bits available for subnet IDs and 3 bits reserved for host IDs for each subnet. As we will see, since an entire octet has not been reserved for the subnet ID, it will not be as immediately evident as in previous

| | Network Prefix | Subnet Number | Reserved for Host ID | Decimal with Extended Network Prefix |
|---|---|---|---|---|
| Assigned Network ID | 11000000.11010010.10100101 | 00000 | 000 | 192.210.165.0/24 |
| Subnet 0 | 11000000.11010010.10100101 | 00000 | 000 | 192.210.165.0/29 |
| Subnet 1 | 11000000.11010010.10100101 | 00001 | 000 | 192.210.165.8/29 |
| Subnet 2 | 11000000.11010010.10100101 | 00010 | 000 | 192.210.165.16/29 |
| Subnet 3 | 11000000.11010010.10100101 | 00011 | 000 | 192.210.165.24/29 |
| Subnet 31 | 11000000.11010010.10100101 | 11110 | 000 | 192.210.165.240/29 |
| Subnet 32 | 11000000.11010010.10100101 | 11111 | 000 | 192.210.165.248/29 |

*Figure 8-8*    Subnet Definition with Less Than an Octet

examples. Also notice in Figure 8-8 that with just 5 bits to work with, we are able define only 32 total subnets, two of which are reserved.

Figure 8-9 defines Host IDs for Subnet 1 from Figure 8-8. Since there are only 3 bits reserved for host ID, we can only define eight different host IDs, two of which are reserved. Notice how the extended network prefix does not increase when we define host IDs for a given subnet the way it did when we defined additional subnet levels to existing subnets.

In the case of subnet 1 (subnet address 8), if we were to choose one of the full host IDs as defined Figure 8-9, we don't immediately see the subnet address of 8 in the full dotted decimal address of the host IDs. Where is the subnet address of 8 hiding? Why is the subnet address of subnet 1 defined as 8? As illustrated in Figure 8-10, it is due to the decimal place values of the binary digits used to define the subnet number.

Routers need to know the real subnet address of every piece of packetized data that they encounter in order to properly forward that data toward its ultimate destination. To do this, routers must be given the subnet mask or extended network

| | Extended Network Prefix | Host ID | Decimal |
|---|---|---|---|
| Host 1—Reserved | 11000000.11010010.10100101.00001 | 000 | 192.210.165.8/29 |
| Host 2 | 11000000.11010010.10100101.00001 | 001 | 192.210.165.9/29 |
| Host 3 | 11000000.11010010.10100101.00001 | 010 | 192.210.165.10/29 |
| Host 4 | 11000000.11010010.10100101.00001 | 011 | 192.210.165.11/29 |
| Host 5 | 11000000.11010010.10100101.00001 | 100 | 192.210.165.12/29 |
| Host 6 | 11000000.11010010.10100101.00001 | 101 | 192.210.165.13/29 |
| Host 7 | 11000000.11010010.10100101.00001 | 110 | 192.210.165.14/29 |
| Host 8—Reserved | 11000000.11010010.10100101.00001 | 111 | 192.210.165.15/29 |

*Figure 8-9*    Defining Host IDs

| Decimal Value | 128 | 64 | 32 | 16 | 8 | 4 | 2 | 1 |
|---|---|---|---|---|---|---|---|---|
| Power of 2 | 7 | 6 | 5 | 4 | 3 | 2 | 1 | 0 |
| Subnet 1 Binary | 0 | 0 | 0 | 0 | 1 | Reserved | For | Host ID |
| Subnet 1 Decimal | 0+ | 0+ | 0+ | 0+ | 9 = 8 | Reserved | For | Host ID |
| Subnet 31 Binary | 1 | 1 | 1 | 1 | 0 | Reserved | For | Host ID |
| Subnet 31 Decimal | 128+ | 64+ | 32+ | 16+ | 0 = 240 | Reserved | For | Host ID |

*Figure 8-10*    Hidden Subnet IDs

prefix of the address in question and then use a type of binary arithmetic known as a logical AND. If a one is present in a given place in both the IP address and the subnet mask, then a one is placed in the result, otherwise a zero is placed in the result. This operation is illustrated in Figure 8-11. In this case, we will use the host ID defined in Figure 8-9 for Host ID 6 on Subnet 1, with the full dotted-decimal address of 192.210.165.13/29.

As illustrated in Figure 8-11, although the last octet of the full address had a value of 13, by using binary arithmetic the router is able to determine the actual subnet ID of the address as long as it also knows the subnet mask or extended network prefix.

If the subnet ID of the destination address on the data packet is the same as the subnet of the router interface, the router will do nothing. Since it is a local delivery, the router does not need to get involved. If after determining the real subnet ID of the destination address it turns out that the destination subnet is not the same as the local router interface's subnet, then the router needs to go to work consulting its

| **IP Address** | **192.210.165.13/29** | | | | |
|---|---|---|---|---|---|
| Subnet Mask | 255.255.255.248 | | | | |

| | First Octet | Second Octet | Third Octet | Subnet Portion of Fourth Octet | Host ID Portion of Fourth Octet |
|---|---|---|---|---|---|
| 192.210.165.13 | 11000000 | 11010010 | 10100101 | 00001 | 101 |
| 255.255.255.248 | 11111111 | 11111111 | 11111111 | 11111 | 000 |
| Result Binary from logical AND | 11000000 | 11010010 | 10100101 | 00001 | 101 |
| Result Decimal | 192 | 210 | 165 | 8 | 5 |

*Figure 8-11*    Determining if IP Addresses Are Part of the Same Subnet

routing tables and determining the address of the next hop router that will help this data packet on its way to its ultimate destination.

## Limitations of Classful Addressing and Fixed-Length Subnet Masks

Before moving on to classless addressing and variable-length subnet masks, it is important to understand the problems that these techniques are attempting to fix:

- Wasted addresses because only one subnet mask can be used for a network prefix
- A shrinking pool of available IPv4 addresses

Routing protocols such as RIP—which are unable to transmit subnet masks or extended network prefix information along with network IDs and IP addresses—force all routers, servers, and workstations within a given network to all have the same subnet mask. Recalling that a subnet mask is the logical portion that relates to a physical network topology, it should be evident that a fixed subnet mask implies a fixed subnet size for all subnets of a given network ID. Naturally, subnets must be sized to accommodate the largest required subnet within a given network ID. As a result, all subnets, regardless of their requirements, are sized to this largest required size, resulting in wasted host addresses that cannot be recovered or used by other subnets.

Internet traffic is doubling every three to six months. class A addresses are exhausted. class B addresses are either exhausted, or nearly so. All that remains is class C addresses. However, as was seen in the IP Subnet Definition Chart, class C addresses, with only an 8-bit host ID, don't leave much room for subnet definition.

## ■ CLASSLESS ADDRESSING AND VARIABLE-LENGTH SUBNET MASKS

Clearly, something needed to be done. Two different techniques, described below, seek to mitigate the shortcomings of classful IP addressing.

## Variable-Length Subnet Masks

Variable-length subnet masks, defined in 1987 as RFP1009, specified how a single network ID could have different subnet masks among its subnets. Used correctly, VLSM could minimize the wasted IP addresses forced by a single subnet mask per network ID as defined by the original RFC 950 Subnetting technique.

Benefits   The major benefit of VLSM is that subnets can be defined to different sizes as needed under a single network ID, thereby minimizing, if not eliminating, wasted addresses. As a result, an organization's assigned IP address space is more efficiently used. Second, when correctly defined to match the physical topology of the network, variable-length subnet masks can used to permit router aggregation that minimizes the number of distinct routes that need to be advertised and processed by network backbone or Internet routers. Route aggregation will be explained shortly.

**Implementation Requirements**   In order for VLSM to be successfully implemented, the routers on the network where VLSM is implemented must be able to share subnet masks and/or extended network prefixes along with each router advertisement. Routing protocols such as OSPF and IS-IS are able to do this, whereas RIP and IGRP are not. Without the subnet mask or extended network prefix for each route being shared, the receiving router would have to assume that the received route was using the same subnet mask as the receiving router itself. An improvement to the original RIP (RIPv1), known as RIPv2 (RFC 1388), added support for VLSM.

Second, all routers supporting VLSM must support a longest match routing algorithm. This is particularly important in VLSM networks because subnets can be embedded within subnets. As will be seen in the following sections, the deeper a particular subnet is embedded within the network topology, the greater its extended network prefix, and the more specific its route advertisement.

Finally, the implemented network topology must match the distribution of addresses and definition of subnets. That is to say, the network designers must decide in advance how many levels of subnets are required, and how many hosts per subnet must be supported at each level. As will be seen in the following sections on network design with variable-length subnet masks, at each level of subnetting, all addresses can be summarized or aggregated into a single address block. This reduces the amount of routing information that needs to be shared among the routers on a given network.

**Recursive Division of a Network Prefix with VLSM**   As previously described, VLSM allows an organization's assigned address space to be recursively divided into as many levels and sizes of subnets as required. In order to better understand this process, we will first show how the address space is divided and then show how the routes from that recursively divided address space can be aggregated to effectively reduce the amount of transmitted routing information. In addition to reducing the amount of transmitted and stored routing information, an added benefit is that the associated network topology and structure of one subnet is unknown to other subnets. Figure 8-12 illustrates how a single network prefix can be recursively divided thanks to VLSM.

Notice in Figure 8-12 how subnet sizes can be flexibly defined even on a given subnet level. On the sub-subnet level in Figure 8-12, the 121.1.0.0 subnet is divided into 254 sub-subnets while the 121.253.0.0 subnet is divided into only 6 sub-subnets. Also, notice that subnet IDs can become "hidden" when subnet addresses do not fall evenly on octet boundaries.

**Route Aggregation with VLSM**   While the benefits of flexible subnet size definition is illustrated in Figure 8-12, the route aggregation benefits of VLSM are illustrated in Figure 8-13. Often, the terms **summarization** and **aggregation** are used interchangeably to describe the process of reducing the number of routing advertisements between subnets by only advertising the common portion of subnet IDs. Alternatively stated, summarization and aggregation mean that subnet information is not shared between two networks when a router connects those networks.

In some cases, however, a distinction is made between the two terms. In such cases, the term *summarization* is reserved to describe those circumstances in which subnet addresses have been rolled up all the way to the major network prefix as assigned by the Internet authorities. In Figure 8-13, this would be the 121.0.0.0/8 major network prefix. On the other hand, the term aggregation is used to more

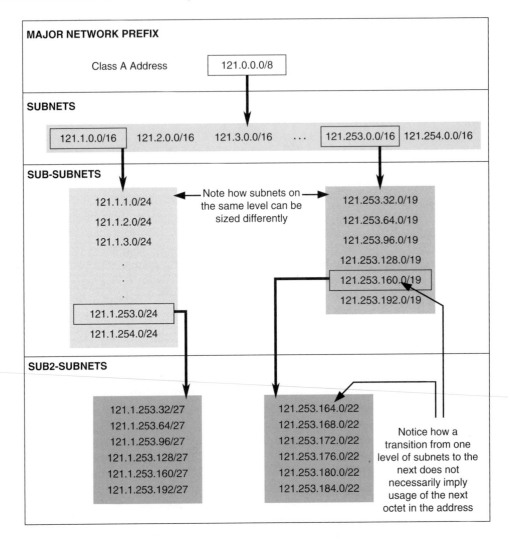

*Figure 8-12*    Recursive Division of a Network Prefix with VLSM

generally describe any circumstance when only only the common portion of those addresses in a routing advertisement can represent a subnet's entire address space. In Figure 8-13, Router 6's advertisement to Router 4 of the 121.253.10.0/19 route to represent six separate networks is an example of aggregation since 121.253.10.0/19 is not the major network prefix.

Notice in Figure 8-13, how each physical network that houses multiple subnet IDs can have its routing information summarized to a single route advertisement to the next higher layer of subnet. Finally, the entire internetwork can be advertised to the Internet routing tables by the single assigned network ID: 121.0.0.0. Such route aggregation and the efficiencies gained therein, are only possible if subnet masks are assigned in a planned manner so that subnet address assignment mirrors the actual topology of the network, as illustrated in Figure 8-13. If assigned addresses are not organized to mirror the physical topology of the network, then address aggregation is not possible and the benefit of reduction of routing table size will not be realized.

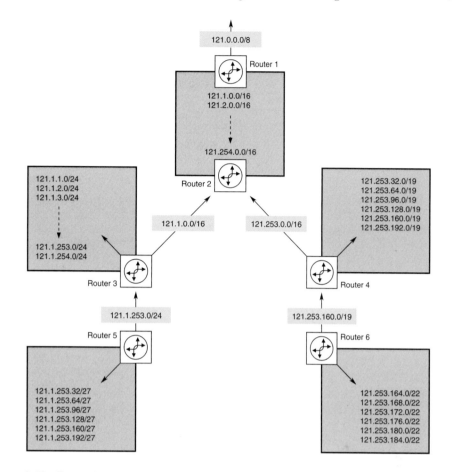

*Figure 8-13*    Route Aggregation with VLSM

**Subnet Design Using VLSM**    Subnet design with variable-length subnet masks is similar to subnet design with fixed-length subnet masks, but the decisions made regarding subnets for the entire network in the fixed-length subnet mask scenario are made independently at each level in the variable-length subnet mask scenario. To elaborate, at each level (subnets, sub-subnets, sub2-subnets, etc.), basically two questions must be answered:

1.  How many subnets are required at this level, both now and in the future?

2.  What is the largest number of host required per subnet on this level, both now and in the future?

The answers to these questions will determine how many subnets with how much host ID capacity need to be defined at each level.

*Defining Sub-Subnet Numbers with VLSM*    Figure 8-14 provides an example of how subnet numbers are defined in VLSM. In this example, it was determined that six sub-subnets were needed beneath the 121.253.0.0/16 subnet. Since two subnets are reserved, we need to really be able to define eight sub-subnets. Two to the third

| | Network Prefix | Sub-Subnet Number | Reserved for Host ID | Decimal with Extended Network Prefix |
|---|---|---|---|---|
| Assigned Network ID | 01111001.11111101 | | | 121.253.0.0/16 |
| Sub-Subnet 0—Reserved | 01111001.11111101 | 000 | 00000.00000000 | 121.253.0.0/19 |
| Sub-Subnet 1 | 01111001.11111101 | 001 | 00000.00000000 | 121.253.32.0/19 |
| Sub-Subnet 2 | 01111001.11111101 | 010 | 00000.00000000 | 121.253.64.0/19 |
| Sub-Subnet 3 | 01111001.11111101 | 011 | 00000.00000000 | 121.253.96.0/19 |
| Sub-Subnet 4 | 01111001.11111101 | 100 | 00000.00000000 | 121.253.128.0/19 |
| Sub-Subnet 5 | 01111001.11111101 | 101 | 00000.00000000 | 121.253.160.0/19 |
| Sub-Subnet 6 | 01111001.11111101 | 110 | 00000.00000000 | 121.253.192.0/19 |
| Sub-Subnet 7—Reserved | 01111001.11111101 | 111 | 00000.00000000 | 121.253.224.0/19 |

*Figure 8-14*    Defining Sub-Subnetwork Numbers with VLSM

power is eight, so it will take 3 additional bits or /19 (/16 + 3 = /19) extended network prefix to provide the required six sub-subnets.

*Defining Sub2-Subnet Numbers with VLSM*    If it was then decided that the 121.253.160.0/19 sub-subnet needed to be recursively divided into six sub2-subnets, so 3 additional bits of variable length subnet mask would be required. This is illustrated in Figure 8-15.

*Defining Host Addresses for a Given Subnet*    With VLSM, defining host addresses involves the same process for subnet, sub-subnets, or sub2-subnets. Figure 8-16 illustrates the host definition process for sub2-subnet 121.253.184.0/22 defined in Figure 8-15. The extended network prefix of /22 tells us that 1022 host IDs can be defined on this sub2-subnet. (32 bit address – 22 reserved bits = 10 bits available for host ID; 2 to the 10th power = 1,024 – 2 reserved host IDs = 1,022 available host IDs.) If 1,022 host IDs are way more than we could ever reasonably use, we would probably want to consider defining another subnet level so as not to strand or waste precious IP addresses. Notice how the extended network prefix does not increase when we define host IDs for a given subnet the way it did when we defined additional subnet levels to existing subnets.

Notice how the third octet has changed from 184 to 187 on the last few host IDs. Does this mean that the subnet ID changed somehow? The answer is no. If you look in the extended network prefix column, you will see that the subnet ID has not changed. The reason the third octet changed is because the extended network prefix was 22, leaving 2 bits of the third octet leftover for use by the host ID. Since the host IDs start using the rightmost bits first, it was only when we got to the last few host IDs that we were forced to use the leftmost bits, which happened to belong in the third octet. As a result, the third octet may have become 187, but the sub2-subnet ID is still 184.

| | Network Prefix | Sub-Subnet Number | Reserved for Host ID | Decimal with Extended Network Prefix |
|---|---|---|---|---|
| Assigned Network ID | 01111001.11111101.101 | | | 121.253.160.0/19 |
| Sub-Subnet 0—Reserved | 01111001.11111101.101 | 000 | 00.00000000 | 121.253.160.0/22 |
| Sub-Subnet 1 | 01111001.11111101.101 | 001 | 00.00000000 | 121.253.164.0/22 |
| Sub-Subnet 2 | 01111001.11111101.101 | 010 | 00.00000000 | 121.253.168.0/22 |
| Sub-Subnet 3 | 01111001.11111101.101 | 011 | 00.00000000 | 121.253.172.0/22 |
| Sub-Subnet 4 | 01111001.11111101.101 | 100 | 00.00000000 | 121.253.176.0/22 |
| Sub-Subnet 5 | 01111001.11111101.101 | 101 | 00.00000000 | 121.253.180.0/22 |
| Sub-Subnet 6 | 01111001.11111101.101 | 110 | 00.00000000 | 121.253.184.0/22 |
| Sub-Subnet 7—Reserved | 01111001.11111101.101 | 111 | 00.00000000 | 121.253.188.0/22 |

*Figure 8-15*    Defining Sub2-Subnet Numbers with VLSM

*Determining if VLSM IP Addresses Are Part of the Same Subnet*    Routers use the same algorithm to determine if IP addresses are part of the same subnet, whether or not VLSM is used. A router must somehow know the extended network prefix or subnet mask, as well as the IP address. In the case of fixed-length subnet masks, the router could use its own interface's subnet mask (since all subnet masks on a given network had to be the same), or it could assume the default subnet mask based on classful address class. In the case of variable-length subnet masks, no such assumptions can be made. Extended network prefixes must accompany every advertised route that is shared between routers. Only certain router-to-router protocols are able to support VLSM's requirement for sharing extended network prefixes. OSPF and IS-IS are link

| | Extended Network Prefix | Host ID | Decimal |
|---|---|---|---|
| Host 0—Reserved | 01111001.11111101.101110 | 00.00000000 | 121.253.184.0/22 |
| Host 1 | 01111001.11111101.101110 | 00.00000001 | 121.253.184.1/22 |
| Host 2 | 01111001.11111101.101110 | 00.00000010 | 121.253.184.2/22 |
| Host 3 | 01111001.11111101.101110 | 00.00000011 | 121.253.184.3/22 |
| Host 1022 | 01111001.11111101.101110 | 11.11111110 | 121.253.187.254/22 |
| Host 1023—Reserved | 01111001.11111101.101110 | 11.11111111 | 121.253.187.255/22 |

*Figure 8-16*    Defining Host IDs

state protocols that are able to support VLSM. RIPv2 is a distance vector protocol that is able to support VLSM. Neither RIPv1 not IGRP are able to support VLSM.

How routers use the extended network prefix or subnet mask to determine if IP addresses are part of the same subnet was illustrated in Figure 8-11.

### Classless Inter-Domain Routing

As previously mentioned, the near exhaustion of class B addresses and rapid depletion of the limited capacity class C addresses, combined with the explosive growth of the Internet and an associated explosive growth in demand for Internet IP addresses, forced the IETF (Internet Engineering Task Force) to take decisive action.

**Classless Inter Domain Routing (CIDR)** was announced in September 1993 and is documented in RFCs 1517, 1518, 1519, and 1520. CIDR is also sometimes referred to as **supernetting.**

**Benefits**    CIDR (often pronounced as "cider") eliminates the traditional concept of class A, B, and C addresses entirely. The first 3 bits of the IP address, which have traditionally been used to determine address class, are meaningless. Likewise first octet address ranges no longer indicate a particular address class. Thus, CIDR allows a more efficient allocation of the remaining Internet IP addresses.

CIDR also supports route aggregation, which allows routing information for multiple network addresses to be represented by a single routing table entry. This can significantly reduce the number of routes that must be processed by Internet routers, thereby making the Internet perform more efficiently.

**Implementation Requirements**    CIDR addresses are issued in blocks known as CIDR blocks. Recall that the first octet is meaningless in determining how many subnets or host IDs can be defined for a given CIDR block. The only factor that determines the capacity of a CIDR block is the network prefix assigned by the Internet authorities when the CIDR block is issued. Just as was the case with classful addressing, the network prefix issued by the Internet authorities indicates the number of bits used for the major network ID. These bits are reserved and cannot be used by the end users for subnet IDs or host IDs. Think of the network prefix number as the "hands off" area. For example, if a CIDR block were issued with a network prefix of /18, that would imply that the first 18 bits from left to right were reserved for the network ID. This would leave 14 bits (32 – 18) for subnet IDs and host IDs. Since 2 raised to the 14th power is 16,384, that is how many host IDs or individual addresses can be defined for a CIDR block with a network prefix of /18.

An important point to remember is that it doesn't matter what the assigned major network ID is: All /18 CIDR blocks are equal in terms of capacity, regardless of network ID. This is where is becomes important to forget the traditional view of classful addressing. As an example, the following three CIDR addresses are equivalent, even though they would not be equal from a classful addressing standpoint:

- 10.46.64.0/18
- 128.210.0.0/18
- 204.17.192.0/18

Figure 8-17 summarizes the key information about the capacity of CIDR blocks with various prefix lengths. Remember that the assigned prefix indicates the number of leftmost reserved bits. Much like subnettting, all bits reserved by the Internet authorities for the network ID prior to assignment to end users are designated with a 1 in the reserved bit positions. These reserved ones can then be converted to dotted-decimal format. Unlike subnetting—where end users assign reserved bits to create a subnet mask—because these ones are assigned to reserved bits in a mask before assignment to end users, this could be called a supernet mask.

Another important implementation issue with CIDR is that the TCP/IP configuration programs on all servers and workstations must be CIDR compliant. That is to say, they must be able to accept classless subnet masks, or masks that would be illegal from a classful addressing standpoint. Many of the TCP/IP configuration programs associated with network operating systems have error-checking routines that assume that only classful addressing is supported and will not allow subnet masks that appear to violate classful addressing rules but are perfectly correct for CIDR.

**Address Allocation Using CIDR**  The impact of address allocation using CIDR is most clearly seen when Internet Service Providers must provide a block of addresses to an organization that wishes to connect to the Internet through its ISP. For example, let's start by assuming that an ISP has been issued the CIDR block of 207.32.128.0/17 by

| CIDR Prefix Length | Supernet Mask | Number of Host Addresses | Number of Bits Available for Subnetting | Equivalent Number of Classful Networks |
|---|---|---|---|---|
| /13 | 255.248.0.0 | 524288 | 19 | 8 Bs or 2048 Cs |
| /14 | 255.252.0.0 | 262144 | 18 | 4 Bs or 1024 Cs |
| /15 | 255.254.0.0 | 131072 | 17 | 2 Bs or 512 Cs |
| /16 | 255.255.0.0 | 65536 | 16 | 1 B or 256 Cs |
| /17 | 255.255.128.0 | 32768 | 15 | 128 Cs |
| /18 | 255.255.192.0 | 16384 | 14 | 64 Cs |
| /19 | 255.255.224.0 | 8192 | 13 | 32 Cs |
| /20 | 255.255.240.0 | 4096 | 12 | 16 Cs |
| /21 | 255.255.248.0 | 2048 | 11 | 8 Cs |
| /22 | 255.255.252.0 | 1024 | 10 | 4 Cs |
| /23 | 255.255.254.0 | 512 | 9 | 2 Cs |
| /24 | 255.255.255.0 | 256 | 8 | 1 C |
| /25 | 255.255.255.128 | 128 | 7 | 1/2 C |
| /26 | 255.255.255.192 | 64 | 6 | 1/4 C |
| /27 | 255.255.255.224 | 32 | 5 | 1/8 C |

*Figure 8-17*  CIDR Block Capacity Chart

the Internet authorities. Referring to the CIDR Block Capacity Chart (Figure 8-17), it should be evident that this block equals 32,768 IP addresses, or the equivalent of 128 separate C addresses. Remember that this is classless addressing and the value in the first octet of the CIDR block address has no significance. Obviously, the ISP wants to allocate these addresses in as efficient a manner as possible.

Suppose an organization needed 1,000 IP addresses from the ISP for Internet connection. If this were strictly a classful environment, the ISP would have two choices:

- Give up a class B address. This would effectively waste 64,534 addresses, since a class B address offers 65,534 and the organization only wanted 1,000.

- Assign four separate class C addresses that support up to 254 addresses each. The disadvantage of this approach is that it will take four additional advertised routes on all Internet routers to reach this organization. Although four additional routes may not sound like much, if multiple class C addresses was the only way to meet any organization's Internet connectivity needs, the impact on Internet routing tables would be significant indeed.

However, thanks to CIDR, the ISP has the flexibility to more closely match the exact needs of the organization in terms of the number of required IP addresses, while adding only a single entry to the Internet routing tables. Referring back to the CIDR Block Capacity Chart, it should be evident that a /22 CIDR block with 1,024 IP addresses would fit the needs of the organization in question quite well. Figure 8-18 illustrates the relationship between the ISP's CIDR block, the client organization's CIDR block, and the equivalent class C Addresses.

**Reducing Route Advertisements with CIDR**    Just as CIDR allowed addresses to be more effectively allotted to meet a given organization' s needs, CIDR allows route aggregation to effectively reduce the number of route advertisements from a given network. Using the example illustrated in Figure 8-18 the client organization could summarize all of the subnet information from its four assigned networks into a single route advertisement: 207.32.168.0/22. Likewise the ISP in the example could summarize all of its routes for all of its client organizations into a single route advertisement: 207.32.128.0/17.

| | Binary | Available for Subnets and Hosts | Dotted Decimal with Extended Network Prefix |
|---|---|---|---|
| ISP CIDR Block | 11001111.00100000.1 | 0000000.00000000 | 207.32.128.0/17 |
| Client Organization's CIDR Block | 11001111.00100000.101010 | 00.00000000 | 207.32.168.0/22 |
| Class C Address 1 | 11001111.00100000.10101000 | .00000000 | 207.32.168.0/24 |
| Class C Address 2 | 11001111.00100000.10101001 | .00000000 | 207.32.169.0/24 |
| Class C Address 3 | 11001111.00100000.10101010 | .00000000 | 207.32.170.0/24 |
| Class C Address 4 | 11001111.00100000.10101011 | .00000000 | 207.32.171.0/24 |

*Figure 8-18*    Address Allocation with CIDR

*CIDR vs. VLSM: Similarities and Differences*    CIDR and VLSM are actually quite similar in that they both allow a given high-level network ID to be divided and subsequently subdivided repeatedly into smaller and smaller pieces. This division into subnets, sub-subnets, sub-sub-subnets, and so on is done in such a way that the addresses that are contained within any lower level subnet can be rolled up, or aggregated into a single address at the next higher level of addressing. This type of address segmentation is sometimes referred to as recursive division or **recursion.**

In terms of implementation, both VLSM and CIDR require that the extended network prefix information is transmitted with every route advertisement. All routers supporting VLSM or CIDR must use a longest match algorithm for determining which route should be chosen from among possible routes in a routing table. In order for router aggregation to effectively limit the number of route advertisements, addresses must be assigned in a manner that mirrors the physical topology of the network.

The key difference between CIDR and VLSM is a matter of when the recursion is performed. In the case of VLSM, the division of the addresses and definition of multiple levels of subnets of various sizes is done *after* the addresses were assigned to the end user. All of the addresses of the nested subnets are aggregated and the Internet has no knowledge of internal network structure of the VLSM environment. In the case of CIDR, the recursion is know as supernetting, and is performed by Internet authorities and higher level ISPs and is done *before* the end user receives assigned addresses.

## ■ IP VERSION 6

IPv4 has been the backbone of the Internet for twenty years. Although it has worked well, the evolution of the Internet from a fairly small network of universities and government installations into the commercial Internet of today have exposed some key limitations in IPv4 that have been addressed by the IETF in a new version of the Internet Protocol, IPv6. For those wondering, IPv5 was the version number given to a project to create a completely different, connection-oriented version of IP that has gone on to become the Internet Stream protocol (ST and ST2).

## Limitations of IPv4

While IPv4 is the most commonly used network layer protocol, there are some key limitations that affect its usage. Recall that connection to the Internet requires use of an IP address that is absolutely unique. Although the current version of IP could theoretically support 4.3 billion host addresses, far fewer addresses than that are actually available.

The recent boom in the use of the Internet by commercial entities has put a serious strain on the availability of IP addresses. As the number of hosts on the Internet grows, the 32-bit address space provided by IPv4 is rapidly running out. Although it provides almost 4.3 billion addresses, the hierarchical nature of IP addressing greatly limits the efficiency with which IP addresses can be used. This is largely due to the IP address classes introduced earlier. class C addresses, with only 256 hosts IDs are too limiting for many corporations, while class B addresses with 65,534 host IDs, provide far more host IDs than necessary, leading to wasted and subsequently unavailable addresses in most cases. Although this appears to be a waste of address spaces, the routing benefits of such a hierarchical addressing approach greatly outweigh the inefficiency of address utilization. Nevertheless some method of increasing the IP address space is required.

The second class of problems with IPv4 is that the design of the protocol results in increased processing at each router. This major problem is the result of several smaller problems. Fragmentation between the network layer and the datalink layer forces each router to carve an IP packet into smaller sections and reassemble them at the next hop. This problem mainly manifests itself when local area networks are interconnected via wide area networks. LANs typically run over fast, relatively error free datalink layer technologies such as Ethernet. With an available payload of 1,508 bytes, it makes sense to set the IP packet size at 1,500 bytes. However, if these packets are required to cross a WAN link, they will be carried on datalink layer technologies that typically can handle only a 576-byte payload; resulting in packet fragmentation and increased router workload.

Another major router processing problem with IPv4 is the variable-length IP packet header. As previously mentioned, the options and padding fields are optional. This forces each router to parse the packet header to determine where the packet header stops and the data begins, wasting router resources.

Other concerns with IPv4 include the need for new functionality that simply isn't included in current version of the protocol. With the advent of streaming media on the Internet, there is a strong need for multicasting to be supported under IP. **Multicasting** allows a single packet to be sent to multiple hosts (but not all hosts) on multiple network segments. In the current unicast model, if five hosts on one network need to receive the same packet of data, it must be sent five times—one packet addressed to each host. In a multicasting model, only a single packet would have to be sent, thus reducing the load on the routers and reducing the bandwidth required to support the transmission. Although IPv4 provides limited support for multicasting most routers do not support it.

The third class of problems with IPv4 has to do with the evolution of data networks. Data networks are now being used to carry data types that the creators of IPv4 couldn't have anticipated. Streaming media, Internet telephone calls, and other time-sensitive data were not considered when the protocol was originally developed. These new applications create another issue that cannot easily be resolved using IPv4: different packets have different levels of importance. Under IPv4 there is no way to indicate that a packet carrying payroll data is more important than a packet carrying a media stream of the radio broadcast of a basketball game. If a router becomes overloaded, it will drop whichever packet comes after the buffer is full. Ideally, the router should make a decision to drop lower-priority packets from the buffer to allow higher-priority packers to reach their destinations. This ability is commonly known as **class of service.**

The final concern with IPv4 is that there are absolutely no security features. Although data in the higher-level protocols can be encrypted, the resulting cipher-text is readily available to anyone who wants to "listen" for it anywhere along the route to the destination. There is also no mechanism in IPv4 to prevent a host from pretending to be someone it is not. This process of deception, known as *spoofing*, presents a serious security threat to IP-based networks.

To address these shortcomings, the Internet Engineering Task Force developed IPv6, also known as IPng (Next Generation), in December 1998.

## Addressing

IPv6 resolves the IPv4 address space problem by expanding IP addresses to 128 bits, an $8 \times 10$ to the $28^{\text{th}}$ power improvement. Instead of the familiar dotted decimal notation,

IPv6 addresses are represented in a manner similar to MAC addresses: as a series of eight 16-bit sections represented by their hexadecimal values, separated by colons. An example, IPv6 address is: FF0E:0:0:A0B9:0:23:9873:212. A section of all zeroes is simply expressed as a single zero. Subnet masks are expressed in a similar manner. An example IPv6 subnet mask would be FFFF:FFFF:FFFF:FFFF:0:0:0:0.

## Other Improvements

Other improvements address the fragmentation problem. For those data streams that require multiple packets to be sent, an explorer packet is sent to the destination to determine the smallest underlying datalink layer payload on the route. The source node then uses this setting as the maximum transmission unit for that connection, thus effectively eliminating packet fragmentation and its resulting processor overhead.

To further reduce the processing load on routers, IPv6 utilizes fixed-length field headers. While the overall packet header for IPv6 is larger than IPv4 due to the increased length of the source and destination addresses, each header is constructed in exactly the same format, thus removing the requirement that routers parse each packet. Packet header error checking has been removed, as it is somewhat redundant: If a packet header had an error, it was somewhat unlikely it would reach its destination in the first place, so why bother to check for errors?

To address the need for classes of service, IPv6 numbers each data stream and labels it as either congestion controlled or noncongestion controlled. Congestion-controlled data streams can tolerate delays while noncongestion-controlled data streams cannot tolerate delays. An example of a congestion-controlled data stream might be a file transfer, while an example of a noncongestion-controlled data stream might be an Internet telephone call. IPv6 also includes support for multicast addresses and a new unicast address method called anycast that streamlines routing through IPv6 networks along with traditional support for broadcast addresses.

Security has been addressed on two fronts: authentication and encryption. IPv6 packets can be set to authenticate their origin. This prevents another node from spoofing an IP address and from fraudulently gaining access to sensitive data. IPv6 packets can also be encrypted at the network layer, thus eliminating the need to each higher level protocol to implement its own encryption methodology.

## Packet Construction

The IPv6 packet header is 40 bytes long. Although this is longer than the 20 to 24 bytes of IPv4, the fixed header structure and field lengths combine to increase routing performance. The packet layout of an IPv6 packet is shown in Figure 8-19. A detailed description of the IPv6 header fields is given in Figure 8-20.

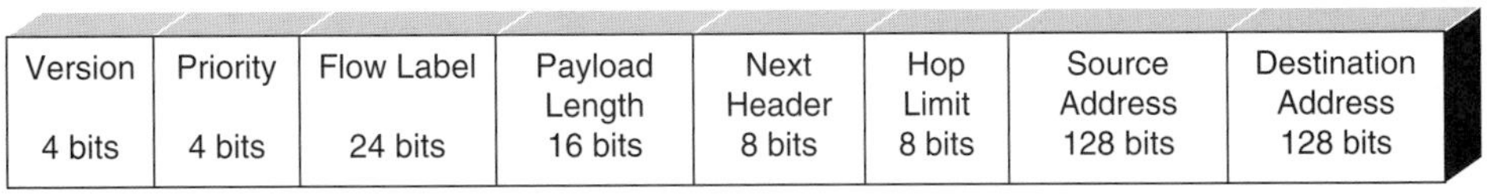

| Version | Priority | Flow Label | Payload Length | Next Header | Hop Limit | Source Address | Destination Address |
|---------|----------|------------|----------------|-------------|-----------|----------------|---------------------|
| 4 bits | 4 bits | 24 bits | 16 bits | 8 bits | 8 bits | 128 bits | 128 bits |

*Figure 8-19*   IPv6 Packet Layout

| IPv6 Header Field | Function/Importance |
| --- | --- |
| **Ver** | It is important for computers and internetwork devices processing this IP packet to know the version of IP with which it was written in order to preclude any potential cross-version incompatibility problems. |
| **Prio** | Priority of the packet. This field indicates the class of service of the packet. |
| **Flow Label** | This field uniquely identifies the stream of data relative to other streams between the same source and destination. |
| **Payload Length** | This field indicated the length of the data in the packet. |
| **Next Hdr** | This field indicates what type of header is contained in the payload of the IP packet. It tells the destination node what protocols are encapsulated in the packet. |
| **Hop Limit** | This field corresponds to the Time to Live counter in IPv4. It is a simple 8-bit (up to 255) hop counter that prevents a packet from wandering around an IPv6 network forever. |
| **Source Address** | This is the 128-bit IP address of source computer. |
| **Destination Address** | This is the 128-bit IP address of ultimate destination computer. |
| **Checksum** | This field is more correctly known as the IP Header Checksum, as it only provides error detection for the IP header. Reliability checks for the IP data are provided by upper-layer protocols. |

*Figure 8-20*    IPv6 Header Fields

## Transition from IPv4 to IPv6

While there are compelling technical reasons to transition all IP-based networks to IPv6 as soon as possible, the actual transition itself is problematic at best. Consider a large corporate private network consisting of 5,000 nodes in seventeen cities spread across six time zones. It is simply not realistic to say that at midnight GMT on a certain date every node will change over to IPv6. The Internet exacerbates the problem with its constituent networks under the control of various organizations spread literally around the globe. What is needed is a mechanism to allow IPv4 and IPv6 to coexist for a period of time until the transition can be completed.

IPv6 provides three such mechanisms. An NIC can be bound to two IP addresses: one IPv4 and one IPv6. Such a dual-addressed node would respond to either IP address as if it were the node's only address. A second approach is to tunnel IPv6 data across IPv4 network backbones. This approach works well for organizations that interconnect their data networks via the Internet. They can transition their internal networks to IPv6, then literally stuff the IPv6 packet into an IPv4 packet payload for delivery across the Internet where the IPv6 packet is removed and routed to its destination.

The third approach provides the most seamless solution to the problem by adding the ability to translate headers between IPv4 and IPv6 at the routers between IPv4 and IPv6 networks. In this manner, an IPv6 node can directly communicate with an IPv4 node. Ironically, this solution increases the load on the routers until all the nodes have been converted to IPv6—the exact opposite of what IPv6 is intended to do. However, it can be thought of as an investment to make the transition as straightforward as possible.

## ■ STRUCTURE OF THE INTERNET

Although it's often referred to as the world's largest network, the Internet cannot really be referred to as a *network,* as that implies a single entity. Instead, the Internet is a collection of independent networks interlinked in such a manner that data can pass from any connected network to any other connected network. The key differentiation is that a single network is under the control of a single authority. The Internet is under the control of no one.

The Internet is a hierarchical network. Individual organizations' networks are connected to ISP's networks, which are, in turn, connected to major ISP's networks, then to major carrier networks. The major carrier's networks are interconnected at **Internet exchange points** (also known as peering points or network access points). A listing of Internet exchange points with links to the points themselves is maintained at http://www.ep.net/ep-main.html. This hierarchy is illustrated in Figure 8-21.

As shown in Figure 8-22, each carrier operates its backbone network independently and offers paths to other carriers through connections to *Internet exchange points.* Each sarrier designs and implements their network to deliver packets

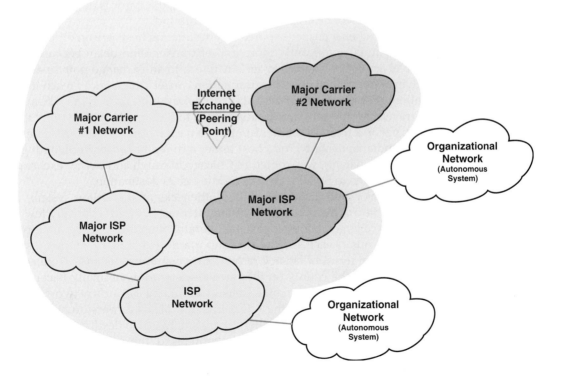

*Figure 8-21*    Hierarchy of the Internet

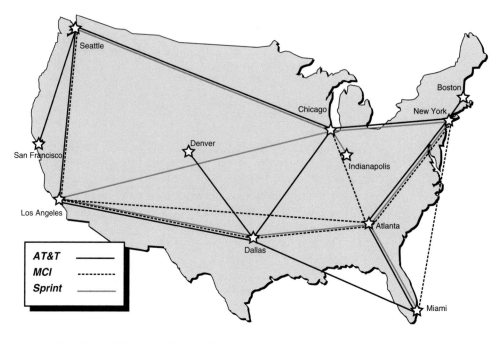

*Figure 8-22*   Carrier Network Geography

between two points as efficiently as possible. When a packet's source and destination host are connected to the same carrier's backbone, the traffic is delivered quickly. An outage on the network can quickly be routed around.

However, when a packet's source and destination hosts are on different carrier's networks there is significantly more risk of transmission delay because the traffic must travel across the source carrier's network to an exchange point, pass through the exchange point, then cross the destination carrier's network to reach its ultimate destination. This is not unlike the hub-and-spoke design used in the U.S. airline system. A traveler wanting fly from Indianapolis to Seattle might have to fly to Atlanta first, then get on a flight to Seattle. Similarly, a packet from the author's home in West Lafayette, Indiana, destined for a host under a different carrier in Bloomington, Illinois (150 miles distant), was routed to Chicago, through an Internet exchange point in Dallas, and then to St. Louis before arriving at its destination.

Just as major hub airports are the bottlenecks of the airline system, Internet exchange points are the bottlenecks of the Internet: there are relatively few of them trying to service large quantities of data. Literally billions of packets attempt to pass through their routers each second. It is important to note that "Internet distance" is best measured in terms of latency rather than geographic distance. Connecting to a destination across the county on the carrier's network is normally faster than connecting to a destination in the same state on a different carrier's network.

A basic business tenet of the Internet is that major carriers do not charge each other to deliver packets from another carrier's network to destination hosts on their network. This business relationship is formalized through peering agreements. Instead of charging each other for packet delivery, they deliver packets for each other and generate their revenue by charging their customer's for access to the Internet through their network. Without these peering agreements, the Internet as we know it would not exist. Either the cost to send data would be prohibitive or there would be added latency to analyze each packet coming across an Internet exchange point to collect billing information.

## ■ IP ROUTING CONCEPTS

Routers serve as intelligent-forwarding devices between subnets and networks. Figure 8-23 illustrates two subnets of the 165.32.0.0 network separated by a router. The router acts as a gateway to each subnet. The router actually has a network interface card that participates in each subnet. The IP address of the router's NIC in subnet 1 is 165.32.1.1 and the IP address of the NIC acting as a gateway to subnet 2 is 165.32.2.1. Associated with the IP address assigned to each NIC on the router is a subnet mask. As we will see shortly, the routers use the subnet mask to determine the subnet IDs of all traffic that the subnet mask is asked to process. Note how the third octet distinguishes between subnets. Also notice the differences in workstation addresses on the respective subnets.

### Static versus Dynamic Routing

Routes to specific networks can be entered into that routing table in two different ways. **A network administrator can manually enter static routes** into a router's routing table. By definition, static routes do not change as network conditions change and are therefore not able to adapt to network failures. As networks grow, configuring and maintaining static routes on multiple routers can become a real challenge.

**Dynamic routing** is achieved when routers are allowed to build their own routing tables based on route advertisements received from other routers. This may be simpler to configure, but runs the risk of having one misbehaving router create a potentially cascading negative impact on other routers. This is a greater concern when

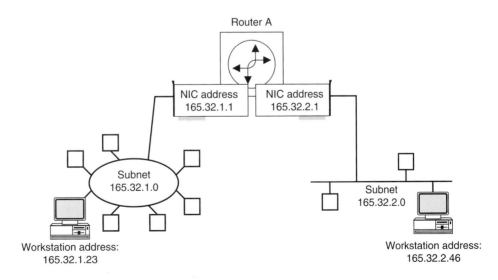

*Figure 8-23*   Single Router Scenario

those other routers are controlled by other unknown organizations as explained further in the section on Hierarchical Networking and Autonomous Systems.

### Longest Match Algorithm and Routing Table Organization

Whenever a router consults its routing table in order to find the proper route on which to forward a given packet, it chooses that route via a method known as the **longest match algorithm.** Simply stated, this means that the more specific the direction, the better. For example, suppose a routing table contained the two entries as illustrated in Figure 8-24.

Now suppose the router received a packet destined for a workstation with the address 192.210.165.32. The router would work its way down the routing table looking for the longest match. Since addresses are sorted from most specific (longest) to least specific, as soon as the router encountered the 192.210.0.0 entry it would have known that it had just passed the most specific or longest match entry. In this manner, the router does not have to read the entire routing table every time for every packet. It only reads until one entry past the longest match and back up one to its most specific entry.

**Gateways of Last Resort** What if a router gets to the bottom of a routing table and still hasn't found a match? Certain routing protocols, such as IGRP, support a feature known as *gateway of last resort*. If a router cannot find a match in a routing table for a destination packet, then it will forward that packet to the address of the gateway of last resort under the assumption that the gateway of last resort may know of additional networks that were unknown to the original router.

The danger in using a gateway of last resort is that the router may be forwarding traffic to destinations that are truly unreachable. Over time, this lost traffic could consume significant amounts of bandwidth. In order to cope with this, routers can be configured with a **null interface,** sometimes referred to as a bit bucket, so that undesirable traffic can be discarded rather than endlessly forwarded.

### IP Routing (Gateway) Protocols

Having gained a basic understanding of how routing works, the importance of router-to-router communication for establishment, maintenance and updates of routing tables should be obvious. In order for IP-based routers to automatically update their routing tables a routing protocol must be implemented. Although they are tied directly to a specific layer three protocol, routing protocols themselves are considered application layer protocols supporting the routing application.

| Network ID | Path |
|---|---|
| 192.210.165.0/24 | Path 1 |
| 192.210.0.0/16 | Path 2 |

*Figure 8-24* Routing Table for Longest Match Algorithm

**Hierarchical Networking and Autonomous Systems**   Thus far, only two layers of network hierarchy have been discussed: the network ID and the subnet ID. These two layers are sufficient for many private organizations. However, global private internetworks or public networks such as the Internet need additional layers of hierarchy in order to organize such massive networks and to keep routing tables of a reasonable size.

The concept of **autonomous systems** was introduced to allow a more structured view of the Internet and to control the growth of Internet routing tables. An autonomous system is rather arbitrarily defined as a network under the authority of a single entity whose interior routing policies or **interior gateway protocols (IGP)** are independent of those of any other autonomous system. Autonomous systems talk to each other via mutually agreed upon **exterior gateway protocols (EGP)**.

**IP Interior Gateway Protocols**   Interior routing protocol function was introduced in chapter 7. To briefly review, Figure 8-25 differentiates between the two major categories of interior gateway protocols: distance vector and link state.

At least some routers are capable of executing multiple routing protocols. This is often necessary as various networks that had been designed and administered independently must subsequently find a way to interoperate transparently. Routers running more than one routing protocol simultaneously and sharing or translating routing information between those routing protocols are able to do so through a process known as **redistribution.**

There are two basic, nonproprietary IP interior gateway protocols: RIP and OSPF. In addition to these nonproprietary protocols, several proprietary protocols have been developed by router vendors such as Cisco System's IGRP that typically offer unique advantages over standard protocols in a single-vendor environment. While the discussion of these proprietary protocols is beyond the scope of this book, they should be considered if you are operating in a homogeneous, single-vendor environment.

*RIP—Routing Information Protocol*   The most basic routing protocol used in the TCP/IP protocol suite is **Routing Information Protocol** or the **RIP.** There are two versions of RIP: RIPv1 and RIPv2 with the key difference being that RIPv2 supports passing the extended network prefixes required for the use of VLSM and CIDR. A routing table in a router serviced by RIP contains multiple records as illustrated in Figure 8-26.

RIP broadcasts its routing tables to all directly connected routers every 30 seconds. Those directly connected routers then propagate the new routing table information to the routers directly connected to them. This pattern continues, and after a matter of about 7 minutes (30 sec. intervals × 15 hop max.), all routing tables have been updated and, for the moment, are synchronized. However, the delay that occurs while all of the routers are propagating their routing tables, known as **slow convergence,** could allow certain routers to think that failed links to certain networks are still viable. In order to reduce the convergence time, the following optional approaches have been added to RIP:

- **Split horizon** prevents routers from wasting time broadcasting routing table changes back to the routers that just supplied them with the same changes in the first place. This can help prevent **routing loops** in which two routers continue to trade routing table updates for a route that is in fact no longer reachable. In this case, each router thinks the other router can still reach the unreachable network and continues to add an additional hop to its own routing table to that network and rebroadcast this erroneous information to the

|  | **Distance Vector** | **Link State** |
|---|---|---|
| **Examples** | RIPv1, RIPv2, IGRP | OSPF, NLSP, ISIS |
| **Updates** | Entire routing table is exchanged with neighbor every 30–90 seconds, dependent on protocol. | Updates to routing table are sent out only as needed. |
| **Processing** | After receiving the neighboring router's routing table, each router recomputes all routing table entries based on its distance from the sending router. | Link State Packets are processed immediately. Information contained therein is added to update the overall view of the network. |
| **Extent of View** | Only can see its neighboring routers, whom it depends on for broader view of network. | Each router has a view of the entire network, since all link state packets are received and incorporated by all routers. |
| **Bandwidth usage** | More | Less |
| **Processor and Memory usage** | Less | More |
| **Metric** | • RIP: Hop count.<br>• IGRP: bandwidth, delay, load, reliability, max. transmission unit. | Cost, shortest path algorithm. |
| **Advantages** | • Low processing and memory usage.<br>• Simpler to implement. | • No routing table exchange.<br>• No hop count limit.<br>• Link bandwidth and delay are considered in routing decisions.<br>• Fast convergence.<br>• Support for VLSM and CIDR.<br>• Hierarchical view of network scales better for large internetwork. |
| **Disadvantages** | • Doesn't consider bandwidth of links when making routing decisions.<br>• Slow convergence.<br>• Hop count limit of 15, 16 is unreachable.<br>• Exchanging entire routing tables is inefficient.<br>• Doesn't support variable-length subnet masks and classless inter domain routing (RIPv1).<br>• No hierarchy to network view, can't scale to large internetworks. | • More processor and memory intensive.<br>• More complicated to implement. |

*Figure 8-25*    Distance Vector versus Link State Protocols

other router caught in this routing loop. When traffic destined for this unreachable network is received by either of these routers, they continually forward the traffic back and forth, each thinking the other router knows how to reach the unreachable network. Eventually, one of the routers will reach a *hop count of 16* to the unreachable network. In distance vector protocols, a hop count of 16 means the network is unreachable. This is an important limitation

| Field | Description and Purpose |
|-------|------------------------|
| Address | IP address of the network about which this record contains information. |
| Gateway | IP address of the next hop router, or directly reachable router along the path to the network identified in the Address field. It is to these directly connected routers to which RIP broadcasts its routing table every 30 seconds. In larger networks, these routing table broadcasts can amount to a substantial amount of network traffic. |
| Interface | The MAC layer address or port number of the physical interface on this router which is connected to the link that leads to the next hop gateway identified in the previous field. |
| Metric or Hop Count | Total number of hops, or intermediate routers, between this router and the destination network. RIP limits the number of intermediate hops between any two networks to 15, thereby limiting the physical size of RIP-supported networks. Hop counts of 16 are used to indicate that a network is unreachable. |
| Timer | Age of this entry. Two separate timers are actually used. One is usually set to 180 seconds when an entry is first updated and counts down until the 0 when the entry is marked for deletion. Remember that entries are normally updated every 30 seconds. The second timer controls when the entry is physically deleted from the table. |

*Figure 8-26*   RIP Routing Table Fields

to the physical design limitations of networks using distance vector protocols. The slow process of routers caught in a routing loop eventually figuring out that a network is unreachable is sometimes referred to as *counting to infinity*. As previously mentioned, enabling split horizon on a router interface will prevent routing loops.

- Instead of just waiting for the counting to infinity process to eventually identify and shut down routing loops, **reverse poison** allows a router to immediately set a hop count on a given route to 16 (unreachable) as soon as it senses that it and a neighboring router are incrementing hop counts by 1 to a given network on successive routing table exchanges.

- **Triggered updates** allow routers to immediately broadcast routing table updates regarding failed links rather than having to wait for the next 30 second update.

However, it should be pointed out that even with these improvements, RIP is still not as efficient as other routing protocols that will be explored shortly. For this reason, many people now say that RIP stands for *Rest in Peace*.

Figure 8-27 illustrates the layout of the RIP protocol, and field descriptions are given in Figure 8-28.

| UDP Header | RIP Protocol Layout | | | | | | | | | |
|---|---|---|---|---|---|---|---|---|---|---|
| | Command | Version | reserved | Family of NET 1 | NET 1 Address | Number of Hops to NET 1 | and so on | Family of NET25 | NET25 Address | Number of Hops to NET25 |
| | 8 bits | 8 bits | 16 bits | 16 bits | 112 bits | 32 bits | ... | 16 bits | 112 bits | 32 bits |
| | | | | ——— 1st tuple ——— | | | | ——— 25th tuple ——— | | |

*Figure 8-27*   RIP Protocol Layout

| RIP Packet Field | Function/Importance |
|---|---|
| Command | This field identifies if this RIP packet is an explicit request for routing information (1) or the associated response (2), as opposed to the default 30-second interval broadcasts. |
| Version | This field identifies the version of RIP supported in order to avoid possible incompatibilities due to RIP upgrade versions. |
| Family of Net 1 | This field is used to identify the network layer protocol used in the network described in this routing table entry. RIP is able to build routing table entries for networks with network layer protocols other than IP. Net 1 refers to the first network entry in the routing table update being broadcast by RIP. RIP is limited to either 25 network entries per RIP packet or a maximum packet length of 512 bytes. |
| Net 1 Address | The network address of this network entry in the RIP routing table update. The address format will correspond to the network layer protocol identified in the Family of Net 1 field. |
| Number of Hops to Net 1 | This field indicates the number of hops, or intermediate routers, between the router broadcasting this routing table update and Net 1. |

*Figure 8-28*  RIP Header Fields

*OSPF—Open Shortest Path First*  **OSPF** or **Open Shortest Path First** is an IP link state routing protocol developed to overcome some of RIP's shortcomings such as the 15 hop limit, full routing table broadcasts every 30 seconds, and slow network convergence. Introduced in the late 1980s, OSPF is specified in RFCs 1311, 1247, 1583, 2178, and 2328. As an interior gateway protocol, OSPF is used to share routing information inside of an autonomous system.

Each OSPF-enabled router in an autonomous system maintains an identical database consisting of link states, router states, usable interfaces, and known-reachable neighbors. Each router uses this information to construct a tree-like image of the network where the router is at the root of its tree and the branches of the tree represent shortest paths to destinations.

For large internal networks the address space can be broken into sub-sections, or **OSPF Areas,** to reduce the amount of traffic required to converge the network. All OSPF networks have at least one area—known as Area 0 or the backbone area—configured. Depending on the size of the network, in order to keep the topological databases of managable size and to reduce the amount of OSPF information that needs to be transmitted between routers, additional areas can be defined. All areas would communicate with each other through Area 0, the backbone area. Areas are distinguished by the OSPF Area ID field. The Area ID field is a 32-bit number that yields a theoretical limitation of around 4.3 billion areas, although in practice it is best to limit the number of areas to as few as possible to ensure rapid convergence of the network.

There are three classifications of routers within an OSPF network: backbone routers which have at least one interface in area 0, area border routers that have interfaces in two different areas (other than area 0), and internal routers that have all of their interfaces in the same area. When routing from a network segment in one area to a segment in another area the traffic must pass through area 0 via backbone routers. The hierarchy of an OSPF area implementation has four tiers: autonomous systems, OSPF area, network ID, and subnet ID as illustrated in Figure 8-29.

Unlike RIP, which only transmits tuples of routing data, OSPF sends several different types of **link-state announcements** (**LSAs**). LSA types include Hello packets

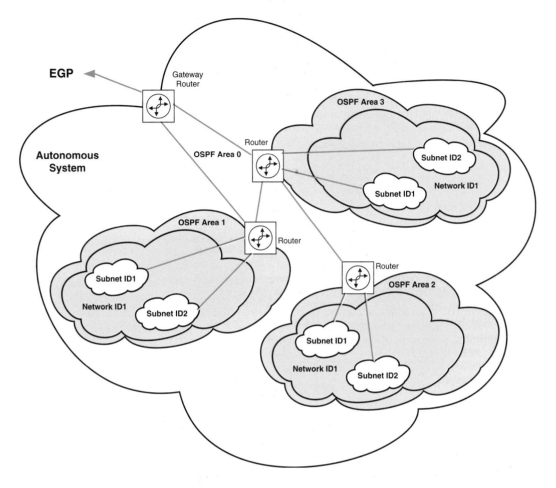

*Figure 8-29*    OSPF Hierarchy

that are used to discover other adjacent OSPF nodes within an area, database description packets that are used to define the structure of the link-state database, link-state request packets that allow a router to request record from a neighbor's link-state database, link-state updates that send in response to link state requests that contain information about networks and routers, and link-state acknowledgments that are used to acknowledge receipt of a link-state update packet. These LSAs are carried in OSPF packets encapsulated in IP packets. Figure 8-30 shows the layout of an OSPF packet, and field descriptions are detailed in Figure 8-31.

**IP Exterior Gateway Protocols**    As previously mentioned, the purpose of an exterior gateway protocol is to share information about autonomous units among gateway

| Version | Type | Length | Router ID | Area ID | Checksum | Authentication Type | Authentication | LSA Type Data |
|---------|------|--------|-----------|---------|----------|---------------------|----------------|---------------|
| 8 bits | 8 bits | 16 bits | 32 bits | 32 bits | 16 bits | 16 bits | 72 bits | Variable number of bits |

*Figure 8-30*    OSPF Protocol Layout

| Field | Description and Purpose |
|---|---|
| Version Number | States the version of OSPF for the advertisement. |
| Type | The type of message: hello, database description, link-state request, link-state update, link-state acknowledgment. |
| Gateway | IP address of the next hop router, or directly reachable router along the path to the network identified in the Address field. It is these directly connected routers to which RIP broadcasts its routing table every 30 seconds. In larger networks, these routing table broadcasts can amount to a substantial amount of network traffic. |
| Length | Total length of the packet. including header and payload. |
| Router ID | A unique value assigned to each router within the autonomous system. |
| Area ID | The area for the packet. |
| Checksum | Used to detect messages that may have gotten corrupted in transit between the source and destination. |
| Authentication Type | Defines which type of authentication code is contained in the authentication field. Supported authentication types include: none, simple, and MD5 among others. |
| Authentication | Authentication credential. |
| LSA Data Type | Any data required for the message. Data may be a single or multiple fields. |

*Figure 8-31*   OSPF Header Fields

routers. In order for an autonomous unit to effectively participate in the Internet, it must be able to speak to all other gateway routers. For this reason, there is only one major exterior IP gateway protocol in widespread use: BGP4.

*BGP4 (Border Gateway Protocol Version 4)*   Currently, the most commonly used exterior gateway protocol is **BGP4 (Border Gateway Protocol Version 4)**. BGP4, as specified in RFCs 1654 and 1771, is an exterior gateway protocol that performs routing between multiple autonomous systems or domains and exchanges routing and reachability information with other BGP systems. To the outside world, the AS is seen as a single entity. Each AS runs its own IGP (interior gateway protocol) independent of any other AS. Simply stated, any network can talk to any other network via the Internet because, regardless of what routing protocols those networks may speak internally, they all speak the same language (BGP) externally. Strictly speaking, BGP is a **path vector protocol.** This means that BGP routers exchange path information, which is a series of AS numbers, to indicate paths between autonomous systems. Routing policy in BGP can be finely defined by manipulating BGP attributes and by setting route filtering. Figure 8-32 is a simple diagram illustrating these concepts.

BGP depends on TCP for path vector information delivery, and is therefore considered a reliable protocol.

BGP works on the concept of neighboring autonomous systems. Once a neighbor to a given autonomous system is discovered, keep-alive messages are continuously exchanged between neighboring autonomous systems to assure the viability of advertised paths. In this manner, BGP routers know when neighboring routers fail and when path information becomes invalid. Each BGP router on an autonomous

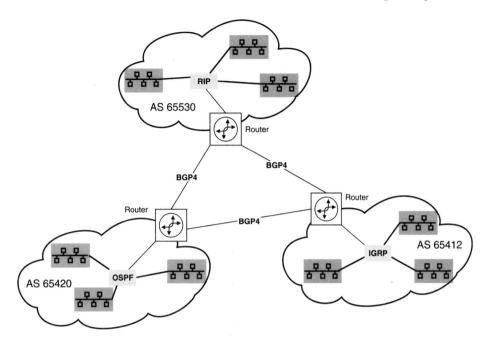

*Figure 8-32*    Autonomous Systems and Exterior Gateway Protocols

system is configured to advertise the summarized networks within that autonomous system, and to define which routers on neighboring autonomous systems it will exchange path vector information with. Administrative weights can be assigned to different paths to make one path more attractive than another.

There are four types of messages available in BGP4: open, update, notification, and keep-alive. An *open* message opens a BGP session between peers and is the first message sent when two BGP routers begin transacting. The open message must be confirmed before any other messages can be sent.

An *update message* is used to share routing information between the BGP routers so they can construct a consistent view of the network. An *update message* can be used to add, modify, or delete routing information. A *notification message* is used to terminate a BGP session when an error condition is detected. The notification includes the type of error along with the termination notice. *Keep-alive messages* are sent between BGP nodes to ensure that they are still active. If a node stops sending keep-alive messages, other nodes will terminate the connection and re-route traffic accordingly.

BGP messages are encapsulated in IP packets. Figure 8-33 shows the layout of a BGP packet and field descriptions are detailed in Figure 8-34.

Since routing information is not shared over the link connecting the various autonomous systems, the danger of having a misbehaving router from another

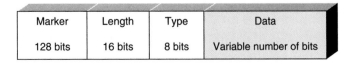

*Figure 8-33*    BGP4 Protocol Layout

| Field | Description and Purpose |
|---|---|
| Marker | Authentication value used to ensure the message is valid |
| Length | Total length of the packer in bytes—including the header and payload |
| Type | The type of message: open, update, notification, keep-alive |
| Data | Additional data for each message type |

*Figure 8-34* BGP4 Header Fields

autonomous system negatively affect the routers within a given autonomous system is minimized.

## Routing Evolution

With the advent of faster LAN and WAN technologies such as gigabit Ethernet (see chapter 4) and dense wave division multiplexing (see chapter 6), the performance bottleneck has shifted from LAN capacity (bandwidth) to router capacity. As the raw data transmission speed across the wire increases, routers have struggled to keep up. Fortunately, routing has evolved to address these speed issues through the development of layer three switching and the evolution of wire speed routers.

**Virtual LANs** Before we can address layer three switching, we must define the concept of a **virtual LAN** and understand how virtual LANs integrate with layer three switches.

In a traditional shared media or layer two switching environment, every host connected to the switch is in the same broadcast domain. As explained in chapter 4, a broadcast domain represents all of the hosts that will receive a layer two broadcast message on the network segment. Because ARP utilizes layer two broadcasts to resolve IP addresses with MAC addresses, there is a one-to-one correlation between IP subnetworks and layer two broadcast domains. Therefore, if you are using shared media hubs or layer two switches, you would have to have a separate device for each IP subnetwork.

All routing between subnets would take place in separate, stand-alone routers. These routers were actually specialized computers that performed the routing function in software. By using software to implement the routing algorithm, it is easy to update the router to support newer protocols or repair errors in the code. The downside to software-based routers is that they are relatively slow despite ever-increasing speed of both processors and memory. This approach is shown in the first scenario in Figure 8-35.

As discussed in chapter 4, the key difference between a shared media hub and a layer two switch is that a switch can dynamically create connections between two ports independent of the other ports. Although this approach goes a long way to solve bandwidth capacity issues, it has a key limitation: It cannot control broadcast traffic or segment hosts into workgroups. Broadcast traffic has traditionally represented a high level of traffic overhead from ARP, RIP, and SAP broadcasts. Occasionally, network nodes would error and propagate these broadcast packets repeatedly, wasting significant bandwidth. The control of broadcast activity was

**Distinct Layer 2 Switching and Layer 3 Routing**

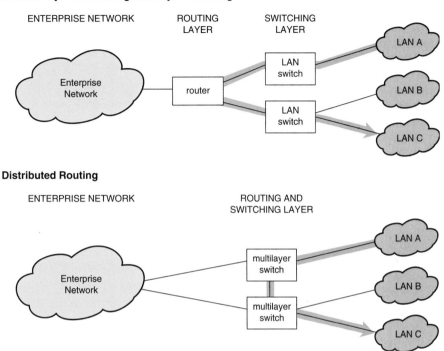

*Figure 8-35*    Distinct Switching and Routing Devices

important due to the fact that network bandwidth was very limited. In addition to the network capacity issue, each broadcast packet sent causes the network stack of each node on the network segment to analyze the packet, generating interrupts and using CPU cycles.

To add control over broadcast traffic to layer two switches, the concept of a *virtual LAN (VLAN)* was created. Virtual LANs are group of hosts defined in the switch by associating their MAC address to a VLAN ID. LAN switches that support virtual LANs use OSI layer two bridging functionality to logically segment the traffic within the switch into distinct virtual LANs.

Any message received by a LAN switch destined for a single workstation is delivered to that destination workstation via an individual switched network connection. The key difference between a LAN switch that does not support virtual LANs and one that does is the treatment of broadcast and multicast messages. In a virtual LAN, broadcasts and multicasts are limited to the members of that virtual LAN only, rather than to all connected devices. This prevents propagation of data across the entire network and reduces network traffic.

When members of the same virtual LAN are physically connected to separate LAN switches, the virtual LAN configuration information must be shared between multiple LAN switches so that broadcast messages are transmitted to the correct hosts. Figure 8-36 illustrates the differences between a LAN switch, a virtual LAN, and a multiswitch virtual LAN.

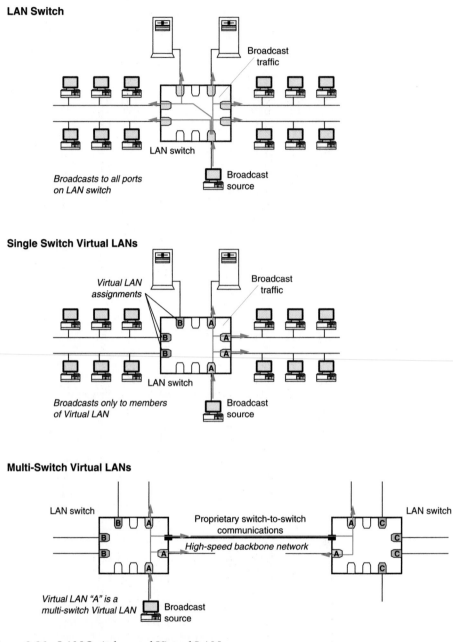

*Figure 8-36* LAN Switches and Virtual LANs

In Sharper Focus

## TRANSMISSION BETWEEN LAYER TWO LAN SWITCHES

When members of the same virtual LAN are physically connected to separate LAN switches, the virtual LAN configuration information must be shared between multiple LAN switches. Currently, no interoperability standards exist for transmitting or sharing virtual LAN information between layer two LAN switches. As a result, only proprietary switch-to-switch protocols between a single vendor's equipment is possible for multiswitch virtual LANs.

Among the alternative methods used by switch vendors to share virtual LAN information across layer two LAN switches are the following:

- Signaling message—Switches inform each other whenever new workstations come on line as to the MAC address and virtual LAN number of that workstation. In order to keep all switches' information synchronized, each switch's virtual LAN tables are broadcast periodically to all other switches. In larger switched networks, this virtual LAN table transfer can introduce significant amounts of broadcast traffic.

- Frame tagging—A tag indicating the virtual LAN number of the source workstation is appended to every datalink layer frame that must travel between LAN switches. In this way, the recipient switch knows immediately to which virtual LAN workstations the received frame must be forwarded. One difficulty with frame tagging is that the added bits may exceed the maximum frame length of the datalink layer protocol, thereby requiring additional proprietary methods to cope with this limitation.

- Time division multiplexing—Each virtual LAN is assigned a specific portion of the bandwidth available on the LAN switches' backplanes. Only the assigned virtual LAN is allowed to use designated bandwidth. In this way, each virtual LAN has a virtual private backplane, and traffic from various virtual LANs does not interfere with each other. However, assigned but unused bandwidth cannot be shared among other virtual LANs.

One possibility for standardization of switch-to-switch communication in support of virtual LANs that span multiple switches is **IEEE 802.10.** Originally conceived as a standard for secure data exchange on LANs that would allow workstations to set encryption and authentication settings, this standard is of interest to virtual LAN switch vendors because of the addition of a 32-bit header to existing MAC sublayer frames. Instead of just holding security information, this additional 32-bit header could hold virtual LAN identifiers. In order to overcome the limitation on maximum datalink layer frame length, IEEE 802.10 also includes specifications for segmentation and reassembly of any frames that should exceed maximum length due to the addition of the 32-bit header.

As shown in Figure 8-37, regardless of the number of switches in the VLAN environment layer two, virtual LANs still require the use of an external, stand-alone router to route traffic from one VLAN to another—even if the source and destination are both connected to the same physical switch. All of the characteristics and limitations of stand-alone routers discussed earlier apply.

**Layer Three Switching**   To remove the requirement for external routers in VLANs routing capabilities were added to LAN switches. These layer three or **routing switches** not only eliminate the need for external routers to connect LAN segments, but also provide a significant performance boost by operating at both layers two and three of the OSI network reference model. A layer three switch performs the traditional routing process for the first packet in a series, adds the layer two addresses (MAC addresses) to an address table, then switches the remaining packets in the data flow at layer two. Because the majority of the data is handled at layer two routing switches can provide connectivity between IP

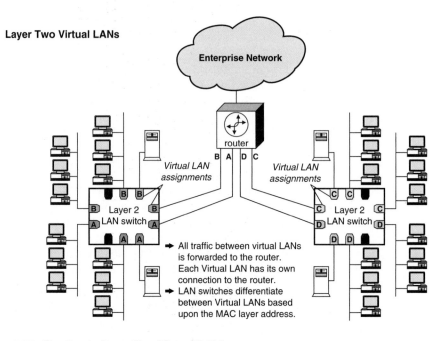

*Figure 8-37*   Routing in Layer Two Virtual LANs

segments at speeds much faster than traditional routers. This approach is detailed in Figure 8-38.

Unlike layer two VLANs layer three VLANs do not require any complicated data tagging to share VLAN definitions between switches. Since the attached hosts have previously assigned IP addresses, the layer three switch are can simply query the attached hosts and automatically them to virtual LANs based on their subnet number.

In Sharper Focus

### LAYER 4+ SWITCHES

In addition to layer three (routing) switches, newer "switches" have arrived in the marketplace that claim to operate at layer four or higher in the OSI stack. As a quick review of the OSI model shows no routing of data occurs higher than layer three. So what is a layer 4/5/6/7 switch?

As layer three switching technologies matured, the ability to analyze traffic flows based on the type of flow (as defined by the port number) was added. The resulting layer four switches provide a means to prioritize traffic flows based on traffic type, increase security by filtering, and collect application level traffic statistics on a per port basis. Although not technically a "switch" these devices are very useful in controlling bandwidth and managing the network.

**Wire Speed Routers**   Although layer three switches can eliminate the need for stand-alone routers to connect LAN segments, they cannot eliminate the need for all routers. There is still a need for stand-alone routers to serve as gateway and boundary routers between networks or between a network and the Internet and to provide routing at the core of the Internet itself.

The speed of the Internet is currently limited by the speed at which routers can move packets between networks at the Internet Exchange Points. As the load on

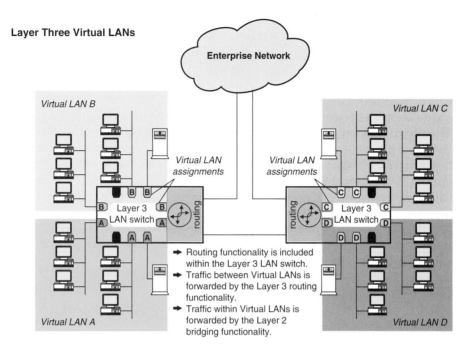

*Figure 8-38*    Routing in Layer Three Virtual LANs

these core routers continues to increase the need to increase their performance become paramount.

Fortunately router vendors have developed extremely fast routers for this purpose. Such routers are referred to by a variety of names including terabit routers, wire-speed routers or wire-rate routers. Such routers can perform millions of route lookups per second and possess aggregate throughput rates ranging upwards of 250 Gbps. Theoretical maximum capacity of such devices are measured in hundreds of Terabits per second. However, in order to compute the actual maximum usable capacity, one should the maximum number of ports on a single chassis by the maximum port speed. They are able to support a variety of interfaces including gigabit and 10 gigabit Ethernet, ATM, and SONET.

## SUMMARY

The purpose of this chapter was to provide readers with an understanding of how to correctly use IP addressing when designing networks. Two key characteristics in which different IP network design techniques differ are the efficiency with which addresses can be allocated to minimize wasted IP addresses and the level to which route advertisements can be aggregated to minimize both router to router traffic and the size of routing tables.

Classful addressing is a simple technique for both people and routers to understand but has the undesirable effect of not allowing subnets. classful or fixed length Subnet masking allows the creation of subnets but has the undesirable characteristic of wasting precious IP addresses. Variable length subnet masking allows more efficient allocation of IP addresses by allowing subnets of appropriate sizes to be defined through an internetwork. The rapid depletion of classful IP addresses is another issue of major concern.

Classless Inter Domain Routing allows blocks of addresses to be assigned in a flexible manner that supports both efficient allocation of addresses as well as reduction of route advertisements. Both variable length subnet masking and classless inter domain routing are dependent on the ability of routers to support these protocols most specifically through the ability to forward extended network prefixes with all route advertisements.

A new version of the IP protocol, IPv6, has been developed. IPv6 addresses many of the limitations of IPv4 including security, fragmentation, and address space.

The Internet consists of the networks of major ISPs that are interconnected at internet exchange points. Traffic bound from one ISP's network to anther must pass through an Internet exchange point. Due to the traffic going through these large routers, they add considerable latency to Internet traffic.

There are two types of IP routing procotols: interior gateway protocols and exterior gateway protocols. Interior gateway protocols are used to handle the transmission of routing information within an organization's network. Commonly used IP interior gateway protocols include RIP, RIPv2, and OSPF. Exterior gateway protocols are used to connect various organization's networks together on an internetwork such as the Internet. The most commonly used IP exterior gateway protocol is BGP4.

## KEY TERMS

| | | |
|---|---|---|
| aggregation | Internet exchange point | RIPv2 |
| area 0 | IPv6 | routing loop |
| autonomous systems | layer three switching | routing switch |
| border gateway protocol (BGP) | longest match algorithm | slow convergence |
| border gateway protocol version 4 (BGP4) | major network ID | split horizon |
| CIDR block | network address translation | static routes |
| classful IP addressing | null interface | static routing |
| classless inter domain routing (CIDR) | OSPF area | subnet |
| dynamic routing | OSPF | subnet mask |
| extended network prefix | reverse poison | summarization |
| exterior gateway protocols (EGP) | path vector protocol | supernetting |
| gateway of last resort | peering point | triggered updates |
| IGRP | private addressing | variable length subnet masking (VLSM) |
| interior gateway protocols (IGP) | recursion | virtual LAN |
| | redistribution | wire speed router |
| | RIP | |

## REVIEW QUESTIONS

1. What are some of the situations that led to the need for subnetting?
2. What is the difference between a major network ID, a network prefix, and an extended network prefix?
3. How does subnetting work?
4. How do routers use classful IP address information?
5. How do routers determine if IP addresses are part of the same subnet?

6. What is the difference between static routing and dynamic routing?
7. What is the longest match algorithm and how is it implemented in routers?
8. What are the major differences between distance vector and link state protocols?
9. Give examples of distance vector and link state protocols.
10. What is redistribution?

11. What is a gateway of last resort?
12. What is a null interface?
13. What is the cause of slow convergence?
14. How does split horizon seek to reduce convergence time?
15. What are routing loops and how are they prevented?
16. How does reverse poison deal with routing loops?
17. How do triggered updates seek to nullify slow convergence?
18. What is the purpose of private addressing?
19. How does network address translation work?
20. What is an autonomous system?
21. What is the difference between interior gateway protocols and exterior gateway protocols? Give an example of each.
22. What are the key functional characteristics of BGP4?
23. What is meant by a path vector protocol?
24. How does a path vector protocol differ from a distance vector protocol?
25. What are OSPF areas?
26. What special role is reserved for OSPF area 0?
27. What are some of the limitations of classful addressing?
28. What are some of the limitations of fixed length subnet masks?

29. How does VLSM overcome the limitations of fixed length subnet masks?
30. How does CIDR overcome the limitations of classful addressing?
31. What are some of the implementation requirements of VLSM?
32. What are some of the implementation requirements of CIDR?
33. How is address allocation done with CIDR?
34. How can route advertisements be reduced with CIDR?
35. What are the similarities and differences between CIDR and VLSM?
36. What is recursive division of a network prefix?
37. How are routes aggregated with VLSM?
38. What is the difference between route aggregation and route summarization?
39. What is an internet exchange point?
40. What is a virtual LAN?
41. List advantages of using virtual LANs.
42. What is a layer three switch?
43. How does a layer three switch differ from a router?
44. What is the longest match algorithm?
45. What is a wire speed router?

**Case Study:** For a business case study and questions on the data communications industry, go to www.wiley.com/college/goldman.

# LOCAL AREA NETWORK OPERATING SYSTEMS AND REMOTE ACCESS

## *Concepts Reinforced*

OSI model
Protocols and standards
Network architectures

Top-down model
Hardware/software compatibility

## *Concepts Introduced*

Network operating system
    functionality
Peer-to-peer network operating
    systems
Network technology analysis
Client network operating systems
Remote access
Mobile computing

Functional network analysis
Client/server network operating
    systems
Network operating systems
    architectures
Server network operating systems
Remote control
Remote access security

## OBJECTIVES

After mastering the material in this chapter you should:

1. Understand the compatibility issues involved with implementing LAN software.

2. Understand the basics of network operating system functionality.

3. Understand the important differences between peer-to-peer and client/server network operating systems architectures.

4. Understand the emerging role of the client network operating system and the universal client.

5. Understand how to analyze functional networking requirements and match those requirements to available technology.

## ■ INTRODUCTION

Network operating systems, like most other aspects of data communications, are undergoing tremendous change. As a result, before examining the operational characteristics of a particular network operating system, it is important to gain an overall perspective of network operating systems in general. In particular, network operating systems architectures are in a state of transition from closed environments in which only clients and servers running the same network operating system could interact, to open environments in which universal clients are able to inter-operate with servers running any network operating system.

In this chapter network operating system functionality is examined for both client and server network operating systems. This functionality is representative of current network operating systems in general rather than any particular product.

With the evolution of portable computers and the Internet, users need to gain access to an organization's data from a variety of locations other than the traditional office setting. One of the most important things to understand about such remote access is the relatively limited bandwidth of the wide area network links that individuals will use to connect to the main office information resources. Although the goal of remote access may be to offer transparent remote connectivity, decreases in bandwidth by a factor of 100 on WAN links as compared to LAN links cannot be ignored.

The overall goal of the second half of this chapter is to outline a methodology for the proper design of remote access solutions based on a thorough understanding of user needs, network architecture alternatives, and available technology.

## ■ NETWORK OPERATING SYSTEMS OVERVIEW

Traditionally, there were two major product categories of network operating systems: peer-to-peer and client/server. In a peer-to-peer network operating system, individual workstations can be configured as a service requester (client), a service provider (server), or both. The terms *client* and *server* in this case describe the workstation's functional role in the network. The installed network operating system is still considered a peer-to-peer network operating system, because all workstations in the network use the same networking software. Designed as a low cost, workgroup solution, peer-to-peer network operating systems lacked the ability to offer centralized authentication and authorization and suffered from exponential performance decreases as the number of users increased. As a result, peer-to-peer network operating systems were often characterized as lacking scalability.

In contrast to the homogeneous, peer-to-peer software environment, traditional client/server network operating systems require two distinct software products for client and server computers. The specialized client software required less memory and disk space, and was less expensive than the more complicated and expensive server software. The client software was made to interact with the corresponding server software. As a result, although traditional client/server network operating systems overcame the scalability limitation of peer-to-peer network operating systems, they did not necessarily overcome the interoperability limitation. Functionally, client/server network operating systems offered faster, more reliable performance than peer-to-peer LANs and well as improved administration, scalability, and security.

## Functional Requirements of Today's Network Operating Systems

Although traditional peer-to-peer and client/server network operating systems successfully met the functional requirements for workgroup and departmental computing, as these departmental LANs needed to be integrated into a single, cohesive, interoperable, enterprise-wide information system, the limitations of these traditional **NOS (network operating system)** architectures became evident.

In order to understand the architectural specifications of today's network operating systems, it is first necessary to understand the functional requirements that these network operating systems must deliver. In taking a top-down approach to network operating system requirements analysis, one might ask, "What are users of an enterprise-wide information system demanding of a network operating system in terms of services?" The answer to this question lies in the application layer of the top-down model. Given that it is distributed applications that will enable enterprise-wide productivity and decision making, the underlying network operating systems must support these distributed applications by supplying the message services and global directory services required to execute these applications in an enterprise-wide, multiple server environment.

Figure 9-1 illustrates these functional requirements and contrasts them with the requirements traditionally demanded of client/server and peer-to-peer network operating systems.

As illustrated in Figure 9-1, the new or emerging demands being put on network operating systems are application services, directory services, and integration and migration services. In order to successfully meet these functional requirements, network operating system architectures have shifted from integrated, single-vendor client/server network operating systems to independent, distinct, multivendor, client and server network operating systems. The functional characteristics of these distinct client and server network operating systems are described in detail later in this chapter. Figure 9-2 illustrates this architectural shift in network operating system development.

| Traditional Requirements | | All services delivered seamlessly across multiple server platforms regardless of installed network operating system | | |
| --- | --- | --- | --- | --- |
| | | Emerging Requirements | | |
| FILE SERVICES | PRINTER SERVICES | APPLICATION SERVICES | DIRECTORY SERVICES | INTEGRATION/MIGRATION SERVICES |
| | | ➡ Database back-end engines<br>➡ Messaging and communication back-end engines<br><br>***SUPPORT FOR:***<br>➡ 32 bit symmetrical multi-processing<br>➡ Pre-emptive multi-tasking<br>➡ Applications run in protected memory mode<br>➡ Multithreading | ➡ Global directory or naming services<br>➡ All network objects defined in single location and shared by all applications<br>➡ Directory information is stored in replicated, distributed databases for reliability, redundancy, fault tolerance | ➡ Allow multiple different client network operating systems to transparently interoperate with multiple, different server network operating systems<br>➡ Provide easy-to-implement paths for upgrades to more recent versions or migration to different network operating systems |

*Figure 9-1*   Required Network Operating System Services: Traditional vs. Current

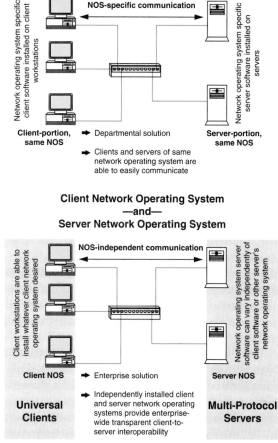

*Figure 9-2*    Client/Server NOS vs. Client *and* Server NOS

**Client Network Operating Systems: The Universal Client**    **Client network operating systems,** as illustrated in Figure 9-2, integrate traditional operating system functionality with highly configurable networking features to enable communication with a variety of network operating system servers. The client workstation's ability to interoperate transparently with a number of different network operating system servers without the need for additional products or configurations breaks the traditional hard linkage between client and server NOS. This ability is commonly referred to as **universal client** capability.

**Server Network Operating Systems**    Because the client and server platforms have been de-coupled, **server network operating systems** can be selected based on their performance characteristics for a given function. For example, Windows servers are often employed as file and print servers while UNIX servers are most likely to be employed as database and application servers. Because the universal client has the ability to communicate with any server, and the server has the ability to communicate with any client, the choice of server network operating system can be based on optimizing functional performance rather than whether the system simply provides interoperability.

### ■ CLIENT NETWORK OPERATING SYSTEM FUNCTIONALITY

Having gained an understanding of the new architectural arrangement of network operating systems consisting of distinct, interoperable, multivendor, client and server network operating systems, the functional aspects of client network operating systems categories can be examined.

Client network operating systems such as Microsoft Windows and the Macintosh OS offer three major categories of functionality:

1. Operating system capabilities

2. Peer-to-peer networking capabilities

3. Client software for communicating with various network operating systems

The logical relationship of these three distinct yet complementary categories of functionality is illustrated in Figure 9-3. Figure 9-3 also points out potential areas for compatibility and protocol consideration where the various software and hardware layers interface.

The following sections cover the importance of each of these three functional categories to the overall network operating system, as well as key implementation differences between technologies. Following this overview, a network analyst should be able to construct a logical network design listing the functionality required to meet the business objectives.

This logical network design is then used as an evaluation mechanism for selecting available technologies. Logical network design functionality can be compared to available technology's delivered functionality in a technology analysis grid such as Figure 9-7 ("Client Network Operating System Technology Analysis Grid"). As stated in previous chapters, the advantage to employing a technology analysis grid in such an endeavor is that it assures that purchase decisions or recommendations are made based on facts rather than creative packaging or effective marketing.

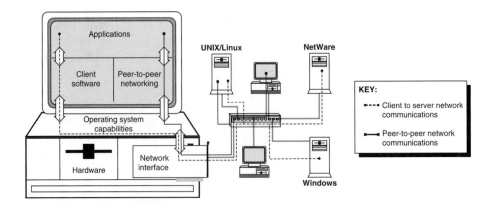

*Figure 9-3*   Logical Relationship of Client NOS Functional Categories

## Operating System Capabilities

The following operating systems characteristics are listed and briefly explained here from the perspective of each characteristic's importance to overall network operating system performance.

- *32-bit operating system.* 32-bit operating systems will allow more sophisticated and higher-performance 32-bit applications to execute more quickly. Although 64-bit hardware is coming to market, operating systems have yet to move to a 64-bit platform.

- *Pre-emptive multitasking.* Pre-emptive multitasking prevents misbehaving programs from monopolizing systems resources at the expense of the performance of other applications.

- *Protected memory space.* Protected memory space prevents application programs from accidentally writing into each other's or the operating system's memory space thereby causing general protection faults and/or system crashes.

- *Support for symmetrical multiprocessing.* SMP support is especially important for server network operating systems due to the processing load imposed by multiple simultaneous requests for services from clients. Some high-powered client applications such as 3-D modeling or simulation software may warrant SMP support on client platforms as well.

- *Multithreading.* Multithreaded applications are only able to achieve performance increases if they are executed by an operating system that supports multithreaded applications, allowing more than one sub-process to execute simultaneously.

**Application Program Support**    A very important aspect of any migration plan to a new client network operating system is the extent of support for **backward compatibility** in terms of application support, also known as **legacy application** support. It should stand to reason that most companies cannot afford to replace or re-write all of their application software in order to upgrade to a new client network operating system.

Although 32-bit client network operating systems are desirable and most current network-based applications are 32-bit, many custom software solutions are still 16-bit. In addition, many of these 16-bit application programs bypass supported **application program interface** (**API**) calls and commands in favor of directly addressing hardware devices. Initially done in the interest of increasing performance, these applications significantly limit multitasking and interoperability. Programs or subroutines that write directly to computer hardware are sometimes referred to as employing **real-mode device drivers.**

Many 32-bit network operating systems do not allow application programs to address or control hardware directly in the interest of security and protecting applications from using each other's assigned memory spaces and causing system crashes. Instead, these more secure 32-bit operating systems control access to hardware and certain system services via **virtual device drivers,** otherwise known as **VxDs**. Windows XP is a good example of a 32-bit network operating system that prevents direct hardware addressing. As a result, many 16-bit applications, particularly highly graphical computer games, will not execute over the Windows XP operating system. On the other hand, Windows XP is extremely stable.

Another issue concerning the execution of 16-bit applications is whether those applications execute in a shared memory address space, sometimes referred to as a **16-bit sub-system.** If this is the case, then a single misbehaving 16-bit application can crash the 16-bit subsystem and all other executing 16-bit applications. Some 32-bit operating systems allow each 16-bit application to execute in its own protected memory execution area.

When it comes to 32-bit applications, client network operating systems may execute these applications in their own address space, otherwise known as **protected memory mode.** However, all of these protected-mode 32-bit applications may execute over a single 32-bit sub-system, in which case a single misbehaving 32-bit application can crash the entire 32-bit subsystem and all other associated 32-bit applications.

Whether or not an application is executable over a particular network operating system is dependent upon whether that application issues commands and requests for network-based services in a predetermined format defined by the network operating system's API. Each network operating system has a unique API or variation. For example, Microsoft 2000/XP and Windows '9x both support variations of the Win32 API.

Some client network operating systems, such as Windows 2000/XP, have the ability to support multiple APIs and multiple different operating system subsystems, sometimes known as **virtual machines.** This feature allows applications written for a variety of operating systems such as OS/2, DOS, or POSIX, to all execute over a single client network operating system.

Figure 9-4 illustrates some of the concepts of Application Program Support by Client Network Operating Systems.

**Plug-n-Play**   Traditionally, one of the largest problems with installing new devices into a computer was configuring the hardware's resource usage. **Plug-n-play (PnP),** included in most modern client network operating systems, is designed to free users from having to understand and worry about such things as IRQs (Interrupt Requests), DMA (Direct Memory Access) channels, memory addresses, COM ports, and manually editing configuration files to add a device to their computer.

Although the goal of completely automatic hardware configuration has not been fully realized, definite progress has been made. Ideally, PnP functionality will automatically detect the addition or removal of PnP devices, configure them so that they do not conflict with other devices, and automatically load necessary drivers to enable the particular device

Compatibility issues are important to the achievement of full PnP functionality. To be plug-n-play compliant, the following are required:

- A **PnP BIOS** (Basic Input Output System) is required to interface directly to both PnP and non-PnP compliant hardware.

- PnP capabilities must be supported by the operating system through interaction with the PnP BIOS.

- The devices installed must be PnP compliant. This basically means that the manufacturers of these devices must add some additional software and processing power so that these devices can converse transparently with the PnP operating system and BIOS. In some cases, PnP compliant device drivers may also be required.

**Real Mode Drivers vs. API and VXD**

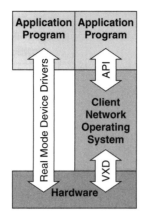

**Shared 16-bit Subsystems vs. Individual 16-bit Address Spaces**

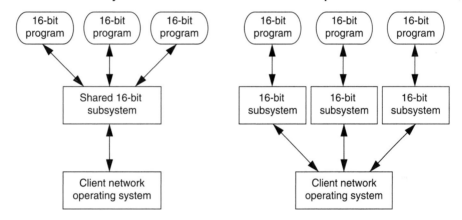

A single misbehaving program can crash the entire subsystem.

A single misbehaving program crashes only its own 16-bit subsystem.

*Figure 9-4*   Application Program Support by Client Network Operating Systems

Devices are detected by the client operating system through an assistant agent program, sometimes referred to as a hardware wizard, which walks the user through the configuration routine. Such programs are often capable of detecting and displaying IRQs and DMA addresses used by other devices, allowing users to accept supplied default answers in this semi-automatic configuration scenario.

## Peer-to-Peer Networking Capabilities

Most current network client operating systems also include peer-to-peer networking capability. These features allow each client to interact at a basic level with other clients. By utilizing these features, many small businesses can avoid the expense of implementing a large-scale server environment.

**File and Printer Sharing**    Perhaps the most basic peer-to-peer network function is file and printer sharing. In many cases, other resources such as CD-ROM drives and fax modems can also be shared. Network operating systems supporting peer-to-peer networking can vary widely in terms of file access security features. The level at which access can be controlled (disk, directory, or file level) is sometimes referred to as the **granularity** of the access control scheme. Access is controlled on a per-user or per-group basis. Sophistication of the printer management facility can also vary from one client network operating system to another.

**Workgroup Applications**    Striving to find new ways to differentiate themselves from the competition, client network operating systems are usually offered with bundled workgroup application software such as these:

- Terminal emulation
- Calculator
- Clock
- Games
- Paintbrush
- Sound recorder
- Remote access software
- CD player
- Backup
- Chat

- Phone dialer
- Performance and network monitors
- Diagnostic software
- Screen savers
- Web browsers
- Internet telephony
- Instant messenger clients
- Fax access software

Managerial Perspective

**JUST BECAUSE SOMETHING IS FREE DOES NOT NECESSARILY MAKE IT VALUABLE**

The network operating system that offers the greatest number of workgroup applications is not necessarily the best or most appropriate choice. Although free application software is nice, priority should be given to client network operating systems characteristics:

- Application program support and operating system characteristics

- Networking capabilities

- Flexibility and ease of installation and use in acting as a client to a variety of different server network operating systems

Client network operating systems that are able to connect to many different server operating systems are sometimes referred to as a universal client. In support of multivendor, multiplatform, distributed information systems, this is probably the most important evaluation criteria when selecting a client network operating system.

## Client Networking Capabilities

As illustrated architecturally in Figure 9-5, there are three distinct elements of client network functionality in addition to the previously mentioned required application support capabilities. In some cases, more than one alternative is offered for each of the following elements:

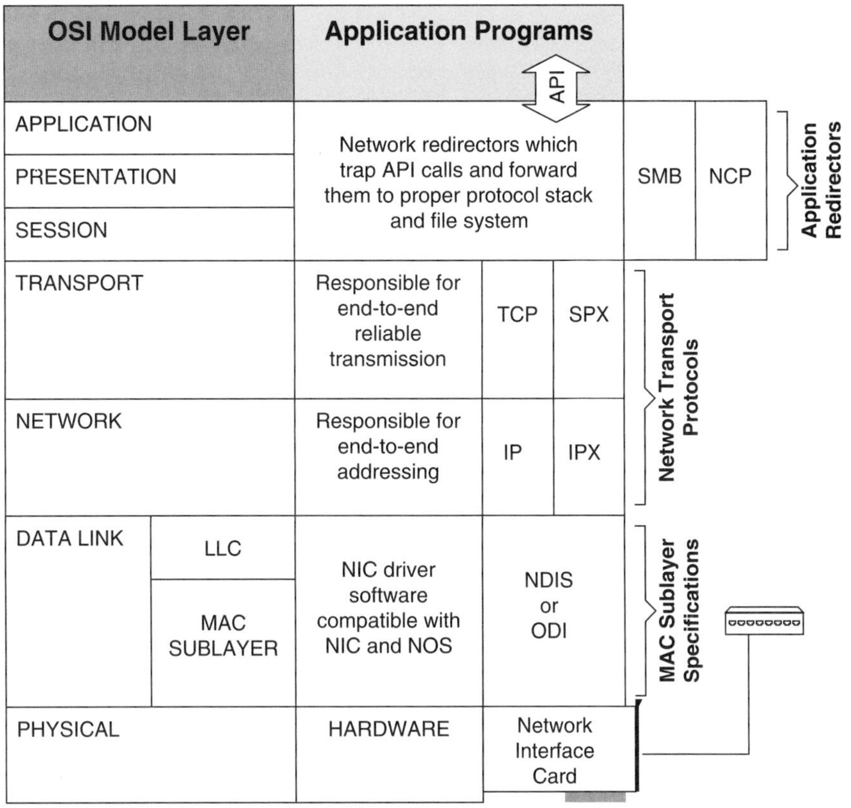

| OSI Model Layer | | Application Programs | | | | | |
|---|---|---|---|---|---|---|---|
| APPLICATION | | Network redirectors which trap API calls and forward them to proper protocol stack and file system | | | SMB | NCP | Application Redirectors |
| PRESENTATION | | | | | | | |
| SESSION | | | | | | | |
| TRANSPORT | | Responsible for end-to-end reliable transmission | | TCP | SPX | | Network Transport Protocols |
| NETWORK | | Responsible for end-to-end addressing | | IP | IPX | | |
| DATA LINK | LLC | NIC driver software compatible with NIC and NOS | | NDIS or ODI | | | MAC Sublayer Specifications |
| | MAC SUBLAYER | | | | | | |
| PHYSICAL | | HARDWARE | | Network Interface Card | | | |

*Figure 9-5*   Client Network Functionality

- *Client software and network drivers* allow a particular client to communicate with a compatible server.

- *Network transport protocols* package and transport messages between clients and servers. These protocols correspond to the network and transport layers of the OSI model.

- *Network redirectors* trap API (application program interface) calls and process them appropriately. Redirectors are concerned with providing file system related services in support of application programs.

More than one protocol may be provided in a given client network operating system for each of the three network protocol categories. Figure 9-6 displays the protocol stacks Windows '9x, Windows XP, and Linux. Rather than organize protocols according to the OSI Network Reference Model, Figure 9-6 divides the protocols into layers according to networking functionality.

**Connecting Clients to Multiple Servers**   In most client network operating systems, the combination of these three elements of network functionality allows client platforms to automatically find and connect to servers. For example, a properly configured Windows client will be able to automatically display network connections and connect to Windows and NetWare servers that are physically reachable and

| | Windows XP | | | | | Windows '9x | | | | | Linux | | |
|---|---|---|---|---|---|---|---|---|---|---|---|---|---|
| Application Support | WIN32 API 32-bit and some 16-bit Windows applications supported | | | | | WIN32 API 32-bit and most 16-bit Windows applications supported | | | | | POSIX compliant applications UNIX compliant applications | | |
| Application Redirectors and File Systems | NCP Netware Core Protocol Redirector (Novell) | SMB Server Message Block Redirector (Microsoft) | FAT File Allocation Table File System (DOS/Windows) | NTFS NT File System | | NCP Netware Core Protocol Redirector (Novell) | SMB Server Message Block Redirector (Microsoft) | FAT File Allocation Table File System (DOS/Windows) | | | NFS Network File System (UNIX) | SMB Server Message Block (SAMBA) | EFS Extended File System |
| Network Transport Protocols | IPX/SPX | NETBEUI NetBIOS Extended User Interface (Microsoft) | TCP/IP | Apple-Talk | | IPX/SPX | NETBEUI NetBIOS Extended User Interface (Microsoft) | TCP/IP | | | TCP/IP | | |
| MAC Sublayer Specifications | NDIS Network Data-Link Interface Specification (Microsoft/3Com) | | | | | NDIS Network Data-Link Interface Specification (Microsoft/3Com) | | | ODI Open Data-Link Interface (Novell) | | UNIX KERNEL DRIVER | | |

*Figure 9-6* Supported Protocol Stacks for Major Client Network Operating Systems

to which the client has been assigned access privileges. The client software does not have to be preconfigured with any information about these servers. The server discovery and access is all handled transparently by the client network operating system.

In addition to network operating system client software for specific server network operating systems such as NetWare and Windows NT Server, specialized application-oriented client software is often also included in client network operating systems. Examples of such network applications include the following:

- Web browsers
- FTP (file transfer protocol) client software
- E-mail client software
- Scheduling systems client software

In the case of the e-mail and scheduling clients, maximum benefit is attained only when compatible e-mail and scheduling application servers are available. The client portion is merely the front-end to a back-end application engine executing in some other network-accessible location. Most e-mail clients do support the POP3 and SMTP protocols required to connect to generic Internet mail servers.

**Mobile Computing Synchronization**   As mobile computing on notebook computers has grown exponentially, a need to synchronize versions of files on laptops and desktop workstations became quickly apparent. Such **file synchronization software** was initially available as a stand-alone product or included as a feature on remote access or file transfer packages. Also known as **version control software** or **directory synchronization software,** this valuable software is now often included as a standard or optional feature in client network operating systems. Laptop synchronization should happen automatically when the laptop computer is docked in its docking station. E-mail clients and scheduling system client software should automatically synchronize with the LAN-attached e-mail and scheduling application servers.

Some of the important functional characteristics or differences among laptop synchronization options include:

- *Copy by date option.* Files and directories can be selectively synchronized by selected data range.

- *Bidirectional option.* File synchronization can occur just from laptop to desktop, desktop to laptop, or both (bi-directional).

- *Cloning option.* This guarantees that the contents of a directory on one system exactly matches the contents of the same directory on another system.

- *Refresh option.* This copies only newer versions of files that are already located on both systems from one system to another.

- *Delta file synchronization.* This is perhaps the most significant file synchronization option in terms of its potential impact on reducing required bandwidth and file transfer time to accomplish the synchronization. Rather than sending entire files across the dial-up or LAN link, delta file synchronization only transfers the changes to those files.

## CLIENT NETWORK OPERATING SYSTEM TECHNOLOGY ANALYSIS

Applied Problem
Solving

Figure 9-7 is a technology analysis grid comparing key architectural and functional characteristics of Windows '9x, Windows XP, and Linux.

This grid is included as an example of how technology analysis grids can be used to effectively map required networking functional requirements to available technology solutions in an objective manner. This technology analysis grid is not meant to be absolutely authoritative or all-inclusive. Its primary purpose is to provide a concrete example of the type of analysis tool used in a professional, top-down, network analysis and design methodology. It is expected that network analysts will create new technology analysis grids for each networking analysis opportunity based on their own networking functional requirements and the latest technology specifications available from buyer's guides or product reviews.

The client network operating system technology analysis grid is divided into the following major sections:

- Hardware/platform-related characteristics
- Operating system capabilities
- Peer-to-peer networking capabilities
- Client networking capabilities

| Category | Client Network Operating System | | |
| --- | --- | --- | --- |
| | Windows 9x | Windows XP | Linux |
| **Hardware and Platform** | | | |
| Required-Recommended Memory | 32–64 MB | 64–128 MB | 32–128 MB |
| 16 or 32 bit | 32 bit | 32 bit | 32 bit |
| **Operating System Capabilities** | | | |
| Preemptive Multitasking | yes | yes | yes |
| Supports SMP | no | yes (professional version) | yes |
| Protected Memory Program Execution | yes | yes | yes |
| Multithreading | yes | yes | yes |
| Runs 32-bit apps | yes | yes | yes |
| Runs 16-bit apps | yes | Some; won't support real mode drivers | no |
| **Peer-to-Peer Networking** | | | |
| File & Printer Sharing | yes | yes | yes |
| Workgroup Applications | yes | yes | yes (most distributions) |
| **Client Networking** | | | |
| Network Clients | Windows Servers, NetWare | Windows, NetWare, UNIX (NFS) | Windows (Samba), UNIX (NFS) |
| Network Transport Protocols | NetBEUI, TCP/IP, IPX/SPX | NetBEUI, TCP/IP, IPX/SPX, AppleTalk | TCP/IP IPX.SPX |
| Remote Access | yes | yes | yes (most distributions) |
| Laptop Synchronization | yes | yes | no |

*Figure 9-7*   Client Network Operating System Technology Analysis Grid

# ■ SERVER NETWORK OPERATING SYSTEM FUNCTIONALITY

## Changing Role of the Server Network Operating System

Traditionally, file and printer sharing services were the primary required functionality of server-based network operating systems. However, as client/server information systems have boomed in popularity, **application services** have become one of the most important criteria in server network operating system selection. The distributed applications of the client server model require distinct client and server portions applications to interact in order to perform the required task as efficiently as possible. The server network operating system is responsible for not only executing the back-end portion of the application, but also supplying the messaging and communications services that enable interoperability between distributed clients and servers. Figure 9-8 illustrates the evolving role of the server network operating system from an architectural perspective.

The remainder of this section will focus on server network operating system functionality—specifically, those aspects of functionality that are most important to the support of distributed applications and their associated distributed clients and users.

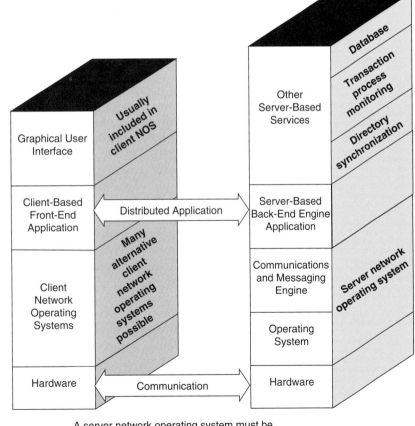

A server network operating system must be
capable of communicating transparently
with many different client network operating
system platforms.

*Figure 9-8*  Role of Server Network Operating Systems in Distributed Applications

Novell NetWare and Microsoft Windows Server are the predominate server network operating systems. When comparing these two network operating systems, it is important to note the historical strong points of each. NetWare has traditionally been stronger in file and print services than in the area of application services. Microsoft Windows Server has traditionally been stronger in terms of application services than file and print services. With the release of the latest versions of each product, both are rapidly making progress at improving on their weaknesses.

Various flavors of UNIX, combined with TCP/IP as a network protocol and NFS as a file system, have also been a popular choice of an applications server platform. However, this combination of operating system, network protocols, and file system is not as integrated or feature-rich as either NetWare or Windows NT Server and probably does not deserve the label of "next-generation" NOS. To resolve issues with NFS, newer UNIX implementations have co-opted the SMB protocol from Windows through the use of Samba to allow them to appear as a Windows NT Server on the network. The combination of UNIX and Samba makes an attractive NOS solution.

## Directory Services

Network operating systems depend on some sort of naming service or directory in which to store information about users and system resources such as disks, servers, and printers. Traditionally each individual server maintained this list separately. However, as distributed client/server systems became more prevalent a means of sharing this information was required. There are two approaches to accomplishing this: domains and directory services.

**Directory Services vs. Domains**    Domains and directory services differ primarily in the organization of information concerning network users and resources. Directory services organize all network user and resource data into a single hierarchical database, providing a single point of user and resource management. The hierarchical database is based on a hierarchical tree structure. All servers that participate in the directory are part of the global hierarchy and can see all other parts of the network. In this sense, the hierarchical directory database is merely a reflection of the hierarchical network itself. Examples of directory services include Novell's Netware Directory Service (NDS) and Microsoft's Active Directory (AD).

The directory service database is often **distributed;** different portions of the data are physically stored on different servers connected via the network. In addition, the directory service database is often **replicated** among multiple servers for redundancy and fault tolerance. In terms of a logical view of the network, directory services provide a view of a single, enterprise network.

In contrast, **domains** see the network as a series of linked subdivisions. Domain's associate network users and resources with a special server known as a **Domain Controller.** Each domain's directory must be individually established and maintained. Domains can be individually maintained and controlled in terms of how much of other domains can be seen. The key weakness with the domain model is that there is limited granularity: You are in the domain or you are not. There is no hierarchy within the domain. Examples of domain solutions include Microsoft Windows NT and Samba running on UNIX.

Directory services can also vary in what types of information are stored in the directory services database. In some cases, all users and network resources are considered **network objects** with information concerning them stored in a single database, arranged by object type. Object attributes can be modified and new network objects can be defined. In other cases, network users and network resources are kept in separate databases. Frequently, separate databases are maintained for network user account information and e-mail user account information.

In Sharper Focus

## DIRECTORY SERVICES COMMUNICATION

In a directory service implementation, a remote server performs a lookup in the directory database to authenticate the user's right to the requested service. This database lookup is repeated for every request for service from remote users. Recalling that the database is distributed, the physical location of the server which contains the rights information of the requesting user may be located anywhere in the hierarchical distributed network.

In the case of a domain solution such as Samba, the remote or foreign server receives the user authentication from the user's domain controller (local server) in a process known as **Inter-domain Trust** (**IT**). By having servers act on behalf of their local users when verifying authenticity with remote and foreign servers, every user ID does not have to be entered and maintained in every domain's directory service. In addition, once the interdomain trust has been established for a particular user, the remote domain server does not repeat the request for authentication.

The current trend is toward directory services and away from domain solutions. While each vendor's directory services solution is proprietary, all are loosely based on the OSI **X.500** directory service standard. A subset of the X.500 standard, known as the **Lightweight Directory Access Protocol or LDAP** and standardized by both OSI and the IETF, provides a means of achieving some degree of interoperability between various vendors directory services offerings. LDAP runs over TCP/IP on ports 389 and 636. Any client that supports LDAP can access information in any LDAP compliant directory service. All major vendors support LDAP in their various directory services offerings.

## Application Services

Recalling that the primary objective of the next-generation server NOS is to provide high-availability, high-performance application services, the most important NOS characteristic is the ability to support symmetrical multiprocessing. As numbers of users and sophistication of application programs continue to increase, the only real solution is for the application to be able to utilize more processing power simultaneously. Not all server network operating systems support symmetrical multiprocessing and those that do might vary in the maximum number of processors supported. Other server network operating system characteristics that are essential to optimization of application program performance:

- Preemptive multitasking

- 32-bit execution

- Multithreaded application support

- Program execution in protected memory space

**File Services** Applications programs are stored in a particular file system format. In addition, when these application programs execute, they may request additional services from the resident file system via API calls. Server network operating systems vary in the types and number of supported file systems. Some network operating systems can have multiple partitions on a disk drive supporting multiple file systems. Figure 9-9 lists file systems supported by the various server network operating systems in the marketplace.

Other file services offered by some server network operating systems include file compression utilities and **data migration** utilities that manage the migration of data among different types of storage devices as part of a comprehensive hierarchical storage management (HSM) program.

**Application Integration** Application integration refers to the extent to which applications program are able to integrate or take advantage of the capabilities of the operating system in order to optimize application program performance. Successful applications integration with operating system can yield both increased convenience and performance.

From a convenience standpoint:

- Does the application integrate with the operating system's security system, allowing single-user accounts, or must two separate security databases be maintained?

- Does the application integrate with the operating system's monitoring capabilities, allowing it to be monitored from within the operating system?

- Can the application be configured and maintained from within the operating system's control panel or setup subsystem?

From a performance standpoint:

- Can the application take advantage of the multithreaded capabilities of the operating system?

- Can the application automatically detect the presence of multiple processors and respond accordingly?

| File System Name | Associated Network Operating System |
|---|---|
| EFS | UNIX/Linux |
| EFS2 | UNIX/Linux |
| FAT 32—File Allocation Table/32 | Windows '9x, 2000, XP, and Linux |
| NetWare File System | NetWare 3 and 4 |
| NetWare Storage System | NetWare 5 and 6 |
| NTFS—NT File System | Windows NT, 2000, XP, server 2003, and Linux |
| VFS | UNIX/Linux |

*Figure 9-9* File Systems and Associated Server Network Operating Systems

- Can the application use the multitasking capabilities of the operating system, or does it supply its own multitasking environment?

- How easily, and to what extent, can adjustments be made to the operating system in order to optimize the performance of the application?

## Networking and Connectivity Services

**Network Client Support**    In addition to the client network operating systems that were previously reviewed, server network operating systems may also have to communicate with client platforms with the following operating systems installed:

- Windows '9x

- Windows NT/XP

- Macintosh

- UNIX

Many of these operating systems provide built-in client software that will allow for it to connect to the server. However, often this built-in software is rather limiting in terms of its overall functionality and ability to integrate cohesively. It is usually best to ensure that the latest client software available from the server vendor is installed on the client.

**Network Protocol Support**    One of the key questions concerning network protocols and server network operating systems is how many different network protocols are supported and how many network protocols can be supported simultaneously? Although the standardization on TCP/IP as the network protocol of choice in recent years has made this process easier, it is still important to ensure that the systems can support all protocols that may be required.

Related to the ability of a server network operating system to simultaneously support multiple protocols is the ability of a server network operating system to support multiple network interface cards. If a single NIC is the bottleneck to network communications, additional NICs can be added, provided the NOS and computer bus supports them.

**Remote Access and Gateway Services**    Just as client network operating systems supplied the client portion of a remote access communication, server network operating systems can supply the server side of remote access communication. These remote access servers may be included with the server NOS or may be available for an additional fee. It is important that these remote access servers be tightly integrated into the server network operating system to assure reliable performance, full functionality as offered to locally connected users, and tight security. Remote access solutions are detailed later in this chapter.

## Management and Administration Services

**Installation, Configuration and Administration**    Reviews of server network operating systems consistently list **auto-detection and configuration** of installed controllers, interface cards and peripherals as the most important installation-related feature. The ability of a server network operating system to automatically configure a controller, adapter, or peripheral is dependent on the network operating system possessing a compatible driver for that device. It should stand to reason that the greater the number of drivers supported by a given network operating system, the greater the probability that auto-configuration will be successful.

In order to appreciate the differences in ease of administration offered by server network operating systems, it is important consider enterprise network serving hundreds, if not thousands, of users. Simple items that are merely a nuisance on a smaller network can easily become major issues in such a large implementation. With this scenario in mind, there are some pertinent questions:

- How many steps are involved in creating a new user account?

- What is involved in giving a user access to remote servers?

- How easily can a user profile be copied and used as a template to automatically generate other user profiles? (This feature is particularly important in academic settings where user profiles must be constantly generated in large numbers.)

- What tools are available to assist in managing multiple servers simultaneously?

Server network operating systems can vary widely in the sophistication of the **performance monitoring** software included or available as an add-on. Ideally, the monitoring software should offer the ability to set thresholds for multiple system performance parameters. If these thresholds are exceeded, alerts or alarms should notify network management personnel of the problem, and offer advice as to possible diagnoses or solutions. Event logging and audit trails are often included as part of the performance monitoring package.

In multiple-server environments, it is particularly important that all servers can be monitored and managed from a single management console. Desktop and server management software offers capabilities beyond the monitoring software included in server network operating systems. For example, performance statistics are often gathered and stored in databases known as **MIBs** (**Management Information Base**). In addition, this performance management information can be communicated to Enterprise Management Systems such as HP OpenView, Computer Associates UniCenter, or Tivoli's Management Framework using **SNMP** (**Simple Network Management Protocol**). In addition to these enterprise network management platforms, both Microsoft and Novell offer tools designed to ease system administration across large network installations such as Microsoft System Management Server (SMS) and Novell ManageWise. Network Management is covered in more detail in chapter 11.

**Integration and Migration**  **Migration** features are aimed at easing the transition from one server NOS to another. Key among the migration concerns is the conversion of the directory services information. Utilities are available from third-party software vendors as well as from the NOS vendor's themselves to help automate directory data conversion. **Integration** refers to the transition period of time in the migration process when both network operating systems are running simultaneously and interacting to some degree.

**Monitoring**  As more mission-critical applications are deployed on LAN-attached servers, server operating systems must offer more sophisticated management tools in order to manage those applications effectively. Monitoring ability is essential in determining where potential performance bottlenecks might occur and to react accordingly. Server attributes that should capable of being monitored and logged include the following:

- Processor utilization
- Network I/O
- Disk I/O
- Memory usage including L2 cache
- Individual application performance and system impact
- Process and thread performance

The monitor tool should be able to display data in a variety of ways:

- As a graph
- As a report
- As alarms or alerts if pre-set thresholds are crossed

A strong and flexible alert system is essential to keeping applications running and users happy. Some alert systems have the ability to dial particular pagers for particular alerts and can forward system status information to that pager as well.

A monitoring tool should support multiple open monitoring windows simultaneously so that multiple attributes or applications can be observed. The monitoring or management tool should be open and support industry standard management protocols and APIs so that application-specific management tools can be easily integrated into the overall operating system monitor.

## Performance

In order to take advantage of the increased processing powers of multiple processors, server operating systems must be specially written to operate in a symmetrical multiprocessing (SMP) environment. Server operating systems can differ as to the maximum number of processors that they can support.

RISC-based UNIX systems such as Solaris and AIX have been offering SMP capabilities for many more years than Intel-based operating systems. As a result, UNIX-based server operating systems tend to be more stable, with larger number of processors.

*Clustering* is another performance-enhancing solution now available for LAN-based servers as more powerful and performance-hungry applications migrate from the mainframe environment to client/server architectures. By truly distributing applications on a thread level, as well as associated data over multiple CPUs physically located on multiple machines, clustering-capable operating systems can truly harness all of the available computing power in a client/server environment.

## Security

Security will be covered in detail in chapter 12, but a review of basic security concepts is appropriate here. Overall security features fall into three broad categories:

- Authentication

- Authorization

- Encryption

Authentication    **Authentication** is concerned with determining which user is attempting to access the system. There are two key components to authentication: identification and proof of identification. In most network operating system environments, identification is provided by a UserID and proof of identification is provided by a password. Collectively, the UserID and password are known as a set of **Authentication Credentials.** In the login process, the server NOS checks the supplied authentication credentials against the directory service to determine if the credentials are valid. If so, the user is allowed to log into the system.

Most server network operating systems have the facility to support a guest user that is not authenticated. Although such a user usually is assigned minimal access rights to network resources, some situations, such as Internet publishing, require that a nonauthenticated user be given access to files and resources on a network server. When browsing the Web, a user typically doesn't need to log onto each server they wish to access.

Authorization    **Authorization** is the process of controls access rights to network resources. **Access Control Lists** (**ACLs**) are the most commonly used authorization technique for local area network operating systems. In an ACL-based authorization scheme, a list of users and groups is attached to each network resource along with their permitted access level. When a user attempts to access a network resource, the server checks the supplied authentication credentials against the access control list. If the credentials support the desired access level, the action is completed. If the credentials do not support the desired access level, the action is prohibited and an error is displayed to the user. A second authorization method is Kerberos, a multiserver authorization method that provides increased security for large client/server applications. Although traditionally used only in mainframe type applications, Kerberos is rapidly being integrated into PC local area network operating systems to increase the level of available security as more high end applications are ported to these platforms.

In addition to individual user accounts, it is also possible to create user *group accounts.* A group account is a place holder that allows for a single change in user permissions or rights to affect a multiple users at a time. By assigning all authorization rights to groups rather than users, it is possible to greatly reduce the amount of effort required to administrate a system while increasing consistency and alleviating potential security holes. When creating user accounts, considerable time can be saved if UserIDs can be created or modified using a template or group name instead of having to answer numerous questions for every individual UserID.

Encryption    **Encryption** is the process of "scrambling" data before data are sent across a network and "unscrambling" it at the destination. Encrypting dataprotects the data from anyone who may make a copy along the way. There are multiple methods of data encryption in the marketplace. The two most common are DES and RSA public key encryption. DES is a single key system, whereby a single key is used to encrypt and decrypt the message. In RSA public key encryption a combination of private and public keys are used to encrypt and decrypt the message, effectively eliminating potential problems with the transmission of a single key from the source to the destination.

Applied Problem
Solving

## SERVER NETWORK OPERATING SYSTEM TECHNOLOGY ANALYSIS

A network analyst's job is to always seek out the latest information that the industry has to offer before making recommendations for purchases which could have a significant bearing on the company's prosperity as well as personal job security. The following "Server Networking Operating System Technology Analysis Grid" (Figure 9-10) is

| | Server Network Operating System Characteristic | | |
| --- | --- | --- | --- |
| | **Windows Server** | **NetWare** | **UNIX** |
| **Hardware/Platform** | | | |
| Required Memory | 128–512 MB | 128–512 MB | 64 MB + |
| CPUs | Intel | Intel | Intel, Sparc, Power PC, DEC/Compaq Alpha, MIPS, etc. |
| Symmetrical Multiprocessing | yes | yes | yes |
| Pre-emptive multitasking | yes | yes | yes |
| Multithreading | yes | yes | yes |
| Protected memory app execution | yes | yes | yes |
| **Installation and Configuration** | | | |
| Automatic detection & configuration of adapters & peripherals | yes | no | no |
| Requires a separate administrator console | no | yes | yes |
| **Networking and Connectivity** | | | |
| Clients supported | Windows, Macintosh, UNIX | Windows, Macintosh, UNIX | Windows, Macintosh, UNIX |
| Network Protocols supported | TCP/IP, IPX/SPX, NetBEUI, Appletalk, TCP/IP encapsulated NetBIOS | TCP/IP, IPX/SPX, Appletalk, TCP/IP encapsulated IPX, IPX encapsulated NetBIOS | TCP/IP, IPX/SPX |
| Routing supported | TCP/IP, IPX/SPX | TCP/IP, IPX/SPX, AppleTalk | TCP/IP, IPX/SPX |
| Remote access services | Windows RAS | Novell BorderManager | Optional |
| E-Mail gateways | Mail server optional | MHS included | SendMail |
| Clients able to access remote resources | yes | yes | yes |
| **Management and Administration** | | | |
| Can act as SNMP agent for enterprise mgmt system | yes | Optional | yes |
| Can set performance thresholds & alerts | yes | yes with ManageWise (optional) | yes |
| Central mgmt of multiple servers | yes | yes | yes |
| Audit trails & event logs | yes | yes | yes |

*Figure 9-10*  Server Network Operating System Technology Analysis Grid

given as an example but is not meant to be either authoritative or all-inclusive. The technology analysis grid is divided into the following major categories:

- Hardware/platform characteristics
- Installation and configuration
- Networking and connectivity
- Management and administration

Managerial
Perspective

## SERVER NETWORK OPERATING SYSTEM SELECTION

New versions of server operating systems are released on an annual basis, if not more frequently. When in the market for a server operating system, it is important to consider all currently available products. You will want to consider current technology invest-ments, cost of deploying the new technology, business objectives, required applications, as well as the stability and strategic product development direction of the operating sys-tem vendor. After completing this analysis, the best solution should be apparent.

## ■ REMOTE ACCESS

As the computing power available in portable formats has increased and the Internet has matured, the number of portable computers has increased. Combined with the evolution of *n*-tier client/server solutions, the need for these portable computers to gain remote access to corporate resources at off-site locations has also increased.

One of the most important things to understand about LAN remote access is the relatively limited bandwidth of the wide area network links that individuals will use to connect to corporate information resources. Although the goal of LAN remote access may be to offer transparent remote LAN connectivity, decreases in bandwidth by a factor of 100 on WAN links as compared to LAN links cannot be ignored.

Managerial
Perspective

## BUSINESS ISSUES OF REMOTE ACCESS

As information has come to be seen as a corporate asset to be leveraged to competitive advantage, the delivery of that information to users working at remote locations has become a key internetworking challenge. Corporate downsizing has not only increased remaining employees' responsibilities, but pushed those responsibilities ever closer to the corporation's customers. As a result, the voice mail message, "I'll be virtual all day today," is becoming more and more common. The business-oriented motivations for remote access to local LAN resources fall into about three general categories.

The first category of remote LAN access is often referred to as **telecommuting,** or more simply, working from home with all the information resources of the office LAN at one's fingertips. This category of connectivity and computing is often referred to as **SOHO,** or **Small Office Home Office.**

Studies have indicated some of the ways in which telecommuting can increase overall worker productivity:

- Better, quicker, more effective customer service
- Increased on-time project completion and quicker product development

- Increased job satisfaction among highly mobile employees, which can lead to both greater productivity and employee retention

- Decreased worker turnover, which leads to decreased training and recruiting budgets

- Increased sales

A variation of telecommuting, **mobile computing,** addresses the need for field representatives to be able to access corporate information resources in order to offer superior customer service while working on the road. These field reps may or may not have a corporate office PC into which to dial.

Although some of the positive results of enabling remote access to corporate data for mobile workers are similar to those of telecommuters, the increased customer focus of the mobile worker is evident in the following benefits:

- Faster responses to customer inquiries

- Improved communications with co-workers and support staff at corporate offices

- Better, more effective customer support

- Increased personal productivity by the mobile workers such as being able to complete more sales calls

- Increased ability to be "on the road" in front of customers

- Allowing service personnel to operate more efficiently

The third major usage of remote computing is for **technical support.** Organizations must be able to dial in to client systems with the ability to appear as a local workstation, or take control of those workstations, in order to diagnose and correct problems remotely. Being able to diagnose and solve problems remotely can have significant impacts:

- Quicker response to customer problems

- Increased ability to avoid having to send service personnel for on-site visits

- More efficient use of subject matter experts and service personnel

- Increased ability to avoid re-visits to customer sites due to a lack of proper parts

- Greater customer satisfaction

Managerial
Perspective

## THE HIDDEN COSTS OF TELECOMMUTING

In order to fully understand the total costs involved in supporting telecommuters, it is first essential to understand which employees are doing the telecommuting. Telecommuting employees generally fall into either one of the following categories:

- Full-time, day shift, at-home workers

- After-hours workers who have a corporate office but choose to extend the workday by working remotely from home during evenings and weekends

Most studies indicate that more than 75 percent of telecommuters are of the occasional, after-hours variety. However, corporate costs to set up and support these occasional users are nearly equal to the costs for setting up and supporting full-time at-home users—more than $4,000 per year. Among the hidden costs to be considered when evaluating the cost/benefit of telecommuting are the following:

- Workers might not be within local calling area of corporate resources, thereby incurring long-distance charges.

- The telephone company might have to add wiring from street to home or within home to support additional phone lines.

- If existing phone lines are used, personnel time is used to sort personal calls from business calls.

- In order to provide sufficient bandwidth, alternative access technologies such as ISDN, DSL, or cable modems are often installed, if available, because some applications, especially those not optimized for remote access, run very slowly over dial-up lines, leading to decreased productivity.

## Architectural Issues of Remote Access

There are four steps to designing remote access capability for a network:

- Needs analysis

- Logical topology choice

- Physical topology choice

- Current technology review and implementation

**Needs Analysis** As dictated by the *top-down model,* before designing network topologies and choosing technology, it is essential to first determine what is to be accomplished in terms of LAN-based applications and use of other LAN-attached resources. Among the most likely possibilities for the information-sharing needs of remote users are the following:

- Exchanging e-mail

- Uploading and downloading files

- Running interactive application programs remotely

- Utilizing LAN-attached resources

- Attend virtual meetings via Internet telephony and conferencing

The purpose in examining information-sharing needs in this manner is to validate the need for the remote PC user to establish a connection to the local LAN that offers all of the capabilities of locally attached computers.

In other words, if the ability to upload and download files is the extent of the remote PC user's information sharing needs, then file transfer software, often included in asynchronous communications software packages, would suffice at a very reasonable cost. A network-based bulletin-board service (BBS) package is another way in which remote users can easily share information. Likewise, if e-mail exchange is the total information sharing requirement, then e-mail gateway software loaded on the LAN would meet that requirement.

However, in order to run LAN-based interactive application programs or utilize LAN-attached resources such as high-speed printers, CD-ROMs, mainframe connections, or FAX servers, a full-powered remote connection to the local LAN must be established. From the remote user's standpoint, this connection must offer transparency: The remote PC should behave as if it were connected locally to the LAN. From the LAN's perspective, the remote user's PC should virtually behave as if it were locally attached.

**Logical Topology Choice: Remote Node vs. Remote Control**   In terms of logical topology choices, two different logical methods for connection of remote PCs to LANs are possible. Each method has advantages, disadvantages, and proper usage situations. The two major remote PC operation mode possibilities are remote node and remote control.

The term **remote access** is most often used to generally describe the process of linking remote PCs to local LANs without implying the particular functionality of that link (remote node versus remote control). Unfortunately, the term *remote access* is also sometimes more specifically used as a synonym for remote node. Figure 9-11 outlines some of the details, features, and requirements of these two remote PC modes of operation, while Figure 9-12 highlights the differences between remote node and remote-control installations.

**Remote node** or remote client computing implies that the remote client PC should be able to operate as if it were locally attached to network resources. In other words, the geographic separation between the remote client and the local LAN resources should be transparent. In practice, the comparative bandwidth of a typical remote access link (ranging from 34–42 Kbps for a dial-up link to 512 Kbps for a DSL connection) compared with the Mbps bandwidth of the LAN is anything

| Functional Characteristic | Remote Node | Remote Control |
| --- | --- | --- |
| **Also Called** | Remote client<br>Remote LAN node | Modem remote control |
| **Redirector hardware/<br>software required?** | Yes | No |
| **Traffic characteristics** | All client/server traffic | Keystrokes and screen images |
| **Application Processing** | On the remote PC | On the LAN-attached local PC |
| **Relative Speed** | Slower | Faster |
| **Logical role of WAN link** | Extends connection to an NIC | Extends keyboard and monitor cables |
| **Best Use** | With specially written remote client applications that have been optimized for execution over limited bandwidth WAN links | DOS applications; graphics on Windows apps; can make response time unacceptable |

*Figure 9-11*   Remote Node vs. Remote Control Functional Characteristics

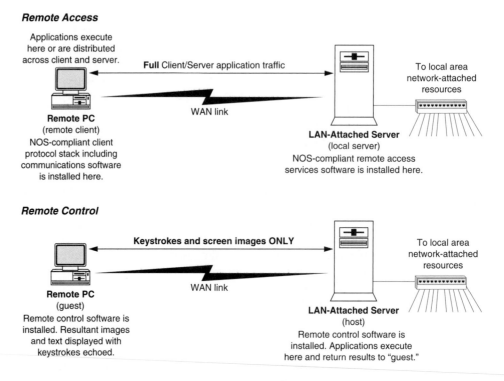

*Figure 9-12*   Remote Node vs. Remote Control Installations

but transparent. Where a NIC would normally plug directly into an expansion slot in a computer, a remote node connection merely extends that link via a relatively low speed connection. In remote node mode, client applications run on the remote client rather than a local LAN-attached client.

Client/server applications which require large transfers of data between client and server will not run well in remote node mode. Most successful remote node applications are rewritten to minimize large data transfers. For example, modified remote node e-mail client software allows just the headers of received messages, which include sender, subject, and date/time, to be transferred from the local e-mail server to the remote client. The remote client selects which e-mail messages should have the actual e-mail message body and attachments transferred. Local e-mail client software, which assumes plenty of LAN bandwidth, does not bother with such bandwidth conserving modifications. Other client/server applications must be similarly modified if they are to execute acceptably in remote node mode.

Although transparent interoperability was discussed as one of the goals of remote access, that does not necessarily mean that a worker's mobile computer programs must be identical to those running on one's desktop at the price of terrible performance. One of the most commonly overlooked aspects in deploying remote access solutions is the need to customize applications for optimal performance in a remote access environment.

Remote node mode requires a full client network operating system protocol stack to be installed on the remote client. In addition, wide area network communication software must be incorporated with the remote client NOS protocol stack. Remote node software often also includes optional support of remote control functionality.

**Remote control** differs from remote node mode both in the technology involved and the degree to which existing LAN applications must be modified. In remote control mode, the remote PC is merely supplying input and output devices for the local client that interacts as normal with the server and other LAN resources. Client applications still run on the local client that is able to communicate with the local server at native LAN speeds, thereby precluding the need to rewrite client applications for remote client optimization.

Remote control mode requires only remote control software to be installed at the remote PC rather than a full NOS client protocol stack compatible with the NOS installed at the local LAN. The purpose of the remote control software is only to extend the input/output capabilities of the local client out to the keyboard and monitor attached to the remote PC. The host version of the same remote control package must be installed at the host or local PC. There are no interoperability standards for remote control software.

One of the most significant difficulties with remote control software is confusion by end users as to logical disk assignments. Recalling that the remote PC only supplies the keyboard and monitor functionality, remote users fail to realize that a C: prompt refers to the C: drive on the local LAN-attached PC and not the C: drive of the remote PC that they are sitting in front of. This can be particularly confusing with file transfer applications.

*Protocols and Compatibility*    At least some of the shortcomings of both remote node and remote control modes are caused by the underlying transport protocols responsible for delivering data across the WAN link. In the case of remote control, the fact that proprietary protocols are used between the guest and host remote control software is the reason that remote control software from various vendors is not interoperable. In the case of remote node, redirector software in the protocol stack must take LAN based messages and convert them into proper format for transmission over WAN links.

Figure 9-13 illustrates the protocol related issued of typical remote control and remote node links as well as TCP/IP based links for a dial-up environment. If a different access technology is used the required client to server communication technology would change accordingly (Cable Modem/CMTS, DSL Modem/DSLAM, etc.) per chapter 3.

*Virtual Private Networks*    In order to provide virtual private networking capabilities using the Internet as an enterprise network backbone, specialized **tunneling protocols** needed to be developed that could establish private, secure channels between connected systems. By using these tunneling protocols, a virtual private network (VPN) can be built between the remote workstation and the organization's private network. A VPN creates an encrypted tunnel across a public network (typically the Internet) and passes the data destined for the remote location across the tunnel. The remote workstation gets a local IP address and appears to all computers on the local network as if it were local.

The two most commonly implemented VPN technologies are PPTP and L2TP/IPSec. **L2TP/IPsec** is largely supported by the firewall vendor community and is intended to provide interoperability between VPN firewalls from different vendors. **PPTP** is Microsoft's tunneling protocol that is specific to Windows Servers and remote access servers. It has the backing of several remote access server vendors. Figure 9-14 illustrates the use of tunneling protocols to build virtual private networks across the Internet.

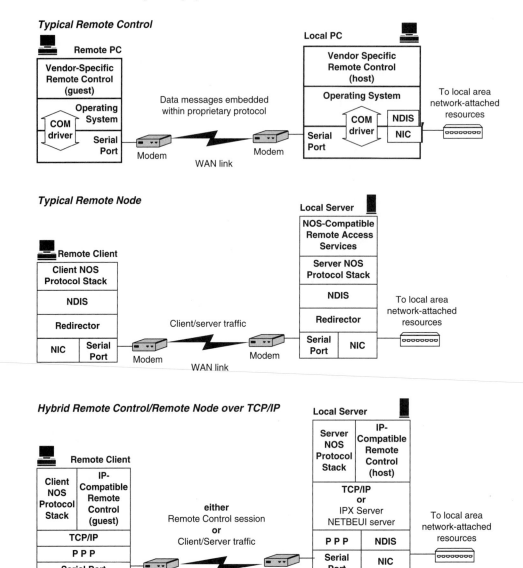

*Figure 9-13* Protocol Issues of Remote Control and Remote Node Links

- *L2TP/IPSec.* Layer two tunneling protocol (L2TP) is an IETF standard based on Cisco Systems layer-two forwarding (L2F). L2TP is typically uses IPSec (secure IP) as an underlying encrypting protocol to secure the connection between the remote workstation and the VPN server. Once an encrypted IPSec connection is established across the public network, L2TP is used to create the actual VPN redirection and encapsulation.

- *PPTP—Point-to-point tunneling protocol.* PPTP is essentially just a tunneling protocol that allows managers to choose whatever encryption or authentication technology they wish to hang off either end of the established tunnel.

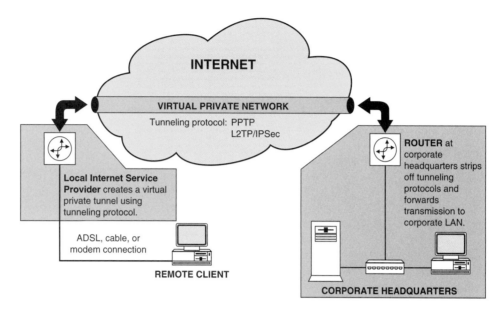

*Figure 9-14*    Tunneling Protocols Enable Virtual Private Networks

PPTP supports multiple network protocols including IPX, NetBEUI, and IP. PPTP is primarily concerned with secure remote access in that PPP enabled clients would be able to dial in to a corporate network via the Internet.

**Remote Access Security**    Although security from an enterprise-wide perspective will be dealt with in chapter 12, security issues specifically related to remote access of corporate information resources are briefly summarized here. Security related procedures can be logically grouped into the following categories:

- *Password assignment and management.* Change passwords frequently, even considering single-use passwords. Passwords should not be actual words found in a dictionary, but should ideally be a random or meaningless combination of letters and numbers.

- *Intrusion responses.* User accounts should be locked after a pre-set number of unsuccessful logins. These accounts should only be able to be unlocked by a system administrator.

- *Logical/physical partitioning of data.* Separate public, private, and confidential data onto separate physical servers to avoid users with minimum security clearances gaining unauthorized access to sensitive or confidential data.

- *Encryption.* Although it is important for any sensitive or proprietary corporate data to be encrypted, it is especially important that passwords be encrypted to avoid interception and unauthorized re-use.

- *Dial-back systems.* After remote users enter proper UserID and passwords, these systems terminate the call and dial the authorized user back at pre-programmed phone numbers.

- *Remote client software authentication protocols.* Remote client protocol stacks often include software-based authentication protocols such as PAP (Password Authentication Protocol) or CHAP (Challenge Handshake Authentication Protocol).

- *Remote client authentication devices.* Although exact implementation details may vary from one vendor to the next, all token authentication systems include server components linked to the communications server, and client components which are used with the remote access clients. Physically, the token authentication device employed at the remote client location may be a hand-held device resembling a calculator or just a small LCD screen capable of displaying six digits, a floppy disk, or it may be an in-line device linked to either the remote client's serial or parallel port. Token authentication devices are explained further in chapter 12.

**Physical Topology: Alternative Access Points**   As Figure 9-15 illustrates, there are two basic ways in which a remote PC user can gain access to the local LAN resources.

- *Serial port of a LAN-attached PC.* Perhaps the simplest physical topology or remote access arrangement is to establish a communications link to a user PC located in the corporate office. However, many field representative or mobile computing users no longer have permanent offices and workstations at a corporate building and must depend on remote access to shared computing resources

- *Communications-server.* As an alternative to having a dedicated PC at the corporate office for each remote user to dial into, remote users could attach to a dedicated multi-user server, known as a **remote access server** or **communications server** through one or more modems or via a VPN connection across the Internet. Depending on the software loaded on the communications server, it may deliver remote node functionality, remote control functionality, or both. As telecommuting and demand for internet access have increased, remote access servers have become the dominant means for accessing networks remotely.

The physical topology using the communications server (Figure 9-15, Illustration 2) actually depicts two different possible remote LAN connections. Most communications servers answer the modem, validate the UserID and password, and log the remote user onto the network. Some communications servers go beyond this to allow a remote user to access and/or remotely control a particular networked workstation. This scenario offers the same access capabilities as if the networked workstation had its own modem and software, but also offers the centralized management, security, and possible financial advantage of a network attached communications server.

The access arrangements illustrated are examples of possible physical topologies and do not imply a given logical topology such as remote node, remote control, or both. It is important to understand that the actual implementation of each of these LAN access arrangements may require additional hardware and/or software. They may also be limited in their ability to utilize all LAN attached resources.

**Network Topology: Alternative Network Access Services**   While Figure 9-15 illustrated alternative access points within an enterprise network, numerous network access

**Access Point 1: Serial Port of LAN-Attached PC**

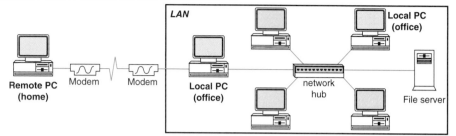

**Access Point 2: Communications Server**

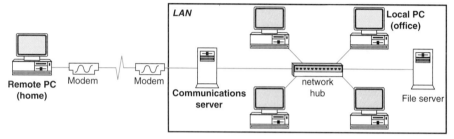

*Figure 9-15*    Physical Topology—Alternative Access Points

service alternatives exist that a remote access client can employ to reach an enterprise network's access point. Among these alternatives are the following, many of which were introduced in chapter 3.

- *Public Switched Telephone Network (PTSN).* Switched analog service, requires a modem. The highest current modem standard is V.90, theoretically 56 Kbps, closer to 33 Kbps in reality.

- *Integrated Services Digital Network (ISDN).* Switched digital service, requires an ISDN "modem,, 64 Kbps per B channel; it may be able to combine 2 B channels for 128 Kbps.

- *Digital Subscriber Line (xDSL).* This fixed point-to-point digital service rides over PSTN circuit. Requires DSL "modem." Bandwidth ranges from 64 Kbps to 1.5 Mbps; may be symmetrical or asymmetrical.

- *Cable modems.* This Internet access technique provides high bandwidth at a low price point. However many providers block the ability to use VPN technologies over the link, thereby reducing their usefulness for remote access solutions.

- *Virtual Private Network (VPN).* Builds secure communication channels through the Internet to connect remote corporate sites with the regional or headquarters sites. Requires VPN hardware and software and access to an Internet service provider.

Figure 9-16 illustrates alternative Network Access Services that might be used to construct a remote access network topology.

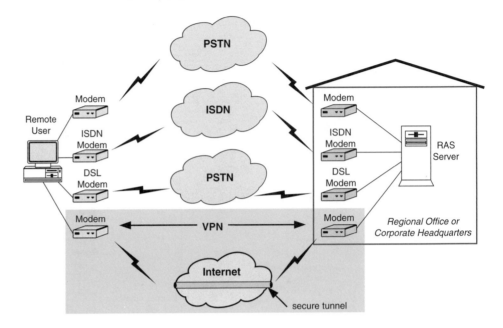

*Figure 9-16*   Alternative Network Access Services

## Remote Access Technology

There are two key components to a remote access solution: software and hardware. Remote access software consists of communications servers and remote access servers. Required hardware includes NICs and any other hardware required to provide a connection from the server to the client. The following sections provide a closer look at these required components.

**Communications Servers and Remote Access Servers**    As is often the case in the wonderful but confusing world of data communications, communications servers are also known by many other names. In some cases these names may imply, but don't guarantee, variations in configuration, operation, or application. Among these varied labels for the communications servers include access servers, remote access servers, and remote node servers.

A communications server offers both management advantages as well as financial payback when large numbers of users wish to gain remote access to and from a LAN. Besides the cost savings of a reduced number of computers, modems, phone lines and other access hardware, there is a significant gain in control of remote access to the LAN and its attached resources.

Multiple remote users can access a communications server simultaneously. Exactly how many users can gain simultaneous access will vary with the type of connection being used (dial-up modem, Internet, or VPN). Most communications servers service at least four simultaneous users—as many as 1,000 are possible.

**Remote Control Software**    **Remote control software,** especially designed to allow remote PCs to "take-over" control of local PCs, should not be confused with the asynchronous communications software used for dial-up connections to asynchronous hosts via modems. Modem operation, file transfer, scripting languages and terminal emulation are the primary features of asynchronous communications software.

Taking over remote control of the local PC is generally only available via remote control software. Remote control software allows the keyboard of the remote PC to control the actions of the local PC with screen output being reflected on the remote PC's screen. The terms *remote* and *local* are often replaced by **guest** (remote) and **host** (local).

Operating remote control software requires installation of software programs on both the guest and host PCs. Various remote control software packages do not interoperate. The same brand of remote control software must be installed on both guest and host PCs. Both the guest and host pieces of the remote control software may or may not be included in the software package price. Remote control software must have modem operation, file transfer, scripting language and terminal emulation capabilities similar to those of asynchronous communications software. However, in addition, remote control software should perform the following functions:

- Avoid lockups of host PCs

- Allow the guest PC to disable the keyboard and monitor of the host PC

- Add security precautions to prevent unauthorized access

- Include virus detection software

Additionally, Windows-based applications pose a substantial challenge for remote control software. The busy screens of this graphical user interface can really bog down communications links, especially if large screen resolutions or color depths are specified. Some remote control software solutions have included the capability to reduce the number of bits of color depth to reduce the amount of data that must be sent across the communication link. Figure 9-17 summarizes the important features of remote control software, as well as their potential implications.

The Remote Control Software loaded onto a communications server for use by multiple simultaneous users is not the same as the remote control software loaded onto single remote (guest) and local (host) PCs. Communications Servers' remote control software has the ability to handle multiple users, and in some cases, multiple protocols.

**Remote Node Software**   Traditionally remote node client and server software were supplied by the vendor of the network operating system on the server to be remotely accessed. **Windows RAS** (Remote Access Service) and **NetWare BorderManager** are two examples of NOS-specific **remote node server** software. It is important to note that these are software-only solutions, installed on industry standard, Intel application servers, as opposed to the proprietary hardware of specialized remote access or communications servers.

Some of the important functional characteristics of remote node server software other than operating system/network operating system compatibility are listed in Figure 9-18.

| Feature Category | Feature | Importance/Implication |
|---|---|---|
| **Protocol Compatibility** | • Network Operating System Protocols | • Which network operating system protocols are supported? (IP, IPX, NetBIOS) |
| **LAN Compatibility** | • LAN versions<br>• Host/guest<br>• Operating system | • Are specific multi-user LAN server versions available or required?<br>• Are both host and guest (local & remote) versions included?<br>• Some remote control packages require the same operating system at host and guest PCs while others do not. |
| **Operational Capabilities** | • Printing<br>• File transfer<br><br><br><br>• Scripting language<br>• Color depth/resolution<br>• Simultaneous connections | • Can remote PC print on local or network attached printers?<br>• Which file transfer protocols are supported?<br>• Delta file transfer allows only changes to files to be transferred.<br>• Automated File and directory synchronization is important to mobile workers who also have desktop computers at home or at the office.<br>• Allows repetitive call set-ups and connections to be automated.<br><br>• Can the software dynamically reduce the color depth to save bandwidth?<br>• Some packages allow more than one connection or more than one session per connection, for example, simultaneous file transfer and remote control. |
| **Security** | • Password access<br>• Password encryption<br>• Keyboard disabling<br>• Monitor blanking<br><br><br>• Call-back system<br><br><br>• Access restriction<br><br><br>• Remote access notification<br>• Remote host reboot<br>• Limited logon attempts<br>• Virus protection<br><br><br>• Logoff after inactivity time-out | • This should be the minimum required security for remote login.<br>• Since passwords must be transmitted over WAN links it would be more secure if they were encrypted.<br>• Since the local PC is active but controlled remotely, it is important that the local keyboard be disabled to prevent unauthorized access.<br>• Similar to rationale for keyboard disabling, since output is being transmitted to the remote PC it is important to blank the local monitor so that processing cannot be viewed without authorization.<br>• If a dial-in solution is being implements call back can add security. Although not hacker-proof, the server hangs up on dial in, and calls back at pre-programmed or entered phone number.<br>• Are remote users able to be restricted to certain servers, directories, files, or drives? Can the same user be given different restrictions when logging in locally or remotely?<br>• Can system managers or enterprise network management systems be notified when remote access or password failures have occurred?<br>• Can the remote PC (guest) reboot the local host if it becomes locked up?<br>• Are users locked out after a given number of failed login attempts?<br>• This feature is especially important given file transfer capabilities from remote users.<br>• Can remote users be restricted to read-only access?<br>• In order to save on long distance charges, can users be logged off (and calls dropped) after a set length of time? |

*Figure 9-17*   Remote Control Software Technology Analysis

| Remote Node Server Software Functional Characteristic | Importance/Implication |
|---|---|
| NOS protocols supported | • While most remote node server software supports IP, support for legacy protocols such as IPX, NetBIOS, NetBEUI, and AppleTalk is more limited.<br>• If IP is supported, is the full IP protocol stack including applications and utilities supplied? |
| WAN Data-link layer protocol | • Most remote node server software now supports PPP, while others support proprietary protocols. Proprietary protocols are fine in single-vendor environments. |
| Management | • How is the remote node server managed? Via a specialized console or any attached workstation with proper software?<br>• Does the remote node server software output management information in SNMP format?<br>• Can remote users be limited as to connect time or by inactivity time-out? |
| Security | • Is forced password renewal (password aging) supported?<br>• Are passwords encrypted?<br>• Is the remote node server software compatible with third party security servers such as token authentication servers? |
| Client support | • Which types of client platforms are supported? (Macintosh, Windows, UNIX/Linux) |

*Figure 9-18*  Remote Node Server Software Functional Characteristics

**Mobile-Aware Operating Systems**  The mobile computer user requires flexible computing functionality in order to easily support at least three possible distinct computing scenarios:

• Stand-alone computing on the laptop or notebook computer

• Remote node or remote control computing to corporate headquarters

• Synchronization of files and directories with desktop workstations at home or in the corporate office

Operating systems that are able to easily adapt to these different computing modes with a variety of included supporting accessory programs and utilities are sometimes referred to as **mobile-aware operating systems.** Most modern client operating systems offer some sort of native mobile-awareness. Among the key functions offered by such mobile-aware operating systems are the following:

• *Auto-detection of multiple configurations.* If external monitors or full-size keyboards are used when at home or in the corporate office, the operating system should automatically detect these and load the proper device drivers.

- *Built-in multi-protocol remote node client.* Remote node software should be included which can automatically and transparently connect to the network via any available connection including: wired network connections, wireless LAN connections, and dial-up modem connections.

- *File transfer and file/directory synchronizations.* Once physical connections are in place, software utilities should be able to synchronize files and directories between either the laptop and the desktop or the laptop and the corporate server.

- *Deferred printing.* This features allows printed files to be spooled to the laptop disk drive and saved until the mobile user is next connected to corporate printing resources. At that point, instead of having to remember all of the individual files requiring printing, the deferred printing utility is able to automatically print all of the spooled files.

- *Power management.* Since most mobile computing users depend on battery-powered computers, anything that the operating system can do to extend battery life would be very beneficial. The demand for higher-resolution screens has meant increased power consumption in many cases. Power management features offered by operating systems have been standardized as the **Advanced Power Management (APM)** and **Advanced Configuration and Power Interface (ACPI)** specification.

## SUMMARY

Network operating systems have traditionally provided shared file and print services among networked clients. With the increase in client/server architectures and the associated increase in distributed applications, network operating systems are now also providing application services, directory services and messaging and communications services in support of these distributed applications.

Client network operating systems functionality can be categorized into operating systems capabilities, peer-to-peer networking capabilities, and client networking capabilities. Client networking capabilities are largely measured by the number of different server network operating systems with which the client can transparently interoperate. Remote access capability is also important.

Server network operating systems are now primarily concerned with high performance application services for back-end application programs. Enterprise-wide directory services must also be provided. The two major approaches to enterprise directory services are global directory services and domain directory services.

In order to communicate with numerous client platforms, server network operating systems must support a variety of different network clients as well as a variety of different network transport protocols. Multi-protocol routing and remote access services are also essential to deliver transparent interoperability to the greatest number of client platforms. In the multiple server environments of the enterprise network, monitoring, management and administration tools play a critical role.

Remote access to LANs has taken on increased importance in response to major changes in business conditions. As indicated by the top-down model, network functionality must respond to changing business conditions. Expectations of LAN remote access are significant. Remote users expect the same level of data accessibility, application services, and performances on the road as they receive at the office. Delivering this equivalent functionality is the challenge faced by networking professionals today. The major obstacle to this objective is bandwidth, availability, and quality of the wide area network services which are expected to deliver remote connectivity to mobile users.

There are two basic logical topologies for remote access. Remote control allows a remote PC to take over or control a local PC. Processing occurs on the local PC and only keyboard strokes and screen images are transported over the WAN link. Remote node allows the remote PC to act as a full-fledged LAN client to the local LAN server. In this case, full client/server traffic travels over the WAN link as the application executes on the remote client PC. One of these logical topologies is not preferable in all cases. Each situation must be analyzed on an individual basis.

Physical topologies include accessing a local LAN-attached PC directly via modem, accessing a shared communications server via a dedicated wide area network connection, or connecting to the LAN via a virtual private network across a public access network such as the Internet.

## KEY TERMS

16-bit sub-system
access control list (ACL)
access server
application program interface
application services
authentication
authentication credentials
authorization
auto-detection & configuration
Challenge/Handshake
   Authentication Protocol (CHAP)
client network operating systems
client/server network operating
communications server
delta file transfer
dial-in server
dial-up server

directory services
directory synchronization software
domain services
domains
encryption
file synchronization software
lightweight directory access
   protocol (LDAP)
NetWare directory services (NDS)
network objects
password authentication protocol
   (PAP)
peer-to-peer network operating
   systems
performance monitoring
plug-n-play
PnP

PnP BIOS
RAS
remote access
remote control
remote control software
remote node
remote node client software
remote node server
remote node server software
remote node software
screen caching
server network operating
small office home office (SOHO)
telecommuting
universal client
virtual machines

## REVIEW QUESTIONS

1. Differentiate between peer-to-peer network operating systems and client/server network operating systems.
2. How does the combination of today's client and server network operating systems differ from a traditional client/server network operating system implementation?
3. What is a universal client?
4. Why is a universal client important to enterprise computing?
5. What new demands for services are being put on today's server network operating systems?
6. Describe the importance of the following service categories in more detail: directory services, applications services, integration/migration services.

7. Describe the major categories of functionality of client network operating systems.
8. What is the objective of PnP standards?
9. Describe the components required to deliver a PnP solution, and the relationship of the described components.
10. Describe the three elements of networking functionality belonging to client network operating systems paying particular attention to the relationship between the elements.
11. Why is it important for a client network operating system to be able to support more than one network transport protocol?
12. Describe the importance of laptop synchronization as a client network operating system feature.

13. Describe the major differences between global directory services and domain services in terms of architecture and functionality.
14. What is LDAP?
15. What is the relationship between file systems, APIs, and application services?
16. What are the two basic parts of an authentication credential set?
17. What is the difference between authentication and authorization?
18. What is the purpose of an ACL?
19. Why might it be important for a network operating system to support more than one file system?
20. What is the role of NCP, SMB, and NFS redirectors in offering application services?
21. What are some important functional characteristics of server network operating systems related to installation and configuration?
22. What are some important functional characteristics of server network operating systems related to integration and migration?
23. Name and describe the issues surrounding at least four areas of NOS functionality which must be addressed when designing interoperability solutions.

24. What are some of the key business trends which have led to an increased interest in LAN remote access?
25. What is the importance of needs analysis to LAN remote access design?
26. Differentiate between remote node and remote control in terms of functionality and network impact.
27. What is the major limitation in terms of delivering transparent access to remote LAN users?
28. Describe how it is possible to run remote control software via a remote node connection. What are the advantages of such a setup?
29. What are some of the security issues unique to remote access situations?
30. What is the relationship between the guest and host remote control software?
31. Differentiate between remote control and remote node software in terms of transport protocols and client protocol stacks.
32. What are some of the unique functional requirements of remote node server software?

**Case Study:** For a business case study and questions that relate to network services, go to www.wiley.com/college/goldman.

# THE NETWORK DEVELOPMENT LIFE CYCLE

*Concepts Reinforced*

Top-down model            Cost/benefit analysis
Business process reengineering

*Concepts Introduced*

Network development life cycle      Physical network design
Comprehensive systems and          Logical network design
     networking budget model        Total cost of ownership
Integrated computer assisted        Return on investment
     network engineering            IT project portfolio management
Network analysis and design
     methodology

## OBJECTIVES

Upon successful completion of this chapter, you should:

1. Understand how the network development life cycle (NDLC) relates to other systems development architectures and life cycles and, consequently, how the network analyst/designer must interact with analyst/designers involved in these related processes.

2. Understand the network development life cycle including: overall issues, process structure, detailed activities for each step of the process, coping with the reality of today's multiprotocol, multivendor environments.

3. Understand how one remains focused with a business perspective throughout the network development life cycle.

4. Understand what automated tools are available to assist in the NDLC process as well as the cost justification necessary for the acquisition of such tools.

5. Understand the current shortcomings of these automated tools as well as possible proposals for solutions to these shortcomings.

6. Understand the role of vendors at various stages of the NDLC and how to maximize the effectiveness of these vendors.

## ■ INTRODUCTION

This chapter is perhaps the most important chapter in this entire book. Although a process-orientation and top-down approach have been taken throughout the entire text as data communications concepts and technology have been introduced, the focus of this chapter is solely on the data communications process known as the network development life cycle. All of the concepts and technology mastered in previous chapters will serve as available resources for the actual network development process outlined in this chapter. Simply stated, this chapter should tie together much of the material covered to this point in the text, which talked *about* data communications by explaining how to *do* data communications.

In addition, this chapter provides a business context for the technically oriented network development life cycle. Important concepts such as alignment of IT projects with strategic business initiatives and the calculation of total cost of ownership and return on investment are stressed.

This chapter does not include instruction in network traffic engineering. Although this is an introductory text, an appropriate level of complexity will be presented for the more technical aspects of network design. Reemphasizing the practical aspect of this chapter, techniques for effective interaction with consultants and vendors who possess the technical expertise to perform network traffic engineering are stressed.

## ■ WHERE DOES NETWORK DESIGN FIT IN OVERALL INFORMATION SYSTEMS DEVELOPMENT?

To be able to fully understand the importance of a properly designed network to a smoothly operating information system, one must first understand how the network design process relates to other information system development processes. The top-down model, which has been a constant strategic framework throughout the text, is an appropriate way to portray the relationship between the network development process and other information systems-related development processes. This relationship is illustrated in Figure 10-1.

As can be seen in Figure 10-1, the network development life cycle depends on previously completed development processes such as strategic business planning, applications development life cycle, and data distribution analysis. If an implemented network is to effectively deliver the information systems that will, in turn, fulfill strategic business goals, then a top-down approach must be taken to the overall information systems development process, as well as to the network development life cycle.

### Cooperative Application and Network Development

As applications have been increasingly deployed on a globally distributed basis over network links of limited bandwidth or uncertain reliability, it has become essential for application developers and networking specialists to work more closely together during the early stages of the application development process. Automated application monitoring and simulation tools discussed later in the chapter are now available to show application developers how distributed applications will actually perform

| Top-Down Model | Information Systems Development Process |
|---|---|
| **Business** | • Strategic business planning<br>• Business process reengineering |
| **Application** | • Systems development life cycle<br>• Systems analysis and design<br>• Application development life cycle |
| **Data** | • Database analysis and design<br>• Database distribution analysis |
| **Network** | • Network development life cycle<br>• Network analysis and design<br>• Logical network design |
| **Technology** | • Physical network design<br>• Network implementation<br>• Technology analysis |

*Figure 10-1*   The Top-Down Model and the Network Development Life Cycle

over a variety of different network conditions. In this manner, application developers and networking specialists can cooperatively ensure that applications are developed in a proactive manner with assurance that the deployed application will operate successfully and meet stated business objectives.

## Understanding Systems Development: Process and Product

Two key components to any systems development effort are the **process** and the **product** of each stage of that development life cycle. Simply stated, the process describes activities that should be taking place at any point during the development cycle, and the product is the outcome or deliverable from a particular stage of the overall cycle.

A focus on the process allows one to visualize what they will be or should be doing at any point in the development life cycle. The product, meanwhile, could be interpreted as a milestone or deliverable, indicating completion of one stage of the development cycle and a readiness to proceed with subsequent stages.

A focus on product and process facilitates understanding of any systems development life cycle, not only the network development life cycle. Alternatively stated, by staying focused on the questions "What are we supposed to be doing?" and "How will we know when we are done?", we are more likely to be productive. Identification of process and product can be beneficial on high-level or summarized development cycles as well as on more detailed methodologies. Figure 10-2 takes the high-level processes identified in Figure 10-1 and lists possible products, or outcomes, from each of the corresponding processes.

Figure 10-2 clearly points out the need for significant analysis and design, and associated products or deliverables, before the commencement of any network analysis and design activities. As has been stated many times in this text, network analysis and design cannot be successfully performed in a vacuum. Rather, network analysis and design is but one step in an overall comprehensive information systems development

| Information Systems Development Process | Product or Milestone |
|---|---|
| Strategic business planning<br>Business process reengineering | • Strategic business plan<br>• Long-range business goals<br>• Business process models, methods, or rules |
| Systems development life cycle<br>Systems analysis and design<br>Application development life cycle | • Information systems design<br>• Applications program design |
| Database analysis and design<br>Database distribution analysis | • Database design<br>• Database distribution design |
| Network development life cycle<br>Network analysis and design<br>Logical network design | • Network requirements document<br>• Network design proposal |
| Physical network design<br>Network implementation<br>Technology analysis | • Detailed network diagram<br>• Network product specifications<br>• Network circuit diagrams |

*Figure 10-2*   Understanding Systems Development: Process and Product

cycle, commencing with business layer analysis and concluding with an analysis of the technology currently available to implement the system as designed.

## ◼ THE NETWORK DEVELOPMENT LIFE CYCLE

The key model behind the network design process is known as the **network development life cycle (NDLC)** as illustrated in Figure 10-3.

The word "cycle" is a key descriptive term of the network development life cycle as it clearly illustrates the continuous nature of network development. A network designed "from scratch" clearly has to start somewhere, namely with an analysis phase.

Existing networks, however, are constantly progressing from one phase to another within the network development life cycle. For instance, the monitoring of

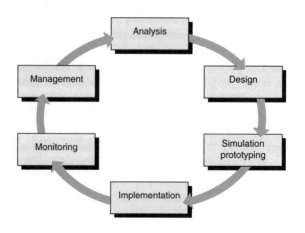

*Figure 10-3*   Network Development Life Cycle

existing networks would produce management and performance statistics perhaps using a network management protocol such as SNMP. Qualified network analysts would then analyze these performance statistics of this existing network. Design changes may or may not be implemented based on the analysis of these performance statistics. As will be described later in the chapter, network designs may be physical or logical in nature. **Physical network designs** involve the arrangement and interconnection of the physical network circuits and devices, whereas **logical network designs** involve configuration and definition of services that will run over that physical network such as addressing schemes, routing schemes, traffic prioritization, security, and management. Many times, proposed network design changes are first simulated using sophisticated network simulation software packages or prototyped in a test environment, safely removed from a company's production network, before being deployed or implemented.

This cycle of monitoring, management, analysis, design, simulation, and implementation is ongoing. Just as demands on a network are in a constant state of change due to changes in business, application, or data requirements, so must the network design itself be of a dynamic nature to successfully support these changing requirements. The network development life cycle serves as a logical framework in which this dynamic network design is able to thrive.

## STRATEGIC ALIGNMENT OF THE NETWORK DEVELOPMENT LIFE CYCLE

It is important to understand the business-oriented nature of the environment in which the network development life cycle must operate. Network design projects are not undertaken at random or on the whim of any network manager. Rather, network design projects must be aligned with strategic business initiatives and/or the strategic development of the overall corporate IT infrastructure. Figure 10-4 illustrates the overall alignment of the network development life cycle with strategic business and IT infrastructure initiatives.

### IT Project Portfolio Management

All networking projects or IT projects are not of equal strategic importance to the enterprise. Some projects may depend on other projects. Some projects may be focused on basic infrastructure improvements, whereas others may be tied to specific business units or projects. Funding for network projects is limited and must be budgeted with a view toward those projects that can have the greatest positive impact on the enterprise and that are most closely aligned with corporate business strategy and the overall strategy of the IT infrastructure. Given the multitude of projects seeking, funding, today's chief information officer (CIO) often views individual projects as potential investments and the sum total of all potential projects as a project portfolio, much like a stock portfolio. Some percentage of investment must be with "blue chip" conservative projects with more likely but more modest returns, whereas another percentage of investment must be with more risky projects with potentially greater payback to the enterprise. Determining how much to invest in which types of projects is a difficult job with serious consequences.

From a strategic process standpoint, as illustrated in Figure 10-4, a given network design project must be aligned with the overall strategic plan of the IT infrastructure as a whole, as well as with the strategic business initiatives of the

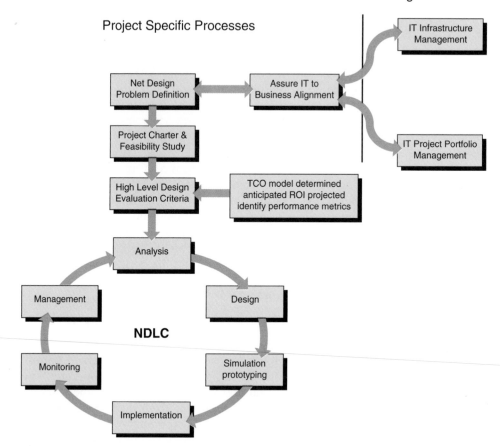

*Figure 10-4*  Alignment of Network Design Projects with Strategic Business and
IT Infrastructure Initiatives

corporation. A process known as **IT project portfolio management** often manages
the overall strategic development direction of the IT infrastructure. In such a process,
all potential IT-related projects from component architectures such as network,
application development, computing platforms, or data management are evaluated
for potential support and funding. In today's business climate, it is simply unrealis-
tic for all IT-related projects to be funded. Tough choices must be made according to
a defined process using justifiable criteria. The exact process used for IT portfolio
management varies from one organization to another. Some processes are more
quantitative and others are more subjective. Figure 10-5 illustrates one potential
strategy for IT portfolio management.

As illustrated in Figure 10-5, the two criteria chosen in this case to evaluate
potential IT projects are "alignment with business initiatives" and "projected return
on investment." The actual criteria chosen vary from one situation to another
depending on corporate circumstances and priority. Other possible choices include:

- Maturity level of technology
- Alignment with current IT infrastructure

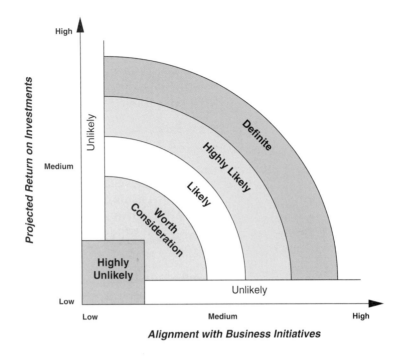

*Figure 10-5*    IT Project Portfolio Management

- Required support and management
- Initial investment cost
- Long-term expense

Each potential project is evaluated according to each of the chosen criteria in a qualitative manner by assigning a value of low, medium, or high. Quantitative methods can be used as a justification for the assignment of these values. Once each project is evaluated in terms of both criteria, the intersection of those assigned values will place each project in one of the portfolio management ranges of the grid. Again, the exact number, arrangement, and assigned names of each section of the grid will vary by organization. In the example shown in Figure 10-5, this organization has decided that if projects score low in either alignment *or* return on investment, then it is unlikely that these projects will be pursued. Furthermore, any project that scores low in alignment *and* return on investment is highly unlikely to be pursued. Other categories of recommended actions are arranged according to relative strengths of alignment with business initiatives and return on investment.

## Project-Specific Processes

As illustrated in Figure 10-4, once a project has been deemed as properly aligned with both the overall IT infrastructure and with the strategic business initiatives of the corporation, it goes through a number of project management steps before the initiation of actual network design activity. Each of these project-specific processes and the overall critical success factors are explained next.

### Critical Success Factors of the Network Development Life Cycle

Also associated with the overall network development process, rather than with any specific step of the process, are several key behaviors or things to remember that can be of critical importance to the overall successful outcome of the network development life cycle. These **critical success factors** are summarized in Figure 10-6 and explained next.

**Identification of All Potential Customers**  The best source of information for system performance requirements is the people who must use the system most frequently. However, all user groups and levels of management must be consulted during the analysis and design phase to ensure that no individuals or groups feel left out of the development process. Although one would like to think it isn't true, the best designed systems can be doomed to failure owing to the effective internal sabotage of disenchanted users.

**Political Awareness**  At the very least, it is imperative to be aware of the so-called corporate culture of an organization. Corporate culture is sometimes described in terms related to network design. For instance, corporate cultures can be described as "hierarchical" or "distributed" or "open." If the corporate culture of the organization in which a network analyst is working is hierarchical, then it would be a mistake to make an appointment to interview an end-user without first interviewing and seeking approval of the required levels of management. On the other hand, "open-door" corporate cultures are less concerned with hierarchies of authority, thereby allowing quicker and simpler access to end-users.

| Critical Success Factor | Explanation |
|---|---|
| **Identification of All Potential Customers and Constituencies** | No one likes to feel left out or that his/her input does not matter. It is better to include too many as representative user groups than to inadvertently exclude anyone. |
| **Political Awareness** | Awareness of the corporate political environment as well as the overall corporate culture can have a large impact on a project's success. |
| **Buy-In** | As each stage is concluded, buy-in or agreement as to conclusions from all effected customer groups is of critical importance. |
| **Communication** | Do not assume others know what is going on with the project. Write memos or newsletters, send e-mail, or communicate with key people in person. |
| **Detailed Project Documentation** | Document every phone call and every meeting. Keep the project well organized from day one with copies of all correspondence. |
| **Process/Product Awareness** | As a simple means of staying focused and on track, keep in mind the process and product for each step in the network analysis and design methodology. |
| **Be Honest with Yourself** | Be your own harshest critic. Identify weak points in your proposal and address them accordingly. Play "devil's advocate" with your proposal and prepare for the possible objections. |

*Figure 10-6*  Critical Success Factors of the Network Development Life Cycle

Unfortunately, so-called "back-room" politics can play an important role in systems design as well. The best researched and planned network design may go unimplemented if the company president's brother-in-law or golf partner is in the computer business and has a different idea. Sad, but true. The best way to defend against such situations is to first be aware of any such possible political situations. Specific strategies for ensuring the objectivity of the analysis and design process will be highlighted as the overall network analysis and design methodology is described further.

**Buy-In** All of the critical success factors listed in Figure 10-6 are important. However, one of the most important yet easiest to accomplish is **buy-in.** After having chartered the project and identified all potential customers and constituencies, it is imperative to gain buy-in from each of these groups for the deliverable or product of each stage of the overall network analysis and design methodology.

By reaching consensus on the acceptability of the results or deliverables of each and every stage, one avoids having initial assumptions or work on earlier stages brought into question during the presentation of the final proposal. In other words, the approved results of one stage become the foundation or starting point for the next stage. If buy-in from all affected parties is ensured at each stage, the presentation of the final proposal should be much smoother with a minimum of back-tracking or rework required.

**Communication** Many of the other critical success factors listed in Figure 10-6 depend on effective communication, both verbal and written. Often in network or systems development projects, it is assumed that because network analysts and designers are aware of the project status, everyone must be fully informed as well. Unfortunately, this is not the case. As previously pointed out, no one likes to feel left out. More important, networks often cross the "territory" or authority of numerous individuals and departments. To keep these people supportive of the project, it is imperative to keep them informed and to make them feel that they are an important part of the process.

Communication can take many forms. Newsletters, project status reports, web sites, and e-mail are all suitable means of keeping people informed and up-to-date. More ambitious communications schemes such as videoconferencing or the production of a VCR tape or CD-ROM might be appropriate for critical tasks, public relations, or training opportunities.

**Detailed Project Documentation** A project manager must not only manage the overall network analysis and design project effectively with task schedules, project lists, and to-do lists, but also document every aspect of the project. During every conversation, by phone or in person, notes should be entered into a log book indicating such things as date, time, persons involved, topics of conversation, and required follow-up. E-mail messages should be printed and filed. Meetings should be documented in a similar fashion, with agendas and action item assignments included in a project binder as well as being sent to responsible parties and key managers.

Organization of this project documentation is of equal importance. A large binder with several sections for different portions of the project can be a very effective way to be able to quickly access any piece of project documentation required.

This documentation is of particular importance in the latter stages of the project when consultants and vendors become a part of the project. Document everything in writing and take no action on any agreement until it has been presented in writing.

**Process/Product Awareness**    As a facilitator in meetings of end-users trying to define system requirements, it is the network analyst's job to keep the participants focused and the meeting on track. To accomplish this goal, it is important to have a clear understanding of the process involved at that particular stage of the network analysis and design methodology as well as the nature of the product or deliverable that is to be the outcome of this process.

Meetings can easily get off on tangents and aggressive users can easily sway meetings toward personal agendas. By remaining focused on the proper topics of discussion and a clear visualization of the product of that discussion, a facilitator can maximize the effectiveness of the analysis and design process. As the leader of the meeting, it is important not to go overboard on controlling the discussion of the meeting however. With practice and patience, experienced facilitators can direct meetings that foster imaginative solutions and proposals without either stifling creativity or allowing discussion to wander ineffectively.

**Be Honest With Yourself**    One of the greatest advantages of being totally honest with oneself is that no one else knows the potential weaknesses or areas for improvement in a proposal better than the person who wrote it. The difficulty comes when forcing oneself to be totally honest and acknowledging the potential weaknesses in a proposal to either correct them or be prepared to defend them.

Peer review and egoless programming are other systems development techniques employed to identify potential weaknesses in programs or proposals before implementation. Not all weaknesses can necessarily be corrected. Financial or time constraints may have restricted potential solutions. If that is the case, an honest self-review of the proposal will allow one to prepare an objective explanation of such weaknesses in advance.

**Critical Success Factors Are Learned Behaviors**    Although many of the critical success factors listed in Figure 10-6 may seem to be nothing more than common sense, it has been the author's experience that more network analysis and design projects suffer from difficulties caused by a failure to address one or more of these critical success factors than from any other cause of failure. These critical success factors must be applied throughout the entire life of the network development project and are therefore best seen as habits or behaviors, rather than discrete events to be scheduled or planned.

### ■ NETWORK ANALYSIS AND DESIGN METHODOLOGY

Although the Network Development Life Cycle is useful as a logical model of the overall processes involved in network development, it is not at all specific as to how the various stages within the life cycle are to be accomplished. What is required is a more detailed step-by-step methodology which compliments the overall logical framework as outlined by the Network Development Life Cycle.

The **Network Analysis and Design Methodology** is a practical, high-level, step-by-step approach to network analysis and design and is illustrated in a summarized fashion in Figure 10-7.

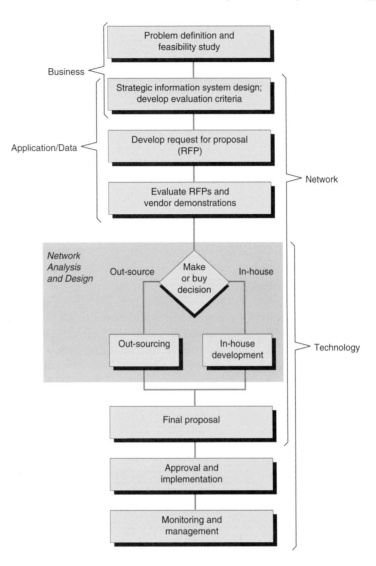

*Figure 10-7*   Network Analysis and Design Methodology

## Overall Characteristics

Before describing each of the major categories of the methodology as illustrated in Figure 10-7 in detail, a few important characteristics of the overall methodology are worth noting.

- First, the Network Analysis and Design Methodology is consistent with previous information systems development models in that business, application, and data requirements definition are prerequisites to network design activities.

- Second, this methodology treats both in-house personnel as well as outside consultants as potential service providers by clearly documenting requirements in a formalized RFP (Request for Proposal) and expecting compliance with those requirements by whomever may be eventually chosen to perform network development duties.

- Finally, although any diagram of a systems development methodology would indicate that activities are of a serial nature, occurring one after another, with discrete starting and ending points, such is very often not the case. In fact, activities from various stages of the methodology often take place simultaneously. In addition, network analysts often must backtrack to previous activities when new or contradictory information is uncovered as the development process progresses.

Thus, the network analysis and design methodology as illustrated in Figure 10-7 should be looked upon as an overall guideline to the network development process rather than a step-by-step cookbook-style set of instructions.

## Net Design Problem Definition

A network cannot very well provide effective solutions to problems that have not been clearly defined in objective terms. To attempt to implement networks before everyone agrees to (buy-in) the exact nature of the problem to be solved is somewhat akin to hitting a moving target. The network will never satisfy all constituencies' needs because no one agreed what those needs were in the first place. All network development efforts start with a problem as perceived by someone, be they management or end-users. At some point, management agrees that a problem exists that is worth expending resources to at least investigate. The responsibility for conducting the investigation may be given to in-house personnel or to an outside consultant or facilitator.

The first job of the facilitator is to identify all parties potentially affected by the perceived problem. Next, representatives of each of these constituencies are selected and convened for brainstorming sessions to determine the nature of the problem and perhaps, the requirements of a solution. To make these problem definition sessions as productive as possible, it is important that representatives do their "homework" before the meetings.

## Project Charter and Feasibility Study

To effectively control multiple projects simultaneously in large organizations, it is essential that all projects requiring allocation of manpower, technical, or financial resources be carefully planned. A **project charter** is the mechanism by which a project is organized and initial expectations are documented and agreed on. Network-related projects are likely to interact with numerous business units and other areas of IT such as application development. It is important to get involvement and buy-in from all affected organizations in the form of project sponsorship. When all parties can agree before the project is launched what the expected outcomes of the project are and what it will take to reach those objectives in a given amount of time, then that project stands a much greater chance of success.

Among the sections that could be included in a project charter are the following:

- Description: Two or three sentences briefly describing what, why, how, and when this project will be accomplished.

- Objectives: Often divided into separate categories of business and technical objectives. Objectives should be measurable and serve as the evaluation criteria for the completed project.

- Scope: Often divided into "within scope" and "out of scope" sections to assure that the project remains on target and is not subjected to "scope creep," where side issues and amendments to the project charter cause the project to lose focus.

- Phases: What are the major logical sections of the project? Give some thought as to what must be accomplished in each phase in order to move on to the next phase. This is where initial thought to overall process design for the project is considered.

- Deliverables: Can be either presented as overall project deliverables or phase by phase deliverables. What tangible work or documents will the project team actually be producing?

- Stakeholders and Key Reporting Relationships: Which departments or business units within an organization or corporation will be impacted by this project? Which departments will have to supply personnel to complete this project? Which individuals have budget responsibility for these departments and will have to approve the participation of team members? Who will provide technical leadership, project management, and technical team participation?

- Project Schedule: When will milestones, phases, and overall project be completed?

- Project Budget: What is the anticipated budget for the project?

- Assumptions, Concerns, and Constraints: Any other issues (technical, business, political) that could have an impact on the project that should be shared with all concerned before project kick-off.

- Sponsor Approval Signatures: Executive level approval to proceed with the project as described in the previous charter.

**Understand Strategic Business Objectives** Once the group has been assembled, it is time to remember the top-down model. To keep the problem definition session and the subsequent solution proposal session on track, it is vital to start with the strategic business goals of the organization as articulated by senior management. Whenever the author consulted as a user group facilitator, he always strived to have either the chief executive officer or chief financial officer (or both) present at the initial meeting to say a few words about the importance of the user group's work and the strategic direction of the corporate business goals. In addition, if strategic corporate goals had been prepared in writing, these were shared with the group, as allowed by company policy. In this way, the whole group starts off with the same focus and strategic business direction with the proper attitude about the overall process.

**Importance of Baseline Data**    To measure the eventual impact, hopefully positive, of the installed network, one has to have baseline data, or the current status of the system and network, from which to measure that eventual network impact. This baseline data can often be collected from the various customer groups or constituencies of the information system and network who are chosen to attend the problem definition sessions. Depending on the extent, in terms of both geography and sophistication, to which current systems have been implemented, a structured framework may be required to record this systems information in a standardized manner. Fortunately, the top-down model is an excellent example of such a framework. Chapter 11, Network Management, provides more detailed information on the technology and processes involved with network performance baselining.

**Top-Down Model Organizes Baseline Data**    Using the top-down model as a framework for organizing the baseline data to reflect the current system and network status does not necessarily imply that a separate top-down model must be completed for every corporate location attached to the network or that every layer of the top-down model must be filled in for every location. Just enough data should be collected at this point in the network analysis and design methodology to clearly define the problem in measurable terms.

Information that is gathered in the top-down models at this stage should relate directly to the problems as perceived by the user groups. It is hoped that the problems have some business layer impact; otherwise this whole process may be a waste of time. In other words, although the source of the problem may be in the application, data, network, or technology layers, if it has no impact on the business layer, why should time be spent studying it?

Questions should deal with business problems or situations. Once these business problems are identified, the sources of these business problems within the lower layers of top-down model would be subsequently investigated as part of the problem definition process. Conversely, these same lower layers of the top-down model will be redesigned to become the source of business solutions as delivered by the new network.

**Feasibility Studies and Buy-In**    Once sufficient information has been gathered to document the current status of the systems and networks in objective, measurable terms, the required product for this process, the problem definition, has been completed and it is time to ensure buy-in. The problem definition and its associated alternative recommendations for further study are sometimes referred to as a **feasibility study.**

The need for buy-in on a problem definition or feasibility study will vary from one case to another. Much of the need for management buy-in and the associated approval to proceed depend on the nature of the original charge from management.

In other words, if management's initial charge were, "Look into this problem and get back to me," then a feasibility study followed by management buy-in and approval before further study is clearly appropriate. Conversely, if management's charge were, "Figure out what's wrong and fix it," then a formalized feasibility report with formal presentation may not be called for. However, remember one of the key critical success factors—communications. Even if a formal feasibility report is not required, timely management reports should be completed and submitted on a regular basis to keep management abreast of progress and in tune with overall project strategic direction. Figure 10-8 summarizes the key points (process and product) of the problem definition phase.

| Process | | |
|---------|---|---|
| | 1. | Problem is perceived. |
| | 2. | Management perceives problem as worth investigating. |
| | 3. | Management delegates responsibility for problem definition. |
| | 4. | User/constituency groups are identified and representatives chosen. |
| | 5. | Representative groups are convened. |
| | 6. | Senior management commitment and priorities are conveyed to representative group. |
| | 7. | Representative groups produce baseline data of current system status. |
| | 8. | Depending on the extent of the current system and network implementation, the top-down model may be used to organize this baseline data into a standardized format. |
| | 9. | Buy-in. |
| Product | | |
| | 1. | Baseline data describing current system status in objective, measurable terms. Can be organized into multiple top-down models. |
| | 2. | A formalized feasibility study may be required depending on the initial charge/direction from management. |

*Figure 10-8*   Key Points of Problem Definition and Feasibility Study

## High-Level Design Evaluation Criteria

The problem definition phase provided a starting point of baseline data for the new system, and the strategic information systems design provides the operational goals for the new system to attain. Just as the baseline data have to be objective and measurable, so must the evaluation criteria associated with these operational goals.

These goals may have a direct impact on network design when defined in terms such as maximum response time, transactions/second, or mean time between failures. By producing objective, measurable goals or performance evaluation criteria and getting subsequent management buy-in on those goals, one helps to ensure the objectivity of the entire network analysis and design process. For example, if a substandard system is suggested solely because of "back-room" politics, it is simply evaluated against the evaluation criteria as previously agreed on by all appropriate levels of management. Figure 10-9 summarizes the key points of the strategic information system design phase in terms of both process and product.

## Total Cost of Ownership

Evaluation criteria based on performance are an important starting point for an overall assessment of a project's relative success or failure. However, performance criteria consider only whether the project was successful from a technical perspective. It is equally important to consider a project's relative success from a financial perspective. Cost-oriented evaluation criteria must also be established. Today, IT projects are often evaluated from a financial standpoint in terms of **total cost of ownership.** Total cost of ownership implies that all cost aspects of a project are properly identified including ongoing costs such as support, management, and maintenance. Hidden costs such as those included in budgets other than the IT department are also an important component of an accurate total cost of ownership. Projected total cost of ownership figures should be completed for every proposed project and used as a financially oriented set of evaluation criteria during project development and after project implementation.

| Process | | |
|---|---|---|
| | 1. | Review strategic corporate objectives. |
| | 2. | Define the overall characteristics of an information system that can successfully support/achieve these objectives. |
| | 3. | Break the overall business down into major functional areas. |
| | 4. | List the business processes performed under each functional area. |
| | 5. | Highlight the decision points in the listed business processes and list information required to make informed decisions at each decision point. |
| | 6. | Highlight the opportunities for improvement in listed business processes and list information required to take advantage of these opportunities for improvement. |
| | 7. | Prepare performance evaluation criteria. |
| | 8. | Prioritize the various aspects of the strategic information system as designed. |
| | 9. | Buy-in. |
| **Product** | | |
| | 1. | Strategic information systems design. |
| | 2. | Performance evaluation criteria in objective measurable terms. |

*Figure 10-9*    Key Points of Strategic Information System Design

A **comprehensive systems and networking budget model,** presented in Figure 10-22, would be a suitable instrument for developing a total cost of ownership model for a network development project. Costing models for ongoing network services provided to business units or end-user organizations require a different type of costing model. Such an activity-based costing model is introduced in Chapter 11, as part of the discussion of service management and costing.

## Return on Investment

Increasingly, networking and information systems professionals are being called on to quantify the positive impact of their projects and implemented systems in financial terms. A variety of options exist for this quantification. **Return on investment (ROI)** is perhaps the most traditional approach to measuring cost/benefit and is well suited to incremental upgrades of existing systems. However, for entirely new or innovative projects, although costs may be accurately projected, projected benefits are more intangible and are far more difficult to quantify in real terms. **Return on opportunity (ROO)** attempts to quantify benefits that may be unanticipated or indirectly related to the immediate investment. This methodology recognizes the fact that improvements in IT infrastructure aimed at one project may enable unanticipated benefits and uses not related to that initiating project.

In a similar manner, **total benefit of ownership (TBO)** tries to quantify the usability and associated benefits of technological options. TBO attempts to quantify productivity increases as well as cost reduction. However, to properly quantify increased productivity, one must first measure current levels of productivity by developing evaluation criteria so that baseline data can be gathered.

## Performance Metrics

Performance metrics refer to quantifiable, measurable performance criteria by which the success of an implemented system can be judged. Performance metrics must be defined in both business terms and IT infrastructure terms. Given that the alignment of a given IT project with a strategic business initiative has already been assured, the performance metrics required to validate that alignment should be able to be defined. Business-oriented performance metrics that reflect the achievement of the intended business outcomes must first be defined. The ability to report on the status of these business performance metrics should be embedded within the components of the IT infrastructure supporting this new initiative.

On a technical level, the performance levels required from each element of the IT infrastructure, in order for the overall system to achieve its business objectives, must be individually identified. Technology-specific performance metrics must be identified for each technical component of the overall system. The definition, monitoring, and management of these performance metrics are part of an area of IT known as service management. Definitions of required levels of service from the IT infrastructure to achieve intended business goals are delineated in service level agreements. Service management and service level agreements are explained further in Chapter 11.

## ■ DESIGN AND ANALYSIS PROCESSES

### Identify Overall System Characteristics

The word *strategic* is used in the context of information systems design to portray the top-down, strategic business goal orientation of the entire information design process. As can be seen in Figure 10-9, the strategic information systems design process starts with a review of the strategic business goals as articulated by senior management.

With these strategic business goals in mind, the next step in the process is to describe the overall characteristics of an information system that could fulfill these strategic business goals. Examples might be the following. To fulfill our corporation's strategic business goals, this information system must:

1. Enable delivery of improved customer service
2. Enable improved inventory control
3. Allow for more flexible pricing
4. Enable shorter shelf restocking cycles
5. Allow for more efficient use of manpower

Many other examples could have been included. The point of these overall characteristics, in terms of the top-down model, is to ensure and specify that the application layer solutions will deliver on the business layer requirements. As can be seen from Figure 10-9, one of the key products of this strategic information system design phase is the performance evaluation criteria. The overall required system characteristics as listed previously serve as one set of evaluation criteria for proposed information systems designs. Other more objective evaluation criteria will be developed further along in the overall design process. However, the importance of the strategic system performance evaluation criteria lies in their ability to measure the extent to which proposed information systems designs deliver on strategic business goals.

### Identify Major Business Functional Areas

Once overall system performance characteristics have been established, the overall business can be broken down into large functional areas. These functional areas may correspond to corporate departments or divisions. Examples might include manufacturing, inventory control, project management, customer service, accounting and payroll, and human resources.

In practice, each of these identified major **business functional areas** can be written on a separate large sheet of flip-chart paper and taped over the walls of the room in which the user groups were meeting. It is not important to argue about which functional areas deserve their own sheet of paper at this point. Consolidation and editing take place later in the process.

### Identify Business Processes Associated with Each Business Functional Area

Once the major functional areas of the business have been established, the business processes that take place in each major functional area are listed. This presents a wonderful opportunity for **business process reengineering.** Oftentimes, user groups are made up of individuals from various business units who have not had the time to really understand each other's jobs and responsibilities. As business processes are described, brainstorming quickly takes over and problems that seemed deeply imbedded in current systems are solved as new or modified business processes are defined for the new strategic information system design. This process is repeated for every major business functional area identified in the previous step.

It is important for the facilitator of this process to keep the discussions on a fairly strategic level, thereby avoiding lower level implementation issues such as screen design and report layouts. Continuing with the flip chart scenario, each major business functional area should now have its own flip chart(s) with detailed business processes described for each large business functional area.

Managerial
Perspective

### THE NETWORK ANALYST AND BUSINESS PROCESS REENGINEERING

As current business processes are discussed during the network development life cycle, opportunities abound for improvement of those business processes. It is important, however, to take an organized approach to business process improvement, more popularly known as business process reengineering. Part of that required organized approach hinges on maintaining one's common sense. For example:

- If it isn't broken, don't fix it: In searching for opportunities for improvement, concentrate on the processes that are in the greatest need of improvement.

- How will you know if the new process is better if you never measured how bad the old process was? Baseline data must be gathered to document the performance of current processes before redesign takes place. These same evaluation criteria and methods must be used to evaluate the new processes to objectively evaluate improvement levels.

- Learn from others' mistakes: Pay attention to other business process reengineering efforts, especially those in closely related industries that have failed. What lessons can be learned and what mistakes can avoid being repeated?

- Don't be afraid to admit mistakes: If the reengineered business process does not produce anticipated results based on objective evaluation criteria, don't be afraid to admit the mistake early and make corrections as soon as possible to minimize negative impact.

As information systems and networking professionals are increasingly called on to justify their budgets and corporate contributions in the face of outsourcing alternatives, it is imperative that network analysts understand the importance of a realistic approach to business process reengineering.

## Identify Decision Points and Opportunities for Improvement

Recalling that one of the primary goals of a well-designed strategic information system is to deliver the right information to the right decision-maker, the next logical step in the design process is to identify the key **decision points** in all of the documented business processes where decision-makers must make decisions.

Once identified, each decision point is then analyzed as to what information (the "right" information) is required for the decision-maker to make an informed decision at each respective decision point. This analysis process often brings out the fact that decision-makers are getting much more information than they need to make informed decisions. Entire reports that are hundreds of pages long may contain only one or two pieces of information that are of critical importance to a decision-maker at any given decision point.

One of the key areas in which user group members can contribute is in the identification of **opportunities for improvement** that can be enabled by this strategic information system design. Opportunities for improvement may imply improvement in any one of a number of areas: financial, productivity, inventory control, accounts receivable collections, customer service, customer satisfaction, repeat customers, employee retention, etc.

The important thing to remember is that if these opportunities for improvement support the strategic business goals of the corporation then they should be identified along with the information required to turn these opportunities into reality. Figure 10-10 illustrates the relationship of the various processes described thus far in the strategic information system design.

## Prioritization

Once the strategic information system has been designed as described previously, priorities can be assigned to each of the major functional areas, business processes, decision points, and opportunities. These priorities may assist in the evaluation process by identifying those systems that exhibit the most important elements of the strategic information systems design. A simple yet effective approach to systems design prioritization is known as the **three-pile approach.** In this prioritization scheme, there are only three priorities, defined as follows:

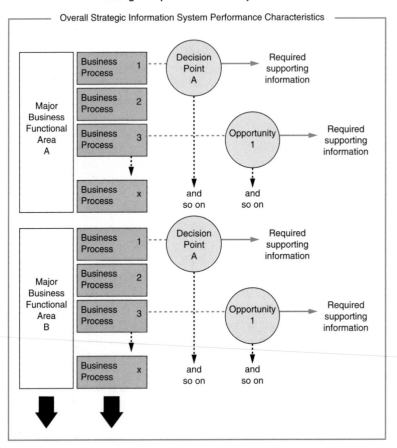

*Figure 10-10*    Process Relationship of Strategic Information System Design

- Priority 1 items are so important that the system is simply not worth implementing without them.

- Priority 2 items can be lived without or "worked around" but really need to be implemented as soon as possible.

- Priority 3 items would be nice to have but can be lived without.

One important point to remember is that these priorities should be considered in terms of business impact. At this point, a strategic, or high-level, information system design has been completed. Many details need to be added to this requirements document before proposals can accurately reflect their ability to meet not only the business and application layer system requirements, but the data and networking requirements that must support this strategic information system as well.

## Finding and Managing Required Technical Talent

Once a clear understanding of system requirements and evaluation criteria have been established, the next major task is to find the technical talent required to produce the designed system. This talent may be either in-house or may be hired from the outside, often referred to as outsourcing. The overall process for finding system development talent is illustrated in Figure 10-11 and explained in the following sections.

## Request for Information (RFI)

Before sending out a detailed request for proposal to numerous potential vendors, it is often prudent to narrow the field of potential respondents by issuing a **request for information (RFI).** The purpose of an RFI is to gather enough information about potential vendors that they can be quickly and easily evaluated as to their suitability for further consideration. The RFI should be easy to comply with for the potential vendors and easy to evaluate the responses from for the corporation issuing the RFI.

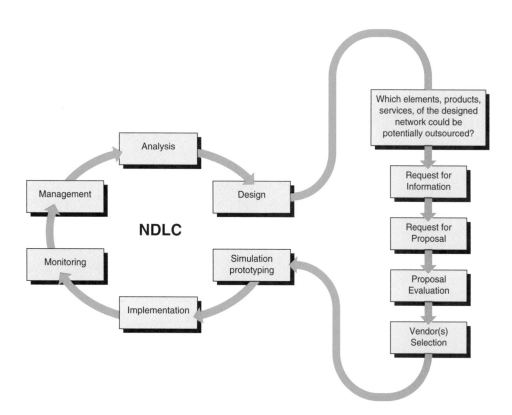

*Figure 10-11*   NDLC and the Proposal Process

Among the sections that could be included in a request for information are the following:

- Technical requirements: A high-level description of technical performance requirements that must be met by the proposed technology or system. These requirements should be of high importance to the overall system. In other words, vendors that cannot meet these technical requirements will not be considered further.

- Business requirements: Ask for price structure of technology or services in order to gauge whether or not potential vendors are even in the ballpark of your budget. Do not share your budget with potential vendors at this point.

- References: The purpose of this section is to gauge the experience of this vendor in supplying this technology or service. How many have been sold or installed? Will you be their first customer for this new technology or service?

Remember, the overall purpose of the RFI is to narrow the field of vendors that will be sent the RFP so that you are not wasting time with nonqualified vendors. Keep the RFI short, to the point, and ask questions regarding those system or business requirements that you regard as absolute necessities or "show-stoppers."

## Request for Proposal (RFP)

By organizing the strategic information system design information into an understandable format and by adding detailed information concerning performance evaluation criteria for the data and network layers, a document known as a **request for proposal (RFP)** is produced. It is important to understand the benefits of an RFP to be able to justify the work that goes into it.

By taking the time to prepare a detailed RFP, a company ensures that its priorities and unique business processes and requirements are fulfilled by the information system and network that is eventually installed. All vendor proposals are measured against the users' predefined requirements regardless of whom the vendor may be related to. If a vendor's proposal does not meet minimum standards for meeting the requirements of the RFP, it is dropped from further consideration regardless of how nice the screens look or how colorful the brochures are. The RFP ensures that the delivered system, whether developed in-house or purchased from an outside vendor, will be flexible enough to change as business needs and requirements change. Unfortunately, the alternative is all too often the case, in which businesses are forced to mold their business practices according to the constraints of the purchased information system and network. Figure 10-12 summarizes both the processes and products involved in the RFP preparation phase of the network design.

**Examine Each Corporate Location**   Now that the strategic information system design has been completed, the next step is to carefully examine each corporate location at which the information system will eventually be deployed. The purpose of gathering all of this data about each of the corporate locations is to compile an accurate representation of the scope and requirements of the network over which this strategic information system will be implemented.

As each location is examined, the information gathered will help determine the unique data and processing requirements for those locations. This detailed

| **Process** | 1. Examine each corporate location |
| | 2. Produce evaluation criteria for application and data layer considerations as required |
| | 3. Survey all existing system resources: people, hardware-software-media, data, network, physical plant |
| | 4. Prepare preliminary overall project schedule |
| | 5. Determine information required from vendor |
| | 6. Determine potential vendors |
| | 7. Determine percent-of-fit goal |
| | 8. Compile and distribute RFP to selected vendors |
| **Product** | 1. Formalized request for proposal |
| | 2. Percent-of-fit goal |

*Figure 10-12*   Preparing the Request for Proposal

location-specific information is distinct from the high-level information gathered in top-down model format as part of the problem definition phase.

Some corporate locations may be regional offices, concentrating data or transactions from several branch offices. These, along with many other facts must be recorded to accurately define data and network layer requirements for the overall information system. Although each company may differ in what location-specific statistics are important in terms of strategic network design, many of the points in Figure 10-13 may warrant consideration.

The information gathered in such location-by-location surveys adds to the evaluation criteria of any potential system proposal. Any need identified must be met by a proposed system solution in accordance with the determined priority of each of these requirements. It is of critical importance that this survey is done as accurately as possible because this is the data upon which the initial network design will largely be based. Buy-in by all affected groups at this stage is especially important, as outside vendors and in-house staffs will be using this data to prepare detailed application, database, and network designs.

**Final RFP Preparation**   The two major components of the RFP that should have been completed at this point are:

1. Strategic information systems design

2. Corporate location survey results

To put the finishing touches on the RFP, a few more pieces of information must be either supplied to or requested from potential system and network suppliers. This additional information is often included in a section of the RFP known as the **management abstract** or executive summary. Figure 10-14 illustrates a sample table of contents from an RFP including the items that might be included in a management abstract.

**Information Supplied to Vendors**   Among the information included in the management abstract that should be supplied to potential vendors to give them as accurate a description as possible of the opportunity are the following items:

| Category | Questions/Issues |
| --- | --- |
| **People** | • Number of total employees<br>• Number of employees performing each business function as listed in strategic information system design<br>• Feeling about the "new" system<br>• Key political situations<br>• Number of network-oriented/technically-oriented employees<br>• Training needs |
| **Hardware-Software-Media** | • Current level of computerization<br>• Current applications software<br>• Current networking status<br>• Local phone company<br>• Availability of data services from local phone company<br>• Software performance requirements<br>  ○ Maximum time for customer look-up<br>  ○ Maximum time for part number or pricing look-up<br>  ○ Maximum time for order entry<br>• How "mission-critical" is each application?<br>• Must backup systems be ready at a moment's notice? |
| **Data** | • Number of customers<br>• Number of inventory items<br>• Number of open orders<br>• Need for sharing data with other locations, regional offices, corporate headquarters<br>• Special security needs for data or transmission |
| **Network** | • Current network configuration<br>• Network traffic volumes<br>• Network protocols<br>• Network monitoring and management technology<br>• Current problems with network to be corrected<br>• Expected growth of network, traffic volume, user community |
| **Physical Plant** | • What is the condition of each remote site?<br>• Will additional electrical, heating, data wiring, space, or security systems be required at any sites to accommodate the new systems? |

*Figure 10-13*   Possible Location-Specific Statistics

- Company profile: A brief description of the company issuing the request for proposal. Number of corporate locations, approximate annual sales, anticipated growth rate, and a brief statement concerning the current state of computerization or networking could all be elements of this section.

- Statement of the problem: From a business perspective, what was the source of the initiation of the problem definition process and what did the problem definition team conclude?

- Overall system characteristics: It is important to include overall system characteristics at the beginning of the RFP as some of these requirements may be beyond the capabilities of possible vendors and their systems. In this way, these vendors won't waste their time or yours in submitting a

| Management Abstract | • Company profile |
|---|---|
| | • Statement of the problem |
| | • Overall system characteristics—anticipated outcomes |
| | • Project phase prioritization |
| | • Proposed project schedule summary |
| | • Constraints |
| | • Contact information |
| | • Evaluation criteria for proposals |
| | • Legal-terms and nondisclosure agreements |
| | • Information requested from vendor; system development experience; hardware, software, networking experience; references; pricing; support; training and documentation; vendor background |
| System Design | • Summary review |
| | • Details of geographic locations |
| | • System requirements of each software module |

*Figure 10-14*   Sample RFP Table of Contents

proposal that can't meet these basic overall requirements. Figure 10-15 lists some possible overall system characteristics that might be included in an RFP. Although some of the requirements listed in Figure 10-15 may seem obvious or unnecessary, it is important not to assume anything when shopping for information systems.

- Project phase prioritization: If some modules (business area computerization plans) of the overall strategic information systems design are more critical than others, this prioritization should be conveyed to potential vendors. Often, a vendor may be able to supply some, but not all, of the information systems modules. If the vendors have a sense of which modules are most important, they will be better able to know whether or not to submit a proposal.

- Proposed project schedule summary: Figure 10-16 illustrates a sample proposed project schedule with key events that may be of concern to potential vendors listed. Before taking the time to prepare detailed proposals, many vendors appreciate knowing the implementation timetable of the proposed project. If the vendor already has projects underway or anticipated, he/she may lack sufficient staff to meet this RFP's proposed implementation schedule.

**Information Requested from Vendors**   At least as important as the information supplied to potential vendors is the information required from potential vendors. To avoid being sent standard proposals with preprinted product literature and brochures, it is advantageous to list specific information required from vendors and to evaluate only those proposals that supply the requested information.

Figure 10-17 lists some of the information that may be requested of vendors, although the list is by no means authoritative or exhaustive. Information requested

1. Source code must be owned by the client company.

2. The system must be easy to use and maintain and must contain on-line help as well as extensive input editing and verification to help prevent errors.

3. The system must require a minimum of training.

4. The system must be easy to install (hardware and software) to expedite installation throughout all corporate locations.

5. The system must allow multiple users simultaneous access to information. The system must have the capability to ensure information integrity through record locking and must have adequate security to ensure against unauthorized access to information.

6. The system must have windowing capabilities allowing drop-down menus and screens to allow simultaneous access to multiple files and/or modules.

7. The system must be easily transportable to numerous hardware and operating system platforms on both minicomputers and microcomputers.

8. The system must have the ability to output and input ASCII data files to ensure necessary informational ties to regional centers.

9. The system must have database/file rollback capabilities to ensure data integrity in the event of a system failure or power outage.

*Figure 10-15*    Possible Required Overall System Characteristics

should satisfy corporate policies as well as business layer concerns from initial problem definition analysis. The overall purpose of this section is to ensure that:

- The vendor has significant experience in developing and implementing systems of a similar nature to the one described in the RFP.

- The vendor has a sufficiently large organization to support the smooth and successful implementation of such a system.

- The vendor is financially solvent so as not to be likely to declare bankruptcy in the middle of the project implementation.

| Event | Proposed Completion Date |
|---|---|
| **Requests for Proposals Sent to Selected Vendors** | 07/29/04 |
| **Proposals Due to Consultant from Vendors** | 08/29/04 |
| **Selection and Notification of Vendor Finalists** | 09/14/04 |
| **Presentation/Demonstration by Vendor Finalists** | 09/21/04–10/07/04 |
| **Make-or-Buy Decision** | 10/14/04 |
| **Pilot Test** | 12/14/04 |
| **Projected System Implementation Date** | 04/01/05 |

*Figure 10-16*    Proposed Project Schedule Summary

| System Development | • Vendor's experience in client's industry<br>• Number of installed systems<br>• Date of first installation<br>• Integration with related manufacturing and financial modules<br>• Scope of installed systems |
|---|---|
| Hardware/Operating Systems/Software | • Which hardware platforms does system run on?<br>• Multiuser?<br>• Operating systems<br>• Programming languages<br>• 4GL/DBMS experience<br>• Ease of/availability of customization<br>• Source code availability |
| References | • Names, addresses, and phone numbers of three customers with similar systems implemented |
| Pricing | • Hardware: If vendor will supply hardware, list cost by component including manufacturer and model number<br>• Software: List cost per module, additional per user license costs, source code costs, cost for software customization, cost for maintenance and support agreements, cost for operating or runtime systems |
| Training | • Include information regarding: facilities, courses, materials, instructor availability, schedule, media used, cost |
| Support | • Hours—hotline available?<br>• Cost—800 number?<br>• Experience of support personnel<br>• Software guarantees<br>• Bug fixes—turnaround time<br>• Software updates—maintenance |
| Vendor Background | • Number of employees<br>• Annual sales (approximate)<br>• Growth pattern<br>• Strategic direction<br>• Research and development |

*Figure 10-17*   Information Requested From Vendor

**Percent-of-Fit Goal**   The RFP should now be fairly complete and ready to send to prospective system vendors. In addition to the RFP itself, one other important product of this phase of the overall network analysis and design methodology is known as the **percent-of-fit goal.** This is an especially important element if in-house development of the system and network is a possibility. The percent-of-fit goal is a rather arbitrary percentage that is determined by the user representative group preparing the RFP and is subject to the same overall buy-in as the RFP itself.

The purpose of the percent-of-fit goal is to set a minimum threshold of compliance for vendor proposals to warrant further consideration and invitations for demonstrations. As an example, perhaps the users group feels that any proposal that meets at least 50% of the priority 1 features deserves further consideration.

This percent-of-fit goal offers an element of objectivity to the proposal evaluation process. The percent-of-fit goal, combined with the specific descriptions of required features in the RFP, constitutes an objective, comprehensive evaluation mechanism for evaluating proposals according to what is important to the corporation. By having this evaluation mechanism clearly defined before receipt of the first proposal, evaluators are less likely to be swayed by fancy brochures or systems' "bells and whistles."

If an in-house systems development group feels that they should rightfully be developing and/or implementing this system, they must submit a proposal in compliance with the requirements outlined in the RFP. Their proposal will be evaluated along with all of the outside vendors' proposals.

The percent of fit of a particular proposal can be easily calculated. Recalling that all features or requirements of the RFP were given a priority of 1, 2, or 3, by merely counting how many features of each priority are present in a given proposal, an overall objective "score" can be determined for each proposal. The process is fair, objective, and, to a large extent, eliminates politics from the proposal evaluation process.

## Proposal Evaluation and Vendor Selection

Having determined a percent-of-fit score for each proposal as well as a percent-of-fit goal for proposals to warrant further consideration, invitations to selected vendors might be the next logical step. However, before selected vendors are invited for demonstrations, it is important once again to gain buy-in from all affected parties, especially management, on not only the selected vendors, but perhaps more important, the vendor selection process. Only when all groups agree that the vendor screening and proposal process has been fair and objective should the overall process move forward to the vendor demonstration stage.

At vendor demonstrations, it is important once again for the users, rather than the vendors, to be in charge. Have a copy of the vendor's proposal at the demonstration and ask to see each and every feature demonstrated that was described as included or supported in the vendor's initial proposal. Score should be kept on those features successfully demonstrated, and this score should be compared to the score received based on the proposal evaluation.

After all of the vendor demonstrations, it is time for the **make-or-buy decision.** Were any of the vendors' systems worth further consideration, or should the system be developed in-house? Once again, before proceeding, buy-in of the vendor demonstration evaluation and the make-or-buy decision should be assured.

Managerial
Perspective

## OUTSOURCING

Outsourcing allows information systems and networking administrators to hire outside contractors to operate and maintain corporate information systems and networks. This option has become increasingly popular with companies whose primary business is not related to information systems or networking. Early ventures into outsourcing were not always ideal, as corporations and outsourcing vendors wrestled with where one entity's control terminated and the other's began.

As corporations have gained more experience with outsourcing, the delineation of control has become clearer. Corporations should maintain control over which services can be subcontracted by the outsourcing vendor and should maintain the right to exclude certain subcontractors. The relationship between the corporation and the outsourcing company should be viewed as a strategic partnership rather than as a typical supplier–customer relationship. Partnership agreements can be written to include mutual benefits for mutually achieved goals or shared successes. In this manner, both the client and outsourcing company stand to gain by working together to reach mutually beneficial goals—truly a win–win situation.

## ■ NETWORK ANALYSIS AND DESIGN

Although it may seem as if a great deal of analysis and design have been done already, it is important to note that the network layer requirements are now ready to be addressed, having designed satisfactory solutions for business, application, and data requirements. As stated several times before, a network cannot be designed in a vacuum, but rather must be designed to deliver solutions and performance in response to specific and well-defined data, application, and business layer requirements.

The term *network analysis and design* really refers more specifically to wide area network analysis and design. LAN design considerations and internetworking (LAN to LAN) connectivity issues were covered in their respective chapters. In this chapter, a more corporate-wide view of networking is taken by designing a network that will effectively support the strategic information system design across geographically dispersed corporate locations. Figure 10-18 illustrates the key points, both process and product, of the network analysis and design phase. Each of these steps is explained in detail.

The overall network analysis and design process can be broken down into three major steps:

1. **Data traffic analysis** examines all aspects and characteristics of the traffic that will be passed between corporate locations over the proposed network. Since this data traffic is what the network must carry effectively, it is important to start with a thorough analysis of the data traffic to design an effective network. As an analogy, it would be equally wise to understand the driving

---

| | |
|---|---|
| **Process** | 1. Data traffic analysis |
| |    • Flow Analysis |
| |    • Payload type analysis |
| |    • Transaction analysis |
| |    • Protocol stack analysis |
| |    • Time studies |
| |    • Mission critical analysis |
| |    • Traffic volume analysis |
| | 2. Circuit analysis and configuration alternatives |
| | 3. Network hardware analysis and configuration alternatives |
| **Product** | 1. Data traffic analysis report for each geographic location |
| | 2. Alternative network configuration diagrams including circuit and network hardware details |

*Figure 10-18*  In-House Network Analysis and Design

patterns and transportation needs of an urban area before designing a new highway system.

2. Once the nature of the data traffic is thoroughly understood, **circuit analysis and configuration alternatives** explores the possibilities for delivering that data traffic in a reliable and effective manner. Although there are often alternative ways to transport data from point A to point B, it is important to document alternative network configurations along with an understanding of the advantages and disadvantages of each alternative.

3. Finally, given the nature of the data traffic, especially its protocol-related characteristics, and the possible circuit configurations over which that data may be transported, **network hardware analysis and configuration alternatives** explores the possible data communications hardware devices that may be required to tie the various circuit configurations together into a reliable, manageable network.

## Baseline Existing Network Infrastructure

In most cases, network design projects are actually upgrades or additions to existing networks. As a result, it is essential to be aware of the existing network infrastructure to which the new network or upgrade must interface. Hopefully, detailed records and network diagrams have been kept up to date, documenting current network configuration and layout. If this is not the case, then the existing network infrastructure must be thoroughly analyzed and documented to ensure accurate baseline information.

## Data Traffic Analysis

The exact types of analysis performed in the major step known as data traffic analysis may vary from one networking design to another. Figure 10-19 details some of the possible types of data traffic analysis. The required outcome from this step is a data traffic analysis report that will form the basis for circuit and networking hardware selection. It is the obligation of the network analyst to perform whatever types of data traffic analysis are necessary to ensure that the data traffic analysis report is as complete as possible while forming the foundation on which to build a network design.

**Flow Analysis**    The first step toward a thorough understanding of data traffic analysis is to analyze the flow of that data. Understanding the source and destination of each data "conversation" and the nature of the data in that conversation is fundamental to a proper network design. Flow analysis may involve the identification and classification of different types or groups of users of information and the sources of the information that they must access. Traffic flow can vary greatly depending on the types of applications or equipment at either end of a traffic flow. Among some of these types are:

- SNA traffic from mainframes to dumb terminals
- Client/server traffic from client applications to back-end servers
- Server-to-server traffic between transaction and/or database servers
- Browser-to-Internet traffic between client browsers and Internet-based servers

| Data Traffic Analysis Category | Description |
| --- | --- |
| Flow Analysis | Flow analysis is concerned with which workstations and servers are talking to each other. In other words, who is talking to whom? Who are the "top-talkers"? It is important to identify not only the amount of traffic to be transmitted but the end-points of these transmissions. Only in this manner can proper traffic consolidation be achieved. |
| Payload Type Analysis | Most locations will require at least voice and data service. Videoconferencing and multimedia also may need to be supported. All payload types should be considered and documented before selecting circuit and networking hardware. |
| Transaction Analysis | Use process flow analysis and document flow analysis to identify each type of transaction. Analyze detailed data requirements for each transaction type. Some types of transactions, database replication for example, may be especially bursty. |
| Time Studies | Once all transaction types have been identified, analyze when and how often each transaction type occurs. |
| Traffic Volume Analysis | By combining all known types of transactions with the results of the time study, a time-sensitive traffic volume requirements profile can be produced. This is a starting point for mapping bandwidth requirements to circuit capacity. |
| Mission-Critical Analysis | Results of this analysis phase may dictate the need for special data security procedures such as encryption or special reliability/fault tolerance features such as redundant circuits and networking components. |
| Protocol Stack Analysis | Each corporate location's data traffic is analyzed as to protocols that must be transported across the corporate wide area network. Many alternatives for the transport of numerous protocols exist, but first these protocols must be identified. |

*Figure 10-19*   Data Traffic Analysis

Only after documenting all flows to be handled by a given network can the various types of flows be summarized or conglomerated in an optimal manner.

**Payload Type Analysis**   For the most cost-effective network design, voice as well as data requirements should be considered during the network analysis and design phase. Videoconferencing, imaging, and multimedia requirements should also be considered due to their bandwidth-intensive transport demands. Digitized video and voice represent streaming data and often require isochronous transmission, whereas inter-LAN data tends to be of a more bursty nature. These data characteristics may have a major impact on network design decisions.

**Transaction Analysis**   To determine the actual data traffic requirements from a given corporate location, the network analyst has to examine the source of that data: transactions of one type or another. Examples might include customer entry or inquiry, order entry, inventory receipt, order fulfillment, part number or pricing lookup, etc.

Each of these different transaction types should be identified from the business process definitions of the strategic information systems design. **Process flow analysis** and **document flow analysis** are also employed to identify and analyze transaction types. Once each transaction type has been identified, the amount of data required to complete that transaction is calculated and documented. Some transactions such as credit card verifications or ATM machine transactions are composed of short bursts of data that must be handled quickly and accurately. Some nightly backup or file transfer applications may not require the same type of high-speed, high-priority transmission. The difference in the characteristics of these transactions may warrant a difference in the network design in each case. Perhaps one type of transaction is better suited to a packet-switched approach, whereas the other may require a leased line.

**Time Studies**   Once all transaction types have been identified, the next step is to analyze when and how often these transactions are executed. One method of determining both the frequency and time distribution of these transactions is through a time study. Simply stated, a time study merely counts how often and at what time of day, week, or month a given transaction or process is executed. For instance, a retail store's daily close-out procedure is executed once per day. However, is it the same time each day and are all stores executing the same process as the same time each day? What are the network implications of month-end closing procedures? The answers to these types of questions can have a major bearing on bandwidth requirements and the resultant network design.

**Traffic Volume Analysis**   Traffic volume analysis could be looked on as the product of transaction analysis and time studies. By knowing the data and network requirements of every transaction type and by further knowing the frequency and time distribution of the execution of a given transaction type, a time-sensitive traffic volume requirements profile can be constructed. Such a profile shows average network bandwidth requirements as well as peak or maximum requirements. Seasonality of transaction volume should not be overlooked. The transaction frequency of retail businesses can easily double or even triple during the Christmas shopping season. An undersized network must not be the cause of poor customer service during important periods of increased customer activity. As another example, power companies must design voice and data networks that can easily accommodate higher than normal demand to provide adequate customer service during power outages or other emergencies.

Traffic volume analysis should also be viewed from a location-oriented perspective. To have an accurate representation of overall traffic volumes, one must consider the average and peak traffic volume levels between all identified corporate locations or network nodes. Such point-to-point traffic volume analysis data can then be fed into network design and simulation software packages for further analysis and what-if scenario development.

**Mission-Critical Analysis**   Although all data could be considered important, some transactions are so important to a business that they are known as mission critical. Electronics funds transfer is a good example of a mission-critical transaction. The mission-critical nature of some transactions can spawn further analysis and design in two other areas. Data security may require investigation. Encryption of data transmitted over wide area networks may be a requirement. If so, this fact should be stated as part of the overall data traffic analysis report.

Second, it is a fact of life that data circuits fail from time to time. If certain mission-critical transactions cannot tolerate an occasional faulty data circuit, then redundant links may need to be designed into the initial network design configuration.

**Protocol Stack Analysis**  As has been seen in both the LAN and internetworking design processes, protocol stack analysis is of critical importance. Some protocols, such as SNA, are extremely time sensitive. Some protocols are routable, but others are not. Others, such as SNA and some LAN protocols are very "chatty," sending constant status-checking and keep-alive messages onto the network and occupying precious bandwidth. As each corporate location's data traffic is analyzed, special attention must be paid to the various protocol stacks of that data.

Will the wide area network be required to support more than one protocol? What are the bandwidth and network hardware implications of a multiprotocol WAN? Is TCP/IP encapsulation an option, or is SDLC conversion a more appealing alternative? Before reaching any conclusions as to how various protocols are to be transported over the corporate network, those protocols must be accurately identified and documented. This is the role of the protocol stack analysis.

The type of network design concerned with the proper accommodation of all necessary protocols is referred to as logical network design.

## Physical Design Concepts

As opposed to logical network design, physical network design is most concerned with the specification of the transmission and switching elements that must be combined to deliver analyzed levels of traffic to its proper destination. Some of the key activities involved with physical network design are described next.

## Circuit Analysis and Configuration Alternatives

A thorough data traffic analysis should produce sufficient information to configure various network design alternatives that will effectively support the strategic information system design to all corporate locations. Evaluating alternative network configurations and computing circuit capacity are beyond the reasonable expectations of a person who may be using this textbook in support of a first course in data communications. Upper level courses in traffic engineering, wide area networking, or network analysis and design would better prepare a person to perform such a task.

Wide area network design software has greatly simplified the design process but is relatively expensive. In most cases, even using the software requires a great deal of network design expertise. As a result, in most cases, only companies that can afford to have full-time network analysts and designers on staff are likely to own copies of network design software. The various categories of network design software are explored in greater detail later in this chapter.

A second alternative for circuit analysis and network configuration would be to hire a data communications/networking consultant. This too may be a very expensive alternative. Furthermore, there is little or no regulation as to the level of expertise required to call oneself a telecommunications consultant.

Third, telecommunications companies, both local carriers and interexchange carriers, have the ability to design networks according to customer data requirements. The network design process is part of preparing a quote and is done at no charge. Therefore, it may be advisable for the small company or novice data communications person to let the experts design the network. Talk to several carriers and get a network design proposal with associated costs from each. If the carriers design the network and quote a price, they can be held accountable for delivering service at a quoted price in accordance with the data traffic analysis and performance evaluation criteria.

## Consideration of Network Alternatives

It is important to consider more than just the data traffic analysis when considering network configuration alternatives. The detailed survey of existing system resources should also be considered. For instance, local carriers servicing some remote corporate locations may be limited in their ability to offer certain data transmission services. This should be documented in the survey of existing system resources.

Regardless of who actually designs the network configuration alternatives, it is important to ensure that sufficient bandwidth has been allocated to handle sudden increases in demand. More gradual increases in bandwidth demand due to expanding business opportunities can usually be accommodated with upgrades to higher capacity lines and their associated data communications equipment.

A second performance evaluation criterion for network configurations involves reliability. Based on the data traffic analysis study, sufficient redundancy should be implemented in the network to properly support mission critical applications. Third, is the data transmission provided by these circuits sufficiently secure? The overall goal of this portion of the network design is to find a network configuration that has sufficient bandwidth to reliably deliver the data as described in the data traffic analysis report in a secure manner at a reasonable cost.

Alternative configurations must be understood in terms of both performance and costs. Comprehensive methodologies for project budgeting are presented later. However, the point remains that the choice of a given network configuration may come down to a business decision. That decision may be that a given network configuration is all a company can afford, and, as a result, that company will have to live with the associated performance and reliability. Conversely, the business decision may be that the business requires optimum network performance, regardless of cost.

In any case, it is not the role of the network analyst to dismiss network design alternatives on the basis of cost. The network analyst's job is to deliver network design alternatives capable of delivering required network functionality. Only senior management should determine the feasibility of any particular network design in terms of its affordability. The person presenting the various network configurations to senior management for buy-in must know the pros and cons of each configuration. The ability of each configuration to handle expansion or business growth should be anticipated.

**Network Hardware Analysis and Configuration Alternatives**    Before describing the process of network hardware analysis, it is important to first reiterate the information gathered thus far that will assist in the decision-making process. Two key products of earlier analysis efforts form the basis of the supporting material for selection of the particular networking devices that will be placed throughout the corporate wide area network. These two key products are:

- Data traffic analysis reports for each corporate location

- Circuit configuration alternatives diagrams

Recall briefly the process involved in producing each of these products. The data traffic analysis report was based on a detailed study of numerous aspects of the data traveling to or from each corporate location. The circuit configuration alternatives were designed, in turn, based on a careful study of the required bandwidth and delay sensitivity of the transactions performed at each corporate location as identified in the data traffic analysis study. If the results of these two analysis efforts are valid, then the networking devices chosen to tie the network together that are based on these results should also be valid.

**Use of the I-P-O Model**    The actual decision-making process for network device selection utilizes a model of data communications that was first introduced very early in the text. By compiling the results of the data traffic analysis report and the circuit configuration diagram in an I-P-O diagram, the required processing ability of the sought-after device can be documented. Once the performance characteristics of the required network device have been identified, product specifications can be reviewed and vendor presentations can be scheduled to find the proper networking device for each location.

As with the data traffic analysis and circuit analysis, the network device analysis were done on a location-by-location basis. Figure 10-20 shows a sample use of an I-P-O diagram as a tool for network device analysis.

Figure 10-20 is not meant to be all-inclusive. Rather, it attempts to portray that by knowing the data characteristics of the local data, with particular attention paid to the protocol stack, and by knowing the circuit alternatives available for carrying that

| Input | Processing | Output |
|---|---|---|
| **Local Data Characteristics** | **Required Network Device Characteristics** | **Wide Area Network Circuit Characteristics** |
| Transport protocols | Host-terminal data | Circuit-switched WAN services |
| SNA | Cluster controllers | POTS |
| TCP/IP | STDMs | ISDN |
| IPX/SPX | T-1 MUXs and switches | Switched 56K |
| Payload types | X.25 MUXs and switches | Leased WAN services |
| LAN data | Frame relay MUXs and switches | DDS |
| Voice | ATM access devices and switches | T-1 |
| Video | LAN data | T-3 |
| Fax | Routers | SONET |
| Imaging/multimedia | Switches | Packet/Cell Switched Services |
| Internet access | Voice | X.25 |
| | T-1 channel banks | Frame relay |
| | Video | ATM |
| | Inverse MUXs | MPLS |
| | Internet access | |
| | Modems | |
| | ADSL devices | |
| | Cable Modems | |

*Figure 10-20*    I-P-O Diagram as Tool for Network Device Analysis

data over the wide area network, the choices among network devices that can join the two are relatively limited.

Careful analysis of the available alternatives that can join the input and output characteristics can then be further analyzed from a business or strategic planning objective. Additional information to assist in this evaluation may come from the detailed reports of each corporate location that were part of the preparation of the RFP.

## Review of Overall Network Analysis and Design Process

Once the network hardware analysis, circuit analysis, and data analysis have been completed, the finishing touches can now be put on the final proposal. Before doing so, a brief review of the network analysis and design process is in order.

Notice that the network design process did not start with a discussion of network hardware device alternatives. To do so would have been to ignore the importance of the top-down model, a central theme of this book. Many so-called data communications experts still start with their favorite hardware alternative and adjust data and circuit characteristics to match the chosen network hardware.

In this case, just the opposite approach was taken:

- Determine data characteristics based on a thorough examination of the transactions that generate the data.

- Determine circuits based on required bandwidth and delay-sensitivity as determined by the data analysis study.

- Determine the networking hardware devices capable of transporting this data over these circuits while remaining responsive to business and location-specific influences.

## Preparing the Final Proposal

Figure 10-21 summarizes the key points of wrapping up the network analysis and design methodology. After preparing and presenting the final proposal, buy-in is sought from all affected constituencies, followed, it is hoped, by final approval and funding by senior management. One element of the final proposal process deserves further explanation.

## Preparing a Comprehensive Budget

It has been the author's experience that senior management can accept well-organized, comprehensive budgets representing large sums of money. What has been found to be unacceptable are the so-called hidden or forgotten costs of network and systems implementation often left out of budgets.

As a result, a comprehensive budget format needed to be developed that would help to identify as many elements of potential implementation and operation costs as possible. Figure 10-22 illustrates a sample budget page from the

| Final Proposal | Process | 1. Prepare a detailed comprehensive budget<br>2. Prepare detailed implementation timetable<br>3. Prepare project task detail<br>4. Prepare formal presentation<br>5. SELL! |
|---|---|---|
| | Product | 1. Comprehensive systems and networking budget model<br>2. Project management details<br>3. Presentation graphics |
| **Approval** | Process | 1. Final buy-in by all affected parties<br>2. Contract negotiation—outsourcing only<br>3. Executive approval |
| **Implementation** | Process | 1. Pilot test<br>2. In-house trial—outsourcing only<br>3. Performance evaluation<br>4. Prepare deployment schedule<br>5. Roll-out |
| | Product | 1. Detailed list of tasks and responsible parties with due dates<br>2. Identify and satisfy needs for management, support, and training on new system/network |

*Figure 10-21*   Final Proposal, Approval, and Implementation

| Proposal Number | Description | | | |
|---|---|---|---|---|
| | **Acquisition** | **Operation** | **Incremental Change/<br>Anticipated Growth** | **TOTALS** |
| **Hardware** | Data center:<br>Network operations:<br>Application development: | Data center:<br>Network operations:<br>Application development: | Data center:<br>Network operations:<br>Application development: | Data center:<br>Network operations:<br>Application development: |
| **Software** | Data center:<br>Network operations:<br>Application development: | Data center:<br>Network operations:<br>Application development: | Data center:<br>Network operations:<br>Application development: | Data center:<br>Network operations:<br>Application development: |
| **Personnel** | Data center:<br>Network operations:<br>Application development: | Data center:<br>Network operations:<br>Application development: | Data center:<br>Network operations:<br>Application development: | Data center:<br>Network operations:<br>Application development: |
| **Communications** | Data center:<br>Network operations:<br>Application development: | Data center:<br>Network operations:<br>Application development: | Data center:<br>Network operations:<br>Application development: | Data center:<br>Network operations:<br>Application development: |
| **Facilities** | Data center:<br>Network operations:<br>Application development: | Data center:<br>Network operations:<br>Application development: | Data center:<br>Network operations:<br>Application development: | Data center:<br>Network operations:<br>Application development: |
| **TOTALS** | Data center:<br>Network operations:<br>Application development: | Data center:<br>Network operations:<br>Application development: | Data center:<br>Network operations:<br>Application development: | Data center:<br>Network operations:<br>Application development: |

*Figure 10-22*   Comprehensive Systems and Networking Budget Model

**comprehensive systems and networking budget model.** Along the vertical axis, major budget categories are listed including:

- Hardware/equipment

- Software

- Personnel

- Communications (carrier services)

- Facilities

There is nothing sacred about these categories. Change them to whatever best reflects your situation. The important point is to organize the budget grid in such a way that all possible costs are identified in advance.

The horizontal access has three columns representing the major categories of costs with respect to time. Networking and systems budgets typically focused only on the **acquisition costs** of the new system. Even within the acquisition category, costs associated with personnel additions, changes, and training were often omitted. Likewise, costs involved with facilities upgrades or changes such as electrical wiring, cabinets, wiring closets, or security systems were also likely to be overlooked or unanticipated. Preventing surprises such as these requires a two-step approach:

- Required or anticipated facilities upgrades and personnel needs are identified during the location-by-location survey as part of the final preparation of the RFP.

- Any legitimate need that was identified in the location-by-location survey should be budgeted for in the comprehensive systems and networking budget model.

Even a budget that identifies all acquisition costs is still neither complete nor accurate. Two other major categories of costs must be accounted for:

- Operations

- Incremental change/anticipated growth

**Operations Costs**    **Operations costs** include estimated monthly costs for leased-line or dial-up line usage, as well as the estimated cost for the additional electricity required to run new equipment. If additional cooling, heating, or environmental control is required as a result of system implementation, these costs should be included as well. Service contracts, maintenance agreements, or budgeted time and materials for repairs should be also be considered as operation costs. Also, don't forget budgeting for taxes, contingency or "rainy day" funds, and other hidden costs.

## ANTICIPATING AND BUDGETING FOR NETWORK GROWTH

Another aspect of project budgeting often overlooked at proposal time is the cost associated with the anticipated growth of the system during the first three to five years after implementation. These **incremental change costs** may be significant if certain elements of the system or network design are not expandable or only moderately so. As an example, perhaps a remote site starts with a four-port STDM as its

Practical Advice
and Information

networking device. To add four more users, an upgrade kit could be installed for $1,300. However, to add a ninth user would require replacing the entire STDM with a higher capacity unit at a cost of $5,000. Although the costs in this example may not be precise, the point of the example remains. Anticipated growth should be budgeted. In some cases, this budgeting process of the anticipated growth may cause changes in the equipment choices at acquisition time.

To accurately budget for anticipated systems and network growth, the network analyst must have access to strategic business plans that outline the anticipated growth of the business. After all, the implemented system and network are a direct result of the business requirements, including the required ability to respond to changing business conditions in accordance with the overall business vision as articulated in a strategic business plan. Depending on the corporate culture, network analysts may not be allowed access to such strategic business planning information.

As shown in Figure 10-22, each budget category that is formed by an intersection of a column and row can be further subdivided if such department budgeting is required within the overall project budget. In Figure 10-22, the three abbreviated categories stand for three typical departments within an overall M.I.S. operation: DC (data center), NO (network operations), and AD (application development). Make this budget grid fit your business. If departmental or cost center budgeting is not required for your business, ignore these subcategories. If other departmental designations are more appropriate, substitute them.

## THE NETWORK IMPLEMENTATION PROCESS

Although specific details of an implementation process will vary from one project to the next, there are a few general points worth making. Perhaps most important, regardless of how well designed an information system or network may be, it is still essential to test that design in as safe a manner as possible. "Safe" in this case could be defined as the least likely to have a tragic effect on production systems or networks.

**Pilot tests** are a popular way to safely roll out new systems or networks. For example, bring one retail store on-line and monitor performance, fix unanticipated problems, and gain management experience before deploying the system on a wider scale. Honest feedback and performance evaluations are essential to smooth system implementations. User groups can be a helpful feedback mechanism if managed skillfully to prevent degeneration into nothing more than gripe sessions.

### Project Management

Another important skill to a smooth implementation process is effective project management. Detailed task lists including task description, scheduled start and finish dates, actual start and finish dates, and responsible parties are at the heart of good project management. Some systems and network professionals use project management software. The author has used project management software on occasion but found, in general, that loading and maintaining all of the project detail in the project management software was more work than managing the project manually. Although perhaps overly simplistic, the general rule of thumb as to when to use project management software is when a project is too complicated to manage manually, then you may benefit from the use of project management software.

### People Are Important

Despite this book's focus on networking hardware and software, people are the most important element of any systems implementation. Buy-in at every stage by all affected parties was stressed throughout the network analysis and design process to ensure that everyone gets behind the new system and network and that everyone feels that they had an opportunity to make their thoughts known. The best designed network will fail miserably without the support of people.

Therefore, a key element of system and network implementation is to ensure that people-related needs such as management, support, and training have been thoroughly researched and appropriately addressed.

### ◼ AUTOMATING THE NETWORK DEVELOPMENT LIFE CYCLE

Sophisticated software packages now exist to assist network analysts in the analysis and design of large and complicated networks. These software tools can vary greatly in sophistication, functionality, scope, and price.

Managerial
Perspective

### THE BUSINESS CASE FOR COMPUTER-ASSISTED NETWORK ENGINEERING

The entire network development life cycle is sometimes referred to as **network engineering.** The use of software tools of one type or another to assist in this process is known as **computer-assisted network engineering (CANE).** Companies must be able to make a strong business case for the payback of this computer-assisted network engineering software when the prices for the software generally range from $10,000 to $30,000 per copy. Besides the obvious use of the software for designing new networks "from scratch," several other uses of computer-assisted network engineering software can offer significant paybacks.

By using analysis and design software to model their current network, companies are able to run **optimization routines** to reconfigure circuits and/or network hardware to deliver data more efficiently. In the case of optimization software, "efficiently" can mean maximized performance, minimized price, or a combination of both.

When current networks have grown over time in a somewhat helter-skelter manner without any major redesigns, network optimization software can redesign networks that can save from thousands of dollars per month to millions of dollars per year depending on the size of the network.

Another important use of analysis and design software on a corporation's current network is for **billing verification.** Most analysis and design packages have up-to-date tariff information from multiple regional and long-distance carriers. By inputting a company's current network design in the analysis and design software and by using the tariff tables to price individual circuits within that network, prices generated from the tariff tables can be compared to recent phone bills. Such verification often uncovers discrepancies in billing amounts, some of which can be significant.

Either of the two previous uses of computer-assisted network engineering software could pay back the cost of that software within six months to one year. Another very common use of this type of software with a less tangible short-term financial payback but significant future benefits is **proactive performance assurance.**

Figure 10-23 illustrates the various categories of computer-assisted network engineering software along with a few examples of each type. Many other software

| Top Category | Examples |
|---|---|
| **Application Monitoring** | • OPNET IT Guru<br>• Compuware Vantage |
| **Network Monitoring** | • Lucent Vitalsuite |
| **Network Management** | • Tivoli/IBM TME<br>• CA—Unicenter<br>• HP—Openview |
| **Network Simulation** | • OPNET Modeler |
| **Network Design** | • OPNET Mainstation<br>• OPNET SP Guru<br>• NetCracker Professional |

*Figure 10-23*    Computer-Assisted Network Engineering Software

packages are available in each category that offer a range of features at a range of prices. Differentiation between network design tools, network simulation tools, and network management tools is not as definitive as Figure 10-23 might imply. In fact, most network design tools now include at least some network simulation and management capabilities, as well as network design intelligence to actively assist in the network design.

In addition, recognizing the interdependence between application performance and network performance, many network-based analysis and monitoring tools are able to monitor and/or simulate application performance on a given network. This capability is essential if applications and networks are to be designed in an optimal fashion. Otherwise, network designers fall prey to the rule of thumb of network design: "when in doubt, over-provision the bandwidth until the application performs acceptably." Unfortunately, for latency-constrained applications, no amount of bandwidth will produce acceptable performance results. However, financial consequences of such a network design philosophy could be disastrous.

## Analysis and Design Tools

Figure 10-24 lists some of the more common elements of network design tools in an input-processing-output model format.

Following is a listing of some of the important features to look for when considering network analysis and design tools:

- Tariff databases: How current are they? How many carriers and types of circuits are included? How often are the tariff databases updated? Is there an additional charge for tariff database updates? Tariff structures have become very complicated and are calculated in a variety of different ways. Confirm that the tariff database in the analysis and design software includes all necessary tariffs.

- Response time calculation: Does the software consider the processing time of the particular host computer that may be a part of the network? Can user-defined elements be taken into account in the response time calculation, for

| Phase | Network Design Tool Features |
|---|---|
| **Input** | • Input requirements definitions |
| | • Drop network objects |
| | • Auto-discovery on existing networks from enterprise network management packages such as HP's Openview, IBM's NetView, or CA-Unicenter |
| | • Assign traffic characteristics and distribution |
| | • Link objects with circuits |
| | • Assign attributes and protocols to network devices and circuits |
| | • Build a computer-assisted network model |
| | • Accept input (traffic data) from network analysis tools or sniffers |
| **Processing** | • Validate the design (which objects can be connected to which other objects) |
| | • Roll up and simulate a fully loaded network |
| | • Ensure protocol compatibility |
| | • Assess reliability and security |
| | • Test alternative configurations for cost and performance optimization |
| | • Conduct what-if testing |
| **Output** | • Detailed network equipment requirements by vendor |
| | • Detailed transmission circuit requirements |
| | • Detailed protocol design |
| | • Bill of materials listing all items to be purchased |

*Figure 10-24*   Input-Processing-Output Model for Network Design Tools

example, applications programs of various types, different types of networking equipment?

- Multiple transport protocols: Can the software consider the effect of various transport protocols on response time? How many protocols are included? SNA, DECNET, ISDN, TCP/IP, X.25, frame relay, ATM, satellite, microwave, cellular?

- Multiple topologies: How many different topologies can the software model? Examples: hierarchical, hub and spoke, mesh, point-to-point multipoint, concentrated, packet-switched, multiple host.

- Circuit design: Can the software configure circuits for a combination of simultaneous voice and data traffic, or must voice and data circuits be designed separately? Can multiplexers be cascaded? Are tail circuits allowed?

- Financial: Can the software roll up costs for network equipment as well as for circuits? Can costs and performance be optimized simultaneously? Can costs be compared across multiple carriers?

- Input/output: Can protocol analyzers or network monitoring or management systems be interfaced directly to the analysis and design software for automatic input of current system performance data? Can analysis and design results be output directly to spreadsheet, database, and word processing packages?

- Operating platforms: What platform does the design software run over? NT, Unix, SunOS, Win'95/98/2000?

- Design platforms: What types of networks can the software design? LAN only, WAN only, LAN/WAN and internetworking?

- Product library: Different network design packages can contain varying numbers of network device objects that contain manufacturer-specific information and specifications.

- Design validation: The software should validate that all devices are accounted for, that all segment lengths conform to standards, and that all hardware is properly matched according to protocols.

## Simulation Tools

Simulation software tools are also sometimes known as **performance engineering** software tools. All simulation systems share a similar trait in that the overall network performance that they are able to model is a result of the net effect of a series of mathematical formulas. These mathematical formulas represent and are derived from the actual performance of the circuits and networking equipment that make up the final network design.

The value of a simulation system is in its ability to predict the performance of various networking scenarios otherwise known as **what-if analysis.** Simulation software uses the current network configuration as a starting point and applies what-if scenarios. The benefits of a good network simulation package include:

- Ability to spot network bottlenecks such as overworked servers, network failures, or disk capacity problems.

- Ability to test new applications and network configurations before actual deployment. New applications may run well in a controlled test environment, but may perform quite differently on the shared enterprise network.

- Ability to recreate circumstances to reproduce intermittent or occasional network problems.

- Ability to replicate traffic volume as well as traffic transaction type and protocol mix.

The key characteristics that distinguish simulation software are as follows:

- Network types: Which different types of networks can be simulated? Circuit-switched, packet-switched, store-and-forward, packet-radio, VSAT, microwave?

- Network scope: How many of the following can the simulation software model either individually or in combination with one another: modems and multiplexers, LANs, Internetworks, WANs, MANs?

- Network services: How many of the following advanced services can be modeled: frame relay, ISDN (BRI and PRI), X.25, ATM, SONET, MPLS?

- Network devices: Some simulation systems have developed performance profiles of individual networking devices to the point where they can model particular networking devices (bridges, routers, switches, MUXs) made by particular manufacturers.

- Network protocols: In addition to the network transport protocols listed in the analysis and design section, different router-to-router protocols can have a dramatic impact on network performance. Examples: RIP, OSPF, PPP, BGP.

- Different data traffic attributes: As studied in previous chapters, all data traffic does not have identical transmission needs or characteristics. Can the software simulate data with different traits? For example: bursty LAN data, streaming digitized voice or video, real-time transaction-oriented data, batch-oriented file transfer data.

- Traffic data entry: Any simulation needs traffic statistics to run. How these traffic statistics may be entered can make a major difference in the ease of use of the simulation system. Possibilities include manual entry by users of traffic data collected elsewhere, traffic data entered "live" through a direct interface to a protocol analyzer, a traffic generator that generates simulated traffic according to the user's parameters or auto-discovery from enterprise network management systems.

- User interface: Many simulation software tools now offer easy-to-use graphical user interfaces with point-and-click network design capability for flexible "what-if" analysis. Some, but not all, produce graphical maps that can be output to printers or plotters. Others require users to learn a procedure-oriented programming language.

- Simulation presentation: Some simulation tools have the ability to animate the performance of the simulated network in real time, and others perform all mathematical calculations and then play back the simulation when those calculations are complete.

**Object-Oriented Technology Meets Network Engineering**    As network simulation software has shifted its intended audience from network engineers well versed in the intricacies of network performance optimization to network analysts most familiar with networking requirements, the designers of that software have had to make some fairly radical changes in the ease of use as well as the sophistication of the software.

The mathematical formulas representing the performance characteristics of individual networking elements become the methods of the network objects, and the attributes describe the details such as manufacturer, model, price, and capacity. By merely clicking on one of these network objects representing a particular network device or circuit, the user automatically adds all of the associated methods and attributes of that network object to the network simulation. Particular applications programs or transport protocols can also be represented as network objects and be clicked on to be added to the overall network simulation. In this way, all seven layers of the OSI model can be included in the final simulation run.

## Management: Proactive LAN Management

Sophisticated proactive network management software has the ability to monitor network performance on an ongoing basis and to report unusual network conditions or activities to a network management workstation. The term *unusual network conditions* is really user definable. **Thresholds,** or desired limits of certain performance characteristics, are set by the user. In some cases, the user may have no idea where to set these thresholds. To aid in such a situation, some management systems can record "normal" performance characteristics over an extended time to gather valid **baseline data.**

Some management software systems even have the ability to feed this "alarm data" back to certain simulation systems that can simulate the "threshold crossing" and allow what-if analysis to be performed in order to diagnose the cause of the problem and propose a solution.

## ■ THE FUTURE OF THE AUTOMATED NETWORK DEVELOPMENT LIFE CYCLE

Some of the trends mentioned in previous sections will continue as computer-assisted network engineering software tools continue to evolve and mature. The key word in terms of the future of these various tools that make up the automated network development life cycle is integration. The real potential of network engineering software integration has just barely scratched the surface and only in a few vendor-specific cases.

For instance, certain protocol analyzers such as Network General's Distributed Sniffer have the ability to interface directly into certain network simulation systems. In such a scenario, actual traffic statistics from the current network configuration are fed directly into the mathematical engines underlying the simulation software. Such vendor-specific, product-specific integration is significant. However, to have true transparent integration of all computer-assisted network engineering tools, a more open and standardized approach must be undertaken.

### Horizontal Integration

Figure 10-25 illustrates, on a conceptual level, how such a standardized open architecture offering seamless **horizontal integration** might be constructed. Rather than having to know the intricacies and, in some cases, the trade secrets of how each other's products work, vendors of computer-assisted network engineering software merely pass the output from their particular software product to a "neutral" data platform known as **common network information platform** or **CNIP.** Any other CANE tool that could use that output to provide transparent integration with other CANE tools would import the standardized, formatted data from the common network information platform. The end result of the use of such a standardized platform for CANE tool data output and retrieval is the seamless integration of a variety of CANE tools spanning all phases of the network development life cycle.

### The Final Frontier: Vertical Integration

Integration implies not only horizontal integration with software from other categories of the CANE family but also **vertical integration** with applications development platforms such as computer assisted software engineering (CASF) tools.

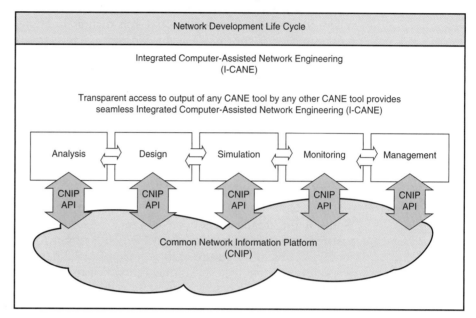

*Figure 10-25*   The Future of the Automated Network Development
Life Cycle—Horizontal Integration

Integrated CASE (I-CASE) tools could generate code for a new corporate-wide application and could download key information concerning that new application to the CANE suite of software products to predict network impact of the new proposed application.

Proactive network management is the result when the network implications of the deployment of new network-intensive applications are known before the actual release of the software.

As can be seen in Figure 10-26, the actual gateway between the I-CASE and **I-CANE** tools may not be a simple API. Because of the sophistication of the interface between these two platforms, expert systems may be required to dynamically model the relationships between the objects underlying the CASE tools and those underlying the CANE tools.

Extending the vertical integration above the CASE tools and the strategic information systems that they produce, expert systems could again maintain the relationships between major software platforms. Applications layer objects used by the CASE tools could be dynamically linked via expert systems to the objects representing the business rules and processes that, in turn, support strategic business goals and objectives.

Thus, although current technology may not possess the capability, the business information system of the future may interface to the strategic business planning person who amends strategic business goals and objects via a graphical user interface and point-and-click manipulation of business process objects. The changes caused by this business process reengineering are immediately forwarded via an expert system interface to the strategic information systems design that supports

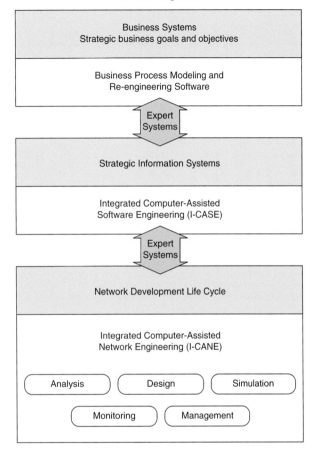

*Figure 10-26*   The Future of the Automated Network Development
Life Cycle—Vertical Integration

these business processes. Changes to application programs would be automatically generated by integrated CASE tools.

Resultant changes in the applications programs produced by the CASE tools are immediately forwarded via expert systems to the integrated computer-assisted network engineering platform. Finally, network objects, circuits, and networking devices are amended as necessary due to the impact of the new applications programs. Network simulation programs are automatically run to assess network impact while network design optimization programs automatically reconfigure the network design to adjust most appropriately to the new network impacts. The amazing part of this whole process is that it was initiated originally by a change in strategic business objectives. The future of computer-assisted network engineering software represents one of the most exciting opportunities in data communications and networking while adhering to the overall top-down model philosophy of network design.

## SUMMARY

As has been stated throughout the text, network design cannot be done in a vacuum. Effective network designs will only result from strict adherence to the top-down model by beginning with an analysis of business objectives rather than networking technology. Strategic information systems design must be conducted after business objectives and processes have been thoroughly examined. The importance of strategic information systems design lies not only in its delivery of business objectives but also in its role as a template for network design.

Information systems may be developed in-house or may be outsourced. In either case, it is essential to have a thorough and accurate RFP (request for proposal). Data traffic analysis is a multi-step process that assures that all potential sources of network traffic are identified and accurately quantified. Circuit analysis and configuration alternatives match the proper WAN service to each location's data delivery needs, while network hardware analysis and configuration alternatives match the proper networking hardware with the location's input data and the installed WAN service.

Comprehensive budgets go beyond the typical proposal focus of acquisition costs to include categories for operations and anticipated network growth for a variety of cost centers and categories. Finally, although network design has been a manual process for many years, automated network design and simulation tools are beginning to become more popular as network scope and complexity make "back of the napkin" network design both impractical and unwise.

## KEY TERMS

acquisition costs
baseline data
billing verification
business functional areas
business process reengineering
buy-in
CANE optimization routines
circuit analysis and configuration
    alternatives
CNIP
common network information
    platform
comprehensive systems and
    networking budget model
computer assisted network
    engineering
critical success factors
data traffic analysis
decision points
document flow analysis
evaluation criteria
feasibility study
flow analysis
horizontal integration
I-CANE

incremental change costs
IT project portfolio management
logical network design
make-or-buy decision
management abstract
mission-critical analysis
NDLC
network analysis and design
    methodology
network development life cycle
network engineering
network hardware analysis and
    configuration alternatives
operations costs
opportunities for improvement
payload type analysis
percent of fit goal
performance engineering
performance metrics
physical network design
pilot tests
proactive performance assurance
process
process flow analysis
project charter product

protocol stack analysis
request for information
request for proposal
return on investment
return on opportunity
RFI
RFP
ROI
ROO
strategic information system
    design
TBO
TCO
three-pile approach
thresholds
time studies
total benefit of ownership
total cost of ownership
traffic volume analysis
transaction analysis
vertical integration
what-if analysis

## REVIEW QUESTIONS

1. Explain how one can assure that IT projects are aligned with strategic business initiatives.
2. Explain how IT project portfolio management works and how it is able to adapt to different corporate business situations.
3. What is the difference between total cost of ownership and total benefit of ownership?
4. What is the difference between return on investment and return on opportunity?
5. Why does total cost of ownership calculation not lend itself easily to IT projects?
6. What is flow analysis and why is it important?
7. Explain how the NDLC interacts with strategic level business and IT infrastructure alignment.
8. Explain how the NDLC interacts with project specific activities such as RFP generation.
9. What are performance metrics and how can they help to assure IT/business alignment?
10. Where does the network development life cycle fit in the overall systems development life cycle?
11. How can one insure that a network design will meet strategic business requirements?
12. How can a company cost justify the expense of network analysis and design software?
13. What does optimization accomplish in network design software?
14. What are the two major characteristics on which networks are optimized?
15. Can these two optimization characteristics conflict with each other?
16. How is horizontal integration of CANE tools likely to be enabled?
17. How is vertical integration of CANE tools likely to be enabled?
18. What is so significant about the comprehensive systems and networking budget model?
19. What is meant by the term critical success factor? Discuss three.
20. What is the significance of process and product in the network analysis and design methodology?
21. What are the important elements of data traffic analysis?
22. Explain the relationship of data traffic analysis, circuit analysis, and network hardware analysis.
23. Explain the importance of evaluation criteria and percent of fit goals to the overall network design process.
24. What is the purpose of an RFP?
25. What are the major components of an RFP?
26. How can the RFP process be kept as objective and non-political as possible?
27. What types of information must be gathered about each corporate location?
28. How can a network analyst assure widespread support of new systems or network implementations?
29. What is cyclic about the network development life cycle?
30. How can computer-assisted network engineering software products exhibit the same cyclic nature?
31. Why are seasonal or occasional differences in transaction volumes or processes so important to network design?
32. What are some of the potential advantages and disadvantages of outsourcing network analysis and design functions?
33. How can so-called backroom politics affect network development and how can a network analyst minimize such effects?
34. What does corporate culture have to do with the method in which a network development project is carried out?
35. What does buy-in imply beyond simple agreement and why is it important to the network development life cycle?
36. How can responses to RFPs be objectively evaluated to determine those vendors worthy of further consideration?
37. What is the role of protocol analyzers in the network development life cycle and in the functionality of network optimization tools?
38. How do network analysts assure that they have a clear understanding of a business problem before proceeding to a network solution?
39. What is the importance of baseline data to the ability to articulate the eventual success or failure of a network development effort?
40. How can too much information be as detrimental as too little information for decision makers? What effect on network design might this have?
41. What is the danger in not starting the network development life cycle with an examination of business layer issues but merely networking business operations as they currently exist?
42. How can the amount of work invested in the development of an RFP be justified?
43. Why is the customer's proposed project schedule important to potential vendors?
44. What is the importance of the corporate location by location survey?
45. Although specific questions asked of vendors in an RFP may vary, what are the overall objectives in asking for this information?

46. How can a network analysis project leader assure that vendor demonstrations are objective and useful and don't revert to "dog and pony" shows?

47. What are some of the difficulties in transporting voice and data simultaneously?

48. What are some of the promising network technologies for transmission of video and data on both the LAN and WAN?

49. How can an I-P-O diagram be used to assist in the proper selection of network hardware devices?

50. Describe those items beyond acquisition costs which should be included in a network budget as well as the importance of those items.

51. What impact has object-oriented programming had on network design and simulation tools?

52. What is so proactive about proactive LAN management? What is the likely business impact of proactive LAN management?

53. Differentiate between ROI, TCO, and TBO is terms of methodology as well as appropriateness for network development projects.

**Case Study:** For a business case study and questions that relate to network development, go to www.wiley.com/college/goldman.

# NETWORK MANAGEMENT

*Concepts Reinforced*

OSI model
Enterprise network architectures
Distributed information systems

Top-down model
Network development life cycle
Protocols and interoperability

*Concepts Introduced*

Enterprise network management
Server management
Desktop management
Distributed applications management
Internetwork device management
Distributed network management
Service management
Traffic shaping

Systems administration
Help desk management
Consolidated services desk
LAN management
Internet/WWW management
Network management technology
Quality of service
Bandwidth management

## OBJECTIVES

Upon successful completion of this chapter, you should:

1. Understand the business motivations and forces at work in the current systems administration and network management arena.

2. Understand the relationship between network management processes, personnel, and technology to produce a successful network management system.

3. Understand the differences between systems administration processes and network management processes.

4. Understand the protocols and technology associated with each area of systems administration and network management.

5. Understand how systems administration and network management technology can be most effectively implemented.

## ■ INTRODUCTION

At this point in the text, it should be clear to all readers that a network is a complex combination of hardware and software technologies linked by networking technologies. Once these various categories of technologies are successfully integrated, they must be properly managed. The purpose of this chapter is to expose the reader to how each of the elements of a network can be managed to achieve stated business objectives. Although entire texts are written on network and information systems management, this chapter provides an overview of the key issues surrounding the management of several aspects of networks including business alignment, standards and protocols, interoperability issues, currently available technology, key vendors, and market trends.

## ■ SERVICE MANAGEMENT PROVIDES BUSINESS ALIGNMENT WITH NETWORK MANAGEMENT

To ensure that networks and their associated information systems are delivering expected levels of service to achieve strategic business initiatives, a verifiable methodology to measure service performance levels must be developed. **Service management** is concerned with the management of IT services and the business processes that depend on them. Service management is achieved through the controlled operation of ongoing service by formalized and disciplined processes. Because of the predictable service environment enabled by strictly defined service processes, the following benefits or characteristics of IT services can be realized:

- Higher quality
- Lower cost
- Greater flexibility and responsiveness
- More consistent service
- Faster responses to customer needs
- Proactive rather than reactive service definition

A service management architecture is developed to map required IT services to specific business unit or customer needs.

### Service Management Architecture

**Service management architectures** provide metrics for service evaluation on both a business and IT infrastructure level. Business expectations as stated by business unit management, the customer, are translated into business performance metrics. These business performance metrics are then mapped to the IT infrastructure expected levels of service that will be required to meet the previously mentioned business expectations. These IT infrastructure expected levels of service are then mapped to IT performance metrics that will objectively measure the IT infrastructure's ability to meet expected levels of service. Figure 11-1 provides a high level view of the components and interaction of a service management architecture.

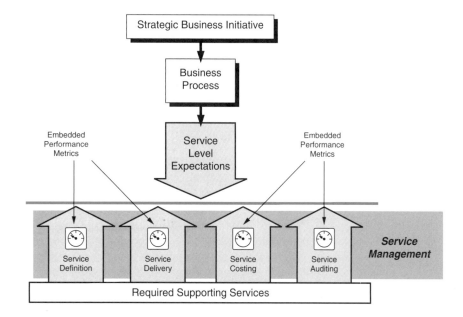

*Figure 11-1*    Service Management Architecture

## Service Definition and Frameworks

Services are defined in terms of the processes, technical expertise (people), and technology that are required to deliver those services. A given service can vary in terms of several characteristics contributing to measurable differences in cost and price:

- Complexity
- Risk (or lack thereof)
- Required service or support level
- Level of deviation from "basic" service

Service definition implies that a baseline level of service and the costs associated with that level of service are first determined. Modifications or upgraded levels of that service are available at customer specification for a predetermined cost above the baseline service.

Defined services and their associated processes are often organized into categories. Workflow and document flow analysis defines the interaction among these various categories of service management processes. Although network management is only one element of overall IT infrastructure and service management, the OSI Network Management Framework can serve as the basis for a larger list of management services incorporating the broader service management category.

The Network Management Forum associated with the OSI Reference Model has divided the field of network management into five major categories in a document known as the **ISO Management Framework** (ISO 7498-4). This categorization is somewhat arbitrary as standards and network management technology apply to multiple categories, and even the categories themselves are interdependent. However, it is important for the network analyst to be aware of this categorization, as it is often referred to when discussing network management architectures and technology. Figure 11-2 lists and explains the five OSI categories of network management.

Other service management frameworks may include other categories of management that further expand the list presented in Figure 11-2. Many of these categories are concerned with the definition, costing, reporting, support, management, and auditing of the services that must be collectively delivered by the combined elements of the IT infrastructure. Some of the potential additional categories of service management include:

- Service level management: Concerned with the definition and management of offered service levels.

- Incident management: Reactive process to resolve issues as quickly as possible.

- Problem management: Proactive process that attempts to prevent incidents from recurring.

| OSI Category of Network Management | Explanation/Importance |
|---|---|
| **Fault Management** | • Monitoring of the network or system state<br>• Receipt and processing of alarms<br>• Diagnosis of the causes of faults<br>• Determination of the propagation of errors<br>• Initiation and checking of error recovery measures<br>• Introduction of trouble ticket system<br>• Provision of a user help desk |
| **Configuration Management** | • Compile accurate description of all network components<br>• Control updating of configuration<br>• Control of remote configuration<br>• Support for network version control<br>• Initiation of jobs and tracing of their execution |
| **Performance Management** | • Determination of quality of service parameters<br>• Monitor network for performance bottlenecks<br>• Measure system and network performance<br>• Process measurement data and produce reports<br>• Capacity planning and proactive performance planning |
| **Security Management** | • Monitor the system for intrusions<br>• Provide authentication of users<br>• Provide encryption in order to assure message privacy<br>• Implement associated security policy |
| **Accounting Management** | • Record system and network usage statistics<br>• Maintain usage accounting system for chargeback purposes<br>• Allocation and monitoring of system or network usage quotas<br>• Maintain and report usage statistics |

*Figure 11-2*    OSI Categories of Network Management

- Change management: Concerned with the management and documentation of changes to the IT infrastructure.

- Capacity management: Proactive management practice concerned with ensuring that the IT infrastructure has sufficient capacity to support current service level agreements as well as unforeseen sudden increases in demand.

- Asset management: Concerned with the monitoring and management of the hardware and software technology that comprises the IT infrastructure.

- Availability management, risk management, and contingency planning: All are related to the desire to be able to meet or exceed system availability commitments as contained in service level agreements.

Many of these categories of management are described in more detail in the remainder of the chapter. Another network management model or framework that is more specifically focused on public telecommunications networks owned by carriers, as opposed to privately owned enterprise networks, is the **Telecommunication Management Network (TMN).** Standards for TMN are issued by the ITU-T (International Telecommunications Union–Telecommunications Standardization Sector). TMN standards are organized according to the particular focus areas such as: architecture, functional requirements, information models, protocols, conformance, profiles, and methodology. Overall TMN management functionality can be organized into a four-layer TMN model consisting of the following four functional layers, following an overall top-down model approach:

- Business management: Focus on high-level business aspects of telecomm management including strategic business and financial planning.

- Service management: Focus on the implementation, support, and management of telecommunications services that will meet business and financial strategic goals described in the business management layer. This layer includes all customer service interaction with end users of services. Quality assurance and billing processes are included on this layer.

- Network management: Focus on the end-to-end management of the network infrastructure that will be delivering the services described in the service management layer. Functionality on this layer is considered vendor independent.

- Element management: In TMN, all networks are comprised of a combination of network elements (NE). The element management layer is concerned with the management of the distributed individual network elements that comprise the networks that deliver the services. Functionality on this layer is considered vendor dependent, based on the vendor of a particular network element.

## Service Level Agreements

Once services are defined and a given level of service is agreed upon between the customer and the IT services department, a formally documented **service level agreement** is negotiated. The service level agreement clearly describes expected levels of service, how that service will be measured, what that service will cost, and what the consequences will be if the agreed upon service levels are not met.

Measurements defined in service level agreements must be able to clearly show how effective services are in meeting business objectives, not how much of an IT commodity was used. For example, it is no longer appropriate to report bandwidth consumed, CPU cycles consumed, or amount of disk space consumed. What really matters is whether or not the total IT infrastructure was able to support the success of the business initiative. Among the network management tools capable of monitoring service level agreements, especially with carriers for wide area network services, are the following:

| Service Level Monitoring Tool | Vendor |
| --- | --- |
| Visual Uptime | Visual Networks |
| Vital Suite | Lucent |
| OpenLANE | Paradyne |

## Service Costing

Once services have been defined, they must be assigned a cost. Costing IT services is not a simple matter. Initially costs can be differentiated as follows:

- Direct costs: Those that can be directly attributed to the provision of a given service.

- Indirect costs: Those that go to support the overall IT infrastructure on which all services depend.

- Variable costs: Those that vary directly with the amount or level of service required or purchased.

- Fixed costs: Those that do not vary as additional amounts or levels of service are required or delivered.

Figure 11-3 provides a simple model of how variable levels of services can be effectively costed.

As illustrated in Figure 11-3, different types of customers from different business units or business initiatives would interact with IT account managers to assist them in defining their IT service needs. This represents a customercentric approach to IT services. Conversely, a systemcentric approach requires the customer to interact individually with all of the managers of the various components of the IT infrastructure (e.g., network, application development, data management, systems management). The systemcentric approach requires the customer to act as a general contractor, whereas the customercentric approach offers the customer one-stop shopping for business-oriented IT services.

Customers are free to choose distinct levels of different services to meet their IT needs. The variable levels of service imply variable, direct costs associated with the chosen level of service. A given level of service requires a combination of technical expertise, defined processes, and requisite technology. The IT infrastructure represents a fixed or indirect cost to the services purchased by the customer. An allocation formula, sometimes called a cost generator, must be calculated to determine how much of the fixed IT infrastructure costs should be passed to the service level cost.

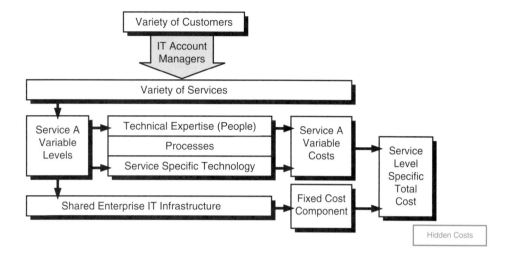

*Figure 11-3*    Service Costing Model

Hidden costs are those costs that must still be covered by organizations other than IT. Informal support of systems and applications by end-user departments or business units is a commonly cited source of hidden costs.

## IT INFRASTRUCTURE MANAGEMENT

Whereas service management provides the methodology to measure business performance expectations, the achievement of these expectations depends on properly managed components of the IT infrastructure. An IT infrastructure is made of a combination of separately managed and monitored elements. This presents a challenge as these different management tools often do not interoperate or share data. As a result, multiple different categories of management and monitoring tools are required to ensure end-to-end performance of the overall IT infrastructure. Figure 11-4 illustrates some of the different categories of IT infrastructure management that are explained further in the remainder of the chapter.

## APPLICATION AND DATABASE MANAGEMENT

### Distributed Application Management

Although distributed applications can be developed for local area networks that possess the power equivalent to those deployed on mainframes, distributed applications have not yet matched mainframe applications in terms of reliability and manageability. This is primarily due to a lack of effective application management tools and underlying application management protocols that can expose an application's dependencies and measure numerous aspects of performance. This lack of application management tools can make it impossible to diagnose and correct application problems ranging from poor performance to system crashes.

Fortunately, an effort is underway to build self-diagnosing intelligence into applications during the development stage. By having these predefined events and

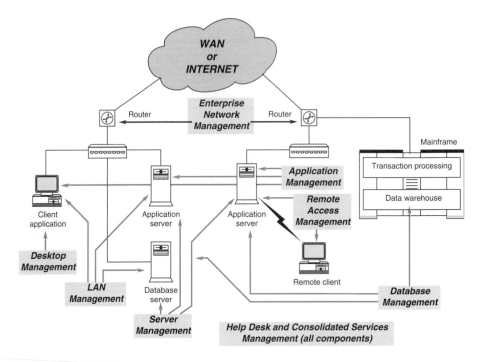

*Figure 11-4*   Elements of IT Infrastructure That Must Be Managed

**performance metrics** included within the application, management consoles will be able to detect problems with application performance and take corrective action. These embedded performance metrics are sometimes referred to as **instrumentation.** Two such development environments are Unify VISION and Sun One Studio. In between the intelligent application, reporting on event conditions and performance metrics, and the management console is an autonomous piece of software known as an **agent** that collects these performance statistics and properly formats them for transmission to the application management console. In turn, these agents are able to communicate with a variety of application management consoles or any SNMP-based administrative program. Examples of agents include AgentWorks from Computer Associates and AppMan from Unify. Eventually, it is hoped that such application management information can be consolidated into enterprise management frameworks such as CA-Unicenter and Tivoli Management Environment.

Application monitoring tools such as Application Expert from OPNET provide real-time statistics on application behavior and network impact as well as the ability to perform "what-if" simulation analysis on captured applications. The two primary network-related variables that can affect distributed application performance are bandwidth and **latency.** It should be obvious at this point in the text how network bandwidth can have a significant impact on application performance. The effect of latency on applications performance, however, is not as widely understood. Latency is simply the delay introduced by any computer or processing node that takes part in the execution of a distributed application. Downloading the client portion of an application from a server, processing SQL queries, or server-to-server queries all introduce latency to an application. The part of application optimization that is surprising to some people is that more bandwidth is not always the answer. If an application is constrained by latency, introducing more bandwidth will have little or no impact on application performance. Application monitoring and simulation tools are extremely valuable in their ability to pinpoint bandwidth and latency constraints before distributed applications are deployed throughout a global enterprise.

An alternative to developing your own applications with embedded management intelligence is to purchase a prewritten **event management tool** that has been written to monitor specific commercially available applications such as Lotus Notes, SAP R2/R3, Oracle Financials, or a variety of databases including IBM DB2, Oracle, Informix, and Sybase. An event can be thought of as a transaction or database update. PATROL from BMC Software, Inc. is an example of such an event management tool.

One of the key stumbling blocks to widespread deployment and support of distributed application management is the lack of a standard of what application performance information should be gathered and how that information should be reported. One proposal for standardizing how instrumentation should be developed within applications is known as the **applications management specification (AMS).** AMS defines a set of management objects that define distribution, dependencies, relationships, monitoring and management criteria, and performance metrics that can subsequently be processed by agents and forwarded to management consoles. These AMS agents are placed into applications through the use of the ARM software developers kit. An API that can be used by applications developers is known as **application response measurement (ARM)** and can measure several key application statistics. Agents are able to forward application performance statistics to ARM-compatible application management consoles. ARM 2.0 added the capability to track applications to multiple servers, to track business-specific transaction information, and to more effectively explain application performance problems. Vendors such as Hewlett Packard, Tivoli, Oracle, and Compuware have committed to supporting the ARM specification. Figure 11-5 illustrates some of the key concepts involved in a distributed application management architecture.

Another possible standard for distributed application management is a proposed IETF standard known as **Web-based enterprise management (WBEM),** which integrates SNMP, HTTP, and DMI (desktop management interface) into an application management architecture that can use common Web browser software as its user interface. Another IETF initiative is developing a two-part applications MIB, the first part of which is known as the SysAppl MIB dealing with collection of applications performance data without the use of instrumentation, and the second part of which

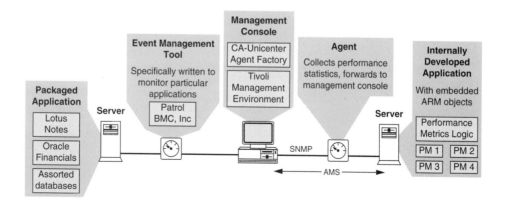

*Figure 11-5*   Distributed Application Management Architecture

deals with the collection of performance data that requires instrumentation (performance metrics). The RMON Application MIB is explained in more detail later in this chapter. As can be seen from the previous paragraph, when it comes to application management, the standards arena is anything but decided.

### Enterprise Database Management

Distributed database management is also important to overall enterprise information system management. Although most distributed data management platforms provide their own management system for reporting performance statistics, there is currently no way to consolidate these separate management systems into a single enterprise-wide view. As a result of corporate mergers and the need to consolidate once isolated departmental databases, it is a very common phenomenon for a corporation to have data stored in a wide variety of incompatible database systems. The IETF has been working on a **database MIB** specification that would allow any enterprise data management system to report performance statistics back to any SNMP-compliant enterprise network management system.

Enterprise database management tools that are able to manage a variety of different databases should include the following important major functional areas:

- Global user administration: User and group authorization and security management across a variety of different databases are important characteristics for an enterprise-wide database management system.

- Heterogeneous data schema and content manipulation: In other words, from one console, an administrator can change the database record layout or the contents of those records, regardless of the particular database management system. In some cases, these changes can be automated across an entire enterprise's databases, scheduled to be run at a later time, or saved for future reuse. Such systems should be able to add columns to or otherwise modify database tables automatically across a variety of different databases. In some cases, databases may need to be replicated from one platform to another or one databases schema, or a portion thereof, may need to be copied to a different database platform.

- Effective troubleshooting: Enterprise database management systems must be able to monitor a variety of different databases for such critical events as inadequate free space, runaway processes, high CPU utilization, or low swap space. Events and alarms should be able to trigger e-mail, pagers, or on-screen events. In some cases, the enterprise database management system can take corrective action as defined by user-supplied script files.

- Among the databases such an enterprise database management system should support are Oracle, Informix, SQL Server, adaptive server, and DB2.

### ■ CLIENT AND DESKTOP MANAGEMENT

### Desktop Management

Desktop management is primarily concerned with the configuration and support of desktop workstations or client computers. In most cases, this management is more concerned with the assorted hardware and operating systems software of the desktop machines than with the applications or database software discussed in the previous section.

**Desktop Management Architecture and Protocols**    Desktop management systems rely on an architecture and associated protocols proposed by the **desktop management task force (DMTF),** which is composed of over fifty companies including Intel, Microsoft, IBM, Digital, Hewlett-Packard, Apple, Compaq, Dell, and Sun. The overall desktop management architecture is known as the **desktop management interface (DMI)** and is illustrated in Figure 11-6.

Although they differ in both strategic intent and governing standards-making organizations, desktop management and enterprise management systems must still be able to transparently interoperate. Since DMI-compliant desktop management systems store performance and configuration statistics in a **management information format (MIF),** and enterprise management systems employ a MIB, a MIF-to-MIB mapper is required to link desktop and enterprise management systems. The DMI architecture is composed of four primary components:

- **DMI services layer** is the DMI application that resides on each desktop device to be managed. The DMI services layer does the actual processing of

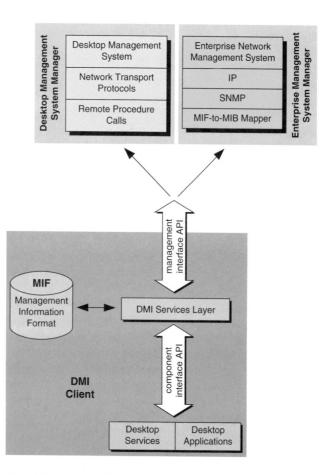

*Figure 11-6*    Desktop Management Interface Architecture

desktop management information on the client platform and serves as an interface to two APIs.

- The **management interface API** is designed to interface to the desktop system management program that will consolidate the information from this client with all other desktop information.

- The **component interface API** is designed to interface to the individual application programs or desktop components that are to be managed and monitored on the local client.

- Information about the local desktop components is stored locally in a MIF or **management information format.**

**Desktop Management Technology**   Desktop management technology offerings from different vendors are best characterized as suites of associated desktop management applications. Current offerings differ in the variety of management modules within a given suite as well as the extent of integration between suite modules. Among the modules that some, but not necessarily all, desktop management suites include are the following:

- Hardware and software inventory
- Asset management
- Software distribution
- License metering
- Server monitoring
- Virus protection
- Help desk support

Key functional characteristics of desktop management systems are listed in Figure 11-7. Many of the functional areas described briefly in Figure 11-7 are explained in further detail later in the chapter.

**Mobile Desktop Management**   Extending desktop management functionality such as software distribution, change analysis, job scheduling, asset monitoring, and backup to mobile laptop computers linked only occasionally to corporate headquarters over relatively low bandwidth network links presents some unique challenges. Mobile users have a need to receive not only updates to their application software but also corporate data such as product and pricing information. It is equally important for support personnel at corporate headquarters to know exactly what is installed on each laptop computer in terms of hardware and software technology.

XcelleNet, Inc. produces a series of remote management modules known collectively as RemoteWare that are able to manage software distribution, antivirus protection, backup, and inventory management for laptop computers. RemoteWare differs from traditional desktop management software packages in that all files transmitted between the management software and the remote laptop computers are in a compressed format. If the transmission is interrupted midstream, the transmission is able to restart where it left off, rather than having to start over from the beginning. Once received at the remote laptop computer after disconnection from the transmission line, the installation application is executed locally on the laptop. Backup management software saves time and bandwidth by only transmitting changes to files rather than the entire file in a process known as delta file synchronization.

In terms of standardized protocols for mobile desktop management, the desktop management task force has created a **mobile MIF** as an extension to the desktop management interface (DMI) 2.0. Among the types of information that management software supporting the Mobile MIF will be able to gather from compliant laptops are the following:

- Battery levels
- AC lines
- Docking status
- Infrared ports
- Video display types
- Pointing devices
- Device bays

## Configuration Management

**Single Sign-On**  Providing single sign-on services for distributed applications deployed across multiple servers is a benefit to users as well as systems administrators. By establishing a distributed security directory housed on a central security server, single sign-on software is able to provide a single login location for multiple, different types of computing platforms. This precludes users from having to remember multiple passwords and allows systems administrators to maintain user accounts and privileges for an entire enterprise from a single location. Single sign-on software is ideally deployed as part of the consolidated service desk.

Among the single-sign-on technology available are the following:

| Single Sign On Technology | Vendors |
|---|---|
| V-GO-PRO | Passlogix |
| VPN–1 | Checkpoint Software |
| SafeWord Plus | Secure Computing |

**Configuration or Policy-based Management Tools**  Once hardware and software desktop configuration standards have been established and enforced, ongoing maintenance and monitoring of those standards can be ensured by configuration management tools such as electronic software distribution tools, license metering tools, and automated inventory tools. To more easily integrate configuration management tools with corporate policy and standards regarding desktop configurations, a new breed of **policy-based management tools** has emerged. These desktop-oriented, policy-based management tools should not be confused with policy-based network management tools, discussed later in the chapter, which are designed to ensure end-to-end quality of service via bandwidth management.

| Functional Category | Importance/Implication |
|---|---|
| **Integration** | • Are all desktop management applications tied together through a single interface to a single console?<br>• Do all desktop management applications share information with each other via a single database?<br>• Can software modules be added individually as needed? Suites may be either modular or tightly integrated in design.<br>• Does the system support the DMI architecture? Output data in MIF format? |
| **Network Operating System Compatibility** | • Which network operating system must the desktop management console or server run over?<br>• Which network operating systems is the desktop management system able to monitor? Some desktop management systems can monitor only a single NOS. For example, Novell ManageWise is able to monitor only NetWare networks and Microsoft's System Management Server is able to manage only Microsoft networks, although this may not always be the case. |
| **Desktop Compatibility** | • Since the primary objective of this software category is to manage desktops, it is essential that as many desktop platforms as possible are supported.<br>• Examples of supported client platforms include Macintosh, Windows 95/98, Windows NT, Windows 2000, or Windows XP. |
| **Hardware and Software Inventory (Asset Management)** | • Can the inventory software auto-detect client hardware and software?<br>• Can changes in files or configuration be tracked?<br>• Can versions of software be detected and tracked?<br>• How many applications can be identified? Libraries of 6,000 are not uncommon.<br>• Can CPU types and speeds be correctly identified?<br>• Is a query utility included to identify workstations with given characteristics? |
| **Server Monitoring** | • Does the software support the setting of threshold limits for CPU activity, remaining disk space, etc.?<br>• What server attributes can be tracked? CPU activity, memory usage, free disk space, number of concurrent logins or sessions. |
| **Network Monitoring** | • Can data-link layer traffic be monitored and reported on?<br>• Can network layer protocol traffic activity be monitored and reported on?<br>• Can MAC layer addresses be sensed and monitored?<br>• Can activity thresholds be established for particular datalink or network layer protocols? |

*Figure 11-7*  Functional Categories of Desktop Management Systems (*Continues*)

| Functional Category | Importance/Implication |
|---|---|
| **Software Distribution** | • Can software be distributed to local client drives as well as network servers?<br>• Can updates be automatically installed?<br>• Can the system track which software needs to be updated through ties with the software inventory system?<br>• Can updates be uninstalled automatically?<br>• Can progress and error reports be produced during and after software distribution? |
| **License Metering** | • Where can software licenses be tracked?<br>  ○ Clients<br>  ○ Server<br>  ○ Across multiple servers<br>• Can license limit thresholds be set?<br>• Will the manager be notified before the license limit is reached?<br>• Will users be notified if license limit has been reached?<br>• Will users be put into a queue for next available license after license limit has been reached? |
| **Virus Protection** | • Can virus protection be provided for both clients and servers?<br>• Can both diskette drives and hard drives be protected?<br>• Can viruses embedded within application programs be detected? |
| **Help Desk Support** | • Are trouble ticketing and call tracking utilities included?<br>• Are query capabilities included to search for similar problems and solutions?<br>• Are reports available to spot trends and track help desk effectiveness and productivity? |
| **Alarms** | • Can managers be notified of changes to files or configuration?<br>• Can violations or preset thresholds be reported?<br>• Can alarms be sent by e-mail, pager, fax, cellular phone? |
| **Remote Control Management** | • Can managers take over remote client workstations for monitoring or troubleshooting purposes?<br>• Can this be done via modem as well as over the local LAN?<br>• Can files be transferred to/from the remote client?<br>• Can files on remote client be viewed without taking over complete control of the remote client?<br>• Can remote reboots be initiated? |
| **Reporting Capabilities** | • How many predefined reports are available?<br>• Can users define their own reports?<br>• Can information be exported to documents, spreadsheets, or databases?<br>• Which export file formats are supported? |

*Figure 11-7*   Functional Categories of Desktop Management Systems (*Continued*)

Policy-based management tools in their simplest form are able to automate certain tasks by using job scheduling utilities to schedule background and after-hours jobs. Another key point about these tools is that they are able to administer multiple different types of client platforms such as Windows 2000, Windows XP, Windows NT, HP-UX, AIX, and Solaris, to name but a few. More advanced tools not only automate administrative tasks, but also provide an interface for managing the corporate desktop configuration policies themselves. Administrators are able to set policies for an entire global enterprise, for specified domains, or for individual workstations. For example, some policy-based management software can store policies in a knowledge base that arranges the policies in a hierarchical fashion to identify policy conflicts. However, once again, mere throwing technology at a problem will not provide an adequate solution. First, internal policies must be developed within the corporate environment before they can be entered into the policy-based management system. This policy development may involve a tremendous amount of work before the software can ever be implemented. Examples of the types of policies that might be enforced by policy-based management tools are the following:

- User access rights to files, directories, servers, and executables.
- Desktop start-up applications and background colors, or corporate-approved screen savers.
- Deny user access to network if desktop virus checking or metering has been disabled.
- Facilitate changes when applications move or devices are added to the network.
- Prevent users from trying to install and run programs their desktops can't support.

## Help Desks

As processing power has moved from the centralized mainframe room to the user's desktop, the support organization required to facilitate that processing power has undergone significant changes. When mission-critical business applications are shifted to distributed architectures, effective help desk operations must be in place and ready to go.

Although some help desk management technology is aimed at setting up small help desks on a single PC or workstation to provide simple trouble ticketing and tracking, the higher end of help desk technology supports such additional processes as:

- Asset management
- Change management
- Integration with event management systems
- Support of business-specific processes and procedures

The basic objective of this higher end technology is to proactively manage system and network resources to prevent problems rather than merely reacting to system or network problems.

Because the help desk is held accountable for its level of service to end-users, it is essential that help desk management technology be able to gather the statistics necessary to measure the impact of its efforts. Since a significant amount of the interaction with a help desk is via the phone, it is important for help desk management software to be able to interact with call center management technology such as **automatic call distributors (ACD)** and **interactive voice response units (IVRU)**. The overall integration of computer-based software and telephony equipment in known as **computer telephony integration (CTI)**.

The heart of any help desk management software package is the **knowledge base** that contains not just the resolutions or answers to problems, but the logic structure or decision tree that takes a given problem and leads the help desk staff person through a series of questions to the appropriate solution. Interestingly, the knowledge bases supplied with help desk management software may be supplied by third parties under license to the help desk management software vendor. Obviously, the knowledge base is added to by help desk personnel with corporate-specific problems and solutions, but the amount of information supplied initially by a given knowledge base can vary. The portion of the software that sifts through the knowledge base to the proper answer is sometimes referred to as the **search engine**.

Figure 11-8 summarizes some of the other key functional areas for help desk management software.

## Asset Management

Asset management is a broad category of management software that has traditionally been divided into three subcategories:

- Electronic software distribution
- License metering software
- LAN inventory management software

**Electronic Software Distribution**   As the distributed architecture has taken hold as the dominant information systems paradigm, the increased processing power possessed by client workstations had been matched by increasing amounts of sophisticated software installed on these client workstations. The distribution of client software to multiple locally and remotely attached client workstations could be a very personnel-intensive and expensive task were it not for a new category of LAN-enabled software known as **electronic software distribution** or **ESD**. ESD software can vary widely in the types of services and features offered as well as the costs for the convenience offered. For example, in addition to simply delivering software to LAN-attached clients, ESD software may also:

- Update configuration files
- Edit other files
- Capture commands entered during a manual software installation and convert the captured text into an automated script to control subsequent electronic software distribution

Figure 11-9 summarizes some of the key functional characteristics of ESD software.

| Help Desk Management Software Functionality | Explanation/Importance |
|---|---|
| **Administration, Security and Utilities** | • What types of adds, deletes, and changes can be made with the system up and running and what types require a system shutdown?<br>• Must all help desk personnel be logged out of the system to perform administrative functions?<br>• Can major changes be done on a separate version off-line, followed by a brief system restart with the new version?<br>• Can changes be tested in an off-line environment before committing to live installation?<br>• Is security primarily group level or individual? Can agents belong to more than one group?<br>• Can priorities and response times be flexibly assigned?<br>• Can information be imported and exported in a variety of formats? |
| **Call Logging** | • How easy is it to log calls?<br>• Can call logging link to existing databases to minimize amount of data that must be entered?<br>• Can number of steps and keystrokes required to add a user or log a call be controlled?<br>• Can multiple calls be logged at once?<br>• Can one call be suspended (put on hold) while another one is logged?<br>• Can special customers or users be flagged as such? |
| **Call Tracking and Escalation** | • How flexible are the call escalation options?<br>• Are escalation options able to support internally defined problem resolution and escalation policies and processes?<br>• Can the system support both manual and automatic escalation?<br>• Can automatic escalation paths, priorities, and criteria be flexibly defined?<br>• Can calls be timed as part of service level reporting?<br>• How flexibly can calls be assigned to individual or groups of agents?<br>• Is escalation system tied to work schedule system?<br>• Can subject area or problem experts be identified and used as part of the escalation process? |
| **Customizability** | • Customizability is an issue at both the database level and the screen design level<br>• How easy is it to add knowledge and new problems/solutions to the knowledge base?<br>• Does the software offer customizability for multinational companies?<br>• Can entire new screens or views be designed?<br>• Do existing screens contain undefined fields? |

*Figure 11-8*    Help Desk Management Software (*Continues*)

| Help Desk Management Software Functionality | Explanation/Importance |
|---|---|
| **Integration with Other Products** | • Computer telephony integration with automatic call distributors and interactive voice response units<br>• Which other integrated modules are included: asset management, change management, scheduling, training, workstation auditing?<br>• Does the software link to enterprise network management software such as HP Open View or IBM System View? |
| **Performance** | • Variables to consider when evaluating performance: number of simultaneous users on-line, number of calls per hour, required platform for database/knowledge base and search engine, required platform for agents.<br>• Which SQL-compliant databases are supported?<br>• Can searches be limited to improve performance? |
| **Problem Resolution** | • Products can differ significantly in how they search knowledge bases. This can have a major impact on performance. Decision trees, case-based retrieval, troubleshooting tools and embedded expert systems or artificial intelligence are the most intelligent, most complicated, and most expensive options for problem resolution methodologies.<br>• Many products provide more than one search engine or problem resolution method.<br>• Some problem resolution products learn about your environment as more problems are entered.<br>• Some problem resolution methods can use numerous different knowledge sources or problem databases. |
| **Reporting** | • How many standard reports are included?<br>• How easily can customized reports be created?<br>• How easily can data (especially agent performance data) be exported to spreadsheet or database programs for further analysis? |

*Figure 11-8*   Help Desk Management Software (*Continued*)

License Metering Software   Although **license metering software** was originally intended to monitor the number of executing copies of a particular software package vs. the number of licenses purchased for that package, an interesting and beneficial side effect of license metering software has occurred. In recognition of this beneficial side effect, this category of software is now sometimes referred to as **license management software.** The previously mentioned beneficial side effect stems from the realization that at any one point in time, less than 100% of the workstations possessing legitimate licenses for a given software product are actually executing that software product.

As a result, with the aid of license management software, fewer licenses can service an equal or greater number of users, thereby reducing the numbers of software licenses purchased and the associated cost of software ownership. License management software is able to dynamically allocate licenses to those users wishing to execute

| ESD Software Functional Category | Description/Implication |
|---|---|
| **NOS Support** | • Since ESD software distributes software via the LAN, it is important to know which network operating systems are supported. |
| **Update Control** | • Can updates be scheduled?<br>• Can updates be selectively done based on hardware configuration?<br>• Can updates be done only on selected machines?<br>• Can only certain files be searched for and replaced?<br>• Can files be edited or updated?<br>• Can files in use be replaced?<br>• Can files be moved and renamed?<br>• Can the update be done in the background on client workstations?<br>• How secure is the update control?<br>• Can updates be scripted?<br>• Can update keystrokes be captured and converted to an automated update control file?<br>• Can users perform their own selected updates from a distribution server?<br>• Are unattended updates possible?<br>• Are in-progress status screens available?<br>• Can outside distribution lists be imported?<br>• Can remote workstations be shut down and rebooted?<br>• How extensive are the update reporting and logging capabilities? |
| **Interoperability** | • Is the ESD software integrated with license metering or LAN hardware/software inventory software?<br>• Are other software packages required in order to execute the ESD software? |
| **Licensing** | • Are licensing fees based on numbers of clients or numbers of distribution servers? |

*Figure 11-9*   Electronic Software Distribution Functionality

a particular software package in a process known as **license optimization.** Popular license optimization techniques include:

- **Dynamic allocation** gives out either single user or suite licenses based on the number of suite applications used. As an example, a user who starts a word processing package within an application suite would be issued a single user license for the word processing package. However, if the user were to subsequently also execute a spreadsheet package within the same suite, he/she would be issued a suite license rather than a second single user license.

- **Load balancing** shifts licenses between servers to meet demands for licenses put on those servers by locally attached users. Licenses are loaned between servers on an as-needed basis. In this way, every server does not need to have a full complement of licenses to meet all anticipated user demands. This technique is also known as **license pooling.**

- **Global license sharing** recognizes the opportunity for license sharing presented by the widely distributed nature of today's global enterprise networks.

While users on one side of the globe are sleeping, users on the other side of the globe are sharing the same pool of licenses.

License metering and management software has traditionally been supplied as add-on products written by third-party software developers. However, this trend may change abruptly. Novell and Microsoft have cooperated (an unusual circumstance in itself) on a **licensing server API (LSAPI).** This API would build license metering capability into Microsoft and Novell's network operating systems and would eliminate the need for third-party license metering software.

LSAPI-compliant applications would communicate with a specialized **license server** that would issue **access tokens,** more formally known as **digital license certificates,** based on the license information stored in the license server database. Applications wishing to take advantage of the NOS-based license metering service would need only to include the proper commands as specified in the LSAPI.

LAN Inventory Management Software    **LAN Inventory Management Software** is often included or integrated with electronic software distribution or license metering software. However, it has a unique and important mission of its own in a widely distributed architecture in which hardware and software assets are located throughout an enterprise network. A quality LAN inventory management software system is especially important when it comes to the planning efforts for network hardware and software upgrades. An enormous amount of human energy, and associated expense, can be wasted going from workstation to workstation figuring out what the hardware and software characteristics of each workstation are when LAN inventory management software can do the job automatically and can report gathered data in useful and flexible formats. Figure 11-10 highlights some of the key functional capabilities of LAN Inventory Management software.

## ■ DISTRIBUTED IT INFRASTRUCTURE ARCHITECTURE

Having covered the issues involved in the management of client workstations whether mobile or desktop oriented, it is now time to look at what is involved with the management of the remainder of the distributed IT infrastructure. To delineate the processes and technology involved with the management of the infrastructure that underlies an enterprise-wide local area network, one must first define those components that make up the infrastructure to be managed. Traditionally, a distributed IT infrastructure is composed of a wide variety of servers and the various networks that connect those servers to each other and to the clients that they serve. There is no single right or wrong way to divide the processes or responsibility for the management of these various components. For the purposes of this chapter, the topic of distributed IT infrastructure management is segmented into the following components:

- **Systems administration** focuses on the management of client and server computers and the operating systems and network operating systems that allow the client and server computers to communicate. This could also be considered as local area network administration.

- **Enterprise network management** focuses on the hardware, software, media, and network services required to seamlessly link and effectively manage distributed client and server computers across an enterprise. This could also be considered internetwork (between LANs) administration.

| LAN Inventory Management Functional Category | Description/Functionality |
|---|---|
| Platforms | • Client platforms supported<br>• Server platforms supported |
| Data Collection | • Scheduling: How flexibly can inventory scans be scheduled?<br>• Can inventory scans of client workstations be completed incrementally during successive logins?<br>• Does the inventory software flag unknown software which it finds on client workstations?<br>• How large a catalog of known software titles does the inventory software have? 6,000 titles is among the best.<br>• Can software titles be added to the known software list?<br>• Are fields for data collection user-definable?<br>• Can the inventory management software audit servers as well as client workstations?<br>• Are hardware and software inventory information stored in the same database?<br>• What is the database format?<br>• Can the inventory management software differentiate between and track the assets of multiple laptop computers that share a single docking bay? |
| Reporting | • How many predefined reports are available?<br>• Are customized reports available?<br>• How easy is it to produce a customized report?<br>• Can reports be exported in numerous formats such as popular word processing, spreadsheet, and presentation graphics formats? |
| Query | • How user-friendly and powerful are the query tools?<br>• Can queries be generated on unique hardware and software combinations?<br>• Can inventory information be gathered and displayed on demand? |

*Figure 11-10* LAN Inventory Management Software Functionality

Both systems administration and enterprise network management are comprised of several subprocesses as illustrated in Figure 11-11.

As local area networks, internetworks, and wide area networks have combined to form enterprise networks, the management of all of these elements of the enterprise has been a key concern. LANs, internetworks, and WANs have traditionally each had their own set of management tools and protocols. Once integrated into a single enterprise, these disparate tools and protocols do not necessarily meld together into an integrated cohesive system.

Figure 11-12 summarizes the key functional differences between enterprise network management and systems administration and lists some representative technologies of each category as well.

### Consolidated Service Desk

Although the division of distributed IT infrastructure management processes into systems administration and enterprise network management is helpful in terms of distinguishing between associated function, protocols, and technology, how are these various processes actually supported or implemented in an enterprise? Reflective of the evolution of information systems in general, distributed IT infrastructure management has undergone an evolution of its own. The current trend in distributed IT infrastructure

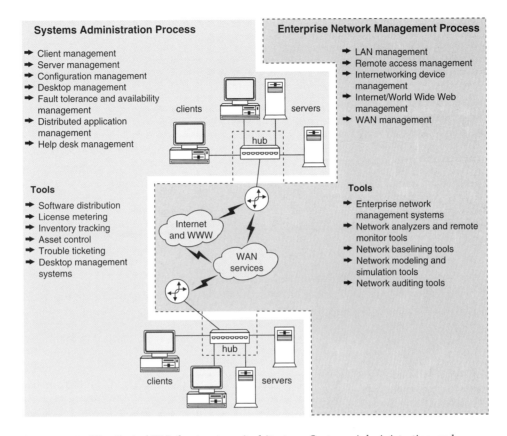

*Figure 11-11*    Distributed IT Infrastructure Architecture: Systems Administration and Enterprise Network Management

|  | Functionality | Technology |
|---|---|---|
| **Enterprise Network Management** | • Monitor and manage internetwork technology: switches, routers, hubs<br>• Monitor and manage WAN links | • HP Openview<br>• Tivoli TME/IBM<br>• Sun Solstice Enterprise Manager<br>• CA Unicenter |
| **Systems Administration Also Known As Desktop Management** | • Track hardware and and software inventory<br>• Perform license metering<br>• Monitor LAN and server activity<br>• Software distribution<br>• Asset management<br>• Server monitoring | • LANDesk Suite—Intel<br>• Norton Administrator for Networks—Symantec<br>• Utilities for Desktops—Seagate<br>• System Management Server—Microsoft<br>• Manage Wise—Novell |

*Figure 11-12*    Systems Administration vs. Enterprise Network Management

management is to offer a **consolidated service desk** (CSD) approach to end-user and infrastructure support. Such an approach offers a number of benefits:

- As a single point of contact for all network and application problem resolution, appropriate personnel processes can be matched with associated network management technologies. This match of standardized processes with technology yields more predictable service levels and accountability. CSD software should include features to support problem escalation, trouble ticketing and tracking, and productivity management reporting. Users should be able to easily check on the status of the resolution of reported problems.

- The consolidation of all problem data at a single location allows correlation between problem reports to be made, thereby enabling a more proactive rather than reactive management style. Incorporated remote control software will allow CSD personnel to take over end-user computers and fix problems remotely in a swift manner.

- Resolutions to known user inquiries can be incorporated into intelligent help desk support systems to expedite problem resolution and make the most effective use of support personnel. On-line knowledge bases allow users to solve their own problems in many cases.

- The consolidated services desk can also handle other processes not directly related to problem resolution such as inventory and asset tracking and asset optimization through the use of such technology as license metering software. It can also coordinate hardware and/or software upgrades. Software upgrades could be centrally handled by electronic software distribution technology. The management of these systems changes is referred to as change management.

- Network security policies, procedures, and technology can also be consolidated at the CSD.

- The consolidated services desk eliminates or reduces "console clutter" in which every monitored system has its own console. In large multinational corporations, this can lead to well over 100 consoles. Recalling that all of these consoles must be monitored by people, console consolidation can obviously lead to cost containment.

Figure 11-13 illustrates how policy, procedures, personnel, and technology all merge at the consolidated service desk. It is important to note the inclusion of policy and procedures in the illustration. The formation of a CSD provides a marvelous opportunity to define or redesign processes to meet specific business and management objectives. Any technology incorporated in the CSD should be chosen based on its ability to support the previously defined corporate policies and procedures in its area of influence. It is important not to first choose a CSD tool and let that tool dictate the corporate processes and procedures in that particular area of management.

## ■ SERVER MANAGEMENT AND SYSTEMS ADMINISTRATION

### Server Management

At the heart of systems administration is the administration of the servers that are the workhorses and providers of basic system functionality. As servers are continuing to

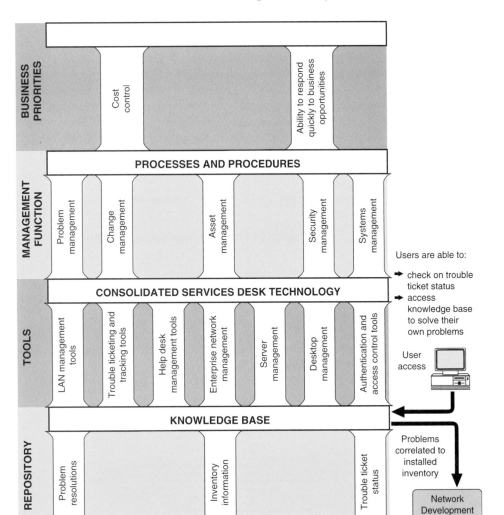

*Figure 11-13*  Consolidated Service Desk

take on increasingly important roles for the entire enterprise such as electronic messaging servers and enterprise directory servers, it is becoming more important to be able to effectively manage, troubleshoot, and remotely configure these critical elements of the enterprise infrastructure. Server management software seeks to ease systems administrators' chores by effectively monitoring, reporting, troubleshooting, and diagnosing server performance. Some server management software is particular to a certain brand of server, whereas other server management software is able to manage multiple different brands of servers. Ultimately, to be especially useful in meeting overall goals of systems reliability and end-user satisfaction, server management software must provide **server capacity planning** capabilities by monitoring server performance trends and making recommendations for server component upgrades in a proactive manner.

An important point to remember about server management software is that it most often requires a software and/or hardware module to be installed on all servers to be monitored and managed. This module will require varying amounts of system resources (CPU cycles, memory) and will have varying degrees of impact on system performance. Some server management systems perform most of the processing on the managed servers, but others perform most of the processing on the server management console or workstation. Likewise, some server management systems require a dedicated management workstation, but others will operate on a multi-function management workstation. Figure 11-14 summarizes some of the key potential functional areas of server management software; Figure 11-15 illustrates the implemented architecture of a server management system.

## ENTERPRISE NETWORK MANAGEMENT

### Quality of Service, Traffic Shaping, and Bandwidth Management

Enterprise network management is no longer limited to ensuring that a network is available and reliable. To provide service management guarantees, networks must be able to ensure that individual applications are delivered according to agreed upon service levels. To achieve this, applications must be able to be uniquely identified, and networks must be able to respond to application needs on an individual basis. Providing end-to-end delivery service guarantees is referred to as **quality of service (QoS).**

**Bandwidth management,** often used interchangeably with the term **traffic shaping,** can be defined as the appropriate allocation of bandwidth to support application requirements. Although a wide variety of terms may be used to describe different bandwidth management techniques, nearly all of these techniques and their associated technologies use either **rate control** or **queuing** or a combination of the two. Traffic shaping can provide bandwidth-constrained or time sensitive applications the bandwidth necessary to potentially improve application performance. Traffic shaping devices will not improve the performance of latency-constrained applications. Figure 11-16 compares and contrasts the key characteristics of rate control and queuing while Figure 11-17 introduces several other bandwidth management protocols.

Standards activity would indicate that bandwidth management will be incorporated as a part of an overall **policy-based network management** system. Such policy-based network management systems exist now, although they are largely limited to single-vendor solutions such as CiscoAssure. The vision of policy based networking is the delivery of an integrated, rules-based implementation of traffic prioritization providing end-to-end quality of service and security. Among the required standards being developed are COPS, Dynamic DNS/DHCP, Directory Services Integration, LDAP, and DEN.

### Enterprise Network Management Architecture and Protocols

As illustrated in Figure 11-18, today's enterprise network management architectures are composed of a relatively few elements.

**Agents** are software programs that run on networking devices such as servers, bridges, and routers to monitor and report the status of those devices. Agent software must be compatible with the device that it is reporting management statistics

| Server Management System Function | Importance/Explanation |
|---|---|
| **Diagnose Server Hardware Problems** | • Can alarm thresholds and status be flexibly defined?<br>• How many alarm levels are possible?<br>• Can RAID drive arrays be monitored and diagnosed?<br>• Is predictive hardware failure analysis offered?<br>• Is a diagnostic hardware module required?<br>• Can server temperature and voltage be monitored?<br>• Can bus configuration and utilization be reported? |
| **Diagnose Server Software Problems** | • Does the server management software track version control and correlate with currently available versions?<br>• Can version control indicate potential impacts of version upgrades?<br>• What diagnostics or routines are supplied to diagnose server software problems? |
| **Server Capacity Planning and Performance Enhancement** | • Are performance enhancement and capacity planning capabilities included?<br>• Trend identification routines included?<br>• Are inventory, asset management, and optimization modules included? |
| **Share Data with Other Management Platforms** | • Can data be passed to frameworks and integrated suites such as HP Open View or Tivoli TME?<br>• Can alerts and alarms trigger pagers, e-mail, dial-up?<br>• Can data be exported to ODBC-compliant database? |
| **Remote Configuration Capability** | • Can servers be remotely configured from a single console?<br>• Is out-of-band (dial-up) management supported?<br>• Is remote power cycling supported?<br>• Is screen redirection/remote console control supported? |
| **Report Generation** | • Are alert logs automatically generated?<br>• Can reports be flexibly and easily defined by users? |
| **Protocol Issues** | • Is TCP/IP required for the transport protocol?<br>• Is IPX supported?<br>• Is SNMP the management protocol?<br>• Are any proprietary protocols required? |
| **Server Platforms Managed** | • Possibilities include Windows NT, NetWare, Unix, Linux, Windows 2000, Windows XP. |
| **Console Requirements** | • Is a Web browser interface supported?<br>• Is a dedicated workstation required for the console?<br>• What are the operating system requirements for a console?<br>• Hardware requirements for console? |
| **Statistics Tracked and Reported** | • Logged in users<br>• Applications running<br>• CPU utilization<br>• I/O bus utilization<br>• Memory utilization<br>• Network interface card(s) utilization<br>• Disk(s) performance and utilization<br>• Security management<br>• System usage by application, user |
| **Mapping Capabilities** | • Can the administrator map or group servers flexibly?<br>• Can statistics be viewed across multiple server groups defined by a variety of characteristics?<br>• How effective is the server topology map?<br>• Can screen displays be easily printed? |

*Figure 11-14* Server Management Software Functionality

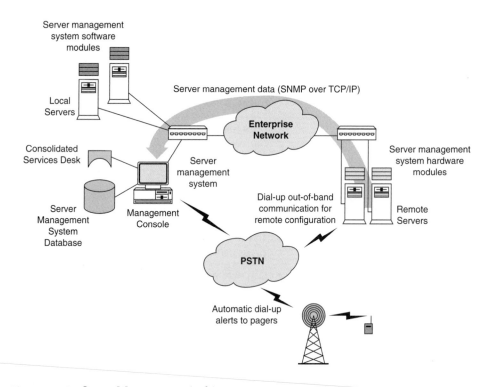

*Figure 11-15*   Server Management Architecture

for as well as with the protocols supported by the enterprise network management system to which those statistics are fed. Agents from the numerous individual networking devices forward this network management information to **enterprise network management systems** that compile and report network operation statistics to the end user, most often in some type of graphical format. Enterprise network management systems are really management application programs running on a management server.

The network management information gathered must be stored in some type of database with an index and standardized field definitions so that network management workstations can easily access these data. A **management information base,** or **MIB** as these databases are known, can differ in the fields defined for different vendor's networking devices. These fields within the MIBs are known as **objects.** One fairly standard MIB is known as the **RMON MIB,** which stands for remote network monitoring MIB. Finally, a protocol is required to encapsulate the management data for delivery by network and transport layer protocols. Partly due to the dominance of TCP/IP as the internetworking protocol of choice, **simple network management protocol (SNMP)** is the de facto standard for delivering enterprise management data.

As originally conceived, the enterprise management console would collect the performance data from all of the devices, or elements, comprising an enterprise network in a single, centralized location. However, as networks grew in both complexity and size, and the numbers of devices to be managed exploded, the amount of management traffic flowing over the enterprise network has begun to reach unacceptable levels. In some cases, management traffic alone can account for 30% of network bandwidth usage, thereby reporting on the problems that it is itself creating.

| | Rate Control | Queuing |
|---|---|---|
| **Otherwise known as** | **Traffic Shaping** | **Flow Control** |
| **Functionality** | • Smooths bursty TCP traffic<br>• Bidirectional including return path<br>• Improves on default behavior of TCP connections by adjusting TCP window size (standard field in TCP header)<br>• Controls flow by TCP window size adjustment<br>• Some traffic shapers can also limit bandwidth based on allocation to a Port ID, or UDP stream | • Not normally bidirectional, but can be if implemented on both routers at the choke point<br>• Algorithms assign traffic with different priorities to different queues |
| **Limitations** | • Due to its dependency on TCP window size adjustment, traffic shaping is ineffective on connectionless networks unless a company has strict service level agreements with its network services provider<br>• Relatively slow reaction to congestion can result in a series of overcorrections that may take several seconds to stabilize | • Traffic classification and queue management may have an impact on router performance<br>• Difficulty of setting admission policies to limit new flows on full links |
| **Requirements** | • Since different applications require different TCP window sizes, round-trip latency and end-to-end bandwidth must be considered<br>• This requires precise measurement of variables in real time and an associated ability to adjust TCP window sizes quickly | • Requires queuing and prioritization functionality in router and switch operating systems<br>• queuing and prioritization must be processed at each hop (router or switch) |
| **Dependencies** | • Future developments in protocols (policy servers, directory enabled networking) will likely interfere with rate control schemes | • If done in routers, depends on level of queuing functionality supported by routers |
| **Deployment Scenarios** | • Use traffic shaping to ensure that traffic flows do not exceed CIR (committed information rate) with network providers to avoid discarded frames and associated retransmissions | • Weighted fair queuing—all queues get an established amount of bandwidth, divides bandwidth across queues of traffic based on weights; prevents low priority traffic from being stranded<br>• Class based queuing—provides support for user defined classes by criteria such as protocol, IP address, access control list, input interfaces; one queue for each class. Queue can be limited by minimum bandwidth, weight, or maximum packet limit |
| **Technology** | • Packet shaper by packeteer—uses TCP for rate control, uses queues for UDP and SNA traffic; provides a hierarchical policy specification architecture in which policies are set, flows are measured for end-to-end latency, and associated with policies; necessary flow rates are predicted and TCP windows sizes are modified to release packets into smooth (shaped) traffic flows | • Xedia access point—dedicated hardware devices work at different maximum throughput levels; include integrated CSU/DSU, interface directly to T1, T3, ATM, Ethernet; popular with ISPs; implements class based queuing algorithm; defines hierarchy of traffic classes, assigns bandwidth commitments and priorities to classes |

*Figure 11-16*    Rate Control vs. Queuing Bandwidth Management Techniques

| Standard | Description/Functionality |
|----------|---------------------------|
| **Diff-Serv** | • Uses type of service field in IP header, can define up to eight priority classes and queues<br>• Must be supported in hardware (multiple queue network interface cards)<br>• Implemented in routers and switches<br>• Based on policy<br>• No per flow state and processing, scales well over large networks |
| **RSVP+** | • Extensions to resource reservation protocol (RSVP)<br>• Intended for use with Diff-Serv<br>• Enables application to identify itself to network devices for prioritization vs. other applications |
| **COPS** | • Common open policy service<br>• Query and response protocol between policy server and clients<br>• Switches and routers are policy clients<br>• Query policy as to proper prioritization of user/applications<br>• Goal is more efficient resource allocation based on business-oriented priorities and rules |
| **Diameter** | • Enables communication between network clients for authorization, authentication, and accounting<br>• Viewed as a replacement for RADIUS<br>• Driven by desire to charge for mobile computing usage |
| **MPLS** | • Multiprotocol label switching<br>• Tags added to routing tables and sent to other network devices<br>• Allows flows to be switched rather than having to route every packet with a routing table lookup<br>• Tag identifies next hop in path<br>• This explicit routing avoids potentially overburdening paths by using only shortest path algorithms |
| **RAP** | • Resource allocation protocol—under development by IETF<br>• Policy-based networking including QOS<br>• Scalable policy control model for RSVP<br>• Defines policy decision points (PDP), policy enforcement points (PEP), policy information base (PIB) for schema and architecture, and policy framework definition language (PFDL); device and vendor independent policy encoding language |
| **DEN** | • Directory enabled networking—DMTF standard; part of the common information model (CIM) specification |

*Figure 11-17*   Bandwidth Management Protocols

An alternative to the centralized enterprise management console approach known as the **distributed device manager (DDM)** has begun to emerge. DDM takes more of an end-to-end full network view of the enterprise network as opposed to the centralized enterprise management console architecture that takes more of an individual device or element focus. A DDM architecture relies on **distributed network probes** that are able to gather information from a variety of network devices

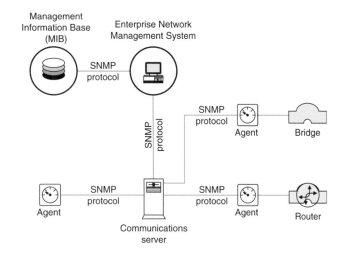

*Figure 11-18*    Enterprise Network Management Architecture

manufactured by multiple vendors and relay that information to numerous distributed device manager consoles. Probes are strategically placed throughout the enterprise network, especially at junctions of LAN and WAN segments to isolate the source of network traffic problems. Management traffic is minimized and remains localized rather than monopolizing enterprise network bandwidth supplying the centralized enterprise management console. Figure 11-19 provides a conceptual view of a distributed device manager architecture.

**Web-Based Management**    Another possible evolutionary stage in enterprise network management architectures is Web-based enterprise management, first mentioned in the section on distributed application management. The WBEM logical architecture is illustrated in Figure 11-20. The overall intention of the architecture is that the network manager could manage any networked device or application from any location on the network, via any **HMMP (hypermedia management protocol)**-compliant browser. Existing network and desktop management protocols such as SNMP and DMI may either interoperate or be replaced by HMMP. Current plans call for HMMP to communicate either via Microsoft's DCOM (distributed component object model) or by CORBA (common object request broker architecture). Management data from a variety of software agents would be incorporated into the Web-based enterprise management architecture via the **HMMS (hypermedia management schema).** All Web-based management information is stored and retrieved by the request broker formerly known as **HMOM (hypermedia object manager),** now known simply as Object Manager.

A proposed protocol currently under development by the DMTF (desktop management task force) that would support HMMS is known as **CIM** or **common information model.** CIM would permit management data gathered from a variety of enterprise and desktop voice and data technology to all be transported, processed, displayed, and stored by a single CIM-compliant Web browser. Management data to be used by CIM would be stored in **MOF (modified object format)** as opposed to DMI's MIF format or SNMP's MIB format. Figure 11-21 illustrates the interaction of the various types of management data.

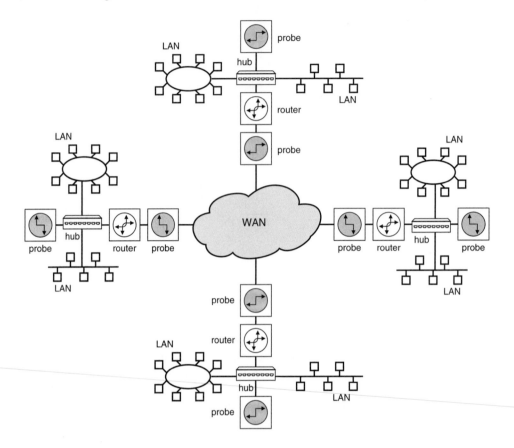

*Figure 11-19*  Distributed Device Manager Architecture

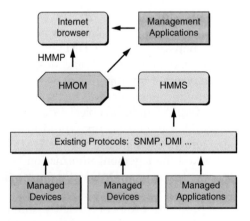

*Figure 11-20*  Web-Based Enterprise Management Logical Architecture

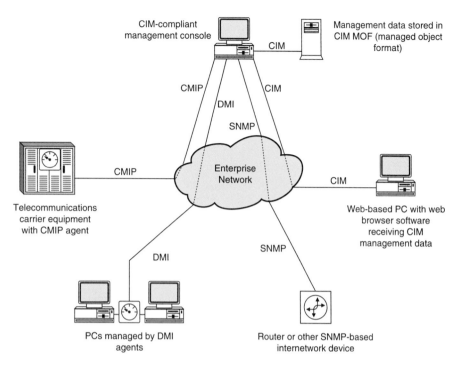

*Figure 11-21*    Management Data: CIM, CMIP, DMI, and SNMP

Managerial
Perspective

## IS CIM A SOLUTION, OR JUST ANOTHER PART OF THE PROBLEM?

Some would argue that CIM is the answer to finally being able to achieve transparency of enterprise management technology. Others would argue that CIM is nothing more than an added layer of complexity on top of an enterprise management system that is already overly complex. An alternative would be to make existing management protocols such as SNMP, DMI, and CMIP more interoperable without the need for additional layers of protocols. However, because of political issues and turf wars, achieving such interoperability is easier said than done, thereby creating opportunities for new all-encompassing protocols such as CIM.

From a practical standpoint, Web-based management could benefit both vendors and users:

- Users would have to deal with only one common interface regardless of the enterprise network device that was to be managed.

- Vendors could save a tremendous amount of development costs by only having to develop management applications for a single platform.

However, the fact that a management tool is Web-based is not enough. It must deliver all of the functionality of the proprietary management software packages written for specific devices. Some of the most important functions for such software are listed in Figure 11-22.

| Functional Category | Importance/Explanation |
|---|---|
| **Configuration** | • Ability to remotely configure network attached devices<br>• Ability to detect changes to remote device configurations |
| **Polling** | • Ability to poll network attached devices for performance and traffic statistics |
| **Analysis** | • Ability to consolidate and analyze statistics from multiple devices across the network<br>• Ability to discern initial errors from cascading errors<br>• Ability to detect trends<br>• Ability to proactively predict potential trouble spots |
| **Response** | • Ability to respond in an appropriate manner to alarms and preset thresholds<br>• Ability to detect false alarms<br>• Ability to escalate problems as appropriate<br>• Ability to notify proper personnel by a variety of means |

*Figure 11-22* Web-Based Management Tool Functionality

Web-based network management technology is relatively new, and the market is still being defined. Current technology in this category provides a Web browser interface to the user in one of two ways:

- A Web server application is embedded with the enterprise network management platform and the user accesses that embedded Web server via a Web browser. Communications between the actual network devices being managed and the enterprise network management platform is still via SNMP as illustrated in Figure 11-18.

- A Web server application is embedded within a given network device, thereby giving a user direct access to the management data of that device via any client-based Web browser. Communication between the user and the network device is via HTTP.

**Which SNMP Is the Real SNMP?**   The original SNMP protocol required internetworking device specific agents to be polled for SNMP encapsulated management data. Alarm conditions or exceptions to preset thresholds could not be directly reported on an as-needed basis from the agents to the enterprise network management software. The lack of ability of agents to initiate communications with enterprise network management systems causes constant polling of agents to transpire. As a result of the constant polling, considerable network bandwidth is consumed.

Also, the original SNMP protocol did not provide for any means of manager-to-manager communication. As a result, only one enterprise network manager could be installed on a given network, forcing all internetworked devices to report directly to the single enterprise network manager. Hierarchical arrangements in which regional managers are able to filter raw management data and pass only exceptional information to enterprise managers is not possible with the original SNMP.

Another major shortcoming of the original SNMP is that it was limited to using TCP/IP as its transport protocol. It was therefore unusable on NetWare (IPX/SPX),

Macintosh (AppleTalk), or other networks. Finally, SNMP does not offer any security features that would authenticate valid polling managers or encrypt traffic between agents and managers.

The need to reduce network traffic caused by the SNMP protocol and to deal with other aforementioned SNMP shortcomings led to a proposal for a new version of SNMP known as **SNMP2,** or **SMP (simple management protocol).**

SNMP2's major objectives can be summarized as follows:

- Reduce network traffic

- Segment large networks

- Support multiple transport protocols

- Increase security

- Allow multiple agents per device

Through a new SNMP2 procedure known as **bulk retrieval mechanism,** managers can retrieve several pieces of network information at a time from a given agent. This precludes the need for a constant request and reply mechanism for each and every piece of network management information desired. Agents have also been given increased intelligence that enables them to send error or exception conditions to managers when request for information cannot be met. With SNMP, agents simply sent empty datagrams back to managers when requests could not be fulfilled. The receipt of the empty packet merely caused the manager to repeat the request for information, thus increasing network traffic.

SNMP2 allows the establishment of multiple manager entities within a single network. As a result, large networks that were managed by a single manager under SNMP can now be managed by multiple managers in a hierarchical arrangement in SNMP2. Overall network traffic is reduced as network management information is confined to the management domains of the individual network segment managers. Information is passed from the segment managers to the centralized network management system via manager-to-manager communication only on request of the central manager or if certain predefined error conditions occur on a subnet. Figure 11-23 illustrates the impact of SNMP2 manager-to-manager communications.

SNMP was initially part of the internet suite of protocols and therefore was deployed only on those networks equipped with the TCP/IP protocols. SNMP2 works transparently with AppleTalk, IPX, and OSI transport protocols.

Increased security in SNMP2 allows not just monitoring and management of remote network devices, but actual **remote configuration** of those devices as well. Furthermore, SNMP2 allows users to access carriers' network management information and incorporate it into the wide area component of an enterprise network management system. This ability to actually access data from within the carrier's central office has powerful implications for users and enables many advanced user services such as SDN, or software defined network.

Perhaps the most significant SNMP2 development in terms of implication for distributed IT infrastructure management is the ability to deploy multiple agents per device. As a practical example, on a distributed server, one agent could monitor the processing activity, a second agent could monitor the database activity, and a third could monitor the networking activity, with each reporting back to its own manager. In this way, rather than having merely distributed enterprise network management, the entire distributed information system could be managed, with

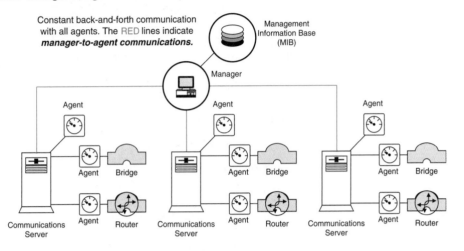

**Before:  Manager-to-Agent Communications**

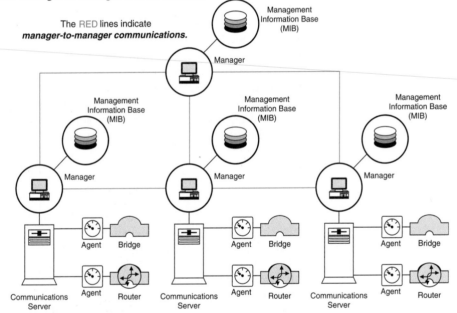

**After:  Manager-to-Manager Communications**

*Figure 11-23*   SNMP2 Supports Manager-to-Manager Communications

each major element of the client-server architecture managed by its own management infrastructure.

Unfortunately, considerable debate over portions of the SNMP2 protocol has delayed its deployment for years. Some people believe that features of SNMP2, especially the security aspects, are too difficult to implement and use, whereas others blame the delay on concerns over marketing position and competitive advantage from technology vendors. In the interim, alternative upgrades to SNMP have been proposed by both officially sanctioned organizations such as the IETF and ad hoc forums.

**MIBs**    Management information bases serve as repositories for enterprise network performance information to be displayed in meaningful format by enterprise network management systems. The original RMON MIB standard that was developed in 1991 has been updated as **RMON2.** Whereas the original RMON MIB only required compatible technology to be able to collect and analyze statistics on the physical and data-link layers, RMON2 requires collection and analysis of network layer protocols as well. In addition, RMON2 requires compatible technology to be able to identify from which applications a given packet was generated. RMON2-compatible agent software that resides within internetworking devices and reports performance statistics to enterprise network management systems is referred to as an **RMON probe.** Overall, RMON2 should enable network analysts to more effectively pinpoint the exact sources and percentages of the traffic that flows through their enterprise networks. Figure 11-24 summarizes some of the key functional areas of the RMON 2 specification.

To implement RMON2-based monitoring, a network manager would purchase RMON2 probes and associated RMON2 management software.

Besides differing in the number of RMON2 options and groups implemented, probes and RMON2 management software also differ significantly in their ability to integrate transparently with enterprise network management systems such as HP Openview, IBM/Tivoli TME 10, and CA Unicenter.

One shortcoming of RMON2 is its inability to collect and provide data regarding wide area network (WAN) performance. **RMON3** is expected to provide much needed standards for the WAN monitoring and management technology category.

| RMON2 Function | Explanation/Importance |
|---|---|
| Protocol Distribution | • Tracks and reports data-link layer protocols by percentage<br>• Tracks and reports network layer protocols by percentage<br>• Tracks and reports application source by percentage |
| Address Mapping | • Maps network layer addresses to MAC layer addresses<br>• Maps MAC layer addresses to hub or switch port |
| Network Layer Host Table | • Tracks and stores in table format network layer protocols and associated traffic statistics according to source host |
| Network Layer Matrix Table | • Tracks and stores in a matrix table format network layer protocols and associated traffic statistics according to sessions established between two given hosts |
| Application Host Table | • Tracks and stores in table format application-specific traffic statistics according to source host |
| Application Matrix Table | • Tracks and stores in a matrix table format application-specific traffic statistics according to sessions established between two given hosts |
| Probe Configuration | • Defines standards for remotely configuring probes that are responsible for gathering and reporting network activity statistics |
| History | • Tracks and stores historical traffic information according to parameters determined by the user |

*Figure 11-24*    RMON2 Specifications

RMON3 would provide a way for many of the current proprietary WAN management tools to interoperate and share data. In addition, RMON3 is supposed to offer management and statistics gathering support for switched networks and virtual LANs, as well as the ability to measure application program response times to monitor distributed applications for degraded performance. Another effort to monitor distributed applications is known as the **application MIB.** Proposals for such an application MIB identify three key groups of variables for proper application tracking and management:

- **Definition variables** would store background information concerning applications such as application name, manufacturer, version, release, installation date, license number, and number of consecutive users.

- **State variables** would report on the current status of a given application. Three possible states are up, down, and degraded.

- **Relationship variables** would define all other network attached resources on which a given distributed application depends. This would include databases, associated client applications, and other network resources.

One of the major difficulties with developing and implementing an application MIB is the vast difference that exists among distributed applications.

## Enterprise Network Management Technology

**Technology Architectures**    All of the systems administration and network management processes reviewed in this chapter can be enabled by associated technology. In most cases, network management products offer functionality across more than one category of network or systems management. One way to distinguish between network management technology is to focus on the architecture of that technology. In general, network management technology can be categorized into one of three possible architectures:

- **Point products,** also known as **element managers,** are specifically written to address a particular systems administration or network management issue. The advantage of point products is that they are narrow in scope, provide the sought after solution, and are usually relatively easy to install and understand. The disadvantage to point solutions is that they do not necessarily integrate with other systems administration and network management tools. Any necessary correlation between point products must be done by network management personnel. Backup and restoral tools, license optimization tools, and management tools specifically written for a particular vendor's equipment are examples of point solutions.

- **Frameworks** offer an overall systems administration or network management platform with integration between modules and a shared database into which all alerts, messages, alarms, and warnings can be stored and correlated. Perhaps more important, most frameworks also offer open APIs or an entire application development environment so that third-party application developers can create additional systems administration or network management modules that will be able to plug-in to the existing framework and share management information with other modules. The advantage of a well-integrated framework is that it can offer the network administrator a single, correlated view of all systems and network resources. The disadvantage of frameworks is the development or integration of modules within the framework can be difficult and time consuming. In addition, not all management modules may be compatible with a given framework.

- **Integrated suites** could perhaps be looked upon as a subset of frameworks, although the two terms are often used interchangeably. The difference between integrated suites and frameworks is that integrated suites are filled with their own network management and systems administration applications rather than offering the user an open framework into which to place a variety of chosen applications. The advantage of integrated suites is that the applications are more tightly integrated and linked by a set of common services that tend to offer the user a more consolidated view of network resources. The disadvantage of integrated suites is that they usually do not offer the open pick-and-choose architecture of the framework. Some products in this category offer an integrated suite of applications but also support open APIs to accommodate third-party systems administration and network management applications.

Managerial
Perspective

## FRAMEWORKS VS. POINT PRODUCTS

The original intention of frameworks was to provide a standards-based shell into which both the framework vendor and independent third-party software vendors could offer framework compatible applications for sale. The idea behind the framework was that all of these various applications would be able to talk to each other and share data. From a functional standpoint, frameworks have often fallen short of this goal. From a financial standpoint, although the frameworks themselves were expensive enough, they provide little functionality without the proper combination of added-cost applications. The other major problem faced by framework adopters is the complexity of framework configuration. Delivered with a pricetag of as much as $500,000, frameworks can add little value without a significant amount of complex setup and configuration. This configuration requires highly specialized skills, often brought in on a consulting basis. These consulting and training costs should be considered when purchasing a framework.

As an alternative to frameworks, point products can offer specific solutions at a more reasonable price, with far less configuration complexity. However, point products do not provide the integration capability afforded by the frameworks. The bottom line to the frameworks vs. point products debate is that each is appropriate in certain circumstances. However, network managers would be wise to clearly understand their needs and the characteristics of the various product categories before making a purchasing decision.

**Desired Functionality**   Beyond the choices of architecture, systems administration and network management technology also differ in the level of functionality offered. For example, although most network management software can report on network activity and detect abnormal activities and report alarms, fewer packages can diagnose or fix problems. Among the commonly listed functions that network administrators would like to see delivered by systems administration and network management technology are the following:

- The ability to track the operational status of distributed applications.
- The ability to automate reporting of system status information.
- The ability to automate repetitive system management tasks.
- The ability to integrate application management and systems administration information with network management information.
- The ability to improve application performance by properly responding to system status messages.

**Currently Available Technology** Enterprise network management systems must be able to gather information from a variety of sources throughout the enterprise network and display that information in a clear and meaningful format. Furthermore, enterprise network management systems are being called on to monitor and manage additional distributed resources such as:

- Workstations and servers
- Distributed applications
- Distributed data management systems

One of the current difficulties with actually implementing enterprise network management systems is a lack of interoperability between different enterprise network management systems and third-party or vendor-specific network management systems. Popular enterprise network management systems that could be considered frameworks or integrated suites include:

- HP Openview
- Computer Associates' CA-Unicenter TNG (The Next Generation)
- TME 10—IBM/Tivoli Systems (includes IBM System View)
- PatrolView—BMC Software Inc.

Examples of third-party or vendor-specific network management systems, sometimes known as element managers or point products include:

- 3Com Transcend Enterprise Manager
- Cisco Cisco Works
- American Power Conversion PowerNet

Among the manifestations of the lack of interoperability between third-party applications and enterprise network management systems are:

- Separate databases maintained by each third-party application and enterprise network management system.
- Redundant polling of agent software to gather performance statistics.
- Multiple agents installed and executed on networked devices to report to multiple management platforms.

The lack of interoperability between different enterprise network management systems makes it difficult if not impossible to:

- Exchange network topology information and maps.

- Exchange threshold performance parameter and alarm information.

The major cause of all of this lack of interoperability is the lack of common APIs, both between different enterprise network management systems, and between a given enterprise network management system and a variety of third-party network management systems. Figure 11-25 illustrates an architectural view of how enterprise network management systems interface to other enterprise network components. Interoperability APIs included in Figure 11-25 are either proposed or under development.

In addition to interoperability issues previously discussed, key functional areas of enterprise network management software are listed in Figure 11-26.

## Analysis—Network Analyzers

The only really effective way to diagnose problems with network performance is to be able to unobtrusively peer into the network transmission media and actually see the characteristics of the packets of data that are causing performance problems. LAN and WAN **network analyzers** are able to capture network traffic in real time without interrupting normal network transmission. In addition to capturing packets of data from the network, most network analyzers are able to decode those packets, monitor packet traffic statistics, and simulate network traffic through traffic generators. Filtering provided

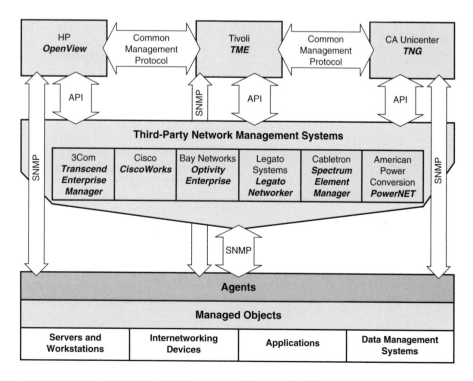

*Figure 11-25*   Enterprise Network Management System Architecture

| Functional Category | Importance/Implication |
|---|---|
| **Operating System Compatibility** | • Which operating systems does the enterprise network management system run over?<br>• HP UX<br>• Sun OS<br>• Solaris SPARC<br>• IBM AIX<br>• Windows NT/2000<br>• How many simultaneous operators of the enterprise network management system are supported?<br>• Can multiple operators be distributed across the enterprise network? |
| **Database Compatibility** | • With which databases can the enterprise network management system interoperate?<br>• Oracle<br>• Ingres<br>• SyBase<br>• Informix<br>• Proprietary<br>• DB2<br>• Flat file |
| **Network Size and Architecture** | • Is there a limit to the number of nodes supported?<br>• Can the software map all network architectures (Ethernet, token-ring, FDDI, switched LANs, WANs, ATM)?<br>• Can mainframes be integrated into the enterprise network management system?<br>• Can IPX and IP devices be managed? |
| **Third-Party Application Support** | • How many third-party applications are guaranteed to interoperate with this enterprise network management system? |
| **MIB and Management Protocol Support** | • How many different MIBs are supported? MIBs can be both IETF sanctioned or vendor specific. Enterprise network management systems can easily support over 200 different MIBs.<br>• Are management protocols other than SNMP supported? CMIP (common management information protocol), proprietary, SNMP2. |
| **Self-Configuration** | • To what extent is the enterprise network management software able to self-configure or auto-discover the enterprise network topology?<br>• Can the self-configuration process be customized or controlled? |
| **Cascading or Effect Alarms** | • Is the system able to identify and report alarms triggered by other alarms to more easily pinpoint the cause of problems? This capability may be known as event correlation. |

*Figure 11-26*  Functional Categories of Enterprise Network Management Systems

by network analyzers can isolate certain types of protocols or traffic from only particular workstations or servers. Given the multitude of protocols and the tidal wave of packets on a given network, effective filtering capabilities are enormously important to network analyzer usefulness.

Some network analyzers are software based (you supply the PC), hardware-based (come fully installed in their own dedicated PC), or hybrid in which an add-on hardware device with installed software is linked to the notebook PC via the parallel port. Still other analyzers, such as the Network General Sniffer are shipped with a PCMCIA (PC card) Ethernet adapter and software for installation on a limited number of supported notebook computers. Preconfigured sniffers are also available. Network analyzers can also differ in the number of LAN and WAN protocols that can be analyzed, the number of nodes from which traffic can be captured, and the ease of use, understanding, and flexibility of the user interface. Some network analyzers include expert systems that are able to predict oncoming problems based on observed traffic trends.

Network analyzer capabilities are most easily compared and categorized according to the seven-layer OSI model as outlined in Figure 11-27. In some cases, devices are specific to particular layers. For example, layer 1 testers are more commonly known as **cable scanners** or cable testers, whereas devices that test layers 2 through 7 are often called **protocol analyzers.**

## Monitoring—Network Baselining Tools

By combining the ability to monitor and capture SNMP, RMON, and RMON2 data from multivendor networking technology with the abilities to analyze the captured data and report on trends and exceptions, **network baselining tools** are able to track network performance over extended periods of time and report on anomalies or deviations from the accumulated baseline data. Also known as **proactive network management tools** or **network trending products,** such tools usually need several weeks of SNMP data to establish realistic baseline network performance averages. Network baselining tools may possess auto-discovery or auto-DNS capabilities that allow them to build graphical representations of networks by monitoring network management traffic. Such tools also exhibit characteristics such as flexible polling and event correlation that allow them to proactively seek information from network-attached devices and assimilate that information with previously collected data to form conclusions and make recommendations. Most network baselining tools share the results of their efforts through a wide variety of predefined and user-defined reports.

Typical reports would offer such statistics such as:

- Current network volume by day, week, and month compared to historical averages

- Network traffic volume leaders by node, actual vs. expected in terms of utilization, errors, or collisions

- Nodes that are in violation of a variety of user-defined thresholds

- Predicted number of days before a node will cross a user threshold

- Nodes whose performance is degrading

| OSI Model Layer | Network Analyzer Functionality |
|---|---|
| **Layer 7—Application** | • Some analyzers are able to display actual text and numbers being transmitted across a medium. Since passwords and credit card numbers can be displayed by such a device, it is understandable why network analyzers are sometimes considered a security threat. Displaying protocols from layers 4 through 7 is referred to as embedded protocol decodes. |
| **Layer 6—Presentation** | • Embedded protocol decodes |
| **Layer 5—Session** | • Embedded protocol decodes |
| **Layer 4—Transport** | • Embedded protocol decodes |
| **Layer 3—Network** | • Network layer protocols: X.25, ISDN Q.931, IP, IPX, AppleTalk |
| **Layer 2—DataLink** | • Hardware Interface Modules (LAN): Ethernet, token ring, switched Ethernet, fast Ethernet, FDDI <br> • Hardware interface modules (WAN): ISDN BRI, DDS, ATM <br> • DataLink WAN Protocols: BiSync, HDLC, SDLC, PPP, LAPB, LAPD, SLIP, frame relay, SNA |
| **Layer 1—Physical** <br><br> **(Also Known As Cable Scanners or Cable)** | • Cable scanners are able to pinpoint cable problems including locations of breaks, short-circuits, mis-wiring, and polarity problems <br> • Although a variety of different media types might be tested, the two most popular are Category 5 unshielded twisted pair and fiber optic cable <br> • Layer 1 protocols: V.35, RS-232, RS-449, 423, 422, 530, T-1 (variety of interfaces) |
| **Testers** | Among the key features and measurements of cable testers are the following: <br> • Ambient noise: level of external noise (from fluorescent lights, motors) where a cable is installed <br> • Attenuation: loss of signal strength over the distance traveled through media <br> • Attenuation-to-crosstalk: extent to which a medium resists crosstalk <br> • BERT (bit error rate tester): able to determine percent of received bits received in error <br> • Capacitance: capacity of the medium to store an electrical charge <br> • Continuity: an uninterrupted electrical path along the medium <br> • Impedance: opposition to flow of a signal within a medium, measured in ohms; the lower the impedance, the better the conductor <br> • Loopback device: cable tester function that sends transmitted signal out through medium and back into device for test and measurement <br> • Loop resistance: resistance encountered in completing a full electrical circuit <br> • Injector device: part of cable tester that creates signal, verifies transmission, and manages testing |

*Figure 11-27*   Network Analyzer Functional Capabilities by OSI Model Layer (*Continues*)

| OSI Model Layer | Network Analyzer Functionality |
|---|---|
| **Testers (continued)** | • NeXT (near-end crosstalk): signals being transmitted on one end overcoming and interfering with the weaker signals being received on the same end |
| | • NVP (nominal velocity of propagation): the speed of the data transmission through the tested media compared to speed of light transmission through a vacuum |
| | • OTDR (optical time division reflectometer): device that measures the time it takes for light to be reflected through a medium to detect breaks, crimps, etc. |
| | • SNR (signal to noise ratio): comparison of signal strength to background noise measured in dB (decibels) |
| | • Split pair: when a wire of one pair gets spliced to the wire of an adjacent pair |
| | • TDR (time domain reflectometer): able to measure cable lengths, distance to breaks, etc. by reflected electrical signals through a medium |
| | • Two way NeXT: measures near-end crosstalk as well as far-end crosstalk, which is crosstalk in same direction as signal |
| | • Wire map: verifies pin-to-pin continuity and checks for polarity reversal, short-circuits, and open circuits; displayed graphically |

*Figure 11-27*   Network Analyzer Functional Capabilities by OSI Model Layer (*Continued*)

## Simulation—Network Modeling and Simulation Tools

Simulation software tools are also sometimes known as **performance engineering** software tools. All simulation systems share a similar trait in that the overall network performance they are able to model is a result of the net effect of a series of mathematical formulas. These mathematical formulas represent and are derived from the actual performance of the circuits and networking equipment that compose the final network design.

The value of a simulation system is in its ability to predict the performance of various networking scenarios otherwise known as **what-if analysis.** Simulation software uses the current network configuration as a starting point and applies what-if scenarios. The benefits of a good network simulation package include:

- Ability to spot network bottlenecks such as overworked servers, network failures, or disk capacity problems.

- Ability to test new applications and network configurations before actual deployment. New applications may run well in a controlled test environment, but may perform quite differently on the shared enterprise network.

- Ability to recreate circumstances to reproduce intermittent or occasional network problems.

- Ability to replicate traffic volume as well as traffic transaction type and protocol mix.

The key characteristics that distinguish simulation software are listed in Figure 11-28.

| Network Simulation Software Characteristic | Importance/Explanation |
|---|---|
| **Network Types** | • Which different types of networks can be simulated: Circuit-Switched, Packet-Switched, Store-and-Forward, Packet-Radio, VSAT, Microwave? |
| **Network Scope** | • How many of the following can the simulation software model either individually or in combination with one another? modems and multiplexers, LANs, Netware only, Internetworks, WANs, MANs? |
| **Network Services** | • How many of the following advanced services can be modeled: frame relay, ISDN (BRI and PRI), SMDS, X.25, SONET, ATM? |
| **Network Devices** | • Some simulation systems have developed performance profiles of individual networking devices to the point where they can model particular networking devices (bridges, routers, MUXs) made by particular manufacturers. |
| **Network Protocols** | • In addition to the network transport protocols listed in the analysis and design section, different router-to-router or WAN protocols can have a dramatic impact on network performance. Examples: RIP, OSPF, PPP, BGP. |
| **Different Data Traffic Attributes** | • As studied in previous chapters, all data traffic does not have identical transmission needs or transmission needs or characteristics. Can the software simulate data with different traits? For example: bursty LAN data, streaming digitized voice or video, real-time transaction-oriented data, batch-oriented file transfer data. |
| **Traffic Data Entry** | • Any simulation needs traffic statistics to run. How these traffic statistics may be entered can make a major difference in the ease of use of the simulation system. Possibilities include: manual entry by users of traffic data collected elsewhere, traffic data entered "live" through a direct interface to a protocol analyzer, a traffic generator that generates simulated traffic according to the user's parameters, or auto discovery from SNMP, and RMON data generated by enterprise network management systems. |
| **User Interface** | • Many simulation software tools now offer easy to use graphical user interfaces with point-and-click network design capability for flexible "what-if" analysis. Some, but not all, produce graphical maps that can be output to printers or plotters. Others require users to learn a procedure-oriented programming language. |
| **Simulation Presentation** | • Some simulation tools have the ability to animate the performance of the simulated network in real time, whereas others perform all mathematical calculations and then play back the simulation when those calculations are complete. |

*Figure 11-28* Network Simulation Software Functionality

## ■ BUSINESS ISSUES

The successful implementation of a network management strategy requires a combination of policy, process, people, and technology. Merely throwing management technology in a vacuum at a management opportunity will not produce the desired results. What these desired results are may be a matter of perspective.

From the top-down, or business-first perspective, senior management may look to the proper management of information resources to enable a competitive advantage and to be able to deploy new network services quickly and as needed at a reasonable cost. Meanwhile, the desired result of business unit management might be that end users can successfully execute those applications that have been implemented to enable business processes and achieve business objectives. Successful execution of applications can be quantified in terms such as transactions per second, mean time between failures, and average response time to database queries. Such guarantees of proper execution and delivery of end-user applications are sometimes quantified in terms of a quality of service (QoS) guarantees. Network management personnel tend to take a more infrastructurecentric approach by concentrating on those elements of the network infrastructure that support the enterprise applications. Examples of such infrastructure components could be server performance, network traffic analysis, internetwork device performance, and WAN analysis.

How can network managers simultaneously deploy new services, control costs, provide competitive advantage, and provide guaranteed quality of service in an increasingly complicated, multivendor, multiplatform, multiprotocol environment? To a great extent, the answer is to combine the processes embedded in the top-down model and the network development life cycle. The top-down model forces the network manager to constantly evaluate business objectives, the nature of the applications that will meet those business objectives, the nature of the data that will support those applications, the functional requirements of the network that will deliver that data, and finally, the configuration of the technology that will provide the required network functionality. The network development life cycle forces the network manager to engage in an ongoing process of network monitoring, planning, analysis, design, modeling, and implementation based on network performance.

Network infrastructures must be both flexible and reliable. The ability to have networks change in response to changing business conditions and opportunities is of critical importance to the successful network manager.

### Cost Containment

Before a network manager can contain or reduce costs, it is first necessary to have an accurate representation of the source of those costs. Although this may sound like simple common sense, it is easier said than done, and sometimes not done at all. Figure 11-29 lists some practical suggestions for systems administration and network management cost containment.

### Outsourcing

In terms of cost control, one of the key weapons in the arsenal of network managers is **outsourcing,** or the selective hiring of outside contractors to perform specific network management duties. Outsourcing is also becoming increasingly necessary for

| Cost Containment Issue | Importance/Explanation |
|---|---|
| **Take Inventory** | • Gather accurate statistics and information as to every device, including hardware and software configuration information, that is currently requiring support<br>• This initial inventory will produce an overall accounting of how many different platforms and standards must be supported |
| **Determine Support Costs** | • Perform task analysis on network support personnel to determine how costly personnel are spending their time<br>• Are there too many fires?<br>• Are networking personnel being managed effectively?<br>• What is the cost of supporting multiple platforms and standards?<br>• Are networking personnel required at all corporate sites?<br>• Are more networking personnel required as networks become more complex? |
| **Consolidate and Centralize** | • Consolidate support personnel and deliver one-stop-support for end-users<br>• Centralize purchasing authority<br>• Pool network support personnel to optimize use of costly personnel<br>• Implement centralized license metering and software distribution to help standardize software platforms deployed throughout the enterprise<br>• How can network management functions and technology be centralized to cap or reduce the number of network personnel required to support enterprise networks?<br>• Centralize standardized applications on a server rather than allowing desktops to install a wide variety of applications |
| **Support Process Redesign** | • Once task analysis has been performed on network support personnel, redesign network support processes to optimize end-user support while minimizing support costs<br>• Use consolidated help desk and trouble ticketing systems to organize user support efforts while minimizing fire-fighting mentality |
| **Standardize** | • Standardize on hardware and software platforms, network architectures, network protocols, and network management platforms to simplify management tasks and reduce costs<br>• Standardized desktop platforms will lead to reduced support and maintenance costs<br>• Implement a software version control program so that network support people don't have to deal with multiple versions of multiple software packages |

*Figure 11-29*   Systems Administration and Network Management Cost Containment

global corporations to cost effectively secure required systems and network support personnel throughout the world. There are several keys to outsourcing success:

- The successful identification of those processes that can be most appropriately outsourced is the first key issue. Which processes do the company really need to manage themselves and which could be more cost effectively managed by a third party? Which skills are worth investing in for the strategic needs of the corporation itself, and which skills are better hired on an as-needed basis? Which tasks can an outsourcer do more cheaply than internal personnel? Which tasks can outsourcers supply new or on-demand expertise for? Which tasks can be outsourced to free corporate personnel for more strategically important issues? Are there tasks that could be more effectively managed by outside experts?

- The successful management of the outsourcing process is required once network management activities have been outsourced as appropriate. It is a good idea to establish communication and evaluation mechanisms as part of the contract negotiation. Issues to be discussed include reporting requirements from the outsourcer to the customer. Among these issues are performance reports on systems the outsourcers are responsible for problem resolution mechanisms, change negotiation mechanisms, performance criteria to be used for outsourcer evaluations, and penalties or bonuses based on outsourcer performance.

- Choosing the right outsourcing provider for the right job. For example, any or all of the following areas may be outsourced, although it is unlikely that any one outsourcer could be considered as expert in all areas: application development, application maintenance, client/server systems migration, data center operation, server management, help desk operations, LAN management, end-user support, PC and workstation management, network monitoring, off-site backup and recovery, remote network access, user training and support, and WAN management. The two most common outsourcing areas are application development and data center operation. Among the key evaluation criteria that could be used to narrow the choices of outsourcing vendors are the following: financial stability, networking skill set, geographic coverage, customer references, and pricing structure.

## Flexibility

Delivering network flexibility at a reasonable cost to respond quickly to pending business opportunities has become a priority for many network managers. Most network managers that have achieved success in this area cite a few key underlying philosophies:

- Remove dependencies on customized or proprietary hardware and software.

- Move toward adoption of open protocols and off-the-shelf hardware and software technologies. Examples of open protocols include TCP/IP for network transport and SNMP for management information.

- Adopt network management and systems administration packages that support open APIs and can easily accommodate add-in modules.

How can such an acquisition process be managed? Again the top-down model provides the framework to build the technology analysis grid in which technologies to be considered are measured against requirements as dictated by the upper layers of the top-down model.

## SUMMARY

Network management, like other network-related, technology-based solutions, can only be effectively implemented when combined with the proper processes, people, and procedures. As information technology departments have had to become more business-oriented, network management has become more focused on cost containment. Outsourcing is one way in which costs may be contained. However, outsourcing opportunities must be properly analyzed and managed to ensure the delivery of quality network management.

The overall field of network management can be logically segmented into systems administration, which is most concerned with the management of clients, servers, and their installed network operating systems, and enterprise network management, which is more concerned with the elements of the enterprise network that connect these distributed systems. One solution to providing comprehensive systems administration and enterprise management services is known as the consolidated service desk.

Server management, help desk management, configuration management, desktop management, LAN management, and distributed application management are all segments of systems administration. Although each of these segments may contain unique functionality and require unique technology, there is a great deal of integration of functionality and overlap of technology.

Enterprise network management architectures and protocols can vary from one installation to the next. New architectures and protocols are under development to bring some order to the multiplatform, multivendor, multiprotocol mix of today's enterprise networks.

A variety of enterprise network management technology is available to allow network managers to be proactive rather than reactive. Besides a wide variety of enterprise network management integrated suites and element managers, other enterprise network management tools include network analyzers, network baselining tools, network modeling and simulation tools, and network auditing tools.

## KEY TERMS

access to kens
ACD
agents
AMS
application MIB
application response measurement
applications management
  specification
ARM
automatic call distributors
bandwidth management
bulk retrieval mechanism
cable scanners
CIM
common information model
component interface API

computer telephony integration
consolidated service desk
CTI
database MIB
DDM
definition variables
desktop management interface
desktop management task force
digital license certificates
distributed device manager
distributed network probes
DMI
DMI services layer
DMTF
dynamic allocation
electronic software distribution

element managers
enterprise network management
enterprise network management
  systems
ESD
event management tool
frameworks
global license sharing
HMMP
HMMS
HMOM
hypermedia management protocol
hypermedia management schema
hypermedia object manager
instrumentation
integrated suites

interactive voice response unit
ISO Management Framework
IVRU
knowledge base
LAN Inventory Management
    Software
latency
license management software
license metering software
license optimization
license pooling
license server
licensing server API (LSAPI)
load balancing
management information base
management information format
management interface API
MIB
MIF
mobile MIF
modified object format
MOF
network analyzers
network auditing tools

network baselining tools
network modeling and simulation
    tools
network trending products
objects
outsourcing
performance engineering
performance metrics
point products
policy-based management tools
policy-based network
    management
proactive network management
    tools
protocol analyzers
queuing
QoS
quality of service
rate control
relationship variables
remote configuration
RMON MIB
RMON probe
RMON2

RMON3
search engine
secure SNMP
server capacity planning
service level agreement
service management
service management architectures
simple management protocol
simple network management
    protocol
SMP
SNMP
SNMP2
state variables
systems administration
telecommunication management
    network
traffic shaping
TMN
WBEM
Web-based enterprise
    management
what-if analysis

## REVIEW QUESTIONS

1. Differentiate between rate control and queuing as traffic-shaping techniques.
2. Describe circumstances in which bandwidth management could help application performance and those in which it could not.
3. What is service management and how does it differ from IT infrastructure management?
4. What are some of the various categories of service management and what are the roles of each category?
5. How can IT services be effectively costed?
6. What is a service level agreement and why is it important?
7. What is quality of service and how does it relate to IT infrastructure management?
8. Describe some of the business-oriented pressures faced by network managers as well as some of the responses to those pressures.
9. What are some of the advantages and disadvantages to outsourcing?
10. Differentiate between systems administration and enterprise network management.
11. Differentiate between the various layers of management defined by the OSI management framework.
12. What is a consolidated service desk and what unique functionality or advantages does it offer?

How does it differ from previous network management technologies?
13. What are some of the important advantages and disadvantages of server management software?
14. Why is it important for help desk software to be able to integrate with call center technology?
15. What is the difference between a knowledge base and a search engine and why is each important?
16. What are the unique features of policy-based management tools and what is the significance of such features?
17. What is the purpose and structure of the DMI?
18. How does desktop management software functionality differ from enterprise network management software functionality?
19. What are the key limitations of distributed application management and how are these limitations overcome?
20. What is the difference between distributed device management and centralized enterprise network management?
21. What disadvantage of centralized network management does distributed network management attempt to overcome?
22. Differentiate among the following terms: agent, MIB, RMON, object, SNMP.

23. What is a distributed network probe and how does it differ from an SNMP agent or an RMON probe?
24. What is CIM and what interoperability issues does it hope to overcome?
25. Describe the relationship between the various components of WBEM.
26. What are some of the shortcomings of SNMP and how are they overcome in SNMP2?
27. Why has SNMP2 not been widely accepted and implemented?
28. Differentiate between RMON and RMON2.
29. Differentiate between point products, frameworks, and integrated suites as alternate enterprise network management technology architectures.
30. What are some of the most important functional characteristics of enterprise network management systems?
31. What are some of the important functional characteristics of network analyzers?
32. What is the difference between a cable scanner and a protocol analyzer?
33. What is the overall purpose or value of a network baselining tool?
34. What is the overall purpose or value of a network modeling and simulation tool?
35. What are some of the ways in which current network configuration information can be loaded into a network modeling and simulation package?
36. What is the overall purpose of network auditing tools?
37. Why are network auditing tools becoming more popular than they once were?

**Case Study:** For a business case study and questions that relate to network management, go to www.wiley.com/college/goldman.

# NETWORK SECURITY

*Concepts Reinforced*

| | |
|---|---|
| OSI model | Internet suite of protocols model |
| Top-down model | Standards and protocols |

*Concepts Introduced*

| | |
|---|---|
| Security policy development | Virus protection |
| Security architecture | Security principles |
| Firewalls | Authentication |
| Encryption | Applied security technology |
| Active content monitoring | Intrusion detection |

## OBJECTIVES

Upon successful completion of this chapter, you should:

1. Understand the many processes involved with the development of a comprehensive security policy and security architecture.

2. Understand the importance of a well-developed and implemented security policy and associated people processes to effective security technology implementation.

3. Understand the concepts, protocols, standards, and technology related to virus protection.

4. Understand the concepts, protocols, standards, and technology related to firewalls.

5. Understand the concepts, protocols, standards, and technology related to authentication.

6. Understand the concepts, protocols, standards, and technology related to encryption.

## ■ INTRODUCTION

As interest and activity concerning the Internet has mushroomed, and as telecommuters and remote users are increasingly in need of access to corporate data, network security has become a dominant topic in data communications. As the various processes, concepts, protocols, standards, and technology associated with network security are reviewed in this chapter, it is important to remember the importance of people and their basic honesty and integrity as the underlying foundation for any successful network security implementation. Merely throwing network security technology at a problem without the benefit of a comprehensive, vigorously enforced network security policy including sound business processes will surely not produce desired results. As the saying goes, such action "is like putting a steel door on a grass hut."

## ■ BUSINESS IMPACT

What is the impact on business when network security is violated by on-line thieves? Consider these facts:

- According to federal law enforcement estimates, more than $10 billion worth of data is stolen annually in the United States.

- In a single incident, 60,000 credit and calling card numbers were stolen.

- Fifty percent of computer crimes are committed by a company's current or ex-employees.

One of the problems with gauging the true business impact of security breaches is that many companies are understandably reluctant to publicly admit that they have suffered significant losses due to failed network security. Network security is a business problem. It is not merely a network problem or an information technology problem. The development and implementation of a sound network security policy must start with strategic business assessment followed by strong management support throughout the policy development and implementation stages.

However, this management support for network security policy development and implementation cannot be assumed. For example, 71% of executives surveyed stated that they lacked confidence in the ability of their company's network security to fend off attacks from within or without. This stated lack of confidence has not translated into an infusion of support for network security efforts. From the same survey previously referenced, 73% of responding companies had three or fewer employees dedicated to network security, and 55% of respondents said that less than 5% of their information technology budgets went to network security. Enterprise network security goals must be set by corporate presidents and/or board of directors. The real leadership of the corporation must define the vision and allocate sufficient resources to send a clear message that corporate information and network resources are valuable corporate assets that must be properly protected.

## ■ SECURITY POLICY DEVELOPMENT

### The Security Policy Development Life Cycle

One methodology for the development of a comprehensive network security policy is known as the **security policy development life cycle (SPDLC).** As illustrated in

Figure 12-1, the SPDLC is aptly depicted as a cycle since evaluation processes validate the effectiveness of original analysis stages. Feedback from evaluation stages causes renewed analysis with possible ripple effects of changes in architecture or implemented technology. The feedback provided by such a cycle is ongoing, but will work only with proper training and commitment from the people responsible for the various processes depicted in the SPDLC.

Each of the processes identified in the SPDLC is explained further in Figure 12-2.

A successful network security implementation requires a marriage of technology and process. Roles and responsibilities and corporate standards for business processes and acceptable network-related behavior must be clearly defined, effectively shared, universally understood, and vigorously enforced for implemented network security technology to be effective. Process definition and setting of corporate security standards must precede technology evaluation and implementation.

## Security Requirements Assessment

Proper security requirements assessment implies that appropriate security processes and technology have been applied for any given user group's access to/from any potential corporate information resource. The proper development and application of these security processes and technology require a structured approach to ensure that all potential user group/information resource combinations have been considered.

To begin to define security requirements and the potential solutions to those requirements, a network analyst can create a matrix grid mapping all potential user groups against all potential corporate information resources. An example of such a security requirements assessment grid is illustrated in Figure 12-3. Whereas the user groups and corporate information resources form the row and column headings of the grid, the intersections of these rows and columns are the suggested security processes and policies required for each unique user group/information resource combination.

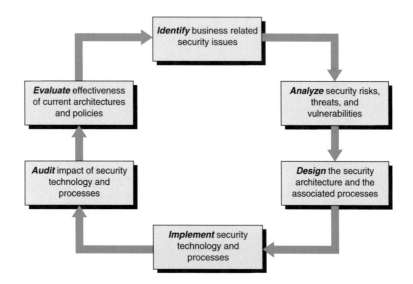

*Figure 12-1* The Security Policy Development Life Cycle

| SPDLC Process | Explanation/Importance |
|---|---|
| **Identification of Business-Related Security Issues** | • Security requirements assessment<br>• What do we have to lose?<br>• What do we have worth stealing?<br>• Where are the security holes in our business processes?<br>• How much can we afford to lose?<br>• How much can we afford to spend on network security? |
| **Analysis of Security Risks, Threats, Vulnerabilities** | • Information asset evaluation—what do you have that's worth protecting?<br>• Network architecture documentation—What is the current state of your network?<br>• How many unauthorized modems are dialing in?<br>• Identify all assets, threats, and vulnerabilities<br>• Determine risks and create protective measures |
| **Architecture and Process Design** | • Logical design of security architecture and associated processes<br>• What must be the required functionality of the implemented technology?<br>• What business processes implemented and monitored by people must complement this security architecture? |
| **Security Technology and Process Implementation** | • Choose security technology based on logical design requirements<br>• Implement all security technology with complementary people processes<br>• Increase the overall awareness of network security and implement training<br>• Design ongoing education process for all employees including senior management |
| **Audit Impact of Security Technology and Processes** | • Ensure that implemented policy and technology are meeting initial goals<br>• Institute a method to identify exceptions to security policy standards and deal with these exceptions swiftly |
| **Evaluate Effectiveness of Current Architecture and Processes** | • Based on results of ongoing audits, evaluate effectiveness of current policy and architecture of meeting high-level goals<br>• Adjust policy and architecture as required and renew the cycle |

*Figure 12-2* Processes of the Security Policy Development Life Cycle

These security processes refer to not just restrictions to information access imposed on each user group, but also the responsibilities of each user group for security policy implementation and enforcement. Another category of information for each intersection is the security technology to be applied to each unique user group/information resource combination to implement the documented security processes.

| User Group | Legacy Data Access | Intranet Access | Internet Inbound Access | Internet Outbound Access | Global E-mail Access |
|---|---|---|---|---|---|
| **Corporate HQ employees** | | | | | |
| Executives | | | | | |
| I.S. development staff | | | | | |
| Network management | | | | | |
| Network technicians | | | | | |
| Dept. management | | | | | |
| End-users | | | | | |
| **Remote branch employees** | | | | | |
| **Telecommuters** | | | | | |
| **Trading partners** | | | | | |
| Customers | | | | | |
| Vendors | | | | | |
| **Browsers** | | | | | |
| Casual browsers | | | | | |
| Prospective customers | | | | | |
| **Consultants and outsourcers** | | | | | |

*Figure 12-3*    Security Requirements Assessment Grid

The security requirements assessment grid is meant to provide only an example of potential user groups and information resource categories. The grid should be modified to provide an accurate reflection of each different corporate security environment. Furthermore, the grid should be used as a dynamic strategic planning tool. It should be reviewed on a periodic basis and should be modified to reflect changes in either user groups or information resources. Only through on-going auditing, monitoring, evaluation, and analysis, can a security requirements assessment plan remain accurate and reflective of a changing corporate network environment.

## Scope Definition and Feasibility Studies

Before proceeding blindly with a security policy development project, it is important to properly define the scope or limitations of the project. In some cases, this scope may be defined in advance due to a management edict to develop a corporate-wide security policy, perhaps in response to an incident of breached security. In other cases, feasibility studies may be performed in advance of the decision that determines the scope of the full security policy development effort.

The pilot project or feasibility study provides an opportunity to gain vital information on the difficulty of the security policy development process as well as the assets (human and financial) required to maintain such a process. In addition, vital information concerning corporate culture, especially management attitudes, and its readiness to assist in the development and implementation of corporate network security can be gathered. Only after the feasibility study has been completed can one truly assess the magnitude of the effort and assets required to complete a wider scope policy development effort.

One of the key issues addressed during scope definition or feasibility studies is deciding on the balance between security and productivity. Security measures that are too stringent can be just as damaging to user productivity as can a total lack of enforced security measures. The optimal balance point that is sought is the proper amount of implemented security process and technology that will adequately protect corporate information resources while optimizing user productivity. Figure 12-4 attempts to graphically depict this balance.

Another issue that is commonly dealt with during the scope definition stage is the identification of those key values that a corporation expects an implemented security policy and associated technology to be able to deliver. By defining these key values during scope definition, policy and associated architecture can be developed to assure that each of these values are maintained. These key values represent the objectives or intended outcomes of the security policy development effort. Figure 12-5 lists and briefly explains the five most typical fundamental values of network security policy development.

Yet another way to organize an approach to security policy and architecture development is to use a model or framework such as **ISO 7498/2,** the **OSI Security Architecture.** This framework maps fourteen different security services to specific layers of the OSI 7 Layer Reference Model. The OSI Model Security Architecture can be used as an open framework in which to categorize security technology and protocols, just as the OSI 7 Layer Model can be used to categorize internetworking technology and protocols. Although more specific and varying slightly in terminology from the five fundamental

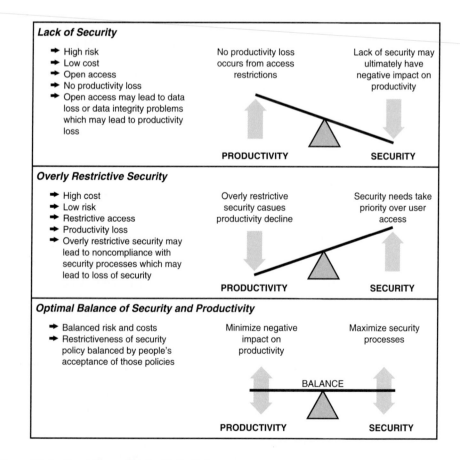

*Figure 12-4*    Security vs. Productivity Balance

| Value of Network Security Policy Development | Explanation/Implication |
|---|---|
| **Identification/Authentication** | Want to be assured that users can be accurately identified and that only authenticated users are allowed access to corporate resources |
| **Access Control/Authentication** | Want to be assured that even authenticated users are only allowed access to those information and network resources that they are supposed to access |
| **Privacy/Confidentiality** | Want to be assured that network based communication is private and not subject to eavesdropping |
| **Data Integrity** | Want to be assured that data is genuine and cannot be changed without proper controls |
| **Nonrepudiation** | Want to be assured that users cannot deny the occurrence of given events or transactions |

*Figure 12-5*   Fundamental Values of Network Security Policy Development

values listed in Figure 12-5, the OSI Security Architecture is consistent with and includes all of these fundamental values. As illustrated in Figure 12-6, the ISO 7498-2 Security Architecture could be used as a grid or checklist to assess whether or not the listed security service has been provided for each associated OSI Model layer protocols and by what technologies each service is to be provided. Not all services will necessarily be provided to all suggested layers in all corporate settings. This does not diminish the values of the OSI Security Architecture as a planning framework, however.

## Assets, Threats, Vulnerabilities, and Risks

Although Figure 12-4 graphically illustrates the theoretical goal of the security policy development process, balance between productivity, and security, how can such a balance actually be delineated within the context of a structured methodology such as the security requirements assessment grid? Most security policy development methodologies boil down to the following six major steps:

1. Identify assets
2. Identify threats
3. Identify vulnerabilities
4. Consider the risks
5. Identify risk domains
6. Take protective measures

The terms used within these six major steps are related in a process-oriented manner.

**Assets** are corporate property of some value that require varying degrees of protection. In the case of network security, assets most often include corporate data and the network hardware, software, and media used to transport and store that data.

| ISO 7498-2 Security Architecture | Associated OSI Model Layer(s) |
|---|---|
| **Peer entity authentication:** Verifies that a peer entity in an association is the one claimed; verification is provided to the next layer | Application, transport network |
| **Data origin authentication:** Verifies that the source of the data is as claimed; verification is provided to the next layer | Application, transport network |
| **Access control service:** This service protects against unauthorized access of network resources, including by authenticated users | Application, transport network |
| **Connection confidentiality:** Provides for the confidentiality of all data at a given layer  for its connection to a peer layer elsewhere, provided primarily by encryption technology | Application, transport network, datalink |
| **Connectionless confidentiality:** Same security as above applied to a connectionless communication environment | Application, transport network, datalink |
| **Selective field confidentiality:** Provides for the confidentiality of selected fields of application level information on a connection; for example, a customer's PIN (personal ID number) on an ATM transaction | Application, transport network, datalink |
| **Traffic flow confidentiality:** Protects against unauthorized traffic analysis such as capture of source and destination addresses | Application, network physical |
| **Connection integrity with recovery:** Provides for data integrity for data on a connection at a given time and detects any modifications with recovery attempted | Application, transport |
| **Connection integrity without recovery:** Same as above except no recovery attempted | Application, transport network |
| **Selective field connection integrity:** Provides for the integrity of selected fields transferred over a connection and determines whether the fields have been modified in any manner | Application |
| **Connectionless integrity:** Provides integrity assurances to the layer above it, and may also determine if any modifications have been performed | Application, transport network |
| **Selective field connectionless integrity:** Provides for the integrity of selected fields and may also determine if any modifications have been performed | Application |
| **Nonrepudiation, origin:** The recipient of the data is provided with proof of the origin of the data; provides protection against the sender denying the transmission of the data | Application |
| **Nonrepudiation, delivery:** The sender is provided with proof that the data was delivered; protects against attempts by the recipient to falsify the data or deny receipt of the data | Application |

*Figure 12-6*   OSI 7498-2 Security Architecture

**Data or Information Classification**   Because the most common asset to be protected in an information systems environment is the information or data itself, it is important for an organization to adopt an information classification scheme that is easily understood and globally implemented. As will be seen in the discussion of security architectures, properly classified data are an input assumption for a security architecture. If information is not properly classified, the security architecture will be unable to protect it appropriately. Most information classification schemes are based on some variation of the classification scheme used by the Department of Defense:

- Unclassified or public: Information that is readily available to the public. No restrictions as to storage, transmission, or distribution.

- Sensitive: Information whose release could not cause damage to the corporation but could cause potential embarrassment or measurable harm to individuals. Salary and benefits data would be examples of sensitive data.

- Confidential: Information whose release could cause measurable damage to the corporation. Corporate strategic plans and contracts would be considered confidential.

- Secret: Information whose release could cause serious damage to a corporation. Trade secrets or engineering diagrams would be examples of secret information.

- Top Secret: Information whose release could cause grave or permanent damage. Release of such information could literally put a company out of business. Secret formulas for key products would be considered top secret.

**Threats** are processes or people that pose a potential danger to identified assets. A given asset can be potentially threatened by numerous threats. Threats can be intentional or unintentional, natural or man-made. Network-related threats include hackers, line outages, fires, floods, power failures, equipment failures, dishonest employees, or incompetent employees.

**Vulnerabilities** are the manner or path by which threats are able to attack assets. Vulnerabilities can be thought of as weak links in the overall security architecture and should be identified for every potential threat/asset combination. Vulnerabilities that have been identified can be blocked.

Once vulnerabilities have been identified, how should a network analyst proceed in developing defenses to these vulnerabilities? Which vulnerabilities should be dealt with first? How can a network analyst determine an objective means to prioritize vulnerabilities? By considering the **risk,** or probability of a particular threat successfully attacking a particular asset in a given amount of time via a particular vulnerability, network analysts are able to quantify the relative importance of threats and vulnerabilities. A word of caution, however. Risk analysis is a specialized field of study, and quantification of risks should not be viewed as an exact science. In identifying the proper prioritization of threats and vulnerabilities to be dealt with, network analysts should combine subjective instincts and judgment with objective risk analysis data.

A **risk domain** consists of a unique group of networked systems sharing both common business function and common elements of exposure. These common business functions and risks are identified during initial risk analysis or assessment. Risk domains are differentiated or isolated from each other based on the differences in risks associated with each risk domain. Because each risk domain has unique business functions and risks, it would stand to reason that each should have a uniquely designed set of technology control processes and technology to offer the required level of security for that particular risk domain. The column headings in Figure 12-3 could potentially be considered as risk domains. Risk domains are important to security analysts because of their use as a means to organize security strategies and technology.

Once the order in which threats and vulnerabilities will be attacked has been determined, **protective measures** are designed and taken that effectively block the vulnerability to prevent threats from attacking assets. Recalling that multiple vulnerabilities (paths) may exist between a given asset and a given threat, it should be obvious that multiple protective measures may need to be established between given threat/asset combinations. Among the major categories of potential protective measures are:

- Virus protection
- Firewalls
- Authentication
- Encryption
- Intrusion detection

An explanation of each of these categories of protective measures and examples and applications of each category are supplied in the remainder of this chapter. Figure 12-7 illustrates the relationships between assets, threats, vulnerabilities, risks, and protective measures.

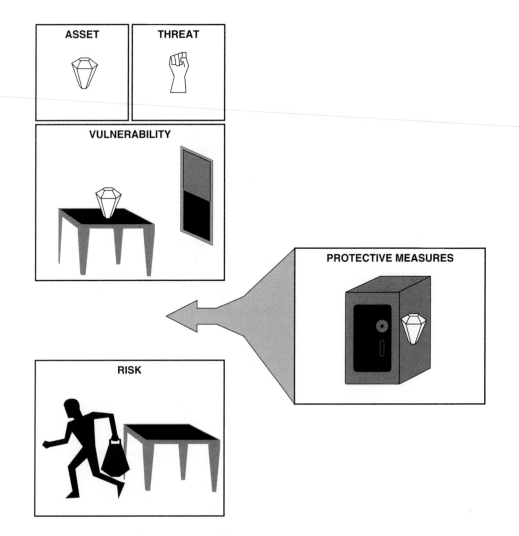

*Figure 12-7* Assets, Threats, Vulnerabilities, Risks, and Protective Measures

## Attack Strategies

Attack strategies often concentrate on vulnerabilities of specific network operating systems. For example, attack strategies for NetWare servers differ from those intended for Windows NT or Unix servers. Often, such attack strategies are openly shared on the Internet. To understand how to properly protect servers, it is important to use all possible means to discover the server's vulnerabilities. Paying attention to hackers' forums on the Internet is one way to stay on top of these issues.

Figure 12-8 lists some of the more common attack strategies and potential protective measures.

Rather than attacking a specific network operating system, some hackers choose to attack the underlying transport protocols that are used to communicate between servers. The most common transport protocol is **transmission control protocol** or **TCP.** When two servers that are communicating via TCP wish to set up a connection to each other, they engage in a three-step exchange of addresses and confirmations known as a **three-way handshake.** The following two attack strategies take advantage of this three-way handshake in slightly different ways:

- **Denial of service attack:** In the denial of service attack, the hacker flooded the server with requests to connect to other servers that did not exist. The server would try to establish connections with the nonexistent servers and wait for a response while being flooded with thousands of other bogus connection requests. This caused the server to deny service to legitimate users because it was overwhelmed trying to handle the bogus requests

- **Land attack:** The land attack is a variation on the denial of service attack in which the hacker substitutes the targeted server's own address as the address of the server requesting a connection. This causes the attacked server to constantly try to establish connections to itself, thereby often crashing the server.

| Network/Information System Attack Strategies | Protective Measure |
|---|---|
| Masquerading | Authentication |
| Eavesdropping | Encryption |
| Man-in-the-Middle-Attack | Digital certificates, digital signatures |
| Address Spoofing | Firewalls |
| Data Diddling | Encrypted message digest |
| Dictionary Attack | Strong passwords, intruder detection |
| Replay Attack | Time stamping or sequence numbering |
| Virus Attack | Virus management policy |
| Trojan Horse Attack | Firewalls |
| Denial of Service Attack | Authentication, service filtering |

*Figure 12-8*  Network/Information System Vulnerabilities and Protective Measures

Web-Specific Attack Strategies    All Web servers employ some type of operating or network operating system and are subject to any of the previously mentioned attack strategies. In addition, there are other Web specific vulnerabilities and associated attack strategies. To minimize the possibility of attack the following techniques should be considered:

- Eliminate all unused user accounts, especially default accounts such as GUEST.

- Remove or disable all unused services such as FTP, Telnet, and Gopher. If such services must be enabled, consider installing a proxy server or application layer firewall.

- Remove unused Unix command shells and interpreters so that hackers can't access the Web server's operating system directly.

- Be sure that permission levels on files and directories are properly set. Default permissions often grant access to too many user groups or individual user accounts.

- Consult WWW security frequently asked questions (FAQ) sites on an ongoing basis to stay up-to-date with current attack strategies and defenses.

- Common gateway interface (CGI) programs are capable of extracting a Unix-based Web server's password file.

- Server side includes (SSIs) can be embedded in Web pages such as guest books and can instruct a Web server to remove an entire directory's contents.

## Management Roles and Responsibilities

Once the scope of the security policy development effort has been determined and assets, threats, vulnerabilities, risks, and protective measures have been identified, it is time to secure management buy-in for the security policy development process before proceeding. Results of the feasibility study form the basis of the presentation for management.

Be certain that this presentation for management is objective and that any estimates of financial losses caused by security threats can be substantiated. You will be asking for financial and moral support from management. Your success at securing this success will be a simple matter of management's perception of the cost/benefit analysis of your threat/asset/protective measure scenarios. In other words, have you clearly proven that the costs involved to provide protective measures for corporate assets are outweighed by the benefits of ensuring proper protection of those assets?

Once you have substantiated the existence of security threats and vulnerabilities, propose your plan of action to develop and implement a solution. It is important not to underestimate the manpower and time requirements necessary to scale up your security analysis from a limited scope feasibility study to a full-fledged, enterprise-wide security policy development and implementation process.

What are the responsibilities of executives and managers beyond merely approving budgets and providing policy enforcement? Figure 12-9 provides a brief listing of key executive responsibilities, and Figure 12-10 provides a brief list of management responsibilities. Each of these lists was summarized from publications available from

**Executive's Responsibilities for Protection of Information Resources** (excerpted from NIST Special Pub. SP 500:169 Executive Guide to the Protection of Information Resources)

| | |
|---|---|
| 1. | Set the security policy (acceptable use policy) of the entire organization. |
| 2. | Allocate sufficient staff, funding, and positive incentives to successfully implement policy. |
| 3. | State the value of information as a corporate resource to your organization. |
| 4. | Demonstrate your organization's commitment to the protection of its information resources. |
| 5. | Make it clear that the protection of the corporate information resources is everyone's responsibility. |
| 6. | Assign ultimate responsibility for information and network security to specific individuals. |
| 7. | Require computer and network security and awareness training. |
| 8. | Hold employees personally responsible for the resources in their care including network access and corporate information. |
| 9. | Monitor and assess security through external and internal audits (overt and covert). |
| 10. | State and follow through on penalties for nonadherence to network security policies. |
| 11. | Lead by example. |

*Figure 12-9*   Executive's Responsibilities for Protection of Information Resources

**Management's Responsibilities for Protection of Information Resources** (excerpted from NIST Special Pub. SP 500-170, Management Guide to the Protection of Information Resources)

| | |
|---|---|
| 1. | Assess the consequences of a security breach in the area for which you are responsible. Risks include inability or impairment to perform necessary duties; waste, misuse, or theft of funds or resources; and internal or external loss of credibility. |
| 2. | Find the optimal balance between security needs and productivity needs. |
| 3. | Assess vulnerabilities. How long can each information resource be unavailable before business processes become threatened?. |
| 4. | Assure data integrity within the systems for which you are responsible. |
| 5. | Maintain required confidentiality and data privacy. |
| 6. | Ensure that nonrepudiation and auditing are present in the systems for which you are responsible. |
| 7. | Adhere by and enforce corporate acceptable use policies. |

*Figure 12-10*   Management's Responsibilities for the Protection of Information Resources

the National Institute of Standards and Technology. The NIST publishes a series of Federal Information Processing Standards (FIPS) as well as a series of special publications on a variety of computer and network security-related topics.

## Policy Development Process

It is important to reiterate that although technology may well be implemented as part of the protective measures to eliminate vulnerabilities and protect assets from their associated threats, it is the processes and policies associated with each of those protective measures that really determine the success or failure of a network security policy implementation.

Be sure that all effected user groups are represented on the policy development task force. Start from a business perspective with a positive philosophy and a universally supportable goal: "The purpose of this policy is to protect our vital corporate resources to ensure that we can all keep our jobs. This is in our collective best interests...." The emphasis should be on corporate-wide awareness and shared values as to the importance of protecting corporate resources such as information and network access. The policy should not be portrayed as administrative edicts to be obeyed under consequence of termination.

Areas that may be considered for development of acceptable use policies are listed in Figure 12-11.

The list of suggested areas for policy development in Figure 12-11 is not meant to be exhaustive or all-inclusive. Each corporation should amend such a list to include

---

**Potential Areas for Development of Acceptable Use Policies**

1. Password protection and management (i.e., it is against corporate policy to write your password on a Post-it note and paste it to your monitor; it is against corporate policy to allow anyone else to use your user ID or password)

2. Software license policy (policies on using illegal or pirated software on corporate machines, policy on use of shareware on corporate machines, policy regarding who is allowed to install any type of software on corporate machines)

3. Virus protection policy (policies regarding use of diskettes on network attached PCs, use of corporate computing resources by consultants and outsource personnel, related to Internet access policies)

4. Internet access policy (policies regarding acceptable use of Internet for corporate business)

5. Remote access policy (policies regarding use of single use passwords, Smart Cards, secure transfer of corporate data)

6. E-mail policy (policies regarding enrollment in e-mail news groups, personal use of e-mail systems)

7. Policies regarding penalties, warnings, and enforcements for violation of corporate acceptable use policies

8. Physical access policies (policies regarding access to locked areas, offices, computer and telecom rooms, combinations for limited access areas, visitor policies, logging out or locking keyboard when leaving office)

---

*Figure 12-11*   Potential Areas for Development of Acceptable Use Policies

those areas of policy development most appropriate to their corporation. Once policies have been developed for those agreed-on areas, those policies should be measured against the user group/information resource matrix produced in the security requirements assessment grid (Figure 12-3) to be sure that all potential needs for acceptable use policies have been met.

## Policy Implementation Process

Once policies have been developed, it is up to everyone to support those policies in their own way. The required support of executives and managers was listed in Figures 12-9 and 12-10, respectively. Having been included in the policy development process, users should also be expected to actively support the implemented acceptable use policies. Users' responsibilities for the protection of information resources are included in Figure 12-12.

---

**Users' Responsibilities for Protection of Information Resources** (excerpted from NIST Special Pub. SP 500-171, Computer Users' Guide to the Protection of Information Resources)

| | |
|---|---|
| 1. | You are ultimately responsible for protecting the data to which you have access. |
| 2. | Know which information is especially sensitive or confidential; when in doubt, ask.. |
| 3. | Information is a valuable, shared corporate asset—as valuable as buildings, stock price, sales, or financial reserves. |
| 4. | The computing resources that the company provides for you are the property of the company and should only be used for purposes that benefit the company directly. |
| 5. | Familiarize yourself with the acceptable use policies of your company and abide by them. |
| 6. | Understand that you will be held accountable for whatever actions you take with corporate computing or networking resources. |
| 7. | If you ever observe anything or anyone unusual or suspicious, inform your supervisor immediately. |
| 8. | Never share your password or user ID with anyone. |
| 9. | If you are allowed to choose a password, choose one that could not be easily guessed. |
| 10. | Always log off before leaving your computer or terminal. |
| 11. | Keep sensitive information, whether on diskettes or on paper, under lock and key. |
| 12. | Don't allow others to look over your shoulder if you are working on something confidential. |
| 13. | Don't smoke, eat, or drink near computer equipment. |
| 14. | Know the location of the nearest fire extinguisher. |
| 15. | Backup your data onto diskettes early and often. |

*Figure 12-12*    Users' Responsibilities for the Protection of Information Resources

**Organizing Policy Implementation: The Security Architecture** Once security policy has been determined, appropriate technology and associated processes must be implemented to execute that policy. It is difficult to organize all security technologies and processes and map them to security policies without overlooking something. What is required is an overall security model or architecture that starts with business drivers and ends with a combination of available security tools, mapping policy to processes and technology controls.

A security architecture implies an open framework into which business-driven security processes and requirements can be quickly and easily organized, now or in the future. Security architectures map clearly justified security functional requirements to currently available security technical solutions. Security architectures imply that standardized security solutions have been predefined for a given corporation's variety of computing and network platforms. In this manner, security solutions are implemented consistently across an enterprise without the need for security personnel to become personally involved in every implementation. The use of a well-designed security architecture should provide both a more secure and a more cost-effective information systems environment.

Information systems architectures in general and information security architectures in particular separate business needs from the logical requirements that meet those business needs and the physically implemented technology that meets those logical requirements. In doing so, the architecture enables security analysts to separately analyze these major elements of the security architecture while understanding the relationship among the various layers of the architecture. This allows the architecture to stand the test of time by allowing changing business drivers to be mapped to changing logical requirements to be mapped to changing security technology without having to change the overall architecture into which all of these changing elements are organized. As new threats or vulnerabilities are discovered, a well-designed security architecture should provide some structure to the manner in which protective measures are designed to counteract these new threats and vulnerabilities.

Information security architectures could, and perhaps should, vary from one organization to the next. Figure 12-13 is a representative example of a security architecture that clearly maps business and technical drivers through security policy and processes to implemented security technology. One or more of the layers of the security architecture could be subsequently expanded into more detailed multilayer models. Figure 12-14 explains each layer of the representative architecture in terms of the significance of each layer, as well as the relationships or impacts between layers.

At this point, an effective security policy, including associated technology and processes, should have been developed and be ready for implementation. If user involvement was substantial during the policy development stage and if buy-in was assured at each stage of the policy development, then implementation stands a better chance of succeeding. However, policy implementation will inevitably force changes in people's behaviors, which can cause resistance. Resistance to change is both natural and to be expected. Handled properly, resistance to change can be just a temporary implementation hurdle. Handled improperly, it can spell disaster for an otherwise effective network security policy. Figure 12-15 summarizes some of the key behaviors and attitudes that can help ensure a successful network security policy implementation.

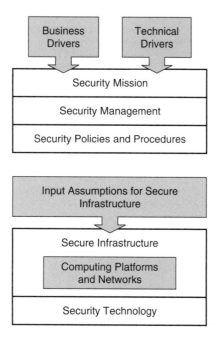

*Figure 12-13*    Representative Security Architecture

## Auditing

**Manual Audits**    To judge whether or not a corporate security policy is successful, it must be audited and monitored on a continual basis. Auditing as it relates to network security policy may be either automated or manual. Manual audits can be done by either internal or external personnel. Manual audits serve to verify the effectiveness of policy development and implementation, especially the extent to which people understand and effectively execute their assigned processes in the overall corporate security policy. Manual audits are also referred to as **policy audits** or **off-line** audits. Consulting firms that specialize in network security have generated some rather startling results during security audits when they were able to gain entry to a corporate president's office, access her e-mail account, and send e-mail to the chief information officer informing him he was fired for his lack of effective security policy. As it turns out, the CIO was not really fired. In fact, it was poorly designed and poorly executed people processes that allowed this incident to occur. A receptionist was solely responsible for physical access security to the executive offices and the president left her PC logged in.

**Automated Audits**    Automated audits, otherwise known as **event detection** or **real-time audits** depend on software that is able to assess the weaknesses of your network security and security standards. Most audit software depends on capturing large amounts of event data and then filtering that data for exceptional or unusual events. Captured events can be telephone calls, login attempts, network server directory access attempts, access to Internet news groups or Web sites, or remote access attempts via dial-up lines. To generate meaningful exception reports, audit software

| Security Architecture Layer | Importance/Implication/Examples |
|---|---|
| **Business and Technical Drivers** | Business drivers are inherited from the corporation's overall strategic business plan. The security architecture must play its part in the achievement of the corporation's overall business mission. Technical drivers are enablers or limiting factors that determine the extent to which technology can contribute to the security architecture's achievement of the overall corporate business mission. |
| **Security Mission** | The security mission is the definition of the role of the security architecture as driven by the business and technical drivers. An example would be: "To enable secure information sharing and protect information resources throughout the corporate enterprise." |
| **Security Management** | Security management bridges the gap between the high-level security mission statement and the policies and procedures that actually implement and achieve the security mission. These are the parts of the security architecture that do not change, even though security policies and procedures may change. Examples include communications mechanisms, educational programs, and other efforts that ensure that security policies and procedures are well understood, widely observed, and strictly enforced. |
| **Security Policies and Procedures** | Security policies and procedures are meant to protect identified assets from identified threats by neutralizing identified vulnerabilities through the implementation of appropriate protective measures. |
| **Input Assumptions for Secure Infrastructure** | Examples of input assumptions might be the following: <br>• All information will be properly classified before entering the secure infrastructure so that the secure infrastructure is able to handle each type of information classification accordingly. <br>• All users will be properly categorized in terms of what resources they have a right to access so that if the secure infrastructure properly authenticates an individual, it will know what resources that individual can access. |
| **Secure Infrastructure** | The secure infrastructure is a combination of technology and associated procedures applied to a corporation's computing platforms and networks. |
| **Computing Platforms and Networks** | Since vulnerabilities are specific to different computing platforms and networks, proper technology controls must be applied to specific computing platforms and networks. Likewise, security analysts must be constantly vigilant, looking for new vulnerabilities on any installed computing platform or network. |
| **Security Technology** | Security technology, sometimes known as the security toolkit, is the constantly changing combination of potential solutions that can be implemented to achieve a secure infrastructure. As vulnerabilities change, security technology constantly changes to keep pace. It is essential for security analysts to be students of security technology, constantly seeking the best and most effective security solutions for their corporations. |

*Figure 12-14*   Layers of the Security Architecture

| Critical Success Factors for Network Security Policy Implementation |
|---|

| 1. | The policy must have been developed in a team effort with all affected parties feeling that they had input to the process. Policy development must be a bottom-up, grassroots effort rather than a top-down, administration imposed effort. |
|---|---|
| 2. | The security policy must be coordinated with and in compliance with other corporate policies re: disaster recovery, employee rights, and personnel policies. |
| 3. | It is important to ensure that no part of the security policy is illegal. This is particularly important for corporations that do business in multiple states or countries. For example, in some localities, it is illegal to monitor phone conversations of employees. |
| 4. | Technology must not be promoted as a security solution. Dedicated people, implementing well-designed processes on a consistent basis, combined with the effective use of technology, are the only means to a true security solution. |
| 5. | The network security policy must not be put on a shelf and forgotten. Security awareness must be a priority, and ongoing auditing and monitoring should ensure that security remains at the forefront of people's thoughts. |
| 6. | An attitude must be fostered that security threats are indeed real and that they can and will happen in the company if people do not follow corporate security procedures. |
| 7. | Management must be ready to impose prescribed penalties on employees who fail to follow corporate security policy. To do otherwise will quickly send the message that the security policy is a farce. |
| 8. | Corporate culture may indeed need to change. This is especially true for growing companies that started out as very open, entrepreneurial cultures. Such companies often have difficulty adjusting to structure and controlled access to corporate resources imposed by corporate security policies. |

*Figure 12-15* Critical Success Factors for Network Security Policy Implementation

allows users to create filters that will allow only those events deemed exceptional by the users to appear on reports.

Some automated audit tools are able to analyze the network for potential vulnerabilities and make recommendations for corrective action, whereas others merely capture events so that you can figure out who did what and when after a security breach has occurred. Other automated tools are able to benchmark or compare events and security-related parameters to a set of government-issued security standards known as C2 or Orange Book standards (officially known as the Trusted Computer System Evaluation Criteria or TCSEC) and issue a report card or "Top 10 Risks" list as to how well a given network measures up. The C2 standards and other security standards are explained later in the chapter. Some audit tools are able to save previous audit data as baseline information so that network analysts and security specialists can measure improvement in network security including the impact of any security improvements that may have been implemented.

**Security Probes and Intrusion Detection Systems** Rather than passively gathering network statistics like auditing tools, **security probes** (otherwise known as vulnerability scanners) actively test various aspects of enterprise network security and report results and suggest improvements. **Intrusion detection systems** (sometimes referred to as host-based intrusion detection systems) monitor systems, ports, files and applications. When an unauthorized access or intrusion is detected, the software can respond with alarms. In addition to merely detecting intrusions, such as unsuccessful login attempts over a preset limit, some tools are also able to provide automated responses, or countermeasures to these intrusion attempts. Also, some of the more sophisticated intrusion detection systems are dynamic or self-learning and are able to become better at detecting intrusions or to adjust exception parameters as they gain experience in a given enterprise network environment. Examples of host-based intrusion detection systems include CyberCop from Network Associates, Kane Security Monitor from Security Dynamics, and Intruder Alert from Axent Technologies.

**Network-based intrusion detection systems** often use network traffic probes distributed throughout a network to identify traffic patterns that may indicate some type of attack may be underway. Rather than wait until such attacks reach a particular host, network-based intrusion detection systems keep a big picture view of overall suspicious network activity. Examples of network-based intrusion detection systems include Cisco Secure from Cisco Systems, NetProwler from Axent Technologies, and RealSecure from Internet Security Systems.

RealSecure also acts as a security probe that looks for as many as 600 known security weaknesses on firewalls, routers, Unix machines, Windows machines, or Windows NT machines or any other device that uses TCP/IP as its transport protocol stack. RealSecure combines network-analyzer, attack signature recognition, and attack response in a single unit. If an attack is detected, RealSecure is able to terminate the connection by spoofing both hosts involved in the communication.

A security probe known as **Security Analyzer Tool for Analyzing Networks (SATAN)** is able to probe networks for security weak spots. The SATAN probe is especially written to analyze Unix- and TCP/IP-based systems, and once it has found a way to get inside an enterprise network, it continues to probe all TCP/IP machines within that enterprise network. Once all vulnerabilities have been found, SATAN generates a report that not only details the vulnerabilities found, but also suggests methods for eliminating the vulnerabilities. SATAN tries to start TCP/IP sessions with target computers by launching applications such as Telnet, FTP, DNS, NFS, and TFTP. It is able to target specific computers because all TCP/IP-based machines use the same 16-bit address or port number for each of these previously mentioned applications. This application-specific port address plus the 32-bit IP address is known as a socket. Although SATAN was developed as a tool for network managers to detect weaknesses in their own networks, it is widely available on the Internet and can easily be employed by hackers seeking to attack weaknesses in target networks of their choice. Because of the potential for unscrupulous use of SATAN, tools such as Courtney, from the Department of Energy's Computer Incident Advisory Capability, and Gabriel, from Los Altos Technologies, are able to detect the use of SATAN against a network and are able to trigger alarms.

## ■ VIRUS PROTECTION

Virus protection is often the first area of network security addressed by individuals or corporations. A comprehensive virus protection plan must combine policy, people, processes, and technology to be effective. Too often, virus protection is thought to be a technology-based quick fix. Nothing could be further from the truth. A survey conducted by the National Computer Security Association revealed the following:

- Computer viruses are the most common microcomputer security breach.

- Ninety percent of the organizations surveyed with 500 or more PCs experience at least one virus incident per month.

- Complete recovery from a virus infection costs an average of $8,300 and 44 hours over a period of 22 working days.

## Virus Categories

Although definitions and parameters may vary, the term *computer virus* is generally used to describe any computer program or group of programs that gains access to a computer system or network with the potential to disrupt the normal activity of that system or network. Virus symptoms, methods of infection, and outbreak mechanisms can vary widely, but all viruses do share a few common characteristics or behaviors:

- Most viruses work by infecting other legitimate programs and causing them to become destructive or disrupt the system in some other manner.

- Most viruses use some type of replication method to get the virus to spread and infect other programs, systems, or networks.

- Most viruses need some sort of trigger or activation mechanism to set them off. Viruses may remain dormant and undetected for long periods.

Viruses that are triggered by the passing of a certain date or time are referred to as **time bombs,** and viruses that require a certain event to transpire are known as **logic bombs.** Logic bombs in event-driven or visual programs may appear as a button supposedly providing search or some other function. However, when the button is pushed, the virus is executed, causing a wide range of possibilities from capturing passwords to wiping out the disk drive. One of the ways in which viruses are able to infect systems in the first place is by a mechanism known as a **trojan horse.** In such a scenario, the actual virus is hidden inside an otherwise benign program and delivered to the target system or network to be infected. The Microsoft Word Macro (or Concept) Virus is an example of a trojan horse virus because the virus itself is innocently embedded within otherwise legitimate Word documents and templates. **Macro viruses** can infect Macintosh as well as Windows-based computers and are not limited to Word, but can also infect files through such programs.

A particular disruptive variation of the macro virus affecting Microsoft documents was known as the Melissa virus. The Melissa virus arrived via e-mail with the message, "Here is the document you asked for … don't show anyone else.;-)." Once opened, the virus would replicate itself and e-mail itself via mail servers to the first fifty users in the Microsoft Outlook local address book with the subject line "Important message from [username]." Because the username was probably known to the intended recipient, it was more likely to be opened, thereby perpetuating the virus infection. Before long, an estimated 100,000 computer systems were infected, and entire corporate e-mail systems were forced to shut down. Virus protection experts quickly posted fixes for the virus, and the FBI launched the largest Internet suspect hunt ever. David Smith of Aberdeen, NJ, was arrested for and has admitted to creating the Melissa virus but contends that he never intended to do anything wrong.

Although new types of viruses will continue to appear, Figure 12-16 lists the major virus categories and gives a brief explanation of each.

| Virus Category | Explanation/Implication |
|---|---|
| **File Infectors** | • Attach themselves to a variety of types of executable files.<br>• Subcategories of file infectors include the following:<br>  ○ Direct action file infectors infect a program each time it is executed<br>  ○ Resident infectors use the infected program to become resident in memory from where they attack other programs as they are loaded into memory<br>  ○ Slow infectors infect files as they are changed or created thus assuring that the infection is saved<br>  ○ Sparse infectors seek to avoid detection by striking only certain programs on an occasional basis<br>  ○ Companion viruses create new infected programs that are identical to the original uninfected programs<br>  ○ Armored viruses are equipped with defense mechanisms to avoid detection and antivirus technology. **Polymorphic viruses** change their appearance each time an infected program is run to avoid detection. |
| **System/Boot Infectors** | • Attack the files of the operating system or boot sector rather than application programs<br>• System/boot sector viruses are memory resident |
| **Multipartite Viruses** | • Also known as boot-and-file viruses, attack both application files and system and boot sectors |
| **Hostile Applets** | • Although specific to Web technology and Java-embedded programs, hostile applets could still be considered viruses. **Attack applets** are intent on serious security breaches, whereas **malicious applets** tend to be annoying rather than destructive. Hostile applets are unknowingly downloaded while Web surfing. Hostile ActiveX components present a similar threat. Some people would argue that such malicious code is not technically a virus. However, there is little doubt as to the potential destructiveness of the code. |
| **E-mail Viruses** | • Some sites report that 98% of viruses are introduced through e-mail attachments<br>• Antivirus software must be version specific to the e-mail messaging system (i.e., Exchange Server 5.5)<br>• Such software scans files after decryption before releasing the files to the users, and questionable files are quarantined |
| **Cluster/File System Viruses** | • Attack the file systems, directories, or file allocation tables so that viruses can be loaded in to memory before requested files |

*Figure 12-16*   Virus Categories

## Antivirus Strategies

An effective antivirus strategy must include policy, procedures, and technology. Policy and procedures must be tied to those vulnerabilities that are specific to virus infection. Viruses can attack systems at the client PC, the server PC, or the network's connection to the Internet. By far, the most common physical transport mechanism for the spread of viruses is the diskette. Effective antivirus policies and procedures must first focus on the use and checking of all diskettes before pursuing technology-based solutions. In fact, 61% of all viral infections are caused by infected diskettes. However, the macro viruses that infect Word documents and Excel spreadsheets are becoming a predominant virus transport mechanism because of the frequency at which such documents are shared between co-workers and across networks as e-mail attachments. Figure 12-17 lists some examples of antivirus strategies, although this list should be tailored for each situation and reviewed and updated on a regular basis.

As collaborative applications such as groupware have become more commonplace in corporations, a new method of virus infection and virus reinfection has emerged. Because groupware messages and data are stored in a shared database, and because documents can be distributed throughout the network for document conferencing or workflow automation, the virus is spread throughout the network. Moreover, because groupware servers usually replicate their databases to ensure that all servers on the network are providing consistent information, the virus will continue to spread. Even if the virus is eliminated from the originating server, responses from still-infected replicated servers will reinfect the original server as the infection/reinfection cycle continues. Virus scanning software specially designed for groupware databases has been designed to combat this problem. Norton AntiVirus for

---

**Antivirus Strategies**

1. Identify virus infection vulnerabilities and design protective measures.

2. Install virus scanning software at all points of attack. Assure that network-attached client PCs with detected viruses can be quarantined to prevent the spread of the virus over the network.

3. All diskettes must be scanned at a stand-alone scanning PC before being loaded onto network-attached clients or servers.

4. All consultants and third-party contractors are prohibited from attaching notebook computers to the corporate network until the computer has been scanned in accordance with security policy.

5. All vendors must run demonstrations on their own equipment.

6. Shareware or downloaded software should be prohibited or controlled and scanned.

7. All diagnostic and reference diskettes must be scanned before use.

8. Write protect all diskettes with .exe, .com files.

9. Create a master boot record that disables writes to the hard drive when booting from a floppy or disable booting from a floppy, depending on operating system.

---

*Figure 12-17*   Antivirus Strategies

Microsoft Exchange is an example of such a specialized antivirus tool. Figure 12-18 illustrates the collaboration software infection/reinfection cycle.

Managerial
Perspective

## ANTIVIRUS ISSUES

Antivirus awareness and a mechanism for quickly sharing information regarding new virus outbreaks must accompany the deployment of any antivirus technology. These antivirus awareness and communications mechanisms must be enterprise wide in scope rather than being confined to a relatively few virus-aware departments. Procedures and policies on how and when antivirus technology is to be employed must be universally understood and implemented.

### Antivirus Technology

Since viruses can attack locally or remotely attached client platforms, server platforms, and/or the entrance to the corporate network via the Internet, all four points of attack must be protected. Viruses must be detected and removed at each point of

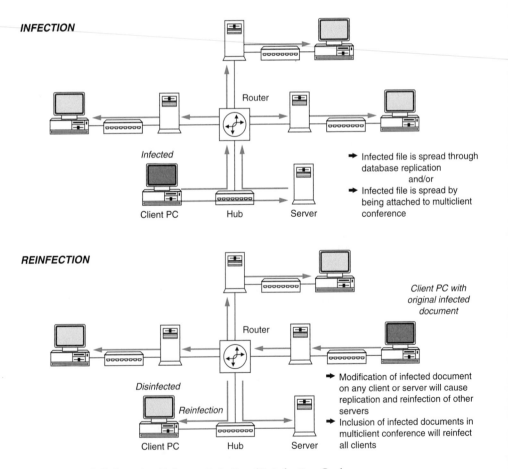

*Figure 12-18*   Collaborative Software Infection/Reinfection Cycle

attack. **Virus scanning** is the primary method for successful detection and removal. However, virus scanning software most often works off a library of known viruses, or more specifically the unique digital signatures of these viruses, but new viruses are appearing at the rate of nearly 200 per month. Because of this, it is important to buy virus scanning software whose vendor supplies updates of virus signatures at least once per month. As virus introduction accelerates, it is likely that virus signature updates to virus scanning software will become more frequent as well. Vendors are currently updating virus signatures files every four hours, with hourly updates expected in the near future. Also, some virus scanners can remove a virus from an infected file, while others merely destroy the infected file as a remedy. Because virus scanners are really scanning for known digital signatures or viruses, they are sometimes referred to as **signature scanners.**

In an effort to be more proactive than reactive, **emulation technology** attempts to detect as yet unknown viruses by running programs with a software emulation program known as a **virtual PC.** In so doing, the executing program can be examined in a safe environment for any unusual behavior or other tell-tale symptoms of resident viruses. The advantage of such programs is that they identify potentially unknown viruses based on their behavior rather than by relying on identifiable signatures of known viruses. Because of their ability to monitor behavior of programs, this category of antivirus technology is also sometimes known as **activity monitors** or **heuristic analysis.** Such programs are also capable of trapping encrypted or polymorphic viruses that are capable of constantly changing their identities or signatures. In addition, some of these programs are self-learning, thereby increasing their knowledge of virus-like activity with experience. Obviously, the key operational advantage is that potentially infected programs are run in the safe, emulated test environment before they are run on actual PCs and corporate networks.

A third category of antivirus technology, known as **CRC checkers** or **hashing checkers,** creates and saves a unique cyclical redundancy check character or hashing number for each file to be monitored. Each time that file is subsequently saved, the new CRC is checked against the reference CRC. If the CRCs do not match, then the file has been changed. These changes are then evaluated by the program to determine the likelihood that the change was caused by a viral infection. The shortcoming of such technology is that it is only able to detect viruses after infection, which may already be too late. Perhaps as a solution to this problem, **decoys** are files that are allowed to become infected to detect and report on virus activity.

To identify viruses and malicious content such as Java applets or Active X controls that may be introduced via Internet connectivity, a new defensive tool category known as **active content monitors** is able examine transmissions from the Internet in real time and identify known malicious content based on contents of reference or definition libraries.

Antivirus software is now available for clients, servers, e-mail gateways, Web browsers, firewalls, and groupware. It is even being installed in the firmware on network interface cards. Overall, the trend is to catch Internet-borne viruses before they reach servers and clients computers by installing virus protection technology at the Internet gateways capable of scanning FTP, HTTP, and SMTP traffic. Antivirus products are now certified by the **National Computer Security Association (NCSA),** which also maintains a list of known or sighted viruses. Figure 12-19 illustrates the typical points of attack for virus infection as well as potential protective measures to the combat those attacks.

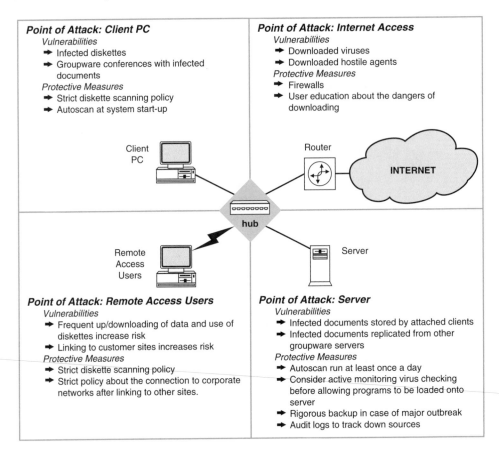

**Point of Attack: Client PC**
*Vulnerabilities*
➡ Infected diskettes
➡ Groupware conferences with infected documents
*Protective Measures*
➡ Strict diskette scanning policy
➡ Autoscan at system start-up

**Point of Attack: Internet Access**
*Vulnerabilities*
➡ Downloaded viruses
➡ Downloaded hostile agents
*Protective Measures*
➡ Firewalls
➡ User education about the dangers of downloading

Client PC

Router

INTERNET

hub

Remote Access Users

Server

**Point of Attack: Remote Access Users**
*Vulnerabilities*
➡ Frequent up/downloading of data and use of diskettes increase risk
➡ Linking to customer sites increases risk
*Protective Measures*
➡ Strict diskette scanning policy
➡ Strict policy about the connection to corporate networks after linking to other sites.

**Point of Attack: Server**
*Vulnerabilities*
➡ Infected documents stored by attached clients
➡ Infected documents replicated from other groupware servers
*Protective Measures*
➡ Autoscan run at least once a day
➡ Consider active monitoring virus checking before allowing programs to be loaded onto server
➡ Rigorous backup in case of major outbreak
➡ Audit logs to track down sources

*Figure 12-19*   Virus Infection Points of Attack and Protective Measures

## ■ FIREWALLS

When a company links to the Internet, a two-way access point out of as well as *into* that company's confidential information systems is created. To prevent unauthorized access from the Internet into a company's confidential data, specialized software known as a **firewall** is often deployed. Firewall software usually runs on a dedicated server that is connected to, but outside of, the corporate network. All network packets entering the firewall are filtered or examined to determine whether those users have authority to access requested files or services and whether the information contained within the message meets corporate criteria for forwarding over the internal network. Firewalls provide a layer of isolation between the inside network and the outside network. The underlying assumption in such a design scenario is that all of the threats come from the outside network. As evidenced by the statistic cited earlier, this is often not the case. In addition, outside threats may be able to circumvent the firewall entirely if dial-up modem access remains uncontrolled or unmonitored. In addition, incorrectly implemented firewalls can actually exacerbate the situation by creating new, and sometimes undetected, security holes.

### Firewall Architectures

Another difficulty with firewalls is that there are no standards for firewall functionality, architectures, or interoperability. As a result, users must be especially aware of how firewalls work to evaluate potential firewall technology purchases. Firewall functionality and architectures are explained in the next few sections.

**Packet Filtering**    Every packet of data on the Internet is uniquely identified by the source address of the computer that issued the message and the destination address of the Internet server to which the message is bound. These addresses are included in a portion of the packet called the header.

A **filter** is a program that examines the source address and destination address of every incoming packet to the firewall server. Network access devices known as routers are also capable of filtering data packets. **Filter tables** are lists of addresses whose data packets and embedded messages are either allowed or prohibited from proceeding through the firewall server and into the corporate network. Filter tables can also limit the access of certain IP addresses to certain directories. This is how anonymous FTP users are restricted to only certain information resources. It obviously takes time for a firewall server to examine the addresses of each packet and compare those addresses to filter table entries. This filtering time introduces **latency** to the overall transmission time. A filtering program that only examines source and destination addresses and determines access based on the entries in a filter table is known as **a port level filter, network level filter,** or **packet filter.**

Packet filter gateways can be implemented on routers. This means that an existing piece of technology can be used for dual purposes. However, maintaining filter tables and access rules on multiple routers is not a simple task, and packet filtering does have its limitations in terms of the level of security it is able to provide. Dedicated packet-filtering firewalls are usually easier to configure and require less in-depth knowledge of protocols to be filtered or examined. Packet filters can be breached by hackers in a technique known as **IP spoofing.** Since packet filters make all filtering decisions based on IP source and destination addresses, if a hacker can make a packet appear to come from an authorized or trusted IP address, then it can pass through the firewall.

**Application Gateways**    **Application level filters,** otherwise known as **assured pipelines, application gateways,** or **proxies,** go beyond port level filters in their attempts to prevent unauthorized access to corporate data. Whereas port level filters determine the legitimacy of the party asking for information, application level filters ensure the validity of what they are asking for. Application level filters examine the entire request for data rather than just the source and destination addresses. Secure files can be marked as such, and application level filters will not allow those files to be transferred, even to users authorized by port level filters.

Certain application level protocols commands that are typically used for probing or hacking into systems can be identified, trapped, and removed. For example, SMTP (simple mail transfer protocol) is an e-mail interoperability protocol that is a member of the TCP/IP family and used widely over the Internet. It is often used to mask attacks or intrusions. MIME (multipurpose Internet mail extension) is also often used to hide or encapsulate malicious code such as Java applets or ActiveX components. Other application protocols that may require monitoring include World Wide Web protocols such as HTTP, as well as Telnet, FTP, Gopher, and Real Audio. Each of these application protocols requires its own proxy and each application-specific proxy must be intimately familiar with the commands within each application that will need to be trapped and examined. For example an SMTP proxy should be able to filter SMTP packets according to e-mail content, message length, and type of attachments. A given application gateway may not include proxies for all potential application layer protocols.

**Circuit-level proxies** provide proxy services for transport layer protocols such as TCP. **Socks** creates a proxy data channel to the application server on behalf of the application client. Since all data goes through Socks, it can audit, screen, and filter all traffic in between the application client and server. Socks can control traffic by disabling or enabling communication according to TCP port numbers. Socks4 allowed outgoing firewall applications, whereas Socks5 supports both incoming and outgoing firewall applications. Socks5 also supports authentication. The key negative characteristic is that applications must be "socksified" to communicate with the Socks protocol and server. In the case of Socks4, this meant that local applications had to literally be recompiled. However, with Sock5, a launcher is employed that avoids "socksification" and recompilation of client programs that don't natively support Socks in most cases. Socks5 uses a private routing table and hides internal network addresses from outside networks.

Application gateways are concerned with what services or applications a message is requesting in addition to who is making that request. Connections between requesting clients and service providing servers are created only after the application gateway is satisfied as to the legitimacy of the request. Even once the legitimacy of the request has been established, only proxy clients and servers actually communicate with each other. A gateway firewall does not allow actual internal IP addresses or names to be transported to the external nonsecure network. To the external network, the proxy application on the firewall appears to be the actual source or destination as the case may be.

An architectural variation of an application gateway that offers increased security is known as a **dual-homed gateway.** In this scenario, the application gateway is physically connected to the private secure network, and the packet filtering router is connected to the nonsecure network or the Internet. Between the application gateway and the packet filter router is an area known as the screened subnet, or DMZ. Also attached to this screened subnet are information servers, WWW servers, or other servers that the company may wish to make available to outside users. However, all outside traffic still goes through the application gateway first, and then to the information servers. TCP/IP forwarding is disabled, and access to the private network is available only through one of the installed proxies. Remote logins are only allowed to the gateway host.

An alternative to the dual-homed gateway that seeks to relieve all the reliance on the application gateway for all communication, both inbound and outbound, is known as a **trusted gateway** or trusted application gateway. In a trusted gateway, certain applications are identified as trusted and are able to bypass the application gateway entirely and establish connections directly rather than be executed by proxy. In this way, outside users can access information servers and WWW servers without tying up the proxy applications on the application gateway. Figure 12-20 differentiates between packet filters, application gateways, proxies, trusted gateways, and dual-homed gateways.

Proxies are also capable of approving or denying connections based on directionality. Users may be allowed to upload files but not download them. Some application level gateways have the ability to encrypt communications over these established connections. The level of difficulty associated with configuring application level gateways vs. router-based packet filters is debatable. Router-based gateways tend to require a more intimate knowledge of protocol behavior, whereas application level gateways deal with more upper level, application layer protocols. Proxies introduce increased latency compared with port level filtering. The key

**Packet Filter Firewall**

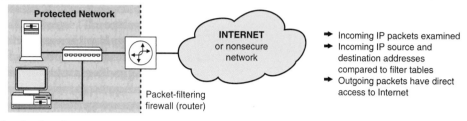

- ➡ Incoming IP packets examined
- ➡ Incoming IP source and destination addresses compared to filter tables
- ➡ Outgoing packets have direct access to Internet

**Application Gateway**

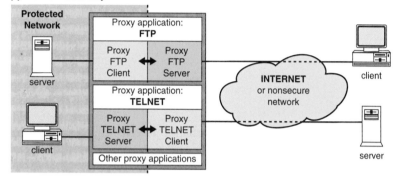

**Trusted Gateway**

**Dual-Homed Gateway**

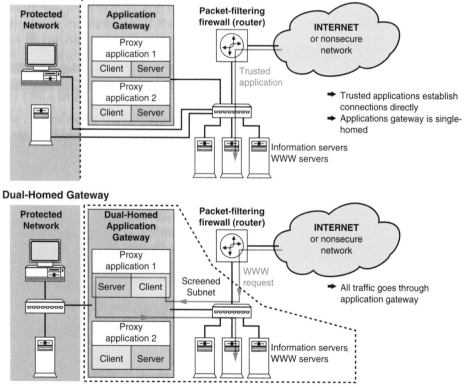

*Figure 12-20*    Packet Filters, Application Gateways, Proxies, Trusted Gateways, and Dual-Homed Gateways

weakness of an application level gateway is its inability to detect embedded malicious code such as trojan horse programs or macro viruses.

**Internal Firewalls**    Not all threats to a corporation's network are perpetrated from the Internet by anonymous hackers, and firewalls are not a stand-alone, technology-based quick fix for network security as evidenced by the following facts:

- Sixty percent of network attacks are made by internal users, people inside the firewall.

- Disgruntled employees, former employees, or friends of employees are responsible for 568 of 600 incidents of network hacking.

- Thirty percent of Internet sites that reported breaches had firewalls in place.

In response to the reality that most episodes of computer crime are inside jobs, a new category of software known as **internal firewalls** has begun to emerge. Internal firewalls include filters that work on the datalink, network, and application layers to examine communications that occur only on a corporation's internal network, inside the reach of traditional firewalls. Internal firewalls also act as access control mechanisms, denying access to any application for which a user does not have specific access approval. To ensure the security of confidential or private files, encryption may also be used, even during internal communication of such files.

## Enterprise Firewall Architectures

The previous section described different approaches to firewall architecture on an individual basis; key decisions are still needed as to the number and location of these firewalls in relation to the Internet and a corporation's public and private information resources. Each of the alternative enterprise firewall architectures explored next is attempting to segregate the following three distinct networks or risk domains:

- The Internet contains both legitimate customers and business partners as well as hackers.

- The demilitarized zone, DMZ, otherwise known as the external private network, contains Web servers and mail servers.

- The internal private network, otherwise known as the secure network or intranet, contains valuable corporate information.

Figure 12-21 illustrates the various ways in which one or two firewalls can be arranged in an enterprise firewall architecture; Figure 12-22 describes the functionality of each alternative.

## Firewall Functionality and Technology Analysis

Commercially available firewalls usually employ either packet filtering or proxies as a firewall architecture and add an easy-to-use graphical user interface to ease the configuration and implementation tasks. Some firewalls even use industry standard

**Single Firewall, Behind DMZ**

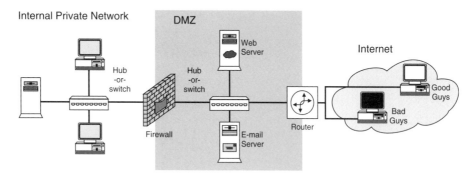

**Single Firewall, In Front of DMZ**

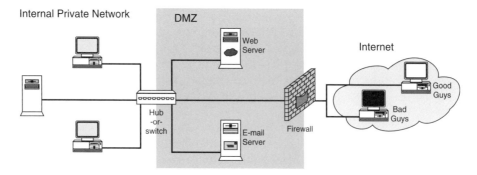

**Dual or Multi-Tier Firewall**

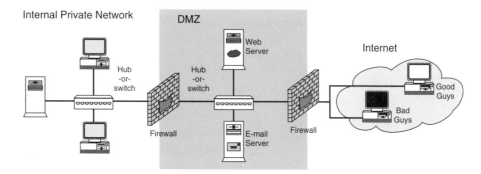

*Figure 12-21*    Enterprise Firewall Architectures

Web browsers as their GUIs. Firewall technology is now certified by the **National Computer Security Association.** The NCSA certifies the following:

- That firewalls meet the minimum requirements for reliable protection
- That firewalls perform as advertised
- That Internet applications perform as expected through the firewall

| Enterprise Firewall Architecture | Key Functional Characteristics |
|---|---|
| **Single Firewall, Behind DMZ** | • Exposes Web servers and mail servers to Internet without protection |
| **Single Firewall, in Front of DMZ** | • Must open paths through single firewall to allow public access to Web server and mail server<br>• No firewall protection to internal private network since it is on the same physical network as the DMZ |
| **Dual or Multitier Firewall** | • Allows controlled access to DMZ while blocking unauthorized access to secure network<br>• Same functionality may be offered in a single product known as a trihomed firewall |

*Figure 12-22*    Comparative Functionality of Enterprise Firewall Architectures

Figure 12-23 summarizes some of the key functional characteristics of firewall technology.

Examples of some of the more popular firewall technology include Firewall-1 from Checkpoint, Gauntlet from Network Associates, Raptor Firewall from Axent Technologies, and AltaVista Firewall from Compaq.

**Small Office Home Office (SOHO) Firewalls**    As telecommuting has boomed and independent consultants have set up shop in home offices, the need for firewalls for the SOHO market has grown as well. These devices are most often integrated with ISDN-based multiprotocol routers that supply bandwidth on demand capabilities for Internet access. Some of these SOHO firewalls offer sophisticated features such as support for virtual private networks and NCSA certification at a reasonable price, less than $100. Some of these devices combine additional functionality such as network address translation, built-in hub/switch ports, and load balancing in a combined hardware/software device known as a **security appliance.**

## ■ AUTHENTICATION AND ACCESS CONTROL

The overall purpose of **authentication** is to ensure that users attempting to gain access to networks are really who they claim to be. Password protection was the traditional means to ensure authentication. However, password protection by itself is no longer sufficient to ensure authentication. As a result, a wide variety of technology has been developed to ensure that users really are who they say they are. Authentication products break down into three overall categories:

- *What you know:* Authentication technology that delivers **single sign-on (SSO)** access to multiple network-attached servers and resources via passwords. Examples of single sign-on technology includes TrustBroker from CyberSafe, PassGo SSO from Axent Technologies, and Global Sign On from IBM.

- *What you have:* Authentication technology that uses one-time or session passwords or other techniques to authenticate users and validate the authenticity of messages or files. This category of technology requires the user to possess some type of smart card or other token authentication device to generate these single-use passwords. Examples of one-time password programs include OPIE and S/Key.

- *What you are:* Authentication technology that validates users based on some physical characteristic such as fingerprints, hand geometry, or retinal scans.

## Token Authentication—Smart Cards

**Token authentication** technology provides one-time-use session passwords that are authenticated by associated server software. This token authentication technology may take multiple forms:

- Hardware-based **smart cards** or Smart IDs that are about the size of a credit card with a numeric keypad, or key fob.
- In-line token authentication devices that connect to the serial port of a computer for dial-in authentication through a modem.
- Software tokens that are installed on the client PC and authenticate with the server portion of the token authentication product transparently to the end user. The user must only enter a personal ID number (PIN) to activate the authentication process.

Token authentication technology is really a system of interacting components that could include any or all of the following:

- A smart card to generate the session password.
- Client software to enter session passwords and communicate with the token authentication server software.
- Server software to validate entries for session passwords and keep track of which smart cards are issued to which users.
- Application development software to integrate the token authentication technology with existing information systems.

There are two overall approaches to the token authentication process:

- **Challenge-response token authentication**
- **Time synchronous token authentication**

Challenge-response token authentication involves the following steps:

1. The user enters an assigned user ID and password at the client workstation.
2. The token authentication server software returns a numeric string known as a challenge.
3. The challenge number and a personal ID number are entered on the handheld smart card.
4. The smart card displays a response number on the LCD screen.

| Firewall Functional Characteristic | Explanation/Importance |
|---|---|
| Encryption | • Allows secure communication through firewall<br>• Encryption schemes supported: DES,<br>• Encryption key length supported: 40, 56, 128 bits |
| Virtual Private Network Support | • Allows secure communication over the Internet in a virtual private network topology<br>• VPN Security protocols supported: IPsec |
| Application Proxies Supported | • How many different application proxies are supported? Internet application protocols (HTTP, SMTP, FTP, Telnet, NNTP, WAIS, SNMP, rlogin, ping traceroute)? Real Audio?<br>• How many controls or commands are supported for each application? |
| Proxy Isolation | • In some cases, proxies are executed in their own protected domains to prevent penetration of other proxies or the firewall operating system if a given proxy is breached. |
| Operating Systems Supported | • Unix and varieties, Windows NT, UnixWare, Windows 2000. |
| Virus Scanning Included | • Since many viruses enter through Internet connections, it would stand to reason that the firewall would be a logical place to scan for viruses. |
| Web Tracking | • To assure compliance with corporate policy regarding use of the World Wide Web, some firewalls provide Web tracking software. The placement of the Web tracking software in the firewall makes sense because all Web access must pass through the firewall. Access to certain URLs can be filtered. |
| Violation Notification | • How does the firewall react when access violations are detected? Options include SNMP traps, e-mail, pop-up windows, pagers, reports. |
| Authentication Supported | • As a major network access point, the firewall must support popular authentication protocols and technology. Options include SecureID, Cryptocard, Enigma Logic, DES, Safeword, Radius, ASSUREnet, FW-1, S/Key, OS Login. |
| Network Interfaces Supported | • Which network interfaces and associated data-link layer protocols are supported? Options include Ethernet, fast Ethernet, Gigabit Ethernet, high speed serial for CSU/DSUs, ATM, ISDN, T-1, T-3, HDLC, PPP. |
| System Monitoring | • Are graphical systems monitoring utilities available to display such statistics as disk usage or network activity by interface? |
| Auditing and Logging | • Is auditing and logging supporting?<br>• How many different types of events can be logged?<br>• Are user-defined events supported?<br>• Can logged events be sent to SNMP managers? |

*Figure 12-23*    Functional Characteristics of Firewall Technology (*Continues*)

| Firewall Functional Characteristic | Explanation/Importance |
|---|---|
| **Attack Protection** | • Following is a sample of the types of attacks that a firewall should be able to guard against: TCP denial-of-service attack, TCP sequence number prediction, Source routing and routing information protocol (RIP) attacks, exterior gateway protocol infiltration and Internet control message protocol (ICMP) attacks, authentication server attacks, finger access, PCMAIL access, domain name server (DNS) access, FTP authentication attacks, anonymous FTP access, SNMP access remote access remote booting from outside networks; IP, media access control (MAC) and address resolution protocol (ARP) spoofing and broadcast storms: trivial FTP and filter to/from the firewall, reserved port attacks, TCP wrappers, Gopher spoofing, and MIME spoofing. |
| **Administration Interface** | • Is the administration interface graphical in nature? Forms-based?<br>• Is a mastery of Unix required to administer the firewall? |

*Figure 12-23*   Functional Characteristics of Firewall Technology (*Continued*)

5. This response number is entered on the client workstation and transmitted back to the token authentication server.

6. The token authentication server validates the response against the expected response from this particular user and this particular smart card. If the two match, the user is deemed authentic and the login session is enabled.

Time-synchronous token authentication uses slightly more sophisticated technology to simplify the challenge-response procedure. The result is that in time-synchronous token authentication, there is no server-to-client challenge step. SecureID tokens from Security Dynamics are examples of time-synchronous token authentication using a protocol known as SecureID ACE (access control encryption).

1. Every 60 seconds, the time-synchronous smart card and the server-based software generate a new access code.

2. The user enters a userID, a personal ID number, and the access code currently displayed on the smart card.

3. The server receives the access code and authenticates the user by comparing the received access code to the expected access code unique to that smart card that was generated at the server in time-synchronous fashion.

Figure 12-24 differentiates between challenge-response token authentication and time-synchronous token authentication.

Besides SecureID from Security Dynamics, other examples of authentication tokens include Praesidium SpeedCard from Hewlett-Packard, PrivateCard from Cylink, CryptCard from Global Technologies Group, TrustBroker from CyberSafe, and Defender from Axent Technologies.

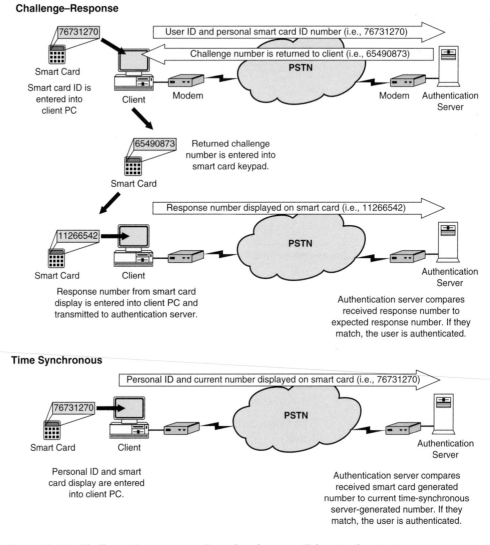

*Figure 12-24*   Challenge-Response vs. Time-Synchronous Token Authentication

## Biometric Authentication

If the security offered by token authentication is insufficient, **biometric authentication** can authenticate users based on fingerprints, palm prints, retinal patterns, hand geometry, facial geometry, voice recognition, or other physical characteristics. Passwords and smart cards can be stolen, but fingerprints and retinal patterns cannot. All biometric authentication devices require that valid users first register by storing copies of their fingerprints, voice, or retinal patterns in a validation database. This gives the biometric device something to reference each time an intended user logs in.

Biometric authentication devices are not yet perfect or foolproof. Most biometric authentication devices must be calibrated for sensitivity. If the biometric device comparison algorithm is set too sensitively, then **false rejects** will occur when valid users are denied access because of slight variations detected between the reference biometric characteristic and the current one. If the biometric device comparison algorithm is not set sensitively enough, then **false accepts** will occur when impostors are allowed access because the comparison was not detailed enough. Users of biometric authentication equipment must calibrate the sensitivity of the equipment to produce acceptable levels of false rejects and false accepts.

## Authorization

Sometimes perceived as a subset of authentication, authorization is concerned with ensuring that only properly authorized users are able to access particular network resources or corporate information resources. In other words, while authentication ensures that only legitimate users are able to log into the network, authorization ensures that these properly authenticated users only access the network resources for which they are properly authorized. This assurance that users are able to log into a network, rather than each individual server and application, and be only able to access only resources for which they are properly authorized is known as **secure single login.**

The authorization security software can be either server-based, also known as **brokered authorization,** or workstation-based, also referred to as **trusted node.** TrustBroker from Cybersafe and AccessMaster from BullSoft are two examples of this category of software.

## Kerberos

Perhaps the most well-known combination authentication/authorization software is **Kerberos,** developed originally at Massachusetts Institute of Technology and marketed commercially by a variety of firms. The Kerberos architecture is illustrated in Figure 12-25.

A Kerberos architecture consists of three key components:

- Kerberos client software
- Kerberos authentication server software
- Kerberos application server software

To be able to ensure that only authorized users are able to access a particular application, Kerberos must be able to communicate directly with that application. As a result, the source code of the application must be "Kerberized" or modified to be compatible with Kerberos. If the source code is not available, perhaps the software vendor sells Kerberized versions of their software. Kerberos is not able to offer authorization protection to applications with which it cannot communicate. Kerberos enforces authentication and authorization through the use of a ticket-based system. An encrypted **ticket** is issued for each server-to-client session and is valid only for a preset amount of time. The ticket is valid only for connections between a designated client and server, thus precluding users from accessing servers or applications for which they are not properly authorized.

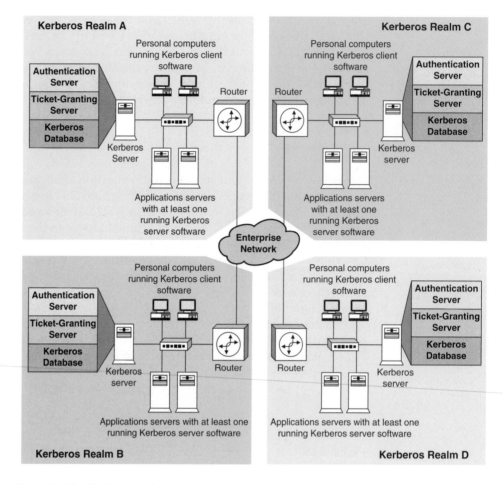

*Figure 12-25*   Kerberos Architecture

Logically, Kerberos works as follows:

1.  Users are first authenticated by the Kerberos authentication server, which consults its database and grants a ticket for the valid user to communicate with the ticket granting server (TGS). This ticket is known as a **ticket-granting ticket.**

2.  Using this ticket, the user sends an encrypted request to the TGS requesting a ticket for access to a particular applications server.

3.  If the TGS determines that the request is valid, a ticket is issued that will allow the user to access the requested server. This ticket is known as a **service-granting ticket.**

4.  The user presents the validated ticket to the application server, which evaluates the ticket's validity. If the application determines that the ticket is valid, a client/server session is established. This session can optionally be encrypted.

Enterprise networks implementing Kerberos are divided into Kerberos **realms,** each served by its own Kerberos server. If a client wishes to access a server in another realm, it requests an **inter-realm** ticket granting ticket from its local ticket granting server to authorize access to the remote ticket granting server that can authorize access to the remote applications server.

Managerial
Perspective

## KERBEROS DEPLOYMENT CONSIDERATIONS

From a network analyst's perspective, concern should be centered on the amount of overhead or network bandwidth consumed by the addition of Kerberos security. Research has indicated that, in fact, the network impact is minimal. However, the additional administrative responsibility of maintaining the Kerberos databases that indicate which users are authorized to access which network resources should not be ignored.

## ■ ENCRYPTION

Encryption involves the changing of data into an indecipherable form before transmission. In this way, even if the transmitted data are somehow intercepted, they cannot be interpreted. The changed, unmeaningful data is known as **ciphertext.** Encryption must be accompanied by decryption, or changing the unreadable text back into its original form.

### DES—Private Key Encryption

The decrypting device must use the same algorithm or method and key to decode or decrypt the data as the encrypting device used to encrypt the data. For this reason **private key encryption** is sometimes also known as symmetric encryption. Although proprietary standards do exist, a standard known as **DES (data encryption standard),** originally approved by the National Institute of Standards and Technology (NIST) in 1977, is often used, allowing encryption devices manufactured by different manufacturers to interoperate successfully. The DES encryption standard actually has two parts, which offer greater overall security. In addition to the standard algorithm or method of encrypting data 64 bits at a time, the DES standard also uses a 64-bit key.

The encryption key customizes the commonly known algorithm to prevent anyone without this private key from possibly decrypting the document. This private key must be known by the both the sending and receiving encryption devices and allows so many unique combinations (nearly 2 to the 64th power), that unauthorized decryption is nearly impossible. The safe and reliable distribution of these private keys among numerous encryption devices can be difficult. If this private key is somehow intercepted, the integrity of the encryption system is compromised.

### RSA—Public Key Encryption

As an alternative to the DES private key standard, **public key encryption** can be utilized. The current standard for public key encryption is known as **RSA,** named after the three founders of the protocol (Rivest-Shamir-Adelman). Public key encryption could perhaps more accurately be named public/private key encryption, as the process actually combines usage of both public and private keys. In public key encryption, the sending encryption device encrypts a document using the intended recipient's public key and the originating party's private key. This public key is readily available in a public directory or is sent by the intended recipient to the message sender. However, to decrypt the document, the receiving encryption/decryption device must be programmed with its own private key and the sending party's public key. In this method, the need for transmission of private keys between sending and receiving parties is eliminated.

## Digital Signature Encryption

As an added security measure, **digital signature encryption** uses this public key encryption methodology in reverse as an electronic means of guaranteeing authenticity of the sending party and assurance that encrypted documents have not been altered during transmission.

With digital signature encryption, a document's digital signature is created by the sender using a private key and the original document. The original document is processed by a hashing program such as Secure Hash Algorithm, Message Digest 2, or Message Digest 5, to produce a mathematical string that is unique to the exact content of the original document. This unique mathematical string is then encrypted using the originator's private key. The encrypted digital signature is then appended to and transmitted with the encrypted original document.

To validate the authenticity of the received document, the recipient uses a public key associated with the apparent sender to regenerate a digital signature from the received encrypted document. The transmitted digital signature is then compared by the recipient to the regenerated digital signature produced by using the public key and the received document. If the two digital signatures match, the document is authentic (really produced by alleged originator) and has not been altered. Figure 12-26 illustrates the differences between private key encryption, public key encryption, and digital signature encryption; Figure 12-27 summarizes some key facts about currently popular encryption standards.

Examples of encryption technology capable of encrypting files either while being stored or transmitted include Secure PC from Security Dynamics, F-Secure Workstation Suite from Data Fellows, and PrivaCD from Global Technologies Group.

## Key Management Alternatives

Before two computers can communicate in a secure manner, they must be able to agree on encryption and authentication algorithms and establish keys in a process known as key management. Two standards for key management are:

- **ISAKMP (Internet security association and key management protocol)** from the IETF: now largely replaced by IKE (internet key exchange) described later in the section on IPSec.

- **SKIP (simple key management for IP)** from Sun.

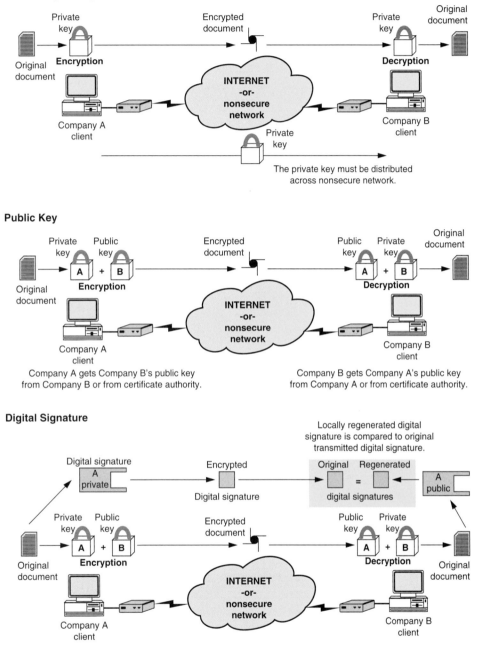

*Figure 12-26*   Private Key Encryption, Public Key Encryption, and
Digital Signature Encryption

Public key dissemination must be managed in such a way that users can be assured that public keys received are actually the public keys of the companies or organizations that they are alleged to be. This added level of assurance is provided by **public key certificates.** The organization required to manage digital keys is generally described as the public key infrastructure (PKI). **PKIX (public**

| Standard | Type | Key Size | Explanation |
|----------|------|----------|-------------|
| **3DES** | Private | 40, 56 bits | Triple DES, uses 2 or 3 keys and multiple passes |
| **DES** | Private | 40, 56 bits | Digital encryption standard, widely used for private key encryption |
| **DSA** | Digital Signature | 1,024 | Digital signature algorithm generates appended digital signatures based on original document to ensure document has not been altered |
| **ECC** | Public | 160 | Elliptical curve cryptography, claims to produce equivalent security of 1,024 bit RSA key in only 160 bits |
| **IDEA** | Private | 128 bit | International data encryption algorithm, generates one-time use session keys, used in PGP (pretty good privacy) |
| **MD5** | Digest | | Produces 128-bit hash number based on original document, can then be incorporated into digital signature, replaced MD4 and MD2 |
| **RSA** | Public | 512 to 2,048 bits | Rivest-Shamir-Adelman, popular public key encryption standard, minimum key length of 1,024 recommended |
| **Skipjack** | Private | 80 | Used for Clipper and Capstone encryption chips and Defense Messaging System (DMS) |

*Figure 12-27*   Encryption Standards

**key infrastructure X.509)** is an international ISO standard for public key certificates. The IETF has been working on an alternative public key infrastructure standard that is oriented toward varying authorization levels rather than personal identities by using what are known as privilege-based certificates. This draft standard, known as **SPKI/SDSI (simple public key infrastructure/simple distributed security infrastructure),** specifies a distributed client/server model in which humanly readable certificates and the authorization levels they represent can be delegated and processed according to user-defined rules.

Public key infrastructures that link a particular user to a particular public key are implemented through the use of server-based software known as **certificate servers.** Certificate server software also supports encryption and digital signatures while flexibly supporting directory integration, multiple certificate types, and a variety of request fulfillment options. Third-party key certification services, or **certificate authorities (CA),** issue the public keys along with a certificate ensuring the authenticity of the key. Such certification authorities issue public keys of other organizations, along with certificates of authenticity, ensured by their own digital signature. VeriSign is one example of a trusted third-party issuer of X.509 public-key certificates. Other certificate authorities include CyberTrust from GTE and CommercePoint from IBM. Interoperability among digital certificates issued by different certificate authorities is now beginning to emerge, but should not be assumed. The U.S. Postal Service has also announced plans to begin issuing public key certificates. Organizations can install their own certificate servers as well. Examples of certificate server software include NetScape Certificate Server from NetScape, Microsoft Certificate Server from Microsoft, and Entrust from Entrust.

Digital certificates or **Digital IDs** issued from CAs such as VeriSign contain an organization's encrypted public key along with a minimal amount of information about the organization such as e-mail address, department, company, state or province, and country. Once a certificate has been issued by a CA, an organization can post its Digital ID on a Web page and be assured that the CA will stand behind the Digital ID's authenticity.

Digital IDs may one day replace passwords for Internet-based communications. Recognizing the potential for electronic commerce vendors to quickly gather demographic data about their customers, VeriSign has enhanced its Class 1 Digital ID format to include additional fields in which to store demographic data such as gender, age, address, zip code, or other personal data. Information stored in the encrypted Class 2 Digital ID could allow customized Web pages to be built based on the information contained therein. The Digital ID service from VeriSign costs $6.00 per year for a Class 1 Digital ID and $12.00 per year for a Class 2 Digital ID.

## ■ APPLIED SECURITY SCENARIOS

### Overall Design Strategies

Although it is impossible to prescribe a network security design that would be appropriate for any given situation, some general guidelines that would apply to most situations are as follows:

- Install only software and hardware that you really need on the network. Every time that hardware or software is installed on a network, potential security vulnerabilities resulting from misconfiguration or design flaws are introduced.

- Allow only essential traffic into and out of the corporate network and eliminate all other types by blocking with routers or firewalls. E-mail and domain name service (DNS) queries are a good place to start.

- Investigate the business case for outsourcing Web-hosting services so that the corporate Web server is not physically on the same network as the rest of the corporate information assets.

- Use routers to filter traffic by IP address. Allow only known authorized users to have access through the router and into the corporate information network.

- Make sure that router operating system software has been patched to prevent denial of service and land attacks by exploiting TCP vulnerabilities, or better still, block all incoming TCP traffic.

- Identify those information assets that are most critical to the corporation, and protect those servers first. It is better to have the most important assets well protected than to have all of the information assets somewhat protected.

- Implement physical security constraints to hinder physical access to critical resources such as servers.

- Monitor system activity logs carefully, paying close attention to failed login attempts and file transfers.

- Develop a simple, effective, and enforceable security policy and monitor its implementation and effectiveness.

- Consider installing a proxy server or applications layer firewall.

- Block incoming DNS queries and requests for zone transfers. This is how hackers are able to map a corporation's internal network resources.

- Don't publish the corporation's complete DNS map on DNS servers that are outside the corporate firewall. Publish only those few servers that the Internet needs to know: e-mail gateway, DNS server, Web site.

- Disable all TCP ports and services that are not essential so that hackers are not able to exploit and use these services.

### Integration with Information Systems and Application Development

Authentication products must be integrated with existing information systems and applications development efforts. APIs (application program interfaces) are the means by which authentication products are able to integrate with client/server applications. Beyond APIs are application development environments or software development kits that combine an application development language with the supported APIs. APIs or application development environments must be compatible with the programming language in which applications are to be developed.

AT&T provides a software development kit that includes a library of C language security APIs and software modules for integrating digital signature and other security functionality into Windows NT and Windows 95 applications.

Security Dynamics, who markets SecurID time-synchronous token authentication products, also provides software development kits known as BSAFE.

Intel, IBM, and Netscape have collaborated on a multi-API security framework for encryption and authentication known as common data security architecture (CDSA) that can be integrated with Java bases objects. Other security APIs may be forthcoming from Sun and Novell also.

An open API which would allow applications to communicate with a variety of security authorization programs is known as **GSS-API (generic security service-applications program interface)** and is documented in RFCs 1508 and 1509. Security products companies such as Nortel, producers of the Entrust file signing and encryption package, and Cybersafe Corporation support the GSS-API. GSS-API is described as open because it interfaces between user applications and a variety of security services such as Kerberos, secure FTP, or encryption services. The applications developer does not need to understand the intricacies of these security services and is able to flexibly choose those security services that best meet the needs of the application under development. The GSS-API can also be integrated with Intel's CDSA.

### Remote Access Security

The biggest challenge facing remote access security is how to manage the activity of all of the remote access users that have logged in via a variety of multivendor equipment and authentication technology. A protocol and associated architecture known as **remote authentication dial-in user service (RADIUS)** (RFC 2058) is supported by a wide variety of remote access technology and offers the potential to enable centralized management of remote access users and technology. The RADIUS architecture is illustrated in Figure 12-28. This architecture is referred to as three-tiered because it enables communication between the following three tiers of technology:

- Remote access devices such as remote access servers and token authentication technology from a variety of vendors, otherwise known as network access servers (NAS).

- Enterprise database that contains authentication and access control information.

- RADIUS authentication server.

In this architecture, users request connections and provide user IDs and passwords to the network access servers, which, in turn, pass the information along to the RADIUS authentication server for authentication approval or denial.

RADIUS allows network managers to centrally manage remote access users, access methods, and logon restrictions. It allows centralized auditing capabilities such as keeping track of volume of traffic sent and amount of time on-line. RADIUS also enforces remote access limitations such as server access restrictions or on-line time limitations. For authentication, it supports **password authentication protocol (PAP), challenge handshake authentication protocol (CHAP),** and SecurID token authentication. RADIUS transmits passwords in encrypted format

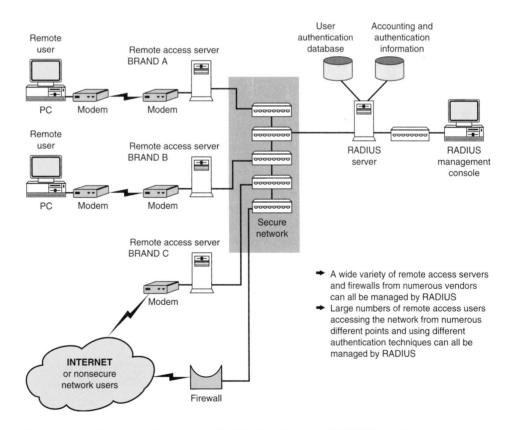

*Figure 12-28*    Remote Authentication Dial-In User Services (RADIUS) Architecture

only. Some RADIUS-based centralized management products may require that a new centralized database of remote access user information be built, whereas others, such as Funk Software's Steel Belted RADIUS, are able to use an existing network operating system's directory services, such as NetWare's NDS, as the management database.

RADIUS is not the only open protocol for communication between centralized remote access management technology and multivendor remote access technology. **Extended terminal access controller access-control system (XTACACS),** also known simply as TACACS or the updated version known as TACACS+ (RFC 1492), is another example of remote access management protocol that supports three-tiered remote access management architectures. The most widely known implementation of TACACS is Cisco System's server-based security protocol. TACACS transmits authentication information in cleartext format, whereas TACACS+ employs MD hashing and encrypts the entire packet. TACACS+ can also handle multiprotocol logins (IP and IPX) and incorporate PAP/CHAP as well.

**PAP/CHAP**   PAP and CHAP, incorporated within RADIUS as previously described, are two other protocols that can be used on a stand-alone basis for remote access authentication. **Password authentication protocol** (RFC 1334) is the simpler of the two authentication protocols designed for dial-in communication. PAP repeatedly sends the user ID and password to the authenticating system in clear text pairs until it is either acknowledged or the connection is dropped. Otherwise known as a two-way handshaking protocol, PAP does not perform encryption.

**Challenge handshake authentication protocol** (RFC 1994) provides a more secure means for establishing dial-in communication. It uses a three-way challenge or handshake that includes the user ID, password and also a key that encrypts the ID and password. The process of sending the pair to the authentication system is the same as with PAP, but the encryption reduces the chance that someone will be able to pick up the ID and password and use it to access a system. CHAP is initiated by the server by issuing a challenge to the client that wishes to log in. The client must calculate a value using a one-time key and the challenge that it just received from the server. The server would then verify the calculated value based on the challenge it had initially sent the client. The problem with this system, and any single key system for that matter, is that some mechanism must be in place for both the receiver and sender to know and have access to the key. To address this problem, a public key technique may be used to encrypt the single private key for transmission. In addition, CHAP repeats the authentication procedure after the link is initially established to ensure that the session or link has not been compromised or taken over by an unauthorized party.

## E-Mail, Web, and Internet/Intranet Security

The two primary standards for encrypting traffic on the World Wide Web are:

- **S-HTTP: secure hypertext transport protocol**
- **SSL: secure sockets layer**

**S-HTTP**   Secure HTTP is a secure version of HTTP that requires both client and server S-HTTP versions to be installed for secure end-to-end encrypted transmission. S-HTTP, based on public key encryption, is described as providing security at the document or application level since it works with the actual HTTP applications to secure documents and messages. S-HTTP uses digital signature encryption to ensure that the document possesses both authenticity and message integrity. The use of S-HTTP has diminished with the growing popularity of Netscape's Secure browser and server as well as other alternatives for secure Web-based transmissions.

**SSL** SSL is described as wrapping an encrypted envelope around HTTP transmissions. Whereas S-HTTP can only be used to encrypt Web documents, SSL can be wrapped around other Internet service transmissions such as FTP, Telnet, and Gopher, as well as HTTP. SSL is a connection level encryption method providing security to the network link itself. SSL Version 3 (SSL3) added support for more key exchange and encryption algorithms as well as separate keys for authentication and encryption.

SSL and S-HTTP are not competing or conflicting standards, although they are sometimes viewed that way. In an analogy to a postal service scenario, SSL provides the locked postal delivery vehicle, and S-HTTP provides the sealed, tamper-evident envelope that allows only the intended recipient to view the confidential document contained within.

Another Internet security protocol directed specifically toward securing and authenticating commercial financial transactions is known as **secure courier** and is offered by Netscape. Secure Courier is based on SSL and allows users to create a secure digital envelope for transmission of financial transactions over the Internet. Secure Courier also provides consumer authentication for the cybermerchants inhabiting the commercial Internet.

**PGP** An Internet e-mail-specific encryption standard that also uses digital signature encryption to guarantee the authenticity, security, and message integrity of received e-mail is known as **PGP,** which stands for **pretty good privacy** (RFC 1991). PGP overcomes inherent security loopholes with public/private key security schemes by implementing a Web of trust in which e-mail users electronically sign each other's public keys to create an interconnected group of public key users. Digital signature encryption is provided using a combination of RSA and **MD5** (message direct version 5) encryption techniques. Combined documents and digital signatures are then encrypted using **IDEA (international data encryption algorithm),** which makes use of one-time 128-bit keys known as **session keys.** PGP is also able to compress data transmissions as well. PGP/MIME overcomes PGP's inability to encrypt multimedia (MIME) objects.

**SET** **Secure electronic transactions (SET)** are a series of standards to ensure the confidentiality of electronic commerce transactions. These standards are being largely promoted by credit card giants VISA and MasterCard. SET standards are specifically aimed at defining how bank-card transactions can be conducted in a secure manner over the Internet. However, the assurance of e-commerce confidentiality is not without costs in terms of processing overhead. A single SET-compliant electronic transaction could require as many as six cryptographic functions, taking from one-third to one-half second on a high-powered Unix workstation. The impact of thousands or millions of transactions per second could be enormous.

A large part of ensuring the authenticity of e-commerce depends on trusting that the e-customers and e-vendors are really who they say they are. An important aspect of the SET standards is the incorporation of digital certificates or digital IDs, more specifically known as SET Digital IDs that are issued by such companies as VeriSign.

**S/MIME**   **Secure multipurpose Internet mail extension** secures e-mail traffic in e-mail applications that have been **S/MIME** enabled. S/MIME encrypts and authenticates e-mail messages for transmission over SMTP-based e-mail networks. S/MIME enables different e-mail systems to exchange encrypted messages and is able to encrypt multimedia as well as text-based e-mail.

## Virtual Private Network Security

To provide virtual private networking capabilities using the Internet as an enterprise network backbone, specialized **tunneling protocols** needed to be developed that could establish private, secure channels between connected systems. Two rival standards are examples of such tunneling protocols:

- Microsoft's **point-to-point tunneling protocol (PPTP)**
- Cisco's **layer two forwarding (L2F)**

An effort is underway to have the Internet Engineering Task Force (IETF) propose a unification of the two rival standards known as **layer 2 tunneling protocol (L2TP).** One shortcoming of the proposed specification is that it does not deal with security issues such as encryption and authentication. Figure 12-29 illustrates the use of tunneling protocols to build virtual private networks using the Internet as an enterprise network backbone.

Two rival specifications currently exist for establishing security over VPN tunnels:

- **IPsec** is largely supported by the firewall vendor community and is intended to provide interoperability between VPN firewalls from different vendors.

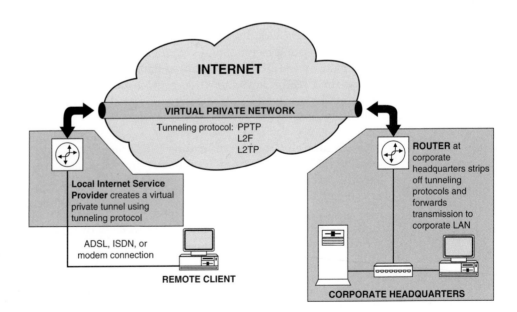

*Figure 12-29*   Tunneling Protocols Enable Virtual Private Networks

- PPTP is Microsoft's tunneling protocol that is specific to Windows NT servers and remote access servers. It has the backing of several remote access server vendors.

Examples of VPN technology include Cisco Secure Integrated VPN Software from Cisco Systems, VPN-1 from Checkpoint, Raptor Power VPN Server from Axent Technologies, Cyberwall PLUS-VPN from Network 1 Security Solutions, and PPTP-RAS from Microsoft.

**IPSec—Secure IP**   IPsec is a protocol that ensures encrypted (56-bit key DES) communications across the Internet via virtual private networks through the use of manual key exchange. IPsec supports only IP-based communications. IPsec is a standard that, in theory at least, should enable interoperability between firewalls supporting the protocol. Although firewalls of the same brand seem to interoperate sufficiently via IPsec, that does not seem to be the case between different brands of firewall technology.

IPsec is also proposed to be able to support both authentication and encryption. These capabilities are optional for IPv4 and mandatory for **IPv6** and are outlined in IETF RFCs 1825 through 1829. In addition to encryption and authentication, IPsec also includes the ISAKMP (Internet security association key management protocol), now largely replaced by IKE. To deliver these functions, two new headers are added to the existing IP header:

- The **authentication header** (RFC 1826) provides data integrity and allows for the authentication of IP packets. It can specify the security association to provide authentication between the source and destination parties, and it can also supply data to be used by the agreed on particular authentication algorithm to be used.

- The **encapsulating security payload header (ESP)** (RFC 1827) ensures the privacy of the transmission. The ESP header can be used in two different modes depending on the user's privacy needs:

  ○ **Transport Mode ESP** is used to encrypt the data carried by the IP packet. The contents of the data field of an IP (network layer) packet are the upper layer or transport layer protocols TCP (connection-oriented) or UDP (connectionless). These transport layer envelopes encapsulate upper layer data.

  ○ **Tunnel Mode ESP** encrypts the entire IP packet including its own header. This mode is effective at countering network analyzers or sniffers from capturing IP address information. Tunnel mode is most often used in a network topology that includes a firewall that separates a protected network from an external nonsecure network.

It is important to note that the mere inclusion of fields in a protocol does not ensure implementation. Applications, authentication products, and trusted security associations would all have to modify hardware and/or software technology to avail themselves of the protocol's new functionality. Figure 12-30 illustrates an IPsec packet with authentication and encryption headers added.

**IKE (Internet key exchange)** is the handshaking portion of the IPSec protocol used to establish sessions across a VPN. It is referred to as a replacement for ISAKMP. However, IKE requires preshared keys and static IP addresses, neither of

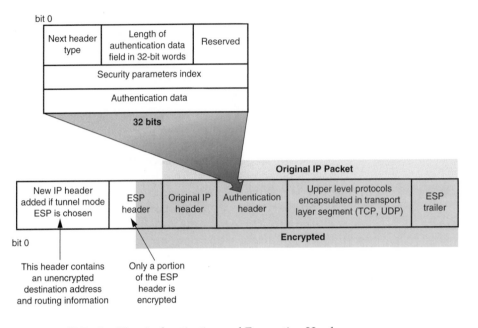

*Figure 12-30*    IP Packet Plus Authentication and Encryption Headers

which may be practical with dial-up users and/or trading partners with whom sharing keys may not be practical. How to get IPSec to work in an interoperable fashion for remote access supporting dynamic IP addresses has generated numerous competing potential standards including the following:

- Use L2TP with IPSec
- Modify IKE to support remote access over the Internet—referred to as IKE/XAUTH (extended authorization) otherwise known as the IKE/RADIUS method; other variations include IKE Mode Config and Hybrid Authentication Mode for IKE
- Modify IKE to support DHCP

Each of these alternatives has technical advantages and disadvantages. Some efforts are being developed within the IETF and others are vendor driven. There are no clear choices and users must educate themselves as to the intricacies of each protocol and force vendors to be truthful as to functionality and interoperability of their products.

## PPTP—Point-to-Point Tunneling Protocol

PPTP is essentially just a tunneling protocol that allows managers to choose whatever encryption or authentication technology they wish to hang off either end of the established tunnel. PPTP supports multiple network protocols including IPX, NetBEUI, and IP. PPTP is primarily concerned with secure remote access in that PPP-enabled clients would be able to dial in to a corporate network via the Internet.

## Enterprise Network Security

To maintain proper security over a widely distributed enterprise network, it is essential to be able to conduct certain security-related processes from a single, centralized, security management location. Among these processes or functions are the following:

- **Single point of registration (SPR)** allows a network security manager to enter a new user (or delete a terminated user) from a single centralized location and assign all associated rights, privileges, and access control to enterprise resources from this single point rather than having to enter this new user's information on multiple resources distributed throughout the enterprise.

- **Single sign-on (SSO),** also sometimes known as secure single sign-on (SSSO), allows the user to login to the enterprise network and to be authenticated from the client PC location. It is not necessary for the user to remember a variety of different user IDS and passwords to the numerous different enterprise servers from which they may request services. Since this is the single entry point onto the enterprise network for this user, auditing software can be used to keep nonrepudiable records of all activities and transactions. Any of the variety of authentication technologies discussed earlier can be used in support of single sign-on.

- **Single access control view** allows the user's access from the client workstation to display only those resources that the user actually has access to. Any differences between server platforms should be shielded from the user. The user should not need to memorize different commands or control interfaces for the variety of enterprise servers that a user may need to access.

- **Security auditing and intrusion detection** is able to track and identify suspicious behaviors from both internal employees and potential intruders. In addition to detecting and reporting these instances, it is essential to be able to respond in an appropriate and automated fashion to these events. Although the intrusions may take place anywhere on the widely distributed network, the detection and response to such events must be controlled from a centralized security management location.

## Tying It All Together—Security Frameworks

An enterprise-wide security solution currently involves the deployment of a wide variety of different security technologies, sometimes referred to as point products, from a multitude of vendors. The centralized management of such a wide array of technology is very challenging. In response to this challenge, **security frameworks** have begun to emerge that attempt to consolidate security management into a single architecture or console, allowing centralized policy management and automated incident response. Obviously, interoperability standards are required to get security tools from various vendors to all interact with a single overall framework. The **OPSEC (open platform for security) alliance** is one example of a multivendor interoperable security architecture. More than 200 vendors of security technology have joined the OPSEC alliance, which offers certification for OPSEC-compliant security products.

## ■ GOVERNMENT IMPACT

Government agencies play a major role in the area of network security. The two primary functions of these various government agencies are:

- Standards-making organizations that set standards for the design, implementation, and certification of security technology and systems

- Regulatory agencies that control the export of security technology to a company's international locations

### Standards-Making Organizations

Although many standards-making organizations are involved to varying degrees in the field of network security, following are some of the most significant ones.

**ANSI**   The American National Standards Institute, or ANSI, is the United States representative to the International Standards Organization, or ISO. Any submissions to the ISO from other U.S. standards organizations must first be submitted to ANSI.

**NIST**   The National Institute of Standards and Technology, or the NIST, was formed in 1987, but it was formerly known as the National Bureau of Standards. This organization issues publications called the Federal Information Processing Standards, or FIPS publications. Category 5 FIPS publications deal with computer security standards and guidelines and include subcategories of access control, cryptography, general computer security, risk analysis and contingency planning, and security labels. The NIST also publishes a series of special publications related to computer security included in the SP500 and SP800 series. The NIST also operates a very useful Computer Security Resource Clearinghouse on the World Wide Web at http://csrc.ncsl.nist.gov.

**IAB**   The Internet Architecture Board is the policy setting and decision review board for the Internet. The IETF or Internet Engineering Task Force is a subgroup of the IAB that is responsible for setting the technical standards that run the Internet. This group is responsible for issuing and gathering the responses to RFC (requests for comments).

**ISO**   The International Standards Organization is a voluntary organization sanctioned by the United Nations. It is responsible for international standards in a variety of fields, not just data communications. Besides the OSI 7 layer reference model, the ISO is also responsible for the security-related addendum to the OSI model known as **ISO 7498/2,** the OSI Security Architecture.

**NSA**   The National Security Agency is a secretive governmental organization that works closely with the NIST and is responsible for the design and use of nonmilitary encryption technology. The NSA also runs the NCSC, or the National Computer Security Center (www.nsa.gov).

**NCSC**   The purpose of this organization is to work with members of the computer industry to provide guidelines that are designed to help them develop trusted systems and computer products. This organization is also known for a security certification program called the Trusted Computer System Evaluation Criteria (TCSEC). It is commonly known as the Orange Book because of the color of the jacket. There is also a Red Book from the NCSC, which was developed in 1987 as a supplement to the Orange Book. These "colored book" security guidelines have been criticized for their focus primarily on computer security rather than network security.

*Orange Book Certification*    The primary focus of the Orange Book is to provide confidential protection of sensitive information based on the following requirements:

- Security policy: An explicit and well-defined security policy must be enforced by the system.

- Marking: Access control labels must be associated with all objects.

- Identification: Individual users must be identified.

- Accountability: Audit information must be kept and protected so that actions affecting security can be traced to the responsible party.

- Assurance: The system must contain hardware and/or software components that can be evaluated independently to provide sufficient assurance that the security policy and accountability criteria can be enforced.

- Continuous protection: The components above that enforce these basic requirements must be continuously protected against tampering and/or unauthorized changes.

The Orange Book is broken into two primary parts. The first part is illustrated in Figure 12-31. It specifies the criteria that must be met to achieve a specific rating. The criteria are defined in hierarchical fashion, with four different ratings possible. The "A" rating is the most secure possible and the "D" rating corresponds to the least secure rating possible. The second portion contains information about the basic objectives, rationale, and government policy behind the development of each of the criteria. It is also intended to provide guidelines for product developers to aid them in achieving a specific criteria.

The Orange Book certification process is both costly and lengthy. Typically, the certification process is projected to take two years to complete at a cost of 17 million dollars. To date, both NetWare and NT Server have achieved the C-2 certification. An important point to be aware of is that many products may advertise a certification compliance with an Orange Book level; however, compliance and certification are two very different terms. Any vendor can claim compliance, but only vendors that have spent the time and money to pursue the certification process can claim that their products are C-2 certified.

## Encryption Export Policy and Key Recovery

Many corporations and organizations depend on the need for private and confidential communication on an international basis. However, in the United States, export of encryption software is tightly controlled. The traditional limit on exportable encryption technology was a 40-bit key. However, 40-bit keys can be cracked in a matter of minutes and do not offer much protection. Businesses conducting operations internationally obviously want to be able to use stronger

| Division | Protection | Class | Protection | Description |
|---|---|---|---|---|
| D | Minimal | D | Minimal | Evaluated but does not meet any higher class requirements |
| C | Discretionary | C1 | Discretionary security | Confidence in hardware and software controls |
| | | | | Isolates and authenticates users and data |
| | | C2 | Controlled access | Encapsulates resources; login and explicit auditing |
| B | Mandatory | B1 | Labeled security | Explicit protection model; execution domains, file labels, system security officer and documentation required |
| | | B2 | Structured | Formal security model, kernelized, covert channel ID, mandatory controls including communication lines required |
| | | B3 | Security domains | Central encapsulation, reference monitor, tamper proof, recovery procedures, protected against authentication attacks |
| A | Verified | A1 | Verified design | Extensive security considerations during all developmental phases; math tools, formal models with explicit math theorems, formal top level specifications, trusted software distribution required |
| | | | Beyond A1 | Developmental; source verification |

*Figure 12-31*    Orange Book Certification Criteria

encryption technology. The government, on the other hand, wishes to gain greater control over international encrypted communication.

U.S. companies can export encryption technology to their own foreign subsidiaries without review or restriction. The new regulations also relax restrictions on publicly available encryption technology posted to the Internet. Exports to Cuba, Iran, Iraq, Libya, North Korea, Sudan, and Syria are still prohibited. Export of encryption technology is now administered by the Commerce Department's Bureau of Export Administration.

Key recovery schemes basically ensure that a spare set of encryption keys is always available. With key recovery, the actual information used to reconstruct a key travels with the message header. However, someone with the key decryption codes (the spare set of keys) must combine the decryption codes with the key information in the message header to decrypt the message. The big question seems to be, "Who will hold the keys?" **Key escrow agencies,** otherwise known as trusted third parties, are the most commonly proposed solution. Other proposals say that large multinational corporations should be able to act as their own key escrow agents. At the moment there are about thirteen different **key recovery mechanisms,** and no single standard has been proposed, although an IBM-led key-recovery alliance with forty corporate members has been formed. If key recovery were to be extended to a domestic basis, the implications could be phenomenal. Everyone who uses the Internet for communication would need a key and a key escrow agent. This could mean tens of millions of keys unless some type of key sharing was initiated.

## SUMMARY

Without question, the overriding theme in this chapter has been that the implementation of security technology in the absence of a comprehensive security policy, including senior management support, is a waste of time and money. Security policy must be developed as part of an overall increase in security awareness on the part of all users. It must be accompanied by a clear understanding of business processes and personal responsibilities as they relate to security policy implementation. Only in the context of a dynamic, constantly audited security policy can security technology implementation be successful.

The first security process that is generally addressed is virus protection, most often in response to a virus incident. Virus scanning technology is of little use without comprehensive, enforced policies regarding use and handling of diskettes and downloaded files. Activity monitors and signature scanners are two major types of virus scanning software.

The next security process that is generally addressed is authentication, ensuring that users attempting to log into network resources are really whom they claim to be. Authentication technology includes challenge response and time synchronous token authentication systems.

Authorization and access control ensure that authenticated users are only able to access those files, directories, and applications to which they are entitled. Kerberos is the best example of a comprehensive authentication/authorization system.

Firewalls are an effective means of shielding private, secure, internal networks from nonsecure external networks. Like other security technology, they must be implemented correctly and in accordance with the overall security policy. Two major categories of firewalls are packet filters, which discriminate between traffic based on source and destination addresses, and application gateways of proxies, which examine individual commands within applications.

Privacy of network communications is ensured by encryption. Private key encryption, public key encryption, and digital signature encryption are the major categories of encryption technology. Encryption sessions are customized through the use of keys. The longer the key, in bits, the more secure the transmission.

## KEY TERMS

active content monitors
activity monitors
application gateways
application level filters
assets
assured pipelines
attack applets
authentication
authentication header
biometric authentication
brokered authorization
C-2 certification
CA
certificate authorities
certificate servers
challenge handshake
    authentication protocol
challenge-response token
    authentication
CHAP
ciphertext

circuit-level proxies
CRC checkers
data encryption standard
decoys
denial of service attack
DES
Digital IDs
digital signature encryption
DMZ
dual firewalls
dual-homed gateway
emulation technology
encapsulating security payload
    header
ESP
event detection
extended terminal access control
    access system
false accepts
false rejects
filter

filter tables
firewall
generic security service-
    applications program interface
GSS-API
hashing checkers
heuristic analysis
IDEA
IKE
inter-realm
internal firewalls
international data encryption
    algorithm
Internet key exchange
Internet security association and
    key management protocol
intrusion detection systems
IP spoofing
IPsec
IPv6
ISAKMP

ISO 7498/2
Kerberos
key escrow agencies
key recovery mechanisms
L2F
L2TP
land attack
latency
layer 2 tunneling protocol
layer two forwarding
logic bombs
macro viruses
malicious applets
MD5
Multi-tiered firewall
National Computer Security
   Association
NCSA
network-based intrusion detection
   systems
network level filter
off-line audits
OPSEC Alliance open platform for
   security
OSI security architecture
packet filter
PAP
password authentication protocol
PCT
PEM
PGP
PKIX
point-to-point tunneling protocol
policy audits
polymorphic viruses
port level filter
PPTP
pretty good privacy

privacy enhanced mail
private communications
   technology
private key encryption
protective measures
proxies
public key certificates
public key encryption
public key infrastructure X 509
RADIUS
real-time audits
realms
remote authentication dial-in user
   service
risk
risk domain
RSA
S-HTTP
S/MIME
SATAN
Secure Courier
Secure Electronic Transactions
secure hypertext transport
   protocol
secure multipurpose Internet mail
   extension
secure single login
secure sockets layer
Security Analyzer Tools for
   Analyzing Networks
security appliance
security auditing and intrusion
   detection
security frameworks
security policy development life
   cycle
security probes
service-granting ticket

session keys
SET
signature scanners
simple distributed security
   infrastructure
simple key management for IP
simple public key infrastructure
single access control view
single point of registration
single sign-on
SKIP
smart cards
Socks
SPDLC
SPKI/SDSI
SPR
SSL
SSO
TCP
threats
three-way handshake
ticket
ticket-granting ticket
time bombs
time-synchronous token
   authentication
token authentication
transmission control protocol
transport mode ESP
trojan horse
trusted gateway
trusted node
tunnel mode ESP
tunneling protocols
virtual PC
virus scanning
vulnerabilities
XTACACS

## REVIEW QUESTIONS

1. What are some recent changes in the business and networking worlds that have brought network security to the forefront?
2. What is the importance of the cyclical nature of the security policy development life cycle?
3. What is the purpose of the security requirements assessment grid?
4. What is the dilemma involved with the security/productivity balance?
5. How do the critical success factors introduced with the network development life cycle apply to security policy development?
6. What is the purpose of the OSI Security Architecture and how does it relate to the OSI 7 layer reference model?
7. Differentiate between and give an example, in a network security context, of each of the following: asset, threat, vulnerability, risk, protective measures.
8. Are all of the entities listed in the previous question related by one-to-one relationships? Give an example to defend your answer.
9. Briefly summarize the roles of executives, management, and users in the successful development and implementation of security policy.

10. What is the difference between off-line audits and real-time audits?
11. What is the difference between event detection technology and intrusion detection technology?
12. What is the difference between security audit tools and security probes?
13. What is a virus?
14. What is the difference between a logic bomb and a time bomb?
15. What is a trojan horse?
16. What is a polymorphic virus?
17. What are hostile applets and which environment are they particular to?
18. Why are collaborative applications such as groupware an especially friendly environment for viruses?
19. Differentiate between virus scanning and activity monitors as antivirus technology.
20. What is the shortcoming of CRC and hashing checkers as antivirus solutions?
21. What is a firewall?
22. Differentiate between packet filtering firewalls and application gateway firewalls.
23. Describe the advantages and disadvantages of proxies.
24. What is a dual-homed gateway?
25. What is a trusted gateway?
26. How does a trusted gateway differ from a dual-homed gateway?
27. What is an internal firewall and what is the motivation for such a device?
28. What is authentication?
29. Differentiate between challenge-response authentication and time-synchronous authentication.
30. What is biometric authentication? Give some examples of biometric authentication technology.
31. What is Kerberos?

32. How does Kerberos ensure both authentication and authorization?
33. Differentiate between private key encryption, public key encryption, and digital signature encryption.
34. Why are public key certificates and certificate authorities necessary?
35. Why are APIs and application development environments required to integrate security services with information systems? What would be the alternative?
36. What is RADIUS and what added functionality does it offer over an environment without a three-tiered approach?
37. Differentiate between S-HTTP and SSL.
38. Differentiate between PAP and CHAP.
39. What is PGP? What are its advantages and disadvantages?
40. What is SET and what industry is it targeted toward?
41. What is a tunneling protocol and why is it necessary?
42. What is the difference between single sign-on, single point of registration, and single access control view? What do they all have in common?
43. What is Orange Book or C-2 certification?
44. What is the purpose of a key recovery mechanism and how does it work?
45. What is the role of key escrow agencies in enabling a key recovery mechanism?
46. What are the potential implications if all Internet users were required to use key recovery mechanisms?
47. Discuss the advantages and disadvantages of the alternative enterprise firewall architectures discussed in the text. Are there other viable alternatives that were not mentioned?

**Case Study:** For a business case study and questions that relate to network security, go to www.wiley.com/college/goldman.

# GLOSSARY

**10/100 NICs** Most 100baseT NICs are called 10/100 NICs, which means that they are able to support either 10baseT or 100baseT, but not simultaneously.

**1000baseCX** Uses copper twinaxial cable and transceivers for distances of only 25 meters; used primarily to link servers within a data center or high speed network devices within a wiring closet.

**1000baseLX** Uses long wavelength (1,300 nanometers) laser fiber optic media, used primarily for high speed campus backbone applications.

**1000baseSX** Uses short wavelength (850 nanometers) laser fiber optic media; used primarily for horizontal building cabling on a given floor.

**1000baseTX** This standard allows gigabit Ethernet to travel over 4 pair of Category 5 unshielded twisted pair at a distance of 100 meters.

**100baseFX** Physical layer standard for 100 Mbps transmission over fiber optic cable.

**100baseT4** Physical layer standard for 100 Mbps transmission over 4 pair of Category 3, 4, or 5 UTP.

**100baseTX** The most common of the three 100baseX standards and the one for which the most technology is available. It specifies 100 Mbps performance over 2 pair of Category 5 UTP (Unshielded Twisted Pair) or 2 pair of Type 1 STP (Shielded Twisted Pair).

**100VG-AnyLAN** A 100 Mbps alternative to 100baseT which replaces the CSMA/CD access methodology with Demand Priority Access or DPA, otherwise known as Demand Priority Protocol or DPP.

**10base2** A 10 Mbps Ethernet standard for thin coaxial cable media.

**10base5** A 10 Mbps Ethernet standard for thick coaxial cable media.

**10baseF** A 10 Mbps Ethernet standard for fiber optic cable media.

**10baseT** A 10 Mbps Ethernet standard for unshielded twisted pair media.

**16-bit subsystem** A shared memory address space, sometimes referred to as a 16-bit subsystem, allows 16-bit applications to execute in a 32-bit operating environment.

**16QAM** A 16-point quadrature amplitude modulation; a modulation scheme with 16 different potential detectable events would allow 4 bits/baud or quadbits to be produced or detected per signaling event. In this case the transmission rate in bps would be 4 times the baud rate.

**1base5** A 1 Mbps Ethernet standard for unshielded twisted pair.

**23B+D** 23 bearer channels (64 Kbps ea.) plus one 64K D channel. Configuration of PRI ISDN.

**2B+D** 2 64 Kbps B channels plus one 16K D channel. Configuration of BRI ISDN.

**30B+D** 30 64 Kbps bearer channels plus one 64K D channel. European PRI which maps to an E-1.

**3270 protocol conversion card** Card inserted into an open expansion slot of a PC. Additional protocol conversion software, which may or may not be included with the protocol conversion card, must be loaded onto the PC in order to make the PC keyboard behave like a 3270 terminal keyboard.

**3G Mobile Telephony Service** This next generation of wireless transmission services is most often grouped under the name of 3G (Third Generation) Mobile Telephony, otherwise known as UWC (Universal Wireless Communications)—136.

**4 conductor station wire** RYGB; the type of phone wire installed in most homes consists of a tan plastic jacket containing four untwisted wires: red, yellow, green, and black.

**7 hop limit** One very important limitation of source routing bridges as applied to large internetworks. Because of the limited space in the RIF (Router Information Field) of the explorer packet, only 7 hop locations can be included in the path to any remote destination.

# A

**AAL** ATM adaptation layer protocols convert user input payloads into ATM cells.

**ABR** Available bit rate; ATM bandwidth management scheme that takes a fixed minimum amount of bandwidth plus whatever VBR (variable bit rate) is not using.

**access charges** RBOCs were allowed to charge access charges for co-location of the alternate carrier's equipment in their COs.

**Access Control List** *See* ACL.

**access line** Local loop from customer premises to network service entry point.

**access methodologies** Because the LAN media is to be shared by numerous PC users, there must be some way to control access by multiple users to that media. These media sharing methods are properly known as access methodologies.

**access server** *See* Communications server.

**ACD** Incoming calls are routed directly to certain extensions without going through a central switchboard. Calls can be routed according to the incoming trunk or phone number. Often used in customer service organizations in which calls may be distributed to the first available agent.

**ACE** Adverse Channel Enhancements; a collection of 4 MNP 10 protocols designed to work with circuits subject to impairment such as cellular.

**ACE/NAK** Acknowledgment/negative acknowledgment, used with ARQ error correction to indicate whether or not retransmission is required.

**acknowledgment** Postive acknowledgment indicating data block was received without error.

**acknowledgment and polling traffic** The first characteristic of SNA that can cause trouble on a LAN is the great amount of acknowledgment and polling traffic between SNA processors and SNA end-user devices. This constant chatter could quickly monopolize the better part of the LAN bandwidth.

**ACL** A list of users authorized to access a given resource. An ACL is located on the server con-

taining the resource and includes the effective rights or permissions that the user has to the resource.

**acquisition costs** Networking and systems budgets typically focused only on the acquisition costs of the new system. Even within the acquisition category, costs associated with personnel additions, changes, and training were often omitted.

**ACR** Attenuation to Crosstalk Ratio—measured in dB or decibels. A decibel is a logarithmic rather than linear measurement of the ratio between two powers, often a data signal and some type of noise or interference.

**active management MAUs** Able to send alerts to management consoles regarding malfunctioning token ring adapters and can also forcibly remove these misbehaving adapters from the ring.

**active monitor** In a token passing access methodology, the token is generated in the first place by a designated PC known as the active monitor and passed among PCs until one PC would like to access the network.

**activity monitors** A category of antivirus technology with the ability to monitor behavior of programs.

**Adaptive Differential Pulse Code Modulation** *See* ADPCM.

**adaptive protocols** Protocols that are able to change transmission characteristics as circuit quality varies.

**Adaptive Size Packet Assembly** A MNP 4 protocol that changes the amount of data transmitted in each block dependent on circuit quality.

**Adaptive switching** *See* Error-free cut-through switches.

**address bit order reversal** In the case of IEEE 802.3, the least significant bit is the right-most bit of the byte and, in the case of IEEE 802.5, the least significant bit is the left-most bit of the byte. This bit order reversal is especially troublesome for translating bridges which must translate between token ring and Ethernet frames.

**address caching** In order to avoid constantly flooding the network with explorer packets seeking destinations, source routing bridges may employ some type of address caching or RIF caching, so that previously determined routes to known destinations are saved and reused.

**address classes**   IP addresses are categorized into address classes A, B, C, D, or E.

**address resolution**   The process of resolving a hardware (MAC) address from a layer three network layer address.

**address resolution protocol**   *See* ARP.

**address resolution server**   LAN emulation is most often implemented by the ATM vendor by the installation of an address resolution server, which provides translation between the ATM addressing scheme and the addressing scheme that is native to a particular emulated LAN.

**ADPCM**   By transmitting only the approximate difference or change in amplitude of consecutive amplitude samples, rather than the absolute amplitude, only 32 Kbps of bandwidth is required for each conversation digitized via ADPCM as opposed to PCM.

**ADSL**   Asymmetric digital subscriber line. Local loop data service able to offer 6 Mbps download and 640 Kbps upload over existing copper pairs without interfering with existing POTS service.

**ADSP**   A connectionless session layer protocol used in the AppleTalk protocol suite.

**advanced intelligent network**   *See* AIN.

**advanced mobile phone service**   *See* AMPS.

**Advanced Parallel Technology**   *See* APT.

**Advanced Peer to Peer Networking**   *See* APPN.

**Advanced Power Management**   *See* APM.

**Adverse Channel Enhancements**   Transmitting data over analog cellular networks requires modems that support specialized cellular transmission protocols on both ends of the cellular transmission in order to maximize throughput. Examples of such protocols are MNP-10 Adverse Channel Enhancements and Enhanced Throughput Cellular (ETC).

**AEP**   A protocol used to test network connectivity on AppleTalk networks through echo-reply packets.

**AFP**   The file sharing application layer protocol used in the AppleTalk protocol suite.

**agent**   In between the intelligent application, reporting on event conditions and performance metrics, and the management console is an autonomous piece of software known as an **agent,** which collects these performance statistics and properly formats them for transmission to the application management console.

**agent event manager**   One of three cooperating components of the agent portion of the client/agent/server architecture. The agent event manager is combined with a customer-written transaction handler to form an entity known as the intelligent agent which resides on the local server. Once the agent event manager receives a request from a mobile client, it acts on behalf of that client in all communications with the local server until the original client request is totally fulfilled.

**agents**   Network statistics and information are gathered in the first place and packetized in SNMP format by specialized software known as agents which reside within the monitored network device and are supplied by the network device's manufacturer.

**AIN**   Signaling System 7 and the intelligent services that it enables are often described as part of an all-encompassing interface between users and the PSTN (Public Switched Telephone Network) known as AIN or Advanced Intelligent Network.

**American Standard Code for Information Interchange**   *See* ASCII.

**amplifier amplitude**   Device used on analog circuits to strengthen and retransmit signals carrier wave characteristic which is manipulated to represent 1s and 0s (wave height).

**amplitude modulation**   A modulation scheme in which amplitude is manipulated in order to represent discrete detectable events which are then interpreted into 1s and 0s.

**AMPS**   The current circuit switched analog cellular network is more properly known by the transmission standard to which it adheres known as Advanced Mobile Phone Service (AMPS) and operates in the 800 MHz frequency range.

**AMS**   Applications management specification; one proposal for standardizing how instrumentation should be developed within applications.

**analog**   Transmission method characterized by continuously varying tones within a given bandwidth or range of frequencies.

**analog simultaneous voice/data**   *See* ASVD.

**ANI**   Automatic number identification; also known as caller ID.

**API**   Application program interface; a set of standard commands supported by both application programs and the operating systems with which they interact.

**APM** Power management features offered by operating systems have been standardized as the Advanced Power Management (APM) specification.

**AppleTalk** Included as a communications protocol in order to support NT's Services for Macintosh (SFM).

**AppleTalk Data Stream Protocol** *See* ADSP.

**AppleTalk Echo Protocol** *See* AEP.

**AppleTalk Filing Protocol** *See* AFP.

**AppleTalk Session Protocol** *See* ASP.

**AppleTalk Transaction Protocol** *See* ATP.

**application gateways** Concerned with what services or applications a message is requesting in addition to who is making that request. Connections between requesting clients and service providing servers are created only after the application gateway is satisfied as to the legitimacy of the request. Even when the legitimacy of the request has been established, only proxy clients and servers actually communicate with each other.

**application level filters** Examine the entire request for data rather than just the source and destination addresses. Secure files can be marked as such and application level filters will not allow those files to be transferred, even to users authorized by port level filters.

**application MIB** Identifies three key groups of variables for proper application tracking and management.

**application program interface** *See* API.

**application response measurement** *See* ARM.

**application services** It is the server network operating system that is responsible for application services, which includes not only executing the back-end engine portion of the application, but also supplying the messaging and communications services to enable interoperability between distributed clients and servers.

**applications layer** The application layer, layer 7 of the OSI Model is also open to misinterpretation. Application layer protocols do not include end-user application programs. Rather, they include utilities that support end-user application programs. Some people include network operating systems in this category. Strictly speaking, the best examples of application layer protocols are the OSI protocols X.400 and X.500.

**applications management specification** *See* AMS.

**APPN** Advanced Peer to Peer Network, IBM's answer to multiprotocol networking on a peer to peer basis using the SNA architecture, rather than a LAN-based network architecture.

**APT** Microcom protocol that allows modems to connect to PCs via parallel port in order to avoid serial port bottlenecks.

**ARM** Application response measurement; an API that can be used by applications developers, and can measure several key application statistics.

**ARP** Address Resolution Protocol (RFC 826); used if an IP address of workstation is known but a data-link layer address for the same workstation is required.

**ARQ** Automatic retransmission request; error correction protocol that requires retransmission of data blocks received in error.

**ASCII** Standardized method for encoding humanly readable characters; uses a series of 7 bits to represent 128 ($2^7 = 128$) different characters.

**ASP** The session layer protocol used in the AppleTalk protocol suite.

**assets** Corporate property of some value that require varying degrees of protection.

**assured pipelines** *See* application gateways.

**ASVD** Analog simultaneous voice/data; does not transmit voice and data in a truly simultaneous manner. Instead, it switches quickly between voice and data transmission. Voice transmission always takes priority, so data transfers are paused during data transmissions. ASVD has been formalized as ITU standard V.61.

**asymmetric digital subscriber line** *See* ADSL.

**asymmetrical transmission** A data transmission where the two directions operate at different speeds.

**asynchronous frames** In FDDI, while synchronous frames are being transmitted, any unused network capacity can still be used by other workstations transmitting asynchronous frames.

**asynchronous transfer mode** *See* ATM.

**asynchronous transmission** Synchronization is reestablished with the transmission of each character in asynchronous transmission via the use of start and stop bits.

**AT&T 5ESS Switch**  One of the switches that supports ISDN.

**ATM**  Asynchronous Transfer Mode; a switch-based WAN service using fixed length frames, more properly referred to as cells. Fixed length cells assure fixed length processing time by ATM switches, thereby enabling predictable, rather than variable, delay and delivery time.

**ATM access switches**  Interface between ATM switches and legacy LANs.

**ATM adaptation layer**  *See* AAL.

**ATM gateway switches** *See* ATM access switches.

**ATM LAN emulation**  ATM service that allows Ethernet or token ring traffic to travel across higher speed ATM networks without requring changes to LAN workstations.

**ATP**  The transport layer protocol used in the AppleTalk protocol suite.

**Attachment Units**  *See* AU.

**attack applets**  Attack applets are Java applets, downloaded from the Web, intent on serious security breaches.

**attenuation**  The decrease in the power of signal over a distance in a particular type of wire or media.

**attenuation to crosstalk ratio**  *See* ACR.

**AU**  Iso-Ethernet hubs are known as Attachment Units (AU) and cost between $400–$500 per port.

**Audiotex**  These systems deliver audio information to callers based on responses on the touch-tone keypad to prerecorded questions. Primarily used for information hotlines.

**authentication**  The process of proving that a user is who they claim to be. Authentication is a two-step process: identification and proof of identification.

**authentication credentials**  The means used to authenticate a user. Most commonly a user ID and a password.

**Authentication Header**  In Secure IP, provides data integrity and allows for the authentication of IP packets.

**authorization**  The process of determining the access rights a user should have for a resource. Authorization is usually accomplished through the use of Access Control Lists.

**auto restoral**  Ability of dial backup units to restore communications to leased lines from dial-up backup lines once the leased lines have been repaired.

**auto-detection and configuration**  Auto-detection and configuration of installed controllers, interface cards, and peripherals by network operating systems are dependent on the network operating system possessing a compatible driver for that device.

**automated attendant**  Allows callers to direct calls to a desired individual at a given business without necessarily knowing that person's extension number.

**automatic call distribution**  *See* ACD.

**automatic number identification**  Service available via either ISDN or in-band signaling.

**Automatic retransmission request**  *See* ARQ.

**available bit rate**  *See* ABR.

**AWG**  American Wire Gauge; wire thickness is measured by gauge and represented with the unit AWG.

## B

**B channel**  In Isochronous Ethernet, the 6.144 Mbps C channel is in fact further subdivided into 96 64 Kbps ISDN B channels, which carry the actual multimedia traffic. Applications are able to aggregate these B channels as needed up to the 6.144 Mbps limit.

**backbone network**  In a hierarchial enterprise network design, the high speed inter-LAN portion of the network is often referred to as the backbone network.

**backbone/data center switch**  Offer high capacity, fault tolerant, switching capacity with traffic management capabilities. These high-end switches are actually a self-contained backbone network that is sometimes referred to as a collapsed backbone network.

**backbone-attached LAN switch**  Offer all of the local switching capabilities of the stand-alone workgroup/departmental LAN switch plus switched access to higher speed backbone networks.

**backplane capacity**  The number of simultaneous point to point connections that a given switch can support.

**backpressure**  In the case of Ethernet switches, backpressure prevents lost frames during overload conditions by sending out false collision detection signals in order to get transmitting clients and servers to time-out long enough to give the switch a chance to forward buffered data.

**backward compatibility**   An important aspect of any migration plan to a new client network operating system is the extent of support for backward compatibility is terms of application support, also known as legacy application support. In other words, will current applications run without modification on the new network operating system?

**backward explicit congestion notification**   *See* BECN.

**bandwdith management**   Often used interchangeably with the term traffic shaping, can be defined as the appropriate allocation of bandwidth to support application requirements.

**bandwidth**   Range of frequencies.

**bandwidth on demand interoperability group**   *See* BONDING.

**Base I/O address**   This address defines a memory location through which the data will flow between the network interface card and the CPU.

**Base memory address**   Not to be confused with Base I/O address, some NICs require a base memory address to indicate the starting location in the computer's memory that can be used by the NIC as a buffer memory.

**baseband transmission**   Means that the entire bandwidth of the media is devoted to one data channel.

**baseline data**   In order to properly quantify increased productivity, one must first measure current levels of productivity by developing evaluation criteria so that baseline data can be gathered.

**basic input output system**   *See* BIOS.

**basic rate interface**   *See* BRI.

**baud**   Timed opportunities to identify ones and zeros by sampling the carrier wave are known as signaling events. The proper name for one signaling event is a baud.

**baud rate**   The number of baud, or signaling events, per second.

**bearer channels**   ISDN channels that actually bear, or carry, data and voice.

**BECN**   Backward explicit congestion notification; a frame relay flow control mechanism.

**Bell 103**   Bell system modem standard for 300 bps modem using FSK modulation.

**Bell 212A**   Bell system modem standard for 1,200 bps modem using 4PSK.

**benchmarking**   A process of demonstrating the impact of implemented technology by tying networking costs to business value.

**BER**   Bit error rate; measurement of errors on a given transmission line.

**BGP**   Border Gateway Protocol; an exterior gateway protocol used to exchange routing information between autonomous systems.

**billing verification**   By inputting a company's current network design in the analysis and design software and by using the tariff tables to price individual circuits within that network, prices generated from the tariff tables can be compared to recent phone bills.

**bindery**   Network operating systems have always depended on some sort of naming service or directory in which to store information about users as well as systems resources such as disks, servers, and printers. NetWare 3.x servers stored this type of information in a bindery.

**binding**   NDIS specifies a binding operation that is managed by a separate program known as the Protocol Manager, which combines separate NDIS compliant driver software supplied by NIC and NOS vendors.

**biometric authentication**   Can authenticate users based on fingerprints, palm prints, retinal patterns, voice recognition, or other physical characteristics.

**BIOS**   Basic input system; interface between operating system and PC hardware components.

**B-ISDN**   Broadband ISDN; ATM switching plus SONET transmission.

**bit**   A binary digit, a 1 or 0.

**bit error rate**   *See* BER.

**Block Sequence Number**   Used in ARQ error control to identify which data blocks were received in error.

**Bluetooth**   A wireless transmission standard for linking mobile phones, computers, and other devices using unlicensed 2.45 GHz frequency for transmission rates of up to 1 Mbps over 10 meters. Supported by more than 700 vendors.

**BONDING**   Bandwidth on demand interoperability group Inverse multiplexing standard.

**BootP**   Originally designed to configure local diskless workstations that were unable to store IP configuration information locally. In the case of BootP, the MAC address of the BootP client had to be known beforehand, entered into a database in the BootP server, and permanently associated with an IP address.

**boundary router**   In the case of boundary or branch office routers, all routing information is kept at the central site router. This allows the boundary router to require less technical configuration and to be available for a lower cost than central site routers.

**bps**   Bits per second.

**breakout boxes**   A device used to monitor and manipulate transmission signals.

**BRI**   Basic rate interface; 2B+D ISDN.

**bridge**   Uses MAC layer addressing to logically segment traffic between attached LANs.

**Broadband ISDN**   *See* B-ISDN.

**broadband transmission**   In general, any transmission service at the T-1 level or greater is considered broadband.

**broadcast**   In a broadcast logical topology, a data message is sent simultaneously to all nodes on the network. Each node decides individually if the data message was directed toward it. If not, the message is simply ignored.

**broadcast address**   A special network address that identifies all nodes on a network segment rather than a single node.

**broadcast filtering**   Instead of allowing explorer packets onto the internetwork, routers can filter these broadcast packets out of the traffic, read the destination address to which the PC is seeking a route, and supply the PC directly with that information after consulting its own routing tables.

**broadcast storm**   In the case of improperly addressed frames or frames destined for nonexistent addresses, frames can be infinitely perpetuated or flooded onto all bridged LANs in a condition known as a broadcast storm.

**brokered authorization**   Authorization security software can be either server-based, also known as brokered authorization, or workstation-based, also referred to as trusted node.

**brouters**   At one time, specialized devices that could either bridge or route were referred to as brouters; today, however, most advanced routers include bridging functionality.

**Buffer Memory**   Memory included in modems to hold transmitted blocks of data in order to implement sliding window or continuous ARQ.

**bulk retrieval mechanism**   A new SNMP2 procedure whereby managers can retrieve several pieces of network information at a time from a given agent.

**bus**   A linear arrangement with terminators on either end and devices connected to the "bus" via connectors and/or transceivers.

**bus and tag**   A standard for high speed data channels between FEPs and IBM mainframes, Bus and Tag has a transmission rate of 4.5 Mbps and has been available since 1967.

**bus mastering DMA**   The CPU on the network adapter card manages the movement of data directly into the PC's RAM memory without interruption of the system CPU by taking control of the PC's expansion bus.

**business functional areas**   Once overall system performance characteristics have been established, the overall business can be broken down into large functional areas. These functional areas may correspond to corporate departments or divisions.

**business process reengineering**   As business processes are described, brainstorming quickly takes over and problems that seemed deeply imbedded in current systems are solved as new or modified business processes are defined for the new strategic information system design.

**buy-in**   As each stage is concluded, buy-in or agreement as to conclusions from all affected customer groups is of critical importance.

**byte**   A collection of 8 bits which represents a character.

## C

**C channel**   In Isochronous Ethernet, A 6.144 Mbps ISDN C channel is reserved for streaming time-sensitive traffic such as multimedia applications.

**C-2 certification**   The Orange Book certification process is both costly and lengthy. Typically, the certification process is projected to take 2 years to complete at a cost of $17 million. To date, both NetWare and NT Server have achieved the C-2 certification.

**C2 level security**   A standard security level required by the U.S. government for stand-alone systems.

**CA**   Third-party key certification services, or certificate authorities (CA), issue the public keys along with a certificate assuring the authenticity of the key.

**cable modem**    A high speed data communications device that encodes digital data onto a cable television distribution system.

**cable scanners**    Layer 1 testers are more commonly known as **cable scanners** or cable testers.

**CAI**    PBX-integrated wireless phones support the CT2 (Cordless Telephony Generation 2) Common Air Interface (CAI) global standard for low-power wireless transmission.

**call accounting system**    Systems that can pay for themselves in a short amount of time by spotting and curtailing abuse as well as by allocating phone usage charges on a departmental basis.

**call control**    Using computer-based applications users can more easily use all of the features of their phone system or PBX, especially the more complicated but seldom used features. Includes use of features like on-line phone books, auto-dialing, click-and-point conference calls, on-line display, and processing of voice mail messages.

**call pickup**    Allows a user to pick up or answer another user's phone without having to actually forward calls.

**call set-up packets**    Used to establish virtual circuits in frame relay networks.

**callback security**    Modem security feature that verifies users and dials them back at predetermined numbers.

**CANE**    Computer Assisted Engineering; the use of software tools of one type or another to assist in network engineering.

**CAP**    A de facto standard, deployed in many trial ADSL units; developed by AT&T Paradyne.

**card and socket services**    *See* CSS.

**card services**    The card services sub-layer of PCMCIA Card and Socket Services is hardware independent and interfaces to the client operating system or network operating system driver software.

**CardBus**    Version 3.0 of the PCMCIA standard; supports bus widths to 32 bits and clock speeds as high as 33 MHz.

**Carrier Sense Multiple Access with Collision Avoidance**    *See* CSMA/CA.

**Carrier Sense Multiple Access with Collision Detection**    *See* CSMA/CD.

**carrier wave**    A reference wave that is manipulated by modems to represent 1s and 0s.

**carrierless amplitude and phase**    *See* CAP.

**carriers**    A carrier, or phone company, that offers phone services to the general public in a given geographic area.

**cascading ports**    Hubs may also be cascadable or stackable via cascading ports which may be specialized ports on the hub or may be switch configurable "normal" ports allowing repeated data to flow out of a cascading port to the next hub rather than the normal inbound-only port traffic flow.

**CAT 5**    Category 5 UTP -22 or 24 AWG; tested for attenuation and near-end crosstalk to 100 MHz. Capable of transmitting up to 100 Mbps when strictly installed to EIA/TIA 568 specifications. Currently the most commonly installed category of UTP.

**CBR**    Constant Bit Rate; voice is currently transmitted across ATM networks using a bandwidth reservation scheme known as CBR, which is analogous to a Frame Relay virtual circuit.

**CBS**    Commited Burst Size; defines the extent to which a user can exceed their CIR over a period of time in a frame relay network.

**CCIS**    Common Channel Interoffice Signaling; a more official name for out-of-band signaling.

**CDDI**    Copper Distributed Data Interface; employs FDDI over twisted pair media. The official ANSI standard for CDDI is known as TP-PMD (Twisted Pair-Physical Media Dependent).

**CDMA**    Code division multiple access; transmits digitized voice packets from numerous calls at different frequencies spread throughout the entire allocated bandwidth spectrum.

**CDPD**    Cellular Digital Packet Data; a service that uses idle capacity in the circuit-switched cellular network to transmit IP-based data packets. The fact that CDPD is IP-based allows it to easily interface to IP-based private networks as well as to the Internet and other e-mail services.

**cell relay**    Fast packet switching technology employing fixed length cells.

**cells**    ATM (Asynchronous Transfer Mode) is a switch-based WAN service using fixed length frames, more properly referred to as cells.

**Cellular Digital Packet Data**    *See* CDPD.

**central clock** A timing device in the TDM that gives each input device its allotted time to empty its buffer into an area of the TDM where the combined data from all of the polled input devices are conglomerated into a single message frame for transmission over the composite circuit.

**Central Directory Server** In APPN, the Central Directory Server can save time as well as network traffic for the Network Nodes. Instead of each Network Node on an internetwork doing its own information gathering and internetwork exploration and inquiry, they can simply consult the Central Directory Server.

**central office** *See* CO.

**central site router** Otherwise known as enterprise or backbone routers; employed at large corporate sites, whereas boundary or branch office routers are employed at remote corporate locations with less routing requirements and fewer technical support personnel.

**certificate authorities** *See* CA.

**certificate servers** Public key infrastructures that link a particular user to a particular public key are implemented through the use of server-based software known as certificate servers. Certificate server software also supports encryption and digital signatures while flexibly supporting directory integration, multiple certificate types, and a variety of request fulfillment options.

**Challenge Handshake Authentication Protocol** *See* CHAP.

**Challenge Response Token Authentication** A token authentication protocol in which a user uses a Smart Card to generate a one-time session key response to a server initiated challenge.

**channel bank** When a bank of codes are arranged in a modular chassis to not only digitize analog voice conversations but also load them onto a shared high capacity (T-1:1.544 Mbps) circuit, the hybrid device is referred to as a channel bank.

**Channel Service Unit/Data Service Unit** *See* CSU/DSU.

**channel-attached gateways** As an alternative to LAN-based gateways, they have the ability to interface directly to the mainframe's high speed data channel, thereby bypassing the FEP entirely. Physically, the channel attached gateways are often modules that are added to enterprise routers.

**CHAP** Challenge Handshake Authentication Protocol; provides a more secure means for establishing dial-in communication. Uses a three-way challenge that includes the user ID, password and also a key that encrypts the ID and password.

**CHAP MD5** A protocol for PPP encrypted authentication included with most PPP clients.

**CHAP MD80** A protocol for authentication for Windows NT RAS included with most PPP clients.

**character encoding** Process required to render humanly readable characters into machine language through representation of characters as a series of 1s and 0s.

**checksums** Error check character calculated using decimal face values of characters in transmitted data blocks.

**CIM** **Common Information Model;** proposed protocol currently under development by the DMTF (Desktop Management Task Force) would support HMMS. CIM would permit management data gathered from a variety of enterprise and desktop voice and data technology to all be transported, processed, displayed, and stored by a single CIM-compliant Web browser.

**ciphertext** In encryption, the changed, meaningless data.

**CIPX** A protocol for compression of IPX headers included with most PPP clients.

**CIR** Committed Information Rate; refers to the minimum bandwidth guaranteed to users for "normal" transmission in a frame relay network.

**circuit analysis and configuration alternatives** Explores the possibilities for delivering data traffic in a reliable and effective manner, once the nature of the data traffic is thoroughly understood.

**circuit-level proxy** Provide proxy services for transport layer protocols such as TCP.

**circuit switched network** A network based on circuit switched services in which users are able to use the entire bandwidth of physical circuits created solely for their transmissions.

**circuit switching** A switching process in which physical circuits are created, maintained, and terminated for individual point-to-point or multi-point connections.

**circuit-switched cellular** Analog cellular service capable of supporting 14.4 Kbps max.

**Class 1 regional center** Highest capacity switching office in PSTN network hierarchy.

**Class 2 sectional center** 2nd highest capacity switching office in PSTN network hierarchy.

**Class 3 primary center** 3rd highest capacity switching office in PSTN network hierarchy.

**Class 4 toll center** 4th highest capacity switching office in PSTN network hierarchy.

**Class 5 office** Local switching office.

**class of service** A method of prioritizing traffic to ensure that important packets are not delayed at routers or switches.

**classful address** An IP address that is broken into network segment and node portions at octet boundaries.

**classical IP** *See* IP over ATM.

**classless address** An IP address that is broken into network segment and node portions at locations other than octet boundaries.

**clear request packet** In frame relay networks, the special packet that terminates virtual circuits.

**CLEC** Competitive Local Exchange Carriers; companies that seek to offer local access service in competition with RBOCs.

**client network operating systems** Integrate traditional operating system functionality with advanced network operating system features to enable communication with a variety of different types of network operating system servers.

**client/server CTI** In this CTI architecture, a CTI server computer interfaces to the PBX or ACD to provide overall system management while individual client-based CTI applications execute on multiple client PCs.

**client/server network operating systems** Offer the ability to support hundreds of users, and the ability to interact with other network operating systems via gateways. These client/server network operating systems are considerably more expensive and considerably more complicated to install and administer than peer-to-peer network operating systems.

**client-agent-server** The overall objective of a client-agent-server architecture, as opposed to the more common LAN-based client/server architecture, is to reduce the amount of mobile client-to-server network traffic by building as much intelligence as possible into the server-based agent so that it can act on behalf of the mobile client application.

**Clipper Chip** An initiative proposed that every phone and data communications device in the United States would be equipped with a Clipper Chip to support encryption.

**cluster controller** A device that allows connection of both 3270 terminals as well as LANs with possible wide area links to packet switched networks (X.25) or high speed leased lines. Concentrates the transmissions of its numerous input devices and directs this concentrated data stream to the FEP either locally or remotely.

**CNIP** Common Network Information Platform. Rather than having to know the intricacies, and, in some cases, the trade secrets, of how each other's products work, vendors of computer assisted network engineering software merely pass the output from their particular software product to a "neutral" data platform known as CNIP.

**CO** Central office; a facility belonging to the local phone company in which calls are switched to their proper destination.

**code division multiple access** *See* CDMA.

**codec** Coder/decoder used to digitize analog voice signals.

**collapsed backbone network** A switched network architecture that employs backbone/data center switches to offer high capacity, fault tolerant, switching capacity with traffic management capabilities.

**co-location** A mandated process through which RBOCs had to allow alternate local loop carriers to install their equipment in the RBOC's central office.

**committed burst size** *See* CBS.

**committed information rate** *See* CIR.

**Common Air Interface** *See* CAI.

**common channel interoffice signalling** *See* CCIS.

**Common Control Area** Software programs that reside in and are executed on specialized computers within the PBX in an area sometimes referred to as the PBX CPU, Stored Program Control or Common Control Area.

**common information model** *See* CIM.

**common network information platform** *See* CNIP.

**communications server** Remote users could attach to a dedicated multi-user server, known as an access server or communications server through one or more modems. Depending on the software loaded on the communications server, it may deliver remote node functionality, remote control functionality, or both.

**competitive local exchange carrier** *See* CLEC.

**component interface API** Designed to interface to the individual application programs or desktop components that are to be managed and monitored on the local client.

**composite message frame** The frame that is built by combining the contents of individual channel buffers in a multiplexer.

**comprehensive systems and networking budget model** A comprehensive budget format needed to be developed that would help to identify as many elements of potential implementation and operation costs as possible associated with systems and networking implementations.

**computer assisted network engineering** *See* CANE.

**Computer telephony integration** *See* CTI.

**configuration bridge protocol data unit** Spanning Tree Algorithm bridges accomplish path management by communicating with each other via configuration bridge protocol data units (Configuration BPDU).

**connectionless** IP allows each packet to be processed individually within the network and provides no guarantees as to whether packets will arrive at their intended destination in sequence, if at all. As such, IP is described as a connectionless, unreliable protocol.

**connection-oriented** Implying that specific paths known as virtual circuits are explored and determined prior to the first packet being sent. Once the virtual circuit is established directly from the source host or node to destination node, then all packets bound for that address follow each other in sequence down the same physical path.

**consolidated service desk** A single point of contact for all network and application problem resolution, appropriate personnel processes can be matched with associated network management technologies.

**constant bit rate** *See* CBR.

**constellation points** A plotted point on a quadrant that represents a particular phase shift and amplitude of a modulation scheme.

**Continuous ARQ** Also known as sliding window ARQ, continues to transmit data while waiting for ACK/NAK. Slides back to NAK'd block and begins retransmission from there.

**convolutional encoding** Encoding methodology used with trellis coded modulation, a forward error correction protocol.

**Copper Distributed Data Interface** *See* CDDI.

**Cordless Telephony Generation 2** *See* CT2.

**CPE** Customer premises equipment; generic name for customer owned PBX.

**CRC** A 32-bit cyclical redundancy check (CRC) is generated over the address, type, and data fields as a frame check sequence in Ethernet networks.

**CRC Checkers** Category of antivirus technology also known as Hashing Checkers; creates and saves a unique cyclical redundancy check character or hashing number for each file to be monitored.

**CRC-16** 16-bit cyclic redundancy check; traps multiple bit errors up to 15 bits 100% of the time.

**CRC-32** 32-bit cyclic redundancy check; traps multiple bit errors up to 31 bits 100% of the time.

**critical success factors** Several key behaviors or things to remember that can be of critical importance to the overall successful outcome of the network development life cycle.

**CSMA/CA** Carrier Sense Multiple Access with Collision Avoidance; part of the IEEE 802.11 standard. Similar to CSMA/CD except that collisions cannot be detected in wireless environments as they can in wire-based environments. Before transmitting, workstations wait a predetermined amount of time in order to avoid collisions, and set up a point-to-point wireless circuit to the destination workstation.

**CSMA/CD** Carrier Sense Multiple Access with Collision Detection; the access methodology used by Ethernet media sharing LANs.

**CSS** Card and Socket Services; the driver specification for PCMCIA devices that enables the following capabilities and is supposed to be relatively self-configuring: hot swappable devices allowing PCMCIA cards to be removed and inserted while the notebook computer is powered up, automatic PCMCIA card configuration, multiple PCMCIA card management, standby mode, I/O conflict management.

**CSU/DSU** Channel service unit/data service unit; used to interface to carriers' digital transmission services.

**CT2**   PBX-integrated wireless phones support the CT2. (Cordless Telephony Generation 2) Common Air Interface (CAI) global standard for low-power wireless transmission.

**CTI**   It is important for help desk management software to be able to interact with call center management technology such as **automatic call distributors (ACD)** and **interactive voice response units (IVRU).** The overall integration of computer-based software and telephony equipment in known as **computer telephony integration (CTI).**

**CTI application development tool**   Generates application code in a language such as Visual Basic and incorporates TAPI or TSAPI system commands into the program.

**CTI voice card**   Key functions are as follows: Record and playback digitized video, Create and recognize DTMF tones (Dual Tone Multiple Frequency), Answer and place phone calls, Recognize and process incoming Caller ID (Automatic Number Identification) information.

**customer premises equipment**   *See* CPE.

**cut-through switches**   Read only the address information in the MAC layer header before beginning processing. Cut-through switching is very fast. However, because the Frame Check Sequence on the forwarded frame was not checked, bad frames are forwarded.

**cyclical redundancy check**   *See* CRC.

### D

**D channel**   In Isochronous Ethernet, one 64 Kbps ISDN D channel is used for management tasks such as call control and signaling.

**D-4**   A type of T-1 framing in which 24 8-bit time slots are combined with a framing bit to form 193-bit frames.

**DARPA**   TCP/IP was developed during the 1970s and widely deployed during the 1980s under the auspices of DARPA or Defense Advanced Research Projects Agency.

**DAS**   Dual Attachment Station devices attach to both of FDDI's rings.

**data circuit terminating equipment**   *See* DCE.

**data communications**   The encoded transmission of data via electrical or optical means.

**Data Compression**   Procedure in which redundant data are removed from the data stream and represented by shorter codes thereby increasing overall throughput for a given transmission rate.

**data display channel**   *See* DDC.

**Data Encryption Standard**   *See* DES.

**Datalink Control**   *See* DLC.

**Datalink Switching**   *See* DLSw.

**data migration**   Utilities that manage the migration of data among different types of storage devices as part of a comprehensive hierarchical storage management (HSM) program.

**data over voice**   A type of frequency division multiplexer.

**data terminal equipment**   *See* DTE.

**data traffic analysis**   Examines all aspects and characteristics of the traffic that will be passed between corporate locations over the proposed network.

**database MIB**   The IETF has been working on a Database MIB specification that would allow any enterprise data management system to report performance statistics back to any SNMP-compliant enterprise network management system.

**Datagram Delivery**   *See* DDP.

**Protocol datagrams**   Globally addressed message packets found in connectionless frame relay networks.

**datalink layer**   Layer 2 of the OSI model; responsible for providing protocols that deliver reliability to upper layers for the point-to-point connections established by the physical layer protocols. The datalink layer is of particular interest to the study of local area networks because this is the layer in which network architecture standards are defined.

**DB-25**   A 25 pin physical connector associated with both serial and parallel transmission protocols.

**DB-9**   A 9 pin physical connector associated with a variety of serial protocols.

**DCE**   Data circuit terminating equipment; a generic designation to indicate directionality in a serial transmission. Modems are DCE.

**DDM**   Distributed device manager. A DDM architecture relies on distributed network probes that are able to gather information from a variety of network devices manufactured by multiple vendors and relay that information to numerous distributed device manager consoles.

**DDP**   The network layer protocol associated with the AppleTalk protocol suite.

**DDS** Digital data service; a digital carrier transmission service offering speeds up to 56 Kbps.

**DE** Discard eligibility. Flag in frame relay frame indicating those frames that can be discarded in the event of network congestion.

**decision points** Points in all of the documented business processes where decision makers must make decisions.

**de-encapsulation** Each successive layer of the OSI model removes headers and/or trailers and processes the data that were passed to it from the corresponding layer protocol on the source client.

**definition variables** In Application MIB, variables that would store background information concerning applications such as application name, manufacturer, version, release, installation data, license number, number of consecutive users, etc.

**delta file synchronization** Perhaps the most significant file synchronization option in terms of its potential impact on reducing required bandwidth and file transfer time to accomplish the synchronization. Rather than sending entire files across the dial-up or LAN link, delta file synchronization only transfers the changes to those files.

**delta file transfer** Allows only changes to files to be transferred.

**Demand Priority Access** *See* DPP.

**Demand Priority Protocol** *See* DPP.

**demodulation** Conversion of an analog signal to equivalent digital data.

**denial of service attack** The hacker floods the server with requests to connect to other nonexistent servers. The server tries to establish connections with the nonexistent servers and waits for a response while being flooded with thousands of other bogus connection requests. This causes the server to deny service to legitimate users because it is overwhelmed trying to handle the bogus requests.

**deregulation** As a result of deregulation, both AT&T and the RBOCs were allowed to enter into other nonregulated industries by forming additional subsidiaries.

**DES** Data Encryption Standard; a private key encryption standard originally approved by the National Institute of Standards and Technology (NIST) in 1977.

**desktop CTI** In this CTI architecture, individual PCs are equipped with telephony boards and associated call control software. Each Desktop CTI-equipped PC controls only the phone to which it is directly attached.

**desktop management interface** *See* DMI.

**desktop management task force** *See* DMTF.

**destination address** Rather than merely transferring all data between LANs or LAN segments, a bridge reads the destination address (MAC layer address of destination NIC) of each data frame on a LAN, decides whether the destination is local or remote (on the other side of the bridge), and only allows those data frames with nonlocal destination addresses to cross the bridge to the remote LAN.

**DHCP** Dynamic Host Control Protocol; dynamically assigns IP upon requests from clients. With DHCP, IP addresses are leased for a fixed length of time rather than being permanently assigned.

**dial backup** Ability of leased line modems to restore transmission via dial-up circuits in the event of a leased line failure,

**dial-in server** *See* LAN modem.

**dial-up line** Circuit switched connection or local loop used to access PSTN.

**dial-up router** In those cases where the amount of inter-LAN traffic from a remote site does not justify the cost of a leased line, dial-up routers may be the appropriate choice of internetworking equipment.

**dial-up server** *See* Remote node server.

**dibit** Two bits.

**DID** Direct inward dialing allows calls to bypass the central switchboard and go directly to a particular user's phone.

**Diff-Serv** Provides the following functionality: Uses the type of service (ToS) bits already in the IP header to differentiate between different levels of service required by different applications; allows service level agreements between users and service providers to be supported.

**digital** A transmission method characterized by discrete voltage levels used to represent logical 1s and 0s.

**digital data services** *See* DDS.

**Digital IDs** Digital certificates or Digital IDs issued from CAs such as VeriSign contain an organization's encrypted public key along with a minimal amount of information about the organization such as e-mail address, department, company, state or province, and country.

**digital service hierarchy** Series of standards defining high speed digital services (DS-1 = 1.544 Mbps).

**digital signal processors** Take the digitized PCM code and further manipulate and compress it.

**digital signal processors** *See* DSP.

**Digital Signature Encryption** Provides an electronic means of guaranteeing authenticity of the sending party and assurance that encrypted documents have not been altered during transmission.

**digital simultaneous voice/data** *See* DSVD.

**Digital subscriber line** *See* DSL.

**direct enablers** If compatible CSS drivers are not available for a particular PC Card/Controller combination, or if the amount of memory CSS drivers require is unacceptable, then lower-level drivers known as direct enablers must be configured and installed.

**direct inward dial** *See* DID.

**direct sequence spread spectrum** DSSS; transmits at a particular frequency within the allowable range. In order to distinguish between transmissions from multiple wireless workstations, DSSS adds at least 10 bits to the data message in order to uniquely identify a particular transmission. DSSS receivers must be able to differentiate between these bits, known as chips, in order to properly distinguish transmissions.

**directory services** Network operating systems have always depended on some sort of directory or naming service in which to store information about users as well as systems resources such as disks, servers, and printers.

**directory synchronization software** *See* File synchronization.

**discard eligibility** *See* DE.

**Discrete ARQ** Also known as stop and wait ARQ. Transmitting modem waits for an ACK or NAK for each transmitted block before transmitting the next block.

**discrete multitone** *See* DMT.

**distance vector** RIP uses a distance vector algorithm that only measures the number of hops to a distant router, to a maximum of 16.

**distance vector protocols** Router to router protocols, such as RIP, which only consider the distance between networks in hops as a determination of the best internetwork path.

**distinct layer 2 switching and layer 3 routing** An internetwork evolutionary design scenario in which separate Layer 2 switches and Layer 3 routers cooperatively contribute what each does best in order to deliver internetwork traffic as efficiently as possible.

**distributed database** A database application that consists of a central data repository with separate clients connecting to it.

**distributed device manager** *See* DDM.

**distributed network probes** A DDM architecture relies on **distributed network probes** that are able to gather information from a variety of network devices manufactured by multiple vendors and relay that information to numerous distributed device manager consoles.

**distributed queue dual bus** *See* DQDB.

**distributed routing** An internetwork evolutionary design scenario in which layer 2 switching and layer 3 routing functionality are combined into a single device sometimes referred to as a multi-layer switch.

**divestiture** Broke up the network services of AT&T into separate long-distance and local service companies.

**DLC** Datalink Control; a Windows NT communication protocol that has been traditionally reserved for communication with IBM mainframe computers. Recently, this same communication protocol has been used to communicate between Windows NT servers and printers that are attached directly to the network by network interface cards such as the Hewlett-Packard LaserJet 4Si equipped with a JetDirect card.

**DLSw** Datalink Switching; IBM's version of TCP/IP encapsulation has been proposed as a standard to the IETF (Internet Engineering Task Force) as RFC (Request for Comment) 1434. DLSw does not propose anything radically new but incorporates many vendor-specific TCP/IP encapsulation features into a single standard which, it is hoped, will be widely supported.

**DMI** Desktop management systems rely on an architecture and associated protocols proposed by the Desktop Management Task Force (DMTF), which is comprised of more than 50 companies including Intel, Microsoft, IBM, Digital, Hewlett-Packard, Apple, Compaq, Dell, and Sun. The overall desktop management architecture is known as the DMI or Desktop Management Interface.

**DMI services layer**  The DMI application that resides on each desktop device to be managed.

**DMT**  Discrete multitone; has been approved as an ADSL standard (ANSI Standard T1.413) by the ANSI T1E1.4 working group.

**DMTF**  Desktop management systems rely on an architecture and associated protocols proposed by the Desktop Management Task Force (DMTF), which is comprised of more than 50 companies including Intel, Microsoft, IBM, Digital, Hewlett-Packard, Apple, Compaq, Dell, and Sun. The overall desktop management architecture is known as the DMI or Desktop Management Interface.

**DMZ**  The de-militarized zone, otherwise known as the external private network; contains Web servers and mail servers.

**DNS**  The Domain Name System; has been created to provide the following key services: Uniquely identify all hosts connected to the Internet by name, resolve, or translate, host names into IP addresses (and vice versa), identify which services are offered by each host such as gateway or mail transfer, and to which networks these services are offered.

**DNS server**  DNS is physically implemented in a client/server architecture in which client-based DNS software known as the DNS or name resolver, sends requests for DNS name resolution to a DNS (or name) Server.

**domain directory services**  Network operating systems have always depended on some sort of naming service or directory in which to store information about users as well as systems resources such as disks, servers, and printers. Windows NT uses a domain directory service.

**domain name system**  *See* DNS.

**domains**  Domain directory services see the network as a series of linked subdivisions known as domains.

**DPA**  *See* DPP.

**DPP**  Demand Priority Protocol (Demand Priority Access); the access methodology of 100VG-AnyLAN. Ports can be designated as high priority, thereby giving priority delivery status to time-sensitive types of traffic such as video or voice which require guaranteed delivery times for smooth presentation. This makes 100VG-AnyLAN especially suitable for multimedia traffic.

**DQDB**  Distributed queue dual bus; SMDS network architecture.

**DS**  Digital service; *see* Digital service hierarchy.

**DS-0**  A 64 Kbps digital carrier transmission service.

**DS-1**  1.544 Mbps.

**DSE**  Data Switching Exchanges; otherwise known as packet switched networks.

**DSL**  Digital Subscriber Line services use frequency division multiplexing to analog encode a high speed data channel over a traditional POTS local loop connection.

**DSP**  Digital signal processor; specialized computer chip able to process digital signals quickly; used in echo cancellation.

**DSVD**  Digitizes all voice transmissions and combines the digitized voice and data over the single analog transmission line (ITU V.70).

**DTE**  Data terminal equipment; a generic designation to indicate directionality in a serial transmission. PCs are DTE in a point to point, PC to modem transmission.

**DTMF**  Touch-tone dialing is technically known as DTMF, or Dual Tone Multi-Frequency, because the tone associated with each number dialed is actually a combination of two tones selected from a matrix of multiple possible frequencies.

**Dual Attachment Station**  *See* DAS.

**dual firewalls**  An enterprise firewall architecture that allows controlled access to DMZ while blocking unauthorized access to secure network, Same functionality may be offered in a single product known as a tri-homed firewall.

**dual homing**  In FDDI, a given server may be connected to more than one FDDI concentrator to provide redundant connections and increased fault tolerance. Dual connecting servers in this manner are known as dual homing.

**dual ring of trees**  Multiple concentrators attaching multiple devices to the FDDI rings as illustrated in Figure 7-13.

**dual tone multi frequency**  *See* DTMF.

**dual-homed gateway**  The application gateway is physically connected to the private secure network and the packet filtering router is connected to the nonsecure network or the Internet. Between the application gateway and the packet filter router is an area known as the screened subnet.

**Dynamic Host Configuration Protocol** *See* DHCP.

**dynamic reconfiguration** PnP standards also include support for dynamic reconfiguration which will enable such things as: PCMCIA cards being inserted into and removed from computers without a need to reboot, Hot docking (powered up) of laptop computers into docking bays or stations, Dynamic reconfiguration-aware applications software that could automatically respond to changes in system configuration.

**Dynamic Speed Shifts** MNP 10 protocol that allows modems to automatically raise or lower transmission speeds in response to variable circuit conditions.

# E

**E-1** European standard for high speed digital transmission 2.048 Mbps.

**early token release mechanism** A modified form of token passing access methodology, used by 16 Mbps Token Ring network architectures, in which the token is set free and released as soon as the transmission of the data frame is completed rather than waiting for the transmitted data frame to return to the source workstation.

**EBCDIC** Extended binary coded decimal interchange code; 8-bit encoding scheme, 256 characters.

**echo cancellation** Sophisticated technique that allows some moderms to offer full duplex transmission over two wire circuits.

**edge switches** Edge switches deployed within the LANs will be programmed with minimal routing information. Edge switches will consult distributed route servers for "directory assistance" when they encounter routing situations which they are not equipped to handle.

**EGP** Exterior gateway protocol.

**EIA/TIA 568** Electronics Industry Association/ Telecommunications Industry Association; in addition to specifying UTP specifications, EIA/TIA 568 also specifies: the topology, cable types, and connector types to be used in EIA/TIA 568 compliant wiring schemes; the minimum performance specifications for cabling, connectors, and components such as wall plates, punch down blocks, and patch panels to be used in an EIA/TIA 568 compliant installation.

**element managers Point products** (also known as **element managers**) are specifically written to address a particular systems administration or network management issue.

**EMI** Electro Magnetic Interference.

**emulation technology** Attempts to detect as yet unknown viruses by running programs with a software emulation program known as a virtual PC.

**encapsulating bridges** The encapsulating bridge merely takes the entire Ethernet data-link layer frame and stuffs it in an "envelope" (data frame) that conforms to the FDDI data-link layer protocol.

**Encapsulating Security Payload Header** *See* ESP.

**encapsulation** A process in which a data message emerges from a client front end program and proceeds down the protocol stack of the network operating system installed in the client PC. Each successive layer of the OSI model adds a header according to the syntax of the protocol that occupies that layer.

**encryption** The process of "scrambling" a message for transmission to ensure that it is not intercepted along the way.

**end nodes** In APPN, end nodes are end user processing nodes, either clients or servers without any information on the overall network, available internetwork links, or routing tables.

**end-to-end network links** The network layer protocols are responsible for the establishment, maintenance, and termination of end-to-end network links. Network layer protocols are required when computers that are not physically connected to the same LAN must communicate.

**Enhanced CAT 5 Enhanced Category 5 UTP (EC5),** otherwise known as **Category 5+** or **CAT5e,** offers enhanced performance over CAT5 UTP due to the following improvements in electrical specifications: Attenuation to Crosstalk ratio of 10dB at 155 MHz, a minimum 400% improvement in capacitance, or ability of a wire to store an electrical charge, a 250% improvement in frequency, a 35% improvement in resistance, an average of 5% improvement in attenuation, an average of a 6dB improvement in NEXT.

**enhanced paging**   A pager based wireless service capable of delivering one- or two-way messages of 100 characters or less.

**enhanced throughput cellular**   *See* ETC.

**enterprise hubs**   Modular by design, offering a chassis-based architecture to which a variety of different modules can be inserted. In some cases, these modules can be inserted and/or removed while the hub remains powered-up, a capability known as hot-swappable.

**enterprise network management**   Focuses on the hardware, software, media, and network services required to seamlessly link and effectively manage distributed client and server computers across an enterprise.

**enterprise network management systems**   Systems such as HP OpenView, IBM NetView, and Sun Net Manager are able to manage a variety of multi-vendor network attached devices distributed throughout an enterprise network.

**equal access**   Any other long-distance carrier must be treated equally by the local BOCs in terms of access to the local carrier switching equipment, and ultimately to their customers.

**error correction**   Process of re-transmitting data blocks received in error.

**error detection**   Comparison of CRCs in order to detect transmission errors.

**error prevention**   Process of trying to prevent data errors by either reducing interference on circuits or by employing adaptive protocols that are able to adjust to impairments of varying circuit quality.

**error-free cut-through switches**   Switches that read both the addresses and Frame Check Sequences for every frame. Frames are forwarded immediately to destinations nodes in an identical fashion to cut-through switches. Should bad frames be forwarded, however, the error-free cut-through switch is able to reconfigure those individual ports producing the bad frames to use store-and-forward switching.

**ESCON**   Enterprise System CONnection; a standard for high speed data channels between FEPs and IBM mainframes, ESCON II has a maximum transmission rate of 70 Mbps, has been available since 1990, and is able to transmit up to 30 miles over fiber optic cable.

**ESF**   24 D-4 frames.

**ESMR**   Enhanced specialized mobile radio; currently under development, this wireless WAN service offers one- or two-way voice, paging, or messaging at speeds up to 4.8 Kbps over proprietary integrated voice/data devices.

**ESP**   Encapsulating Security Payload Header; in Secure IP, ESP assures the privacy of the transmission.

**ETC**   Enhanced Throughput Cellular; transmitting data over analog cellular networks requires modems that support specialized cellular transmission protocols on both ends of the cellular transmission in order to maximize throughput. Examples of such protocols are MNP-10 Adverse Channel Enhancements and ETC.

**Ethernet**   Although strictly speaking, Ethernet and IEEE 802.3 are conflicting standards, the term *Ethernet* is commonly used to refer to any IEEE 802.3 compliant network.

**Ethernet II**   The first Ethernet standard was developed by Digital, Intel, and Xerox Corporation in 1981 and was known as DIX 1.0, sometimes referred to as Ethernet I. This standard was superseded in 1982 by DIX 2.0, the current Ethernet standard, also known as Ethernet II.

**evaluation criteria**   These goals may have a direct impact on network design when defined in terms such as maximum response time, transactions per second, or mean time between failures.

**event detection**   Most audit software depends on capturing large amounts of event data and then filtering that data for exceptional or unusual events.

**event management tool**   An alternative to developing your own applications with embedded management intelligence is to purchase a prewritten **event management tool** that has been written to monitor specific commercially available applications.

**exchange sequential**   In a sequential logical topology, also known as a ring logical topology, data are passed from one PC (or node) to another. Each node examines the destination address of the data packet to determine if this particular packet is meant for it. If the data were not meant to be delivered at this node, the data are passed along to the next node in the logical ring.

**explorer packet**   In an internetwork connected via source routing bridges, the PC sends out a special explorer packet that determines the best path to the intended destination of its data message. The explorer packets are continually propagated through all source routing bridges until the destination workstation is finally reached.

**extended binary coded decimal interchange code**  *See* EBCDIC.

**extended superframe**  *See* ESF.

**Extended Terminal Access Control Access System**  *See* XTACACS.

**EZ-ISDN**  In order to try to further simplify the ISDN ordering process, an alternative ordering code scheme known as EZ-ISDN has been proposed by the National ISDN Users Forum.

### F

**fallback**  When an analog circuit, dial-up or leased, degrades or has some kind of transmission impairment, many modems automatically use fallback or lower speeds and continue with data transmissions.

**false accepts**  In biometric authentication, false accepts will occur when impostors are allowed access because the comparison was not detailed enough.

**false rejects**  In biometric authentication, false rejects will occur when valid users are denied access because of slight variations detected between the reference biometric characteristic and the current one.

**fast packet forwarding**  *See* Packet overlapping.

**Fax-on-demand**  By combining computer-based faxing with interactive voice response, users can dial in and request that specific information be transmitted to their fax machine.

**FCS**  Frame check sequence, error detection technique.

**FDDI**  Fiber Distributed Data Interface; a 100 Mbps network architecture that was first specified in 1984 by the ANSI (American National Standards Institute) subcommittee entitled X3T9.5.

**FDM**  Frequency division multiplexing; each channel gets a portion of the bandwidth for 100% of the time.

**feasibility study**  The problem definition and its associated alternative recommendations for further study are sometimes referred to as a feasibility study.

**FECN**  Forward explicit congestion notification; a flow control mechanism in frame relay networks.

**FEP**  Front end processor; a computer that offloads the communications processing from the mainframe, allowing the mainframe to be dedicated to processing activities. A high speed data channel connects the FEP to the mainframe locally although FEPs can be deployed remotely as well.

**Fiber Distributed Data**  *See* FDDI.

**filter**  A program that examines the source address and destination address of every incoming packet to the firewall server.

**filter tables**  Lists of addresses whose data packets and embedded messages are either allowed or prohibited from proceeding through the firewall server and into the corporate network.

**filtering**  A bridge reads the destination address on an Ethernet frame or Token Ring packet and decides whether or not that packet should be allowed access to the internetwork through the bridge.

**filtering rate**  Measured in Packets/sec or Frames/sec, a measure of the filtering performance of a given bridge.

**firewall**  Specialized software often deployed to prevent unauthorized access from the Internet into a company's confidential data. All network packets entering the firewall are filtered, or examined, to determine whether those users have authority to access requested files or services and whether the information contained within the message meets corporate criteria for forwarding over the internal network.

**firewire**  *See* IEEE-1394.

**first-party call control**  Also known as desktop CTI.

**fixed callback**  Callback mechanism that is only able to call remote uses back at predetermined phone numbers entered in a directory.

**flat gray modular**  Wiring, also known as gray satin or silver satin, that contains either 4, 6, or 8 wires which get crimped into either RJ-11 (4 wire), RJ-12 (6 wire), or RJ-45 plugs (8 wire) using a specialized crimping tool.

**flow analysis**  The first step toward a thorough understanding of data traffic analysis is to analyze the flow of that data. Understanding the source and destination of each data "conversation" and the nature of the data in that conversation is fundamental to a proper network design.

**flow control** Mechanism that stops and starts data transmission in order to avoid overflow of buffer memory.

**format converter** A special type of bridge that includes a format converter can bridge between Ethernet and Token Ring. These special bridges may also be called multi-protocol bridges or translating bridges.

**Forward Error Correction** Error correction protocols that seek to avoid the need for retransmission by sending redundant data along with actual data in order to assist the receiving modem in correctly interpreting received signals.

**forward explicit congestion notification** *See* FECN.

**forward if not local** Since only frames with destination addresses not found in the known local nodes table are forwarded across the bridge, bridges are sometimes known as a "Forward-if-not-local" devices.

**forward if proven remote** Once the router is satisfied with both the viability of the destination address as well as with the quality of the intended path, it will release the carefully packaged data packet via processing known as forward-if-proven-remote logic.

**forwarding** Forwarding is the bridge process necessary to load the packet onto the internetwork media whether local or remote.

**forwarding rate** Measured in Packets/sec or Frames/sec, a measure of the forwarding performance of a given bridge.

**four-wire circuit** Comprised of two wires capable of simultaneously carrying a data signal each with its own dedicated ground wire. Typically, four-wire circuits are reserved for leased lines.

**fractional T-1** *See* FT-1.

**Fractional T-1 multiplexers** A T-1 multiplexer that is able to use less than a full T-1 as its composite output channel.

**FRAD** Frame relay access device; the access device to the frame relay network must be able to respond to requests from the frame relay network to "throttle back" or slow down the input to the network or risk losing transmitted packets due to network overload.

**fragmentation** As contiguous blocks of memory of varying sizes are continuously cut out of a finite amount of primary memory, that primary memory suffers from fragmentation where numerous, small leftover pieces of contiguous memory remain unused.

**frame check sequence** FCS; is an error detection mechanism generated by the transmitting Ethernet network interface card.

**frame check sequence** *See* FCS.

**frame relay** A switch based service that packages voice and data into variable length frames.

**frame relay access device** *See* FRAD.

**frame relay switch** Network switch capable of switching frame relay frames.

**frame status flags** In a token passing access methodology, successful delivery of the data frame is confirmed by the destination workstation setting frame status flags to indicate successful receipt of the frame and continuing to forward the original frame around the ring to the sending PC.

**frames** The data-link layer provides the required reliability to the physical layer transmission by organizing the bit stream into structured frames that add addressing and error checking information.

**frameworks** Offer an overall systems administration or network management platform with integration between modules and a shared database into which all alerts, messages, alarms, and warnings can be stored and correlated.

**framing** In T-1 framing, differentiating between channels is accomplished through a technique known as framing, which is an adaptation of the TDM.

**framing bit** The 193rd bit added to the 24 8-bit time slots to indicate the end of one D-4 frame.

**frequency** A wave characteristic that can be manipulated in order represent 1s and 0s.

**frequency division multiplexing** *See* FDM.

**frequency hopping spread spectrum** FHSS hops from one frequency to another throughout the allowable frequency range. The pattern of frequency hopping must be known by the wireless receiver so that the message can be reconstructed correctly.

**frequency modulation** Process of manipulating carrier wave frequency in order to represent 1s and 0s.

**frequency shift keying** *See* FSK.

**front end processor** *See* FEP.

**FSK** Frequency shift keying; shifting carrier wave frequency on analog circuits in order to represent digital 1s and 0s.

**FT-1** Fractional T-1, broadband service that allows customer to access less than the full 24 DS-0s in a T-1.

**full duplex Ethernet** Requires specialized full duplex Ethernet NICs, NIC drivers, and full duplex Ethernet switches. Should allow twice the normal Ethernet performance speed by offering a dedicated 10Mpbs communication channel in each direction for a total available bandwidth 20 Mbps.

**full duplex** Simultaneous transmission in both directions on a given circuit.

# G

**gateway** A LAN server-based, shared protocol converted access to a mainframe is known as a gateway.

**Generic Security Service-Applications Program Interface** *See* GSS-API.

**gigabit Ethernet** Also known as 1000base-X; an upgrade to Fast Ethernet that was standardized as the **IEEE 802.3z** standard by the IEEE on June 25, 1998.

**global address** Address attached to a datagram in a frame relay network that allows it to be properly delivered.

**global directory services** *See* NDS.

**global system for mobile communication** *See* GSM.

**granularity** How finely access can be controlled (by disk, directory, or file level) is sometimes referred to as the granularity of the access control scheme.

**GSM** Global System for Mobile Communication; in Europe and much of the rest of the world, is either currently deployed or planned for implementation as the digital cellular standard.

**GSS-API** An open API that would allow applications to communicate with a variety of security authorization programs.

**guardbands** Portions of the 4000Hz voice bandwidth, reserved to protect against interference.

**guest** The terms *remote* and *local* are often replaced by guest (remote) and host (local), when referring to Remote Control Software.

# H

**half duplex** Transmission in both directions, only one direction at a time on a given circuit.

**handshaking** Modem initialization that takes place in order to allow modems to agree on carrier wave frequency, modulation scheme, error correction protocols, etc.

**Hashing Checkers** Flow control mechanism that uses RS-232 pins CTS/RTS, clear-to-send/request to send, category of antivirus technology known as CRC Checkers or Hashing Checkers. Creates and saves a unique cyclical redundancy check character or hashing number for each file to be monitored.

**Hayes AT Command Set** Series of commands understood by both communications software and modems that allows the communications software to control and respond to modem activity.

**Hayes compatible** Term that indicates a modem is able to understand and respond to commands in the Hayes AT command set.

**HDLC** High level data-link control; data-link layer protocol for X.25.

**header** Additional information added to the front of data.

**heuristic analysis** Because of their ability to monitor behavior of programs, this category of antivirus technology is also sometimes known as **activity monitors** or **heuristic analysis.** Such programs are also capable of trapping encrypted or polymorphic viruses that are capable of constantly changing their identities or signatures.

**hierarchical networking** An internetworking design strategy that isolates local LAN traffic on a local network architecture such as Ethernet or Token Ring while transmitting internetwork traffic over a higher speed network architecture such as FDDI or Fast Ethernet. Servers are often directly connected to the backbone network while individual workstations access the backbone network only as needed through routers.

**high level data link control** *See* HDLC.

**high speed token ring** *See* HSTR.

**HMMP** Hypermedia Management Protocol; The overall intention of the WBEM architecture is that the network manager could manage any networked device or application from any location on the network, via any **HMMP** compliant browser.

**HMMS** Hypermedia Management Schema; management data from a variety of software agents would be incorporated into the Web-based enterprise management architecture via the **HMMS.**

**HMOM** Hypermedia Object Manager; all Web-based management information is stored and retrieved by the request broker known as **HMOM.**

**horizontal integration** A standardized open architecture offering seamless horizontal integration between a variety of CANE products might be constructed. Rather than having to know the intricacies, and, in some cases, the trade secrets, of how each other's products work, vendors of computer assisted network engineering software merely pass the output from their particular software product to a "neutral" data platform.

**host** The terms *remote* and *local* are often replaced by guest (remote) and host (local), when referring to Remote Control Software.

**hot swappable** A capability in which enterprise hub modules can be inserted and/or removed while the hub remains powered-up.

**HPR/AnyNET** Recent enhancements to APPN known as HPR (High Performance Routing)/AnyNET now allow multiple transport protocols such as IP and IPX to travel over the APPN network simultaneously with SNA traffic. In such an implementation, APPN rather than TCP/IP serves as the single backbone protocol able to transport multiple LAN protocols as well as SNA traffic simultaneously.

**HSTR** High Speed Token Ring; a 100 Mbps token ring network architecture, otherwise known as HSTR has been approved by an organization known as the High Speed Token Ring Alliance, which is also supposedly working on a gigabit token ring standard.

**hubs** Wiring centers for network architectures other than token ring.

**Huffman encoding** Encoding mechanism that replaces ASCII code with variable length codes, shorter codes (4 bits) for most frequently used characters, longer (11 bit) codes for least frequently used characters.

**hunting** Hunt groups are established to allow incoming calls to get through on alternate trunks when a primary trunk is busy.

**hypermedia management protocol** *See* HMMP.

**hypermedia management schema** *See* HMMS.
**hypermedia object manager** *See* HMOM.

## I

**IBM3270** In micro-mainframe connectivity, the micro (Standalone or LAN-attached PC) pretends to be or "emulates" a mainframe terminal such as an IBM 3270 attached and logged into the mainframe.

**I-CANE** Integration of CANE software with CASE software and business process expert systems via vertical integration.

**ICMP** Internet Control Message Protocol; although IP is by definition an unreliable transport mechanism, ICMP does deliver a variety of error status and control messages related to the ability of IP to deliver its encapsulated payloads.

**ICP** Intelligent Call Processing service; customers are able to reroute incoming 800 calls among multiple customer service centers in a matter of seconds.

**IDEA** International Data Encryption Algorithm; makes use of one-time 128-bit keys known as session keys.

**IEEE 1394** A high speed multipoint serial bus based solution used in digital video and high speed data applications. Also known as firewire and I-link.

**IEEE 802** Local area network architecture standards are defined, debated, and established by the IEEE (Institute of Electrical and Electronic Engineers) 802 committee.

**IEEE 802.1** *See* Spanning Tree Algorithm.

**IEEE 802.11** A lack of interoperability among the wireless LAN offerings of different vendors is a shortcoming being addressed by a proposal for a new wireless LAN standard known as IEEE 802.11.

**IEEE 802.12** Details of the 100VG-AnyLAN network architecture are contained in the proposed IEEE 802.12 standard.

**IEEE 802.14** The access methodologies for sharing cable bandwidth via cable modems are being standardized as IEEE 802.14 cable network specifications.

**IEEE 802.2** The upper sub-layer of the data-link layer that interfaces to the network layer is known as the logical link control or LLC sub-layer and is represented by a single IEEE 802 protocol (IEEE 802.2).

**IEEE 802.3** Although strictly speaking, Ethernet and IEEE 802.3 are conflicting standards, the term *Ethernet* is commonly used to refer to any IEEE 802.3 compliant network.

**IEEE 802.3u** The details of the operation of 100baseT are in the IEEE 802.3u proposed standard.

**IEEE 802.3x** Full duplex Ethernet has gathered sufficient interest from the networking technology vendor and user communities so as to warrant the formation of the IEEE 802.3x committee to propose standards for full duplex Ethernet.

**IEEE 802.3z** *See* Gigabit Ethernet.

**IEEE 802.5** IBM has been the driving force behind the standardization and adoption of Token Ring with a prototype in IBM's lab in Zurich, Switzerland, serving as a model for the eventual IEEE 802.5 standard.

**IEEE 802.6** IEEE specification for DQDB, the SMDS network architecture.

**IEEE 802.9a** Details of the Iso-Ethernet network architecture are contained in the IEEE 802.9a standard, which is officially known as Isochronous Ethernet Integrated Services.

**IGRP** Interior Gateway Routing Protocol; Cisco's proprietary distance vector protocol.

**i-link hardware flow control** *See* IEEE-1394.

**in-band signaling** Occurs when signal bandwidth is robbed to transport managerial or control information.

**incremental change costs** An important element of the comprehensive systems and networking budget model that highlights costs for anticipated growth over the next five years.

**Infrared Data Association** In order to assure multi-vendor interoperability between laptops and mobile aware operating systems, the infrared transmission should conform to the IrDA standards.

**infrared transmission** A wireless LAN transmission methodology limited by its line-of-sight requirement.

**Institute of Electrical and Electronic Engineers 802 Committee** *See* IEEE 802.

**instrumentation** Embedded performance metrics are sometimes referred to as instrumentation.

**Int14** Interrupt 14; one of the supported dial-out software re-directors and most often employed by Microsoft network operating systems. Int14 is actually an IBM BIOS serial port interrupt used for the purpose of redirecting output from the local serial port.

**integrated service digital network** *See* ISDN.

**Integrated Services Terminal Equipment** *See* ISTE.

**integrated suites** The difference between integrated suites and frameworks is that integrated suites are filled with their own network management and systems administration applications rather then offering the user an open framework into which to place a variety of chosen applications.

**integration** Refers to that transitionary period of time in the migration process when both network operating systems must be running simultaneously and interacting to some degree.

**integration/migration services** Integration refers to that transitionary period of time in the migration process when both network operating systems must be running simultaneously and interacting to some degree. Migration features are aimed at easing the transition from NetWare 3.12 to either NetWare 4.1 or Windows NT.

**intelligent agent** *See* Agent event manager.

**intelligent call processing** *See* ICP.

**interactive voice response** *See* IVR.

**Interdomain Trust** In the case of a domain directory service such as Windows NT 3.51, the remote or foreign server receives the user authentication from the user's primary domain controller (local server) in a process known as Interdomain Trust (IT).

**inter-exchange carriers** *See* IXC.

**interface** The logical gap between two communicating hardware or software components.

**interface file synchronization software** Software that is able to synchronize versions of files on laptops and desktop workstations and is now often included as a standard or optional feature in client network operating systems. Also known as version control software or directory synchronization software.

**interface specification** Bit by bit layout of frames that user data must be transformed into before entering network switches.

**internal firewalls** Include filters that work on the data-link, network, and application layers to examine communications that occur only on a corporation's internal network, inside the reach of traditional firewalls.

**International Data Encryption Algorithm** *See* IDEA.

**Internet Control Message Protocol** *See* ICMP.

**Internet Packet Exchange** *See* IPX.

**Internet protocol** *See* IP.

**Internet Security Association and Key Management Protocol** *See* ISAKMP.

**Internet Suite of Protocols** TCP/IP (Transmission Control Protocol/Internet Protocol); the term generally used to refer to an entire suite of protocols used to provide communication on a variety of layers between widely distributed different types of computers. Strictly speaking, TCP and IP are just two of the protocols contained within the family of protocols more properly known as the Internet Suite of Protocols.

**Internet Suite of Protocols Model** A four-layered communications architecture in which upper layers use the functionality offered by the protocols of the lower layers.

**internetworking** Linking multiple LANs together in such as way as to deliver information more efficiently from cost, business, and performance perspectives.

**inter-realm** In Kerberos, if a client wishes to access a server in another realm, it requests an inter-realm ticket granting ticket from its local ticket granting server to authorize access to the remote ticket granting server which can authorize access to the remote applications server.

**inter-ring gate calls** NLMs executing in Ring 3 access operating systems services in Ring 0 by issuing structured inter-ring gate calls, thereby protecting the operating system from misbehaving NLMs overwriting its memory space.

**Interrupt 14** *See* Int14.

**interrupt request** *See* IRQ.

**intersymbol interference** Interference between constellation points in a given modulation scheme which can cause misinterpretation is known as intersymbol interference.

**intranets** Internet type services available for use by in-house, authorized employees.

**intrusion detection systems** Test the perimeter of the enterprise network through dial modems, remote access servers, Web servers, or Internet access.

**inverse multiplexing** A process in which MLPPP compliant devices are able to deliver "bandwidth on demand."

**IOC** Depending on what combinations of voice, video, or data traffic a user wishes to transmit over ISDN, up to twenty or more ISDN Ordering Codes are possible.

**IP** Internet Protocol; the network layer protocol of the TCP/IP suite of protocols. As such, it is primarily responsible for providing the addressing functionality necessary to assure that all reachable network destinations can be uniquely and correctly identified.

**IP over ATM** Otherwise known as Classical IP, adapts the TCP/IP protocol stack to employ ATM services as a native transport protocol directly. This is an IP specific proposal and is not an option for LANs using other protocol stacks such as NetWare's IPX/SPX.

**IP spoofing** A technique in which packet filters can be breached by hackers. Since packet filters make all filtering decisions based on IP source and destination addresses, if a hacker can make a packet appear to come from an authorized or trusted IP address, then it can pass through the firewall.

**IP Switching** Technology that distinguishes between the length of data streams and switches or routes accordingly on a case-by-case basis.

**IPng** IP next generation, otherwise known as IPv6 (IP version 6), offers significant increases in functionality as well as increased address space in comparison to IPv4 (current version, IP version 4).

**I-P-O model** Provides a framework in which to focus on the difference between the data that came into a particular networked device (1) and the data that came out of that same device(O). By defining this difference, the processing (P) performed by the device is documented.

**IPsec** For establishing security over VPN tunnels. IPsec is largely supported by the firewall vendor community and is intended to provide interoperability between VPN firewalls from different vendors.

**IPv4** Current version, IP version 4.

**IPv6** *See* IPng.

**Ipv6** IPsec is also proposed to be able to support both authentication and encryption. These capabilities are optional for IPv4 and mandatory for **IPv6** and are outlined in IETF RFCs 1825 through 1829.

**IPX** Internet Packet Exchange like most OSI network layer protocols, serves as a basic delivery mechanism for upper layer protocols such as SPX, RIP, SAP, and NCP. It is connectionless and unreliable.

**IrDA** *See* Infrared Data Association.

**IRQ Interrupt request**—The network interface card, like every other hardware device in the computer, must interrupt and request resources such as CPU cycles and memory from the CPU itself. It must be assigned an IRQ or interrupt request number so that the CPU knows that it is the NIC requesting these services.

**ISAKMP Internet Security Association and Key Management Protocol;** a key management protocol from the IETF.

**ISDN** Integrated Services Digital Network; a circuit-switched digital WAN service that is the support network transport service for Isochronous Ethernet.

**ISDN data/voice modem** Not truly a modem, but a ISDN terminal adapter that supports analog phones as well as data transmission.

**ISDN ordering codes** *See* IOC.

**ISDN switch** Switch that supports circuit switching for ISDN services.

**ISDN terminal adapters** Allows analog devices (phones, fax machines) to hook to ISDN services.

**ISO 10646** More commonly known as Unicode, this encoding scheme used 16-bit characters to represent most known languages and symbols (more than 65,000 possible characters).

**ISO 7498/2** This framework maps 14 different security services to specific layers of the OSI 7 Layer Reference Model.

**ISO Management Framework** The Network Management Forum associated with the OSI Reference Model has divided the field of network management into five major categories in a document known as the ISO Management Framework (ISO 7498-4).

**isochronous** Refers to any signaling system in which all connections or circuits are synchronized using a single common clocking reference. This common clocking mechanism allows such systems to offer guaranteed delivery times that are very important to streaming or time-sensitive traffic such as voice and video.

**Isochronous Ethernet** *See* Iso-Ethernet.

**Iso-Ethernet** Isochronous Ethernet; offers a combination of services by dividing the overall 16.144 Mbps bandwidth delivered to each workstation into several service-specific channels.

**ISTE** Integrated Services Terminal Equipment; a workstation with an Iso-Ethernet NIC installed.

**IT** *See* Interdomain Trust.

**IT project portfolio management** A process that often manages the overall strategic development direction of the IT infrastructure.

**ITU H.323** The standard for interoperability among client software for low bandwidth audio (voice) and video conferencing.

**IVR** Interactive voice response; systems that support on-line transaction processing rather than just information hot-line applications.

**IVRU** It is important for help desk management software to be able to interact with call center management technology such as automatic call distributors (ACD) and interactive voice response units (IVRU). The overall integration of computer-based software and telephony equipment in known as **computer telephony integration (CTI).**

**IXC** Inter-Exchange Carrier; any phone traffic destined for locations outside of the local LATA must be handed off to the long distance or IXC of the customer's choice.

## K

**Kerberos** Perhaps the most well-known combination authentication/authorization software; originally developed at Massachusetts Institute of Technology and marketed commercially by a variety of firms.

**Kermit** Kermit is a popular file transfer protocol best known for being available on nearly any computing platform of any type.

**Key Escrow agencies** Otherwise known as Trusted Third Parties, these agencies will hold the keys necessary to decrypt key recovery documents.

**key recovery mechanism** U.S. companies with international subsidiaries may now export 56-bit key-based encryption technology provided that they establish within two years a key recovery mechanism that will offer a back door into encrypted data for the government.

**knowledge base** Contains not just the resolutions or answers to problems, but the logic structure or decision tree that takes a given problem and leads the help desk staff person through a series of questions to the appropriate solution.

**known local nodes**   Data-link protocols such as Ethernet contain source addresses as well as the destination addresses within the predefined Ethernet Frame layout. A bridge checks the source address of each frame it receives and adds that source address to a table of known local nodes.

## L

**L2F**   Cisco's Layer Two Forwarding tunneling protocol for virtual private networks.

**L2TP**   Layer 2 Tunneling Protocol; an effort is underway to have the Internet Engineering Task Force (IETF) propose a unification of the two rival virtual private network tunneling standards known as L2TP.

**LAN caching**   *See* Network caching.

**LAN emulation**   Provides a translation layer that allows ATM to emulate existing Ethernet and token ring LANs and allows all current upper-layer LAN protocols to be transported by the ATM services in an unmodified fashion.

**LAN modem**   Also known as a Dial-In Server; offers shared remote access to LAN resources. LAN modems come with all necessary software preinstalled and therefore require no additional remote control or remote node software. LAN modems are often limited to a single network architecture such as Ethernet or Token Ring, and/or to a single network operating system protocol such as IP, IPX (NetWare), NetBIOS, NetBEUI, or Appletalk.

**LAN switch**   *See* Switching hub.

**Land attack**   A variation on the denial of service attack in which the hacker substituted the targeted server's own address as the address of the server requesting a connection. This caused the attacked server to constantly try to establish connections to itself, thereby often crashing the server.

**Landline telephone network**   PSTN, otherwise known as the Landline Telephone Network.

**LAP-B**   Link access procedure-balanced, data-link layer protocol for X.25.

**LAP-D**   The frame definition for frame relay networks. This frame definition is said to be a subset of the LAP-D protocol. LAP-D stands for Link Access Procedure - D Channel, where the D channel refers to the 16 Kbps Delta Channel in BRI (Basic Rate Interface) ISDN (Integrated Services Digital Network).

**LAP-M**   Link Access Protocol for Modems; V.42 error control protocol that implements selective ARQ.

**Large Internet Packets**   *See* LIP.

**Large Packet IPX**   *See* LIP.

**Large Scale RAS**   **Large Scale Remote Access Servers (RAS)** also known as **Monster RAS** are differentiated from previously mentioned RAS hardware by their scalability (number of modem ports), manageability, and security. These are enterprise class machines boasting modem port counts up to 1,344 per chassis, fast Ethernet LAN interfaces, and ATM DS3 (45 Mbps) or OC3 (155 Mbps) WAN connections.

**LATA**   All local phone traffic within a local access transport area is handled by the local phone company, more formally known as a local exchange carrier or LEC, most often one of the RBOCs.

**latency**   Filtering time introduces latency to the overall transmission time.

**layer 2 switch**   A LAN switch that supports a layer 2 virtual LAN distinguishes only between the MAC addresses of connected workstations.

**Layer 2 Tunneling Protocol**   *See* L2TP.

**layer 3 switch**   Devices able to perform filtering based on network layer protocols and addresses; able to support multiple virtual LANs using different network layer protocols.

**layer 4 switch**   Process TCP port numbers and can distribute multiple requests for a given service to multiple different physical servers, thus providing load balancing.

**Layer Two Forwarding**   *See* L2F.

**LCR**   Using routing and pricing information supplied by the user, the PBX chooses the most economical path for any given call.

**LDAP**   A subset of the X.500 directory service standardized by the IETF for use on TCP/IP networks.

**leased line**   A dedicated phone circuit that bypasses central office switching equipment; no dial tone.

**Least cost routing**   *See* LCR.

**least significant bit**   Both Ethernet and token ring believe that bit 0 on byte 0, referred to as the least significant bit, should be transmitted first.

**LEC**   Local exchange carriers, or local phone company that handles all local phone traffic within a LATA.

**legacy applications**   *See* Backward compatibility.

**Lightweight Directory Access Protocol**   *See* LDAP.

**limited size messaging**   *See* LSM.

**line cards**   PBX cards that attach to users' phones.

**Line conditioning**   Value added service available from carriers in order to reduce interference on analog leased lines.

**link access procedure-D channel**   *See* LAP-D.

**link access procedure-balanced**   *See* LAP-B.

**link access protocol for modems**   *See* LAP-M.

**link state**   OSPF protocol uses a more comprehensive link state algorithm that can decide between multiple paths to a given router based upon variables other than number of hops such as delay, and capacity, throughput, and reliability of the circuits connecting the routers.

**link state packets**   *See* LSP.

**link state protocols**   Routing protocols known as link state protocols take into account other factors regarding internetwork paths such as link capacity, delay, throughput, reliability, or cost.

**link support layer**   A layer of the ODI Architecture; LSL.COM is the program that orchestrates the operation of ODI drivers.

**LIP**   Large Internet Packets; applies only to NetWare 4.1 LANs that are linked to each other via a wide area network through routers. LIP, also known as Large Packet IPX, allows NetWare clients to negotiate with the routers as to the size of the IPX frame. From the NetWare client's perspective, the larger the IPX frame, the larger the IPX frame's data field, and the greater the amount of data that the client can cram into a single IPX frame.

**LLC**   In order for an IEEE 802.3 compliant network interface card to be able to determine the type of protocols embedded within the data field of an IEEE 802.3 frame, it refers to the header of the IEEE 802.2 Logical Link Control (LLC) data unit.

**LLC sub-layer**   The upper sub-layer of the data-link layer that interfaces to the network layer is known as the logical link control or LLC sub-layer and is represented by a single IEEE 802 protocol (IEEE 802.2).

**load balancing**   The effective use of a network's redundant paths allows routers to perform load balancing of total network traffic across two or more links between two given locations.

**local access transport area**   *See* LATA.

**local exchange carrier**   *See* LEC.

**local hub management software**   Usually supplied by the hub vendor and runs over either DOS or Windows. This software allows monitoring and management of the hub from a locally attached management console.

**local loop transmission**   Narrowband transmission services from customer premises to CO.

**local loops**   The circuits between a residence or business and the local Central Office or CO.

**local session number**   A NetBIOS variable that typically limits NetBIOS and NetBEUI clients and servers to a 254 session limit.

**logic bombs**   Viruses that require a certain event to transpire are known as logic bombs.

**logical channel**   Virtual circuit in frame relay network.

**logical channel number**   Identifier assigned to virtual circuit in frame relay network.

**logical link control**   *See* LLC.

**logical network design**   Network performance criteria could be referred to as *what* the implemented network must do in order to meet the business objectives outlined at the outset of this top-down analysis. These requirements are also sometimes referred to as the logical network design.

**Logical Ring Physical Star**   IBM's Token Ring network architecture, adhering to the IEEE 802.5 standard, utilizes a star configuration, sequential message delivery, and a token passing access methodology scheme. Since the sequential logical topology is equivalent to passing messages from neighbor to neighbor around a ring, the token ring network architecture is sometimes referred to as Logical Ring, Physical Star.

**logical topology**   The particular message passing methodology, or how a message will be passed from workstation to workstation until the message ultimately reaches its intended destination workstation, is more properly known as a network architecture's logical topology.

**longitudinal redundancy checks**   *See* LRC.

**LRC** Longitudinal redundancy checks; two-dimensional parity that overcomes simple parity's inability to detect multiple bit errors.

**LSL** *See* Link support layer.

**LSM** By adding a protocol known as LSM (Limited Size Messaging), CDPD will be able to transport two-way messaging that will offer the following key services beyond simple paging: guaranteed delivery to destination mobile users even if those devices are unreachable at the time the message was originally sent, return receipt acknowledgments to the party that originated the message.

**LSP** Link state packets; specialized datagrams used by link state routers to determine the names of and the cost or distance to any neighboring routers and associated networks.

# M

**M block connector** Physical connector most often associated with V. 35 serial transmission standard.

**MAC sub-layer** The media access control or MAC sub-layer is a sub-layer of the data-link layer that interfaces with the physical layer and is represented by protocols that define how the shared local area network media is to be accessed by the many connected computers.

**make or buy decision** Follows all of the vendor demonstrations; will systems and networks be developed in-house or outsourced?

**malicious applets** Java applets downloaded from the Web; tend to be annoying rather than destructive.

**MAN** *See* Metropolitan area networks.

**management abstract** A section of the RFP that includes important information regarding the project other than project specifications.

**management information base** *See* MIB.

**management information format** *See* MIF.

**management interface API** Designed to interface to the desktop system management program which will consolidate the information from this client with all other desktop information.

**MAU** Multistation Access Unit; Token Ring wiring centers.

**Maximum Transmission Unit** *See* MTU.

**MD5** Produces 128-bit hash number based on original document. Can then be incorporated into digital signature. Replaced MD4 and MD2.

**media access control** *See* MAC.

**media sharing LANs** Local area networks that use access methodologies to control the access of multiple users to a shared media.

**message** Transport layer protocols also provide mechanisms for sequentially organizing multiple network layer packets into a coherent message.

**message gateway** One of three cooperating components of the agent portion of the client/agent/server architecture. The message gateway can execute on the local server or on a dedicated Unix or Windows workstation, and acts as an interface between the client's message manager and the intelligent agent on the local server. The gateway also acts as a holding station for messages to and from mobile clients that are temporarily unreachable.

**message manager** One of three cooperating components of the agent portion of the client/agent/server architecture. Executes on the mobile client and acts as an interface between client applications requesting services and the wireless link over which the requests must be forwarded.

**metropolitan area networks** Occasionally, multiple LANs belonging to a single corporate entity that are all located within a single metropolitan area must be internetworked. In such cases, a metropolitan area network or MAN may be used to link these LANs together.

**MIB** Management Information Base; the network management information gathered must be stored in some type of database with an index and standardized field definitions so that network management workstations can easily access this data. An MIB can differ in the fields defined for different vendor's networking devices.

**microcell spread spectrum** Limited to areas such as college and corporate campuses that are served by microcells, this wireless WAN service offers full-duplex transmission at rates up to 104.5 Mbps via proprietary modems.

**Microcom Networking Protocols** *See* MNP.

**micro-mainframe connectivity** In micro-mainframe connectivity, the micro (Standalone or LAN-attached PC) pretends to be or "emulates" a mainframe terminal such as an IBM 3270 attached and logged into the mainframe.

**micro-segmentation** When segmentation is taken to the extreme of limiting each LAN segment to only a single workstation, the internetworking design strategy is known as micro-segmentation. A micro-segmented internetwork requires a LAN switch that is compatible with the NICs installed in the attached workstations.

**MIF** Management Information Format; DMI-compliant desktop management systems store performance and configuration statistics in an **MIF.**

**migration** Migration features are aimed at easing the transition from NetWare 3.12 to either NetWare 4.1 or Windows NT.

**mini-PBX** Offer multiple workers the ability to share a small number of phone lines with integrated advanced features.

**mission-critical analysis** A data traffic analysis process that examines which data must be specially handled due to its mission critical nature.

**MLID** Multi-Link Drivers; Network interface card drivers in an ODI-compliant environment.

**MLPPP** Multilink Point-to-Point Protocol or MLPPP (RFC 1717); able to support multiple simultaneous physical WAN links and also able to combine multiple channels from a variety of WAN services into a single logical link.

**MNP** A series of 10 classes of error control and data compression protocols that have become de facto standards for modem transmission.

**MNP-10** Transmitting data over analog cellular networks requires modems that support specialized cellular transmission protocols on both ends of the cellular transmission in order to maximize throughput. Examples of such protocols are MNP-10 Adverse Channel Enhancements and Enhanced Throughput Cellular (ETC).

**MNP Class 5** MNP protocol that offers data compression at up to a 2:1 ratio.

**mobile computing** Enables field representatives to access corporate information resources in order to offer superior customer service while working on the road. These field reps may or may not have a corporate office PC into which to dial.

**mobile IP** Under consideration by the IETF, may be the roaming standard that wireless LANs require. Mobile IP, limited to TCP/IP networks, employs two pieces of software in order to support roaming: a mobile IP client is installed on the roaming wireless client workstation; a mobile IP home agent is installed on a server or router on the roaming user's home network.

**mobile MIB** The Mobile Management Task Force (MMTF) has proposed a mobile MIB capable of feeding configuration and location information to enterprise network management systems via SNMP. A key to the design of the mobile MIB was to balance the amount of information required in order to effectively manage remote clients while taking into account the limited bandwidth and expense of the remote links over which the management data must be transmitted.

**mobile middleware** The ultimate goal of mobile middleware is to offer mobile users transparent client/server access independent of the following variables: Client or server platform (operating system, network operating system). Applications (client/server or client/agent/server), Wireless transmission services.

**mobile telephone switching office** *See* MTSO.

**mobile-aware applications** The overall objective of mobile-aware applications is to reduce the amount of mobile client to server network traffic by building as much intelligence as possible into the server-based agent so that it can act on behalf of the mobile client application.

**mobile-aware operating systems** Operating systems that are able to easily adapt to these different computing modes with a variety of included supporting accessory programs and utilities.

**modem** Data communications device that modulates/demodulates analog/digital conversion.

**modem cable** Attaches a modem to a PC. Pinned straight through.

**modem setup string** Initialization string of Hayes AT commands that establishes communication between a modem and the local PC's communication software.

**modified object format** *See* MOF.

**modular concentrators** *See* Enterprise hubs.

**modulation** Process of converting discrete digital signals in continuously varying analog signals.

**MOF** Modified Object Format; management data to be used by CIM would be stored in MOF as opposed to DMI's MIF format or SNMP's MIB format.

**monolithic drivers** Network interface card drivers written for specific adapter card/network operating system combinations.

**Monster RAS** *See* Large scale RAS.

**MPLS** Multi-protocol label switching; Cisco's Tag Switching protocol became known as MPLS when it began deliberation by the IETF. Although originally intended for use within a switched internetwork environment, the scope of its application has broadened to include the Internet. MPLS uses labels to provide shortcuts to specific circuits for fast routing of IP packets without the typical packet-by-packet routing table lookups.

**MPOA** Provides support for multiple local area network protocols running on top of the ATM cell switched network.

**MTSO** Mobile Telephone Switching Office; cellular service providers are deploying modem pools of cellular enhanced modems at the MTSO where all cellular traffic is converted for transmission over the wireline public switched telephone network (PSTN).

**MTU** The maximum capacity of a layer two data frame.

**multi-casting** The process of sending a single packet to multiple nodes on one or more network segments.

**multi-function telephony boards** *See* Mini-PBX.

**multi-homed** A node that has NICs on more than one network segment.

**multi-layer switch** A single device in which layer 2 switching and layer 3 routing functionality are combined.

**multi-link interface drivers** *See* MLID.

**Multilink Point-to-Point Protocol** *See* MLPPP.

**multimode** In a Multimode or Multimode Step Index fiber optic cable, the rays of light will bounce off the cladding at different angles and continue down the core while others will be absorbed in the cladding. These multiple rays at varying angles cause distortion and limit the overall transmission capabilities of the fiber.

**multimode graded index** By gradually decreasing a characteristic of the core known as the refractive index from the center to the outer edge, reflected rays are focused along the core more efficiently, yielding higher bandwidth (3 GBps) over several kilometers in a type of fiber optic cable known as Multimode Graded Index Fiber.

**multimode step index** *See* Multimode.

**multiplexing** Process that combines outputs of several channels into a single composite output.

**multiprotocol bridges** *See* Translating bridge.

**Multi-Protocol Over ATM** *See* MPOA.

**multiprotocol routers** Have the capability to interpret, process, and forward data packets of multiple routable and nonroutable protocols.

**multiprotocol routing** Provides the functionality necessary to actually process and understand multiple network protocols as well as translate between them. Without multiprotocol routing software, clients speaking multiple different network protocols cannot be supported.

**Multiprotocol Transport Networking Layer** *See* MPTN.

**multirate ISDN** Uses a technique known as inverse multiplexing in which a collection of 64 Kbps B channels are dialed up and combined into a single logical channel of sufficient bandwidth to meet application needs such as videoconferencing.

**multistation access unit** *See* MAU.

**multi-tier firewall** Allows controlled access to DMZ while blocking unauthorized access to secure network. Same functionality may be offered in a single product known as a tri-homed firewall.

# N

**narrowband digital services** Digital carrier services offering bandwidth of less than 1.544 Mbps.

**narrowband ISDN** A switched digital network service offering both voice and non-voice connectivity to other ISDN end users.

**NASI** NetWare Asynchronous Services Interface; a software interrupt that links to the NetWare shell on NetWare clients. As with the Int14 implementation, a TSR intercepts all of the information passed to the NASI interrupt and forwards it across the network to the dial-out modem pool.

**National Computer Security Association** Now certifies firewall technology.

**National ISDN-1** *See* NISDN-1.

**NBF** NetBEUI Frame; the Windows NT version of the NetBEUI protocol stack included for backward compatibility purposes with such NetBEUI-based network operating systems as

Microsoft LAN Manager and OS/2 LAN Server.

**NCP**  NetWare Core Protocols; provide a standardized set of commands or messages that can be used to communicate requests and responses for services between clients and servers.

**NDIS**  Network Driver Interface Specification; a driver specification that offers standard commands for communications between NDIS-compliant network operating system protocol stacks (NDIS Protocol Driver) and NDIS-compliant network adapter card drivers (NDIS MAC Drivers). In addition NDIS specifies a binding operation that is managed by a separate program known as the Protocol Manager.

**NDLC**  Network development life cycle.

**NDS**  Network operating systems have always depended on some sort of naming service or directory in which to store information about users as well as systems resources such as disks, servers, and printers. NetWare 4.1 employs a global directory service known as NDS or NetWare Directory Services.

**near-end crosstalk**  *See* NExT.

**negative acknowledgment**  NAK; control character sent to the transmitting modem from the receiving modem when a data block is received in error.

**NetBEUI Frame**  *See* NBF.

**NetWare Connect**  Novell's remote node server software.

**NetWare Directory Services**  *See* NDS.

**NetWare Link Services Protocol**  *See* NLSP.

**network analysis and design methodology**  The key model behind the network design process is known as the Network Development Life Cycle. Its major phases include analysis, design, simulation, prototyping, monitoring, and management.

**network analyzers**  LAN and WAN **network analyzers** are able to capture network traffic in real time without interrupting normal network transmission. In addition to capturing packets of data from the network, most network analyzers are able to decode those packets, monitor packet traffic statistics, and simulate network traffic through traffic generators.

**network architecture**  Switching architecture + transmission architecture = network architecture.

**network auditing tools**  All network auditing tools seem to have in common the ability to

provide records of which network files have been accessed by which users.

**network baselining tools**  By combining the ability to monitor and capture SNMP and RMON data with the abilities to analyze the captured data and report on trends and exceptions, network baselining tools are able to track network performance over extended periods of time and report on anomalies or deviations from the accumulated baseline data.

**network byte order**  The IP header can be either 20 or 24 bytes long, with the bits actually being transmitted in network byte order or from left to right.

**network caching**  Network caching or LAN caching software is able to improve overall remote node performance up to five times by caching repetitive applications commands and systems calls. These add-on packages are comprised of both client and server pieces that work cooperatively with cache application commands and reduce network traffic over relatively low-speed WAN links. Network caching software is network operating system and protocol dependent, requiring that compatibility be assured prior to purchase.

**network convergence**  The merging (or converging) of data, voice, and video traffic onto a single physical network. The achievement of network convergence is dependent on a combination of business drivers, technology drivers, and technology industry drivers.

**network development life cycle**  *See* NDLC.

**network device interface specification**  *See* NDIS.

**network engineering**  Field of study concentrated largely on processes represented in the NDLC.

**network hardware analysis and configuration alternatives**  Analysis of networking hardware requirements to link data sources with chosen WAN services.

**network hierarchy**  A hierarchy of switching offices from class 5 to class 1. Higher levels on the network hierarchy imply greater switching and transmission capacity as well as greater expense.

**network interface card**  Data-link layer frames are built within the network interface card installed in a computer according to the predetermined frame layout particular to the network architecture of the installed network interface card. Network interface cards are given a unique address in a format determined by their network architecture.

**network interface card drivers** Small software programs responsible for delivering full interoperability and compatibility between the NIC and the network operating system installed in a given computer.

**network interface cards** *See* NICs.

**network layer** Network layer protocols are responsible for the establishment, maintenance, and termination of end-to-end network links. Network layer protocols are required when computers that are not physically connected to the same LAN must communicate.

**network level filter** A filtering program that only examines source and destination addresses and determines access based on the entries in a filter table is known as a port level filter or network level filter or packet filter.

**network modeling and simulation tools** Simulation software uses the current network configuration as a starting point and applies what-if scenarios.

**network nodes** Processing nodes with routing capabilities in APPN. They have the ability to locate network resources, maintain tables of information regarding internetwork links, and establish a session between the requesting end-node and the internetwork service requested.

**network objects** In some cases, directory services may view all users and network resources as network objects with information concerning them stored in a single database, arranged by object type. Object attributes can be modified and new network objects can be defined.

**network segment address** The portion of a network layer address that determines the network segment upon which the node resides.

**network service** Services offered to customers by carriers dependent upon the capabilities of their network architecture.

**network termination unit-1** *See* NTU-1.

**network trending tools** Tools that are able to track network performance over extended periods of time and report on anomalies or deviations from the accumulated baseline data. Also known as proactive network management tools or network trending products, such tools usually need several weeks of SNMP data in order

to establish realistic baseline network performance averages.

**network-network interface** *See* NNI.

**network-to-network interface** *See* NNI.

**NExT** Near-End Crosstalk; signal interference caused by a strong signal on one-pair (transmitting) overpowering a weaker signal on an adjacent pair (receiving).

**NICs** Network Interface Cards; installed either internally or externally to client and server computers in order to provide a connection to the local area network of choice.

**night mode** Many companies close their switchboard at night but still have employees on duty who must be able to receive and make phone calls.

**NISDN-1** NISDN-1 (National ISDN-1); defines a national standard for ISDN switches as well as inter-switch communication.

**NLSP** NetWare Link Services Protocol; introduced in NetWare 4.1 in an effort to overcome the inefficiencies introduced by RIP. NLSP only broadcasts as changes occur, or every 2 hours at a minimum. Real world implementations of NLSP have reported 15 to 20 times (not %) reduction in WAN traffic with Novell claiming a possibility of up to 40-fold decreases in router-to-router traffic.

**NNI** Network-Network Interface; defines interoperability standards between various vendors' ATM equipment and network services. These standards are not as well defined as UNI.

**node address** The portion of a network layer address that determines to which NIC the network layer address correlates.

**non-routable** Protocols processed by some routers are actually data link layer protocols without network layer addressing schemes. These protocols are considered non-routable.

**non-routable protocol** Non-routable protocols can be processed by routers by either having the routers act as bridges or by encapsulating the non-routable data link layer frame's upper layer protocols in a routable network layer protocol such as IP.

**Northern Telecom DMS100 Switch** One of the switches able to support ISDN services.

**NT-1** *See* NTU-1.

**NTU-1** Network Termination Unit-1 (NTU-1) or (NT-1); required to physically connect the ISDN line to a user's ISDN CPE. Most integrated ISDN equipment includes built-in NT-1s, although stand-alone models are available.

## O

**object-oriented user interfaces**   Present the user with a graphical desktop on which objects such as files, directories, folders, disk drives, programs, or devices can be arranged according to the user's whim.

**objects**   The fields within the MIBs are known as objects.

**OC**   Optical carrier; standards for optical transmission.

**OC-1**   Optical transmission standard, 51.84 Mbps.

**octet**   A unit of data 8 bits long. The term *byte* is often used to refer to an 8-bit character or number. Since today's networks are likely to carry digitized voice, video, and images as well as data, the term *octet* is more often used to refer to these 8-bit packets of digital network traffic.

**ODI**   Open DataLink Interface operates in a manner similar to the basic functionality of NDIS and is orchestrated by a program known as LSL.COM where LSL stands for Link Support Layer.

**open data-link interface**   *See* ODI.

**open shortest path first**   *See* OSPF.

**operations costs**   A cost category from the comprehensive systems and network budget model that focuses on the incremental costs to operate new equipment.

**opportunities for improvement**   During stratgic information systems design, opportunities for improvement of business processes and the associated required information are identified.

**OPSEC   Open Platform for Security Alliance;** one example of a multivendor interoperable security architecture. More than 200 vendors of security technology have joined the OPSEC alliance that offers certification for OPSEC compliant security products.

**optical carrier**   *See* OC.

**optical switching**   A switching process that can be accomplished directly on optical signals without the need to first convert to electronic or digital signals.

**optimization routines**   By using analysis and design software to model their current network, companies are able to run optimization routines to reconfigure circuits and/or network hardware to deliver data more efficiently. In the case of optimization software, "efficiently" can mean maximized performance, minimized price, or a combination of both.

**Oracle Mobile Agents**   Formerly known as Oracle-in-Motion; perhaps the best example of the overall architecture and components required to produce mobile-aware applications. The Oracle Mobile Agents architecture adheres to an overall client-agent-server architecture, as opposed to the more common LAN-based client/server architecture.

**OSI model**   Consists of a hierarchy of seven layers that loosely group the functional requirements for communication between two computing devices. The power of the OSI Model lies in its openness and flexibility. It can be used to organize and define protocols involved in communicating between two computing devices in the same room as effectively as two devices across the world from each other.

**OSI Security Architecture**   A framework that maps fourteen different security services to specific layers of the OSI 7 Layer Reference Model.

**OSI Seven-Layer Model**   Divides the communication between any two networked computing devices into seven layers or categories and allows data communications technology developers as well as standards developers to talk about the interconnection of two networks or computers in common terms without dealing in proprietary vendor jargon.

**OSPF**   Open Shortest Path First (RFC 1247); an example of a link state protocol that was developed to overcome some of RIP's shortcomings such as the 15 hop limit and full routing table broadcasts every 30 seconds. OSPF uses IP for connectionless transport.

**out-of-band signaling**   A process in which interswitch signaling should travel out of the voice conversation's band or channel.

**outsourcing**   The purchase of services from outside vendors rather than supporting internal staffs.

**outsourcing**   The selective hiring of outside contractors to perform specific network management duties.

## P

**P channel** In Isochronous Ethernet, a 10 Mbps ISDN P channel is reserved for Ethernet traffic and is completely compatible with 10baseT Ethernet.

**packet assembler/disassembler** *See* PAD.

**packet filter** A filtering program that examines only source and destination addresses and determines access based on the entries in a filter table. Known as a port level filter or network level filter or packet filter.

**packet layer protocol** *See* PLP.

**packet overlapping** A technology in which the next packet of information is immediately forwarded as soon as its start of frame is detected rather than waiting for the previous frame to be totally onto the network media before beginning transmission of the next packet.

**packet switched network** As opposed to circuit switched networks, physical circuits are shared by numerous users transmitting their own packets of data between switches.

**packet switches** Used to route user's data from source to destination.

**packet switching** As opposed to circuit switching, user's data shares physical circuits with data from numerous other users.

**packetizing** Process of adding overhead or management data to raw user data in order to assure proper delivery.

**packets** Network layer protocols are responsible for providing network layer (end-to-end) addressing schemes and for enabling inter-network routing of network layer data packets. The term *packets* is usually associated with network layer protocols while the term *frames* is usually associated with data-link layer protocols.

**PAD** Device that transforms raw data into properly formatted packets.

**paging** Ability to use paging speakers in a building. May be limited to specific paging zone.

**PAM** Pulse amplitude modulation; a voice digitization technique.

**PAP** The remote network printing protocol used in the AppleTalk protocol suite.

**PAP** Password Authentication Protocol; repeatedly sends the user ID and password to the authenticating system in clear text pairs until it is either acknowledged or the connection is dropped. There is no encryption performed with PAP.

**parallel networks model** A network design in which separate networks for SNA and LAN traffic had to be established between the same corporate locations.

**parallel transmission** Transmission method in which all bits in a given character travel simultaneously through a computer bus or parallel transmission cable.

**parity** Simple error checking mechanism that adds a single bit per character.

**password Authentication** *See* PAP.

**protocol password protection** Modem security mechanism that requires passwords for access to dial-up network resources.

**payload** Generic term referring to data, voice, or video that may be transmitted over WANs.

**payload type analysis** A type of data traffic analysis concerned with whether traffic is data, voice, video, image, or multimedia.

**PBX** Private branch exchange; a customer owned telephone switch.

**PBX CPU** Software program execution area in a PBX.

**PBX-to-host interfaces** Interface between PBXs and host computers for sharing information in order to enable CTI.

**PC Card** Expansion cards that support the PCMCIA standards.

**PCM** Pulse code modulation; voice digitization technique that digitizes voice into 64 Kbps by assigning voice levels to one of 256 eight bit codes.

**PCMCIA** A nonprofit trade association and standards body that promotes PC Card technology along with Miniature Card and SmartMedia cards by defining technical standards and educating the market.

**PCS** Personal Communications Services; will provide national full duplex digital voice and data at up to 25 Mbps via 2-way pagers, PDAs, and PCS devices.

**PCT** Private Communications Technology; Microsoft's version of SSL. The key difference between SSL and PCT is that PCT supports secure transmissions across unreliable (UDP rather TCP based) connections by allowing decryption of transmitted records independently from each other, as transmitted in the individual datagrams.

**PDC** Primary Domain Controller; domain directory services associate network users and resources with a primary server.

**PDM** Pulse duration modulation; a voice digitization technique.

**PDN** Public data network; another name for packet switched network.

**peer-to-peer internetworking** With full peer-to-peer internetworking, the PC can exchange data with any mainframe or any other PC on a host-to-host level rather than acting like a "dumb" terminal as in the case of micro-mainframe connectivity.

**peer-to-peer network operating systems** Also known as DOS-based LANs or low-cost LANs, offer easy to install and use file and print services for workgroup and departmental networking needs.

**PEM** Privacy Enhanced Mail; the application standard encryption technique for e-mail use on the Internet, and used with SMTP, Simple Mail Transport Protocol. It was designed to use both DES and RSA encryption techniques, but it would work with other encryption algorithms as well.

**percent of fit goal** Sets a minimum threshold of compliance for vendor proposals in order to warrant further consideration and invitations for demonstrations.

**performance engineering** Simulation software tools are also sometimes known as Performance Engineering software tools.

**performance metrics** Refer to quantifiable, measurable performance criteria by which the success of an implemented system can be judged. Must be defined in both business terms and IT infrastructure terms.

**performance monitoring** Software that should offer the ability to set thresholds for multiple system performance parameters. If these thresholds are exceeded, alerts or alarms should notify network management personnel of the problem, and offer advice as to possible diagnoses or solutions. Event logging and audit trails are often included as part of the performance monitoring package.

**periodic framing** Framing used in T-1 services to combine 24 DS-0s into a D-4 frame.

**permanent virtual circuit** *See* PVC.

**Personal Communications Services** *See* PCS.

**Personal Computer Memory Card International Association** *See* PCMCIA.

**Personal Handyphone System** *See* PHS.

**PGP** Pretty Good Privacy; an Internet e-mail specific encryption standard that also uses digital signature encryption to guarantee the authenticity, security, and message integrity of received e-mail.

**phase** One characteristic (analogous to the wave's pattern) of a wave that can be manipulated in phase modulation schemes in order to represent logical 1s and 0s.

**phase modulation** Manipulation of a carrier wave's phase via phase shifting in order to represent logical 1s and 0s on an analog transmission circuit.

**phase shift keying** *See* PSK.

**PHS** **Personal Handyphone System;** the digital cellular standard, being implemented in Japan.

**physical layer** Also known as layer 1 of the OSI model; responsible for the establishment, maintenance, and termination of physical connections between communicating devices. These connections are sometimes referred to as point-to-point data links.

**physical network design** The delineation of required technology determining *how* various hardware and software components will be combined to build a functional network that will meet predetermined business objectives is often referred to as the physical network design.

**physical topology** Clients and servers must be physically connected to each other according to some configuration and be linked by the shared media of choice. The physical layout of this configuration can have a significant impact on LAN performance and reliability and is known as a network architecture's physical topology.

**piggyback updates** A dial-up router update mechanism in which updates are performed only when the dial-up link has already been established for the purposes of exchanging user data.

**pilot tests** A popular way to safely roll out new systems or networks. For example, bring one retail store on-line and monitor performance, solve unanticipated problems, and gain management experience, before deploying the system on a wider scale.

**PKIX Public Key Infrastructure X.509** is an international ISO standard for public key certificates.

**Plain Old Telephone Service** *See* POTS.

**PLP** Network layer protocol for X.25.

**Plug-n-play** *See* PnP.

**PnP** The goal of plug-n-play is to free users from having to understand and worry about such things as IRQs (Interrupt Requests), DMA (Direct Memory Access) channels, memory addresses, COM ports, and editing CONFIG.SYS whenever they want to add a device to their computer.

**PnP BIOS** Basic Input Output System required to interface directly to both PnP and non-PnP compliant hardware.

**point of presence** *See* POP.

**point products** Also known as **element managers;** specifically written to address a particular systems administration or network management issue.

**point-to-point datalinks** The physical layer, also known as layer 1 of the OSI model, is responsible for the establishment, maintenance, and termination of physical connections between communicating devices. These connections are sometimes referred to as point-to-point data links.

**Point-to-Point Protocol** *See* PPP.

**Point-to-Point Tunneling Protocol** *See* PPTP.

**policy audits** Manual audits serve to verify the effectiveness of policy development and implementation, especially the extent to which people understand and effectively execute their assigned processes in the overall corporate security policy.

**policy-based management tools** In order to more easily integrate configuration management tools with corporate policy and standards regarding desktop configurations, a new breed of policy-based management tools has emerged.

**poll spoofing** The ability of an internetworking device, such as an SDLC converter or router, to respond directly to, or acknowledge, the FEP's constant polling messages to the remote cluster controller. By answering these status check messages locally, the inquiry and its answer never enter the wide area link portion of the internetwork.

**polling** In TDM multiplexing, the process of emptying each channel's buffer in order to build the composite frame.

**polymorphic viruses** Change their appearance each time an infected program is run in order to avoid detection.

**POP** Point of Presence; competing long-distance carriers wishing to do business in a given LATA maintain a switching office in that LATA known as a POP.

**port cards** Also known as line cards or station cards. PBX cards through which user phones are attached.

**port level filter** A filtering program that only examines source and destination addresses and determines access based on the entries in a filter table is known as a port level filter or network level filter or packet filter.

**port mirroring** Copies information from a particular switch port to an attached LAN analyzer. The difficulty with this approach is that it only allows one port to be monitored at a time.

**ports** Ports are specific addresses uniquely related to particular applications.

**POTS** Plain old telephone service. Analog voice service.

**Powersum crosstalk** Taking into account the crosstalk influence from all pairs in the cable, whether four-pair or 25-pair rather than just crosstalk between adjacent pairs, or pair-to-pair.

**PPM** Pulse position modulation; a voice digitization technique.

**PPN Personal Phone Number;** would become the user's interface to PCS, a number associated with a particular individual regardless of the location, even globally, of the accessed facility.

**PPP** A WAN data-link layer protocol that is able to support multiple network layer protocols simultaneously over a single WAN connection. In addition, PPP is able to establish connections over a variety of WAN services including: ISDN, Frame Relay, SONET, X.25, as well as synchronous and asynchronous serial links.

**PPP clients** Standardized remote clients with the ability to link to servers running a variety of different network operating systems are sometimes referred to as PPP clients. In general, they can link to network operating systems that support IP, IPX, NetBEUI, or XNS as transport protocols.

**PPTP** Microsoft's tunneling protocol that is specific to Windows NT Servers and remote access servers. It has the backing of several remote access server vendors.

**predictive dialing**   Also known as outbound dialing; uses a database of phone numbers, automatically dials those numbers, recognizes when calls are answered by people, and quickly passes those calls to available agents.

**presentation layer**   Protocols that provide an interface between user applications and various presentation-related services required by those applications. For example, data encryption/decryption protocols are considered presentation layer protocols as are protocols that translate between encoding schemes such as ASCII to EBCDIC.

**Pretty Good Privacy**   *See* PGP.

**primary domain controller**   *See* PDC.

**Principle of Shifting Bottlenecks**   Principle that states that as one network bottleneck is overcome, the network bottleneck merely shifts to a different network location (from the modem to the serial port).

**Printer Access Protocol**   *See* PAP.

**prioritization**   Gives priority access to available trunks to certain users.

**Privacy Enhanced Mail**   *See* PEM.

**private branch exchange**   *See* PBX.

**Private Communications Technology**   *See* PCT.

**private key encryption**   The decrypting device must use the same algorithm or method to decode or decrypt the data as the encrypting device used to encrypt the data. For this reason private key encryption is sometimes also known as symmetric encryption.

**private packet radio**   Proprietary wireless WAN service offered by RAM and Ardis in most major U.S. cities. Offers full duplex packet switched data at speeds of up to 4.8 Kbps via proprietary modems.

**proactive network management tool**   Network baselining tools are able to track network performance over extended periods of time and report on anomalies or deviations from the accumulated baseline data. Also known as proactive network management tools or network trending products, such tools usually need several weeks of SNMP data in order to establish realistic baseline network performance averages.

**proactive performance assurance**   For the rapidly growing network, the ability of simula-

tion software to simulate different possible future combinations of traffic usage, circuits, and networking equipment can avoid costly future network congestion problems or failures.

**process**   Network analysts focus on what processes should be taking place at each stage of the NDLC in order to stay on track.

**product**   Network analysts focus on what the deliverables should be at each stage of the NDLC in order to stay on track.

**productivity paradox**   The fact that little if any documented increase in productivity results from massive investments in technology.

**project charter**   The mechanism by which a project is organized and initial expectations are documented and agreed upon.

**promiscuous listen**   Transparent bridges receive all data packets transmitted on the LANs to which they are connected.

**propagation**   Forwarding messages by bridges to all workstations on all intermittent LANs.

**propagation delay**   The time it takes a signal from a source PC to reach a destination PC. Because of this propagation delay, it is possible for a workstation to sense that there is no signal on the shared media, when in fact another distant workstation has transmitted a signal that has not yet reached the carrier sensing PC.

**protected memory mode**   Client network operating systems may execute 32-bit applications in their own address space, otherwise known as protected memory mode.

**protective measures**   Measures designed and taken that effectively block the vulnerability in order to prevent threats from attacking assets.

**protocol**   A set of rules that govern communication between hardware and/or software components.

**protocol analyzers**   Devices that test layers 2 through 7.

**protocol conversion**   Must take place to allow the PC to appear to be a 3270 terminal in the eyes of the mainframe.

**protocol discriminator**   In order to differentiate which particular noncompliant protocol is embedded, any packet with AA in the DSAP and SSAP fields also has a 5 octet SNAP header known as a protocol discriminator following the Control field.

**protocol manager**   The NDIS program which controls the binding operation that combines separate

NDIS compliant software from NOS and NIC vendors into a single compatible driver.

**protocol stack** The sum of all of the protocols employed in a particular computer.

**protocol stack analysis** A data traffic analysis process that focuses on the protocols used at each network node.

**protocols** Rules for how communicating hardware and software components bridge interfaces or talk to one another.

**proxies** *See* Application gateways.

**proxy polling** Emulates the FEP's polling messages on the remote side of the network, thereby assuring the remote cluster controller that it is still in touch with an FEP.

**PSE** Packet switched exchange; another name for packet switched network.

**PSK** A type of phase modulation in which different phase shifts represent different combinations of 1s and 0s.

**PSTN** The Public Switched Network or dial-up phone system through which local access to phone services is gained.

**public data network** *See* PDN.

**public key certificates** A certificate assuring the authenticity of the public encryption key.

**Public Key Encryption** Could perhaps more accurately be named Public/Private Key Encryption since the process actually combines usage of both public and private keys.

**public switched telephone network** *See* PSTN.

**pulse** Older style of dialing with rotary phone that produces pulses of electricity to represent numbers.

**Pulse Amplitude Modulation** *See* PAM.

**Pulse Code Modulation** *See* PCM.

**Pulse Duration Modulation** *See* PDM.

**Pulse Position Modulation** *See* PPM.

**Pulse Width Modulation** *See* PWM.

**PVC** Packet switched equivalent of a leased line.

**PWM** Pulse width modulation; a voice digitization technique.

## Q

**Q.931** An ISDN Standard that allows PBX features to interoperate with Public Switched Network Features.

**Q.sig** Q.Sig standardizes features among different PBX manufacturers and delivers those standardized features within the limitations of the feature set offered by ISDN.

**QAM** Quadrature amplitude modulation; modulation scheme in which both phase and amplitude are manipulated.

**QoS** Quality of Service; general term for being able to differentiate between the level of network performance and reliability required by different applications.

**QPSK** Quadrature phase shift keying; phase shift modulation with four different phases.

**quadrature amplitude modulation** *See* QAM.

**quadrature phase shift keying** *See* QPSK.

**quality of service** *See* QOS.

**quantization error** When an analog signal is converted to a digital signal and back to an analog signal, some data are lost. The difference between the original signal and the final signal is known as quantization error.

**queueing** Bandwidth management technique, otherwise known as flow control that uses algorithms to assign traffic with different priorities to different queues.

## R

**RADIUS** Remote Authentication Dial-In User Service; A protocol and associated architecture supported by a wide variety of remote access technology and offers the potential to enable centralized management of remote access users and technology.

**RADSL** Rate adaptive digital subscriber line; able to adapt its data rate to the level of noise and interference on a given line. Currently, it is unable to support this adaptive rate on a dynamic basis.

**RARP** Reverse Address Resolution Protocol; used if the data-link layer address of the workstation is known but the IP address of the same workstation is required.

**RAS** Windows NT's remote access server software.

**rate adaptive DSL** *See* RADSL.

**rate control** Bandwidth management technique, otherwise known as traffic shaping, that controls flow by TCP window size adjustment.

**RBOC** Regional Bell Operating Company Divestiture; caused the former Local Bell Operating Companies to be grouped into new

Regional Bell Operating Companies (RBOCs) to offer local telecommunications service.

**real-mode device drivers**   Programs or sub-routines that write directly to computer hardware are sometimes referred to as employing real-mode device drivers.

**realms**   Enterprise networks implementing Kerberos are divided into Kerberos realms, each served by its own Kerberos server.

**real-time audits**   Most audit software depends on capturing large amounts of event data and then filtering that data for exceptional or unusual events.

**receiver**   Earpiece on a phone handset.

**recursion**   A process whereby if the local DNS cannot resolve an address itself, it may contact the higher authority DNS server, thereby increasing its own knowledge while meeting the client request.

**regulatory agencies**   State, local, and federal authorities charged with overseeing the operation of companies in the telecommunications industry.

**relationship variables**   In Application MIB, **relationship variables** would define all other network attached resources on which a given distributed application depends. This would include databases, associated client applications, or other network resources.

**reliable**   Reliable transmission for upper layer application programs or utilities is assured through the additional fields contained within the TCP header which offer the following functionality: flow control, acknowledgments of successful receipt of packets after error checking, retransmission of packets as required, proper sequencing of packets.

**remote access**   A term most often used to describe the process of linking remote PCs to local LANs without implying the particular functionality of that link (remote node vs. remote control). Unfortunately, the term *remote access* is also sometimes more specifically used as a synonym for remote node.

**remote access server**   Dedicated LAN-based server that controls remote access via modems to LAN based resources.

**Remote Authentication Dial-In User Service**   *See* RADIUS.

**remote configuration**   Increased security in SNMP2 allows not just monitoring and management of remote network devices, but actual remote configuration of those devices as well.

**remote control**   A mode in which the remote PC is merely supplying input and output devices for the local client which interacts as normal with the local server and other locally attached LAN resources.

**remote control software**   Especially designed to allow remote PC's to "take-over" control of local PCs; should not be confused with the Asynchronous Communications Software used for dial-up connections to asynchronous hosts via modems.

**remote monitoring**   *See* RMON.

**remote node**   Remote node or remote client computing implies that, in theory, the remote client PC should be able to operate as if it were locally attached to network resources. In other words, the geographic separation between the remote client and the local LAN resources should be transparent.

**remote node client software**   Most of the remote node server software packages also include compatible remote node client software. A problem arises, however, when a single remote node client needs to login to a variety of different servers running a variety of different network operating systems or remote node server packages.

**remote node server**   An alternative to server-based remote access software is a standalone device also known as a dial-up server or remote node server. Such a self-contained unit includes modems, communications software, and NOS-specific remote access server software in a turnkey system.

**remote node server software**   Traditionally remote node client and server software were supplied by the vendor of the network operating system on the server to be remotely accessed. Windows NT RAS (Remote Access Service) and NetWare Connect are two examples of such NOS-specific remote node server software.

**remote node servers**   Servers strictly concerned with controlling remote access to LAN attached resources and acting as a gateway to those resources. Applications services are supplied by the same LAN-attached applications servers that are accessed by locally attached clients.

**remote node software** Requires both remote node server and compatible remote node client software in order to successfully initiate remote node sessions.

**Repeater** Device used by carriers on digital transmission lines to regenerate digital signals over long distances. A repeater's job is to: Repeat the digital signal by regenerating and retiming the incoming signal, pass all signals between all attached segments, do not read destination addresses of data packets, allow for the connection of and translation between different types of media, effectively extend overall LAN distance by repeating signals between.

**replicate** The process of automatically copying a database from one server to another.

**request for proposal** *See* RFP.

**resolver** DNS is physically implemented in a client/server architecture in which client-based DNS software known as the DNS or name resolver, sends requests for DNS name resolution to a DNS (or name) Server.

**return on investment** *See* ROI.

**return on opportunity** *See* ROO.

**reverse address resolution protocol** *See* RARP.

**reverse poison** *See* Split horizon.

**RFI** Radio Frequency Interference.

**RFP** Request for proposal; by organizing the Strategic Information System Design information into an understandable format and by adding detailed information concerning performance evaluation criteria for the data and network layers, a document known as a RFP (Request for Proposal) is produced.

**RIF** Router Information Field; one very important limitation of source routing bridges as applied to large internetworks is known as the 7 Hop Limit. Because of the limited space in the RIF of the explorer packet, only 7 hop locations can be included in the path to any remote destination.

**ring logical topology** *See* Sequential.

**ring physical topology** Each PC is actually an active part of the ring, passing data packets in a sequential pattern around the ring. If one of the PCs dies, or a network adapter card malfunctions, the "sequence" is broken, the token is lost, and the network is down.

**RIP** A router-to-router protocol used to keep routers synchronized and up-to-date via broadcasts every 30 seconds.

**risk** Probability of a particular threat successfully attacking a particular asset in a given amount of time via a particular vulnerability.

**risk domains** Consists of a unique group of networked systems sharing both common business function and common elements of exposure.

**RJ48c** Jack in which T-1 services are typically terminated.

**RMON** Remote Monitoring; the most commonly used MIB for network monitoring and management.

**RMON MIB** Remote Network Monitoring MIB.

**RMON probe** RMON2 compatible agent software that resides within internetworking devices and reports performance statistics to enterprise network management systems.

**RMON2** While the original RMON MIB only required compatible technology to be able to collect and analyze statistics on the physical and data-link layers, RMON2 requires collection and analysis of network layer protocols as well.

**RMON3 roaming** One important issue not included in the IEEE 802.11 standard is roaming capability that allows a user to transparently move between the transmission ranges of wireless LANs without interruption. Proprietary roaming capabilities are currently offered by many wireless LAN vendors.

**ROI** Return on investment; a form of cost/benefit analysis commonly used in networking and systems projects.

**ROO Return on Opportunity;** attempts to quantify benefits that may be unanticipated or indirectly related to the immediate investment. This methodology recognizes that improvements in IT infrastructure aimed at one project may enable unanticipated benefits and uses not related to that initiating project.

**round robin polling scheme** In 100VG-AnyLAN, the Demand Priority Protocol access methodology uses a round robin polling scheme in which the hubs scan each port in sequence to see if the attached workstations have any traffic to transmit. The round robin polling scheme is distributed through a hierarchical arrangement of cascaded hubs.

**router** A device that forwards packets between layer three segments based on the layer three network address.

**router servers** An internetwork evolutionary design scenario in which route servers will provide a centralized repository of routing information while edge switches deployed within the LANs will be programmed with minimal routing information.

**Routing Information Field** *See* RIF.

**Routing Information Protocol** *See* RIP.

**Routing Table Maintenance Protocol** *See* RTMP.

**routing tables** Routers consult routing tables in order to determine the best path on which to forward a particular data packet.

**roving port mirroring** Creates a roving RMON (Remote Monitoring) probe that gathers statistics at regular intervals on multiple switch ports. The shortcoming with this approach remains that at any single point in time, only one port is being monitored.

**RS-232-C** An EIA serial transmission standard officially limited to 20 Kbps over 50 ft distance.

**RSA** The current standard for public key encryption.

**RSVP** Resource Reservation Protocol; enables routing software to reserve a portion of network bandwidth known as a virtual circuit.

**RT24** A voice compression algorithm.

**RTMP** A routing protocol used in the AppleTalk protocol suite.

**run length encoding** Encoding mechanism that looks for repeating characters and replaces multiple repeating characters with a repetition count code.

**RYGB** The type of phone wire installed in most homes consists of a tan plastic jacket containing four untwisted wires: red, yellow, green, and black and is also known as 4 conductor station wire or RYGB.

## S

**S/MIME** Secure Multipurpose Internet Mail Extension; secures e-mail traffic in e-mail applications that have been S/MIME enabled. S/MIME encrypts and authenticates e-mail messages for transmission over SMTP-based e-mail networks.

**S/N** Signal to noise ratio; expressed in decibels, measures power of data signal as compared to power of circuit interference or noise.

**SAN** *See* Storage area network.

**SAP** Service Advertising Protocol; used by all network servers to advertise the services they provide to all other reachable networked servers. SAP uses IPX packets as its means of delivering its service advertising requests or responses throughout the network.

**SAP filtering** In order to eliminate the every 60 second broadcast of SAP packets, an associated feature of advanced IPX known as SAP filtering, assures that SAP broadcasts are synchronized to take place only with NLSP updates.

**SAS** Single Attachment Stations; attach to only one of FDDI's two rings.

**SATAN** A probe written especially to analyze Unix and TCP/IP based systems, and once it has found a way to get inside an enterprise network, it continues to probe all TCP/IP machines within that enterprise network.

**SBA** Synchronous bandwidth allocation; in FDDI, frames transmitted in a continuous stream are known as synchronous frames and are prioritized according to a methodology known as SBA, which assigns fixed amounts of bandwidth to given stations.

**screen caching** Allows only changes to screens, rather than entire screens to be transmitted over the limited bandwidth WAN links. Screen caching will reduce the amount of actual traffic transmitted over the WAN link.

**SDLC** IBM SNA's data-link layer protocol. SLDC frames do not contain anything equivalent to the OSI network layer addressing information for use by routers, which makes SDLC a nonroutable protocol.

**SDLC conversion** SDLC frames are converted to Token Ring Frames by a specialized internetworking device known as a SDLC Converter.

**SDLC converter** *See* SDLC conversion.

**SDSL** Symmetric digital subscriber line; differs from ADSL in that it offers upstream and downstream channels of equal bandwidth.

**search engine** The portion of the software that sifts through the knowledge base to the proper answer.

**Secure Courier** Based on SSL; allows users to create a secure digital envelope for transmission of financial transactions over the Internet.

**Secure Electronic Transactions** *See* SET.

**Secure Hypertext Transport Protocol** *See* S-HTTP.

**Secure Multipurpose Internet Mail Extension** *See* S/MIME.

**secure single login** Assurance that users are able to log into a network, rather than each individual server and application, and be able to access only resources for which they are properly authorized.

**secure SNMP** SNMP2 or a variation of SNMP known as **Secure SNMP,** will allow users to access carriers' network management information and incorporate it into the wide area component of an enterprise network management system.

**Secure Sockets Layer** *See* SSL.

**Security Analyzer Tool for Analyzing Networks** *See* SATAN.

**security architecture** Implies an open framework into which business-driven security processes and requirements can be quickly and easily organized, now or in the future.

**Security Auditing and Intrusion Detection** Able to track and identify suspicious behaviors from both internal employees as well as potential intruders.

**security framework** Frameworks that have begun to emerge which attempt to consolidate security management into a single architecture or console allowing centralized policy management and automated incident response.

**security policy development life cycle** *See* SPDLC.

**security probes** Actively test various aspects of enterprise network security and report results and suggest improvements.

**segmentation** Usually the first internetworking approach employed to reduce shared media congestion. By having fewer workstations per segment, there is less contention for the shared bandwidth.

**selective ARQ** ARQ error control mechanism that is able to retransmit only those particular data blocks received in error.

**send window** With an adaptive sliding window protocol, the number of packets allowed to be sent before the receipt of an acknowledgment determines the size of the send window.

**Sequenced Packet** *See* SPX.

**Serial Line Internet Protocol** *See* SLIP.

**serial transmission** Method of transmission in which all bits of a given character are transmitted in linear fashion, one after the other.

**server capacity planning** Server management software must provide server capacity planning capabilities by monitoring server performance trends and making recommendations for server component upgrades in a proactive manner.

**server front-end LAN switch** A switched network architecture in which dedicated LAN switch ports are only necessary for servers, while client workstations share a switch port via a cascaded media-sharing hub.

**server isolation** Instead of assigning all workstations to their own LAN segment as in microsegmentation, only selected high-performance devices such as servers can be assigned to their own segment in an internetworking design strategy known as server isolation. By isolating servers on their own segments, guaranteed access to network bandwidth is assured.

**Server MONitoring** *See* SMON.

**server network operating systems** Able to be chosen and installed based on their performance characteristics for a given required functionality. For example, NetWare servers are often employed as file and print servers, whereas Windows NT, OS/2, or UNIX servers are more likely to be employed as application servers.

**Service Advertising Protocol** *See* SAP.

**service level agreement** Clearly describes expected levels of service, how that service will be measured, what that service will cost, and what the consequences will be if the agreed upon service levels are not met.

**service management** Concerned with the management of IT services and the business processes that depend on them.

**service management architectures** Provide metrics for service evaluation on both a business and IT infrastructure level.

**Service Profile Identifier Numbers** *See* SPID.

**service-granting ticket** In kerberos, if the Ticket Granting Server determines that the request is valid, a ticket is issued that will allow the user to access the requested server.

**session keys** Unique, one-time use keys used for encryption.

**session layer** Protocols responsible for establishing, maintaining, and terminating sessions between user application programs. Sessions are interactive dialogues between networked computers and are of particular importance to distributed computing applications in a client/server environment.

**session limits**   The second major improvement of NBF over NetBEUI involves session limits. Since NetBEUI is NetBIOS-based, it was forced to support the 254 session limit of NetBIOS. With NBF, each client to server connection can support 254 sessions, rather than a grand total for all connections of 254 sessions.

**SET**   Secure Electronic Transactions; a series of standards to assure the confidentiality of electronic commerce transactions. These standards are being largely promoted by credit card giants VISA and MasterCard.

**shared media network architecture**   Architectures that employ media-sharing network wiring centers such as hubs, which offer all attached workstations shared access to a single LAN segment.

**shielding**   Shielding may be a metallic foil or copper braid. The function of the shield is rather simple. It "shields" the individual twisted pairs as well as the entire cable from either EMI (Electromagnetic Interference) or RFI (Radio Frequency Interference).

**S-HTTP**   Secure HTTP is a secure version of HTTP, which requires both client and server S-HTTP versions to be installed for secure end-to-end encrypted transmission.

**signal to noise ratio**   *See* S/N.

**signaling system 7**   *See* SS7.

**signature scanners**   Because virus scanners are actually scanning for known digital signatures or viruses they are sometimes referred to as signature scanners.

**simple key management for IP**   *See* SKIP.

**simple management protocol**   *See* SMP.

**simple network management protocol**   *See* SNMP.

**simultaneous RMON view**   Allows all network traffic to be monitored simultaneously. Such a monitoring scheme is only possible on those switches that incorporate a shared memory multigigabit bus as opposed to a switching matrix internal architecture. Furthermore, unless this monitoring software is executed on a separate CPU, switch performance is likely to degrade.

**Single Access Control View**   Allows the users access from their client workstation to display only those resources to which the user actually has access.

**Single Attachment Station**   *See* SAS.

**single mode**   Fiber optic cable that is able to focus the rays of light so that only a single wavelength can pass through at a time. Without numerous reflections of rays at multiple angles, distortion is eliminated and bandwidth is maximized.

**single point of failure**   Any network attached device or piece of technology whose failure would cause the failure of the entire network.

**Single Point of Registration**   *See* SPR.

**single sign-on**   *See* SSO.

**sinks**   Packet destinations.

**SKIP**   Simple Key Management for IP; a proposed key management protocol from Sun.

**Sliding Window Protocols**   Continuous ARQ, for example, continues to transmit and slides back to NAK'd data blocks when a NAK is received.

**SLIP**   Serial Line Interface Protocol; able to establish asynchronous serial links between two computers that support both SLIP and TCP/IP over any of the following connections: via modems and a dial-up line, via modems and a point-to-point private or leased line, via hardwired or direct connections.

**slot time**   In Ethernet networks, the time required for a given workstation to detect a collision is known slot time and is measured in bits.

**slow convergence**   The delay that occurs while all of the routers are propagating their routing tables using RIP, known as slow convergence, could allow certain routers to assume that failed links to certain networks are still viable.

**Small Office Home Office**   *See* SOHO.

**Smart Cards**   Used in token authentication systems, Hardware-based Smart Cards or Smart IDs that are about the size of a credit card with or without a numeric keypad.

**SMDR**   Station message detail recording. An individual detail record is generated for each call for call accounting systems.

**SMDS**   Switched multimegabit data service; a connectionless high speed data service.

**SMON**   The newest addition to the SNMP family of monitoring standards. SMON expands RMON's monitoring ability by offering a mechanism to collect data from all network segments connected to a LAN switch.

**SMP**   Simple Management Protocol; the need to reduce network traffic caused by the SNMP protocol as well as to deal with other aforementioned SNMP shortcomings, led to a proposal for a new version of SNMP known as **SNMP2,** or **SMP.**

**SNA** Systems Network Architecture; IBM's proprietary network architecture, originally designed to link mainframes.

**SNAP** In order to ease the transition to IEEE 802 compliance, an alternative method of identifying the embedded upper layer protocols was developed, known as SNAP or Sub-Network Access Protocol. Any protocol can use SNAP with IEEE 802.2 and appear to be an IEEE 802 compliant protocol.

**SNMP** Simple Network Management Protocol; partly due to the dominance of TCP/IP as the internetworking protocol of choice, **SNMP** is the de facto standard for delivering enterprise management data.

**SNMP2** The need to reduce network traffic caused by the SNMP protocol as well as to deal with other aforementioned SNMP shortcomings, led to a proposal for a new version of SNMP known as **SNMP2,** or **SMP** (Simple Management Protocol).

**socket** The unique port address of an application combined with the unique 32-bit IP address of the computer on which the application is executing.

**socket services** The socket services sub-layer of the PCMCIA Card and Socket Services driver specification is written specifically for the type of PCMCIA controller included in a notebook computer.

**Socks** Used by Circuit level proxy programs, **Socks** creates a proxy data channel to the application server on behalf of the application client. Since all data go through Socks, it can audit, screen, and filter all traffic in between the application client and server.

**software flow control** Uses control characters XON, XOFF to control data transmission into and out of buffer memory.

**SOHO** New market for mini-PBXs and desktop CTI.

**SONET** Synchronous optical network, dual ring, high speed fiber-based transmission architecture.

**SONET superframe** Rather than fitting 24 channels per frame delineated by a single framing bit, a single SONET frame or row is delineated

by 3 octets of overhead for control information followed by 87 octets of payload. Nine of these 90 octet rows are grouped together to form a SONET superframe.

**source address** Data-link protocols such as Ethernet contain source addresses as well as the destination addresses within the predefined Ethernet Frame layout. A bridge checks the source address of each frame it receives and adds that source address to a table of known local nodes.

**source routing bridge** Used to connect two source-routing enabled Token Ring LANs. Data messages arrive at a source routing bridge with a detailed map of how they plan to reach their destination.

**source routing transparent bridge** Bridges that can support links between source routing Token Ring LANs or transparent LANs.

**Spanning Tree Algorithm** STA; has been standardized as IEEE 802.1 for the purposes of controlling redundant paths in bridged networks, thereby reducing the possibility of broadcast storms.

**SPAP** Shiva's proprietary authentication protocol that includes password encryption and callback capability.

**SPDLC** Security Policy Development Life Cycle; one methodology for the development of a comprehensive network security policy.

**SPE** Synchronous Payload Envelope; the 87 octets of payload per row in each of the time rows or the Superframe.

**SPID** Service Profile Identifier Numbers; in order to properly interface an end-user's ISDN equipment to a carrier's ISDN services, desired ISDN features must be specified. In some cases, end-user equipment such as remote access servers must be programmed with SPIDs so as to properly identify the carrier's equipment with which the user equipment must interface.

**split horizon** In order to reduce slow convergence in RIP based router networks, split horizon and reverse poison prevent routers from wasting time broadcasting routing table changes back to the routers that just supplied them with the same changes in the first place.

**spoofing** A method of filtering chatty or unwanted protocols from the WAN link while assuring that remote programs that require ongoing communication from these filtered protocols are still reassured via emulation of these protocols by the local dial-up router.

**SPR** Single Point of Registration; allows a network security manager to enter a new user (or delete a terminated user) from a single centralized location and assign all associated rights, privileges, and access control to enterprise resources from this single point rather than having to enter this new user's information on multiple resources distributed throughout the enterprise.

**spread spectrum transmission** Spreads a data message across a wide range or spectrum of frequencies. This technique was originally employed as a security measure since a receiver would need to know exactly how the message was spread across the frequency spectrum in order to intercept the message in meaningful form.

**SPX** NetWare's connection-oriented, reliable transport layer protocol.

**SS7** Signaling system 7; a common inter-switch signaling protocol for call management and control.

**SSL** A connection level encryption method providing security to the network link itself. SSL Version 3 (SSL3) added support for more key exchange and encryption algorithms as well as separate keys for authentication and encryption.

**SSO** Authentication technology that delivers single sign-on (SSO) access to multiple network attached servers and resources via passwords.

**stackable hubs** Add expandability and manageability to the basic capabilities of the stand-alone hub. Can be linked together, or cascaded, to form one larger virtual hub of a single type of network architecture and media.

**stand-alone hubs** Fully configured hubs offering a limited number (12 or fewer) ports of a particular type of network architecture (Ethernet, Token Ring) and media.

**stand-alone LAN switches** Stand-alone Workgroup/Departmental LAN switches; offer dedicated connections to all attached client and server computers via individual switch ports.

**standards** An agreed-upon protocol as determined by officially sanctioned standards-making organizations, market share, or user group concensus.

**star** The star physical topology employs some type of central management device. Depending on the network architecture and sophistication of the device, it may be called a hub, a wiring center, a concentrator, a MAU (Multiple Access Unit), a repeater, or a switching hub.

**state variables** In Application MIB, **state variables** would report on the current status of a given application. Three possible states are: up, down, or degraded.

**station cards** PBX cards that attach to users' phones.

**station message detail recording** *See* SMDR.

**statistical time division multiplexing** *See* STDM.

**STDM** Advanced form of TDM multiplexing that seeks to overcome TDM inefficiencies by dynamically adapting polling of channels.

**Storage area network** Seek to separate data storage from particular application-oriented servers (sometimes referred to as storage islands) by consolidating storage systems such as disk arrays or tape libraries and attaching them to the enterprise network via redundant, high capacity network connections.

**store-and-forward switches** Switches that read the entire frame into a shared memory area in the switch. The contents of the transmitted Frame Check Sequence field is read and compared with the locally recalculated Frame Check Sequence. Store-and-forward switching is slower than cut-through switching but does not forward bad frames.

**Stored Program Control** Location in PBX where software is executed.

**strategic information system design** A high level information systems design that will meet agreed upon business objectives and serve as a starting point for network design.

**streaming protocol** File transfer protocol that continues to transmit until it encounters an end of file indicator. Relies on modems to provide error control.

**STS-1** Synchronous Transport Signal: the electrical equivalent of the OC-1, the optical SONET Superframe standard is known as the STS-1.

**subnet mask** By applying a 32-bit subnet mask to a Class B IP address, a portion of the bits that comprises the host ID can be reserved for denoting subnetworks, with the remaining bits being reserved for host IDs per subnetwork.

**subnetwork access protocol** *See* SNAP.

**subnetworking** Subnetworking allows organizations that were issued an IP address with a single network ID to use a portion of their host ID address field to provide multiple subnetwork IDs in order to implement internetworking.

**superframe** 12 D-4 frames.

**SVC** Switched virtual circuit; packet switched equivalent of a circuit switched dial-up line.

**switched LAN network architecture** Architectures that depend on wiring centers called LAN switches or switching hubs which offer all attached workstations access to a switching matrix that provides point-to-point, rather than shared, connections between any two ports.

**switched line** Unlike a leased line, a switched line is connected to a CO switch, provides dial tone, and reaches different destinations by dialing different phone numbers.

**switched multimegabit data service** *See* SMDS.

**switched virtual circuit** *See* SVC.

**switching** Process by which messages are routed from switch to switch en route to their final destination.

**switching architecture** Major component of network architecture along with transmission architecture.

**switching hub** Able to create connections, or switch, between any two attached Ethernet devices on a packet-by-packet basis in as little as 40 milliseconds. The "one-at-time" broadcast limitation previously associated with shared media Ethernet is overcome with an Ethernet switch.

**switching matrix** Location in CPU where circuits are switched to complete calls.

**symmetric DSL** *See* SDSL.

**synchronous bandwidth allocation** *See* SBA.

**Synchronous Data Link Control** *See* SDLC.

**synchronous frames** Frames transmitted in a continuous stream in FDDI; prioritized according to a methodology known as synchronous bandwidth allocation or SBA, which assigns fixed amounts of bandwidth to given stations.

**synchronous optical network** *See* SONET.

**synchronous payload envelope** *See* SPE.

**synchronous TDM** In a technique used in T-1 transmission service known as periodic framing or synchronous TDM, 24 channels of 8 bits each (192 bits total) are arranged in a frame.

**synchronous transmission** Transmission method in which timing is provided by a clocking signal supplied by either modems or the carrier.

**systems administration** Focuses on the management of client and server computers and the operating systems and network operating systems that allow the client and server computers to communicate.

**Systems Network Architecture** *See* SNA.

## T

**T.120** Standard for multipoint audioconferences.

**T-1** 1.544 Mbps digital WAN service adhering to the DS-1 standard.

**T-1 channel bank** Device that can take a variety of voice and data inputs, digitize them, and multiplex them onto a T-1 circuit.

**T-1 CSU/DSU** Device that interfaces between a T-1 circuit and another device such as a mux, bridge, or router.

**T-1 IMUX** Inverse multiplexer that can combine four or more T-1s for bandwidth on demand applications.

**T-1 inverse multiplexer** *See* T-1 IMUX.

**T-1 multiplexers** Multiplexers that combine several digitized voice or data inputs into a T-1 output.

**T-1 switches** Switches able to redirect T-1s or the DS-0s contained therein.

**T-3** A leased line digital broadband service of 44.736 Mbps.

**tandem office** Establishes the intra-LATA circuit and also handles billing procedures for the long-distance call.

**TAPI** CTI API promoted by Microsoft and Intel.

**TBO** Total benefit of ownership; a cost benefit measurement methodology used in networking that concentrates on comparing projects based on perceived benefits.

**TCM** Trellis coded modulation; a forward error correction technique that transmits redundant data in hopes of avoiding retransmission.

**TCO** Total cost of ownership; a cost benefit measurement methodology used in networking that concentrates on comparing projects based on perceived costs.

**TCP** Transmission control protocol, connection oriented transport layer protocol whose 3-way handshake for connection setup is vulnerable to attack.

**TCP/IP** Transmission Control Protocol/Internet Protocol; the term generally used to refer to an entire suite of protocols used to provide communication on a variety of layers between widely distributed different types of computers. Strictly speaking, TCP and IP are just two of the protocols contained within the family of protocols more properly known as the Internet Suite of Protocols.

**TCP/IP encapsulation** Each nonroutable SNA SDLC frame is "stuffed" into an IP "envelope" for transport across the network and processing by routers supporting TCP/IP internetworking protocol.

**TDM** Time division multiplexing; with TDM, from a connected terminal's point of view, 100% of the bandwidth is available for a portion of the time.

**TDMA** Time Division Multiple Access; achieves more than one conversation per frequency by assigning time slots to individual conversations. Ten time slots per frequency are often assigned, with a given cellular device transmitting its digitized voice only during its assigned time slot.

**TDP** Telocator Data Protocol; an alternative two-way messaging architecture is proposed by the PCIA (Personal Communicator Industry Association). Rather than building on existing IP-based networks as the CDPD/LSM architecture did, the TDP architecture is actually a suite of protocols defining an end-to-end system for two-way messaging to and from paging devices.

**technical support** The third major usage of remote computing is for technical support organizations that must be able to dial-in to client systems with the ability to appear as a local workstation, or take control of those workstations, in order to diagnose and correct problems remotely.

**Technology Push/Demand Pull** In a technology push scenario, new technologies may be introduced to the market in order to spawn innovative uses for this technology and thereby generate demand. Conversely, business needs may create a demand for services or technological innovation that are currently unavailable. However, the demand pull causes research and development efforts to accelerate, thereby introducing the new technology

sooner than it would have otherwise been brought to market.

**telecommunications** Usually used to indicate a broader market than data communications, including voice, video, and image services.

**Telecommunications Act of 1996** Seeks to encourage competition in all aspects and markets of telecommunications services, including switched and dedicated local and inter-LATA traffic as well as cable TV companies and wireless services such as paging, cellular, and satellite services.

**telecommuting** Working from home with all the information resources of the office LAN at one's fingertips, is often referred to as SOHO, or Small Office Home Office.

**telephony API** *See* TAPI.

**telocator data protocol** *See* TDP.

**threats** Processes or people that pose a potential danger to identified assets.

**three pile approach** Prioritization method for elements of strategic information systems design.

**three-way handshake** TCP vulnerability that can be exploited for denial of service or land attacks.

**thresholds** Desired limits of certain performance characteristics that are set by the user and monitored by network management software.

**throughput** PC-to-PC data rate, transmission rate × data compression ratio.

**ticket** In Kerberos, an encrypted ticket is issued for each server to client session and is valid only for a preset amount of time.

**ticket-granting ticket** Users are first authenticated by the Kerberos Authentication server which consults its database and grants a ticket for the valid user to communicate with the Ticket Granting Server (TGS). This ticket is known as a ticket-granting ticket.

**time bombs** Viruses triggered by the passing of a certain date or time.

**time division multiple access** *See* TDMA.

**time division multiplexing** *See* TDM.

**time slot** 8 bits of digitized information collected in one sample and assigned to one of 24 channels in a T-1 D-4 frame.

**time studies** A data traffic analysis process that measures how often different types of transactions occur.

**time synchronous authentication** Owing to the time synchronization, the server authentication unit should have the same current random authentication number which is compared to the one transmitted from the remote client.

**Time Synchronous Token Authentication** A token authentication process in which no challenge is sent because both the SecureID card and the server are time synchronized, so only the displayed one-time session key is transmitted.

**timed updates** A dial-up router update mechanism in which updates are performed at regular predetermined intervals.

**timing limitation** The second SNA characteristic that can cause problems when run over a shared LAN backbone is that SNA has timing limitations for transmission duration between SNA hosts and end-user devices. Thus on wide area, internetworked LANs over shared network media, SNA sessions can "time-out," effectively terminating the session.

**token** In a token passing access methodology, a specific packet (24 bits) of data is known as a token.

**token authentication** All token authentication systems include server components linked to the communications server, and client components that are used with the remote access clients. Physically, the token authentication device employed at the remote client location may be a hand-held device resembling a calculator, a floppy disk, or it may be an in-line device linked to either the remote client's serial or parallel port.

**token passing** An access methodology that assures that each PC user has 100% of the network channel available for their data requests and transfers by insisting that no PC accesses the network without first possessing a specific packet (24 bits) of data known as a token.

**token response authentication** Schemes that begin when the transmitted challenge response is received by the authentication server and compared with the expected challenge response number that was generated at the server. If they match, the user is authenticated and allowed access to network attached resources.

**toll quality** The ITU standard for 32 Kbps ADPCM is known as G.721 and is generally used as a reference point for the quality of voice transmission.

**tone** Common name for DTMF dialing.

**top-down model** Insisting that a top-down approach to network analysis and design is undertaken, through the use of the top-down model, should assure that the network design implemented will meet the business needs and objectives that motivated the design in the first place.

**total benefit of ownership** *See* TBO.

**total cost of ownership** *See* TCO.

**TP-PMD** Twisted Pair-Physical Media Dependent; the official ANSI standard for CDDI.

**traffic shaping** Can provide bandwidth-constrained or time sensitive applications with the bandwidth necessary to potentially improve application performance. Traffic shaping devices will *not* improve the performance of latency-constrained applications.

**traffic volume analysis** A data traffic analysis process that combines transaction analysis and time studies to yield a traffic volume profile.

**trailer** Information added to the back of data.

**transaction analysis** A data traffic analysis process that examines the amount of data transmitted for every different type of identified transaction.

**translating bridges** A special type of bridge that includes a format converter which can bridge between Ethernet and Token Ring. These special bridges may also be called multi-protocol bridges or translating bridges.

**transmission architecture** Key component of network architecture along with switching architecture.

**transmission control protocol** *See* TCP.

**Transmission Control Protocol/Internet Protocol** *See* TCP/IP.

**transmission rate** Rate of actual bits transmitted end-to-end measured in bps, equal to bits/baud × baud rate.

**transmitter** Mouthpiece on telephone handset.

**transparent** Bridges are passive or transparent devices, receiving every frame broadcast on a given LAN. Bridges are known as transparent due to their ability to only process data-link layer addresses while transparently forwarding any variety of upper layer protocols safely embedded within the data field of the data-link layer frame.

**transparent bridge** Bridges that connect LANs of similar data-link format.

**transport layer** Protocols responsible for providing reliability for the end-to-end network layer connections. Provide end-to-end error recovery and flow control and also provide mechanisms for sequentially organizing multiple network layer packets into a coherent message.

**Transport Mode ESP**   In Secure IP, used to encrypt the data carried by the IP packet.

**Trellis Coded Modulation**   *See* TCM.

**triggered updates**   In order to reduce slow convergence in RIP based router networks, allow routers to immediately broadcast routing table updates regarding failed links rather than having to wait for the next 30 sec. periodic update.

**trojan horse**   The actual virus is hidden inside an otherwise benign program and delivered to the target system or network to be infected.

**trunk cards**   Cards in PBX that attach to local loops.

**trusted gateway**   Certain applications are identified as trusted and are able to bypass the application gateway entirely and also are able to establish connections directly rather than be executed by proxy.

**trusted node**   Authorization security software can be either server-based, also known as brokered authorization, or workstation-based, also referred to as trusted node.

**Tunnel Mode ESP**   In Secure IP, encrypts the entire IP packet including its own header. This mode is effective in countering network analyzers or sniffers from capturing IP address information.

**tunneling protocols**   In order to provide virtual private networking capabilities using the Internet as an enterprise network backbone, specialized tunneling protocols needed to be developed that could establish private, secure channels between connected systems.

**turnaround time**   Time it takes two half-duplex modems to change from transmit to receive mode by manipulating RTS and CTS signals.

**two-way messaging**   Sometimes referred to as enhanced paging, allows short text messages to be transmitted between relatively inexpensive transmission devices such as PDAs (Personal Digital Assistants) and alphanumeric pagers.

**two-wire circuits**   Common local loop circuit in which one of these two wires serves as a ground wire for the circuit, thereby leaving only one wire between the two ends of the circuit for data signaling.

## U

**UART**   Universal Asynchronous Receiver Transmitter; acts as the interface between the parallel transmission of the computer bus and the serial transmission of the serial port.

**UDP**   User datagram protocol; transport protocol that is part of the Internet suite of protocols, used in IP voice transmission.

**UNI**   User network interface; in ATM, cell format that carries information between the user and the ATM network.

**Unicode**   16-bit character encoding scheme identical to ISO 10646.

**unified messaging**   Also known as the Universal In-Box; will allow voice mail, e-mail, faxes, and pager messages to be displayed on a single graphical screen. Messages can then be forwarded, deleted, or replied to easily in point and click fashion.

**universal asynchronous receiver transmitter**   *See* UART.

**universal client capability**   A client workstation's ability to interoperate transparently with a number of different network operating system servers without the need for additional products or configurations.

**universal in-box**   *See* Unified messaging.

**Universal Serial Bus**   *See* USB.

**unreliable**   An unreliable protocol does not require error checking and acknowledgment of error-free receipt by the destination host.

**unshielded twisted pair**   *See* UTP.

**USB**   A fast multi-point serial interface commonly installed in current generation PCs. USB can be used to support a wide variety of peripherals from network adapters to scanners and digital cameras.

**User Datagram Protocol**   *See* UDP.

**user demands**   The top layer of the wide area network architecture.

**user-network interface**   *See* UNI.

**UTP**   Twisted pair wiring consists of one or more pairs of insulated copper wire that are twisted at varying lengths, from 2 to 12 twists per foot, to reduce interference both between pairs and from outside sources such as electric motors and fluorescent lights. No additional shielding is added before the pairs are wrapped in the plastic covering.

## V

**V.32** ITU standard for modem transmitting at 9600 bps, 4 QAM and TCM modulation.

**V.32bis** ITU standard for modem transmitting at 14.4 Kbps, 6QAM and TCM modulation.

**V.32ter** Proprietary standard for modem transmitting at 19.2 Kbps, 8 QAM and TCM modulation.

**V.34** ITU standard for modem transmitting at 28.8 Kbps, 9QAM and TCM.

**V.42** ITU standard for error control, supports MNP 4 and LAP-M.

**V.42bis** ITU standard for data compression, compression ratios up to 4:1.

**V.90** ITU standard for modems that operate at speeds up to 56 Kbps by using directly connected digital servers.

**variable bit rate** *See* VBR.

**variable callback** Callback security mechanism for modems that supports callback to phone numbers entered at dial-in time after password verification.

**VBR** Variable Bit Rate; provides a guaranteed minimum threshold amount of constant bandwidth below which the available bandwidth will not drop. However, as bursty traffic requires more bandwidth than this constant minimum, that required bandwidth will be provided.

**VDSL** Very High Speed DSL; provides 52 Mbps downstream and between 1.6–2.3 Mbps upstream over distances of up to only 1,000 ft. It is being explored primarily as a means to bring video on demand services to the home.

**vector** Once a NDIS driver is bound and operating, packets of a particular protocol are forwarded from the adapter card to the proper protocol stack by a layer of software known as the vector.

**version control software** *See* File synchronization.

**vertical integration** Integration of CANE software with I-CASE software and business process reengineering software through the use of expert systems.

**vertical redundancy check** *See* VRC.

**very high speed DSL** *See* VDSL.

**virtual circuit** Dedicated path for voiceover frame relay that minimizes or eliminates delay usually associated with frame relay.

**virtual circuit table** Details that relate the LCN to a physical circuit consisting of an actual series of specific packet switches within the packet switched network are stored in a virtual circuit table.

**virtual circuits** Paths set up in connection-oriented packet switched networks.

**virtual device drivers** *See* VxDs.

**virtual machines** Some client network operating systems, such as Windows NT, have the ability to support multiple APIs and multiple different operating system subsystems, sometimes known as virtual machines.

**virtual PC** Emulation technology attempts to detect as yet unknown viruses by running programs with a software emulation program known as a virtual PC.

**virtual tributary** *See* VT.

**virus scanning** The primary method for successful detection and removal.

**VJ** A protocol for compression of IP headers included with most PPP clients.

**voice digitization** Technique by which analog voice is converted into digital signals.

**voiceover IP** Also known as IP-based voice.

**voice/data multiplexers** Device that interfaces to T-1 leased lines to carry voice and data.

**voice-grade leased line** Analog leased line with 3100Hz of bandwidth.

**VRC** Simple parity checking; adds one parity bit per character.

**VT** Virtual tributaries; flexibly defined channels within the SONET payload area.

**VT1.5** SONET virtual tributary equivalent to a mapped T-1.

**vulnerabilities** The manner or path by which threats are able to attack assets.

**VxDs** More secure 32-bit operating systems control access to hardware and certain system services via virtual device drivers. otherwise known as VxDs.

## W

**WAP** *See* Wireless access protocol.

**wavelength** The distance between the same spots on two subsequent waves. The longer the wavelength, the lower the frequency and the shorter the wavelength, the greater the frequency.

**Wavelength Division Multiplexing** *See* WDM.

**WBEM** Web-Based Enterprise Management; another possible standard for distributed application management is a proposed IETF standard (WBEM) that integrates SNMP, HTTP, and DMI (desktop management interface) into an application management architecture that can use common Web browser software as its user interface.

**WDM** Wavelength Division Multiplexing; technique in fiber optic transmission in which multiple bits of data can be transmitted simultaneously over a single fiber by being represented by different light wavelengths.

**Web-based enterprise management** *See* WBEM.

**what-if analysis** A feature of network simulation software that allows users to modify their current network in a variety of hypothetical scenarios.

**Windows NT RAS** Microsoft's remote node server software for Windows NT.

**wireless access protocol** A protocol that brings Web browsing to mobile phones allowing users of WAP 1.1 compliant PDAs to browse the Internet and download bitmap images. In addition, WAP supports secure wireless business transactions.

**wireless bridge** Uses spread spectrum radio transmission between LAN sites (up to 3 miles); at present, primarily limited to Ethernet networks.

**wireless WAN services** A variety of wireless services are available for use across wider geographic spans. These wireless WAN services vary in many ways including availability, applications, transmission speed, and cost.

# X

**X.25** Packet switching standard that defines interface specification for packet switched networks.

**X.500** As enterprise networks become more heterogeneous comprised of network operating systems from a variety of different vendors, the need will arise for different network operating systems to share each other's directory services information. A directory services specification known as X.500 offers the potential for this directory services interoperability.

**X.509** An international standard for public key certificates.

**XMODEM** Public domain file transfer protocol, widely used, 128 bytes/block, checksum error control.

**XON/XOFF** Control characters used in software flow control. XOFF stops data transmission; XON restarts it.

**XTACACS** Extended Terminal Access Control Access System; another example of a remote access management protocol that supports three-tiered remote access management architectures.

# Y

**YMODEM** File transfer protocol, 1KB data blocks, CRC-16 error control, batch execution.

# Z

**zero slot LANs** The name "zero slot" refers to the fact that by using existing serial or parallel ports for network communications, zero expansion slots are occupied by network interface cards.

**ZMODEM** File transfer protocol, dynamically adjusts data packet size, automatic recovery from aborted file transfers.

**zone** The scope of coverage, or collection of domains, for which a given DNS server can resolve names.

# INDEX